to show some of the basic operations using three popular brands of algebraic scientific calculators.

Some keys of the calculator can be used for more than one type of calculation. For example, the $\boxed{\sqrt{x^2}}$ key can also be used to find the *square root* of a number. The second use, or function, of the key is usually indicated by a symbol written on the body of the calculator either above or below the key. To use the key for the second function, you must first depress another key on the calculator labeled *2nd F*, or *shift*, or *inv* (inverse), and then the desired key.

For example, to find the square root of 49, execute the following sequence of steps:

49 $\boxed{\text{2nd F}}$ $\boxed{\genfrac{}{}{0pt}{}{\sqrt{x}}{x^2}}$ and the display will show 7.

While no specific calculator is favored by the authors of this text, the calculator examples in the text use the $\boxed{M\text{ in}}$ and $\boxed{M\text{ out}}$ or $\boxed{RCL}$ memory keys.

Memory	Casio		Sharp		Texas Instruments	
	Keyed Entry	Display	Keyed Entry	Display	Keyed Entry	Display
Store a number in memory and clear out previous numbers stored there: e.g., put 7 in memory.	7 $\boxed{M\text{ in}}$	7	7 $\boxed{x \rightarrow M}$	7	7 $\boxed{\text{Sto}}$	7
Look at what is stored in memory:	$\boxed{M\text{ out}}$	7	$\boxed{RM}$	7	$\boxed{RCL}$	7
Add or accumulate numbers in memory: e.g., add 5, 7, and 20.	5 $\boxed{M\text{ in}}$ 7 $\boxed{M+}$ 20 $\boxed{M+}$		5 $\boxed{x \rightarrow M}$ 7 $\boxed{M+}$ 20 $\boxed{M+}$		5 $\boxed{\text{Sto}}$ 7 $\boxed{\text{Sum}}$ 20 $\boxed{\text{Sum}}$	
Look at the total of the accumulated sum in memory: e.g., 32 from above.	$\boxed{M\text{ out}}$	32	$\boxed{RM}$	32	$\boxed{RCL}$	32

FUNDAMENTALS OF BUSINESS MATHEMATICS

FUNDAMENTALS OF BUSINESS MATHEMATICS

John E. Rogers
Onondaga Community College

Bruce F. Haney
Onondaga Community College

Denise Laird
B.S., M.B.A.

PWS-KENT Publishing Company
Boston

PWS–KENT
Publishing Company

Editor: Timothy L. Anderson
Assistant Editor: Kelle Karshick
Production Editors: Susan Krikorian, Abigail M. Heim
Interior Design: Susan Krikorian
Cover Design: Julie Gecha
Manufacturing Coordinator: Lisa M. Flanagan
Composition and Illustration: G & S Typesetters, Inc.
Cover Art: David Bishop, San Francisco
Cover Printer: Henry N. Sawyer Company, Inc.
Text Printer/Binder: R. R. Donnelley & Sons Company, Crawfordsville

---

PWS-KENT Publishing Company is a division of Wadsworth, Inc.

Printed in the United States of America
1 2 3 4 5 6 7 8 9 — 97 96 95 94 93

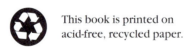 This book is printed on
acid-free, recycled paper.

Library of Congress Cataloging-in-Publication Data

Rogers, John E.
    Fundamentals of business mathematics / John E. Rogers, Bruce F. Haney, Denise Laird.
      p. cm.
    Includes index.
    ISBN 0-534-92476-X
    1. Business mathematics. 2. Business mathematics—Case studies. I. Haney, Bruce F. II. Laird, Denise. III. Title.
HF5691.R57 1992   92-33170
650'.01'513—dc20   CIP

To our students, who through the years have helped us to better understand the teaching and learning process.

To our families.   *J.E.R.*
                    B.F.H.

I dedicate this book to you, the student.   *D.L.*

CONTENTS

PREFACE

Fundamentals of Business Mathematics is designed for students enrolled in any business mathematics course that teaches the fundamental quantitative principles encountered in business. The main objective of the book is to show the importance of business mathematics to the students' personal and professional lives. This goal is accomplished through the use of realistic business applications that require the students to apply problem solving skills of varying complexity. Selected solutions, which are presented clearly in both arithmetic and algebraic form, emphasize the interaction of mental and technical skills required in business today. This dual approach allows the instructor to select the presentation appropriate to the students' abilities.

We advocate the use of calculators and computers, and encourage every student to obtain a scientific calculator with statistical functions and learn to use it properly. We hope that this book will help teach students to think through a problem, develop a reasonable estimate of the answer, and then use their calculators either for the final computations or to check their own mental arithmetic. To this end, calculator steps are provided for many examples presented in the text.

ORGANIZATION OF THE TEXT

The book is divided into sixteen chapters. Each chapter consists of topical units with practice problems and an exercise set. This format provides the necessary flexibility for designing a course syllabus to meet the instructor's teaching objectives. The text distinguishes itself from other business mathematics textbooks in three ways.

- Financial statements and their analysis are presented early because these topics provide an immediate application of the review units and will help the student to better understand the interrelationships of subsequent subjects such as markup, trade discounts, inventory, depreciation, and interest.

- The review of basic arithmetic functions is covered in one chapter. The review includes all the usual topics, such as whole numbers, rounding, fractions, decimals, and percents, but assumes knowledge of the addition, subtraction, multiplication, and division of whole numbers. It is hoped that students have had some work with the basics of algebra, but topics utilizing algebra are treated in such a way that an algebra prerequisite is NOT necessary.

- A seven-step pedagogical approach is used, which includes

  1. an in-depth narrative presentation;
  2. realistic examples;
  3. a set of practice problems after each section;
  4. exercise sets throughout the chapter;
  5. word problems that develop students' critical thinking and provide practice with written expression;
  6. case studies that draw together the main concepts taught in each chapter; and
  7. chapter self-tests that cover terminology as well as quantitative skills.

The authors recommend that chapters be taught in the order presented in the text, but the instructor can change the sequence if desired, after the first three chapters have been completed.

TEXT FEATURES

- **Learning Objectives:** Each chapter opens with a list of skills that the student will be expected to master.
- **Key Terms:** Important terminology is identified at the beginning of each chapter and included in the self-test at the end of that chapter.
- **Introduction:** Each chapter topic is introduced with an explanation of the real-world use and value of the concept in business.

- **Examples and Solutions:** Each section of a chapter contains realistic example problems that illustrate important concepts with detailed step-by-step solutions.

- **Check Your Knowledge:** Practice problems follow every section of a chapter. These problems are similar to the example problems and afford students immediate reinforcement of their newly acquired knowledge. Answers to all Check Your Knowledge activities are provided in each section.

- **Exercises:** Within each chapter are exercises that the instructor can assign as homework to further reinforce comprehension of chapter concepts. The exercises include drill and word problems of varying complexity, many based on actual business data. Numerous exercises allow maximum flexibility to the instructor.

- **For Your Information:** A description of an actual situation, in many cases taken from a business publication or document, appears in each chapter. Each presentation includes both graphic and narrative material illustrating the application of chapter topics and concepts to the real business world.

- **Express Your Thoughts:** These optional exercise sets require students to think critically about the key topics discussed in a chapter and to formulate their responses in well composed written form.

- **Case Exercises:** Beginning with Chapter 3, there is a case study in each chapter that requires students to apply their knowledge to a comprehensive problem-solving activity. The cases also ask students to apply skills and concepts learned in preceding chapters, providing systematic reinforcement throughout the text. The case studies are often based on business data contained in documents that students must use to discuss the facts and support their conclusions with appropriate calculations.

- **Self-Test:** Each chapter ends with a self-test that enables students to evaluate their comprehension of both the terminology and quantitative concepts that have been presented.

INSTRUCTOR RESOURCES

- An *Instructor's Resource Manual* is available to accompany *Fundamentals of Business Mathematics*. The manual includes

    a diagnostic pretest of arithmetic;

    suggested course outlines;

> lecture outlines and teaching suggestions;
>
> complete solutions to all exercises and case study problems; and
>
> transparency masters.

- The *Printed Test Bank* contains multiple chapter tests and final examinations.

- *Transparency Acetates*, printed in two colors, are each keyed to the appropriate section of the lecture outline.

- *EXPTest*, a computerized test bank for IBM PCs and compatibles, allows users to view, edit, add to, or delete any test. Instructors can modify hundreds of existing questions and print all tests. A graphics importation feature permits the display and printing of graphs. Demonstration disks are available.

- *Exambuilder*, a computerized test bank for the Macintosh, is a simple testing program that allows instructors to view and edit existing tests, as well as create new test items. Questions can be stored by objective, and tests can be created using multiple-choice, true/false, fill-in-the-blank, essay, and/or matching formats. Questions can be scrambled to avoid duplicate testing, and graphs can be generated and printed. Demonstration disks are available.

STUDENT RESOURCES

- The *Student's Partial Solutions Manual* contains complete solutions to every odd-numbered exercise.

- *Investigate*, tutorial software created exclusively for this text, gives students an interactive format with which to reinforce their learning. The tutorial software is available for Macintosh and IBM (and compatible) personal computers. Demonstration disks are available.

- Videos by Professor Hope Florence (College of Charleston), a series of five videotapes, reviews topics covered in *Fundamentals of Business Mathematics* including

> arithmetic;
>
> polynomials;
>
> linear equations and inequalities;
>
> graphs and systems of equations; and
>
> intermediate algebra.

A set of practice worksheets, reproducible for student use, is provided with the videotapes.

ACKNOWLEDGMENTS

The process of completing a project of this magnitude involves many individuals. We would like to express our appreciation and gratitude to the following reviewers for their valuable suggestions and comments at various stages of the manuscript's development.

Maryann Birdsall
Ocean County College

Michael Cicero
Highline Community College

Dick J. Clark
Portland Community College

Charles W. Cooper
San Antonio College

Bobbie D. Corbett
Northern Virginia Community College

Ree B. Erickson
Salt Lake Community College

Carolyn H. Goldberg
Niagara County Community College

Doris E. Holland
Houston Community College

Gerald W. Jones
Spokane Community College

Bob Kegel
Cypress College

Robert J. Leonard
Bunker Hill Community College

Shirley A. MacKenzie
Bunker Hill Community College

David C. Mayne
Anne Arundel Community College

Kenneth Schoen
Worcester State College

Richard W. Shapiro
Cuyahoga Community College

Nancy Z. Spillman
Economic Education Enterprises

Kenneth O. Vaughn
Guilford Technical Community College

Mildred L. Williams
Lansing Community College

Nicholas J. Wood
Bryant & Stratton Business Institute

We would also like to thank our colleagues at Onondaga Community College and the Los Angeles City School District who have provided their support and assistance. In particular our appreciation is extended to Kathleen O'Donnell for her review and contributions to the accounting chapters, Jim Carey and Terry Pierce for their reviews and suggestions on the finance and merchandising chapters, and Arnold Gozzi and Fred Kapelewski of Solvay Bank for their assistance with the banking and finance chapters.

We sincerely appreciate the guidance and encouragement that we have received from the many individuals associated with our publisher, PWS-KENT Publishing Company—in particular, our acquisitions editors, Tim Anderson and Al Bruckner, and assistant editor, Kelle Karshick; and our production editors, Abby Heim and Sue Krikorian. This group has kept us focused, provided invaluable feedback and technical expertise, posed challenging questions that forced us to reevaluate our work, and been a continual source of motivation.

The list would certainly not be complete without acknowledging the computer and word processing assistance provided by Dr. Cynthia Kirby, Jane Covillion, Linda Texido, Kathleen Russell, Mary Bryant, and Donna Dalton.

We also want to thank our families for their encouragement and understanding. Throughout the project, they offered their encouragement, expressed their confidence in our abilities, and helped us when needed.

To all of you, we extend a sincere thank-you.

John E. Rogers

Bruce F. Haney

Denise Laird

FUNDAMENTALS OF BUSINESS MATHEMATICS

1

REVIEW OF BASIC ARITHMETIC

Learning objectives

1. Read and write whole numbers and decimals.

2. Round whole numbers or decimals to a specific place value.

3. Identify basic types of fractions.

4. Convert fractions to higher or lower terms.

5. Convert improper fractions to mixed numbers, and mixed numbers to improper fractions.

6. Perform basic arithmetic functions involving fractions, decimals, percents, and whole numbers.

7. Convert fractions to decimals and percents interchangeably.

8. Perform calculations with aliquot parts.

9. Define the key terms.

INTRODUCTION

The focus of Chapter 1 is to review the most important concepts of basic arithmetic, which are essential to your successful completion of this course and other courses in a business curriculum such as accounting, data processing, marketing, and management. Most of the concepts presented will not be new to you, having already encountered them at some point in your education. You may already possess the required proficiency. But you may also find concepts and procedures that are new to you since this text encourages the use of microcomputers and calculators as tools for solving business problems. To make sure you understand each chapter's content, complete the "Check Your Knowledge" exercises at the end of each section. New technology increases the importance of understanding the fundamentals of arithmetic, since the most crucial part of solving a mathematical problem is to set it up properly and to determine the correct quantitative procedures required to analyze the problem data.

1.1   DECIMAL NUMBERS AND ROUNDING

Learning objective
Read and write whole numbers and decimals.

The system that we use for writing numbers is called the *Hindu-Arabic numeration system*; This system is a **decimal system** because it is based on the ten digits (0, 1, 2, 3, 4, 5, 6, 7, 8, 9), which means any **decimal number** can be written using the proper selection and combination of these digits. There are other versions of the Hindu-Arabic system besides the decimal system. For example, computers use the binary system in which all numbers are expressed using two digits (0, 1) and the hexadecimal system in which all numbers are expressed using a set of sixteen digits (0, 1, 2, 3, 4, 5, 6, 7, 8, 9, A, B, C, D, E, F). The letters represent the numbers 10 through 15. Most microprocessors and calculators use the decimal version of the Hindu-Arabic system; this is therefore the system we will emphasize in this text.

The decimal system is a **place value** system because the value of each digit depends on its position relative to the decimal point. As Figure 1.1 shows, each position has a name that indicates its value. The decimal point in a decimal number separates **whole numbers** from their fractional parts. Whole numbers are written to the left of the decimal point and increase by tens from units through trillions in groups. Commas are inserted every three places to the left of the decimal point to facilitate reading the number. Numbers that are not whole numbers are written to the right of the decimal point and decrease by tens from tenths to billionths. Commas are not used for positions to the right of the decimal.

Figure 1.1

The decimal system

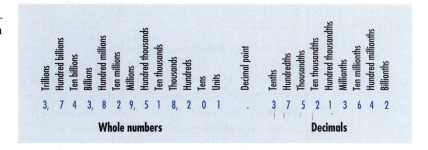

Let us analyze a decimal number using some of the numbers provided in Figure 1.1.

Example 1

Write 8,201.375 in extended place value form.

Solution

$$8,201.375 = (8 \times 1,000) + (2 \times 100) + (0 \times 10) + (1 \times 1) + (3 \times .1) + (7 \times .01) + (5 \times .001)$$

We are often required to write numbers out in word form. For example, legal documents such as negotiable instruments, checks, notes, and bills of sale all require amounts of money to be written in both number and word form. In fact, if there is an error in the presentation of amounts, the written amount is always considered the legal figure.

Decimal numbers are expressed in word form exactly as they are read. To read a decimal number, the whole numbers are read as their place value indicates followed by the name of the group. The decimal point in the number is replaced by the word "and." The fractional parts to the right of the decimal are read as whole numbers followed by the name of the smallest place value position.

Example 2

Write 47,682.52463 in word form.

Solution

Forty-seven thousand, six hundred eighty-two and fifty-two thousand four hundred sixty-three hundred thousandths.

ROUNDING AND ESTIMATING DECIMAL NUMBERS

When working with decimal numbers, it is necessary to express the results of a calculation to the place value most appropriate to the situation. For example, the U.S. monetary system is expressed in dollars and cents, which requires an answer to be expressed to the nearest whole cent (hundredths). Therefore, if a calculation produced a product of $137.4642, the answer would be rounded to $137.46.

Learning objective
Round whole numbers or decimals to a specific place value.

There are also situations where an approximation rather than an exact amount is more appropriate. While an approximation is less accurate it may be more practical and meaningful. To illustrate, an employee receives an hourly wage of $3.87 per hour but expresses the wage as about $4.00 per hour; the population of a city is 249,761 but is expressed as 250,000 by city officials.

The **rounding** of a number is nothing more than the determination of its significant place value. Therefore, any number may be rounded and, quite often, in several ways (thousands, tens, integers, tenths, etc.).

To round a whole number or a decimal number to any place value, complete the following steps:

Rounding a number

Step 1: Identify the place value of accuracy desired in number to be rounded.

Step 2: Evaluate the numerical value of the first digit to the right of the selected place value to be rounded.

Step 3: If the first digit to the right is 5 or greater, increase the selected place value by 1 and change all digits to the right of the place value rounded to 0s.

Step 4: If the first digit to the right of the selected place value to be rounded is 4 or less, simply change all digits to the right of the place value selected for rounding to 0s.

Step 5: If the selected place value for rounding is a decimal, follow steps 1 through 4 and drop all digits to the right of the place value selected for rounding.

The following examples provide a thorough application of the rounding procedure described above. Analyze these examples carefully as you will be required to round answers in all subsequent chapters of this text.

Example 3

Round $5,847,389 to the nearest million.

Solution

Select the place value:

millions position
↓

$5,847,389
↑

digit to the right of selected place value is 8

The selected place value of the accuracy desired is millions. Since the digit to the right of the millions position is 5 or greater (8), we "round up," adding 1 to the 5 and changing all digits to the right of the 5 to 0s.

$5,847,389 = $6,000,000

Example 4

Round 43,275 to the nearest ten thousand.

Solution

Select the place value:

ten thousands position
↓

43,275
↑

digit to the right of selected place value is 3

The selected place value of the accuracy desired is ten thousand. Since the digit to the right of the ten thousands position is 4 or less (3), we "round down": the ten thousand position is not changed, and all digits to the right of the 4 are changed to 0s.

43,275 = 40,000

Example 5

Round $945.2682 to the nearest cent.

Solution

Select the place value:

hundredths position
↓
$945.2682
↑

digit to the right of selected place value is 8

The selected place value of the accuracy desired is hundredths. Since the digit to the right of the hundredths position is 5 or greater (8), we "round up" adding 1 to the 6 in the cents (or hundredths) position and dropping the digits to the right of it.

$945.2682 = $945.27

Example 6

Round 12.4465 to the nearest tenth.

Solution

Select the place value:

tenths position
↓
12.4465
↑

digit to the right of selected place value position is 4

The selected place value of the accuracy desired is tenths. Since the digit to the right of the tenths position is 4 or less (4), we "round down": the tenths position is not changed, and all digits to the right of the 4 are dropped.

12.4465 = 12.4

A practical use of rounding is the process of **estimating** answers. We should mentally estimate answers when we wish to check the accuracy of our calculations or when we want an approximation instead of an exact amount. To estimate sums, differences, products, or quotients we round values to the appropriate place value (10s, 100s, 1,000s, etc.) indicated by the degree of accuracy required. For example, if you purchase items that cost $21.30, $5.69, and $12.15, an estimate of your total cost would be $39.00 ($21 + $6 + $12 = $39). Here we rounded each cost to the nearest whole dollar and then added the rounded values to get an estimate of the actual total cost. We rounded to whole number values because it is mentally easier to sum whole numbers and because the nearest whole dollar is a reasonable degree of accuracy.

To further illustrate estimation, let's say you wish to buy 48 videotapes costing $9.95 each. You can estimate your total cost by rounding $9.95 to $10.00 and 48 to 50 and multiply. ($10 × 50 = $500.) When estimating products, multiply the integers alone (1 × 5) and then add back in the total number of 0s in the multiplier (50) and multiplicand ($10)—in this case two—to the product: $500.

When we estimate a quotient, we round the numbers and then drop the common 0s and divide the remaining numbers. For instance, if we wanted to estimate the average amount of each sale based on total sales of $4,350 from 769 separate sales we would round the total sales to $4,000 and the number of separate sales to 800 and mentally divide, as follows:

$$\frac{\$4,000}{800} = \frac{\$40}{8} = \$5 \text{ per sale.}$$

CHECK YOUR KNOWLEDGE

Decimal numbers and rounding

Write the following numbers in extended place value form.

1. 2,460	*2.* 78,258.931	*3.* 3.00472

Write the following numbers in word form.

4. 6,275	*5.* 265,892,326	*6.* 57.03680

In the number 619,587.325:

7. The 6 is in the ——————— position.

8. The 2 is in the ——————— position.

9. The 8 is in the ——————— position.

Round each of the following values as indicated.

10. $1,279.57 to the nearest dollar

11. 4,627,385 to the nearest hundred thousand

12. 9.78% to the nearest tenth of a percent

13. 3.0005185 to the nearest hundred thousandth

14. $75.0543 to the nearest cent

Estimate each of the following:

15. $1.20 + $.95 + $6.10 + $.65   **16.** 31 × 45

17. $82.50 × 24   **18.** 64 ÷ 17

19. 38 + 71 − 52   **20.** 2,130 ÷ 270

1.1 Exercises

Write each number in extended place value.

1. 1,345   **2.** 10,768

3. 250,345   **4.** 85.667

5. 3.0045

Write each number in words.

6. 2,758   **7.** 75,250

8. 455,685,210   **9.** 64.0327

10. 0.36295

Round each number to the indicated position.

11. 746 to the nearest ten

12. 454,275 to the nearest thousand

13. 1,675 to the nearest hundred

14. 37.673 to the nearest tenth

15. 12,481.3658 to the nearest hundredth

16. 809.75 to the nearest one (unit)

17. 125,645.460 to the nearest hundred thousand

18. 5,785,642,125 to the nearest billion

19. 63.00496 to the nearest ten thousandth

20. $1.339 to the nearest cent

21. 2.125688 to the nearest hundred thousandth

22. $35.0525 to the nearest cent

Estimate each of the following answers.

23. 12 + 38 + 64 + 87

24. 37 × 72

25. 96 − 28

26. $1.22 + $.99 + $11.48 + $3.40

27. 879 × $2.60

28. 3,525 ÷ 485

Solve the following word problems.

29. María Ruìz ran 6.8 miles on Monday, 10.3 miles on Tuesday, 3.6 miles on Wednesday, 8.5 miles on Thursday, and 15.2 miles on Saturday as part of her training program for the Boston Marathon. How many miles did she run during the week?

30. What is the cost of 3,287 board feet of lumber that sells for $1.035 per board foot? (Round your answer to the nearest cent.)

31. The Newton Construction Company completed a 43-mile section of highway at a cost

Answers to CYK: *1.* 2,460 = (2 × 1,000) + (4 × 100) + (6 × 10) + (0 × 1)   *2.* 78,258.931 = (7 × 10,000) + (8 × 1,000) + (2 × 100) + (5 × 10) + (8 × 1) + (9 × .1) + (3 × .01) + (1 × .001)   *3.* 3.00472 = (3 × 1) + (0 × .1) + (0 × .01) + (4 × .001) + (7 × .0001) + (2 × .00001)   *4.* 6,275 = six thousand, two hundred seventy-five   *5.* 265,892,326 = two hundred sixty-five million, eight hundred ninety-two thousand, three hundred twenty-six   *6.* 57.03680 = fifty-seven and three thousand six hundred eighty hundred-thousandths   *7.* hundred thousands   *8.* hundredths   *9.* tens   *10.* $1,280   *11.* 4,600,000   *12.* 9.8%   *13.* 3.00052   *14.* $75.05   *15.* $9 *16.* 1,500   *17.* $1,600   *18.* 3   *19.* 60   *20.* 7

of $8,575,640. What was the cost per mile? (Round your answer to the nearest hundred thousand.)

32. If you spent 26.5% of your income on housing, 10.3% on clothing, and 30.6% on food, what percent of your income could be used for other purposes? (Round your answer to the nearest percent.)

33. Stephen Nichols made a trip to the supermarket to pick up some last minute items for a party. The items he selected were marked $1.89, $.69, $1.09, $2.49, $3.99, and $.39. Stephen realized while he was in the store that he had only brought $10 with him. Estimate the value of Stephen's purchases to the

nearest dollar to determine if he had sufficient funds to pay for the merchandise. (Round each of the values *before* summing them for the "estimated" total.)

34. If an employer pays an average wage of $6.78 an hour, and employees' work hours for the week total 34,689, what is the estimated amount of the weekly payroll to the nearest thousand dollars?

35. A stamping machine produced 23,645 parts during a recent week. Estimate to the nearest hundred how many parts per hour were produced if the machine was in operation 115 hours during the week.

1.2   FRACTIONS

A **fraction** is a numerical expression used to indicate a value that is a part of a whole unit. The fraction ⅝ indicates that the whole consists of eight equal parts and we are interested in five of those eight parts. In Figures 1.2 and 1.3, we have divided graphic illustrations (the whole) each into eight equal parts of which five of the parts are shaded. The unshaded portion represents three-eighths of the whole, or ⅜.

A fraction consists of two numbers separated by a line called a *bar* that indicates a division or a **ratio.** The number above the bar is called the **numerator** and represents the part of the whole under consideration. The number below the bar is called the **denominator** and represents the number of equal parts into which the whole has been divided.

$$\frac{5}{8} \quad \text{or} \quad 5/8 \qquad \frac{\text{numerator}}{\text{denominator}}$$

Figure 1.2

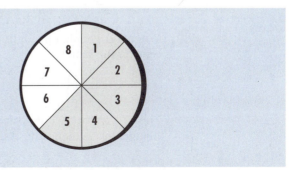

Figure 1.3

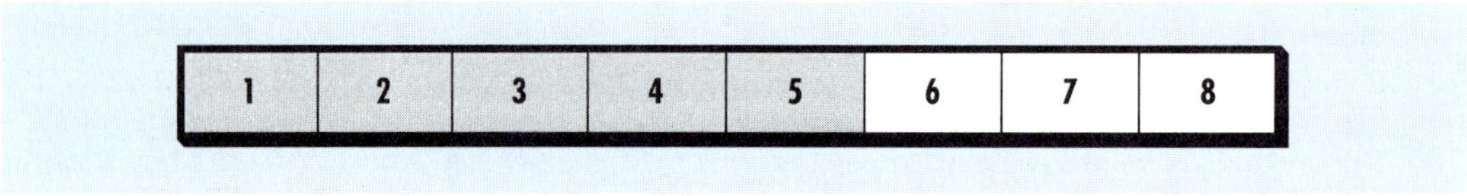

Learning objective
Identify basic types of fractions.

The basic types of fractions are *proper fractions, improper fractions,* and *mixed numbers*. A **proper fraction** has a numerator that is smaller than the denominator, and its value is always less than 1. For example, $\frac{3}{4}$, $\frac{6}{8}$, and $\frac{12}{24}$ are proper fractions. An **improper fraction** has a numerator that is equal to or greater than the denominator. Therefore, $\frac{6}{6}$, $\frac{12}{4}$, and $\frac{25}{8}$ are examples of improper fractions. A **mixed number** is a combination of a whole number and a proper fraction. The following are mixed numbers: $2\frac{1}{2}$, $12\frac{3}{4}$, and $25\frac{2}{5}$. A **complex fraction** has a numerator and/or a denominator containing a fraction or a mixed number. For example, $\frac{1}{2}/\frac{3}{4}$, $3\frac{5}{8}/100$, and $10\frac{2}{5}/50\frac{3}{4}$ are complex fractions.

CONVERTING FRACTIONS TO HIGHER OR LOWER TERMS

Learning objective
Convert fractions to higher or lower terms.

A fraction may be converted to higher terms or lower terms without changing the value of the fraction by multiplying or dividing the terms by the same factor.

Example 7

Raise a fraction to higher terms by converting $\frac{3}{5}$ to a proper fraction with a denominator of 35.

Solution

$$\frac{3}{5} = \frac{3 \times 7}{5 \times 7} = \frac{21}{35}$$

Both numerator and denominator are multiplied by the factor 7 since $5 \times 7 = 35$.

Whenever we multiply by 1, the value of the number (whole or fraction) remains the same:

$$\frac{3}{5} \times 1 = \frac{3}{5}$$

The "1" we've used in Example 7 is written as a fraction with the same number in the numerator and denominator, which always equals 1:

$$\frac{3}{5} \times 1 = \frac{3}{5} \times \frac{7}{7}$$

When we perform the multiplication:

$$\frac{3}{5} \times \frac{7}{7} = \frac{21}{35},$$

so $^{21}\!/_{35}$ has the same value as $^3\!/_5$.

A proper fraction is considered reduced (converted) to its *lowest terms* when there is no factor greater than 1 by which both the numerator and the denominator can be divided evenly.

Example 8

Reduce a fraction to lowest terms by converting $^{27}\!/_{45}$ to lowest terms.

Solution

$$\frac{27}{45} = \frac{27 \div 9}{45 \div 9} = \frac{3}{5}$$ Both numerator and denominator are divided by the factor 9 since 9 produces the lowest terms of $^{27}\!/_{45}$.

We are reducing the fraction by factoring a common factor, 9, out of the numerator and denominator, and reversing the multiplication.

$$\frac{27}{45} = \frac{3 \times 9}{5 \times 9} = \frac{3}{5} \times \frac{9}{9} = \frac{3}{5} \times 1 = \frac{3}{5}$$

Reducing fractions can be challenging because it is not always easy to identify which numbers will divide into another number. The following rules of divisibility will help you with the task of reducing fractions.

Rules of divisibility

A number can be divided evenly by:
  2 if the last digit is an even number.
  3 if the sum of the digits is divisible by 3.
  4 if the last two digits are divisible by 4.
  5 if the last digit is 0 or 5.
  6 if the number is even and the sum of the digits is divisible by 3.
  8 if the last three digits are divisible by 8.
  9 if the sum of the digits is divisible by 9.
  10 if the last digit is 0.

Example 9

Show that 15,384 is divisible by 3.

Solution $1 + 5 + 3 + 8 + 4 = 21$, 21 is divisible by 3.

Example 10

Show that 3,620,560 is divisible by 8.

Solution   The last 3 digits of 3,620,560 (560) form a number divisible by 8.

Learning objective
Convert improper
fractions to mixed
numbers, and mixed
numbers to improper
fractions.

CONVERTING IMPROPER FRACTIONS AND MIXED NUMBERS

Improper fractions can be converted to mixed numbers by dividing the numerator by the denominator, as the following example illustrates.

Example 11

Convert the improper fraction $\frac{25}{4}$ to a mixed number.

Solution $\frac{25}{4} = 6\frac{1}{4}$ The denominator 4 is divided into the numerator 25, producing a quotient of 6 and a remainder of 1.

If an improper fraction can be converted to a mixed number, then a mixed number can be converted to an improper fraction. The procedure is to multiply the denominator by the whole number and add the result to the numerator. This figure becomes the numerator of the improper fraction and is placed over the original denominator.

Example 12

Convert the mixed number $7\frac{5}{8}$ to an improper fraction.

Solution $7\frac{5}{8} = \frac{(7 \times 8) + 5}{8}$ The original denominator is retained as the denominator in the improper fraction.

$= \frac{61}{8}$

A mixed number is really two numbers being added together. $7\frac{5}{8} = 7 +$ $\frac{5}{8}$. The 7 can be written as a fraction with 1 as its denominator: $\frac{7}{1}$. When we add fractions, though, we need a common denominator, so we raise the fraction to $\frac{7}{1} \times \frac{8}{8} = \frac{56}{8}$

$$\frac{7}{1} + \frac{5}{8} = \left(\frac{7}{1} \times \frac{8}{8}\right) + \frac{5}{8} = \frac{56}{8} + \frac{5}{8} = \frac{61}{8}$$

CHECK YOUR KNOWLEDGE

Fractions

Identify each as a proper fraction, improper fraction, or a mixed number.

1. $\frac{8}{12}$ **2.** $1\frac{5}{9}$ **3.** $\frac{12}{6}$ **4.** $15\frac{1}{2}$

Convert each fraction to a new fraction with the indicated denominator.

5. $\frac{1}{3}, \frac{?}{12}$ **6.** $\frac{6}{12}, \frac{?}{60}$ **7.** $\frac{17}{20}, \frac{?}{100}$ **8.** $\frac{3}{30}, \frac{?}{240}$

Reduce each fraction to its lowest terms.

9. $\frac{9}{15}$ **10.** $\frac{26}{98}$ **11.** $\frac{98}{182}$ **12.** $\frac{102}{969}$

Convert each improper fraction to a mixed number.

13. $\frac{19}{8}$ **14.** $\frac{33}{12}$ **15.** $\frac{97}{14}$ **16.** $\frac{300}{9}$

Convert each mixed number to an improper fraction.

17. $2\frac{1}{8}$ **18.** $18\frac{4}{9}$ **19.** $29\frac{11}{15}$ **20.** $4\frac{103}{229}$

1.2 EXERCISES

Raise each fraction to higher terms as indicated.

1. $\frac{1}{2} = \frac{?}{8}$ **2.** $\frac{3}{4} = \frac{?}{28}$ **3.** $\frac{5}{12} = \frac{?}{120}$

4. $\frac{22}{57} = \frac{?}{114}$ **5.** $\frac{2}{21} = \frac{?}{105}$ **6.** $\frac{13}{16} = \frac{?}{256}$

7. $\frac{7}{8} = \frac{?}{40}$ **8.** $\frac{14}{15} = \frac{?}{105}$ **9.** $\frac{5}{8} = \frac{?}{56}$

Reduce each fraction to lowest terms.

10. $\frac{3}{9}$ **11.** $\frac{21}{42}$ **12.** $\frac{15}{40}$

13. $\frac{20}{70}$ **14.** $\frac{64}{80}$ **15.** $\frac{84}{216}$

16. $\frac{625}{1,125}$ **17.** $\frac{110}{121}$ **18.** $\frac{351}{513}$

19. $\frac{32}{196}$ **20.** $\frac{72}{108}$ **21.** $\frac{825}{1,575}$

Answers to CYK: **1.** proper fraction   **2.** mixed number   **3.** improper fraction   **4.** mixed number   **5.** $\frac{4}{12}$ **6.** $\frac{30}{60}$ **7.** $\frac{85}{100}$ **8.** $\frac{24}{240}$ **9.** $\frac{3}{5}$ **10.** $\frac{13}{49}$ **11.** $\frac{7}{13}$ **12.** $\frac{2}{19}$ **13.** $2\frac{3}{8}$ **14.** $2\frac{3}{4}$ **15.** $6\frac{13}{14}$ **16.** $33\frac{1}{3}$ **17.** $\frac{17}{8}$ **18.** $\frac{166}{9}$ **19.** $\frac{446}{15}$ **20.** $\frac{1,109}{229}$

Convert each improper fraction to a mixed number reduced to lowest terms.

Convert each mixed number to an improper fraction.

22. $^{19}\!/_6$ *23.* $^{38}\!/_4$ *24.* $^{85}\!/_{52}$

25. $^{100}\!/_3$ *26.* $^{585}\!/_{248}$ *27.* $^{91}\!/_8$

28. $^{390}\!/_{126}$ *29.* $^{269}\!/_6$ *30.* $^{215}\!/_{12}$

31. $3\frac{1}{3}$ *32.* $15\frac{7}{8}$ *33.* $26\frac{2}{3}$

34. $5\frac{18}{25}$ *35.* $2\frac{9}{10}$ *36.* $135\frac{5}{6}$

37. $40\frac{2}{7}$ *38.* $120\frac{3}{32}$ *39.* $52\frac{3}{4}$

1.3   CONVERTING FRACTIONS TO DECIMALS AND PERCENTS

A fraction is a mathematical expression of a part of the whole. The fractional presentation of a value is very common in business. For example, stock quotations (up $\frac{5}{8}$), interest rates ($10\frac{1}{2}\%$), retailing ($6\frac{3}{4}$ doz. or $1\frac{1}{8}$ gross), and payroll ($48\frac{1}{2}$ hours) are data reported with fractions.

If we are to use technology as a tool to increase the quality and quantity of our productivity, we must possess the arithmetic skills to convert data to appropriate input formats. For example, microcomputers and calculators analyze and print data in decimals; therefore, we must be able to express fractional parts of a whole as decimals or as percents. As students of business mathematics, this section of the chapter is extremely important. If you are to solve business problems successfully, using state-of-the-art technology, you must be capable of converting fractions to decimals or percents.

CONVERTING A FRACTION TO A DECIMAL

At the beginning of this chapter, we discussed the decimal as a numeric part of the whole. We will now look at how to convert a fraction to its **decimal equivalent.** The procedure involves dividing the numerator by the denominator and rounding the answer to the required place value.

Example 13

Convert the fraction $\frac{5}{8}$ to a decimal rounded to the nearest thousandth.

Solution

```
      .6250
  8 )5.0000
     48
     ──
     20
     16
     ──
     40
     40
     ──
      0
```

Add as many 0's as necessary to round your answer to the required place value.

Therefore, ⅝ = .625

CALCULATOR SOLUTION

Keyed entry   Display

[AC] 5 [÷] 8 [=]   0.625

If a fraction can be converted to a decimal, a decimal can be converted to
a **decimal fraction.** (A decimal fraction has a denominator of 1, 10, 100,
1,000, etc.) It is sometimes necessary to report data in fractional form even
though it may be easier to perform the calculations with decimals. To convert a decimal to a decimal fraction, use one of the following methods:

M e t h o d 1   Write the decimal in fractional form exactly the way it
is read and reduce to lowest terms.

E x a m p l e 1 4

Convert the decimal .875 to a fraction and reduce to lowest terms.

S o l u t i o n   .875 = Eight-hundred seventy-five thousandths, or

$$\frac{875}{1,000} = \frac{875 \div 5}{1,000 \div 5} = \frac{175 \div 5}{200 \div 5} = \frac{35 \div 5}{40 \div 5} = \frac{7}{8}$$

Note: By the rules of divisibility, both 875 and 1,000 are divisible by 5, as
are 175, 200, 35, and 40.

M e t h o d 2

Step 1:   Write the decimal as a whole number in the numerator.

Step 2:   Write 1 in the denominator and add as many 0s as the number of digits in the original decimal.

E x a m p l e 1 5

Write .075 as a fraction and reduce to lowest terms.

S o l u t i o n   *Step 1* $.075 = \dfrac{75}{?}$ (drop the 0, write as a whole number)

$$\textit{Step 2} \quad .075 = \frac{75}{1 + 3 \text{ 0s}} = \frac{75}{1,000} = \frac{3}{40}$$

Learning objective
Perform basic arithmetic functions involving fractions, decimals, percents, and whole numbers.

When we convert fractions or mixed numbers to decimal equivalents, the basic arithmetic functions of addition, subtraction, multiplication, and division can be carried out rapidly by calculators and microprocessors as most systems automatically account for the decimal if the data is entered properly.

Example 16

Find the sum of $3\frac{2}{5} + 6\frac{3}{8} + 12\frac{11}{20}$. Round your answer to thousandths.

Solution

Convert each fraction to a decimal and enter the data as decimal numbers with the instructions to add. (Remember that $3\frac{2}{5}$ is $3 + \frac{2}{5}$, or $3 + .40 = 3.40$; $6\frac{3}{8}$ is $6 + \frac{3}{8}$, or $6 + .375 = 6.375$; $12\frac{11}{20}$ is $12 + \frac{11}{20}$, or $12 + .55 = 12.55$.)

Mixed number	Decimal equivalent
$3\frac{2}{5}$	3.400
$6\frac{3}{8}$	6.375
$12\frac{11}{20}$	12.550
Total	22.325

The total is 22.325. If we were required to report the answer as a mixed number, we would convert the decimal number to $22\frac{13}{40}$ using the procedure explained earlier in this chapter.

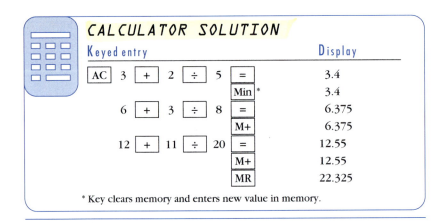

CALCULATOR SOLUTION

Keyed entry	Display
AC 3 + 2 ÷ 5 =	3.4
Min *	3.4
6 + 3 ÷ 8 =	6.375
M+	6.375
12 + 11 ÷ 20 =	12.55
M+	12.55
MR	22.325

* Key clears memory and enters new value in memory.

The same procedure would be followed if we were required to perform calculations involving multiplication or division. Let's look at an example that involves multiplication.

Example 17

Multiply 12⅛ by 4¾. Round to hundredths.

Solution

Mixed number	Decimal equivalent
12⅛	12.125
4¾	4.75
Total	57.59375
	or
	57.59 (rounded to hundredths)

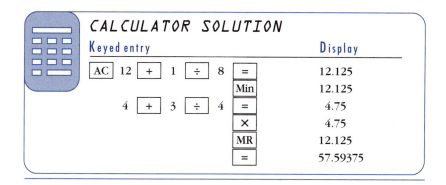

CALCULATOR SOLUTION

Keyed entry	Display
AC 12 + 1 ÷ 8 =	12.125
Min	12.125
4 + 3 ÷ 4 =	4.75
×	4.75
MR	12.125
=	57.59375

CONVERTING A FRACTION TO A PERCENT

Learning objective
Convert fractions to decimals and percents interchangeably.

A **percent** also represents a part of the whole. Percents are hundredths, or parts of a 100. A percent is a numeral written with a percent sign (%). For example, 10% is 10 parts of 100, and 50% is 50 parts of 100. Because 100% refers to the whole, 125% indicates that more than one whole unit (each unit divided into 100 parts) is involved; 125 of those parts are under consideration.

To convert a fraction to its **percent equivalent,** first convert the fraction to a decimal, then move the decimal point two places to the right and add the % sign; or multiply the decimal by 100 and add the percent sign (.50 × 100 = 50 or 50%).

Example 18

Convert the fractions ½, ⅞, and 1¼ to percents.

Solution

Fraction	Decimal equivalent	Percent equivalent
½	.50	50%
⅞	.875	87.5%
1¼	1.25	125%

Note: To change a decimal to a percent, move the decimal point 2 places to the right and add the percent sign. If the decimal number extends beyond the hundredths position (⅞ = .875 or 87.5%), the percent equivalent includes *parts of a percent*.

Any fraction can be converted to a percent, which also means any percent can be converted to a fraction. To convert a percent to a fraction, drop the % sign and move the decimal two places to the left. Then convert the decimal number to a fraction and reduce to lowest terms.

Example 19

Convert the percents 2% and 12.5% to fractions and reduce to lowest terms.

Solution

Percent	Decimal equivalent	Fraction equivalent
2%	.02	²⁄₁₀₀, or ¹⁄₅₀
12.5%	.125	¹²⁵⁄₁₀₀₀, or ⅛

Note: To change a percent to a decimal, drop the percent sign and move the decimal 2 places to the left; or divide the number by 100 and drop the percent sign (50 ÷ 100 = .5).

If the percent also contains a fraction, the conversion is a little more difficult. The procedure explained in Example 19 can be used if the fractional ending of the percent is an aliquot part. An **aliquot part** is defined as any number that will divide evenly into another number. For example, the fraction ¾ is an aliquot part because the numerator (3) can be divided by the denominator (4) evenly. Therefore, if we wished to convert 5¾% to a fraction, we would follow the procedure that was explained in Example 19, as shown next.

Example 20

Convert 5¾% to a fraction and reduce to lowest terms.

Solution

Fractional percent	Decimal percent	Decimal equivalent	Fractional equivalent	
5¾%	5.75%	.0575	$\dfrac{575}{1{,}000}$, or	$\dfrac{23}{400}$

To convert a percent that contains a fractional ending that is not an aliquot part, follow the procedure shown in Example 21.

Example 21

Convert 4²⁄₇% to a fraction and reduce to lowest terms.

Solution

$$4\tfrac{2}{7}\% = \frac{30}{7}\,\%$$ Convert to an improper fractional percent.

$$= \frac{\frac{30}{7}}{100}$$ Divide by 100 to convert to a decimal.

$$= \frac{\frac{30}{7}}{100} \times \frac{\frac{7}{1}}{\frac{7}{1}}$$ Multiply both the numerator and the denominator by 7 to simplify the fraction.

$$= \frac{30}{700} \div \frac{10}{10}$$ Divide both the numerator and the denominator by the largest common factor (10).

$$= \frac{3}{70}$$ Reduce to lowest terms.

Table 1.1 Fraction, decimal, and percentage equivalents

Denominator	1 (1.00 or 100%)	2	3	4	5	6	7	8	9	10	11	12	13	14	15
2	.50 / 50%														
3	.333 / 33$\frac{1}{3}$%	.666 / 66$\frac{2}{3}$%													
4	.25 / 25%	.50 / 50%	.75 / 75%												
5	.20 / 20%	.40 / 40%	.60 / 60%	.80 / 80%											
6	.166 / 16$\frac{2}{3}$%	.333 / 33$\frac{1}{3}$%	.50 / 50%	.666 / 66$\frac{2}{3}$%	.833 / 83$\frac{1}{3}$%										
7	.142 / 14$\frac{2}{7}$%	.285 / 28$\frac{4}{7}$%	.428 / 42$\frac{6}{7}$%	.571 / 57$\frac{1}{7}$%	.714 / 71$\frac{3}{7}$%	.857 / 85$\frac{5}{7}$%									
8	.125 / 12$\frac{1}{2}$%	.25 / 25%	.375 / 37$\frac{1}{2}$%	.50 / 50%	.625 / 62$\frac{1}{2}$%	.75 / 75%	.875 / 87$\frac{1}{2}$%								
9	.111 / 11$\frac{1}{9}$%	.222 / 22$\frac{2}{9}$%	.333 / 33$\frac{1}{3}$%	.444 / 44$\frac{4}{9}$%	.555 / 55$\frac{5}{9}$%	.666 / 66$\frac{2}{3}$%	.777 / 77$\frac{7}{9}$%	.888 / 88$\frac{8}{9}$%							
10	.10 / 10%	.20 / 20%	.30 / 30%	.40 / 40%	.50 / 50%	.60 / 60%	.70 / 70%	.80 / 80%	.90 / 90%						
11	.090 / 9$\frac{1}{11}$%	.181 / 18$\frac{2}{11}$%	.272 / 27$\frac{3}{11}$%	.363 / 36$\frac{4}{11}$%	.454 / 45$\frac{5}{11}$%	.545 / 54$\frac{6}{11}$%	.636 / 63$\frac{7}{11}$%	.727 / 72$\frac{8}{11}$%	.818 / 81$\frac{9}{11}$%	.909 / 90$\frac{10}{11}$%					
12	.083 / 8$\frac{1}{3}$%	.166 / 16$\frac{2}{3}$%	.25 / 25%	.333 / 33$\frac{1}{3}$%	.416 / 41$\frac{2}{3}$%	.50 / 50%	.583 / 58$\frac{1}{3}$%	.666 / 66$\frac{2}{3}$%	.75 / 75%	.813 / 83$\frac{1}{3}$%	.916 / 91$\frac{2}{3}$%				
13	.077 / 7$\frac{9}{13}$%	.153 / 15$\frac{7}{13}$%	.230 / 23$\frac{1}{13}$%	.307 / 30$\frac{10}{13}$%	.385 / 38$\frac{6}{13}$%	.462 / 46$\frac{2}{13}$%	.538 / 53$\frac{11}{13}$%	.615 / 61$\frac{7}{13}$%	.692 / 69$\frac{3}{13}$%	.769 / 76$\frac{12}{13}$%	.846 / 84$\frac{8}{13}$%	.923 / 92$\frac{4}{13}$%			
14	.071 / 7$\frac{1}{7}$%	.142 / 14$\frac{2}{7}$%	.214 / 21$\frac{3}{7}$%	.285 / 28$\frac{4}{7}$%	.357 / 35$\frac{5}{7}$%	.428 / 42$\frac{6}{7}$%	.50 / 50%	.571 / 57$\frac{1}{7}$%	.642 / 64$\frac{2}{7}$%	.714 / 71$\frac{3}{7}$%	.786 / 78$\frac{4}{7}$%	.857 / 85$\frac{5}{7}$%	.929 / 92$\frac{6}{7}$%		
15	.066 / 6$\frac{2}{3}$%	.133 / 13$\frac{1}{3}$%	.20 / 20%	.266 / 26$\frac{2}{3}$%	.333 / 33$\frac{1}{3}$%	.40 / 40%	.466 / 46$\frac{2}{3}$%	.533 / 53$\frac{1}{3}$%	.60 / 60%	.666 / 66$\frac{2}{3}$%	.733 / 73$\frac{1}{3}$%	.80 / 80%	.866 / 86$\frac{2}{3}$%	.933 / 93$\frac{1}{3}$%	
16	.062 / 6$\frac{1}{4}$%	.125 / 12$\frac{1}{2}$%	.1875 / 18$\frac{3}{4}$%	.25 / 25%	.3125 / 31$\frac{1}{4}$%	.375 / 37$\frac{1}{2}$%	.4375 / 43$\frac{3}{4}$%	.50 / 50%	.5625 / 56$\frac{1}{4}$%	.625 / 62$\frac{1}{2}$%	.6875 / 68$\frac{3}{4}$%	.75 / 75%	.8125 / 81$\frac{1}{4}$%	.875 / 87$\frac{1}{2}$%	.9375 / 93$\frac{3}{4}$%

Note: Table 1.1 shows the decimal and percentage equivalents for many fractions used in this text. If your instructor encourages you to use a calculator or a microprocessor as part of the instructional resources of the course, you could use either Table 1.1 or your calculator to find decimal equivalents.

CHECK YOUR KNOWLEDGE

Converting fractions to decimals and percents

Convert each fraction or mixed number to a decimal rounded to the nearest thousandth.

1. $\frac{1}{3}$ *2.* $6\frac{1}{5}$ *3.* $\frac{5}{9}$ *4.* $28\frac{13}{15}$

Convert each decimal to a fraction and reduce to lowest terms.

5. .8 *6.* 3.4166 *7.* .025 *8.* .08

Convert each decimal to a percent.

9. .2 *10.* 5.05 *11.* .0016 *12.* 3

Convert each percent to a decimal.

13. 39% *14.* $12\frac{7}{8}$% *15.* 6.125% *16.* 225%

Convert each percent to a fraction or mixed number and reduce to lowest terms.

17. 50% *18.* 2.25% *19.* .02% *20.* $5\frac{5}{6}$%

Convert each of the following fractions or mixed numbers to decimal and percent equivalents. Round decimals to thousandths.

21. $\frac{3}{8}$ *22.* $18\frac{11}{12}$ *23.* $\frac{2}{50}$ *24.* $3\frac{1}{3}$

Answers to CYK: ***1.*** .333 ***2.*** 6.200 ***3.*** .556 ***4.*** 28.867 ***5.*** $\frac{4}{5}$ ***6.*** $\frac{17,083}{5,000}$ ***7.*** $\frac{1}{40}$ ***8.*** $\frac{2}{25}$ ***9.*** 20% ***10.*** 505% ***11.*** .16% ***12.*** 300% ***13.*** .39 ***14.*** .12875 ***15.*** .06125 ***16.*** 2.25 ***17.*** $\frac{1}{2}$ ***18.*** $\frac{9}{400}$ ***19.*** $\frac{1}{5,000}$ ***20.*** $\frac{7}{120}$ ***21.*** .375; 37.5% ***22.*** 18.917; 1,891.7% ***23.*** .040; 4% ***24.*** 333.333; 333.3%

1.3 EXERCISES

Convert each fraction or mixed number to a decimal rounded to the nearest thousandth where appropriate.

1.	$\frac{2}{3}$	*2.*	$8\frac{1}{3}$	*3.*	$148\frac{9}{64}$
4.	$\frac{13}{16}$	*5.*	$\frac{2}{5}$	*6.*	$15\frac{1}{15}$

Convert each decimal to a fraction reduced to lowest terms.

7.	.5	*8.*	2.4	*9.*	.80
10.	.1875	*11.*	.125	*12.*	.008

Convert the following decimals to percents.

13.	.3	*14.*	.125	*15.*	1.50
16.	.0075	*17.*	.05	*18.*	.032

Convert the following percents to decimals.

19.	6%	*20.*	17.5%	*21.*	$\frac{1}{2}$%
22.	3,500%	*23.*	20%	*24.*	3.33%

Convert the following fractions or mixed numbers to percents.

25.	$\frac{1}{4}$	*26.*	$8\frac{2}{3}$	*27.*	$\frac{22}{32}$
28.	$\frac{8}{24}$	*29.*	$\frac{7}{10}$		

Convert the following percents to fractions or mixed numbers reduced to lowest terms.

30.	12%	*31.*	640%	*32.*	$6\frac{2}{9}$%
33.	.5%	*34.*	5.25%		

Complete the following conversions as indicated. Round decimal answers to thousandths and reduce fractions to lowest terms.

	Fraction	Decimal	Percent
35.	$\frac{1}{5}$	______	______
36.	______	.625	______
37.	______	______	4%
38.	______	1.8	______
39.	$17\frac{1}{2}$	______	______

Convert the following mixed numbers and fractions to decimals and solve as indicated. Round all answers to thousandths.

40.	$6\frac{5}{8} + 9\frac{3}{4}$	*41.*	$\frac{11}{22} \times \frac{3}{6}$
42.	$110\frac{17}{52} - 87\frac{15}{32}$	*43.*	$285 \div 4\frac{1}{3}$
44.	$\frac{3}{8} \times \frac{6}{7} \times \frac{2}{9}$	*45.*	$10\frac{3}{14} + 75\frac{3}{10} + 9\frac{17}{22}$
46.	$(105\frac{2}{8} \div 8\frac{1}{6}) \times 5\frac{2}{21}$		

Solve the following word problems. Express all answers as decimals rounded to hundredths unless otherwise instructed.

47. Ahmed Al-Hindi owns a small farm consisting of six lots of the following acreage: $5\frac{3}{4}$, $10\frac{1}{8}$, $27\frac{1}{2}$, $18\frac{2}{5}$, $15\frac{1}{6}$, and $42\frac{1}{4}$. What is the total acreage of Mr. Al-Hindi's farm?

48. A truck gets $17\frac{1}{8}$ mpg. How many miles will the driver be able to go before stopping for gas if the gas tank contains $12\frac{2}{5}$ gallons?

49. The enrollment this fall at Ourtown Community College is 1,275 of which 969 are local students, 255 are out-of-state students, and 51 are foreign students. Express the student population as fractional parts of the total student enrollment.

50. The Wildcat youth football program is planning a fall picnic. If 266 attend the picnic and each is estimated to eat $1\frac{1}{2}$ hot dogs, how many pounds of hot dogs must be purchased if there are 8 hot dogs per pound? Express your answer as a mixed number.

51. In 1985, Allied Manufacturing employed 368 people. Today the company employs 920. Express as a fraction the number of employees working today compared to 1985.

52. Buildrite Construction Company purchases $20\frac{3}{10}$ acres of land for a housing development. Two and four-fifths acres of the property will be used for roads. If each building lot is to be $\frac{5}{8}$ of an acre, how many houses will be constructed in the tract?

53. Last winter, fuel oil prices averaged $\$1.03\frac{3}{8}$ per gallon. This winter, fuel oil is expected to average 89½ cents. If a homeowner's average fuel oil consumption is 986⅘ gallons per heating season, how much money will be saved this year over last year?

54. Market Research Associates conducted a telephone survey that involved the purchase of a new product being test-marketed in New York, Pennsylvania, and New Jersey. Of the 1,600 households contacted, 573 indicated they had purchased the product, and 250 indicated they would purchase the product regularly. What part of those surveyed would use the new product regularly? Express your answer as a fraction, a decimal, and a percent.

55. Jim, Juan, and Giles formed a business partnership to sell sporting goods. Jim owns ½ of the company, and Juan ⅙. If the ownership is based on the amount of money invested, and the total investment was $90,000, what fractional part of the company is owned by Giles? Also, how much money did he invest?

56. Ann Nolan plans to attend a conference in Buffalo, New York. She lives in Albany and estimates it will take her 2½ hours to drive from Albany to Syracuse, 1¼ more hours to drive from Syracuse to Rochester, and an additional 1¾ hours from Rochester to Buffalo. If the distance from Albany to Buffalo is 288 miles, what is Ann's estimated speed if she makes a nonstop trip?

EXPRESS YOUR THOUGHTS

Compose one or two well-written sentences to express the requested information.

1. Explain how you would round 35.63974 to the nearest hundredth.
2. Identify two practical applications of estimating answers. Include in your response the basic arithmetic function required in each situation.
3. Develop an illustration that shows how to raise a proper fraction to higher terms.
4. How can you be sure that a fraction has been reduced to its lowest terms?
5. Describe the procedure required to convert a fraction to its decimal equivalent.
6. Express in word form .0050 as a decimal fraction reduced to lowest terms.
7. Explain in words the process required to convert a fraction to its percent equivalent.
8. Develop a step-by-step explanation of how to convert 62.5% to a fraction reduced to lowest terms.

SELF-TEST

A. Terminology review

Complete the following items using the key terms presented at the beginning of the chapter. Check your responses against the answer key at the end of the test.

1. The _decimal sys._ is a place value system be-

cause the value of each digit depends on its position relative to the decimal point.

2. In a decimal number, the ~~decimal point~~ separates whole numbers from their fractional parts.

3. One place to the right of the decimal point is the ~~tenths~~ position and three places to the right is the ~~thousandths~~ position.

4. The determination of the significant place value of a whole number or a decimal is called ~~rounding~~.

5. In a fraction, the ~~denomination~~ identifies the number of parts into which the whole has been divided.

6. a. ⅝ is a(n) ~~proper~~ fraction.   b. $^{18}\!/\!_7$ is a(n) ~~improper~~ fraction.   c. $\dfrac{3\frac{2}{5}}{100}$ is a(n) ~~complex~~ fraction.

7. A number that consists of a whole number and a fraction is known as a ~~mixed #~~.

8. When the numerator of a fraction is divided by the denominator, the result is called the ~~decimal equivalent~~ of the fraction.

9. A ~~percent~~ is a part of the whole based on 100 or hundredths.

10. An ~~aliquot~~ is any number that will divide evenly into another number.

B. Calculation review

The following concepts and short problems are designed to test your understanding of the objectives identified at the beginning of the chapter. Answers are provided at the end of the test.

11. Write 37,698.0025 in word form.

12. Write six hundred eighty-five billion, two hundred twenty-nine million, seven hundred eighteen thousand, four hundred ninety-two as a number.

13. Round 78.087625 to the nearest thousandth.

14. Round 10.5% to the nearest whole percent.

15. Round $17.0265 to the nearest cent.

16. Change $^{11}\!/\!_{12}$ to the higher terms with a denominator of 84.

17. Convert $^{28}\!/\!_6$ to a mixed number.

18. Convert $35\frac{7}{9}$ to an improper fraction.

19. Express $40\frac{5}{8}$ as a decimal and as a percent.

20. Convert 6.225 to a fraction reduced to lowest terms.

21. Convert 37½% to a fraction reduced to lowest terms.

22. At a given rate of interest, the final cost (principal + interest) of repaying a home mortgage is estimated to be 3⅛ times the original mortgage amount (principal). If a bank approves a $75,000 mortgage, how much will the owner re-pay for the home, based on the estimate?

23. In a recent election for city mayor, the winning candidate received ⅔ of the ballots cast, and the runner-up ¼ of the ballots cast. What fractional part of the ballots did the other candidates receive in the election?

24. Janet receives 4½ cents per paper for delivering the local newspaper five evenings per week. If she receives $8.55 a week excluding tips, how many customers does Janet have on her route?

25. Alexander's Men's Shop had five-eighths of its in-store inventory destroyed by flooding water. The insurance company has agreed to pay for eight-tenths of the inventory damaged. How much will Alexander's receive from the insurance company if the total inventory was valued at $85,000?

Answers to self-test: *1.* decimal system   *2.* decimal point   *3.* tenths, thousandths   *4.* rounding   *5.* denominator   *6.* a. proper; b. improper; c. complex   *7.* mixed number   *8.* decimal equivalent   *9.* percent   *10.* aliquot part   *11.* thirty-seven thousand, six hundred ninety-eight and twenty-five ten-thousandths   *12.* 685,229,718,492   *13.* 78.088   *14.* 11%   *15.* $17.03   *16.* $^{77}\!/\!_{84}$ *17.* $4\frac{2}{3}$ *18.* $^{322}\!/\!_9$ *19.* 4,062.5%   *20.* $^{249}\!/\!_{40}$ *21.* ⅜   *22.* $234,375.00   *23.* $^{7}\!/\!_{20}$ *24.* 38   *25.* damage cost = $53,125.00, insurance pays = $42,500.00

2

REVIEW OF ALGEBRA AND SOLVING WORD PROBLEMS

Learning objectives

1. Find the sum, difference, product, or quotient of signed numbers.

2. Using algebra, find the value of the unknown variable when given an equation with one unknown variable.

3. Set up an algebraic equation to solve for the unknown variable when given a word problem.

4. Define the key terms.

INTRODUCTION

We all face consumer-oriented problems in our daily lives, whether they occur at work, school, or home, such as: "A business wishes to sell an average of $88,000 per month within a 6-month period. If sales during the 5 months were $90,000, $98,000, $79,000, $80,000, and $87,000, how much should sales be in the sixth month in order to achieve their objective?" Or: "You originally paid $50,000 for your home. Ten years later, you sold it for $80,000. From the money you made selling your house, you must pay the realtor 6% of the selling price and the attorney 1% of the selling price. How much money is left for you?" Would you know how to solve these problems? This chapter provides you with a review of algebra and an easy, systematic way to solve these types of problems.

2.1   SIGNED NUMBERS

Signed numbers are positive and negative numbers where a positive can be thought of as a gain and a negative can be thought of as a loss. To illustrate, suppose a friend gives you five tickets to a concert. This transaction can be thought of as "positive five." If your friend then decides to take two tickets away from you, this transaction can be thought of as "negative two."

Before we look at any concrete examples of how signed numbers are used in our daily lives, let us first look at how signed numbers can be visually represented. The following is a number line used to diagram the use of positive and negative numbers.

When using a number line, numbers are represented by points on the line. Arrows along the line can represent the addition or subtraction of one number to another. The length of the arrow corresponds to the size of the number, and the direction of the arrow is determined by the sign (positive or negative) of the number. For example, the addition of the number 3 can be represented on the number line as the following arrows:

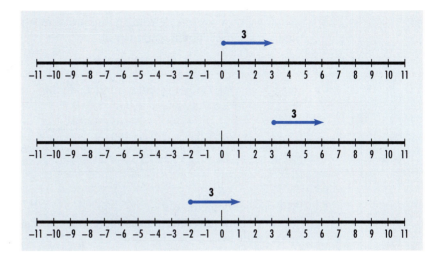

The addition of the number − 3 can be represented on the number line as any of these arrows:

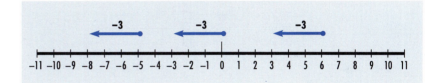

Learning objective

Find the sum, difference, product, or quotient of signed numbers.

The number line can also be used to depict addition and subtraction. If we add 5 and 7, the number line would look like this:

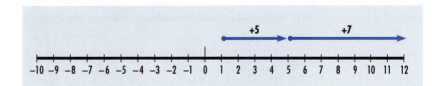

The sum depicted is 12.

If we now subtract 3 from 12, the problem looks like this: $5 + 7 - 3$, and we see the following number line:

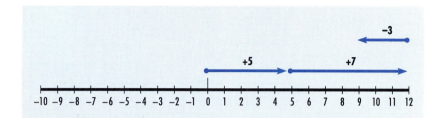

The answer depicted is 9.

Let us now look at Example 1 to see how signed numbers are used in our daily lives.

Example 1

You spent a day at Santa Anita racetrack betting on the horse races. The results of your betting are as follows:

1st race	lose	$ 3
2nd race	lose	15
3rd race	lose	2
4th race	win	16
5th race	win	2

How much did you win or lose at the end of the day?

Solution   If we use negative numbers to represent money lost and positive numbers to represent money won, we get the following number line:

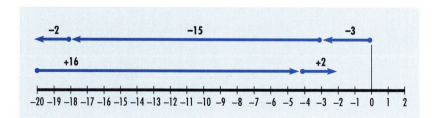

Remember to begin at 0 and follow the direction of the arrow. The answer: You lost $2 by the end of the day.

Using a number line is cumbersome, so instead use a set of rules.

Rule 1:   When adding two numbers with the same sign, add the numbers together, then attach the sign to the sum; for example,

$$(+5) + (+7) = +12$$
$$(-5) + (-7) = -12$$

Rule 2:   When adding two numbers with different signs, subtract the numbers, then attach the sign of the greater number to the sum; for example,

$$(+5) + (-7) = -2$$
$$(-5) + (+7) = +2$$

Rule 3:   When multiplying signed numbers, multiply the two numbers together and attach the sign as follows:

A positive times a positive equals a positive.

A positive times a negative equals a negative.

A negative times a negative equals a positive.

A negative times a positive equals a negative.

For example,

$$(+5) \times (+7) = +35$$
$$(+5) \times (-7) = -35$$
$$(-5) \times (-7) = +35$$

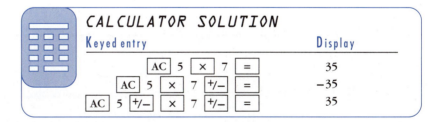

CALCULATOR SOLUTION

Keyed entry	Display
AC 5 × 7 =	35
AC 5 × 7 +/− =	−35
AC 5 +/− × 7 +/− =	35

Rule 4:   When dividing signed numbers, divide the two numbers and attach the sign as follows:

A positive divided by a positive equals a positive.

A positive divided by a negative equals a negative.

A negative divided by a negative equals a positive.

For example,

$$(+35) \div (+7) = +5$$
$$(+35) \div (-7) = -5$$
$$(-35) \div (-7) = +5$$

Here are six more equations for you to refer to:

$$(-10) + (+7) = -3$$
$$(-10) + (+7) + (-4) = -7$$
$$(-10) \times (+7) = -70$$
$$(-10) \times (-7) = +70$$
$$(-10) \div (+2) = -5$$
$$(-10) \div (-2) = +5$$

CHECK YOUR KNOWLEDGE

Signed numbers

Solve the following equations.

1. $(-12) + (+9)$
2. $(-1) + (+9) + (-11)$
3. $(-22) \times (+2)$
4. $(-22) \times (-2)$
5. $(+22) \div (-2)$
6. $(-22) \div (+2)$
7. $(+4) + (+2)$
8. $(+4) + (+2) + (-5) + (-3)$
9. $(+4) \times (-2)$
10. $(-4) \div (-2)$
11. $(+4) \div (-2)$
12. $(-4) \div (+2)$

2.1 EXERCISES

Solve the following equations.

1. $4 - 9$
2. $-4 + 9$
3. $4 \times (-9)$
4. -4×9
5. $-4 \times (-9)$
6. $20 \div 5$
7. $-20 \div 5$
8. $20 \div -5$
9. $-20 \div -5$
10. $-2 - 7$
11. $3 - 4 + 5 - 12$
12. $44 + 21 - 55 - 14$
13. $-30 + 15 + (-45) + 20$
14. $-44 \div (-11)$
15. $50 \div -20$
16. -2.4×10
17. -5.5×-3
18. $-31 \div 6$
19. $-42 \times .05$
20. $50 \div (-.5)$

Answers to CYK: *1.* -3 *2.* -3 *3.* -44 *4.* 44 *5.* -11 *6.* -11 *7.* 6 *8.* -2
   9. -8 *10.* 2 *11.* -2 *12.* -2

2.2   EQUATIONS

A numeric sentence that contains an equals sign is called an **equation**. The left side of the equation must have the same numeric value as the right side. Some examples of equations are as follows:

$$3 + 2 = 5$$
$$4 \times 3 = 12$$
$$-9 + 3 = -6$$
$$\frac{10}{-5} = -2$$

These equations consist entirely of constants. A **constant** is a number that has a fixed value; this value will not change. In other words, the number 3 will always be equal to 3; 5 will always have the value of 5.

Sometimes equations contain variables. A **variable** is a *symbol* that may represent *any* number. The equation $x = -4$ contains one variable called x. In order to make this equation true, we must find the number that x represents. We call this "solving for x." In this case, x must be -4 so that $-4 = -4$.

The following rules are very helpful when solving equations.

Rule of opposite operations

An opposite operation will *undo* the original operation.

addition $\longleftrightarrow$ subtraction
multiplication $\longleftrightarrow$ division

For example, if we multiply 5 by 3, we get 15.

$$5 \times 3 = 15$$

To undo this multiplication, we use division, which is the opposite operation of multiplication: 15 divided by 3 brings us back to the original 5.

$$\frac{15}{3} = 5$$

R u l e s o f
e q u a l s

If equals are added to equals, the sums are equal.

If equals are subtracted from equals, the differences are equal.

If equals are multiplied by equals, the products are equal.

If equals are divided by equals, the quotients are equal.

Always do to the right side of an equation what you do to the left.

An easy way to begin to solve for x is to isolate all the variables on the left side of the equals sign and all the constants on the right. To remove an unwanted variable or constant, perform the opposite operation.

E x a m p l e 2

Using subtraction, remove the quantity 3 from the equation $3 + x = 5$.

S o l u t i o n

$$
\begin{array}{rl}
3 + x = & 5 \\
-3 \quad\; = & -3 \\
\hline
x = & 2
\end{array}
$$

Original equation.

Subtract 3 from both sides of the equation to eliminate $+3$ from the left side of the equation, which will keep all constants to the right of the equals sign.

Check: Always check to make certain your solution is correct. This can be done by substituting the answer you got for x in the original equation.

$3 + x = 5$
$3 + 2 = 5$
$\quad\; 5 = 5$

True; therefore $x = 2$ is the correct solution.

E x a m p l e 3

Using addition, remove the quantity -3 from the equation $x - 3 = 2$.

S o l u t i o n

$$
\begin{array}{rl}
x - 3 = & 2 \\
+3 = & +3 \\
\hline
x = & 5
\end{array}
$$

Original equation.

Add $+3$ to cancel out the -3, which will keep all constants to the right of the equals sign.

Check:

$$x - 3 = 2$$
$$5 - 3 = 2$$
$$2 = 2 \qquad \text{True!}$$

Example 4

Using division, remove the quantity 4 from the equation $4 \times x = 12$.

Solution

$$4 \times x = 12 \qquad \text{Original equation.}$$

$$\frac{4 \times x}{4} = \frac{12}{4} \qquad \text{Divide both sides by 4 to keep all constants to the right of the equals sign.}$$

$$x = 3$$

Check:

$$4 \times x = 12$$
$$4 \times 3 = 12$$
$$12 = 12 \qquad \text{True!}$$

Note: Instead of writing $4 \times x$ to represent 4 multiplied by x, it is common practice to write $4x$.

Example 5

Using multiplication, remove the quantity 4 from the equation $\dfrac{x}{4} = 3$.

Solution

$$\frac{x}{4} = 3 \qquad \text{Original equation.}$$

$$\frac{4}{1} \cdot \frac{x}{4} = \frac{3}{1} \cdot \frac{4}{1} \qquad \text{Multiply both sides of the equation by 4 to keep all variables to the right of the equals sign.}$$

$$x = 12$$

Check:

$$\frac{x}{4} = 3$$

$$\frac{12}{4} = 3$$

$$3 = 3 \qquad \text{True!}$$

Example 6

Solve for x by combining like terms: $2x + 3x = 20$.

Solution

$2x + 3x = 20$	Original equation.
$5x = 20$	$2x$ and $3x$ are *like terms*: they each have a number and the same *letter(s)*; they can be added or combined into the single term $5x$.
$\dfrac{5x}{5} = \dfrac{20}{5}$	Divide both sides of the equation by 5 to isolate the variable.
$x = 4$	

Check:

$$2x + 3x = 20$$
$$2(4) + 3(4) = 20$$
$$8 + 12 = 20$$
$$20 = 20 \qquad \text{True!}$$

Example 7

Solve for x: $4 + 4x - 3 = 11 - 1x$.

Solution

$4 + 4x - 3 = 11 - 1x$	Original equation.
$1 + 4x = 11 - 1x$	Combine like terms in the equation.
$\underline{-1 \qquad\qquad -1}$	Subtract 1 from both sides of the equation to begin isolating all constants to the right of the equals sign.
$4x = 10 - 1x$	
$\underline{+1x \qquad\qquad +1x}$	Add $1x$ to both sides of the equation to isolate all variables to the left of the equals sign.
$5x = 10$	
$\dfrac{5x}{5} = \dfrac{10}{5}$	Divide by 5 to finish isolating all constants to the right of the equals sign.
$x = 2$	

Check:

$$4 + 4x - 3 = 11 - 1x$$
$$4 + 4(2) - 3 = 11 - 1(2)$$
$$4 + 8 - 3 = 11 - 2$$
$$9 = 9$$

ORDER OF OPERATIONS

Occasionally, we encounter expressions that contain several mathematical operations $(+, -, \times, \div)$. For example, the expression $12 - 10 + 6 \times 8 \div 2$ has all four operations. To properly evaluate this expression, we perform all multiplication and division first, and then complete any addition and subtraction.

Order of operations rule	With an expression that has some or all of the operations of addition, subtraction, multiplication, and division, but no parentheses, first complete all multiplication and division operations and then complete any additions and subtractions.

Example 8

Solve for x: $x = 12 - 10 + 6 \times 8 \div 2$.

Solution 1

$x = 12 - 10 + 6 \times \underline{8 \div 2}$ *Step 1:*   Divide 2 into 8.
$x = 12 - 10 + 6 \times \quad 4$

$x = 12 - 10 + \underline{6 \times 4}$ *Step 2:*   Multiply 6 and 4.
$x = 12 - 10 + \quad 24$

$x = \underline{12 - 10} + 24$ *Step 3:*   Subtract 10 from 12.
$x = \quad 2 \quad + 24$

$x = 2 + 24$ *Step 4:*   Add the 2 and 24.
$x = 26$

Note: We can do either division *or* multiplication first; when performing addition and subtraction, we can also do either first.

Solution 2

$x = 12 - 10 + \underbrace{6 \times 8} \div 2$ *Step 1:* Multiply the 6 and the 8.

$x = 12 - 10 + \quad 48 \quad \div 2$

$x = 12 - 10 + \underbrace{48 \div 2}$ *Step 2:* Divide 48 by 2.

$x = 12 - 10 + \quad 24$

$x = 12 + \underbrace{(-10) + 24}$ *Step 3:* Add the -10 and 24.

$x = 12 + \quad\quad 14$

$x = 12 + 14$ *Step 4:* Add the 12 and 14.

$x = 26$

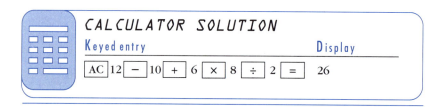

CALCULATOR SOLUTION

Keyed entry	Display
$\boxed{AC}$ 12 $\boxed{-}$ 10 $\boxed{+}$ 6 $\boxed{\times}$ 8 $\boxed{\div}$ 2 $\boxed{=}$	26

This order of operations rule always applies unless parentheses are used to override the rule. Always work inside the parentheses first.

Parentheses rule for operations

When performing operations on expressions that contain parentheses, complete the operations in the innermost parentheses first, then the operations inside the next innermost parentheses, and so forth.

Example 9

Solve for x: $x = ((12 - (10 + 6)) \times 8) \div 2$.

Solution

$x = ((12 - \underbrace{(10 + 6)}) \times 8) \div 2$ *Step 1:* Evaluate the innermost

$x = ((12 - \quad 16 \quad) \times 8) \div 2$ set of parentheses first.

$x = (\underbrace{(12 - 16)} \times 8) \div 2$ *Step 2:* Evaluate the next inner-

$x = (\quad -4 \quad \times 8) \div 2$ most set of parentheses.

$x = \underbrace{(-4 \times 8)} \div 2$ *Step 3:* Evaluate the next inner-

$x = \quad -32 \quad \div 2$ most set of parentheses.

$x = -16$

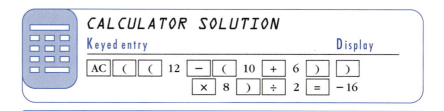

CALCULATOR SOLUTION

Keyed entry   Display

| AC | (| (| 12 | − | (| 10 | + | 6 |) |) |

| × | 8 |) | ÷ | 2 | = | − 16 |

Notice that the answer to Example 9 is different from the answer to Example 8. Both problems are correctly evaluated, but the parentheses used in Example 9 overrode the order of operations rule, which resulted in a different final value.

EXPONENTS

When a quantity is multiplied by itself, we express the multiplication by the use of **exponents**. Exponents are superscripts placed to the right of a quantity to indicate a repeated multiplication of the quantity by itself. The exponent is also referred to as the *power* of the quantity. Each of the following multiplications can be represented by the exponential expression to the right of the equals sign.

$$2 \times 2 = 2^2$$
$$2 \times 2 \times 2 = 2^3$$
$$2 \times 2 \times 2 \times 2 = 2^4$$
$$2 \times 2 \times 2 \times 2 \times 2 = 2^5$$

$$2 \times 2 \times 2 \times 2 \times 2 \times 2 \times \cdots \times 2 = 2^n$$

if there are n 2s multiplied together

Example 10

Solve for x: $x = 3^5$.

Solution

3^5 means there are five 3s multiplied together.

$$x = 3^5$$
$$x = 3 \times 3 \times 3 \times 3 \times 3$$
$$x = 243$$

CALCULATOR SOLUTION

Keyed entry   Display

AC   3 y^x 5   =   243

Example 11

Solve for x: $x = 2^3 + 3^2$.

Solution

2^3 means $2 \times 2 \times 2$; 3^2 means 3×3, so:

$x = 2^3 + 3^2$

$x = 2 \times 2 \times 2 + 3 \times 3$

$x = 8 + 9$

$x = 17$

Recall by our order of operations rule that we multiply first and then add.

Example 12

Solve for x: $x = (4^2 + 2^4)^2$.

Solution

$x = (4 \times 4 + 2 \times 2 \times 2 \times 2)^2$ *Step 1:*   Evaluate inside the paren-

$x = (16 + 16)^2$ theses first.

$x = 32^2$

$x = 32 \times 32 = 1,024$ *Step 2:*   Evaluate this result to get

the solution.

CHECK YOUR KNOWLEDGE

Equations, order of operations, and exponents

Solve the following problems and check your answers.

1. $9 + x = 13$

2. $x - 7 = 5$

3. $5 \times x = 15$

4. $\dfrac{x}{11} = 3$

5. $6x + 2x = 48$
6. $5x - 7x = -10$
7. $8 + 8x - 6 = 22 - 2x$
8. $3.1x + 3.2 = 1.1x - 2.8$
9. $x = 15 + 9 - 6 \times 12 \div 4$
10. $(4x + 8 - 3x) \times 2 = 18$
11. $x = 5^3 - 4^3$
12. $x = (3^3 - 2^2)^3$

2.2 EXERCISES

Solve the following equations.

1. $7 + x = 14$
2. $x - 8 = 11$
3. $5 \times x = 40$
4. $x/11 = 4$
5. $7x + 3 + 2x = 21$
6. $-x - 3 + 6x = 23$
7. $-4 + 6x - 10 = 40$
8. $3x + 7 - 5x + 5 = 22$
9. $\frac{1}{3}x = 8$
10. $\frac{1}{2}x + 1 = 2$
11. $-42 - \frac{1}{2}x + 4 = 1\frac{1}{2}x - 3 + 68$
12. $21 + 3 - 2x = 4x + 5x + 32$

13. $3x - 5 = 5x + 45$
14. $6x - 32 + 8 = 20 - 2x + 8$
15. $-6.5 - \frac{3}{4}x + 14 = -32 - \frac{1}{2}x + 49$
16. $x = .6x + 320$
17. $y - .4y = 7.2$
18. $2z = 1.3z + 66$
19. $b - .5b = 3b + 156$
20. $w + 3.2w = -4.3w + 170$
21. $x = 6^4$
22. $x = 7^2 + 2^5$
23. $x = (2^4 - 3^2)^3$
24. $x = 3^3 + 6^2 - 2^5$
25. $x = (5^2 - 4^2)^2 - 3^4$

2.3 SOLVING WORD PROBLEMS

Normally, the problems we encounter in daily life are not presented in the form of equations; problems are usually presented in the form of words. In this section, we will demonstrate how to systematically solve word problems.

Answers to CYK: *1.* $x = 4$ *2.* $x = 12$ *3.* $x = 3$ *4.* $x = 33$ *5.* $x = 6$ *6.* $x = 5$
7. $x = 2$ *8.* $x = -3$ *9.* $x = 6$ *10.* $x = 1$ *11.* $x = 61$
12. $x = 12,167$

Solving word problems

First:	Read and reread the problem.
Second:	Write down the information given in the problem.
Third:	Write down what the problem is asking for.
Fourth:	Write down any additional information that is needed in order to solve the problem.
Fifth:	Write an equation that states the problem, what information is given, what information is missing, and any additional information.
Sixth:	Solve the equation and check the answer.

Example 13

What is the total cost of a gross of paperback books if the price per book is $5.95?

Solution

Given: Cost per book = $5.95

Asking for: Total cost of a gross of books

Learning objective
Set up an algebraic
equation to solve for
the unknown variable
when given a word
problem.

Additional information: 144 units = one gross

The cost of a gross of books equals the cost per book times 144 books. Let x = total cost of a gross of books.

$$x = \$5.95 \times 144$$
$$x = \$856.80$$

Example 14

A couple bought a house in Colorado for $210,000. One-fifth (20%) of the price of the house was needed for a down payment. What is the dollar amount of the down payment?

Solution

Given: House cost = $210,000
                                Down payment = $\frac{1}{5}$ of house cost

Asking for: Amount of down payment

Additional information: None needed

Amount of down payment needed is $\frac{1}{5}$ of the house cost. Let x = amount of down payment needed.

$$x = \tfrac{1}{5} \times \$210{,}000 \quad \text{or} \quad x = .20 \times \$210{,}000$$
$$x = \$42{,}000 \qquad\qquad\qquad x = \$42{,}000$$

Example 15

The two leading companies in the laundry detergent industry are "Spots Gone" and "Easy Does It." At present, the profits of Easy Does It are four times that of the profits of Spots Gone. If the total profits for these two companies are $120,000, what is the profit for each company?

Solution

Given: Total profits = $120,000
               Total profits = Easy Does It profit + Spots Gone profit
               (Easy Does It profits = 4 × Spots Gone profits)

Asking for: Profit for Spots Gone and profit for Easy Does It

Additional information: None needed

Total profits = Easy Does It profit + Spots Gone profit
$120,000 = 4(Spots Gone profit) + Spots Gone profit
x = Spots Gone profit,
$4x$ = Easy Does It profit

$$\$120{,}000 = 4x + x$$
$$\$120{,}000 = 5x$$
$$\frac{120{,}000}{5} = \frac{5x}{5}$$
$$\$24{,}000 = x = \text{Spots Gone profits}$$
$$\$24{,}000(4) = x(4)$$
$$\$96{,}000 = 4x = \text{Easy Does It profits}$$

Following are two helpful tips for translating word problems into equations.

The word "is" is represented by an equal sign (=); for example, $2x$ is 12.

$$2x = 12$$
$$x = \frac{12}{2}$$
$$x = 6$$

The word "of," especially used with percent, suggests multiplication; for example, ten percent of x is 20.

$$10\% \text{ of } x \text{ is } 20$$
$$.10x = 20$$
$$x = \frac{20}{.10}$$
$$x = 200$$

Some other phrases and their representations are shown below.

Phrases and their mathematical representations

Phrase	Representation (with x as the unknown)
5 more than a number	$x + 5$
7 times a number	$7x$
Subtract 6 from a number	$x - 6$
Four times the sum of a number and 3	$4(x + 3)$
Eight less than a number	$x - 8$
The difference of a number and 9	$x - 9$
The quotient of a number divided by 4	$\dfrac{x}{4}$
One eighth "of" a number	$\dfrac{1}{8}x$

CHECK YOUR KNOWLEDGE

Solving word problems

1. Bob earns $3 per hour less than his father at the local woolens mill. How much does Bob earn per hour if their total hourly wage is $15?

2. After paying a percentage of his earnings to his attorney, his manager, and his agent, Johnny Hollywood receives 13% of the money made by his films. If Johnny received $260,000 from his latest film, how much money did the film make?

3. A florist has found that there are 4¾ times as many red roses purchased for Valentine's Day as white roses. If the total number of roses purchased is 782, find the number of red roses purchased.

4. The top salesperson for Alvarez Realty had sales of $150,000 more than the next salesperson for the month of June. If the total sales of these two people was one-and-a-half million dollars, how much did each sell?

5. The Meadville athletic center has a 48,000-seat capacity, comprised of reserved seats, box seats, and general admission seats. There are three times the number of reserved seats as box seats, and 13,000 more general admission seats than box seats. How many of each type of seat are there in the center?

2.3 EXERCISES

1. Bart cashed his paycheck at the bank, deposited a total of $450 into his checking and savings accounts, and took the remaining $150 with him. If the amount he deposited in checking was $250 more than he deposited in his savings, how much did he deposit in each?

2. Bonita spent $30 less on gasoline for her compact car last week than she spent on gasoline for her minivan. If she spent a total of $86 on gasoline, how much did she spend for each car?

3. Brad's gross pay for one week was $640. He noticed that the amount of his take-home pay was three times the amount withheld for taxes and other benefits. How much did he take home?

4. Mary deposited a total of $1,000 into her two bank accounts. She deposited $300 more into her checking account than into her savings account. How much did she deposit in each?

5. Anwar spent three times as much money on repairing his car as he spent on clothes last week. If he spent a total of $360, how much did he spend on each?

6. If Tom and Jerry win the Million Dollar Lotto, Tom will receive four times the winnings that Jerry will receive. How much money will each of them win?

7. The area of your office is 24 feet by 21 feet. The carpeting you want is $36.99 per square yard. How much will it cost to carpet your new office? (1 square yard = 9 square feet.)

8. You fill your car with gasoline, then travel 271.4 miles. When refilling your car you notice that you put 11.8 gallons of gasoline in the tank. How many miles per gallon did you get?

9. You are about to cook a roast beef that weighs 5 pounds. If the roast needs to be cooked 45 minutes per pound, what's the total cooking time required?

10. Wilbur and JB have $12.00 to spend on fishing bait. If minnows are $.75 each and worms are $.05 each, how many of each can they purchase if they want to buy the same number of minnows as worms?

11. A business wishes its average sales to be $88,000 per month for a six-month period. If sales during the 5 months were $90,000, $98,000, $79,000, $80,000, and $87,000, what should sales be in the sixth month to achieve their objective?

Answers to CYK: *1.* $x = \$6$ *2.* $x = \$2,000,000$ *3.* $x = 136$ white roses; $4\frac{3}{4}x = 646$ red roses   *4.* $x = 675,000$; $x + 150,000 = 825,000$ *5.* $x = \#$ box seats; $x = 7,000$ box seats; $3x = 21,000$ reserved seats; $x + 13,000 = 20,000$ general admission seats

12. You originally paid $50,000 for your home. Ten years later, you sold it for $80,000. From the money you made selling your house, you must pay the realtor 6% of the selling price and the attorney 1% of the selling price. How much money is left for you?

13. The state symphony orchestra has ⅔ the number of men this season as it does women. If the total number of players is 45, how many men are in the orchestra?

14. A computer salesman needs to sell an average of $2 million worth of equipment per month. In January and February, his sales were $2.4 million and $1.2 million, respectively. What do his sales need to be during the month of March in order for him to maintain his average?

15. A local music store sells compact disks and cassette tapes. If there are a total of 38,000 CDs and tapes in inventory, and there are ⁹⁄₁₀ as many tapes as there are CDs, how many tapes are in inventory?

EXPRESS YOUR THOUGHTS

Compose one or two well-written sentences to express the requested information in your own words.

1. Explain how you would add two numbers that have different signs: one positive and the other negative.

2. Express how you would divide (-12) by (-3).

3. Describe how you would multiply (-3), $(+5)$, and (-8) together.

4. Describe the steps you would take to solve the equation

$$3x - 9 = 4x - 11$$

5. Explain how you would evaluate the expression

$$4 + 9 \times 8 + 5 \times (3 - 5) + 3^2$$

6. Write the rule for order of operations.

7. If x = Dick's age and $x - 5$ = Mike's age, write the following expressions in words with no mention of x.

$$2x - 5 = x + x - 5$$
$$2x - 5 = 11$$

8. Write the expression

$$.35x = 105$$

as a phrase in terms of a percentage of the unknown.

9. If x represents Juan's daily wage and $(x + 15)$ represents Mario's daily wage, state how the two daily wages compare.

10. Describe the steps you would follow to evaluate

$$(5^2 + 4^3)^2$$

SELF-TEST

A. Terminology review

Complete the following items using the key terms presented at the beginning of the chapter. Check your responses against the answer key at the end of the test.

1. A numeric sentence in which the values on the left of the equals sign must equal the values on the right is called an _equation_

2. Positive and negative numbers are often called _signed_ numbers.

3. A number whose value is fixed is called a _constant_

4. A symbol that represents any number is called a _variable_

B. Calculation review

The following concepts and short problems are designed to test your understanding of the objectives identified at the beginning of the chapter. Answers are provided at the end of the test. Solve for each.

5. $-32 \times (-3)$

6. $42 \div (-2)$

7. $-1.5 \div .5$

8. $30 \div 10 + 7.5 - 29$

9. $4x + 10 = 20$

10. $-2 + 6x = 24 - 8x$

11. $4.5x - 12.5 = -44 - 10.5x$

12. $100x + 3 + 4x = -200 - 50x + 303$

13. The sum of two numbers is 102. One of the numbers is five times the other number. Find the two numbers.

14. A car salesman wishes to sell an average of $11,000 a day. If his sales during the first four days of the week are $6,900, $10,500, $18,500, and $13,000, what do his sales need to be on the fifth day of the week?

15. Millie's Fast-Fill gas station had a total of $30,000 in gasoline sales for the month of August. Unleaded gasoline sold for $1.15 per gallon and super unleaded gasoline sold for $1.33 per gallon. If credit sales accounted for 40% of the sales and the remaining were cash sales, determine the amount of each type of sale.

Answers to self-test: **1.** equation **2.** signed **3.** constant **4.** variable **5.** 96 **6.** -21 **7.** -3 **8.** -18.5 **9.** 2.5 **10.** $1\frac{3}{7}$ **11.** -2.1 **12.** .649 **13.** first = 17, second = 85 **14.** $6,100 **15.** credit sales = $12,000, cash sales = $18,000

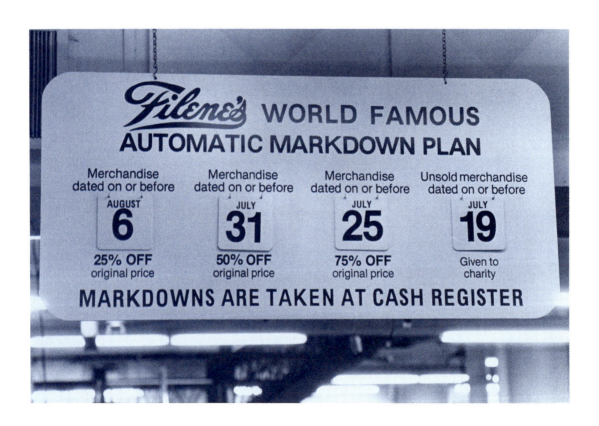

3

BASE, RATE, AND PART

Learning objectives

1. Define the elements of the percent formula.

2. Identify the base, rate, and part of a percent problem.

3. Use the percent formula to solve for the part, base, and rate.

4. Calculate the rate of increase and the rate of decrease.

5. Calculate the rate of inflation using the Consumer Price Index and other price indexes.

6. Define the key terms.

INTRODUCTION

This chapter is one of the most important in the text because the concepts we discuss will reappear as part of the quantitative procedures in subsequent chapters. Percentage computations are used by every segment of our society to express the degree of efficiency and/or effectiveness achieved between objectives and performance. As consumers, we are concerned with the percent change in the cost of living when compared to our annual income and the percent of interest on home mortgages, saving accounts, and taxes. Governments report the percents of economic growth and unemployment, and express population demographics as percentages. Businesses summarize their percent increases or decreases in sales, costs, expenses, and profits. Managers of today's businesses are evaluated on their applications of percent calculations when making decisions.

3.1   THE PERCENT FORMULA

Learning objective
Define the elements of the percent formula.

All percent problems can be solved by using the *percent formula*. The formula consists of three key variables: the *base*, the *rate*, and the *part*.

The percent formula

part = base × rate

or

$$P = B \times R$$

The **base** (*B*) in the formula is the *total*, or *whole*, and always equals 100%. For example, the base in the equation shown in Figure 3.1 is net sales, which equals $15,000. In word problems, you can usually identify which quantity is the base by looking for the quantity preceded by the preposition "of" or expression "part of."

Learning objective
Identify the base, rate, and part of a percent problem.

The **rate** (*R*) is the **percent**, decimal, or fractional part of the base to be calculated. It is easy to identify when it is expressed with the symbol % (percent). For example, in Figure 3.1, 40% of net sales is cost and 60% is gross profit.

The **part** (*P*) is the *portion* of the base that is determined by the rate. The base can be divided into as many parts as required by the data. The

Figure 3.1 The percent formula

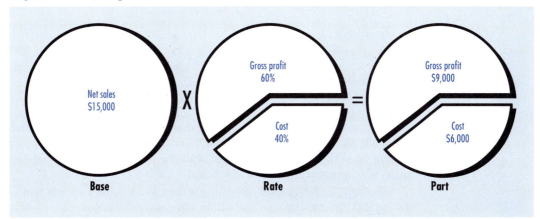

part is always expressed as a number and is generally a value less than the base. Returning to Figure 3.1, net sales of $15,000 (the base) multiplied by .40 (the rate of 40% converted to a decimal) equals $6,000 (the part, or portion, of net sales that represents cost).

Now that we understand the key variables of the percent formula, we can begin solving percent problems. A number of examples will help to differentiate between the given variables and the unknown variables that must be calculated.

3.2 COMPUTING THE PART

Learning objective
Use the percent formula to solve for the part.

We find the part (portion) by multiplying the base times the rate as expressed by the basic **percent formula**.

part = base × rate

Example 1

The student body of a university is 23,000, and 54% of it is female. How many female students attend the university?

Solution

Step 1: To solve this problem we must first identify the variables given.

base = 23,000   total student body

rate = 54%   percent of female students

part = unknown   number of female students

Step 2: We insert the variables into the formula and solve for the unknown part.

$P = B \times R$

$P = 23{,}000 \times .54$ (change percent to decimal)

$P = 12{,}420$ female students

The base can be divided into more than one part, however, as shown
in Figure 3.1: Net sales of $15,000 included a gross profit of $9,000 and a
cost of $6,000. Therefore, you must read the problem carefully to deter-
mine which part you are required to find.

Example 2 contains the same information as Example 1 except that in
Example 2 you are asked to find a different part of the base.

Example 2

The student body of a university is 23,000, and 54% of it is female. What
portion of the student body is male?

Solution

Step 1: The first step in solving this problem is to identify the variables
provided.

base = 23,000   total student body

rate = 46% (100% − 54%)   percent of male students

part = unknown   number of male students

The rate given in the example refers to the part of the student body that is
female. We are asked to find the portion that is male; therefore, we must
subtract the rate of those students who are female (54%) from the rate of
the base (100%) to find the rate of those students who are male (46%).

Step 2: Now insert the values into the equation and solve for the
unknown.

$P = B \times R$

$P = 23{,}000 \times .46$ (change percent to decimal)

$P = 10{,}580$ male students

Check:

$P = B \times R$

$10{,}580 = 23{,}000 \times .46$

$10{,}580 = 10{,}580$

It should be noted that although the part is usually smaller in value than the base, it can also be larger. The numerical value of the part is smaller than the base when the rate is less than 100%, and larger than the base when the rate exceeds 100%.

Example 3

What is 18¼% of 12,000?

Solution

$$P = B \times R$$
$$P = 12,000 \times .1825$$
$$2,190 = 12,000 \times .1825$$

The part (2,190) is smaller than the base (12,000).

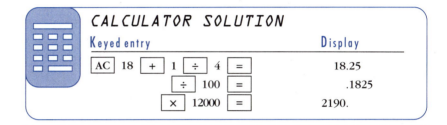

```
CALCULATOR SOLUTION
Keyed entry                          Display
AC  18  +  1  ÷  4  =                 18.25
              ÷  100  =                .1825
              ×  12000  =             2190.
```

Example 4

What number is 115% of 500?

Solution

$$P = B \times R$$
$$P = 500 \times 1.15$$
$$575 = 500 \times 1.15$$

The part (575) is larger than the base (500).

CHECK YOUR KNOWLEDGE

Calculate the part

1. What is 45% of 300?

2. A worker's gross pay for the week was $500. If 23% was withheld for various payroll deductions, how much did the worker take home?

3. Sales for Rojon Enterprises in September were $250,000. What will be the dollar amount of October's sales if they are estimated to be 120% of September's sales?

4. A local hospital estimates that approximately 5¾% of its billed services are uncollectable each year. If the hospital billed patients a total of $3,785,260 for medical services, what amount will be uncollectable?

5. Find the sales tax on an automobile priced at $12,345.00 if the rate of sales tax is 6¼% of the sales price.

3.3   COMPUTING THE BASE

Learning objective
Use the percent formula to solve for the base.

Many business transactions provide the given variables rate (*R*) and part (*P*). In such problems, the base (*B*) is the unknown. We can find the base (*B*) by using a *variation* of the basic formula, $P = B \times R$. We develop the formula by dividing both sides of the equation by *R* as explained in Chapter 2.

$$\frac{P}{R} = \frac{B \times \cancel{R}}{\cancel{R}} \quad or \quad \frac{P}{R} = B \quad or \quad P \div R = B$$

Now let's solve a base problem with the formula. We will use the data provided in Example 1.

Example 5

At a local university, 10,580 male students (46% of the student body) are enrolled. What is the total number of students?

Solution 1

Step 1: Identify the given variables.

base = unknown   total number of students
rate = 46% (.46)   percent which are male
part = 10,580   number of male students

Step 2: Insert the variables into the formula and solve. Because the base is the unknown, use the formula variation and divide.

$$B = \frac{P}{R}$$

$$B = \frac{10,580}{.46} \quad (or\ 10,580 \div .46)$$

$$B = 23,000 \text{ students}$$

Answers to CYK: *1.* 135   *2.* $385   *3.* $300,000   *4.* $217,652.45   *5.* $771.56

Check:

$$P = B \times R$$
$$10{,}580 = 23{,}000 \times .46$$

In Chapter 2, we learned how to solve for the unknown, which we called x. We also know that we can change the order of numbers when we multiply. To solve percent problems algebraically, we must apply this knowledge to the percent formula. When computing the base, we will substitute the letter B for x as the unknown and we will change the order of the variables as follows:

$$BR = P$$

To solve Example 5 with algebra, we will use the same analysis.

Solution 2

Step 1: Identify the given variables.

B = unknown   total student body

R = 46% (.46)   % of students male

P = 10,580   number of male students

Step 2: Insert variables into equation and solve.

$$BR = P$$
$$(B)\,(.46) = 10{,}580$$
$$.46B = 10{,}580$$
$$\frac{.46B}{.46} = \frac{10.580}{.46}$$
$$B = 23{,}000 \text{ total students}$$

We can use algebra to solve all percent problems reducing the number of formulas you must learn to one: the basic equation ($BR = P$).

Example 6

Fred Chang has a new yearly salary that is 8% more than last year's salary. If Fred's new salary is $37,962, what was his salary last year?

Solution

Step 1: Identify the given variables.

base = unknown   last year's salary

rate = 108% (100% + 8% = 108%)

part = $37,962   current year's salary

Step 2: Insert the variables into the equation and solve.

$$BR = P$$
$$(B) \times (1.08) = \$37,962$$
$$1.08B = \$37,962$$
$$\frac{1.08B}{1.08} = \frac{37,962}{1.08}$$
$$B = \$35,150$$

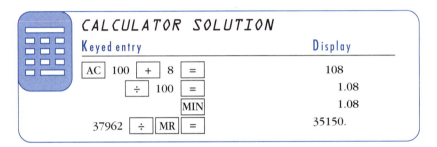

CALCULATOR SOLUTION

Keyed entry	Display
AC 100 + 8 =	108
÷ 100 =	1.08
MIN	1.08
37962 ÷ MR =	35150.

The part ($37,962) is greater than the base ($35,150) because the rate (8%) represents the size of increase to be added to the base amount. In other words, the part (new salary) is 108% of the base (last year's salary) as illustrated below.

Check:

$$P = B \times R$$
$$\$37,962 = \$35,150 \times 1.08$$
$$\$37,962 = \$37,962$$

Example 7 illustrates how to calculate the base when the rate given indicates a decrease. In this type of problem, the part (which is given) has a value less than the base (the unknown).

Example 7

Peco Products employed 396 people after implementing a 12% reduction in the workforce (a layoff). How many people were employed by Peco before the layoff?

Solution

Step 1: Identify the given variables.

base = unknown   number of employees before layoff

rate = 88% (100% − 12% = 88%)

part = 396   employees currently employed

Step 2:   Insert the variables into the equation and solve.

$$BR = P$$
$$(B) \times (.88) = 396$$
$$.88B = 396$$
$$\frac{.88B}{.88} = \frac{396}{.88}$$
$$B = 450$$

Check:

$$P = B \times R$$
$$396 = 450 \times .88$$
$$396 = 396$$

The rate 88% (100% $-$ 12%) must be used because the base is unknown and the part (396) represents 88% of the base as shown in the check above.

CHECK YOUR KNOWLEDGE

Calculate the base

1. 640 is 20% of what number?
2. If 12½% of a number is 800, what is the number?
3. 338 is 130% of what number?
4. 80 is 25% more than what number?
5. 266 is 24% less than what number?
6. Stephen Francis earns 10.5% on a certificate of deposit. He received his first annual statement showing interest of $525.00. How much money did he originally invest?
7. An employee has $41.30 withheld for social security. This amount represents 7.51% of total wages for the week. What was the employee's weekly wage?
8. The student tuition of a community college amounted to $2.5 million. If the tuition revenue amounts to 33.3% of the college operating budget for the year, what is the amount of the operating budget? (Round your answer to nearest tenth of a million dollars.)
9. Jill Clark's commissions this year are 20% more than last year's commissions. If her commissions this year are $12,000, what were her last year's commissions?
10. The food concession sales at the Fireman's Field Days this year were

4% less than last year. If this year's sales were $15,260, what were last year's sales?

3.4   COMPUTING THE RATE

Learning objective
Use the percent for-
mula to solve for the
rate.

Like the base, the rate can be found by using a variation of the basic per-cent formula. In problems where the rate (R) is the unknown, we will be given the base (B) and part (P). To convert the basic formula $P = B \times R$ into the rate formula, we divide both sides of the equation by B.

$$\frac{P}{\cancel{B}} = \frac{\cancel{B} \times R}{B} \qquad or \qquad \frac{P}{B} = R \qquad or \qquad P \div B = R$$

The result of the calculation is a decimal value that must be converted to a percent or decimal percent. For example, .25 is 25% and .075 is 7.5%. (This procedure was explained in Chapter 1.)

Example 8

A university has a total student body of 23,000 of which 10,580 are male students. What percent of the student body is male?

Solution 1

Step 1:   Identify the given variables.

base = 23,000   total number of students
rate = unknown   % of male students
part = 10,580   number of male students

Step 2:   Insert the variables into the formula and solve.

$$R = \frac{P}{B}$$

$$R = \frac{10,580}{23,000} \quad (or\ 10,580 \div 23,000)$$

$$R = .46, or\ 46\% \qquad \text{Always express the rate as a percent (\%).}$$

Check:

$$P = B \times R$$
$$10,580 = 23,000 \times .46$$
$$10,580 = 10,580$$

Solution 2

Step 1:   Now use algebra to solve Example 8. Identify the given variables.

Answers to CYK: *1.* 3,200   *2.* 6,400   *3.* 260   *4.* 64   *5.* 350   *6.* $5,000   *7.* 549.93   *8.* 7.5 million   *9.* $10,000   *10.* $15,895.83

For Your Information

Federal taxes: sources and outlays

Approximately 30 cents out of every $1.00 spent by American families is for some type of federal tax. This is nearly twice the amount spent on the next biggest item, housing, at 16 cents. In 1990, the federal government collected $1,031.3 billion in federal taxes and spent $1,251.7 billion, increasing the deficit by $220.4 billion. The budget deficit is financed largely by government borrowing from the public. The government borrows from the public by selling bonds and other debt securities to private citizens, banks, businesses, and other governments.

The pie charts show how base, rate, and part are used by the federal government to illustrate the relative sizes of the major categories of federal tax sources and outlays.

Source: Tax Foundation, I.R.S. Form 1040 Instruction booklet (U.S. Government Printing Office).

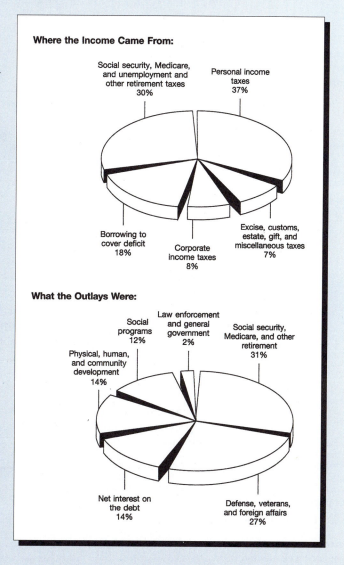

Where the Income Came From:

Social security, Medicare, and unemployment and other retirement taxes
30%

Personal income taxes
37%

Borrowing to cover deficit
18%

Corporate income taxes
8%

Excise, customs, estate, gift, and miscellaneous taxes
7%

What the Outlays Were:

Social programs
12%

Law enforcement and general government
2%

Social security, Medicare, and other retirement
31%

Physical, human, and community development
14%

Net interest on the debt
14%

Defense, veterans, and foreign affairs
27%

$$B = 23{,}000 \qquad \text{total number of students}$$
$$R = \text{unknown} \qquad \text{\% of male students}$$
$$P = 10{,}580 \qquad \text{number of male students}$$

Step 2: Insert the variables into the equation.

$$BR = P$$
$$(23{,}000)(R) = 10{,}580$$
$$23{,}000R = 10{,}580$$
$$\frac{23{,}000R}{23{,}000} = \frac{10{,}580}{23{,}000}$$
$$R = .46, \text{ or } 46\%$$

CHECK YOUR KNOWLEDGE

Calculate the rate

1. 1,500 is what percent of 6,000?

2. What percent is 780 of 600?

3. In a recent basketball game, Matthew Ryan scored 20 points. If he made 8 of 12 field goal attempts and 4 of 9 free throws, what is his rate of accuracy in each category?

4. Rick's Appliance Store reported sales of console TVs at 30 units and portable TVs at 90 units for the month of December. What percentage of total sales is represented by portable TVs?

5. A real estate agent received a sales commission of $5,525 for selling a house to a client for $85,000. What was the rate of commission paid to the real estate agent?

6. Outdoor Sports purchased 40 snowmobiles for the season. If they sold 25 of the snowmobiles, what percent of the snowmobiles remain in inventory?

3.4 EXERCISES

Solve for the part (round answers to the nearest whole cent or hundredth).

1. What is 15% of 500?

2. 35.5% of $1,200 is _____.

3. What is 7¾% of $89.45?

4. 125% of 52,785 is _____.

5. 13.2% of 12,856 is _____.

Answers to CYK: *1.*   25%   *2.*   130%   *3.*   66⅔%; 44.4%   *4.*   75%   *5.*   6.5%   *6.*   37.5%

Solve for the base (round answers to the nearest whole cent or hundredth).

6. 30 is 60% of what number?

7. 120% of what number is 19,200?

8. 33.125 is 6⅝% of what number?

9. 325 is 30% more than what number?

10. 500 is 5% of what number?

Solve for the rate (round answers to the nearest tenth of a percent).

11. 45 is what percent of 150?

12. What percent is 924 of 560?

13. 1,200 is what percent of 1,800?

14. 15.4 is what percent of 48?

15. .33 is what percent of 3?

Solve the following problems and express your answers to the nearest tenth of a percent, nearest whole cent, or nearest whole number.

Supply the missing information in the table.

	Part	Base	Rate
16.	_____	1,500	20%
17.	240	_____	30%
18.	$3,267.00	$9,900	_____
19.	$2.38	_____	.7%
20.	_____	3,000	⅕%
21.	$817.50	$6,540	_____
22.	$58.50	_____	130%
23.	15	60	_____
24.	_____	$640	.8%
25.	$15.60	$240	_____

Calculate the base, rate, or part.

26. What percent of 336 is 112?

27. 425 is 12.5% of what number?

28. 7.9% of $6,379 equals what number?

29. 15% of what number is 120?

30. .2 is what percent of .8?

31. What number is 12¾% of $35,000?

32. 6 is ½% of what number?

33. What percent of .25 is 4?

34. 150% of what number is 1,275?

35. 1,500% of .5 is what number?

Solve problems 36–45 using the percentage equation. Round your answers to the nearest tenth of a percent or nearest whole number.

36. Bill's Sub Shop reported profits of $12,000 in 1991. What will the profit be for 1992 if profits are estimated to be 130% of the 1991 profits?

37. A car dealer sold 125 cars last month to people entering his showroom. How many customers visited the dealership if the 125 who purchased cars represent 2½% of those who visited the showroom?

38. If an investment of $12,000 earned $1,260 in annual interest, what was the rate of interest earned?

39. Ann Randall's annual salary was $15,000 before she received a promotion to head teller. The bank has a policy of allowing employees to select a minimum dollar increase of $1,000 or 6% of their annual salary. Which type of raise would Ann have selected? Why?

40. A real estate salesperson receives 3½% commission on gross sales per month. What would be the amount of commission if the salesperson sold three properties during August for the following amounts: $54,900, $89,000, $70,600?

41. Sally Zimmerman sells automobiles for Eastside Imports. Sales records show that she sold 15% more cars in June than she sold in May. If Sally sold 46 cars in June, how many cars did she sell in May?

42. An inspector rejected 15 units due to defective assembly, which represented 1½% of the total day's production. How many units passed inspection?

43. Kyle Bush sold his 4-year-old automobile for $5,550, which was 62.5% less than what he paid for it. How much did Kyle pay for the car?

44. Mrs. Adams, Miss Ramìrez, and Ms. Elliott are business partners. Mrs. Adams invested

$5,000, which represented 12% of the total investment. How much money was invested by Miss Ramìrez and Ms. Elliott if they invested 38% and 50%, respectively?

45. A house contains 1,800 square feet of living space. If the family room measures 12 feet by 20 feet, what percent of the total living space is devoted to other living areas?

3.5   COMPUTING THE RATE OF INCREASE OR DECREASE

Learning objective
Calculate the rate of increase and the rate of decrease.

In the preceding section, we discussed how to calculate the rate. The rate (%) is an important measure of performance because it can be used to reflect the rate of increase or decrease in just about every type of business activity. To calculate the rate of increase or decrease we use the rate formula $R = P/B$. However, the variables must be adapted in the following manner:

Calculating the rate of increase or decrease

$$\text{rate (increase or decrease)} = \frac{\text{part (difference)}}{\text{base (original value)}}$$

In the above formula, the **difference** is found by subtracting the **original value** from the **current value**. The original value is always the base; when divided into the difference, the base produces the rate of change. If the current value is greater than the original value (positive difference), the rate reflects an **increase**. A **decrease** results when the current value is less than the original value (negative difference). When the rate is converted to a percent, we refer to the change as a **percent increase** or a **percent decrease**.

The following example illustrates the logic in calculating the rate of increase or decrease.

Example 9

Country Pride Foodservice reported profits for the first and second quarters of 1991 as $15,000 and $12,000, respectively. What was the percent of change if profits for the same quarters of 1992 were $18,000 and $10,000, respectively?

Solution

First Quarter

Step 1: Identify the given variables.

base = $15,000   earlier period profits

rate = unknown   percent of change

part = $3,000   the difference in profits between the two periods

$$\underset{\uparrow}{\$18,000} \quad - \quad \underset{\uparrow}{\$15,000} \quad = \quad \underset{\uparrow}{\$3,000}$$

current value   original value   difference

Step 2: Insert variables into the formula.

$$\text{rate (increase)} = \frac{\text{part (difference)}}{\text{base (original value)}}$$

$$R = \frac{\$3,000}{\$15,000}$$

$$R = .20, \text{ or } 20\% \text{ increase}$$

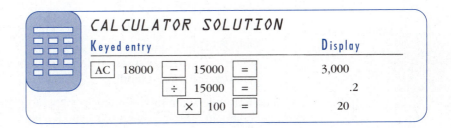

CALCULATOR SOLUTION

Keyed entry					Display
AC	18000	−	15000	=	3,000
		÷	15000	=	.2
		×	100	=	20

Second Quarter

Step 1: Identify the given variables.

base = $12,000   earlier period profits

rate = unknown   percent of change

part = − $2,000   the difference in profits between the two periods

$$\underset{\uparrow}{\$10,000} \quad - \quad \underset{\uparrow}{\$12,000} \quad = \quad \underset{\uparrow}{-\$2,000}$$

current value   original value   difference

Step 2: Insert variables into the formula.

$$\text{rate (decrease)} = \frac{\text{part (difference)}}{\text{base (original value)}}$$

$$R = \frac{\$2,000}{\$12,000}$$

$$R = .1666, \text{ or } 16.7\% \text{ decrease}$$

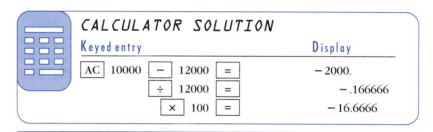

CALCULATOR SOLUTION

Keyed entry						Display
AC	10000	−	12000	=		− 2000.
		÷	12000	=		− .166666
		×	100	=		− 16.6666

Notice that the answer in the above solution was rounded to the nearest tenth of a percent (.1666 becomes 16.66%, rounded to 16.7%). Unless otherwise indicated, apply the following rules when rounding your answers to percentage problems:

1. When an answer is expressed in monetary form, round to the nearest cent.

2. When an answer is expressed in basic number form (decimal), round to the nearest tenth.

If you do not understand the rounding of values explained in this presentation, you should refer to page 6 of Chapter 1 before proceeding to the next section.

Example 10

The Grinding Department of Santos Manufacturing Company produced 40,000 units of part no. 1385 during the month of May. If the total units produced in May represent an increase of 5,000 units more than were produced in April, what was the rate of increase for the period?

Solution

Step 1: Identify the given variables.

base = 35,000   April's production

$$\begin{array}{ccccc} 40{,}000 & - & 5{,}000 & = & 35{,}000 \\ \uparrow & & \uparrow & & \uparrow \\ \text{current value} & & \text{difference} & & \text{original value} \end{array}$$

rate = unknown   percent of change

part = 5,000 units   the difference in production between the two periods

Step 2:   Insert the variables into the formula.

$$\text{rate (increase)} = \frac{\text{part (difference)}}{\text{base (original value)}}$$

$$R = \frac{5,000}{35,000}$$

$$R = .1428, \text{ or a } 14.3\% \text{ increase}$$

CHECK YOUR KNOWLEDGE

Calculate the rate of increase or decrease

1.   If you reported taxable income of $15,000 in 1991 and $17,000 in 1992, what was the percent change in your taxable earnings?

2.   A coat that you have been interested in buying has been advertised for $79.00. The advertised price is $19.95 less than the original price. What percent of savings will you realize if you purchase the coat during the sale?

3.   Last month, the average price for unleaded gasoline was $1.25%₁₀. This month the average price dropped to $1.19%₁₀. What was the percent of change during this period?

4.   If the Miller Paper Company reported net sales of $142,600 this year, which was $15,800 less than net sales for the same period last year, what was the percent change in sales for the period?

5.   A student received a grade of 65 on a recent math exam. On a makeup exam, the student achieved a score of 90. Calculate the percent of change in test scores.

6.   Last month the number of unemployed workers in the central region of the state was 18,500. This month the number of unemployed workers was reported to be 20,750. What was the percent of change in unemployment during this period?

Answers to CYK: *1.* 13.3% increase   *2.* 20.2% decrease   *3.* 4.8% decrease   *4.* 10% decrease
5. 38.5% increase   *6.* 12.2% increase

PRICE INDEXING — APPLYING PERCENT OF CHANGE

Learning objective
Calculate the rate
of inflation using
the Consumer Price
Index and other price
indexes.

Price indexes provide businesses and individuals with information necessary to measure the impact of inflation on the purchasing power of the dollars they spend for goods and services. For example, a business may determine the percent increase or decrease in the prices they charge for their goods or the wages to be paid to their employees based on changes in price indexes. An individual might use a price index to measure the extent his purchasing power improves or diminishes each year by comparing his change in income to the change in the index.

There are many different types of price indexes; however, the most widely used index is the *Consumer Price Index*. The U.S. Bureau of Labor Statistics compiled the first Consumer Price Index (CPI) in 1967 by pricing a representative sample of goods generally purchased by households throughout the United States. The total cost of those goods selected in 1967 (the base year) is compared annually to the total cost of similar goods to update the CPI and report the rate of inflation for the current year. Using the data provided in the Consumer Price Index (see Table 3.1) we can find the rate of inflation between 1967 and 1990 by subtracting the index for the base year (1967) from the 1990 index (362.7 − 100 = 262.7). This means that prices have increased 262.7% between 1967 and 1990. An index number is a percent, but the percent sign is omitted in the index. We can convert the index to monetary terms by moving the decimal point two places to the left. (362.7 ÷ 100) = 3.627) Therefore, we had to pay $3.63 to purchase the same quantity and value of goods in 1990 that would have cost us $1.00 in 1967.

If we want to use the CPI to compare the price changes for any two of the years presented in the index, we use the percent of increase or decrease procedure presented in the preceding section of this chapter. First, we find the difference between the two index values; then we divide the difference by the index value of the earlier year.

Example 11

Verify the rate of inflation between 1987 and 1988 in the Consumer Price Index (Table 3.1).

Solution

Step 1:   Identify the given variables.

base = 346.1   earlier period index

rate = unknown   percent of inflation

part = 16.6   difference in indexes between the two periods
(current period − earlier period = difference)

$$362.7 - 346.1 = 16.6$$

Step 2:   Insert the variables into the formula and solve.

$$R = \frac{part\ (difference)}{base\ (earlier\ period\ value)}$$

$$R = \frac{16.6}{346.1}$$

$$R = .047963, \text{ or } 4.8\% \text{ increase}$$

A 4.8% increase in inflation suggests that a person would need to have had at least a 4.8% wage increase in 1988 to maintain the same purchasing

Table 3.1

Consumer Price
Index

Year	Index	% of in-flation
1967	100.0	2.9
1968	104.2	4.2
1969	109.8	5.4
1970	116.3	5.9
1971	121.3	4.3
1972	125.3	3.3
1973	133.1	6.2
1974	147.7	11.0
1975	161.2	9.1
1976	170.5	5.8
1977	181.5	6.5
1978	195.3	7.6
1979	217.7	11.5
1980	245.5	12.8
1981	272.3	10.9
1982	288.6	10.6
1983	298.4	3.4
1984	311.1	4.3
1985	322.2	3.6
1986	331.1	2.8
1987	346.1	4.5
1988	362.7	4.8
1989	379.4	4.6
1990	402.5	6.1
1991	415.0	3.1

power he or she had in 1987. Any percent less would have resulted in a loss of purchasing power; any percent greater would have indicated a gain in purchasing power.

Example 12 illustrates another useful application of the CPI.

Example 12

If the CPI for 1 ounce of gold was 242.8 in 1980 compared to a CPI of 386.4 in 1990, how much would it cost in 1990 for an ounce of gold that would have cost $240 in 1980?

Solution

Step 1:   Identify the given variables.

base = 242.8   earlier period index

rate = unknown   rate of inflation for the period

part = 143.6   difference in indexes between two periods

Step 2:   Insert the variables into the formula and solve.

$$R = \frac{\text{part (difference)}}{\text{base (earlier period index)}}$$

$$R = \frac{143.6}{242.8}$$

$$R = .5914332, \text{ or } 59.1\% \text{ increase}$$

Step 3:   Multiply the earlier cost (base) by the rate of increase plus 1 to find the current cost.

$$P = B \times R$$

$$P = \$240 \times 1.591 \qquad (1.00 + .591)$$

$$P = \$381.84$$

Because the part is greater than the base, we add the percent of increase (59.1%) to the base percent (100%) to accurately state the rate (159.1%). The part ($381.84) then represents 159.1% of the base.

CHECK YOUR KNOWLEDGE

Price indexes

1. Calculate the rate of inflation on a textbook that sold for $57 in 1990 compared to $32 in 1985.

2. What is the rate of inflation of an item with a CPI of 120.8 in 1980 and a CPI of 238.4 in 1990?

3. Compute the yearly inflation rate of a half-gallon of milk for each of the following years:

Year	Price
1989	$1.10
1990	1.18
1991	1.24
1992	1.39

4. The price index for a 19-inch color television set was 172.6 in 1975 and 365.8 in 1990. How much would a comparable set cost in 1990, if the 1975 price was $129?

5. If the price index for a gallon of unleaded gasoline was 162.9 in July of 1987 compared to 120.3 in July of 1988, what was the rate of inflation for the period?

3.5 EXERCISES

For problems 1 through 5, calculate the difference and the percent increase or decrease from original to current amounts. Round your answers to the nearest tenth percent.

Item	Original amount	Current amount
1. Gasoline (per gal.)	$1.31%10	$.89%10
2. Automobile	$8,399	$8,785
3. Student enrollment	6,480	7,695
4. Personal computer	$1,499	$1,029
5. Fixed-interest rate	12.95	9.50

For problems 6 through 10, provide the missing information where indicated. Round answers to nearest tenth percent, whole cent, or number.

Item	Original amount	Current amount	Amount of difference	Percent change
6. Sport coat	$79.00	_____	− $20.00	_____
7. Common stock share	_____	67⅞	2¼	_____
8. Net profit	$128,600.00	~~166 60.8~~	~~11450 60.8~~	12.8%
9. Units of production	250,000	233,750	_____	_____
10. Hourly wage	$10.50	_____	_____	− 3%

Answers to CYK: *1.* 78.1%   *2.* 97.4%   *3.* 1989 = 0%; 1990 = 7.3%; 1991 = 5.1%; 1992 = 12.1%
4. $273.35   *5.* 26.2% decrease

Using the following prices, calculate the rate of inflation for each year. Round your answers to tenths.

	Year	Price
11.	1988	17.00
12.	1989	21.50
13.	1990	18.75
14.	1991	20.45
15.	1992	24.00

Solve the following percent increase or decrease problems and round your answers to the nearest tenth of a percent.

16. Maria Torres's annual salary was $15,000 before she received a promotion to head teller. She now receives an annual salary of $16,500. What is the rate of change in her salary?

17. Last season, Silver Bluffs Ski Association was open for business a total of 50 days. This season, weather conditions were more favorable, which permitted the association to offer 65 days of skiing. What is the percent change in the number of days Silver Bluffs was open for business?

18. The property tax in Richland County increased this past year to $180.00 per $1,000 of assessed evaluation. What is the percent change if last year's rate was $160.00?

19. Agri-Mart sold 340 lawnmowers this year, which was 60 more than they sold last year during the same period. What is the percent change in sales of mowers for the period?

20. In 1991, the Dudick family received utility bills amounting to $1,345.00, which included $960 for natural gas to heat their home. This year the Dudick's heating costs decreased to $840 after their home was insulated. What was the percent change in heating costs?

21. The Allied Manufacturing Company recently reduced its workforce from 5,200 to 3,700. Allied intends to recall 500 of the laid-off workers over the next two weeks. What is the percent change in the size of the workforce as a result of these decisions?

22. Over the past 2 years, the liability insurance premiums for the West End Football Association increased from $1,600 per year to $2,400 per year. What was the percent change in insurance premiums during the 2-year period?

23. Bart's Service Station sold 3,200 fewer gallons of gasoline during the month of December than it sold in November. If gasoline sales for December were 62,845 gallons, what was the rate of change in gasoline sales for the month?

24. A pair of sneakers cost $60.00. This same pair of sneakers sold for $25.00 5 years ago. What was the rate of inflation over the 5-year period?

25. The CPI for 1985 was 322.2, compared with a CPI of 379.4 for 1989. What was (a) the rate of inflation during the 5-year period, (b) the cost of an item in 1989 if that same item cost $45.00 in 1985?

EXPRESS YOUR THOUGHTS

Compose one or two well-written sentences to express the requested information.

1. Identify and briefly define the three key variables of the percent formula.

2. If a percentage problem contained the numbers 20 and 80, and you were asked to find the rate, how would you determine which of those two numbers is the base?

3. Explain how you would solve the following:

15 is 25% of what number?

4. Develop a step-by-step procedure to determine which variables are given and which variable is missing in the following:

What number is 120% of 400?

5. Explain in detail the procedure required to calculate the rate of increase or decrease.

6. Describe how you would use the Consumer Price Index to determine the rate of inflation between 1967 and 1980.

7. Explain how to convert an index of 298.4 to monetary terms.

8. Describe how you would develop a price index for an item that sold for $1.25 in 1989, $1.32 in 1990, and $1.44 in 1991.

Case exercise   Family medical services

Family Medical Services allows its patients 30 days to make payment for services that are not covered by insurance. Any payments not received within 90 days are considered bad debts and are turned over to Healthcare Collections.

This year, Family Medical Services billed patients a total of $289,000 compared to $237,000 last year. Family Medical Services declared 2½% of its current year billing's as bad debts, which was ⅜% less than last year's rate.

Healthcare Collections charges its clients 3¾% of the amount they are able to collect as their fee for services. Healthcare Collections promotes a collection success rate of 96% of the accounts they accept.

Answer the following questions using the information in the case. Express your answers to the nearest tenth percent, or whole cent.

A. What was the amount of the bad debts remitted by Family Medical Services this year to Healthcare Collections?

B. What is the percent change in both billed services and bad debts?

C. How much money would Healthcare Collections receive this year for its services if they were able to collect an amount equal to their success rate?

D. What was the amount of bad debts declared by Family Medical Services last year?

E. How much money did Healthcare Collections remit to Family Medical Services last year if they were successful in collecting 92% of the bad debts?

SELF-TEST

A. Terminology review

Complete the following items using the key terms presented at the beginning of the chapter. Check your responses against the answer key at the end of the test.

1. The ___rate___ is the percent of the base to be calculated.

2. We use the terms "whole" and "total" when we are referring to the ___Base___.

3. The __part__ is a portion of the base and is always expressed as a number.

4. The expression $P = B \times R$ is referred to as the __%equation__

5. The rate is also referred to as a __%__ of the base.

6. When the current value is larger than the original value, the rate will be stated as a __% increase__

7. A __% decrease__ results when the current value is less than the original value.

8. We are solving for the __base__ when we divide the part by the rate.

9. The __Rate__ is found by dividing the part by the base.

10. The difference in a percent-of-change problem is found by subtracting the __original__ value from the __current__ value.

B. Calculation review

The following concepts and short problems are designed to test your understanding of the objectives identified at the beginning of the chapter. Answers are provided at the end of the test. Solve for each.

11. A community college employs 630 people. If 30% of the employees are faculty, how many faculty members are employed by the college?

12. If you are required to make a down payment of 5% on the purchase of a new home that amounts to $4,250 of the selling price, what is the selling price?

13. The budget of the Reddy Corporation consists of the following items and respective amounts: salaries $250,000, equipment $85,000, supplies $12,000, administrative expenses $25,000, maintenance $10,000, advertising $18,000, and production material inventory $600,000. What percent of the budget is allocated for salaries, supplies, advertising expense, and equipment collectively?

14. If you earned $30,000 this year, which represents a 6% increase over last year's annual income, what was your annual income last year?

15. If a manufacturer sells an item for $40 per unit, which includes a unit labor cost of $8, what percent of the unit price is the labor cost?

16. Find the percent change in sales for Lakeside Marina if they sold six more Lazer sailboats this year than last year. Last year, the marina sold 24 sailboats.

17. If an employee's absences last year accounted for 4,000 lost work-hours compared to 5,500 lost work-hours this year, what was the percent change?

18. Last month you paid $.89 for a head of lettuce at the grocery store. This month the selling price for a head of lettuce is $.69. What is the rate of inflation?

19. If sales are $1,250,000 after a 15% decrease, what were sales before the decrease?

20. A hamburger at Art's Diner cost 75 cents in 1975. Art adjusts his prices based on the CPI. If the CPI was 161.2 in 1975, how much did Art charge for a hamburger in 1985 with a CPI of 322.2?

Answers to self-test: *1.* rate   *2.* base   *3.* part   *4.* percent equation   *5.* percent   *6.* percent increase   *7.* percent decrease   *8.* base   *9.* rate   *10.* original, current   *11.* 189   *12.* house cost = $85,000; salary = $28,333.33   *13.* 36.5%   *14.* $28,301.89   *15.* 20%   *16.* 25%   *17.* 27.27%   *18.* −22.47%   *19.* 1,470,588.20   *20.* $1.50

4

Key terms

wages
gross earnings
overtime rate
regular rate
time-and-a-half
double time
shift differential
incentive rate
piece rate
task and bonus plan
salary
exempt
nonexempt
commission
take-home pay
mandatory deductions
state disability insurance
   (SDI)
Federal Insurance Contri-
   butions Act (FICA)
Social Security Fund
medicare tax
federal income withhold-
   ing tax (FWT)
wage bracket method
percentage method
Employer's Tax Guide
   Circular E
state income withholding
   tax (SWT)
elective deductions
Federal Unemployment
   Tax Act (FUTA)
State Unemployment Tax
   Act (SUTA)

PAYROLL SYSTEMS

Learning objectives

1. Calculate gross earnings based on hourly, incentive, or salary payroll systems.

2. Identify and calculate the various types of employee payroll deductions.

3. Identify and calculate the various types of employer payroll taxes.

4. Complete payroll records and quarterly payroll tax returns.

5. Define the key terms.

INTRODUCTION

The payroll is an extremely important subsystem of the accounting system because most organizations expend close to one-third of their revenues for labor costs and associated taxes. Expressed another way, generally, the largest single expense for many businesses is the payroll. Control of a cost as significant as payroll is vital to the achievement of the profit goals of an enterprise.

Employees of a firm provide services for which they expect and are guaranteed under legal statutes to receive compensation at established intervals. Therefore, the payroll system must be accurate and capable of processing data within the required time limitations. In addition, the system must provide internal audits of the procedures and technology to assure the proper use of funds.

Municipal agencies at the federal, state, and local levels have established laws that require employers to collect data in their payroll records concerning compensation, deductions, and taxes. This information is then used by the employer to prepare periodic reports for government agencies that identify the payments required for amounts withheld from employees and for employer payroll taxes.

Employees generally are compensated on the basis of time and work performed. For example, managerial or administrative personnel usually receive a compensation for their services expressed in terms of a week, month, or year. Most skilled and unskilled workers receive compensation for their labor based on hours of working time or piecework. Employees may receive other forms of compensation in addition to their base earnings such as overtime premiums, cost-of-living adjustments (COLA), profit-sharing plans, commissions, shift differentials, bonuses, and compensatory time. The payment of compensation to an employee is generally in the form of a check or cash. However, an employee may also be compensated in other forms such as merchandise, services, or property, based on the fair value of cash in payment for the employee's services. In this chapter, we will present the most common methods used to determine an employee's gross earnings, the procedures required to calculate deductions and net earnings, and the computations necessary to complete payroll tax records.

4.1   GROSS EARNINGS: HOURLY WAGES

When an employee receives compensation for his or her services by the hour, the employee's **wages** are determined by the number of hours worked during the pay period and the hourly rate paid by the employer

F or **Y** our **I** nformation

Changing American work hours

Americans are working longer and harder than ever before. Instead of creating more leisure time, as Europeans have done, Americans today have less leisure time. In the last 20 years, the amount of time spent on the job has increased approximately 9 hours per year, or slightly more than 1 additional day of work per year. While the annual change is small, the accumulated increase over the 20-year period amounts to 160 hours, or 1 extra month. The

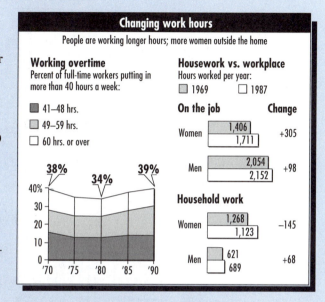

Changing work hours

People are working longer hours; more women outside the home

Working overtime
Percent of full-time workers putting in more than 40 hours a week:

- ▉ 41–48 hrs.
- ▨ 49–59 hrs.
- ☐ 60 hrs. or over

Housework vs. workplace
Hours worked per year:
☐ 1969   ☐ 1987

On the job   **Change**

Women   1,406 / 1,711   +305

Men   2,054 / 2,152   +98

Household work

Women   1,268 / 1,123   −145

Men   621 / 689   +68

increase in work hours is attributed in part to the decline in real wages since 1973, coupled with the increased cost of health care and housing, and to women taking jobs covering a greater part of the year. Time spent on household work did decrease but not enough to stem the loss in leisure time. (Women are devoting more hours to the workplace and fewer hours to the household, and men are devoting more time to the household *and* to the workplace.)

The trends in work and leisure time are the direct inverse of the predictions that experts made 30 years ago. Automation, productivity, growth, and consumer satiation have not increased leisure time as expected.

Source: Knight-Ridder Tribune Graphics (based on data from Julliet Schor, "The Overworked American," U.S. Bureau of Labor Statistics), as it appeared in the Syracuse *Herald-Journal*, March 15, 1992. Used with permission.

Learning objective
Calculate gross earnings based on hourly payroll systems.

for the job. These two variables, time and rate, are the basis of determining the employee's **gross earnings** under the hourly wage method. Gross earnings is the total compensation earned by an employee during a pay period before mandatory and elective deductions are withheld by the employer. The computation of gross earnings can be expressed by the following equation.

Figure 4.1

Sample payroll time card

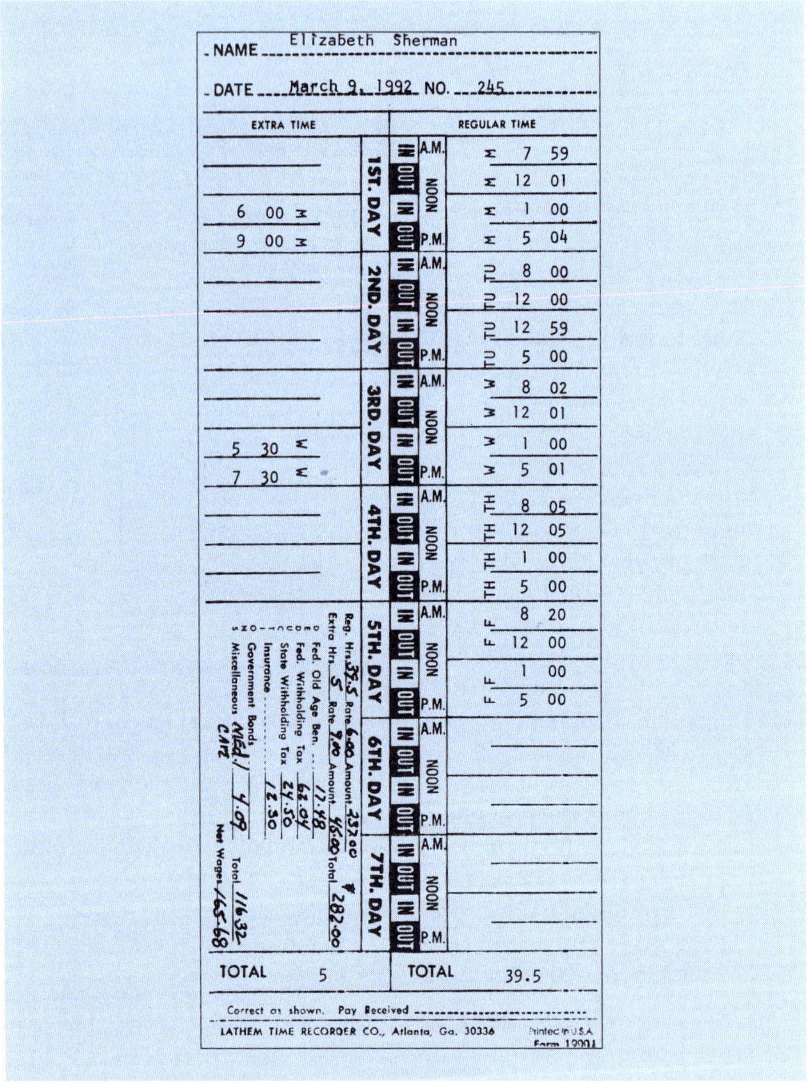
NAME Elizabeth Sherman

DATE March 9, 1992 NO. 245

EXTRA TIME			REGULAR TIME
	1ST. DAY	IN A.M.	M 7 59
		OUT NOON	M 12 01
6 00 M		IN NOON	M 1 00
9 00 M		OUT P.M.	M 5 04
	2ND. DAY	IN A.M.	TU 8 00
		OUT NOON	TU 12 00
		IN NOON	TU 12 59
		OUT P.M.	TU 5 00
	3RD. DAY	IN A.M.	W 8 02
		OUT NOON	W 12 01
5 30 W		IN NOON	W 1 00
7 30 W		OUT P.M.	W 5 01
	4TH. DAY	IN A.M.	TH 8 05
		OUT NOON	TH 12 05
		IN NOON	TH 1 00
		OUT P.M.	TH 5 00
	5TH. DAY	IN A.M.	F 8 20
		OUT NOON	F 12 00
		IN NOON	F 1 00
		OUT P.M.	F 5 00
	6TH. DAY	IN A.M. / OUT NOON / IN NOON / OUT P.M.	
	7TH. DAY	IN A.M. / OUT NOON / IN NOON / OUT P.M.	
TOTAL 5		TOTAL	39.5

Reg. Hrs. 39.5 Rate 6.00 Amount 237.00

Extra Hrs. 5 Rate 9.00 Amount 45.00 Total 282.00

DEDUCTIONS

Fed. Old Age Ben. 17.48

Fed. Withholding Tax 62.04

State Withholding Tax 24.50

Insurance 12.30

Government Bonds

Miscellaneous Med./CAFE 4.09 Total 116.32

Net Wages 165.68

Correct as shown. Pay Received

LATHEM TIME RECORDER CO., Atlanta, Ga. 30336 Printed in U.S.A. Form 1900J

Source: Latham Time Recorder Co. Used with permission.

Gross earnings for regular time

gross earnings = hours worked × rate per hour

Hourly employees are usually required to maintain *time cards* similar to the one shown in Figure 4.1. The data on the time card is later recorded on an *employee earnings record* (Figure 4.2) and in the *payroll register* (Figure 4.3), which is a record of all employees' payroll information.

Figure 4.2

Sample employee earnings record

EMPLOYEE'S INDIVIDUAL EARNINGS RECORD

2nd Quarter of 19 9X

Name __George Anderson__   Social Security No. __364-56-8573__   Phone No. __487-2406__
Address __136 First Street__   City __Detroit__   State __Michigan__   ZIP __48226__
Position __QC Inspector__   Pay Rate __$10.50__   Pay Period __Weekly__
Male _X_ Female ____ Married X Single ____   Number of Exemptions _3_   Date Employed ___9/12/86___

| | EARNINGS | | | DEDUCTIONS | | | | | | | | | Check | Year-to- |
Wk	Regular	Overtime	Total	FICA	MEDCR	FIT	SIT	SDI	INS	RET	MISC	NET PAY	number	date
1	$420		$420.00	26.04	6.09	92.40	28.60	3.20	8.40	24.00		231.27	1549	5,482.35
2	420	85.00	505.00	31.31	7.32	99.80	34.25	3.20	8.40	28.50		292.22	1638	5,987.35
3	420	52.00	472.00	29.26	6.84	95.75	31.10	3.20	8.40	26.30		271.50	1789	6,459.35
4	420		420.00	26.04	6.09	92.40	28.60	3.20	8.40	24.00		231.27	1854	6,879.35
5	420	78.75	498.75	30.92	7.23	97.60	32.80	3.20	8.40	27.45		298.90	1931	7,378.10
6														
7														
8														
9														
10														
11														
12														
13														
QUARTER TOTALS														

Example 1

Compute the gross earnings for Elizabeth Sherman based on the regular time and rate data on the time card shown in Figure 4.1.

Solution

Insert the total hours worked for the week and the regular rate of pay into the equation and multiply as shown.

$$\text{gross earnings} = \text{hours worked} \times \text{regular rate per hour}$$
$$= 39.5 \qquad \times \$6.00$$
$$= \$237.00$$

OVERTIME AND PREMIUM WAGES

Salary and hourly wage rates are determined by a number of factors; one is the *Fair Labor Standards Act*, commonly known as the *wage and hour*

Figure 4.3

Sample payroll register

Payroll Register

Week no. 7   Beginning 2/10   Ending 2/16

Record for 1st Quarter of 199X

Name	Status	Exemptions	Rates Reg.	Rates O.T.	Hrs. worked Reg.	Hrs. worked O.T.	Earnings Reg.	Earnings O.T.	Gross earnings	FICA	MEDCR	FWT	SWT	RET	Net earnings
Adams, T	S	1	6.50	9.75	40	0	260.00		260.00	16.12	3.77	46.80	24.45	12.00	156.86
Butler, G	M	3	9.40	14.10	40	10	376.00	141.00	517.00	32.05	7.50	98.40	42.55	24.00	312.50
Duncan, L	M	2	10.00	15.00	35	0	350.00		350.00	21.70	5.08	62.40	28.50	14.00	218.32
Ford, Z	S	1	8.60	12.90	40	5	344.00	64.50	408.50	25.33	5.92	73.44	34.50	18.20	251.11
Harter, P	M	4	12.25	18.38	40	12	490.00	220.56	710.56	44.05	10.30	134.90	58.30	30.50	432.51
Jordan, R	M	2	10.00	15.00	40	0	400.00		400.00	24.80	5.80	72.20	33.10	15.00	249.10
Kowalski, G	S	1	8.60	12.90	40	0	344.00		344.00	21.33	4.99	60.25	26.75	12.80	217.88
Martino, J	M	2	9.40	14.10	40	6	376.00	84.60	460.60	28.56	6.68	82.80	37.40	20.00	285.16
Nowak, J	S	2	8.60	12.90	40	0	344.00		344.00	21.33	4.99	52.40	24.50	12.80	227.98
Potter, S	M	3	12.25	18.38	40	0	490.00		490.00	30.38	7.11	88.20	39.60	22.40	302.31
Reddy, M	S	1	6.50	9.75	40	0	260.00		260.00	16.12	3.77	46.80	24.45	12.00	156.86
Sawyer, T	M	2	10.00	15.00	40	8	400.00	120.00	520.00	32.24	7.54	84.40	38.30	25.00	332.52
Williamson, F	M	3	9.40	14.10	40	0	376.00		376.00	23.31	5.45	58.20	25.60	16.00	247.44
Pay period total							4,810.00	630.66	5,440.66	337.32	78.90	961.19	438.00	234.70	3,390.55

law. This legislation, which covers the majority of full-time hourly wage employees, establishes the minimum hourly wage ($4.25 as of March 31, 1991) and sets the regular workweek at 40 hours. While the law has been expanded in recent years to include state, county, and city hourly workers, it continues to exclude business executives, administrators, employees of small retail organizations, specified seasonal agricultural workers, and those in professional occupations like teachers, lawyers, and medical doctors. The 40-hour workweek requires the employer to pay an **overtime rate** (for hours worked in excess of 40 per week) of at least one and one-half the **regular rate**. This overtime rate is expressed as **time-and-a-half** ($1\frac{1}{2}$) and can be determined by one of the two methods presented in Example 2 using the equation below.

Formula for gross earnings with overtime

gross earnings = regular earnings + overtime earnings
$$(H \times R) + (H \times 1.5R)$$

Example 2

Todd Marshall's time card indicated that he worked 8 hours Monday; 10 hours Tuesday; 9½ hours Wednesday; 7 hours Thursday; and 10¾ hours Friday. Todd receives a regular rate of $8.50 per hour and time-and-a-half for overtime. Determine his gross earnings for the week.

Solution 1

Standard Overtime Method

Step 1: Determine total number of hours worked and overtime hours.

$$8 + 10 + 9.5 + 7 + 10.75 = \quad 45.25 \text{ total hours}$$
$$\underline{-40.00} \text{ regular hours}$$
$$5.25 \text{ overtime hours}$$

Step 2: Determine the overtime rate.

$$8.50 \times 1.5 = \$12.75 \text{ per hour}$$

Step 3: Insert the data into the earnings equation and solve.

gross earnings = regular earnings + overtime earnings
$$= (40 \times 8.50) \quad + (5.25 \times 12.75)$$
$$= \$340.00 \quad\quad + \$66.9375$$
$$= \$406.94$$

Note: When computing gross earnings, round your answer to the nearest whole cent in the final calculation.

CALCULATOR SOLUTION

Keyed entry	Display
AC 40 × 8.5 =	340
Min	340
5.25 × 1.5 × 8.50 =	66.9375
M+	66.9375
MR	406.9375

Some companies prefer the *overtime premium method* to calculate gross wages with overtime. This method produces the same gross wage but is computed by adding the total hours worked at the regular rate to the overtime hours at the premium rate (one-half regular rate).

Solution 2

Overtime Premium Method

Step 1:   Determine the total hours worked and overtime hours.

$$8 + 10 + 9.5 + 7 + 10.75 = \quad 45.25 \text{ total hours}$$
$$-\underline{40.00} \text{ regular hours}$$
$$5.25 \text{ overtime hours}$$

Step 2:   Determine the overtime premium rate.

$$\$8.50 \times .5 = \$4.25$$

Step 3:   Insert the data into the earnings equation and solve.

$$\begin{aligned} \text{gross earnings} &= \text{regular earnings} & &+ \text{ overtime earnings} \\ &= (45.25 \times 8.50) & &+ (5.25 \times 4.25) \\ &= \$384.625 & &+ \$22.3125 \\ &= \$406.9375 \text{ or } \$406.94 \end{aligned}$$

The overtime premium method provides a more distinct analysis of labor costs since it considers $4.25 (one-half the regular rate) to be the actual additional cost of each overtime hour, compared to the $12.75 (time and one-half) rate used with the standard overtime method.

Many companies pay the time-and-a-half rate for all time worked over eight hours in one day regardless of how many hours are worked during a week. This *daily overtime* exceeds the requirements of the Fair Labor

Standards Act and is usually determined through collective bargaining and stated in the labor agreement. The next example shows how to calculate gross earnings using the daily overtime method to determine the premium wage.

Example 3

Lynette Elbert worked 8½ hours on Monday, 8 hours on Tuesday, 10 hours on Wednesday, 9 hours on Thursday, and was absent from work on Friday. Her regular hourly rate of pay is $10.20. Find her gross earnings for the week.

Solution

Step 1: Determine the regular hours and overtime hours worked.

	M	T	W	T	F	Total hours
Regular	8	8	8	8	0	32.0
Overtime	.5	0	2	1	0	3.5

Step 2: Determine the overtime rate.

$10.20 \times 1.5 = \$15.30$

Step 3: Insert the rate into the earnings equation and solve.

$$\begin{aligned}
\text{gross earnings} &= \text{regular earnings} + \text{overtime earnings} \\
&= (32 \times \$10.20) + (3.5 \times \$15.30) \\
&= \$326.40 \qquad\quad + \$53.55 \\
&= \$379.95
\end{aligned}$$

Elbert is paid time-and-a-half for the .5 hour of overtime Monday, 2 hours of overtime Wednesday, and 1 hour of overtime Thursday because she worked more than 8 hours each of these 3 days. For the week, she worked a total of 35.5 hours of which 3.5 hours were overtime and 32 were regular time.

The labor agreement is also the basis for other premium wage payments such as **double time** and **shift differentials**. Double time (twice the regular hourly rate) is paid for holidays and sometimes weekend work. A shift-differential is an additional amount per hour paid to employees who work other than the day shift, such as the second shift (4 P.M. to 12 A.M.) and the graveyard shift (12 A.M. to 8 A.M.). Example 4 illustrates how to calculate gross earnings when an employee receives both double time and a shift differential.

Example 4

Debbie Gonski works the 4 P.M.– 12 A.M. shift at Rexford Handling. She is paid $7.58 per hour and a 20-cent shift differential for her work. Last week, she worked five 8-hour shifts. Find her gross earnings for the week if she is paid double-time for one of her 8-hour shifts because she worked a holiday.

Solution   *Step 1:*   Determine the regular hours and premium hours worked.

$4 \times 8 = 32$ regular hours
$1 \times 8 = \underline{8}$ premium hours
$ 40$ total hours

Step 2:   Determine the premium rate.

$(7.58 + .20) \times 2 = \$15.56$

Step 3:   Insert the data into the earnings equation and solve.

gross earnings = regular earnings + premium earnings
$ = (32 \times \$7.78) \quad + (8 \times \$15.56)$
$ = \$248.96 + \$124.48$
$ = \$373.44$

The $7.78 is the regular rate even though it includes the shift differential because this is the amount the employee regularly receives for each hour of work. Some employers will consider the extra 20-cent shift differential as premium earnings and record it separately on the employee's earnings record.

CHECK YOUR KNOWLEDGE

Calculating hourly wage earnings and overtime earnings

1. Robin Anderson is paid $4.50 an hour as a nurse's aid. Find her gross earnings for the current week if she worked a total of 38 hours.

2. Last week, Ed Ramsey worked 48 hours. Find his (a) regular earnings, (b) overtime earnings, and (c) gross earnings for the week if he is paid $6.40 per hour and receives time-and-a-half for hours worked in excess of 40. (Use the standard overtime method.)

3. Using the information in problem 2, recalculate parts a, b, and c based on the overtime premium method.

R = 38 = 220.40
1½ = 5.25 = 8.70 = 45.68
D = 5 = 11.60 = .58

4. Rick LaValle earns $5.80 per hour and is paid time-and-a-half for all time over 8 hours in any 1 day. His company also pays double time for holidays and Sundays. Find his gross earnings for a week in which he works the following hours: Monday, 10½; Tuesday, 8; Wednesday, 9; Thursday, 6; Friday, 9¾; and Sunday, 5 hours. (Use the standard over-time method.)

5. Tad Nichols works the third shift (12:00 A.M.–8:00 A.M.) at Rapid Waters Chemical Company and is paid $9.62 per hour. Rapid Waters Chemical Company pays its hourly workers an additional $.28 per hour for the third-shift hours and time-and-a-half for all overtime hours. Calculate Tad's gross earnings for the week if his time card shows that he worked 40 regular hours and 6 overtime hours.

4.2 GROSS EARNINGS: PIECEWORK

Learning objective
Calculate gross earnings based on incentive payroll systems.

Organizations in the manufacturing of goods, agriculture, and building construction may compensate some of their employees with **incentive rates** instead of *time rates*. When incentive rates are used, an employee's gross earnings are based on job performance instead of time worked. Piecework encourages employees to increase their productivity in order to increase their gross earnings. A **piece rate** is determined through a time and motion study of a job, and that rate is paid to the employee for each acceptable unit produced. Employees may also receive a premium rate for all units produced beyond established quotas. Employers are generally willing to pay higher wages for such increases in productivity as long as the units meet quality control requirements. Defective units often increase cost and decrease profits because of the loss of labor time and material. An employer, therefore, may require an employee to reimburse the company for part of the loss related to his or her defective units through a charge-back. *Chargebacks* reduce an employee's earnings; they are considered a penalty and are usually set at a rate lower than what was paid to produce the unit. There are a number of piecework plans in use in today's businesses. We will discuss the most commonly used plans in this section.

The basic *straight piecework* plan pays the employee a fixed amount for each unit of production. Under this plan the gross earnings are found using the following formula:

Answers to CYK: *1.* $171.00 *2.* a. $256.00; b. $76.80; c. $332.80 *3.* a. $307.20; b. $25.60; c. $332.80 *4.* $324.08 *5.* $485.10

Gross earnings for straight piecework

gross earnings = (number of units × rate per unit)

Example 5

Jorge Swensen works in an electrical manufacturing firm and is paid $.75 for each switch he assembles that passes quality control inspections. His production card for the week indicated that he assembled 120 switches on Monday; 118 on Tuesday; 126 on Wednesday; 105 on Thursday; and 96 on Friday. Fifteen of those switches had been rejected by inspectors. If the company uses a chargeback of $.50 per defective unit, calculate Jorge's gross earnings for the week.

Solution

First, determine the total number of units produced.

Monday	120
Tuesday	118
Wednesday	126
Thursday	105
Friday	96
	565 units produced

Now, insert the appropriate variables into the equation and solve.

$$\begin{aligned}
\text{gross earnings} &= (\text{number of units} \times \text{rate per unit}) \\
&\quad - (\text{defective units} \times \text{defective rate}) \\
&= (565 \times \$.75) - (15 \times \$.50) \\
&= \$423.75 - \$7.50 \\
&= \$416.25
\end{aligned}$$

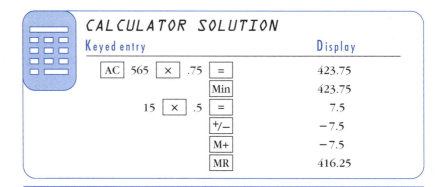

CALCULATOR SOLUTION

Keyed entry	Display
AC 565 × .75 =	423.75
Min	423.75
15 × .5 =	7.5
+/−	−7.5
M+	−7.5
MR	416.25

Many companies use the *differential piece-rate plan*, which incorporates a premium rate for units produced above established standards. Differential piece-rate schedules are prepared that identify the required level of production and the corresponding rate paid per unit. The schedule can be based on a 40-hour workweek, 8-hour workday, or hourly productivity. This plan provides the incentive to produce more because the employee's gross earnings increase more in proportion to units produced than with the straight piece-rate plan. The reason being, the employee receives higher rates of pay per unit for different levels of production. To illustrate this concept, let's compare the information in Example 5 to that in Example 6.

Example 6

The electrical manufacturing firm's differential piece-rate schedule is as follows:

Weekly net standard units	Rate per unit
0–300	$ .70
301–400	.85
401–500	.95
501–600	1.05
Over 600	1.15

Determine Jorge Swensen's gross earnings using this schedule.

Solution

The gross earnings for Jorge would be calculated in the following manner.

first	300 units at $ .70	$210.00
next	100 units at .85	85.00
next	100 units at .95	95.00
last	65 units at 1.05	68.25
	565 total units accepted	$458.25 piecework earnings

gross earnings = piecework earnings − chargeback
= $458.25 − (15 × $.50)
= $458.25 − $7.50
= $450.75

As you can see, using the differential piece-rate plan, Jorge receives $34.50 ($450.75 − 416.25) more in gross earnings for the 565 units he produced.

CALCULATOR SOLUTION

Keyed entry	Display
AC 300 × .7 =	210
Min	210
100 × .85 =	85
M+	85
100 × .95 =	95
M+	95
65 × 1.05 =	68.25
M+	68.25
MR	458.25
15 × .5 =	7.5
+/−	−7.5
M+	−7.5
MR	450.75

In Section 4.1, we discussed the Fair Labor Standards Act, which sets the minimum wage for employees. To conform with this law, a company will provide an *hourly rate/piecework plan*, which includes an hourly rate guarantee if gross earnings from piecework is less than the required minimum wage rate. While the hourly rate cannot be below the minimum wage level, it can be as high as that determined by management and labor. Whatever the hourly rate, the employer must pay either the hourly rate or the piece rate, whichever is higher. This plan can be based on each hour of work, each job order, or each 8-hour workday. For example, if the hourly base is used, a worker who is paid $.55 per unit or $6.60 per hour would be paid $6.60 for any hour that 12 or fewer units were produced ($6.60 ÷ .55 = 12 units) and straight piece-rate for any hour that 13 or more units were produced (13 × $.55 = $7.15). Let's look at an example based on an 8-hour day.

Example 7

The Armstrong Manufacturing Company pays its production workers $8.40 an hour or $.30 per unit of production, whichever is higher. Find the weekly gross earnings for an employee, based on the following production record, if the employee worked 8 hours each day.

Day	Units of production
Monday	210
Tuesday	235
Wednesday	220
Thursday	240
Friday	215

Solution

We must calculate the pay for each day based on the piece rate and compare it to the hourly rate ($8 \times \$8.40 = \$67.20$).

Day	Piece rate	Hourly rate	Gross earnings
Monday	$210 \times .30 = \$63.00$	$ 67.20	$ 67.20 hourly
Tuesday	$235 \times .30 = 70.50$	67.20	70.50 piece
Wednesday	$220 \times .30 = 66.00$	67.20	67.20 hourly
Thursday	$240 \times .30 = 72.00$	67.20	72.00 piece
Friday	$215 \times .30 = 64.50$	67.20	67.20 hourly
		$336.00	$344.10 total gross earnings

Another approach to solving Example 7 would be to divide the daily hourly wage by the piece rate, which will give you the daily task standard ($\$67.20 \div \$.30 = 224$ units). Any units produced above this daily task standard will result in higher daily wages that must be calculated, such as Tuesday's 235 and Thursday's 240 units of production.

The final piecework plan we will discuss in this section is called the **task and bonus plan**. Under this plan, the task (productivity per time period) is established and, if the worker produces less than task, the hourly rate is paid similar to the hourly ÷ piece-rate plan. If, however, the worker performs equal to or greater than task, a *bonus* (additional compensation) is paid. The following equation can be used to calculate gross earnings when a bonus is to be paid.

Gross earnings when bonus is paid

gross earnings = (bonus factor) × (hourly rate) × (hours) × (production task)

The *bonus factor* in the equation is a percentage agreed upon by management and labor as the additional monetary reward paid to the worker for equaling or exceeding the task requirement.

Example 8

Lisa Jarrett packages small appliances and has a task requirement of 120 units during an 8-hour period. Her job pays a bonus factor of 115%. Find her gross earnings for an 8-hour day in which she packaged 162 appliances. Lisa's hourly rate is $4.87 an hour.

Solution

Insert the required variables into the equation and solve. Note: Convert the bonus factor and the production ratio to decimals.

$$
\begin{aligned}
\text{gross earnings} &= \text{bonus factor} \times \text{hourly rate} \times \text{hours} \\
&\qquad \times \text{production task} \\
&= 115\% \ \times \$4.87 \times 8 \times 162/120 \\
&= 1.15 \ \ \times \$4.87 \times 8 \times 1.35 \\
&= \$60.49
\end{aligned}
$$

If Lisa had packaged less than 120 appliances, her daily gross earnings would be $38.96 (8 × $4.87).

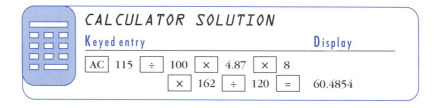

CALCULATOR SOLUTION

Keyed entry   Display

| AC | 115 | ÷ | 100 | × | 4.87 | × | 8 | | |
| | | | × | 162 | ÷ | 120 | = | 60.4854 |

Employers must pay time-and-a-half for overtime to piecework employees if their earnings are regulated by the 40-hour workweek. The overtime rate is usually 1½ times the regular rate for each hour worked over 40 in the workweek. The regular rate of pay is computed by adding together earnings for the week from piecework, other hours worked, waiting time, and bonuses. This total is then divided by the total number of hours worked during the pay period to determine the regular rate for the week. The gross earnings for the pay period will be the total of the regular earnings and overtime earnings (gross earnings = regular earnings + overtime earnings). Example 9 illustrates how to calculate overtime based on the piece-rate method.

Example 9

Luis Santiago is paid $.62 per unit produced under his company's straight piece-rate plan and $5.00 per hour for waiting time. His production record for a recent week showed that he produced 390 units during a 50-hour work period with 6 hours of waiting time. What were Luis's gross earnings for the week if he receives time-and-a-half for overtime?

Solution

Step 1: Determine the regular earnings from piecework and waiting time.

$241.80 (390 × $.62) piecework
  30.00 (6 × $5.00) waiting time
$271.80 regular earnings

Step 2: Compute the regular hourly rate.

regular hourly rate = regular earnings ÷ total hours worked
= $271.80/50
= $5.436

Step 3: Determine the overtime rate.

overtime rate = regular rate × 1.5
= $5.436 × 1.5
= $8.154

Step 4: Calculate the gross earnings based on the piece rate.

gross earnings = regular earnings + overtime earnings
= $271.80   + (10 × $8.154)
= $271.80   + $81.54
= $353.34

CHECK YOUR KNOWLEDGE

Calculating piecework earnings

1. John Michels is paid $.86 for each subassembly he produces and is charged back $.60 for defective units. Calculate his gross earnings for the week if he produced 478 subassemblies of which 12 were considered defective.

2. Rolling Hills Orchards pays its apple pickers daily based on a differential rate plan that provides $.50 per box for the first 20 boxes; $.75 for the 21st through 35th box; and $1.00 per box above 35 per day. Find the gross earnings for a picker who picked 47 boxes on a given day.

3. Find the gross earnings for a worker who is paid $5.80 per hour or $.20 per unit, whichever is greater. The worker produced 238 units on Monday; 226 units on Tuesday; 218 units on Wednesday; 232 units on Thursday; and 247 units on Friday. In addition, calculate the daily task standard.

4.   Robert Emerson is a machine operator at a local manufacturing facility and is paid by the terms of a task/bonus plan as follows. He receives a bonus of 130% for a task requirement of 150 units per 8-hour shift. If his hourly wage is $6.58, find his gross earnings for 2 days in which he produced 190 and 148 units, respectively.

5.   Lucy Cooper is paid $.82 for each toy truck she assembles and $5.50 for each hour she has to wait to have her machine set up or repaired. During a recent week, she assembled 296 trucks in 42 hours including 3 hours of waiting time. What were her gross earnings for the week if she is paid time-and-a-half for overtime?

4.2   EXERCISES

Calculate the gross earnings for each of the following employees.

	Name	M	T	W	Th	F	Total hours	Hourly rate	Gross wage
1.	Adams, P.	8	7	8	6	8	_____	$10.42	_____
2.	Bedell, R.	8	0	8	8	8	_____	7.78	_____
3.	Kane, J.	3	8	8	8	8	_____	9.65	_____
4.	Peters, D.	8	8	8	8	8	_____	6.87	_____
5.	Watson, R.	0	0	8	8	8	_____	8.90	_____

Complete the following payroll record. Employees receive time-and-a-half for all hours over 40 hours per week. Use the standard overtime method to calculate overtime rates.

								Hours	
	Name	M	T	W	Th	F	S	Reg. hrs.	O.T. hrs.
6.	Abboud, C.	8		8	6	6	6		34	0
7.	Bacon, R.	8		8.5	8	10	8	4	40	6.5
8.	Choi, G.	8		8	8	8	8		40	0
9.	Healy, S.	8.25		12	7	8	9	3.75	40	8
10.	Montone, J.	9		3	8	8	8	6	40	2
11.	Regan, W.	8		9.5	8	10	8	3.25	_____	_____

Answers to CYK: *1.* $403.88   *2.* $33.25   *3.* $236.20; 232 units task standard   *4.* $139.32
                      5. $277.74

	Rate				
Name	Reg. rate	O.T. rate	Regular earnings	Overtime earnings	Total earnings
Abboud, C.	$ 6.40	0	47.65	+ ____	27.60
Bacon, R.	8.10	12.15	324	78.98	402.84
Choi, G.	10.50	0	420	0	420
Healy, S.	6.80	12.20	272	81.60	282.60
Montone, J.	9.30	13.95	372	27.00	299.9
Regan, W.	7.60	____	____	____	____

Complete the following payroll record. Employee earnings are based on the straight piecework plan with time-and-a-half over 40 hours and $6.00 per hour waiting time.

	Units produced							
Employee	M	T	W	Th	F	Total units	Hours worked	Waiting time
12. Ackley, F.	270	268	279	283	186	_____	36	4
13. Didziak, F.	950	937	896	943	960	_____	44	0
14. Eberle, D.	188	174	168	190	179	_____	47	3
15. Jenkins, M.	112	85	102	98	87	_____	40	6
16. Riccardo, T.	889	925	963	972	987	_____	40	0
17. Shirtz, A.	250	237	261	278	290	_____	43	2

	Rates			Earnings		
Employee	Piece rate	Regular hourly rate	O.T. rate	Regular	Overtime	Total
Ackley, F.	$.248	_____	_____	_____	_____	_____
Didziak, F.	.0866	_____	_____	_____	_____	_____
Eberle, D.	.485	_____	_____	_____	_____	_____
Jenkins, M.	.7972	_____	_____	_____	_____	_____
Riccardo, T.	.0675	_____	_____	_____	_____	_____
Shirtz, A.	.375	_____	_____	_____	_____	_____

Calculate the gross earnings for each employee based on the following differential pay scale. Assume a chargeback of $.95 per unit.

Units	Rate
0 – 150	$ .85
151 – 300	.97
301 – 450	1.10
451 – 600	1.22
Over 600	1.30

18.	Aiello, M.	520	5	_____		_____	_____
19.	Guckert, T.	348	12	_____		_____	_____
20.	Lutz, N.	625	21	_____		_____	_____
21.	Quilty, D.	290	0	_____		_____	_____
22.	Teachout, P.	487	8	_____		_____	_____

23. Robin Evans's time card shows she worked a 48½-hour week during the current pay period. She is paid a regular rate of $8.38 per hour and time-and-a-half for all hours over 40 per week. Calculate her gross earnings for the week based on the standard overtime method.

24. From the payroll information in problem 23, calculate the employee's gross earnings using the overtime premium method.

25. Philip Vannelli earns $9.20 per hour and is paid time-and-a-half for all time over 8 hours in any 1 day. His company also pays double time for Sundays and holidays. Calculate his gross earnings for the week based on the following hours: Monday, 8; Tuesday, 10½; Wednesday, 8; Thursday, 4; Friday, 8; Saturday, 6; and Sunday, 4 (use the standard overtime method).

26. An employee at Omni Engineering is paid $11.40 per hour and a $.10 shift differential for working the second shift. The employee is paid time-and-a-half for overtime, and he worked a total of 46 hours this pay period. Find the employee's gross earnings.

27. Find the gross earnings for a packer who is paid $.63 for each case she packs that passes inspection. Calculate her gross earnings if her production for the week is 780 cases of which 58 were rejected. She is charged $.40 per rejection.

28. Betty Wright operates a drill press and is paid $6.45 per hour or $.15 per unit, whichever is greater. Her production record for the week shows that she produced 380 units Monday, 368 units Tuesday, 330 units Wednesday, 390 units Thursday, and 340 units Friday. Determine her gross earnings based on a daily task standard for the pay period.

29. Custom Fabricating pays its production worker by the terms of a task/bonus plan agreement. The plan provides a 125% bonus and a task requirement of 200 units per 8-hour workday. Find the gross earnings of an employee who produced 258 units during an 8-hour day and is paid $7.15 an hour.

30. An employee is paid $.75 per unit produced and $5.75 per waiting time hour. During the weekly pay period, the employee produced 450 units over a 45-hour period and had 5 hours of waiting time. Find the employee's gross earnings for the week if time-and-a-half is paid for overtime.

4.3 GROSS EARNINGS: SALARY AND COMMISSION

Employees who are engaged in administrative, managerial, and sales positions are most often paid a salary for their services. A **salary** is a fixed amount of compensation usually expressed in terms of a year or a month. For example, a manager may receive an annual salary of $30,000, where an office supervisor may be paid $1,800 per month. The actual payment

Table 4.1

Prorated annual
pay periods

Period	Number of paychecks
Weekly	52
Biweekly	26; one every 2 weeks
Semimonthly	24; two each month
Monthly	12; one every month

Learning objective
Calculate gross earnings based on salary payroll systems.

of annual and monthly salaries to employees is prorated into *pay periods* that identify the time between paychecks. Most companies pay their employees weekly or biweekly; however, some still prefer semimonthly or monthly. Table 4.1 contains the prorated pay periods for an annual salary. Let's look at an example that explains how to prorate an annual salary into various pay periods.

Example 10

Elaine Smart is the Director of Patient Services at Community Hospital and receives an annual salary of $28,000. Determine her gross earnings if she is paid (a) weekly, (b) biweekly, or (c) semimonthly.

Solution

a. annual salary   pay periods   weekly salary
     $28,000   ÷   52   = $538.46
b. annual salary   pay periods   biweekly salary
     $28,000   ÷   26   = $1,076.92
c. annual salary   pay periods   semimonthly salary
     $28,000   ÷   24   = $1,166.67

Many salaried employees are classified **exempt** and are compensated for their work, not the number of hours worked; hourly wage employees are **nonexempt**. The exempt status provides for payment of earnings under conditions that hourly employees may not be paid, such as leaving the workplace early or missing work due to illness. On the other hand, exempt salaried employees may not receive overtime compensation for additional hours worked beyond the required workday or workweek. There are, however, some salaried positions covered by the terms of the Fair Labor Standards Act that are paid overtime. When overtime is paid to salaried workers they usually receive time-and-a-half for all hours worked in excess of 40 hours per week. For example, if a salaried employee's regular workweek is 35 hours, he would receive an overtime rate equal to 1½ times his prorated regular hourly rate for all hours worked over 40 in a given week plus his regular salary for all hours worked up to 40 hours per week. Examples 11 and 12 further illustrate this concept.

Example 11

Harold Jurkiewicz is an account clerk; he is paid a weekly salary of $280 and time-and-a-half for all hours over 40 worked in a week. Find Harold's gross earnings for the week if he worked 45 hours and his regular workweek is 35 hours.

Solution

Step 1:   Prorate the weekly salary to an hourly rate based on the hours worked during the pay period.

$$\frac{\text{weekly salary}}{\text{regular workweek}} \quad \frac{\$280}{35} = \$8 \text{ prorated hourly rate}$$

Step 2:   Determine the overtime rate, which is $12 (1.5 × $8) and the overtime hours (45 − 40 = 5).

Step 3:   Then calculate the gross earnings for the week as follows:

$$
\begin{aligned}
\text{gross earnings} &= \text{regular earnings} + \text{overtime earnings} \\
&= (40 \times \$8) \quad\quad + (5 \times \$12) \\
&= \$320 \quad\quad\quad\quad + \$60 \\
&= \$380
\end{aligned}
$$

Notice that the employee's regular earnings are based on the prorated regular hourly rate ($8.00) for the first 40 hours worked. In other words, any hours worked beyond the number of hours that the salary is intended to compensate for (40 − 35 = 5) are paid at the prorated regular hourly rate. The overtime rate ($12) is paid for each hour worked over 40 (45 − 40) during the pay period.

There are some salaried employees who receive a fixed salary for working hours that fluctuate week to week. The fixed salary is paid whatever the number of hours worked during the pay period; however, the employee must receive additional overtime compensation for each hour over 40 hours worked in the pay period at a rate not less than one-half the prorated regular rate.

Example 12

Janet Willis is a police sergeant and has working hours that are subject to change. Find her gross earnings for the week if she worked 48 hours and is paid an annual salary of $29,952.

Solution

Step 1: Prorate the annual salary to a weekly salary ($29,952 ÷ 52 = $576 per week) and then to a prorated hourly rate by dividing the weekly salary by the hours worked.

$$\frac{\$576}{48} = \$12 \text{ prorated hourly rate}$$

Step 2: Determine the overtime rate (.5 × $12 = $6) and the overtime hours (48 − 40 = 8).

Step 3: Calculate the gross earnings.

gross earnings = regular earnings + overtime earnings
  = $576   + (8 × $6)
  = $576   + $48
  = $624

COMMISSIONS

The ultimate success of any business can be measured in its ability to sell its goods and services. The sales force, therefore, is often compensated by **commission**, which is an incentive payment designed to generate a high volume of sales. The commission paid to the employee is always based on *net sales* and is usually expressed as a percent. Net sales is the result of deducting from gross sales all sales returns (returned merchandise) and sales discounts (reduction in the price of merchandise).

Formula for determining net sales

net sales = gross sales − sales returns − sales discounts

There are two basic commission plans, namely: *straight commission* and *variable*, or *graduated*, *commission*. In either case, the gross earnings based on commission can be calculated with the following equation:

Formula for determining gross earnings

gross earnings = (value of net sales) × (commission rate)

When a salesperson is paid a straight commission, he or she receives a fixed percent of net sales for a given pay period. As commission earnings are usually based on monthly sales figures, many companies allow their salespersons to draw against their commissions during the pay period. A *draw* is an advance on projected earnings, which is deducted from the employee's commission at the time the employee's earnings are normally determined. If the draw exceeds the employee's commission, the employee owes the company the difference, which is charged against future commissions.

Example 13

Matthew Higgins recorded gross sales of $25,750 for October. Determine his gross earnings for the period if his company offered a 5% discount to all customers. Matthew is paid a straight commission of 8½% of net sales and received a draw of $800 in October.

Solution

Step 1: Calculate the discount ($25,750 × .05 = $1,287.50) and subtract the discount amount from gross sales to find the net sales amount.

$$\text{net sales} = \text{gross sales} - \text{allowances and discounts}$$
$$= \$25,750 \quad - \$1,287.50$$
$$= \$24,462.50$$

Step 2: Insert the required variables into the equation and find the gross earnings.

$$\text{gross earnings} = \text{net sales} \quad \times \text{commission rate}$$
$$= \$24,462.50 \times .085$$
$$= \$2,079.31$$

Step 3: Subtract the draw from the commission to determine the gross earnings that remain unpaid by the employer.

$$\text{unpaid gross earnings} = \text{commission} - \text{draw}$$
$$= \$2,079.31 \quad - \$800$$
$$= \$1,279.31$$

Some businesses elect to pay a fixed amount as the commission, based on the number of units sold. If this is the case, the gross earnings would be calculated in a manner similar to an hourly employee's piecework wages. The equation would be modified as shown in the next example.

Example 14

Martha Deinhart works for a mailing service company and receives a commission of $.04 for each piece of mailing she prepares. Find her gross earnings if she prepared 5,625 mailings during a recent pay period.

Solution

$$\text{gross earnings} = \text{number of units} \times \text{commission rate per unit}$$
$$= 5,625 \qquad \times .04$$
$$= \$225.00$$

The variable, or graduated commission, plan is similar in motive to the differential-piecework plan for hourly workers as it pays higher commission rates for increased net sales levels. A *commission rate schedule* identifies the net sales range and the corresponding commission rate to be paid, as shown in Example 15.

Example 15

Salespersons employed by International Frozen Foods are paid a graduated commission on sales per month as follows:

Sales	Rate
$0 – $8,000	8%
$8,001 – $12,000	9%
$12,001 – $15,000	10%
Over $15,000	12%

Find the gross earnings for Kara Andrews whose net sales amounted to $16,840 for the month.

Solution

Insert the variables into the equation and solve for gross earnings.

gross earnings = net sales × commission rate

gross earnings on first	$ 8,000 =	$8,000 × .08 =	$ 640.00
gross earnings on next	4,000 =	4,000 × .09 =	360.00
gross earnings on next	3,000 =	3,000 × .10 =	300.00
gross earnings on remaining	1,840 =	1,840 × .12 =	220.80
total net sales	$16,840	total gross earnings	$1,520.80

Many large retail stores and industrial firms pay their sales personnel a *salary plus commission*. This method of payment requires a fixed salary per pay period plus a commission on net sales. This plan eliminates the additional record keeping required by the draw system and provides the salesperson with a regular income as well as an incentive. The following equation is used to determine gross earnings with the salary-plus-commission plan.

Formula for gross earnings on salary-plus-commission plan

gross earnings = fixed salary + (net sales × commission rate)

Example 16

Lisa Shrank is paid a salary of $2,000 per month plus 4¾% commission on net sales over $10,000. Calculate her gross earnings for the month if her net sales were $18,000.

Solution

Insert the required variables into the equation and solve.

gross earnings = fixed salary + (commission sales × commission rate)
= $2,000   + ($8,000   × .0475)
= $2,000   + $380
= $2,380

The net sales figure ($8,000) in the example is the amount of commission sales over the required standard sales ($10,000) that the employee must sell before she can earn the commission ($18,000 − $10,000 = $8,000).

CHECK YOUR KNOWLEDGE

Calculating Salary and Commissions

1. Eileen Hyde receives an annual salary of $17,680. What is her (a) biweekly salary? (b) semimonthly salary?

2. Ray Jewell is paid a weekly salary of $420. He is paid time-and-a-half for all hours over 40 hours a week. Find his gross earnings for a week in which he worked 45 hours.

3. Christie Halloran is compensated on a fluctuating workweek basis at an annual salary of $19,500. Find her gross earnings for two separate pay periods if she worked (a) 44 hours and (b) 35 hours during each pay period.

4. Last month Jason Novak had net sales of $40,250. What were his gross earnings for the period if he is paid a 5⅜% straight commission rate and his drawing account totaled $1,250?

5. The student association of Northeast State College recently conducted a fund-raiser involving the sale of boxed candies. The club is paid a

$1.25 commission on each box of candy sold. Calculate the club's gross earnings if they sold 2,687 boxes during the fund-raiser.

6. Maria Rodriguez is a sales representative for an industrial machinery manufacturer. Her earnings are based on a graduated commission as follows: 3% of the first $10,000 in sales; 4¼% of the next $25,000; 6% of the next $30,000; and 8% of all sales over $65,000. Find her gross earnings for the month if her sales for the period amounted to $72,500.

7. Midtown Automobile Emporium pays its salespersons a base salary of $500 biweekly plus a commission of 2½% on all sales. Determine Mark Edsall's gross earnings for the period; he sold $48,750 in cars for the dealership.

4.3 EXERCISES

Determine the prorated earnings for each of the following salaries based on the given amounts.

	Weekly 52	Biweekly 26	Semimonthly 24	Monthly 12	Annual
1.	$200.00				
2.			$850.00		
3.		$645.00			
4.				$1,500.00	
5.					$40,800

Using the graduated straight commission schedule below, calculate the monthly gross earnings for the following salespeople.

Net sales	Commission rate
$1 to $20,000	3%
$20,001 to $35,000	4.5%
$35,001 to $50,000	6%
Over $50,000	6.5%

Employee	Gross sales	Total discounts / returns	Net sales	Gross earnings
6. Carey, P.	$38,500	$1,260		
7. Melnick, T.	52,750	1,525		
8. Sansone, R.	21,250	980		
9. Valentine, H.	43,375	1,325		

Answers to CYK: **1.** a. $680; b. $736.67 **2.** $498.75 **3.** a. $392.05; b. $375 **4.** $913.44 **5.** $3,358.75 **6.** $3,762.50 **7.** $1,718.75

Hitchcock Interiors pays its salespeople a weekly salary of $275 plus a commission of 1⅝% on net sales over $1,200 each pay period. Calculate the biweekly gross earnings for each salesperson using the payroll information provided in the table.

	Name	Gross sales	Returns	Net sales	Commission sales
10.	Abbott, D.	$ 8,500	$375	_____	_____
11.	Butler, G.	22,250	245	_____	_____
12.	North, R.	15,620	430	_____	_____
13.	Smith, J.	39,875	605	_____	_____
14.	Zeigler, H.	26,460	240	_____	_____

Name	Commission	Regular earnings	Gross earnings
Abbott, D.	_____	_____	_____
Butler, G.	_____	_____	_____
North, R.	_____	_____	_____
Smith, J.	_____	_____	_____
Zeigler, H.	_____	_____	_____

15. Carol Ryan, a radiologist, is paid an annual salary of $18,850. She is paid on a weekly basis with a regular workweek of 35 hours; she is paid overtime at the rate of time-and-a-half for hours worked over 40 per week. During recent pay periods, she worked 43 and 46 hours, respectively. Find her gross earnings for each of the pay periods.

16. Carl Costello's salary is $23,842 per year. His company pays him weekly and his hours vary as conditions require. Find his gross earnings for the week if he worked 54 hours during the current pay period.

17. This past month, Alex Marshall had gross sales of $87,250, subject to a 2% trade discount. What were his gross earnings if he is paid a 5% straight commission rate on net sales and had draws totaling $1,350 for the period?

18. Clara Kassler sells cookware door to door. She receives no salary but earns $42.50 for each set of cookware sold. What is her gross earnings for the month if she sold 67 sets?

19. Luber Corporation pays its salespersons on a graduated commission basis: 2% of the first $25,000 net sales; 3½% on net sales above $25,000 to $40,000; and 4⅝% on net sales over $40,000. If Frank Walls had net sales of $68,450 for the month, what would be the amount of his commission based on his gross earnings?

20. Christine Dunn sells microcomputers for Smart Office Systems. She receives a semi-monthly salary of $600 plus a commission of 3¼% on all net sales over $2,500 per period. If she had sales of $10,620 and $840 in merchandise returns, what are her gross earnings for the pay period?

4.4   EMPLOYEE PAYROLL DEDUCTIONS

The preceding sections of this chapter are devoted to the various methods used by employers to determine gross earnings. Gross earnings, however, is not what the employee actually receives for his or her work. *Net earnings*, *net pay*, or **take-home pay** is generally less than gross earnings due

Learning objective
Identify and calculate the various types of employee payroll deductions.

to the *deductions* that are subtracted. This section of the chapter will focus on a discussion of the various mandatory and elective deductions that reduce an employee's gross earnings. The relationship between the principal variables can be expressed by the following equation.

Formula for net earnings

net earnings = gross earnings − total deductions

MANDATORY DEDUCTIONS

Mandatory deductions are those deductions usually required by federal, state, and/or local governments and include *social security tax (FICA)*, *medicare tax*, *income withholding taxes*, and contributions to state *unemployment compensation* programs in the form of **state disability insurance**.

Most employers are required by the **Federal Insurance Contributions Act (FICA)** to withhold from an employee's earnings a tax at a specified rate based on a taxable amount of accumulated gross earnings paid during the calendar year. This tax is sent by the employer to the *Internal Revenue Service (IRS)* to be used by the federal government to finance the **Social Security Fund**. The fund provides to qualified individuals payments for retirement, disability, survivor benefits, and health insurance for the elderly. The portion of the tax that is used to fund health insurance for the elderly (medicare) is called the **medicare tax**. The schedule of tax rates and wage bases subject to tax has been revised periodically by the federal government to reflect economic conditions. Prior to 1991, the social security and medicare tax rates were combined into one rate with a single wage base. Since 1991, social security and medicare taxes have been withheld separately and have different tax rates and wage bases. Table 4.2 shows the tax rates for employees, employers, and self-employed individ-

Table 4.2   Social security and medicare tax rates

Year	Wage base	Employer tax rate	Employee tax rate	Self-employed tax rate
1992 Social security	55,500	6.20	6.20	12.4
1992 Medicare	130,200	1.45	1.45	2.9
1991 Social security	53,400	6.20	6.20	12.4
1991 Medicare	125,000	1.45	1.45	2.9
1990 Social security	51,300	7.65	7.65	15.30
1989 Social security	48,000	7.51	7.51	13.20

uals as well as the wage bases for the years 1989–1992. Notice in Table 4.2 that self-employed persons are required to pay a self-employment FICA tax and a medicare tax equal to the combined rate of the employee–employer FICA tax. The employer is required to pay a FICA tax equal to the employee's for each employee as part of its total payroll taxes. These employer taxes will be discussed in more detail in Section 4.5.

Using the rates given in Table 4.2, an employer in 1992 would deduct from an employee's earnings 6.20% on the first $55,500 of wages earned in the calendar year for a maximum social security tax of $3,441.00 ($55,500 × .0620 = $3,441.00). If an employee earns more than $55,500, the additional earnings are exempt from the tax. Whatever the tax rate and wage base subject to the tax, the procedure used to calculate the tax has remained unchanged. Consequently, we can use the same procedure to calculate the medicare tax that we used to determine the social security tax. For example, in 1992, an employer had to withhold 1.45% of an employee's earnings up to $130,200 paid during the calendar year for a maximum medicare tax of $1,887.90 ($130,200 × .0145 = $1,887.90). There are two methods for determining the amount of FICA tax and medicare tax to be deducted from an employee's gross earnings.

> *Method 1:*   Use the social security and medicare tax tables for the wage bracket method.

> *Method 2:*   Use the following equations, which are an application of the percentage equation ($BR = P$) presented in Chapter 3, for the percentage method.
>
>   FICA tax = taxable earnings × tax rate
>   Medicare tax = taxable earnings × tax rate

We will illustrate both methods in the following example.

Example 17

The gross earnings of Frank Taylor this pay period are $915.50 and his payroll record indicates he has year-to-date earnings of $50,624.75. How much of his current earnings must his employer withhold for FICA tax and medicare tax? (Use the tax tables from Figures 4.4 and 4.5.)

Solution 1

Tax Table Method

Step 1:   Determine the taxable FICA and medicare earnings.

     $55,500.00   maximum taxable earnings
   − 50,624.75   year-to-date earnings

      4,875.25   earnings subject to FICA tax

$130,200.00 maximum taxable earnings
− 50,624.75 year-to-date earnings

79,575.25 earnings subject to medicare tax

The $915.50 earned is entirely taxable for both FICA and medicare taxes since the current gross earnings is less than the earnings still subject to the taxes.

Figure 4.4 Social security tax table

6.2% Social Security Employee Tax Table for 1992

Note: *Wages subject to social security are generally also subject to the Medicare tax. See page 51.*

Wages at least	But less than	Tax to be withheld	Wages at least	But less than	Tax to be withheld	Wages at least	But less than	Tax to be withheld	Wages at least	But less than	Tax to be withheld	Wages at least	But less than	Tax to be withheld
$0.00	$0.09	$0.00	14.60	14.76	.91	29.28	29.44	1.82	43.96	44.12	2.73			
.09	.25	.01	14.76	14.92	.92	29.44	29.60	1.83	44.12	44.28	2.74			
.25	.41	.02	14.92	15.09	.93	29.60	29.76	1.84	44.28	44.44	2.75			
.41	.57	.03	15.09	15.25	.94	29.76	29.92	1.85	44.44	44.60	2.76			
.57	.73	.04	15.25	15.41	.95	29.92	30.09	1.86	44.60	44.76	2.77			
.73	.89	.05	15.41	15.57	.96	30.09	30.25	1.87	44.76	44.92	2.78			
.89	1.05	.06	15.57	15.73	.97	30.25	30.41	1.88	44.92	45.09	2.79			
1.05	1.21	.07	15.73	15.89	.98	30.41	30.57	1.89	45.09	45.25	2.80			
1.21	1.38	.08	15.89	16.05	.99	30.57	30.73	1.90	45.25	45.41	2.81			
1.38	1.54	.09	16.05	16.21	1.00	30.73	30.89	1.91	45.41	45.57	2.82			
1.54	1.70	.10	16.21	16.38	1.01	30.89	31.05	1.92	45.57	45.73	2.83			
1.70	1.86	.11	16.38	16.54	1.02	31.05	31.21	1.93	45.73	45.89	2.84			
1.86	2.02	.12	16.54	16.70	1.03	31.21	31.38	1.94	45.89	46.05	2.85			
2.02	2.18	.13	16.70	16.86	1.04	31.38	31.54	1.95	46.05	46.21	2.86			
2.18	2.34	.14	16.86	17.02	1.05	31.54	31.70	1.96	46.21	46.38	2.87			
2.34	2.50	.15	17.02	17.18	1.06	31.70	31.86	1.97	46.38	46.54	2.88			
2.50	2.67	.16	17.18	17.34	1.07	31.86	32.02	1.98	46.54	46.70	2.89			
2.67	2.83	.17	17.34	17.50	1.08	32.02	32.18	1.99	46.70	46.86	2.90			
2.83	2.99	.18	17.50	17.67	1.09	32.18	32.34	2.00	46.86	47.02	2.91			
2.99	3.15	.19	17.67	17.83	1.10	32.34	32.50	2.01	47.02	47.18	2.92			
3.15	3.31	.20	17.83	17.99	1.11	32.50	32.67	2.02	47.18	47.34	2.93			
3.31	3.47	.21	17.99	18.15	1.12	32.67	32.83	2.03	47.34	47.50	2.94			
3.47	3.63	.22	18.15	18.31	1.13	32.83	32.99	2.04	47.50	47.67	2.95			
3.63	3.80	.23	18.31	18.47	1.14	32.99	33.15	2.05	47.67	47.83	2.96			
3.80	3.96	.24	18.47	18.63	1.15	33.15	33.31	2.06	47.83	47.99	2.97			
3.96	4.12	.25	18.63	18.80	1.16	33.31	33.47	2.07	47.99	48.15	2.98			
4.12	4.28	.26	18.80	18.96	1.17	33.47	33.63	2.08	48.15	48.31	2.99			
4.28	4.44	.27	18.96	19.12	1.18	33.63	33.80	2.09	48.31	48.47	3.00			
4.44	4.60	.28	19.12	19.28	1.19	33.80	33.96	2.10	48.47	48.63	3.01			
4.60	4.76	.29	19.28	19.44	1.20	33.96	34.12	2.11	48.63	48.80	3.02			
4.76	4.92	.30	19.44	19.60	1.21	34.12	34.28	2.12	48.80	48.96	3.03			
4.92	5.09	.31	19.60	19.76	1.22	34.28	34.44	2.13	48.96	49.12	3.04			
5.09	5.25	.32	19.76	19.92	1.23	34.44	34.60	2.14	49.12	49.28	3.05			
5.25	5.41	.33	19.92	20.09	1.24	34.60	34.76	2.15	49.28	49.44	3.06			
5.41	5.57	.34	20.09	20.25	1.25	34.76	34.92	2.16	49.44	49.60	3.07			
5.57	5.73	.35	20.25	20.41	1.26	34.92	35.09	2.17	49.60	49.76	3.08			
5.73	5.89	.36	20.41	20.57	1.27	35.09	35.25	2.18	49.76	49.92	3.09			
5.89	6.05	.37	20.57	20.73	1.28	35.25	35.41	2.19	49.92	50.09	3.10			
6.05	6.21	.38	20.73	20.89	1.29	35.41	35.57	2.20	50.09	50.25	3.11			
6.21	6.38	.39	20.89	21.05	1.30	35.57	35.73	2.21	50.25	50.41	3.12			
6.38	6.54	.40	21.05	21.21	1.31	35.73	35.89	2.22	50.41	50.57	3.13			
6.54	6.70	.41	21.21	21.38	1.32	35.89	36.05	2.23	50.57	50.73	3.14			
6.70	6.86	.42	21.38	21.54	1.33	36.05	36.21	2.24	50.73	50.89	3.15			
6.86	7.02	.43	21.54	21.70	1.34	36.21	36.38	2.25	50.89	51.05	3.16			
7.02	7.18	.44	21.70	21.86	1.35	36.38	36.54	2.26	51.05	51.21	3.17			
7.18	7.34	.45	21.86	22.02	1.36	36.54	36.70	2.27	51.21	51.38	3.18			
7.34	7.50	.46	22.02	22.18	1.37	36.70	36.86	2.28	51.38	51.54	3.19			
7.50	7.67	.47	22.18	22.34	1.38	36.86	37.02	2.29	51.54	51.70	3.20			
7.67	7.83	.48	22.34	22.50	1.39	37.02	37.18	2.30	51.70	51.86	3.21			
7.83	7.99	.49	22.50	22.67	1.40	37.18	37.34	2.31	51.86	52.02	3.22			
7.99	8.15	.50	22.67	22.83	1.41	37.34	37.50	2.32	52.02	52.18	3.23			
8.15	8.31	.51	22.83	22.99	1.42	37.50	37.67	2.33	52.18	52.34	3.24			
8.31	8.47	.52	22.99	23.15	1.43	37.67	37.83	2.34	52.34	52.50	3.25			
8.47	8.63	.53	23.15	23.31	1.44	37.83	37.99	2.35	52.50	52.67	3.26			
8.63	8.80	.54	23.31	23.47	1.45	37.99	38.15	2.36	52.67	52.83	3.27			
8.80	8.96	.55	23.47	23.63	1.46	38.15	38.31	2.37	52.83	52.99	3.28			
8.96	9.12	.56	23.63	23.80	1.47	38.31	38.47	2.38	52.99	53.15	3.29			
9.12	9.28	.57	23.80	23.96	1.48	38.47	38.63	2.39	53.15	53.31	3.30			
9.28	9.44	.58	23.96	24.12	1.49	38.63	38.80	2.40	53.31	53.47	3.31			
9.44	9.60	.59	24.12	24.28	1.50	38.80	38.96	2.41	53.47	53.63	3.32			
9.60	9.76	.60	24.28	24.44	1.51	38.96	39.12	2.42	53.63	53.80	3.33			
9.76	9.92	.61	24.44	24.60	1.52	39.12	39.28	2.43	53.80	53.96	3.34			
9.92	10.09	.62	24.60	24.76	1.53	39.28	39.44	2.44	53.96	54.12	3.35			
10.09	10.25	.63	24.76	24.92	1.54	39.44	39.60	2.45	54.12	54.28	3.36			
10.25	10.41	.64	24.92	25.09	1.55	39.60	39.76	2.46	54.28	54.44	3.37			
10.41	10.57	.65	25.09	25.25	1.56	39.76	39.92	2.47	54.44	54.60	3.38			
10.57	10.73	.66	25.25	25.41	1.57	39.92	40.09	2.48	54.60	54.76	3.39			
10.73	10.89	.67	25.41	25.57	1.58	40.09	40.25	2.49	54.76	54.92	3.40			
10.89	11.05	.68	25.57	25.73	1.59	40.25	40.41	2.50	54.92	55.09	3.41			
11.05	11.21	.69	25.73	25.89	1.60	40.41	40.57	2.51	55.09	55.25	3.42			
11.21	11.38	.70	25.89	26.05	1.61	40.57	40.73	2.52						
11.38	11.54	.71	26.05	26.21	1.62	40.73	40.89	2.53						
11.54	11.70	.72	26.21	26.38	1.63	40.89	41.05	2.54						
11.70	11.86	.73	26.38	26.54	1.64	41.05	41.21	2.55						
11.86	12.02	.74	26.54	26.70	1.65	41.21	41.38	2.56		**Wages**			**Taxes**	
12.02	12.18	.75	26.70	26.86	1.66	41.38	41.54	2.57		100			$6.20	
12.18	12.34	.76	26.86	27.02	1.67	41.54	41.70	2.58		200			12.40	
12.34	12.50	.77	27.02	27.18	1.68	41.70	41.86	2.59		300			18.60	
12.50	12.67	.78	27.18	27.34	1.69	41.86	42.02	2.60		400			24.80	
12.67	12.83	.79	27.34	27.50	1.70	42.02	42.18	2.61		500			31.00	
12.83	12.99	.80	27.50	27.67	1.71	42.18	42.34	2.62		600			37.20	
12.99	13.15	.81	27.67	27.83	1.72	42.34	42.50	2.63		700			43.40	
13.15	13.31	.82	27.83	27.99	1.73	42.50	42.67	2.64		800			49.60	
13.31	13.47	.83	27.99	28.15	1.74	42.67	42.83	2.65		900			55.80	
13.47	13.63	.84	28.15	28.31	1.75	42.83	42.99	2.66		1,000			62.00	
13.63	13.80	.85	28.31	28.47	1.76	42.99	43.15	2.67						
13.80	13.96	.86	28.47	28.63	1.77	43.15	43.31	2.68						
13.96	14.12	.87	28.63	28.80	1.78	43.31	43.47	2.69						
14.12	14.28	.88	28.80	28.96	1.79	43.47	43.63	2.70						
14.28	14.44	.89	28.96	29.12	1.80	43.63	43.80	2.71						
14.44	14.60	.90	29.12	29.28	1.81	43.80	43.96	2.72						

Source: U.S. Dept. of the Treasury, Internal Revenue Service (U.S. Government Printing Office).
See Appendix C for the remainder of the 6.2% Social Security employee tax table for 1992.

Figure 4.5

Medicare tax table

1.45% Medicare Tax Table for 1992

Wages at least	But less than	Tax to be withheld	Wages at least	But less than	Tax to be withheld	Wages at least	But less than	Tax to be withheld	Wages at least	But less than	Tax to be withheld
$0.00	$0.35	$0.00	28.63	29.32	.42	57.59	58.28	.84	86.56	87.25	1.26
.35	1.04	.01	29.32	30.00	.43	58.28	58.97	.85	87.25	87.94	1.27
1.04	1.73	.02	30.00	30.69	.44	58.97	59.66	.86	87.94	88.63	1.28
1.73	2.42	.03	30.69	31.38	.45	59.66	60.35	.87	88.63	89.32	1.29
2.42	3.11	.04	31.38	32.07	.46	60.35	61.04	.88	89.32	90.00	1.30
3.11	3.80	.05	32.07	32.76	.47	61.04	61.73	.89	90.00	90.69	1.31
3.80	4.49	.06	32.76	33.45	.48	61.73	62.42	.90	90.69	91.38	1.32
4.49	5.18	.07	33.45	34.14	.49	62.42	63.11	.91	91.38	92.07	1.33
5.18	5.87	.08	34.14	34.83	.50	63.11	63.80	.92	92.07	92.76	1.34
5.87	6.56	.09	34.83	35.52	.51	63.80	64.49	.93	92.76	93.45	1.35
6.56	7.25	.10	35.52	36.21	.52	64.49	65.18	.94	93.45	94.14	1.36
7.25	7.94	.11	36.21	36.90	.53	65.18	65.87	.95	94.14	94.83	1.37
7.94	8.63	.12	36.90	37.59	.54	65.87	66.56	.96	94.83	95.52	1.38
8.63	9.32	.13	37.59	38.28	.55	66.56	67.25	.97	95.52	96.21	1.39
9.32	10.00	.14	38.28	38.97	.56	67.25	67.94	.98	96.21	96.90	1.40
10.00	10.69	.15	38.97	39.66	.57	67.94	68.63	.99	96.90	97.59	1.41
10.69	11.38	.16	39.66	40.35	.58	68.63	69.32	1.00	97.59	98.28	1.42
11.38	12.07	.17	40.35	41.04	.59	69.32	70.00	1.01	98.28	98.97	1.43
12.07	12.76	.18	41.04	41.73	.60	70.00	70.69	1.02	98.97	99.66	1.44
12.76	13.45	.19	41.73	42.42	.61	70.69	71.38	1.03	99.66	100.00	1.45
13.45	14.14	.20	42.42	43.11	.62	71.38	72.07	1.04			
14.14	14.83	.21	43.11	43.80	.63	72.07	72.76	1.05			
14.83	15.52	.22	43.80	44.49	.64	72.76	73.45	1.06			
15.52	16.21	.23	44.49	45.18	.65	73.45	74.14	1.07			
16.21	16.90	.24	45.18	45.87	.66	74.14	74.83	1.08			
16.90	17.59	.25	45.87	46.56	.67	74.83	75.52	1.09	Wages	Taxes	
17.59	18.28	.26	46.56	47.25	.68	75.52	76.21	1.10	100	$1.45	
18.28	18.97	.27	47.25	47.94	.69	76.21	76.90	1.11	200	2.90	
18.97	19.66	.28	47.94	48.63	.70	76.90	77.59	1.12	300	4.35	
19.66	20.35	.29	48.63	49.32	.71	77.59	78.28	1.13	400	5.80	
20.35	21.04	.30	49.32	50.00	.72	78.28	78.97	1.14	500	7.25	
21.04	21.73	.31	50.00	50.69	.73	78.97	79.66	1.15	600	8.70	
21.73	22.42	.32	50.69	51.38	.74	79.66	80.35	1.16	700	10.15	
22.42	23.11	.33	51.38	52.07	.75	80.35	81.04	1.17	800	11.60	
23.11	23.80	.34	52.07	52.76	.76	81.04	81.73	1.18	900	13.05	
23.80	24.49	.35	52.76	53.45	.77	81.73	82.42	1.19	1,000	14.50	
24.49	25.18	.36	53.45	54.14	.78	82.42	83.11	1.20			
25.18	25.87	.37	54.14	54.83	.79	83.11	83.80	1.21			
25.87	26.56	.38	54.83	55.52	.80	83.80	84.49	1.22			
26.56	27.25	.39	55.52	56.21	.81	84.49	85.18	1.23			
27.25	27.94	.40	56.21	56.90	.82	85.18	85.87	1.24			
27.94	28.63	.41	56.90	57.59	.83	85.87	86.56	1.25			

Source: U.S. Dept. of the Treasury, Internal Revenue Service (U.S. Government Printing Office).

Step 2:   Calculate FICA and medicare tax from the tax tables.

FICA tax	Taxable earnings	Medicare tax
$55.80	$900.00	$13.05
.96	15.50	.22
$56.76	$915.50	$13.27

The tax on the $900 of earnings is $55.80, which is taken from the multiple-of-$100 portion of the table. As the remaining $15.50 of taxable earnings is less than $100, we must find the *tax to be withheld* by locating this amount within the appropriate limits under the columns headed *wages at least, but less than.* In this case, the tax to be withheld is $.96 because the taxable wage of $15.50 is *at least* $15.41, *but less than* $15.57. The amounts are then added, which results in the FICA tax for the pay period ($55.80 + .96 = $56.76).

We use the same procedure to calculate the Medicare tax except that we use the tax table in Figure 4.5.

Solution 2

Percentage Method

Step 1: Determine the taxable earnings.

$55,500.00	maximum taxable earnings
− 50,624.75	year-to-date earnings
4,875.25	earnings subject to FICA tax

$130,200.00	maximum taxable earnings
− 50,624.75	year-to-date earnings
79,575.25	earnings subject to medicare tax

Step 2: Insert the required variables into the percentage equations and solve.

$$\text{FICA tax} = \text{taxable earnings} \times \text{tax rate}$$
$$= \$915.50 \times .0620$$
$$= \$56.76$$

$$\text{medicare tax} = \text{taxable earnings} \times \text{tax rate}$$
$$= \$915.50 \times .0145$$
$$= \$13.27$$

Both the wage bracket method and the percentage method produce the same amount of tax to be withheld because the tax to be withheld in the tables is determined by using the same rates. Computerized payroll systems use the percentage method, whereas smaller businesses with fewer employees may use the tables as a matter of convenience. However, due to the increasing use of microprocessors and payroll software by smaller businesses, the tables are not used as much today as in the past.

The **federal income withholding tax (FWT)**, another mandatory deduction required by the federal government, is applied to the employee's federal income tax. The amount to be withheld by the employer from each employee is based on the following primary factors:

1. the type of pay period
2. the amount of the employee's gross earnings
3. the marital status of the employee
4. the number of exemptions claimed by the employee.

The employees are required by their employer to fill out a W–4 form as shown in Figure 4.6. This form provides the employer with the information regarding each employee's marital status and the number of exemptions claimed so that the federal income withholding tax can be calculated. The employer can use one of two methods to determine the federal withholding tax to be deducted from the employee's gross earnings. The **wage bracket method** is a single-step operation using tables of amounts to be withheld. The **percentage method** uses tax rates and taxable earnings to calculate the amounts to be withheld. The tables that employers use to determine the FWT and the FICA tax are provided in the Internal Revenue Service's **Employer's Tax Guide Circular E**. The guide contains tables for both single and married employees paid daily, weekly, biweekly, semimonthly, monthly, and so forth. The tax tables presented in this text (Figures 4.7, 4.8, 4.9, and 4.10) are excerpts from that publication. The rates and tables will change, but the procedures required to use these tables have remained unchanged.

To illustrate both methods, we will continue to develop the calculation of Frank Taylor's deductions based on his earnings in Example 17.

Example 18

The gross earnings of Frank Taylor during this weekly pay period is $915.50. Using the information provided on his W–4 (Figure 4.6), determine the amount of federal withholding tax to be deducted from his gross earnings.

Solution 1

Wage-Bracket Method

Since Frank's W–4 indicates that he is married and claims four exemptions, we can use the table in Figure 4.8 to determine his FWT deduction. We find his gross earning amount, $915.50, in the wage-bracket columns headed *at least* $910 *but less than* $920 and move to the right across the table to the *withholding allowances claimed* column headed *4* to find the required FWT of 100 as follows:

At least	But less than	0	1	2	3	4	5	etc.
$910	$920	147	134	122	110	100	93	

Frank's employer should withhold $100 from his weekly gross earnings for federal withholding tax.

Figure 4.6

Form W-4: Employee withholding allowance certificate

1992 Form W-4

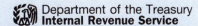

**Department of the Treasury
Internal Revenue Service**

Purpose. Complete Form W-4 so that your employer can withhold the correct amount of Federal income tax from your pay.

Exemption From Withholding. Read line 7 of the certificate below to see if you can claim exempt status. *If exempt, complete line 7; but do not complete lines 5 and 6.* No Federal income tax will be withheld from your pay. Your exemption is good for one year only. It expires February 15, 1993.

Basic Instructions. Employees who are not exempt should complete the Personal Allowances Worksheet. Additional worksheets are provided on page 2 for employees to adjust their withholding allowances based on itemized deductions, adjustments to income, or two-earner/two-job situations. Complete all worksheets that apply to your situation. The worksheets will help you figure

the number of withholding allowances you are entitled to claim. However, you may claim fewer allowances than this.

Head of Household. Generally, you may claim head of household filing status on your tax return only if you are unmarried and pay more than 50% of the costs of keeping up a home for yourself and your dependent(s) or other qualifying individuals.

Nonwage Income. If you have a large amount of nonwage income, such as interest or dividends, you should consider making estimated tax payments using Form 1040-ES. Otherwise, you may find that you owe additional tax at the end of the year.

Two-Earner/Two-Jobs. If you have a working spouse or more than one job, figure the total number of allowances you are entitled to claim on all jobs using worksheets from only one Form

W-4. This total should be divided among all jobs. Your withholding will usually be most accurate when all allowances are claimed on the W-4 filed for the highest paying job and zero allowances are claimed for the others.

Advance Earned Income Credit. If you are eligible for this credit, you can receive it added to your paycheck throughout the year. For details, get Form W-5 from your employer.

Check Your Withholding. After your W-4 takes effect, you can use Pub. 919, Is My Withholding Correct for 1992?, to see how the dollar amount you are having withheld compares to your estimated total annual tax. Call 1-800-829-3676 to order this publication. Check your local telephone directory for the IRS assistance number if you need further help.

Personal Allowances Worksheet

For 1992, the value of your personal exemption(s) is reduced if your income is over $105,250 ($157,900 if married filing jointly, $131,550 if head of household, or $78,950 if married filing separately). Get Pub. 919 for details.

A Enter "1" for **yourself** if no one else can claim you as a dependent . . . . **A** _1_

B Enter "1" if:
- You are single and have only one job; or
- You are married, have only one job, and your spouse does not work; or
- Your wages from a second job or your spouse's wages (or the total of both) are $1,000 or less.

B _0_

C Enter "1" for your **spouse.** But, you may choose to enter -0- if you are married and have either a working spouse or more than one job (this may help you avoid having too little tax withheld) . . . . **C** _0_

D Enter number of **dependents** (other than your spouse or yourself) whom you will claim on your tax return . . . . **D** _2_

E Enter "1" if you will file as **head of household** on your tax return (see conditions under "Head of Household," above) . **E** _0_

F Enter "1" if you have at least $1,500 of **child or dependent care expenses** for which you plan to claim a credit . . **F** _1_

G Add lines A through F and enter total here. **Note:** *This amount may be different from the number of exemptions you claim on your return* ▶ **G** _4_

For accuracy, do all worksheets that apply.
- If you plan to **itemize or claim adjustments to income** and want to reduce your withholding, see the Deductions and Adjustments Worksheet on page 2.
- If you are **single** and have **more than one job** and your combined earnings from all jobs exceed $29,000 OR if you are **married** and have a **working spouse or more than one job,** and the combined earnings from all jobs exceed $50,000, see the Two-Earner/Two-Job Worksheet on page 2 if you want to avoid having too little tax withheld.
- If **neither** of the above situations applies, **stop here** and enter the number from line G on line 5 of Form W-4 below.

- - - - - - - - - - - - **Cut here and give the certificate to your employer. Keep the top portion for your records.** - - - - - - - - - - - -

---

Form W-4
Department of the Treasury
Internal Revenue Service

Employee's Withholding Allowance Certificate

▶ **For Privacy Act and Paperwork Reduction Act Notice, see reverse.**

OMB No. 1545-0010

1992

1 Type or print your first name and middle initial	Last name	2 Your social security number
FrANK E.	TAylor	000 - 00 - 0000

1 Type or print your first name and middle initial   FrANK   E.   Last name   TAylor   **2** Your social security number   000 - 00 - 0000

Home address (number and street or rural route)
122 WANdering WAy

3 ☐ Single ☒ Married ☐ Married, but withhold at higher Single rate.
Note: *If married, but legally separated, or spouse is a nonresident alien, check the Single box.*

City or town, state, and ZIP code
ANywhere   USA

4 If your last name differs from that on your social security card, check here and call 1-800-772-1213 for more information ▶ ☐

5 Total number of allowances you are claiming (from line G above or from the Worksheets on back if they apply) | **5** 4

6 Additional amount, if any, you want deducted from each paycheck | **6** $ 0

7 I claim exemption from withholding and I certify that I meet **ALL** of the following conditions for exemption:
- Last year I had a right to a refund of **ALL** Federal income tax withheld because I had **NO** tax liability; **AND**
- This year I expect a refund of **ALL** Federal income tax withheld because I expect to have **NO** tax liability; **AND**
- This year if my income exceeds $600 and includes nonwage income, another person cannot claim me as a dependent.

If you meet all of the above conditions, enter the year effective and "EXEMPT" here . . ▶ | **7** 19

8 Are you a full-time student? (**Note:** *Full-time students are not automatically exempt.*) . . . . **8** ☐ Yes ☒ No

Under penalties of perjury, I certify that I am entitled to the number of withholding allowances claimed on this certificate or entitled to claim exempt status.

Employee's signature ▶ *Frank E. Taylor*   **Date** ▶ Jan 3   , 19 92

9 Employer's name and address (Employer: Complete 9 and 11 only if sending to the IRS) | **10** Office code (optional) | **11** Employer identification number

Cat. No. 10220Q

Source: U.S. Dept. of the Treasury, Internal Revenue Service (U.S. Government Printing Office).

Figure 4.7

Employer's tax guide: single person paid weekly

(For Wages Paid After December 1991)

And the wages are—		And the number of withholding allowances claimed is—										
At least	But less than	0	1	2	3	4	5	6	7	8	9	10
		The amount of income tax to be withheld shall be—										
$0	$30	$0	$0	$0	$0	$0	$0	$0	$0	$0	$0	$0
30	35	1	0	0	0	0	0	0	0	0	0	0
35	40	2	0	0	0	0	0	0	0	0	0	0
40	45	3	0	0	0	0	0	0	0	0	0	0
45	50	3	0	0	0	0	0	0	0	0	0	0
50	55	4	0	0	0	0	0	0	0	0	0	0
55	60	5	0	0	0	0	0	0	0	0	0	0
60	65	6	0	0	0	0	0	0	0	0	0	0
65	70	6	0	0	0	0	0	0	0	0	0	0
70	75	7	0	0	0	0	0	0	0	0	0	0
75	80	8	1	0	0	0	0	0	0	0	0	0
80	85	9	2	0	0	0	0	0	0	0	0	0
85	90	9	3	0	0	0	0	0	0	0	0	0
90	95	10	3	0	0	0	0	0	0	0	0	0
95	100	11	4	0	0	0	0	0	0	0	0	0
100	105	12	5	0	0	0	0	0	0	0	0	0
105	110	12	6	0	0	0	0	0	0	0	0	0
110	115	13	6	0	0	0	0	0	0	0	0	0
115	120	14	7	1	0	0	0	0	0	0	0	0
120	125	15	8	1	0	0	0	0	0	0	0	0
125	130	15	9	2	0	0	0	0	0	0	0	0
130	135	16	9	3	0	0	0	0	0	0	0	0
135	140	17	10	4	0	0	0	0	0	0	0	0
140	145	18	11	4	0	0	0	0	0	0	0	0
145	150	18	12	5	0	0	0	0	0	0	0	0
150	155	19	12	6	0	0	0	0	0	0	0	0
155	160	20	13	7	0	0	0	0	0	0	0	0
160	165	21	14	7	1	0	0	0	0	0	0	0
165	170	21	15	8	1	0	0	0	0	0	0	0
170	175	22	15	9	2	0	0	0	0	0	0	0
175	180	23	16	10	3	0	0	0	0	0	0	0
180	185	24	17	10	4	0	0	0	0	0	0	0
185	190	24	18	11	4	0	0	0	0	0	0	0
190	195	25	18	12	5	0	0	0	0	0	0	0
195	200	26	19	13	6	0	0	0	0	0	0	0
200	210	27	20	14	7	0	0	0	0	0	0	0
210	220	29	22	15	9	2	0	0	0	0	0	0
220	230	30	23	17	10	3	0	0	0	0	0	0
230	240	32	25	18	12	5	0	0	0	0	0	0
240	250	33	26	20	13	6	0	0	0	0	0	0
250	260	35	28	21	15	8	1	0	0	0	0	0
260	270	36	29	23	16	9	3	0	0	0	0	0
270	280	38	31	24	18	11	4	0	0	0	0	0
280	290	39	32	26	19	12	6	0	0	0	0	0
290	300	41	34	27	21	14	7	1	0	0	0	0
300	310	42	35	29	22	15	9	2	0	0	0	0
310	320	44	37	30	24	17	10	4	0	0	0	0
320	330	45	38	32	25	18	12	5	0	0	0	0
330	340	47	40	33	27	20	13	7	0	0	0	0
340	350	48	41	35	28	21	15	8	2	0	0	0
350	360	50	43	36	30	23	16	10	3	0	0	0
360	370	51	44	38	31	24	18	11	5	0	0	0
370	380	53	46	39	33	26	19	13	6	0	0	0
380	390	54	47	41	34	27	21	14	8	1	0	0
390	400	56	49	42	36	29	22	16	9	2	0	0
400	410	57	50	44	37	30	24	17	11	4	0	0
410	420	59	52	45	39	32	25	19	12	5	0	0
420	430	60	53	47	40	33	27	20	14	7	0	0
430	440	62	55	48	42	35	28	22	15	8	2	0
440	450	64	56	50	43	36	30	23	17	10	3	0
450	460	67	58	51	45	38	31	25	18	11	5	0
460	470	70	59	53	46	39	33	26	20	13	6	0
470	480	72	61	54	48	41	34	28	21	14	8	1
480	490	75	63	56	49	42	36	29	23	16	9	3
490	500	78	66	57	51	44	37	31	24	17	11	4
500	510	81	68	59	52	45	39	32	26	19	12	6
510	520	84	71	60	54	47	40	34	27	20	14	7
520	530	86	74	62	55	48	42	35	29	22	15	9
530	540	89	77	64	57	50	43	37	30	23	17	10
540	550	92	80	67	58	51	45	38	32	25	18	12

Figure 4.7

(*Continued*)

(For Wages Paid After December 1991)												
And the wages are—		And the number of withholding allowances claimed is—										
At least	But less than	0	1	2	3	4	5	6	7	8	9	10
		The amount of income tax to be withheld shall be—										
$550	$560	$95	$82	$70	$60	$53	$46	$40	$33	$26	$20	$13
560	570	98	85	73	61	54	48	41	35	28	21	15
570	580	100	88	76	63	56	49	43	36	29	23	16
580	590	103	91	78	66	57	51	44	38	31	24	18
590	600	106	94	81	69	59	52	46	39	32	26	19
600	610	109	96	84	72	60	54	47	41	34	27	21
610	620	112	99	87	74	62	55	49	42	35	29	22
620	630	114	102	90	77	65	57	50	44	37	30	24
630	640	117	105	92	80	68	58	52	45	38	32	25
640	650	120	108	95	83	70	60	53	47	40	33	27
650	660	123	110	98	86	73	61	55	48	41	35	28
660	670	126	113	101	88	76	64	56	50	43	36	30
670	680	128	116	104	91	79	66	58	51	44	38	31
680	690	131	119	106	94	82	69	59	53	46	39	33
690	700	134	122	109	97	84	72	61	54	47	41	34
700	710	137	124	112	100	87	75	62	56	49	42	36
710	720	140	127	115	102	90	78	65	57	50	44	37
720	730	142	130	118	105	93	80	68	59	52	45	39
730	740	145	133	120	108	96	83	71	60	53	47	40
740	750	148	136	123	111	98	86	74	62	55	48	42
750	760	151	138	126	114	101	89	76	64	56	50	43
760	770	154	141	129	116	104	92	79	67	58	51	45
770	780	156	144	132	119	107	94	82	70	59	53	46
780	790	159	147	134	122	110	97	85	72	61	54	48
790	800	162	150	137	125	112	100	88	75	63	56	49
800	810	165	152	140	128	115	103	90	78	66	57	51
810	820	168	155	143	130	118	106	93	81	68	59	52
820	830	170	158	146	133	121	108	96	84	71	60	54
830	840	173	161	148	136	124	111	99	86	74	62	55
840	850	176	164	151	139	126	114	102	89	77	65	57
850	860	179	166	154	142	129	117	104	92	80	67	58
860	870	182	169	157	144	132	120	107	95	82	70	60
870	880	184	172	160	147	135	122	110	98	85	73	61
880	890	187	175	162	150	138	125	113	100	88	76	63
890	900	190	178	165	153	140	128	116	103	91	79	66
900	910	193	180	168	156	143	131	118	106	94	81	69
910	920	196	183	171	158	146	134	121	109	96	84	72
920	930	198	186	174	161	149	136	124	112	99	87	75
930	940	201	189	176	164	152	139	127	114	102	90	77
940	950	204	192	179	167	154	142	130	117	105	93	80
950	960	207	194	182	170	157	145	132	120	108	95	83
960	970	210	197	185	172	160	148	135	123	110	98	86
970	980	212	200	188	175	163	150	138	126	113	101	89
980	990	215	203	190	178	166	153	141	128	116	104	91
990	1,000	218	206	193	181	168	156	144	131	119	107	94
1,000	1,010	221	208	196	184	171	159	146	134	122	109	97
1,010	1,020	224	211	199	186	174	162	149	137	124	112	100
1,020	1,030	226	214	202	189	177	164	152	140	127	115	103
1,030	1,040	230	217	204	192	180	167	155	142	130	118	105
1,040	1,050	233	220	207	195	182	170	158	145	133	121	108
1,050	1,060	236	222	210	198	185	173	160	148	136	123	111
1,060	1,070	239	225	213	200	188	176	163	151	138	126	114
1,070	1,080	242	228	216	203	191	178	166	154	141	129	117
1,080	1,090	245	231	218	206	194	181	169	156	144	132	119
1,090	1,100	248	234	221	209	196	184	172	159	147	135	122
1,100	1,110	251	238	224	212	199	187	174	162	150	137	125
1,110	1,120	254	241	227	214	202	190	177	165	152	140	128
1,120	1,130	257	244	230	217	205	192	180	168	155	143	131
1,130	1,140	261	247	233	220	208	195	183	170	158	146	133
1,140	1,150	264	250	236	223	210	198	186	173	161	149	136
1,150	1,160	267	253	239	226	213	201	188	176	164	151	139
1,160	1,170	270	256	242	229	216	204	191	179	166	154	142
1,170	1,180	273	259	246	232	219	206	194	182	169	157	145
1,180	1,190	276	262	249	235	222	209	197	184	172	160	147
1,190	1,200	279	265	252	238	224	212	200	187	175	163	150

$1,200 and over   Use Table 1(a) for a **SINGLE** person on page 26. Also see the instructions on page 24.

Source: Circular E: *Employer's Tax Guide*, U.S. Dept. of the Treasury, Internal Revenue Service (U.S. Government Printing Office).

Figure 4.8

Employer's tax guide: married person paid weekly

(For Wages Paid After December 1991)

And the wages are—		And the number of withholding allowances claimed is—										
At least	But less than	0	1	2	3	4	5	6	7	8	9	10
		The amount of income tax to be withheld shall be—										
$0	$75	$0	$0	$0	$0	$0	$0	$0	$0	$0	$0	$0
75	80	1	0	0	0	0	0	0	0	0	0	0
80	85	2	0	0	0	0	0	0	0	0	0	0
85	90	2	0	0	0	0	0	0	0	0	0	0
90	95	3	0	0	0	0	0	0	0	0	0	0
95	100	4	0	0	0	0	0	0	0	0	0	0
100	105	5	0	0	0	0	0	0	0	0	0	0
105	110	5	0	0	0	0	0	0	0	0	0	0
110	115	6	0	0	0	0	0	0	0	0	0	0
115	120	7	0	0	0	0	0	0	0	0	0	0
120	125	8	1	0	0	0	0	0	0	0	0	0
125	130	8	2	0	0	0	0	0	0	0	0	0
130	135	9	3	0	0	0	0	0	0	0	0	0
135	140	10	3	0	0	0	0	0	0	0	0	0
140	145	11	4	0	0	0	0	0	0	0	0	0
145	150	11	5	0	0	0	0	0	0	0	0	0
150	155	12	6	0	0	0	0	0	0	0	0	0
155	160	13	6	0	0	0	0	0	0	0	0	0
160	165	14	7	0	0	0	0	0	0	0	0	0
165	170	14	8	1	0	0	0	0	0	0	0	0
170	175	15	9	2	0	0	0	0	0	0	0	0
175	180	16	9	3	0	0	0	0	0	0	0	0
180	185	17	10	3	0	0	0	0	0	0	0	0
185	190	17	11	4	0	0	0	0	0	0	0	0
190	195	18	12	5	0	0	0	0	0	0	0	0
195	200	19	12	6	0	0	0	0	0	0	0	0
200	210	20	13	7	0	0	0	0	0	0	0	0
210	220	22	15	8	2	0	0	0	0	0	0	0
220	230	23	16	10	3	0	0	0	0	0	0	0
230	240	25	18	11	5	0	0	0	0	0	0	0
240	250	26	19	13	6	0	0	0	0	0	0	0
250	260	28	21	14	8	1	0	0	0	0	0	0
260	270	29	22	16	9	3	0	0	0	0	0	0
270	280	31	24	17	11	4	0	0	0	0	0	0
280	290	32	25	19	12	6	0	0	0	0	0	0
290	300	34	27	20	14	7	0	0	0	0	0	0
300	310	35	28	22	15	9	2	0	0	0	0	0
310	320	37	30	23	17	10	3	0	0	0	0	0
320	330	38	31	25	18	12	5	0	0	0	0	0
330	340	40	33	26	20	13	6	0	0	0	0	0
340	350	41	34	28	21	15	8	1	0	0	0	0
350	360	43	36	29	23	16	9	3	0	0	0	0
360	370	44	37	31	24	18	11	4	0	0	0	0
370	380	46	39	32	26	19	12	6	0	0	0	0
380	390	47	40	34	27	21	14	7	1	0	0	0
390	400	49	42	35	29	22	15	9	2	0	0	0
400	410	50	43	37	30	24	17	10	4	0	0	0
410	420	52	45	38	32	25	18	12	5	0	0	0
420	430	53	46	40	33	27	20	13	7	0	0	0
430	440	55	48	41	35	28	21	15	8	2	0	0
440	450	56	49	43	36	30	23	16	10	3	0	0
450	460	58	51	44	38	31	24	18	11	5	0	0
460	470	59	52	46	39	33	26	19	13	6	0	0
470	480	61	54	47	41	34	27	21	14	8	1	0
480	490	62	55	49	42	36	29	22	16	9	2	0
490	500	64	57	50	44	37	30	24	17	11	4	0
500	510	65	58	52	45	39	32	25	19	12	5	0
510	520	67	60	53	47	40	33	27	20	14	7	0
520	530	68	61	55	48	42	35	28	22	15	8	2
530	540	70	63	56	50	43	36	30	23	17	10	3
540	550	71	64	58	51	45	38	31	25	18	11	5
550	560	73	66	59	53	46	39	33	26	20	13	6
560	570	74	67	61	54	48	41	34	28	21	14	8
570	580	76	69	62	56	49	42	36	29	23	16	9
580	590	77	70	64	57	51	44	37	31	24	17	11
590	600	79	72	65	59	52	45	39	32	26	19	12
600	610	80	73	67	60	54	47	40	34	27	20	14
610	620	82	75	68	62	55	48	42	35	29	22	15
620	630	83	76	70	63	57	50	43	37	30	23	17
630	640	85	78	71	65	58	51	45	38	32	25	18

Figure 4.8

(Continued)

		(For Wages Paid After December 1991)										
And the wages are—		**And the number of withholding allowances claimed is—**										
At least	But less than	0	1	2	3	4	5	6	7	8	9	10
		The amount of income tax to be withheld shall be—										
$640	$650	$86	$79	$73	$66	$60	$53	$46	$40	$33	$26	$20
650	660	88	81	74	68	61	54	48	41	35	28	21
660	670	89	82	76	69	63	56	49	43	36	29	23
670	680	91	84	77	71	64	57	51	44	38	31	24
680	690	92	85	79	72	66	59	52	46	39	32	26
690	700	94	87	80	74	67	60	54	47	41	34	27
700	710	95	88	82	75	69	62	55	49	42	35	29
710	720	97	90	83	77	70	63	57	50	44	37	30
720	730	98	91	85	78	72	65	58	52	45	38	32
730	740	100	93	86	80	73	66	60	53	47	40	33
740	750	101	94	88	81	75	68	61	55	48	41	35
750	760	103	96	89	83	76	69	63	56	50	43	36
760	770	105	97	91	84	78	71	64	58	51	44	38
770	780	108	99	92	86	79	72	66	59	53	46	39
780	790	110	100	94	87	81	74	67	61	54	47	41
790	800	113	102	95	89	82	75	69	62	56	49	42
800	810	116	104	97	90	84	77	70	64	57	50	44
810	820	119	106	98	92	85	78	72	65	59	52	45
820	830	122	109	100	93	87	80	73	67	60	53	47
830	840	124	112	101	95	88	81	75	68	62	55	48
840	850	127	115	103	96	90	83	76	70	63	56	50
850	860	130	118	105	98	91	84	78	71	65	58	51
860	870	133	120	108	99	93	86	79	73	66	59	53
870	880	136	123	111	101	94	87	81	74	68	61	54
880	890	138	126	114	102	96	89	82	76	69	62	56
890	900	141	129	116	104	97	90	84	77	71	64	57
900	910	144	132	119	107	99	92	85	79	72	65	59
910	920	147	134	122	110	100	93	87	80	74	67	60
920	930	150	137	125	112	102	95	88	82	75	68	62
930	940	152	140	128	115	103	96	90	83	77	70	63
940	950	155	143	130	118	106	98	91	85	78	71	65
950	960	158	146	133	121	108	99	93	86	80	73	66
960	970	161	148	136	124	111	101	94	88	81	74	68
970	980	164	151	139	126	114	102	96	89	83	76	69
980	990	166	154	142	129	117	104	97	91	84	77	71
990	1,000	169	157	144	132	120	107	99	92	86	79	72
1,000	1,010	172	160	147	135	122	110	100	94	87	80	74
1,010	1,020	175	162	150	138	125	113	102	95	89	82	75
1,020	1,030	178	165	153	140	128	116	103	97	90	83	77
1,030	1,040	180	168	156	143	131	118	106	98	92	85	78
1,040	1,050	183	171	158	146	134	121	109	100	93	86	80
1,050	1,060	186	174	161	149	136	124	112	101	95	88	81
1,060	1,070	189	176	164	152	139	127	114	103	96	89	83
1,070	1,080	192	179	167	154	142	130	117	105	98	91	84
1,080	1,090	194	182	170	157	145	132	120	108	99	92	86
1,090	1,100	197	185	172	160	148	135	123	110	101	94	87
1,100	1,110	200	188	175	163	150	138	126	113	102	95	89
1,110	1,120	203	190	178	166	153	141	128	116	104	97	90
1,120	1,130	206	193	181	168	156	144	131	119	107	98	92
1,130	1,140	208	196	184	171	159	146	134	122	109	100	93
1,140	1,150	211	199	186	174	162	149	137	124	112	101	95
1,150	1,160	214	202	189	177	164	152	140	127	115	103	96
1,160	1,170	217	204	192	180	167	155	142	130	118	105	98
1,170	1,180	220	207	195	182	170	158	145	133	121	108	99
1,180	1,190	222	210	198	185	173	160	148	136	123	111	101
1,190	1,200	225	213	200	188	176	163	151	138	126	114	102
1,200	1,210	228	216	203	191	178	166	154	141	129	117	104
1,210	1,220	231	218	206	194	181	169	156	144	132	119	107
1,220	1,230	234	221	209	196	184	172	159	147	135	122	110
1,230	1,240	236	224	212	199	187	174	162	150	137	125	113
1,240	1,250	239	227	214	202	190	177	165	152	140	128	115
1,250	1,260	242	230	217	205	192	180	168	155	143	131	118
1,260	1,270	245	232	220	208	195	183	170	158	146	133	121
1,270	1,280	248	235	223	210	198	186	173	161	149	136	124
1,280	1,290	250	238	226	213	201	188	176	164	151	139	127
$1,290 and over		Use Table 1(b) for a **MARRIED person** on page 26. Also see the instructions on page 24.										

Source: Circular E: *Employer's Tax Guide*, U.S. Dept. of the Treasury, Internal Revenue Service (U.S. Government Printing Office).

Figure 4.9

Employer's tax guide: single person paid biweekly

(For Wages Paid After December 1991)

And the wages are—		And the number of withholding allowances claimed is—										
At least	But less than	0	1	2	3	4	5	6	7	8	9	10
		The amount of income tax to be withheld shall be—										
$0	$55	$0	$0	$0	$0	$0	$0	$0	$0	$0	$0	$0
55	60	1	0	0	0	0	0	0	0	0	0	0
60	65	2	0	0	0	0	0	0	0	0	0	0
65	70	3	0	0	0	0	0	0	0	0	0	0
70	75	3	0	0	0	0	0	0	0	0	0	0
75	80	4	0	0	0	0	0	0	0	0	0	0
80	85	5	0	0	0	0	0	0	0	0	0	0
85	90	6	0	0	0	0	0	0	0	0	0	0
90	95	6	0	0	0	0	0	0	0	0	0	0
95	100	7	0	0	0	0	0	0	0	0	0	0
100	105	8	0	0	0	0	0	0	0	0	0	0
105	110	9	0	0	0	0	0	0	0	0	0	0
110	115	9	0	0	0	0	0	0	0	0	0	0
115	120	10	0	0	0	0	0	0	0	0	0	0
120	125	11	0	0	0	0	0	0	0	0	0	0
125	130	12	0	0	0	0	0	0	0	0	0	0
130	135	12	0	0	0	0	0	0	0	0	0	0
135	140	13	0	0	0	0	0	0	0	0	0	0
140	145	14	1	0	0	0	0	0	0	0	0	0
145	150	15	1	0	0	0	0	0	0	0	0	0
150	155	15	2	0	0	0	0	0	0	0	0	0
155	160	16	3	0	0	0	0	0	0	0	0	0
160	165	17	4	0	0	0	0	0	0	0	0	0
165	170	18	4	0	0	0	0	0	0	0	0	0
170	175	18	5	0	0	0	0	0	0	0	0	0
175	180	19	6	0	0	0	0	0	0	0	0	0
180	185	20	7	0	0	0	0	0	0	0	0	0
185	190	21	7	0	0	0	0	0	0	0	0	0
190	195	21	8	0	0	0	0	0	0	0	0	0
195	200	22	9	0	0	0	0	0	0	0	0	0
200	205	23	10	0	0	0	0	0	0	0	0	0
205	210	24	10	0	0	0	0	0	0	0	0	0
210	215	24	11	0	0	0	0	0	0	0	0	0
215	220	25	12	0	0	0	0	0	0	0	0	0
220	225	26	13	0	0	0	0	0	0	0	0	0
225	230	27	13	0	0	0	0	0	0	0	0	0
230	235	27	14	1	0	0	0	0	0	0	0	0
235	240	28	15	2	0	0	0	0	0	0	0	0
240	245	29	16	2	0	0	0	0	0	0	0	0
245	250	30	16	3	0	0	0	0	0	0	0	0
250	260	31	17	4	0	0	0	0	0	0	0	0
260	270	32	19	6	0	0	0	0	0	0	0	0
270	280	34	20	7	0	0	0	0	0	0	0	0
280	290	35	22	9	0	0	0	0	0	0	0	0
290	300	37	23	10	0	0	0	0	0	0	0	0
300	310	38	25	12	0	0	0	0	0	0	0	0
310	320	40	26	13	0	0	0	0	0	0	0	0
320	330	41	28	15	1	0	0	0	0	0	0	0
330	340	43	29	16	3	0	0	0	0	0	0	0
340	350	44	31	18	4	0	0	0	0	0	0	0
350	360	46	32	19	6	0	0	0	0	0	0	0
360	370	47	34	21	7	0	0	0	0	0	0	0
370	380	49	35	22	9	0	0	0	0	0	0	0
380	390	50	37	24	10	0	0	0	0	0	0	0
390	400	52	38	25	12	0	0	0	0	0	0	0
400	410	53	40	27	13	0	0	0	0	0	0	0
410	420	55	41	28	15	2	0	0	0	0	0	0
420	430	56	43	30	16	3	0	0	0	0	0	0
430	440	58	44	31	18	5	0	0	0	0	0	0
440	450	59	46	33	19	6	0	0	0	0	0	0
450	460	61	47	34	21	8	0	0	0	0	0	0
460	470	62	49	36	22	9	0	0	0	0	0	0
470	480	64	50	37	24	11	0	0	0	0	0	0
480	490	65	52	39	25	12	0	0	0	0	0	0
490	500	67	53	40	27	14	0	0	0	0	0	0
500	520	69	56	42	29	16	3	0	0	0	0	0
520	540	72	59	45	32	19	6	0	0	0	0	0
540	560	75	62	48	35	22	9	0	0	0	0	0
560	580	78	65	51	38	25	12	0	0	0	0	0

Figure 4.9

(Continued)

(For Wages Paid After December 1991)

And the wages are—		And the number of withholding allowances claimed is—										
At least	But less than	0	1	2	3	4	5	6	7	8	9	10
		The amount of income tax to be withheld shall be—										
$580	$600	$81	$68	$54	$41	$28	$15	$1	$0	$0	$0	$0
600	620	84	71	57	44	31	18	4	0	0	0	0
620	640	87	74	60	47	34	21	7	0	0	0	0
640	660	90	77	63	50	37	24	10	0	0	0	0
660	680	93	80	66	53	40	27	13	0	0	0	0
680	700	96	83	69	56	43	30	16	3	0	0	0
700	720	99	86	72	59	46	33	19	6	0	0	0
720	740	102	89	75	62	49	36	22	9	0	0	0
740	760	105	92	78	65	52	39	25	12	0	0	0
760	780	108	95	81	68	55	42	28	15	2	0	0
780	800	111	98	84	71	58	45	31	18	5	0	0
800	820	114	101	87	74	61	48	34	21	8	0	0
820	840	117	104	90	77	64	51	37	24	11	0	0
840	860	120	107	93	80	67	54	40	27	14	1	0
860	880	123	110	96	83	70	57	43	30	17	4	0
880	900	128	113	99	86	73	60	46	33	20	7	0
900	920	134	116	102	89	76	63	49	36	23	10	0
920	940	139	119	105	92	79	66	52	39	26	13	0
940	960	145	122	108	95	82	69	55	42	29	16	2
960	980	150	126	111	98	85	72	58	45	32	19	5
980	1,000	156	131	114	101	88	75	61	48	35	22	8
1,000	1,020	162	137	117	104	91	78	64	51	38	25	11
1,020	1,040	167	142	120	107	94	81	67	54	41	28	14
1,040	1,060	173	148	123	110	97	84	70	57	44	31	17
1,060	1,080	178	154	129	113	100	87	73	60	47	34	20
1,080	1,100	184	159	134	116	103	90	76	63	50	37	23
1,100	1,120	190	165	140	119	106	93	79	66	53	40	26
1,120	1,140	195	170	146	122	109	96	82	69	56	43	29
1,140	1,160	201	176	151	126	112	99	85	72	59	46	32
1,160	1,180	206	182	157	132	115	102	88	75	62	49	35
1,180	1,200	212	187	162	138	118	105	91	78	65	52	38
1,200	1,220	218	193	168	143	121	108	94	81	68	55	41
1,220	1,240	223	198	174	149	124	111	97	84	71	58	44
1,240	1,260	229	204	179	154	130	114	100	87	74	61	47
1,260	1,280	234	210	185	160	135	117	103	90	77	64	50
1,280	1,300	240	215	190	166	141	120	106	93	80	67	53
1,300	1,320	246	221	196	171	146	123	109	96	83	70	56
1,320	1,340	251	226	202	177	152	127	112	99	86	73	59
1,340	1,360	257	232	207	182	158	133	115	102	89	76	62
1,360	1,380	262	238	213	188	163	139	118	105	92	79	65
1,380	1,400	268	243	218	194	169	144	121	108	95	82	68
1,400	1,420	274	249	224	199	174	150	125	111	98	85	71
1,420	1,440	279	254	230	205	180	155	131	114	101	88	74
1,440	1,460	285	260	235	210	186	161	136	117	104	91	77
1,460	1,480	290	266	241	216	191	167	142	120	107	94	80
1,480	1,500	296	271	246	222	197	172	147	123	110	97	83
1,500	1,520	302	277	252	227	202	178	153	128	113	100	86
1,520	1,540	307	282	258	233	208	183	159	134	116	103	89
1,540	1,560	313	288	263	238	214	189	164	139	119	106	92
1,560	1,580	318	294	269	244	219	195	170	145	122	109	95
1,580	1,600	324	299	274	250	225	200	175	151	126	112	98
1,600	1,620	330	305	280	255	230	206	181	156	131	115	101
1,620	1,640	335	310	286	261	236	211	187	162	137	118	104
1,640	1,660	341	316	291	266	242	217	192	167	143	121	107
1,660	1,680	346	322	297	272	247	223	198	173	148	124	110
1,680	1,700	352	327	302	278	253	228	203	179	154	129	113
1,700	1,720	358	333	308	283	258	234	209	184	159	135	116
1,720	1,740	363	338	314	289	264	239	215	190	165	140	119
1,740	1,760	369	344	319	294	270	245	220	195	171	146	122
1,760	1,780	374	350	325	300	275	251	226	201	176	151	127
1,780	1,800	380	355	330	306	281	256	231	207	182	157	132
1,800	1,820	386	361	336	311	286	262	237	212	187	163	138
1,820	1,840	391	366	342	317	292	267	243	218	193	168	143
1,840	1,860	397	372	347	322	298	273	248	223	199	174	149
1,860	1,880	402	378	353	328	303	279	254	229	204	179	155

$1,880 and over — Use Table 2(a) for a **SINGLE** person on page 26. Also see the instructions on page 24.

Source: Circular E: *Employer's Tax Guide*, U.S. Dept. of the Treasury, Internal Revenue Service (U.S. Government Printing Office).

Figure 4.10

Employer's tax guide: married person paid biweekly

(For Wages Paid After December 1991)

At least	But less than	0	1	2	3	4	5	6	7	8	9	10
$0	$145	$0	$0	$0	$0	$0	$0	$0	$0	$0	$0	$0
145	150	1	0	0	0	0	0	0	0	0	0	0
150	155	2	0	0	0	0	0	0	0	0	0	0
155	160	2	0	0	0	0	0	0	0	0	0	0
160	165	3	0	0	0	0	0	0	0	0	0	0
165	170	4	0	0	0	0	0	0	0	0	0	0
170	175	5	0	0	0	0	0	0	0	0	0	0
175	180	5	0	0	0	0	0	0	0	0	0	0
180	185	6	0	0	0	0	0	0	0	0	0	0
185	190	7	0	0	0	0	0	0	0	0	0	0
190	195	8	0	0	0	0	0	0	0	0	0	0
195	200	8	0	0	0	0	0	0	0	0	0	0
200	205	9	0	0	0	0	0	0	0	0	0	0
205	210	10	0	0	0	0	0	0	0	0	0	0
210	215	11	0	0	0	0	0	0	0	0	0	0
215	220	11	0	0	0	0	0	0	0	0	0	0
220	225	12	0	0	0	0	0	0	0	0	0	0
225	230	13	0	0	0	0	0	0	0	0	0	0
230	235	14	0	0	0	0	0	0	0	0	0	0
235	240	14	1	0	0	0	0	0	0	0	0	0
240	245	15	2	0	0	0	0	0	0	0	0	0
245	250	16	3	0	0	0	0	0	0	0	0	0
250	260	17	4	0	0	0	0	0	0	0	0	0
260	270	18	5	0	0	0	0	0	0	0	0	0
270	280	20	7	0	0	0	0	0	0	0	0	0
280	290	21	8	0	0	0	0	0	0	0	0	0
290	300	23	10	0	0	0	0	0	0	0	0	0
300	310	24	11	0	0	0	0	0	0	0	0	0
310	320	26	13	0	0	0	0	0	0	0	0	0
320	330	27	14	1	0	0	0	0	0	0	0	0
330	340	29	16	2	0	0	0	0	0	0	0	0
340	350	30	17	4	0	0	0	0	0	0	0	0
350	360	32	19	5	0	0	0	0	0	0	0	0
360	370	33	20	7	0	0	0	0	0	0	0	0
370	380	35	22	8	0	0	0	0	0	0	0	0
380	390	36	23	10	0	0	0	0	0	0	0	0
390	400	38	25	11	0	0	0	0	0	0	0	0
400	410	39	26	13	0	0	0	0	0	0	0	0
410	420	41	28	14	1	0	0	0	0	0	0	0
420	430	42	29	16	3	0	0	0	0	0	0	0
430	440	44	31	17	4	0	0	0	0	0	0	0
440	450	45	32	19	6	0	0	0	0	0	0	0
450	460	47	34	20	7	0	0	0	0	0	0	0
460	470	48	35	22	9	0	0	0	0	0	0	0
470	480	50	37	23	10	0	0	0	0	0	0	0
480	490	51	38	25	12	0	0	0	0	0	0	0
490	500	53	40	26	13	0	0	0	0	0	0	0
500	520	55	42	29	15	2	0	0	0	0	0	0
520	540	58	45	32	18	5	0	0	0	0	0	0
540	560	61	48	35	21	8	0	0	0	0	0	0
560	580	64	51	38	24	11	0	0	0	0	0	0
580	600	67	54	41	27	14	1	0	0	0	0	0
600	620	70	57	44	30	17	4	0	0	0	0	0
620	640	73	60	47	33	20	7	0	0	0	0	0
640	660	76	63	50	36	23	10	0	0	0	0	0
660	680	79	66	53	39	26	13	0	0	0	0	0
680	700	82	69	56	42	29	16	3	0	0	0	0
700	720	85	72	59	45	32	19	6	0	0	0	0
720	740	88	75	62	48	35	22	9	0	0	0	0
740	760	91	78	65	51	38	25	12	0	0	0	0
760	780	94	81	68	54	41	28	15	1	0	0	0
780	800	97	84	71	57	44	31	18	4	0	0	0
800	820	100	87	74	60	47	34	21	7	0	0	0
820	840	103	90	77	63	50	37	24	10	0	0	0
840	860	106	93	80	66	53	40	27	13	0	0	0
860	880	109	96	83	69	56	43	30	16	3	0	0
880	900	112	99	86	72	59	46	33	19	6	0	0
900	920	115	102	89	75	62	49	36	22	9	0	0
920	940	118	105	92	78	65	52	39	25	12	0	0

Figure 4.10

(Continued)

(For Wages Paid After December 1991)

And the wages are—		And the number of withholding allowances claimed is—										
At least	But less than	0	1	2	3	4	5	6	7	8	9	10
		The amount of income tax to be withheld shall be—										
$940	$960	$121	$108	$95	$81	$68	$55	$42	$28	$15	$2	$0
960	980	124	111	98	84	71	58	45	31	18	5	0
980	1,000	127	114	101	87	74	61	48	34	21	8	0
1,000	1,020	130	117	104	90	77	64	51	37	24	11	0
1,020	1,040	133	120	107	93	80	67	54	40	27	14	0
1,040	1,060	136	123	110	96	83	70	57	43	30	17	3
1,060	1,080	139	126	113	99	86	73	60	46	33	20	6
1,080	1,100	142	129	116	102	89	76	63	49	36	23	9
1,100	1,120	145	132	119	105	92	79	66	52	39	26	12
1,120	1,140	148	135	122	108	95	82	69	55	42	29	15
1,140	1,160	151	138	125	111	98	85	72	58	45	32	18
1,160	1,180	154	141	128	114	101	88	75	61	48	35	21
1,180	1,200	157	144	131	117	104	91	78	64	51	38	24
1,200	1,220	160	147	134	120	107	94	81	67	54	41	27
1,220	1,240	163	150	137	123	110	97	84	70	57	44	30
1,240	1,260	166	153	140	126	113	100	87	73	60	47	33
1,260	1,280	169	156	143	129	116	103	90	76	63	50	36
1,280	1,300	172	159	146	132	119	106	93	79	66	53	39
1,300	1,320	175	162	149	135	122	109	96	82	69	56	42
1,320	1,340	178	165	152	138	125	112	99	85	72	59	45
1,340	1,360	181	168	155	141	128	115	102	88	75	62	48
1,360	1,380	184	171	158	144	131	118	105	91	78	65	51
1,380	1,400	187	174	161	147	134	121	108	94	81	68	54
1,400	1,420	190	177	164	150	137	124	111	97	84	71	57
1,420	1,440	193	180	167	153	140	127	114	100	87	74	60
1,440	1,460	196	183	170	156	143	130	117	103	90	77	63
1,460	1,480	199	186	173	159	146	133	120	106	93	80	66
1,480	1,500	202	189	176	162	149	136	123	109	96	83	69
1,500	1,520	205	192	179	165	152	139	126	112	99	86	72
1,520	1,540	210	195	182	168	155	142	129	115	102	89	75
1,540	1,560	215	198	185	171	158	145	132	118	105	92	78
1,560	1,580	221	201	188	174	161	148	135	121	108	95	81
1,580	1,600	226	204	191	177	164	151	138	124	111	98	84
1,600	1,620	232	207	194	180	167	154	141	127	114	101	87
1,620	1,640	238	213	197	183	170	157	144	130	117	104	90
1,640	1,660	243	218	200	186	173	160	147	133	120	107	93
1,660	1,680	249	224	203	189	176	163	150	136	123	110	96
1,680	1,700	254	230	206	192	179	166	153	139	126	113	99
1,700	1,720	260	235	210	195	182	169	156	142	129	116	102
1,720	1,740	266	241	216	198	185	172	159	145	132	119	105
1,740	1,760	271	246	222	201	188	175	162	148	135	122	108
1,760	1,780	277	252	227	204	191	178	165	151	138	125	111
1,780	1,800	282	258	233	208	194	181	168	154	141	128	114
1,800	1,820	288	263	238	214	197	184	171	157	144	131	117
1,820	1,840	294	269	244	219	200	187	174	160	147	134	120
1,840	1,860	299	274	250	225	203	190	177	163	150	137	123
1,860	1,880	305	280	255	230	206	193	180	166	153	140	126
1,880	1,900	310	286	261	236	211	196	183	169	156	143	129
1,900	1,920	316	291	266	242	217	199	186	172	159	146	132
1,920	1,940	322	297	272	247	222	202	189	175	162	149	135
1,940	1,960	327	302	278	253	228	205	192	178	165	152	138
1,960	1,980	333	308	283	258	234	209	195	181	168	155	141
1,980	2,000	338	314	289	264	239	215	198	184	171	158	144
2,000	2,020	344	319	294	270	245	220	201	187	174	161	147
2,020	2,040	350	325	300	275	250	226	204	190	177	164	150
2,040	2,060	355	330	306	281	256	231	207	193	180	167	153
2,060	2,080	361	336	311	286	262	237	212	196	183	170	156
2,080	2,100	366	342	317	292	267	243	218	199	186	173	159
2,100	2,120	372	347	322	298	273	248	223	202	189	176	162
2,120	2,140	378	353	328	303	278	254	229	205	192	179	165
2,140	2,160	383	358	334	309	284	259	235	210	195	182	168
2,160	2,180	389	364	339	314	290	265	240	215	198	185	171
2,180	2,200	394	370	345	320	295	271	246	221	201	188	174
2,200	2,220	400	375	350	326	301	276	251	227	204	191	177
2,220	2,240	406	381	356	331	306	282	257	232	207	194	180

$2,240 and over   Use Table 2(b) for a **MARRIED person** on page 26. Also see the instructions on page 24.

Source: Circular E: *Employer's Tax Guide*, U.S. Dept. of the Treasury, Internal Revenue Service (U.S. Government Printing Office).

Percentage method income tax with-holding table

Payroll Period	One with-holding allowance
Weekly	$44.23
Biweekly.	88.46
Semimonthly	95.83
Monthly	191.67
Quarterly.	575.00
Semiannually	1,150.00
Annually	2,300.00
Daily or miscellaneous (each day of the payroll period)	8.85

Source: U.S. Dept. of the Treasury, Internal Revenue Service (U.S. Government Printing Office).

Solution 2

Percentage Method

Step 1: Determine the amount of the withholding allowance. Multiply the amount of one withholding allowance for the pay period from the table in Figure 4.11 by the number of allowances claimed by the employee on the W-4 form.

$$\text{withholding allowance} = 44.23 \times 4$$
$$= \$176.92$$

Step 2: Determine the earnings subject to withholding tax. Subtract the total withholding allowance found in step 1 from the total earnings to determine the amount of earnings subject to withholding tax.

$$\text{earnings subject to tax} = \$915.50 - 176.92$$
$$= \$738.58$$

Step 3: Calculate the FWT from the tables for the percentage method of withholding. Using the table in Figure 4.12, locate in part b, married person paid weekly, the wage amount *over $71 but not over $760* and calculate the FWT in the following manner:

$$\text{withholding tax} = \text{taxable earnings} \times \text{tax rate}$$
$$= \$667.58 \times .15$$
$$= \$100.14$$

There is no tax withheld on the first $71 after subtracting withholding allowances. Therefore, the tax is calculated on $667.58 ($738.58 − $71 = $667.58) at the 15% rate provided in the table. The percentage method produced a higher amount to be withheld ($100.14) compared to the wage-bracket method ($100). The difference is generally minimal (as in

Figure 4.12

Tables for percentage method of withholding (for wages paid after December 1991)

TABLE 1—If the Payroll Period With Respect to an Employee is Weekly

(a) SINGLE person—including head of household:

If the amount of wages (after subtracting withholding allowances) is:		The amount of income tax to be withheld shall be:	
Not over $25.		0	
Over—	**But not over—**		**of excess over—**
$25	—$438 . . .	15%	—$25
$438	—$1,023 . .	$61.95 plus 28%	—$438
$1,023.		$225.75 plus 31%	—$1,023

(b) MARRIED person

If the amount of wages (after subtracting withholding allowances) is:		The amount of income tax to be withheld shall be:	
Not over $71		0	
Over—	**But not over—**		**of excess over—**
$71	—$760 . . .	15%	—$71
$760	—$1,735 . . .	$103.35 plus 28%	—$760
$1,735		$376.35 plus 31%	—$1,735

TABLE 2—If the Payroll Period With Respect to an Employee is Biweekly

(a) SINGLE person—including head of household:

If the amount of wages (after subtracting withholding allowances) is:		The amount of income tax to be withheld shall be:	
Not over $50.		0	
Over—	**But not over—**		**of excess over—**
$50	—$875 . . .	15%	—$50
$875	—$2,046 . .	$123.75 plus 28%	—$875
$2,046.		$451.63 plus 31%	—$2,046

(b) MARRIED person

If the amount of wages (after subtracting withholding allowances) is:		The amount of income tax to be withheld shall be:	
Not over $142		0	
Over—	**But not over—**		**of excess over—**
$142	—$1,519 . . .	15%	—$142
$1,519	—$3,469 . . .	$206.55 plus 28%	—$1,519
$3,469		$752.55 plus 31%	—$3,469

TABLE 3—If the Payroll Period With Respect to an Employee is Semimonthly

(a) SINGLE person—including head of household:

If the amount of wages (after subtracting withholding allowances) is:		The amount of income tax to be withheld shall be:	
Not over $54.		0	
Over—	**But not over—**		**of excess over—**
$54	—$948 . . .	15%	—$54
$948	—$2,217 . .	$134.10 plus 28%	—$948
$2,217.		$489.42 plus 31%	—$2,217

(b) MARRIED person—

If the amount of wages (after subtracting withholding allowances) is:		The amount of income tax to be withheld shall be:	
Not over $154		0	
Over—	**But not over—**		**of excess over—**
$154	—$1,646 . . .	15%	—$154
$1,646	—$3,758 . . .	$223.80 plus 28%	—$1,646
$3,758		$815.16 plus 31%	—$3,758

TABLE 4—If the Payroll Period With Respect to an Employee is Monthly

(a) SINGLE person—including head of household:

If the amount of wages (after subtracting withholding allowances) is:		The amount of income tax to be withheld shall be:	
Not over $108		0	
Over—	**But not over—**		**of excess over—**
$108	—$1,896 . .	15%	—$108
$1,896	—$4,433 . .	$268.20 plus 28%	—$1,896
$4,433.		$978.56 plus 31%	—$4,433

(b) MARRIED person—

If the amount of wages (after subtracting withholding allowances) is:		The amount of income tax to be withheld shall be:	
Not over $308		0	
Over—	**But not over—**		**of excess over—**
$308	—$3,292 . . .	15%	—$308
$3,292	—$7,517 . . .	$447.60 plus 28%	—$3,292
$7,517		$1,630.60 plus 31%	—$7,517

Source: U.S. Dept. of the Treasury, Internal Revenue Service (U.S. Government Printing Office).

this example) and is adjusted when the employee prepares his or her individual income tax returns.

The employer must provide each employee with a W-2 (Figure 4.13) by January 31 of the following year, which shows the total wages paid, federal income tax withheld, state and local income taxes withheld, as well as FICA and medicare taxes withheld. If the employee's tax liability on the tax return is less than the FWT withheld on the W-2, the employee will receive a refund. On the other hand, if the tax liability is greater than the FWT withheld, the employee will have to pay the additional amount when filing the tax return. As a rule, the amount of FWT withheld should closely approximate the employee's income tax liability for the year.

Another mandatory deduction withheld from some employees' gross earnings is **state withholding tax (SWT)**. The methods used to collect state income tax when applicable are similar to the methods used to collect federal withholding tax. Many states use tables to determine the amount of withholding based on wage-brackets and withholding allow-

Figure 4.13   Form W-2: wage and tax statement

1 Control number			OMB No. 1545-0008	**Copy B To be filed with employee's FEDERAL tax return**	
2 Employer's name, address, and ZIP code				6 Statutory employee Deceased Pension plan Legal rep. 942 emp. Deferred compensation	
				7 Allocated tips	8 Advance EIC payment
				9 Federal income tax withheld	10 Wages, tips, other compensation
3 Employer's identification number	4 Employer's state I.D. number			11 Social security tax withheld	12 Social security wages
5 Employee's social security number				13 Social security tips	14 Medicare wages and tips
19 Employee's name, address, and ZIP code				15 Medicare tax withheld	16 Nonqualified plans
				17 See Instrs. for Box 17	18 Other
20		21		22 Dependent care benefits	23 Benefits included in Box 10
24 State income tax	25 State wages, tips, etc.	26 Name of state		27 Local income tax 28 Local wages, tips, etc. 29 Name of locality	

Source: U.S. Dept. of the Treasury, Internal Revenue Service (U.S. Government Printing Office).

ances claimed. Some states prefer to use a fixed percentage rate to determine the employee's SWT deduction. The *flat tax rate method* requires the employer to apply the same tax rate to all taxable income up to a specified amount of gross earnings paid during the calendar year. The calculation of this tax is similar to the method used in computing FICA tax, which we discussed in Section 4.4. Again, we will use Frank Taylor's example to further illustrate the calculation of his mandatory payroll deductions.

Example 19

Frank Taylor's gross earnings for the week are $915.50 and his year-to-date earnings amount to $50,624.75. Frank works in a state that has a flat tax rate of 3½% on gross earnings with maximum taxable earnings of $52,000. How much of Frank's gross earnings will be deducted for state withholding tax?

Solution

Step 1:   Determine the taxable earnings.

$52,000.00   maximum taxable earnings
$-50,624.75$ year-to-date earnings

$ 1,375.25   earnings subject to tax

Since the current earnings ($915.50) is less than the earnings still subject to tax ($1,375.25), the total amount of gross earnings is used to calculate the state withholding tax.

Step 2:   Use the percentage equation to calculate the amount of tax withheld.

SWT = taxable earnings × tax rate
SWT = $915.50 × .035
    = $32.04

ELECTIVE DEDUCTIONS

Elective deductions are amounts withheld from an employee's gross earnings that have been authorized by the employee and agreed upon by the employer. Elective deductions may include payments for insurance premiums, union dues, retirement annuities, charitable contributions, U.S. savings bonds, personal savings or loan payments, and work uniform expenses. The elective as well as the mandatory deductions comprise the total deductions to be subtracted from gross earnings, which result in net pay or take-home pay.

Net pay formula

net pay = gross earnings − total deductions

To continue the analysis of the Frank Taylor example, let's look at the elective deductions he has authorized his employer to subtract from his gross earnings; then we can develop a summary of his total deductions for the pay period.

Example 20

Frank Taylor has requested his employer to deduct from his gross earnings of $915.50 the following amounts for company benefits and personal expenditures per pay period: group health insurance, $12.50; credit union savings, $25.00; dental insurance, $5.75; charitable contribution, $10.00; and retirement annuity, $40.75. His mandatory deductions for the period were: FICA tax, $56.76; medicare tax, $13.27; federal withholding tax, $100.00; and state withholding tax, $32.04. Find his net pay for the pay period.

Solution

Gross earnings for period			$915.50
Mandatory deductions:			
FICA tax	$ 56.76		
Medicare tax	13.27		
Federal withholding tax	100.00		
State withholding tax	32.04	$202.07	
Elective deductions:			
Health insurance	$ 12.50		
Credit union savings	25.00		
Dental insurance	5.75		
Charitable contribution	10.00		
Retirement annuity	40.75	94.00	
Total deductions			296.07
NET PAY			$619.43

or

net pay = gross earnings − total deductions
net pay = $915.50   − $296.07
        = $619.43

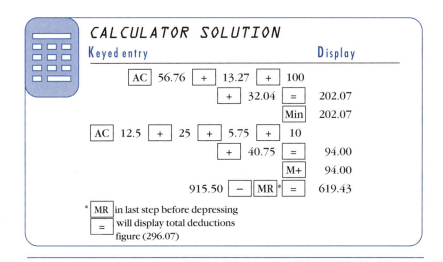

CALCULATOR SOLUTION

Keyed entry   Display

AC	56.76	+	13.27	+	100		
				+	32.04	=	202.07
						Min	202.07
AC	12.5	+	25	+	5.75	+	10
					+	40.75	=	94.00
							M+	94.00
				915.50	−	MR *	=	619.43

* MR in last step before depressing
= will display total deductions
figure (296.07)

CHECK YOUR KNOWLEDGE

Employee deductions

1. Sharon Reynolds, a physician's assistant, is single and claims three withholding allowances. She has year-to-date earnings of $19,265, and her current biweekly gross earnings amount to $865. How much of her gross earnings must be withheld for (a) FICA tax and (b) medicare tax? Use Figures 4.4 and 4.5 to calculate the taxes.

2. From the information provided in problem 1, calculate the federal withholding tax for Sharon. Use the (a) wage bracket method as well as the (b) percentage method for computing FWT.

3. If Sharon works in a state that has a flat tax rate of 6¾% on gross earnings up to maximum taxable earnings of $20,000, how much of her gross earnings will be deducted for state withholding tax (SWT)?

4. Sharon's employer, at her request, deducts $10.50 for health insurance, $18.75 for U.S. savings bonds, and $38.50 for her retirement fund. Determine Sharon's total deductions for the pay period.

5. Determine Sharon's net pay for the pay period using the results of your calculations from problems 1 through 4.

6. Vern Beckwith is married and claims five withholding allowances. His year-to-date earnings amount to $53,225 and his current semimonthly gross earnings are $2,800. Use the (a) percent method to calculate the FWT and the (b) wage bracket tables for the FICA and medicare taxes.

Answers to CYK: **1.** a. $53.63; b. $12.54   **2.** a. $83; b. $82.44   **3.** $49.61   **4.** $265.97
5. $599.03   **6.** a. $412.76; b. $141.05

4.4 EXERCISES

Calculate the FICA and medicare tax deductions for each of the following employees using the tax table (Figures 4.4 and 4.5) method.

	Employee	Current gross earnings	Medicare tax	FICA tax
1.	Cooper, L.	$156.20	_____	_____
2.	Bevard, M.	375.80	_____	_____
3.	Hazeltine, M.	420.75	_____	_____
4.	Solomon, B.	694.90	_____	_____

Calculate the FICA tax deduction for each of the following employees based on 1992 tax rates in Table 4.2 (percentage method).

	Employee	Year-to-date earnings	Current gross earnings	FICA tax	Medicare tax
5.	Charles, T.	$18,680	$ 450	_____	_____
6.	Espinoza, C.	53,750	2,280	_____	_____
7.	Sith, P.	60,200	3,145	_____	_____
8.	Willis, R.	38,150	860	_____	_____

Use the wage-bracket method (Figures 4.7, 4.8, 4.9, and 4.10) to find the federal withholding tax (FWT) for each of the following employees.

	Employee	Current gross earnings	Pay period	Marital status	Exemptions	FWT tax
9.	Alhussein, R.	$ 489.70	Weekly	M	4	_____
10.	Hammond, P.	1,265.50	Biweekly	M	8	_____
11.	Keller, J.	620.45	Biweekly	S	1	_____
12.	Norton, B.	572.30	Weekly	M	6	_____
13.	Wong, D.	376.25	Weekly	S	2	_____
14.	Zimmerman, P.	847.80	Biweekly	M	2	_____

Using the percentage method, calculate the FWT tax for each of the following employees (Figures 4.11 and 4.12).

	Employee	Current gross earnings	Pay period	Marital status	Exemptions	FWT tax
15.	Anderson, D.	$ 520.65	Weekly	M	4	_____
16.	Dombowski, T.	748.20	Semimonthly	S	2	_____
17.	Loftus, P.	2,630.45	Monthly	M	2	_____
18.	Ramos, M.	987.30	Biweekly	M	5	_____
19.	Steel, J.	1,238.75	Monthly	S	1	_____

Complete the following biweekly payroll register as indicated. Use the appropriate wage bracket tables provided in the chapter for the FWT, FICA, and medicare tax rates. All earnings are subject to FICA and medicare taxes.

	Employee	Marital status	Exemptions	Gross earnings	FWT tax
20.	Bright, P.	S	2	$ 846.20	_____
21.	Denny, M.	M	4	1,010.50	_____
22.	Hartz, T.	M	2	910.80	_____
23.	Lee, R.	S	1	1,240.75	_____
24.	Udell, S.	M	6	1,418.30	_____

Employee	Medicare tax	FICA	Other deductions	Net pay
Bright, P.	_____	_____	$102.10	_____
Denny, M.	_____	_____	146.80	_____
Hartz, T.	_____	_____	98.75	_____
Lee, R.	_____	_____	162.40	_____
Udell, S.	_____	_____	187.25	_____

Complete the following weekly payroll register. Use the percentage method to calculate the FWT. Assume all earnings paid during the period are subject to a 6.2% FICA tax and 1.45% medicare tax rate.

	Employee	Marital status	Exemptions	Gross earnings	FWT tax
25.	Boco, P.	M	3	$397.60	_____
26.	Deitz, T.	S	1	285.30	_____
27.	Schmidt, P.	M	7	528.97	_____
28.	Zello, E.	S	2	465.40	_____

Employee	Medicare tax	FICA	Other deductions	Net pay
Boco, P.	_____	_____	$28.40	_____
Deitz, T.	_____	_____	10.90	_____
Schmidt, P.	_____	_____	65.50	_____
Zello, E.	_____	_____	42.20	_____

29. Judy Terrell's earnings this pay period are $1,520.75 and her year-to-date earnings are $42,520.80. How much of her current earnings must her employer withhold for (a) FICA tax and (b) medicare tax based on the tax rates given in Figures 4.4 and 4.5?

30. If an employee is paid $6.50 per hour for 46 hours of working time, how much must be deducted for FICA and medicare taxes if the employer uses the percentage method? All wages are taxable and the employee receives time-and-a-half for all hours worked over 40 in a workweek.

31. Martin Prosser is married and claims three exemptions. He receives an annual salary of $21,970. If he is paid on a biweekly basis,

M 3

what is the amount of FWT deducted from his earnings each pay period? (Use the wage bracket method.)

32. Art Rice, a licensed practical nurse (LPN), is single and claims 2 exemptions. He is paid weekly at an hourly rate of $7.80, with time-and-a-half paid for hours in excess of 40 hours a week. He worked 42 hours last week. If his regular workweek is 35 hours, what are his (a) FICA, (b) medicare, and (c) FWT taxes based on the percentage method, assuming all earnings are taxable? (Use 1992 tax rates.)

33. Sarah Fillingham is an electrical engineer and receives a semimonthly salary of $3,250. She is married and claims four withholding allowances. If her year-to-date earnings are $52,875, how much will her employer deduct from her current earnings for (a) FWT, (b) FICA, and (c) medicare taxes.

34. Bob Bigsbee's gross earnings for the week are $523.85, and his year-to-date earnings amount to $29,785.20. He works in a state that has a flat state withholding tax rate (SWT) of 2½% on gross earnings up to $30,000. How much of Bob's gross earnings will be deducted for state withholding tax?

35. Alice Reschke works for the local power authority. She is paid a weekly salary of $420 and is married with 2 exemptions. What is her net pay if her FICA, medicare, and FWT taxes are based on the wage bracket method and her employer deducts the following: group health insurance, $6.50; dental insurance, $2.50; credit union, $25.00; and retirement contribution, $22.00?

4.5   EMPLOYER PAYROLL TAXES AND REPORTS

Learning objective

Identify and calculate the various types of employer payroll taxes.

Employers are required by law to maintain a *payroll register* that indicates how gross earnings are determined, the amount of mandatory and elective deductions withheld, and the net pay of each employee. The payroll register (Figure 4.3) contains the information necessary to calculate the employer's quarterly payroll taxes.

At the end of March, June, September, and December, employers must file *Form 941*, the *Employer's Quarterly Federal Tax Return* (Figure 4.14). Form 941 is used to report the (FWT) federal withholding tax, the social security (FICA), and medicare taxes collected from employees, and the social security and medicare taxes to be paid by the employer.

FICA TAX AND MEDICARE TAX

Employers must pay a FICA tax and medicare tax equal to the FICA medicare taxes withheld from their employees. The amount of these taxes is reported on line 8 of Form 941 and is determined by multiplying the total taxable social security and medicare wages of employees by the combined rate of each tax. The combined FICA rate (12.4%) is found in Table 4.2 by adding the employee rate (6.2%) to the employer's rate (6.2%) for the same period. The combined medicare rate (2.9%) is determined in the same manner (1.45% + 1.45% = 2.9%).

The employer pays the taxes reported in Form 941 each quarter by depositing the required tax with an authorized financial institution or a

Figure 4.14

Form 941: employer's quarterly federal tax return

Form 941
(Rev. January 1991)
Department of the Treasury
Internal Revenue Service

4141

Employer's Quarterly Federal Tax Return
▶ See Circular E for more information concerning employment tax returns.
Please type or print.

OMB No. 1545-0029
Expires: 5-31-93

Your name, address, employer identification number, and calendar quarter of return. (If not correct, please change.)

Name (as distinguished from trade name)
Rojon Enterpirses Inc.
Trade name, if any

Address and ZIP code

Date quarter ended
September 30, 1992

Employer identification number
65244374876

| T |
| FF |
| FD |
| FP |
| I |
| T |

If address is different from prior return, check here ▶ ☐

IRS Use

1 1 1 1 1 1 1 1 1   2   3 3 3 3 3   4 4 4

5 5 5   6   7   8 8 8 8 8   9 9 9   10 10 10 10 10 10 10 10 10

If you do not have to file returns in the future, check here . . . ▶ ☐   Date final wages paid . . . ▶ **9/18**

If you are a seasonal employer, see **Seasonal employers** on page 2 and check here . ▶ ☐

1a Number of employees (except household) employed in the pay period that includes March 12th ▶ | 1a | **58** |

b If you are a subsidiary corporation AND your parent corporation files a consolidated Form 1120, enter parent corporation employer identification number (EIN) . . ▶ | 1b | **—** |

2 Total wages and tips subject to withholding, plus other compensation . . . . ▶	2	$ **485,235** 00
3 Total income tax withheld from wages, tips, pensions, annuities, sick pay, gambling, etc. . ▶	3	**155,275** 20
4 Adjustment of withheld income tax for preceding quarters of calendar year (see instructions) . ▶	4	**0**
5 Adjusted total of income tax withheld (line 3 as adjusted by line 4—see instructions) . . . ▶	5	**155,275** 20
6a Taxable social security wages (Complete line 7) $ **472,585** × 12.4% (.124) =	6a	**58,600** 54
b Taxable social security tips $ **0** × 12.4% (.124) =	6b	**0**
7 Taxable Medicare wages and tips $ **485,235** × 2.9% (.029) =	7	**14,071** 82
8 Total social security and Medicare taxes (add lines 6a, 6b, and 7) . . . . ▶	8	**72,672** 36
9 Adjustment of social security and Medicare taxes (see instructions for required explanation) . .	9	**0**
10 Adjusted total of social security and Medicare taxes (line 8 as adjusted by line 9—see instructions) ▶	10	**72,672** 36
11 Backup withholding (see instructions)	11	**0**
12 Adjustment of backup withholding tax for preceding quarters of calendar year.	12	**0**
13 Adjusted total of backup withholding (line 11 as adjusted by line 12) . . . . ▶	13	**0**
14 Total taxes (add lines 5, 10, and 13)	14	**227,947** 56
15 Advance earned income credit (EIC) payments made to employees, if any . . . . ▶	15	**0**
16 Net taxes (subtract line 15 from line 14). **This should equal line IV below** (plus line IV of Schedule A (Form 941) if you have treated backup withholding as a separate liability)	16	**227,947** 56
17 Total deposits for quarter, including overpayment applied from a prior quarter, from your records. ▶	17	**227,947** 56
18 Balance due (subtract line 17 from line 16). This should be less than $500. Pay to IRS. . . . ▶	18	**0**

19 Overpayment, if line 17 is more than line 16, enter here ▶ $ ___**0**___ and check if to be:
☐ Applied to next return   **OR**   ☐ Refunded.

Record of Federal Tax Liability (You must complete if line 16 is $500 or more and Schedule B is not attached.) See instructions before checking these boxes.
Check only if you made deposits using the 95% rule ▶ ☐   Check only if you are a first time 3-banking-day depositor. . . . ▶ ☐

Show tax liability here, **not deposits.** IRS gets deposit data from FTD coupons.

Date wages paid		First month of quarter		Second month of quarter		Third month of quarter
1st through 3rd	A		I		Q	
4th through 7th	B		J		R	
8th through 11th	C		K		S	
12th through 15th	D		L		T	
16th through 19th	E		M		U	
20th through 22nd	F		N		V	
23rd through 25th	G		O		W	
26th through the last	H		P		X	
Total liability for month	I	**74,223.22**	II	**70,945.17**	III	**82,779.17**

IV Total for quarter (add lines **I, II,** and **III**). This should equal line 16 above . . . . . ▶ **227,947.56**

Do NOT Show Federal Tax Deposits Here

Sign Here
Under penalties of perjury, I declare that I have examined this return, including accompanying schedules and statements, and to the best of my knowledge and belief, it is true, correct, and complete.

Signature ✗ _John Adams_

Print Your Name and Title ▶ **John Adams Controller**

Date ▶

For Paperwork Reduction Act Notice, see page 2.

Source: U.S. Dept. of the Treasury, Internal Revenue Service (U.S. Government Printing Office).

Figure 4.15

Chart B—summary
of deposit rules for
social security and
medicare taxes
and withheld in-
come tax

Deposit Rule	Deposit Due
(1) If at the end of the quarter your total tax liability for the quarter is less than $500:	(1) No deposit is required. You may pay the taxes to IRS with Form 941 (or 941E), or you may deposit them by the due date of the return.
(2) If at the end of any month your total tax liability is less than $500:	(2) No deposit is required. You may carry the tax liability over to the following month within the quarter.
(3) If at the end of any month your total tax liability is $500 or more but less than $3;000:	(3) Within 15 days after the end of the month. (No deposit is required if you were required to make a deposit for an eighth-monthly period during the month under rule 4. However, if you were required to make a deposit under rule 4 in the last month of the quarter, deposit any balance due of less than $3,000 by the due date of the return.)
(4) If at the end of any eighth-monthly period (the 3rd, 7th, 11th, 15th, 19th, 22nd, 25th, and last day of each month) your total tax liability is $3,000 or more but less than $100,000:	(4) Within 3 banking days after the end of that eighth-monthly period.
(5) If at the end of any day during an eighth-monthly period your total tax liability is $100,000 or more:	(5) By the end of the next banking day.

Source: U.S. Dept. of the Treasury, Internal Revenue Service (U.S. Government Printing Office).

federal reserve bank in accordance with the deposit rules shown in Figure 4.15. Notice that if the undeposited taxes at the end of any quarter are less than $500, the employer can pay the taxes directly to the IRS with Form 941. If a deposit is required, the employer must file Form 8109 (Fig-

Figure 4.16   Form 8109: federal tax deposit coupon

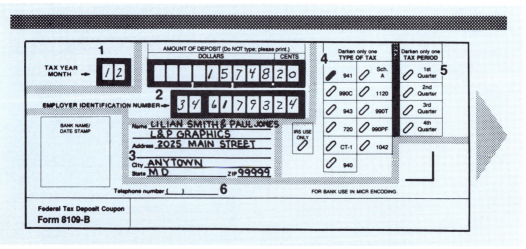

Source: U.S. Dept. of the Treasury, Internal Revenue Service (U.S. Government Printing Office).

ure 4.16) along with the proper amount of money at an authorized financial institution within the allotted time periods. Form 941 must be filed by the end of the month following each quarter. Therefore, if an employer makes deposits within the deposit period, the balance due on line 18 of Form 941 will be 0.

COMPLETING FORM 941

To help you better understand this employer payroll tax, Example 21 will illustrate the calculation procedures necessary to complete selected lines of Form 941 (Figure 4.14) that involve the reporting of employer payroll taxes. It will not be possible to complete the entire form as this report must be prepared from a complete set of payroll records for each quarter.

Learning objective
Complete payroll records and quarterly payroll tax returns.

Example 21

The payroll records of Rojon Enterprises indicate total earnings paid subject to withholding of $485,235 for the quarter ending September 30, 1992. Of the total wages paid, all are subject to medicare tax; $12,650 is exempt from FICA tax because some employees had exceeded the maximum taxable earnings base ($55,500); and $155,275.20 paid to employees was withheld for federal income taxes. Determine the amount of payroll taxes to be reported on Form 941 for the quarter. (Refer to the partially completed Form 941, Figure 4.14.)

Solution

First, enter the total earnings ($485,235) paid during the quarter on line 2. Then, enter the federal income tax withheld ($155,275.20) on line 3. Next, determine the amount of wages reported for the quarter that are subject to FICA tax and medicare tax and enter those on line 6a and line 7 in the calculation columns ($＿＿＿＿ × 12.4% or .124), and ($＿＿＿＿ × 2.9%, or .029).

$$\begin{aligned}
\text{taxable FICA wages} &= \text{total wages reported} - \text{exempt wages} \\
&= \$485,235 \qquad\qquad - \$12,650 \\
&= \$472,585
\end{aligned}$$

As all earnings paid during the period are subject to the medicare tax, $485,235 would be entered on line 7 in the medicare tax calculation column. We can now multiply the taxable FICA wages and the medicare wages by the combined rates (the employer must match the employees' contribution) and enter on lines 6a and 7.

$$FICA \text{ tax} = \text{taxable FICA wages} \times \text{combined rate}$$
$$= \$472,585 \qquad \times \ .124 \ (1992 \text{ rate})$$
$$= \$58,600.54$$

$$medicare \text{ tax} = \text{taxable medicare wages} \times \text{combined rate}$$
$$= \$485,235 \qquad \times \ .029$$
$$= \$14,071.82$$

At this point, we have explained how the entries on lines 2, 3, 6a, and 7 were determined. The other entries follow the instructions provided for each line on the form.

Line 5:   Enter the amount from line 3 on line 5 as there are no adjustments for preceding quarters.

Lines 8, 9, and 10:   Enter the amount from lines 6a, 6b, and 7 on lines 8 and 10 as Rojon Enterprises did not have to make any adjustments for errors in social security taxes reported on line 9.

Lines 11, 12, and 13:   No adjustments necessary, enter 0.

Line 14:   Add the withheld income tax (line 5) to the social security and medicare taxes (line 10) and enter the total.

Lines 16 and 17:   The amounts on these two lines are the same because there is no earned income credit reported on line 15 and the amount of tax owed by Rojon Enterprises for the quarter and the amount deposited are the same. Consequently, no payment is required with the return (line 18), nor is there a refund due for overpayment (line 19).

UNEMPLOYMENT TAXES

Every employer is required by the **Federal Unemployment Tax Act (FUTA)** to pay a tax on each employee's earnings for unemployment insurance. An employer may also be required by a **State Unemployment Tax Act (SUTA)** to pay a similar state tax. The federal and state systems support the unemployment insurance program, which provides payments of unemployment compensation to workers who have lost their jobs. The tax is paid entirely by the employer. The tax rate and wage limits can change. All changes are published annually in the *Employer's Tax Guide*, which can be obtained from the IRS. The problems in this text will be based on the 1992 federal unemployment tax (FUTA) rate of 6.2% of the first $7,000 in earnings paid to employees during the year. The tax guidelines also state that an employer is allowed a credit of up to 5.4% for the state unemployment tax (SUTA) they pay. Therefore, the federal rate can be reduced to .8% by the maximum state experience rate of 5.4%

[handwritten margin notes: "Fed rate", "Fed rate", "if employer state", "pays state unemployment tax", "Unemployment tax"]

(6.2% − 5.4% = .8%). If the state experience rate is less than 5.4%, the employer is allowed the full 5.4% credit. However, if the employer is exempt from state unemployment tax, it must pay the full 6.2% FUTA rate.

Employers are required to file Form 940 (Figure 4.17) annually and make any deposits that may be required quarterly. A deposit is required if an employer has more than a $100 unemployment tax liability at the end of a calendar quarter.

Figure 4.17

Form 940: employer's annual federal unemployment (FUTA) tax returns

continues

Figure 4.17

(Continued)

Page **2**

Part II **Tax Due or Refund** *(Complete if you checked the "Yes" boxes in both questions A and B and did not check the box in C.)*

1	**FUTA tax.** Multiply the wages in Part I, line 5, by .008 and enter here.	1
2	Enter amount from Part I, line 6	2
3	**Total FUTA tax** (add lines 1 and 2) . . . . ▶	3
4	Total FUTA tax deposited for the year, including any overpayment applied from a prior year . .	4
5	**Balance due** (subtract line 4 from line 3). This should be $100 or less. Pay to the Internal Revenue Service. . . . . ▶	5
6	**Overpayment** (subtract line 3 from line 4). Check if it is to be: ☐ **Applied to next return,** or ☐ **Refunded** . . . . ▶	6

Part III **Tax Due or Refund** *(Complete if you checked the "No" box in either question A or B or you checked the box in C.)*

1	Gross FUTA tax. Multiply the wages in Part I, line 5, by .062	1
2	Maximum credit. Multiply the wages in Part I, line 5, by .054. . .	2	
3	Computation of tentative credit	

(a) Name of state	(b) State reporting number(s) as shown on employer's state contribution returns	(c) Taxable payroll (as defined in state act)	(d) State experience rate		(e) State experience rate	(f) Contributions if rate had been 5.4% (col. (c) x .054)	(g) Contributions payable at experience rate (col. (c) x col. (e))	(h) Additional credit (col. (f) minus col.(g)). If 0 or less, enter 0.	(i) Contributions actually paid to the state
			From	To					

3a	Totals . . . ▶	
3b	**Total tentative credit** (add line 3a, columns (h) and (i) only—see instructions for limitations on late payments) ▶	
4	**Credit:** Enter the smaller of the amount in Part III, line 2, or line 3b 4	
5	Enter the amount from Part I, line 6	5
6	**Credit allowable** (subtract line 5 from line 4). (If zero or less, enter 0.)	6
7	**Total FUTA tax** (subtract line 6 from line 1)	7
8	Total FUTA tax deposited for the year, including any overpayment applied from a prior year . .	8
9	**Balance due** (subtract line 8 from line 7). This should be $100 or less. Pay to the Internal Revenue Service. . . . . ▶	9
10	**Overpayment** (subtract line 7 from line 8). Check if it is to be: ☐ **Applied to next return,** or ☐ **Refunded** . . . . ▶	10

Part IV **Record of Quarterly Federal Tax Liability for Unemployment Tax** *(Do not include state liability)*

Quarter	First	Second	Third	Fourth	Total for year
Liability for quarter					

Under penalties of perjury, I declare that I have examined this return, including accompanying schedules and statements, and to the best of my knowledge and belief, it is true, correct, and complete, and that no part of any payment made to a state unemployment fund claimed as a credit was or is to be deducted from the payments to employees.

Signature ▶   Title (Owner, etc.) ▶   Date ▶

Source: U.S. Dept. of the Treasury, Internal Revenue Service (U.S. Government Printing Office).

Example 22

Gancy Chemical Distributors has a state unemployment experience rating of 3.6% for the current year. Using the following payroll information, determine the FUTA tax liability and the SUTA tax liability on earnings paid during the quarter ending June 30.

Employee	First-quarter earnings	Second-quarter earnings
J. Marko	$ 4,270	$ 4,350
B. Netti	6,580	5,785
D. Hills	7,240	6,800
R. Hsu	2,800	4,600
T. Parker	3,200	3,900
L. VanAuken	2,600	4,250
Totals	$26,690	$29,685

Solution

Employee	First-quarter earnings	Unemployment tax wage limit	Second-quarter taxable earnings
J. Marko	$ 4,270	7,000	$ 2,730
B. Netti	6,580	7,000	420
D. Hills	7,240	7,000	0
R. Hsu	2,800	7,000	4,200
T. Parker	3,200	7,000	3,800
L. VanAuken	2,600	7,000	4,250
Totals	$26,690		$15,400

The solution table shows how much of each employee's total earnings for the second quarter are subject to federal unemployment (FUTA) tax. Of the total wages paid during the second quarter ($29,685), only $15,400 is subject to the tax. This is because most of the employees reached the yearly limit ($7,000) during the quarter and only the difference between their first-quarter earnings and the yearly limit can be taxed. One employee (D. Hills) had already reached the taxable limit during the first quarter; therefore, the employer pays no FUTA tax on his second-quarter earnings. Another employee (L. VanAuken) has not yet been paid more than the taxable limit for the year ($2,600 + $4,250 = $6,850). The employer must pay FUTA tax on his total second-quarter earnings. Now that we know the amount of second-quarter earnings subject to unemployment tax, we calculate the FUTA and SUTA tax as follows:

FUTA tax
$$\text{FUTA tax} = \text{taxable earnings} \times \text{tax rate}$$
$$= \$15,400 \qquad \times .008$$
$$= \$123.20$$

SUTA tax
$$\text{SUTA tax} = \text{taxable earnings} \times \text{tax rate}$$
$$= \$15,400 \qquad \times .036$$
$$= \$554.40$$

The FUTA tax rate is .8% because Gancy Chemical Distributors has been assigned a state experience tax rate of 3.6%, which is less than the 5.4% maximum that allows them to take full credit (6.2% − 5.4% = .8%).

Gancy Chemical Distributors must deposit the $123.20 in FUTA tax because the quarterly tax liability exceeds the $100 limit allowed in each quarter. The FUTA tax will be deposited along with any FICA tax or federal withholding tax that is required on June 30 using Form 8109 (Figure 4.16). At the end of the year, the company will file Form 940 (Figure 4.17), the Employer's Annual Federal Unemployment (FUTA) Tax Return.

If the company's state experiential tax rate was higher (4.5%), its SUTA tax would also be higher ($15,400 × .045 = $693), but its FUTA would be the same ($123.20) resulting in a greater total unemployment tax ($123.20 + $693 = $816.20) for the quarter. Therefore, many businesses will keep this concept in mind when they make decisions related to work-force reductions.

Most states use a procedure similar to the federal system presented to report and deposit the state unemployment tax liability (SUTA). Due to a lack of conformity among states, this text will not go into any more detail regarding SUTA than has already been presented. If you are interested in knowing more about your state's employer tax system, guidelines are available from your state tax agency.

CHECK YOUR KNOWLEDGE

Employer payroll taxes and reports

1. Julia Cornish is paid $10.50 an hour and is paid time-and-a-half for all time over 40 hours a week. During the current pay period, Julia worked 46 hours. Her accumulated gross earnings are $6,775.00. Using the following rates: FICA, 6.2%; medicare, 1.45%; SUTA, 2.7%, calculate the following. (You must determine the FUTA rate using the data provided.)
   a. gross earnings
   b. employer's FICA tax
   c. employer's medicare tax
   d. FUTA tax
   e. SUTA tax

2. Using the payroll information of McDowell Company provided on the next page, calculate:
   a. the entries required to complete Form 941, the Employer's Quarterly Federal Tax Return, lines 2, 3, 6a, 7, and 8 as required
   b. the third-quarter FUTA taxes
   c. the third-quarter SUTA taxes
   McDowell has a state experiential rate of 4.2%. Its records indicate no adjustments will be required on their employer tax reports for the

third quarter. Use other rates and wage limits presented in Section 4.5 as they pertain to the required calculations.

Employee	Accumulated gross earnings	Third-quarter gross earnings	Third-quarter FWT
G. Berson	$22,570	$11,310	$3,166.80
F. Castro	15,420	7,735	1,933.75
S. Devall	4,980	6,200	1,488.00
W. LaGrange	26,150	13,050	3,654.20
M. Thayer	2,980	3,650	789.50
P. Wheeler	13,725	6,825	1,638.00

4.5 EXERCISES

Given the first-quarter payroll information for Kleen-All Janitorial Services, calculate the required employer payroll taxes on each employee's earnings for the period. Use the following rates: FICA 6.20%; medicare 1.45%; FUTA .8%; and SUTA 4.2%.

	Employee	First-quarter gross earnings	FICA	Medicare	FUTA	SUTA
1.	Ferry, M.	$6,687.40	_____	_____	_____	_____
2.	Lawson, B.	1,275.00	_____	_____	_____	_____
3.	Orcutt, R.	3,865.20	_____	_____	_____	_____
4.	Romano, F.	5,189.65	_____	_____	_____	_____

Using the first-quarter payroll summary and tax rates provided above, calculate the second-quarter payroll taxes on each employee's earnings.

	Employee	Second-quarter gross earnings	FICA	Medicare	FUTA	SUTA
5.	Ferry, M.	$5,247.20	_____	_____	_____	_____
6.	Lawson, B.	4,865.80	_____	_____	_____	_____
7.	Orcutt, R.	3,990.10	_____	_____	_____	_____
8.	Romano, F.	6,420.00	_____	_____	_____	_____

Answers to CYK: 　*1.* 　a. $514.50; b. $31.90; c. $7.46; d. $1.80; e. $6.08 　　*2.* 　a. line 2 $48,770; line 3 $12,670.25; line 6a $6,047.48; line 7 $1,414.33; line 8 $7,461.81; b. $45.36; c. $238.14

9. Ted Farnholtz is the sole proprietor of Farn-holtz Plumbing. Ted's employees' taxable earnings for the first quarter of 1992 totaled $50,000. Assuming tax rates of 5% SUTA and .8% FUTA, what quarterly payroll tax did Farnholtz Plumbing have to pay for (a) FICA, (b) medicare, (c) FUTA, and (d) SUTA? (Earnings are subject to all taxes.)

10. The Reverend David Griffith is considered to be self-employed as a minister of St. Charles's Church. He was paid $45,000 in 1992 for his services to the church. Assuming a FICA rate of 12.4%, a medicare tax rate of 2.9%, a 3.8% SUTA tax rate, and a .8% FUTA tax rate, how much must the reverend pay in taxes for (a) FICA, (b) medicare, (c) SUTA, and (d) FUTA?

11. Sara Jaynes earned $500 last week, to bring her cumulative earnings to $7,300. Sara works in a state that does not collect state unemployment taxes. How much must Sara's employer pay in payroll taxes on her current earnings based on 1992 tax rates?

12. Marie Penafeather earns a salary of $65,000 per year from Jenkins Modular Homes, a company that has a state unemployment experience rating of 5.2%. Find the amount of payroll taxes paid by Jenkins Modular Homes on Marie's salary for the 1992 fiscal year.

13. Jim Nowicki works on a salary-plus-commission basis. He is paid a monthly base salary of $1,200 and a 2.25% commission on all net sales. If his monthly net sales amounted to $45,000 and the employer tax rates are 6.20% FICA; 1.45% medicare; 4.3% SUTA; and .8% FUTA, calculate the following: (a) gross earnings, (b) employer's medicare tax, (c) employer's FICA tax, (d) FUTA tax, and (e) SUTA.

14. The payroll records of Hartson Enterprises at the end of the quarter indicated that the company had taxable social security wages of $12,689.20; taxable medicare wages of $452,457.80; and that $142,178.50 had been withheld in FWT from employees' earnings. Determine the total amount of taxes Hartson Enterprises reported for the quarter on Form 941, the Employer's Quarterly Federal Tax Return.

15. Given the following payroll information:

Employee	Accumulated gross earnings	Second-quarter gross earnings	Second-quarter federal withholding tax
Butler, D.	$6,420.00	$5,980.75	$1,245.60
Franz, T.	3,175.20	3,250.50	680.25
Hernandez, F.	8,345.10	9,175.60	2,487.90
Taylor, P.	5,680.75	4,245.20	972.50

a. Calculate the employer's FICA tax for the second quarter (assume FICA rate of 6.20% on $55,500).

b. Calculate the employer's medicare tax. (Assume a tax rate of 1.45% on $130,200.)

c. Calculate FUTA tax for the second quarter.

d. Calculate SUTA tax for the second quarter (assume a 3.5% SUTA experience rate on the first $7,000).

e. Determine the total amount of taxes to be deposited for the second quarter indicated on Form 941, the employer's quarterly tax return.

EXPRESS YOUR THOUGHTS

Compose one or two well-written sentences to express the requested information.

1. Explain how gross earnings are calculated for an employee paid by the hour if the employee worked 45 hours in one pay period.

2. Compare the standard overtime method and the premium overtime method of calculating overtime earnings.

3. Describe how gross earnings are determined using the differential piece-rate plan and a chargeback for defective units produced.

4. Identify and describe the methods used to prorate an annual salary into specific pay periods.

5. Explain how you would determine gross earnings for an employee who is paid a straight commission on net sales and is allowed to draw on projected earnings.

6. Describe how you would calculate an employee's net earnings.

7. What factors determine the amount to be withheld by employers from an employee's earnings for federal income taxes?

8. Give a step-by-step description of how to calculate federal withholding tax using the percentage method.

9. Discuss the purpose and content of Form 941, the Employer's Quarterly Federal Tax Return.

10. Illustrate how an employer's state unemployment experience tax rate of 3.5% affects the amount of federal unemployment tax paid by the employer on an employee's earnings.

Case exercise Altman Distributors and Brokers Inc.

Altman Distributors and Brokers is a full-service provider of food products to retailers and restaurants. The company employs a total of 15 people. Nine of the employees are paid various hourly rates and time-and-a-half for all hours worked in excess of 40 hours per week. Four are salespersons who receive a weekly salary of $350 plus commission based on weekly net sales. The company pays its plant manager, Allen Brown, and assistant plant manager, Marie Jordan, an annual salary of $72,800 and $57,200, respectively.

Financial Consultants prepares Altman's payroll and maintains its payroll records. The company's payroll records entering the final payroll period of the first quarter of the year list the following year-to-date totals.

Payroll Register
Altman Distributors and Brokers Inc.

Week no. 12
Beginning 3/18   Ending 3/24

Record for First   Quarter of 1992

Name	Status	Exemptions	Rates Reg.	Rates O.T.	Hrs. worked Reg.	Hrs. worked O.T.	Earnings Reg.	Earnings O.T.	Gross earnings	FICA	MEDCR	FWT	SWT	RET	Net earnings
Akey, M.	M	2	6.25		40	0									
Basile, G.	S	1	5.75		40	5									
Costello, J.	M	3	7.50		40	8									
Erickson, G.	M	4	8.20		40	0									
Martinez, J.	M	2	6.40		40	2									
Purin, T.	M	3	7.50		32	0									
Skinner, G.	S	0	6.25		40										
Testa, V.	M	1	8.20		40	4									
Witowski, S.	M	5	9.40		40	3									

Salespersons	Status	Exemptions	Net sales	Comm. rate	Weekly salary	Comm. amount			Gross earnings	FICA	MEDCR	FWT	SWT	RET	Net earnings
Ford, J.	M	3	10,250	1.0%											
Hart, C.	S	1	12,620	2.0%											
Light, W.	M	2	8,540	1.0%											
McNeeley, K.	M	3	11,875	1.5%											
Brown, A.	M	4	Plant Manager												
Jordan, M.	M	3	Assistant Manager												
Pay period total															

First-quarter payroll tax summary
(totals for an 11-week period)

Name	Gross earnings	FICA taxes	Medicare taxes	Federal with-holding tax
Brown, Allen	$15,000	$954.80	$223.30	$2,772.00
Jordan, Marie	12,100	750.20	175.45	1,815.00
Ford, Jack	7,810	484.22	113.25	937.20
Hart, Carol	8,250	511.50	119.63	990.00
Light, William	7,150	443.30	103.68	858.00
McNeeley, Jill	8,690	538.78	126.01	1,042.80
Akey, Mark	3,440	213.28	49.88	240.80
Basile, Gary	3,500	217.00	50.75	245.00
Costello, Jean	3,680	228.16	53.36	257.60
Erickson, George	4,270	264.74	61.92	298.90
Martinez, Juan	3,816	236.59	55.33	267.12
Purin, Todd	4,300	266.60	62.35	301.00
Skinner, Gail	3,755	232.81	54.45	262.85
Testa, Victoria	4,650	288.30	67.42	325.50
Witowski, Stanley	5,136	318.43	74.47	359.52

The federal tax deductions shown in the above summary are based on 1992 rates. In addition, the company's state unemployment experience tax rate (SUTA) is 2.5%. The company is located in a state that levies a flat state withholding tax of 3% on gross earnings up to $50,000 a year. All employees are required to contribute 1% of their gross earnings for retirement.

You are employed by Financial Consultants as a payroll account specialist and have been assigned the Altman account. Selected payroll data for the last pay period of the first quarter has been entered in the weekly payroll register. As the payroll account specialist, you are to perform the following duties:

A. Complete the weekly payroll register at left using the required payroll data provided. (Base the tax calculations on 1992 federal tax rates.)

B. Prepare Form 941, Employer's Quarterly Federal Tax Return, lines 1a through 16. (Assume no adjustments are required on lines 6b, 11, 12, 13, 15; enter 0s on these lines. Refer to Figure 4.14.)

C. Determine the employer's federal unemployment and state unemployment taxes for the first quarter based on the payroll data provided in the first-quarter payroll tax summary and the weekly payroll register.

SELF-TEST

A. Terminology review

Complete the following items using the key terms presented at the beginning of the chapter. Check your responses against the answer key at the end of the test.

1. A _wage_ is a form of earnings based on an hourly payment for a time period expressed in hours or weeks.

2. The Fair Labor Standards Act requires an employer to pay an _overtime_ rate of

~~Lime and 1½~~ for hours worked over 40 per week.

3. A ~~shift differential~~ is an additional amount per hour paid to employees who work other than day shifts.

4. ~~incentive~~ rates are paid when employees' gross earnings are based on job performance instead of time worked.

5. Under the ~~task + bonus~~ plan, a productivity level is established; when the employee produces less than that level, an hourly rate is paid; when the employee exceeds the production level a ~~bonus~~ is paid.

6. A ~~salary~~ is a fixed amount of compensation usually expressed in terms of a year or a month.

7. An employee who is paid biweekly will receive ~~26~~ paychecks during the year.

8. Employees who are classified ~~exempt~~ are compensated for their work and not the number of hours worked.

9. An incentive payment designed to generate a high volume of net sales is called a ~~commission~~

10. Gross earnings are reduced by ~~total deductions~~ to determine the employee's ~~net earnings~~

11. Mandatory deductions include ~~FICA~~, ~~medicare~~ , ~~FWT~~ and ~~SDI~~ insurance.

12. ~~FICA~~ tax is paid equally by both employee and employer based on the employee's gross earnings for the period.

13. The ~~%~~ method uses tax rates and taxable earnings to calculate the amount of FICA tax and FWT to be withheld from employee earnings.

14. Employer's payroll taxes include ~~FICA~~, ~~med.~~ , _____, and _____; they are based on total taxable earnings and rates reported in the _____ provided by the IRS.

15. Employer reports FWT and FICA taxes withheld from employee earnings each _____ when they file Form _____.

B. Calculation review

The following concepts and short problems are designed to test your understanding of the objectives identified at the beginning of the chapter. Answers are provided at the end of the test.

16. Jodi Larson is a front-desk clerk at the Bayside Motel and receives $6.48 per hour. She is also paid time-and-a-half for hours worked in excess of 40 per week and double time for holidays. Find her gross wage for the current pay period if she worked 57½ hours, of which 6 hours were worked on a holiday.

17. An assembler at the Ace Manufacturing Company produced 42 units per hour on Monday, 56 units per hour on Tuesday, and 30 units per hour on Wednesday. She worked 8 hours each of these days, but did not report to work due to illness the remainder of the week. Find her gross earnings if she is paid $8.50 per hour or $.25 per unit, whichever is greater, based on an hourly task standard.

18. Bill Ford is a machinist at Jenson's Machine Shop and has a task requirement of 200 units per 8-hour shift with a 130% bonus factor. Find his gross earnings if he is paid $12.80 per hour and produced 280 units during an 8-hour period.

19. Louis Pisegna is paid an annual salary of $19,760 on a weekly basis. He also receives time-and-a-half for all hours worked over 40 hours a week. If his regular workweek is 35 hours, find his gross earnings for the week if he worked a total of 46 hours.

20. Ahmad Ashkar is employed as a sales representative for Executive Systems. He is paid a base salary of $300 semimonthly plus a graduated commission of 2% on the first $50,000 net sales, and 1½% on net sales over $50,000. What were his gross earnings for the period if he had gross sales of $68,500 and discounts amounting to 3% of total sales?

21. Kelly Hauser is single and claims two exemptions. She has year-to-date earnings of $18,650 and her current weekly earnings amount to $482.70. What is her net pay if her deductions include FICA tax, medicare tax,

FWT, and SWT of 3% on gross earnings up to maximum taxable earnings of $18,500? Use the wage bracket method to calculate the appropriate payroll taxes.

22. Byron Stone is paid weekly at an hourly rate of $9.40 with time-and-a-half pay over 40 hours. He is married and claims three exemptions. What is his net pay if he worked 48 hours this pay period and his deductions include $15.90 for health insurance; $25.00 for savings; $12.50 for disability insurance; and $32.50 for retirement in addition to his FICA, Medicare, and FWT taxes? Use the percentage method to calculate employee payroll taxes based on 1992 FICA and medicare rates. Assume all earnings are taxable.

23. Jack Winfield is employed at Eastern Community College as a vice president for financial services. He receives an annual salary of $52,650 and is paid biweekly. His year-to-date earnings are $6,075. Using the 1992 FICA and medicare tax rates and a SUTA tax rate of 3.2% with a tax limit of $7,000, calculate the following:
    a. gross earnings
    b. employer FICA tax
    c. SUTA tax
    d. FUTA tax
    e. medicare tax.

24. Given the following payroll summary, calculate the employer's payroll taxes to be reported for the second quarter. Assume a SUTA tax experience rate of 4.2% on the first $7,000. (Use applicable 1992 tax rates.)

Payroll summary

Employee	First-quarter accumulated earnings	Second-quarter accumulated earnings
Bedell, T.	$4,780	$5,960
Hartman, R.	7,200	7,840
Selmon, M.	2,115	4,875

25. The payroll records of Lakeside Marina at the end of the third quarter indicated the company had paid total wages of $132,680.90 of which $124,580.75 were taxable social security wages; the total wages paid during the quarter were also taxable medicare wages. The company had deducted $7,843.20 in FWT tax from employees' earnings. Determine the total amount of employer taxes Lakeside Marina reported for the quarter on Form 941, the Employer's Quarterly Federal Tax Return (Use 1992 tax rates.)

Answers to self-test: *1.* wage *2.* overtime, time-and-one-half *3.* shift differential *4.* incentive rates *5.* task and bonus, bonus *6.* salary *7.* 26 *8.* exempt *9.* commission *10.* total deductions, net earnings *11.* FICA taxes, medicare taxes, FWT, disability (SDI) *12.* FICA (Social Security) *13.* percentage *14.* FICA, medicare, FUTA, SUTA, Circular E Tax Guide *15.* quarter, 941 *16.* $448.74 *17.* $264.00 *18.* $186.37 *19.* $477.74 *20.* $1,546.68 *21.* $389.77 *22.* $322.73 *23.* a. $2,025; b. $125.55; c. $29.60; d. $7.40; e. $29.36 *24.* a. FICA = $1,157.85; b. Medicare = $270.79; c. SUTA = $297.99; d. FUTA = $56.76 *25.* $27,138.96

5

FINANCIAL REPORTING AND ANALYSIS

Learning objectives

1. Explain the purpose and function of financial statements.

2. Prepare a balance sheet.

3. Complete a vertical and horizontal analysis of the balance sheet.

4. Prepare an income statement.

5. Complete a vertical and horizontal analysis of the income statement.

6. Understand the concept and use of ratios.

7. Calculate primary financial statement ratios.

8. Define the key terms.

INTRODUCTION

Learning objective
Explain the purpose
and function of finan-
cial statements.

Financial statements are the "output" of the accounting process. They are composed of financial data summarized from business transactions reported in monetary terms. The financial statements of a business provide a format to communicate economic data concerning its financial status to various segments of the financial community. For example, owners and potential investors use the information on the statements to assess the degree of risk and future ability of a company to report profits. Creditors appraise an organization's debt-paying ability before considering making loans or selling goods on credit. Government agencies are interested in the financial position of a firm for the purposes of regulation and taxation. Labor has become increasingly concerned about a company's stability as it relates to job security and wage increases. The individuals who most actively interact with the financial statements are management. Management uses financial information as an integral part of the decision making process when formulating the short-term and long-term plans of the enterprise.

Every business organization, regardless of its size, periodically prepares four primary financial statements: the income statement, the balance sheet, the owner's equity statement, and the cash flow statement. These reports reflect the financial position and the results of operations. The format of these statements may vary slightly from company to company but their content is somewhat universal.

The focus of this chapter is to familiarize you with the content and purpose of the balance sheet and the income statement. You will also be required to apply basic mathematical processes presented in earlier chapters to analyze and interpret the results of business operations reported in these two financial statements. The information contained in this chapter is very important because future chapters will present concepts and quantitative processes related to financial statements.

5.1 THE BALANCE SHEET

The **balance sheet** consists of three sections and it identifies the financial position of a business at a specific point in time. **Assets** are anything of value owned by a firm such as its cash, equipment, buildings, and land. **Liabilities**, which are debts, include amounts of money owed by a firm to its creditors as a result of buying assets on credit, or borrowing money. The third section, **owner's equity**, represents the owner's right or claim against the net assets of the firm after the total liabilities are deducted (total assets − total liabilities = owner's equity). The owner's equity in the firm's assets consists of items bought and paid for or monies invested in the business by the owner(s). The relationship between the sections of the balance sheet is expressed in an equation known as the **fundamental accounting equation**:

The fundamental accounting equation

assets	**=**	**liabilities**	**+**	**owner's equity**
items of value owned by the business		amounts owed to creditors		owner's claim or investment in the business

The equation can be used to analyze the effect various types of business activity can have on a firm's financial position. To illustrate, suppose you wanted to start a small business and you decided to invest $5,000 of your personal savings in the business. The financial position of your business would appear as follows.

assets   = liabilities + owner's equity
cash $5,000 = $0   + $5,000

Next, you decide to purchase $8,500 worth of office equipment from a supplier who requires you to pay a $1,500 down payment and who will provide credit for the remainder of the purchase ($8,500 − $1,500 = $7,000). The financial position of your business has changed as indicated below.

assets = liabilities + owner's equity

cash	$3,500		
office equipment	8,500		
totals	$12,000 =	$7,000 +	$5,000

Notice that the owner's equity is still $5,000 but your assets and liabilities have changed in value. The assets increased to $12,000, of which $8,500 is the value of the office equipment and $3,500 is cash. The reason cash decreased from $5,000 to $3,500 is because you paid a $1,500 down payment at the time of purchase. You cannot pay your obligations with owner's equity; you must use your assets (cash) to make purchases of other assets or to pay your debts. Your liabilities are now $7,000, which is the amount you owe on the office equipment ($8,500 − 1,500 = $7,000). Your equity in the business at this point remains at $5,000 because you have no additional claim on the business's assets. You can claim ownership of $3,500 in cash and $1,500 of the value of the office equipment ($3,500 + 1,500 = $5,000). Creditors' claims to assets have priority over the owner's claims.

The balance sheet contains a variety of accounts in each of the three sections; therefore, the total assets of a company must always be equal to the total of its liabilities and owner's equity. Let's now look at an example that further explains the relationship between the equation and its variables.

Example 1

The Richland Company has total assets of $135,250, total liabilities of $92,430, and owner's equity of $42,820.

Solution

$$\begin{array}{rcl} assets & = & liabilities + owner's\ equity \\ \$135{,}250 & = & \$92{,}430\ +\ \ \ \ \$42{,}820 \end{array}$$

or

$$\begin{array}{rcl} assets & - & liabilities = owner's\ equity \\ \$135{,}250 & - & \$92{,}430\ =\ \ \ \ \$42{,}820 \end{array}$$

or

$$\begin{array}{rcl} assets & - & owner's\ equity = liabilities \\ \$135{,}250 & - & \ \ \$42{,}820\ \ \ =\ \$92{,}430 \end{array}$$

The report form balance sheet shown in Figure 5.1 for Rojon Enterprises includes accounts listed under the categories of assets, liabilities, and owner's equity. You should analyze, not memorize, the account location with reference to the definitions provided for each category.

Assets are classified in terms of time. *Current assets* are cash or other items of value owned by the company that will be consumed or converted into cash within one year. The current assets in Figure 5.1 are:

- *Cash:* The cash in checking accounts, savings accounts, and any currency on hand on the date identified on the balance sheet.
- *Receivable Accounts:* Money owed by customers of the firm for purchases of goods and/or services sold by the firm on credit. Receivables include accounts receivable and notes receivable. (Notes will be discussed in detail in Chapter 8.)
- *Supply Accounts:* Assets that are used by the firm for operations. Supplies may be broken down into specific-use classifications such as store supplies, office supplies, etc. for better control.
- *Prepaid Accounts:* Money paid in advance by the firm for benefits or services that have not expired or been consumed. Examples of such accounts include prepaid rent and prepaid insurance.

Figure 5.1

Report form balance sheet

Rojon Enterprises
Balance Sheet
December 31, 19XX

Assets

Current assets:			
Cash		$183,250	
Accounts receivable (net)		347,788	
Notes receivable		32,400	
Supplies on hand		14,620	
Prepaid insurance		6,975	
Merchandise inventory		780,000	
Total current assets			1,365,033
Fixed assets:			
Machinery and equipment	$ 872,600		
Less accumulated depreciation	260,780	$611,820	
Buildings	$1,420,000		
Less accumulated depreciation	646,200	773,800	
Land		135,000	
Total fixed assets			1,520,620
Total assets			$2,885,653

Liabilities

Current liabilities:		
Accounts payable	$137,285	
Notes payable	15,200	
Dividends payable	8,300	
Salaries payable	87,495	
Taxes payable	93,470	
Total current liabilities		341,750
Long-term liabilities:		
Mortgage payable, due 1995	265,000	
Debenture 8% bonds payable due December 31, 2008	150,000	
		415,000
Total liabilities		$ 756,750

Stockholders' Equity

Preferred stock	$400,000	
Common stock	750,000	
Retained earnings	978,903	
Total Stockholders' Equity		2,128,903
Total Liabilities and Stockholders' Equity		$2,885,653

- *Merchandise Inventory:* The cost of all inventory the firm has available for sale on the balance sheet date.

- *Fixed assets* (or *long-term assets*, also referred to as *plant assets*): Those assets estimated to be used by the firm for a period longer than one year. They are used in the operation of the business and are not for resale. The cost of fixed assets is charged against income through a process called *depreciation*, which we will discuss in Chapter 13. In Figure 5.1, the fixed assets include:
  Equipment Accounts: The *book value* (original cost less accumulated depreciation) of equipment fixtures, machinery, and other such items owned by the firm on the date of the balance sheet.
  Building Accounts: The book value of buildings owned by the firm. Depreciation is considered in determining a building's net value.
  Land Accounts: The original cost of any land owned by the firm. Land is a fixed asset that does not depreciate.

The liabilities, much like assets, are classified as current or long-term. *Current liabilities* are those debts that must be paid by the firm within a relatively short period of time, generally one year. Current liabilities in Figure 5.1 include:

- *Accounts Payable:* The total of money owed by the firm to creditors for goods and services purchased on credit.

- *Notes Payable:* The amount of money owed by the firm to its creditors in the form of short-term promissory notes. A promissory note is a negotiable financial document that requires the payor to pay the payee an identified amount of money at some specified date, usually less than 1 year.

- *Salaries Payable:* The amount of money owed by the firm to its employees for wages earned but unpaid as of the date of the statement.

Long-term liabilities are those debts that will not be paid within 1 year. Long-term liabilities in Figure 5.1 include:

- *Mortgages Payable:* The total balance of all mortgages for which the firm is liable. Mortgages are loans used to finance buildings and property.

- *Bonds Payable:* The obligation to pay the face amount of a bond at maturity by a firm to bondholders. Bonds are issued by firms to generate funds.

- *Owner's Equity:* As the accounting equation indicates, the difference between total assets (current assets plus fixed assets) and to-

Figure 5.2

Presentation of equity: corporation

Stockholders' Equity

Preferred stock	$500,000
Common stock	700,000
Retained earnings	125,000
Total stockholders' equity	$1,325,000

Figure 5.3

Presentation of equity: sole proprietorship

Owner's Equity

(Company name), capital or individual name	$75,350

tal liabilities (current liabilities plus long-term liabilities). Therefore, the owner's equity section of the balance sheet in Figure 5.1 is determined as follows:

$$owner's\ equity = total\ assets - total\ liabilities$$
$$\$2,128,903\ \ = \$2,885,653 - \ \ \$756,750$$

The ownership section of the balance sheet will vary depending on how a business is organized. For example, corporations identify ownership as *stockholders' equity*, which is the sum of the *stock value* and *retained earnings* (profits not distributed to shareholders). (See Figure 5.2.) A sole proprietorship (owned by an individual) or a partnership (owned by two or more individuals) identifies ownership as **capital**. Figure 5.3 shows the ownership section of a balance sheet for a sole proprietorship.

Example 2

The following account balances are listed in the books of the Village Diner: cash total $4,650; merchandise inventory $18,250; store supplies $500; office supplies $375; and prepaid insurance $1,240. The Village Diner lists equipment at $30,650 with accumulated depreciation of $2,800; a building at $120,000, with accumulated depreciation of $37,500; and land of $30,000. Liabilities include accounts payable totaling $15,300; a note payable of $4,200; and a mortgage balance of $75,860. The owner's equity is listed at $70,005. Prepare a report form balance sheet as of October 31, 199X for the Village Diner.

Solution

Village Diner
Balance Sheet
October 31, 199X

Assets

Current Assets:			
Cash		$ 4,650	
Merchandise inventory		18,250	
Store supplies		500	
Office supplies		375	
Prepaid insurance		1,240	
Total current assets			$ 25,015
Fixed assets:			
Equipment	$ 30,650		
Less accumulated depreciation	2,800	$27,850	
Building	120,000		
Less accumulated depreciation	37,500	82,500	
Land		30,000	
Total fixed assets			$140,350
Total assets			$165,365

Liabilities

Current liabilities:			
Accounts payable		$15,300	
Notes payable		4,200	
Total current liabilities			$ 19,500
Long-term liabilities:			
Mortgage payable			75,860
Total liabilities			$ 95,360

Owner's Equity

Village Diner capital			70,005
Total liabilities and owner's equity			$165,365

CHECK YOUR KNOWLEDGE

The balance sheet

1. Calculate the value of a company's assets if its liabilities total $37,648 and the equity of its owners amounts to $45,376.

2. If a firm has assets of $1,347,275 and owes creditors $649,589, what amount of the firm's assets can be claimed by the owners?

3. If ownership is $72,965 and assets amount to $118,740, what is the value of the company's debt?

4. Prepare a balance sheet for Cohen's Stationery and Book Shop as of December 31, 199X from the financial data below. Use the report form.

Cash	$1,252	Accum. depreciation (fixture)	$ 3,600
Accounts receivable	4,748	Building	80,000
Notes receivable	1,250	Accum. depreciation building	6,500
Supplies	875	Land	35,000
Prepaid insurance	2,400	Accounts payable	8,787
Merchandise inventory	16,479	Notes payable (3/96)	2,500
Equipment	4,200	Salaries payable	1,643
Accumulated		Mortgage payable	56,380
depreciation	1,600	H. Cohen capital	77,944
Store fixtures	12,750		

5.1 EXERCISES

Calculate the missing values in the balance sheet data.

	Assets	=	Liabilities	+	Owner's equity
1.	$85,675		_____		$63,987
2.	$372,460		$118,738		_____
3.	_____		$6,875		$24,920
4.	$1,648,250		$410,298		_____
5.	_____		$12,640		$63,875

Classify each of the following accounts as either a current asset, fixed asset, current liability, long-term liability, or owner's equity.

6. cash

7. accounts payable

8. store equipment

9. R. C. Taylor capital

10. store supplies

11. accumulated depreciation

12. mortgage

13. building

14. retained earnings

15. merchandise inventory

16. wages payable

17. land

Answers to CYK: *1.* $83,024   *2.* $697,686   *3.* $45,775   *4.* $147,254

18. Determine total current assets:

Cash	$ 8,460
Accounts receivable	4,370
Store equipment	12,850
Supplies	1,200
Building	42,800
Prepaid insurance	6,750
Merchandise inventory	21,640

19. Calculate total liabilities:

Accounts payable	$ 6,270
Salaries payable	1,430
Advertising expense	850
Mortgage payable	28,270
Interest expense	550
Notes payable	3,600

20. Calculate the owner's equity:

Common stock	$250,000
Cash	85,600
Preferred stock	175,250
Retained earnings	$105,750

21. Arrange the following accounts as they would appear in the assets section of the balance sheet and determine the value of total assets.

Cash	$12,350
Accounts receivable	4,680
Store equipment	15,200
Accumulated depreciation store equipment	3,600
Supplies	875
Prepaid rent	2,500
Office equipment	6,250
Accumulated depreciation office equipment	1,200
Merchandise inventory	23,950

22. The balance sheet of Leung Associates lists the following items and amounts on June 30, 199X: cash $10,250; accounts receivable $3,875; supplies $475; merchandise inventory $18,500; equipment (book value) $7,250; office furniture (book value) $4,800; accounts payable $2,780; salaries payable $2,350. What is the claim on the assets by the owners of Leung Associates?

23. Ellen Grabowski operates a craft shop. Her balance sheet after 3 years of doing business shows her equity as $8,600, which is one-fourth of the value of total assets. What is the amount of total liabilities at this point in time?

24. Last year, Comstock's Pharmacy reported assets of $62,500. This year, assets increased by $15,850 and liabilities decreased by $4,200. If Comstock capital was $52,650 this year, what was the amount of capital reported on last year's balance sheet?

25. The following is a list of account balances taken from the books of the Axton Company on March 31, 199X. Prepare a report form balance sheet for the Axton Company.

Accounts payable	8,325
Merchandise inventory	35,740
Store equipment	15,250
Retained earnings	28,250
Accounts receivable	12,800
Salaries payable	1,200
Accumulated depreciation— store equipment	4,800
Prepaid insurance	550
Common stock	70,000
Mortgage payable	41,200
Land	22,500
Office supplies	825
Cash	14,260
Office equipment	9,570
Building	85,900
Accumulated depreciation— office equipment	1,200
Store supplies	880
Accumulated depreciation— building	43,300

5.2   THE INCOME STATEMENT

The **income statement** is a summary report that measures the progress of an enterprise by determining its profitability. *Profits* are reported by a business when the *revenue* (inflow of cash from the sale of goods and services) exceeds *expenses* (outflow of cash from costs associated with

Figure 5.4

Multiple-step form
income statement

Rojon Enterprises
Income Statement
December 31, 199X

Revenues:	
Net sales	$1,661,508
Cost of goods sold	710,815
Gross profit	950,693
Operating expenses	863,555
Net income from operations	87,138
Net other income and expenses	6,525
Net income	$ 80,613

Learning objective
Prepare an income
statement.

the activities of the period). The income statement interacts with the balance sheet to give a clear picture of how changing events affect owner's equity from period to period.

The format of the income statement can vary depending on factors specific to an organization. The two most widely used forms are *single-step* and *multiple-step*. The primary difference in the two forms is the amount of detail presented in the main sections of each of the statements. For example, in the single-step income statement form, the total of all expenses is deducted from the total of all revenues to determine the net income; whereas, in the multiple-step income statement form, several sections and subsections with intermediate balances are used to report net income. Figure 5.4 shows one version of the multiple-step form. Notice that only the net totals of the main sections are used to determine net income.

The following example illustrates the relationship between the main sections of an income statement.

Example 3

A company reports net sales of $75,000. It cost the company $26,250 to manufacture the products sold and $33,500 in various expenses. What is the net income?

Solution

net sales	$75,000	
less cost of goods sold	26,250	
gross profit	48,750	(gross profit = net sales
less expenses	33,500	− cost of goods sold)
net income	$15,250	(net income = gross profit
		− operating expenses)

Figure 5.5

Conventional multiple-step income statement

Rojon Enterprises
Income Statement
December 31, 199X

Revenue from sales:			$1,685,795
Sales			
Less: Sales returns and allowances		$ 6,430	
Sales discounts		17,857	24,287
Net sales			$1,661,508
Cost of goods sold:			
Beginning inventory 1/1			$ 635,970
Purchases		$856,250	
Transportation—in		18,775	
Cost of purchases		875,025	
Less: purchase returns	$ 4,860		
purchase discounts	15,320	20,180	
Net purchases		854,845	
Merchandise available for sale		1,490,815	
Less: Merchandise inventory 12/31		780,000	
Cost of goods sold			$ 710,815
Gross profit (net sales − cost of goods sold)			$ 950,693
Operating expenses:			
Selling expenses:			
Sales salaries expenses		$237,300	
Advertising expenses		85,450	
Store supplies expenses		16,250	
Depreciation expenses—Equipment		4,750	
Depreciation expenses—Buildings		7,465	
Total selling expenses			$ 351,215
General expenses:			
Salaries expense		$310,200	
Insurance expense		11,685	
Taxes expense		165,420	
General supplies		12,800	
Depreciation expense—equipment		8,940	
Miscellaneous expenses		3,295	
Total general expenses			$ 512,340
Total operating expenses			$ 863,555

Figure 5.5

(*Continued*)

Net income from operations (gross profit − total operating expenses)		$ 87,138
Other income and expenses:		
Other income:		
Interest income	350	
Other expenses:		
Interest expenses	6,875	
Net other income and expenses		$ 6,525
Net income		$ 80,613

Note: Net other income and expenses reduces net income from operations in this statement because interest expenses (cost) is greater than interest income (revenues). Therefore, to determine net income we must subtract net other income and expenses ($6,525) from net income from operations ($87,138).

The income statement shown in Figure 5.5 is a conventional multiple-step statement, so called because of its additional sections and the use of interim balances to calculate net income.

The various sections of the multiple-step statement as shown in Figure 5.5 will be discussed in detail in the following paragraphs.

In the *revenue from sales* section, *gross sales* to customers for merchandise sold for cash or on account is reported. Sales that are returned and sales discounts that have been accepted are totaled and deducted from gross sales, to arrive at *net sales*. The net sales in Figure 5.5 is determined as follows:

$$\text{net sales} = \text{gross sales} - (\text{sales returns} + \text{sales discounts})$$
$$\$1,661,508 = \$1,685,795 - \qquad (\$6,430 + \$17,857)$$

The section of the income statement that is the most difficult to understand is the **cost of goods sold**, due to the detailed analysis required to determine this important figure. Every merchandising company purchases goods for resale. Therefore, records must be kept of the merchandise that has been purchased (purchases); merchandise that has been purchased but not sold (merchandise inventory); and merchandise that has been purchased and sold (cost of goods sold). Figure 5.6 illustrates how the cost of goods sold in Figure 5.5 is determined.

Note in Figure 5.5 the similarity between net purchases and net sales. *Net purchases* represent purchases plus transportation less purchase returns and purchase discounts.

Figure 5.6

Calculating the cost
of goods sold

Beginning inventory	$ 635,970
Plus net purchases	+ 854,845
Merchandise available for sale	= 1,490,815
Less ending inventory	− 780,000
Cost of goods sold	= $ 710,815

The information you will need to determine the valuation of inventory will be presented in Chapter 14. The focus on inventory in this chapter is its effect on cost of goods sold.

Operating expenses are the costs incurred directly with the sale of merchandise (selling expense) or in the operations of the business (general expense). Figure 5.5 lists examples of expenses in each of the categories. It is not always necessary to classify expenses by category; they can also be listed under the heading "operating expenses."

If a firm generates income from sources other than operations, an additional section of the income statement is required. Other income or expenses can result from nonoperating activities, such as the rental of property, investments in other businesses, or the gain or loss on the sale of fixed assets. *Net other income and expenses* is added to (or deducted from) income from operations to determine **net income**.

Example 4

The Gidget Company reported gross sales of $230,500 on December 31 with sales returns of $8,700. Merchandise inventory on January 1 of the year was $32,400. The company purchased $82,750 worth of goods during the year and paid $1,740 in transportation costs. Inventory on December 31 was $46,250. The company's records indicate they had paid $80,275 in salaries and wages, $2,800 for advertising, $745 for supplies, $12,490 for taxes, $900 for insurance, and depreciated assets of $10,680. Prepare a multiple-step income statement for the Gidget Company for the current year ending December 31.

Solution

Gidget Company
Income Statement
December 31, 199X

Revenue from sales:		
Sales	$230,500	
Less: Sales returns and allowances	8,700	
Net sales		$221,800

Cost of goods sold:		
Beginning inventory January 1, 199X		32,400
Purchases	$82,750	
Transportation—in	1,740	
Net purchases		84,490
Merchandise available for sale		$116,890
Less: Merchandise inventory (12/31)		46,250
Cost of goods sold		70,640
Gross profit		$151,160
Operating expenses:		
Salaries and wages		$ 80,275
Advertising expense		2,800
Supplies expense		745
Taxes expense		12,490
Insurance expense		900
Depreciation expense		10,680
Total expenses		$107,890
Net income		$ 43,270

CHECK YOUR KNOWLEDGE

Income statement sections

1. If net sales are $350,000, expenses are $168,000, and the cost of goods sold is $140,650, what is the gross profit?

2. Northeast Electrical Supply reported the following financial information for the month ending September 30, 199X: net sales $1,675,430, expenses $823,890, and cost of goods sold $703,668. What is the net income?

3. Determine the value of net sales if a firm reports expenses of $724,500, cost of goods sold $661,500, and net income of $189,000.

4. A business reports total sales for the month at $125,750 of which $4,320 was returned for cash or credit refunds. In addition, the business recorded $2,560 in discounts on its sales figure. What is the amount of net sales to be reported for the period?

5. Calculate the cost of goods sold based on the following financial data: beginning inventory $65,800; ending inventory $42,225; and net purchases $120,750.

6. The following information was taken from the records of the Calabria Importing Company: beginning inventory $17,950, purchases

$46,820, purchase discounts $560, transportation—in $835, and ending inventory $23,935. Determine the cost of goods sold.

7. Prepare a multiple-step income statement for the Southside Beverage Center as of December 31, 199X from the following financial data: sales $34,280, sales returns and allowances $375, beginning inventory $3,795, purchases $15,250, purchase returns and allowances $460, ending inventory $7,460, rent expense $6,000, salaries expense $12,250, advertising expense $1,500, supplies expense $480, and miscellaneous expense $220.

5.2 EXERCISES

Calculate the missing values from the income statement data.

	Sales	−	Sales returns	=	Net sales	−	Cost of goods sold	=	Gross profit	−	Operating expenses	=	Net income
1.	$ 28,750		1,250		27,500		18,350		9150		6,480		2670
2.			3,420		65,800				33,270				11,575
3.	$325,845				321,220				168,570		96,430		
4.	$ 7,850		140				2,510				3,670		

Calculate the missing values in the cost of goods sold section of the income statement.

	Beginning inventory	+	Net purchases	=	Merchandise available for sale	−	Ending inventory	=	Cost of goods sold
5.	$12,750		38,625				8,750		
6.			64,260		82,950				61,518
7.	$46,280				120,250				83,730
8.	$ 3,595		12,845				5,970		

9. Reynold's Flower Shoppe reported net sales of $182,400. If it cost the shop $94,700 to buy the products they sold and another $52,480 in expenses to sell them, what is the net income?

10. On June 1, the beginning inventory of Video Sounds was valued at $147,650. The firm's records indicated purchases of $120,380, purchase discounts of $3,475, purchase returns and allowances of $2,960, and transportation

charges of $4,800. The inventory on June 30 was $82,745. Determine Video Sounds' cost of goods sold for the period.

11. Using the information in problem 10, determine Video Sounds' gross profit for June based on sales of $362,740 and sales discounts amounting to $8,960.

12. The Nine-to-Five Daycare Center incurred the following expenses during the month of August 199X: rent $2,250, utilities $875, supplies $585, salaries $3,600, depreciation—equipment $1,200, and miscellaneous expenses $265. If total expenses are 15% of total revenue, determine (a) total revenue and (b) net income.

13. If a firm's net sales are $48,000 and its operating expenses total $22,500, determine the net income with the cost of goods sold being 40% of net sales.

14. Santana Construction Company purchased a single family dwelling for $32,500, which they sold the following year for $68,900. During the year, they invested $12,750 in materials and labor for improvements. The real estate firm who sold the house charged a 6½% commission. What is the company's net profit on the sale of the home?

15. Prepare a multiple-step income statement from the following income data taken from the records of Quick-Stop Foods for the month ended September 30, 199X.

Sales	$15,840
Sales returns	260
Merchandise inventory 9/1	3,950
Purchases	5,270
Transportation	835
Purchase discounts	175
Merchandise inventory 9/30	2,485
Salaries	1,250
Rent	850
Advertising	250
Supplies	480
Depreciation equipment	900
Miscellaneous	340
Interest income	150

5.3 PERCENTAGE ANALYSIS OF FINANCIAL STATEMENTS

The solvency and profitability of a business enterprise are reported in the balance sheet and income statement. These two principal statements provide the basic information needed by individuals both inside and outside the organization to make important economic decisions. A firm's managers, creditors, and investors will assess current statement data in terms of past performance to make projections concerning future performance. This process of analysis provides a clearer picture of the firm's performance because it identifies important relationships, developing trends, and the firm's strengths and weaknesses.

Financial statements are often analyzed by preparing a *comparative statement,* which combines the results of the current year with the results of prior years. Comparative statements are also used to compare the firm's financial data to industry standards and to the financial data of other companies.

The analytical measures generated from the data presented in financial statements are expressed as either percentages or as ratios. In this section we will discuss how financial statements are analyzed both vertically and horizontally.

VERTICAL ANALYSIS

Vertical analysis of financial statements is used by the analyst when the information needed concerns the percentage relationships of the component parts of the statement to either net sales or total assets for a single period. For example, it would be important to a manager to know the percentage relationship between cost of goods sold and net sales. If the cost of goods sold is 40.5% of net sales, then gross profit is 59.5% (net sales − cost of goods sold = **gross profit**). This percentage figure when compared to target criteria of 60% gross profit indicates the effectiveness of management's decisions during the period. A comparative income statement with vertical analysis is shown in Figure 5.7 for Norton Satellite Systems.

Each *item* of the income statement is stated as a percent of *net sales* and expressed to the nearest tenth of a percent. To calculate the percent (rate) we use the rate formula presented in Chapter 3.

$$\text{rate} = \frac{\text{part}}{\text{base}} \quad \text{or} \quad B \times R = P$$

Example 5

Using the data presented in Figure 5.7, calculate the percents for (a) sales and (b) total operating expenses for 1993. Round your answer to the nearest tenth of a percent.

Solution

a. $\dfrac{\text{sales}}{\text{net sales}} = \dfrac{\$85{,}585}{\$84{,}245} = 1.0159 \quad \text{or} \quad 101.6\%$

Note that the sales percent is greater than 100%. This is because the *base* is net sales.

b. $\dfrac{\text{total operating expenses}}{\text{net sales}} = \dfrac{\$24{,}906}{\$84{,}245} = .2956 \quad \text{or} \quad 29.6\%$

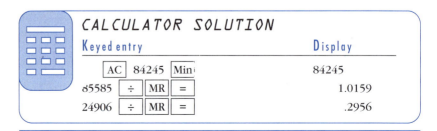

CALCULATOR SOLUTION

Keyed entry	Display
AC 84245 Min	84245
85585 ÷ MR =	1.0159
24906 ÷ MR =	.2956

Figure 5.7

Vertical analysis: comparative income statement

	1993		1992	
Norton Satellite Systems **Comparative Income Statement** **December 31, 1992 and 1993**	Amount	Percent	Amount	Percent
Revenue from sales:				
Sales	$85,585	101.6	$76,187	102.0
Less: sales returns	1,340	1.6	1,480	2.0
Net sales	$84,245	100.0	$74,707	100.0
Cost of merchandise sold:				
Beginning inventory	$12,650	15.0	$14,425	19.3
Net purchases	38,240	45.4	32,500	43.5
Merchandise available	$50,890	60.4	$46,925	62.8
Ending inventory	22,400	26.6	20,200	27.0
Cost of goods sold	$28,490	33.8	$26,725	35.8
Gross profit	$55,755	66.2	$47,982	64.2
Operating expenses:				
Supplies	$ 620	0.8	$ 875	1.1
Wages and salaries	14,356	17.0	12,600	16.9
Advertising	985	1.2	1,400	1.9
Utilities	2,520	3.0	2,535	3.4
Insurance	1,950	2.3	1,500	2.0
Depreciation	4,475	5.3	4,700	6.3
Total operating expenses	$24,906	29.6	$23,610	31.6
Income before taxes	$30,849	36.6	$24,372	32.6
Income taxes	11,105	13.2	8,290	11.1
Net Income	$19,744	23.4	$16,082	21.5

When preparing a vertical analysis of the balance sheet, each *asset* item is stated as a percent of *total assets* and each *liability* and *equity* item is stated as a percent of *total liabilities and equity*.

Example 6

Using the data presented in Figure 5.8, calculate the percents for (a) cash (asset) and (b) accounts payable (liability). Round your answer to the nearest tenth of a percent.

Figure 5.8

Vertical analysis: comparative balance sheet

Norton Satellite Systems
Comparative Balance Sheet
December 31, 1992 and 1993

	1993 Amount	1993 Percent	1992 Amount	1992 Percent
Assets				
Current assets:				
Cash	$ 6,700	7.4	$ 4,250	4.8
Accounts receivable	2,980	3.3	3,470	3.9
Supplies	1,200	1.3	1,275	1.4
Prepaid insurance	700	0.8	1,000	1.1
Merchandise inventory	22,400	24.7	20,200	22.6
Total current assets	$33,980	37.5	$30,195	33.8
Fixed assets:				
Land	$12,000	13.3	$12,000	13.4
Building (net)	32,400	35.8	38,650	43.3
Equipment (net)	12,150	13.4	8,375	9.4
Total fixed assets	$56,550	62.5	$59,025	66.2
Total assets	$90,530	100.0	$89,220	100.0
Liabilities				
Current liabilities:				
Accounts payable	$ 4,600	5.1	$ 8,740	9.8
Wages payable	1,320	1.5	960	1.1
Taxes payable	10,260	11.3	8,785	9.8
Total current liabilities	$16,180	17.9	$18,485	20.7
Long-term liabilities:				
Mortgage payable	$43,800	48.4	$52,200	58.5
Total liabilities	$59,980	66.3	$70,685	79.2
Owner's equity				
Norton B, capital	$30,550	33.7	$18,535	20.8
Total liabilities and equity	$90,530	100.0	$89,220	100.0

Solution

a. $\dfrac{\text{cash}}{\text{total assets}} = \dfrac{\$\ 6{,}700}{\$90{,}530} = .074,$ or 7.4%

b. $\dfrac{\text{accounts payable}}{\text{total liabilities and equity}} = \dfrac{\$\ 4{,}600}{\$90{,}530} = .051,$ or 5.1%

A comparative balance sheet with vertical analysis is presented in Figure 5.8 for Norton Satellite Systems.

CHECK YOUR KNOWLEDGE

Vertical analysis

Complete a vertical analysis of the following partial comparative income statement. Round your answers to nearest tenth of a percent.

		1993		**1992**	
		Amount	Percent	Amount	Percent
1.	Sales	$125,500	_____	$110,200	_____
2	Sales returns	$_____	_____	$_____	_____
	Net sales	122,900	100.0	108,350	100.0
3.	Cost of goods sold	72,750	_____	$_____	_____
4.	Gross profit	50,150	_____	43,850	_____
5.	Operating expenses	45,473	_____	$_____	_____
6.	Net income	$_____	_____	$ 5,200	_____

Complete a vertical analysis of the partial balance sheet given below. Round your answers to the nearest tenth of a percent.

	Assets	Amount	Percent
	Current assets:		
7.	Cash	$ 2,500	_____
8.	Merchandise inventory	8,750	_____
9.	Accounts receivable	_____	_____
10.	Total current assets	14,850	_____
	Fixed assets:		
11.	Equipment	_____	_____
12.	Buildings	20,750	_____
13.	Land	10,000	_____
14.	Total fixed assets	36,950	_____
15.	Total assets	_____	100.0%

Answers to CYK: *1.* a. 102.1; b. 101.7 *2.* a. 2,600; b. 2.1; c. 1,850; d. 1.7 *3.* a. 59.2; b. 64,500; c. 59.5
4. a. 40.8; b. 40.5 *5.* a. 37.0; b. 38,650; c. 35.7 *6.* a. 4,677; b. 3.8; c. 4.8 *7.* 4.8
8. 16.9 *9.* a. 3,600; b. 6.9 *10.* 28.7 *11.* a. 6,200; b. 12.0 *12.* 40.1
13. 19.3 *14.* 71.3 *15.* 51,800

HORIZONTAL ANALYSIS

Learning objective
Complete a horizontal analysis of the balance sheet and income statement.

Financial statements are also analyzed to measure the degree of change (increases or decreases) of a firm's financial data between two time periods. This comparison can reveal important changes that can have either a positive or a negative impact on the firm. For example, the investors of a firm would be pleased to learn that the net income increased 18% over last year while the industry's average increase amounted to 12% and their primary competition reported an increase of 14.5%. On the other hand, management might not be pleased to see an increase in operating expenses at a rate above that considered acceptable in terms of the firm's pricing policies. This percentage analysis of the changes of corresponding items in comparative financial statements is referred to as **horizontal analysis**. Each item of the current period is compared with the corresponding item of one or more earlier periods (base). The increase or decrease in the amount of the item (part) is then listed together with the percent (rate) of increase or decrease. This procedure is illustrated in the comparative balance sheet shown in Figure 5.9 for Norton Satellite Systems.

To calculate the percent increase or decrease for each item we use the rate formula presented in Chapter 3.

$$\text{rate (increase or decrease)} = \frac{\text{amount difference}}{\text{base year (earlier year) amount}}$$

Example 7

In the illustrated balance sheet (Figure 5.9), the cash account totaled $4,250 in 1992 and increased to $6,700 in 1993. Calculate the percent of change.

Solution

The percent change is determined as follows.

Step 1:   Calculate the amount of difference between the 2 years.

$$\text{cash 1993} - \text{cash 1992} = \text{amount difference}$$
$$\$6,700 - \$4,250 \quad = \$2,450 \text{ (increase)}$$

Step 2:   Calculate the percent of change.

$$\text{percent change} = \frac{\text{amount difference}}{\text{base year (earlier year) amount}}$$
$$= \frac{\$2,450}{\$4,250} = .5764$$
$$= 57.6\%$$

Figure 5.9

Horizontal analysis: comparative balance sheet

Norton Satellite Systems
Comparative Balance Sheet
December 31, 1992 and 1993

	1993	1992	Increase/Decrease Amount	Increase/Decrease Percent
Assets				
Current assets:				
Cash	$ 6,700	$ 4,250	$ 2,450	57.6
Accounts receivable	2,980	3,470	(490)	(14.1)
Supplies	1,200	1,275	(75)	(5.9)
Prepaid insurance	700	1,000	(300)	(30.0)
Merchandise inventory	22,400	20,200	2,200	10.9
Total current assets	$33,980	$30,195	$ 3,785	12.5
Fixed assets:				
Land	$12,000	$12,000	-0-	-0-
Building (net)	32,400	38,650	$ (6,250)	(16.2)
Equipment (net)	12,150	8,375	3,775	45.1
Total fixed assets	$56,550	$59,025	$ (2,475)	(4.2)
Total assets	90,530	89,220	1,310	1.5
Liabilities				
Current liabilities:				
Accounts payable	$ 4,600	$ 8,740	$ (4,140)	(47.4)
Wages payable	1,320	960	360	37.5
Taxes payable	10,260	8,785	1,475	16.8
Total current liabilities	$16,180	$18,485	$ (2,305)	(12.5)
Long-term liabilities:				
Mortgage payable	$43,800	$52,200	$(8,400)	(16.1)
Total liabilities	$59,980	$70,685	$(10,705)	(15.1)
Owner's Equity				
Norton B, capital	$30,550	$18,535	$12,015	64.8
Total liabilities and equity	$90,530	$89,220	$ 1,310	1.5

Note: Figures in ( ) are decreases.

```
CALCULATOR SOLUTION
Keyed entry                          Display

AC  6700  −  4250  =                 2450
          ÷  4250  =                       .5764705
```

Horizontal analysis can be used to compare the results of business activity reported in any type of financial report provided the same items are being analyzed over multiple periods of time. Example 8 illustrates the same calculation on data taken from the income statement shown in Figure 5.7.

Example 8

Use the data in Figure 5.7 (comparative income statement) to calculate the percent of change in advertising expenses between 1992 and 1993. Round your answer to the nearest tenth of a percent.

Solution

Step 1:   Calculate the amount of difference between the two periods.

$$\text{difference} = \text{advertising expenses 1993}$$
$$- \text{ advertising expenses 1992}$$
$$-\$415 = \$985 - \$1,400$$

Step 2:   Calculate the percent of change.

$$\text{percent change} = \frac{\text{amount difference}}{\text{base year (earlier year) amount}}$$
$$= \frac{-\$415}{\$1,400} = -.2964$$
$$= 29.6\% \text{ (decrease)}$$

When the difference between the two periods results in a negative number (− $415) the percent of change must be identified as a decrease either by placing parentheses ( ) around the number (as shown in Figure 5.9) or by labeling the answer a "decrease."

CHECK YOUR KNOWLEDGE

Horizontal analysis

Complete a horizontal analysis of the following partial comparative balance sheet. Round your answers to nearest tenth of a percent.

	Assets	1993	1992	Increase/Decrease Amount	Percent
1.	Current assets	$18,260	$10,475	a. _____	b. _____
2.	Fixed assets	$29,150	$32,640	a. _____	b. _____
3.	Total assets	a. _____	b. _____	c. _____	d. _____
4.	Current liabilities	a. _____	$5,340	b. _____	c. _____
5.	Long-term liabilities	$17,120	a. _____	b. _____	c. _____
6.	Total liabilities	$23,260	$27,635	a. _____	b. _____
7.	Owner's equity	a. _____	$15,480	b. _____	c. _____

Prepare a horizontal analysis of the partial comparative income statement shown below. Round answers to the nearest tenth of a percent.

		1993	1992	Amount	Percent
8.	Gross sales	$278,000	$245,540	a. _____	b. _____
9.	Net sales	276,500	243,300	a. _____	b. _____
10.	Cost of goods sold	134,150	98,750	a. _____	b. _____
11.	Gross profit	142,350	144,550	a. _____	b. _____
12.	Total expenses	114,022	112,825	a. _____	b. _____
13.	Total net income	28,328	31,725	a. _____	b. _____

5.3 EXERCISES

1. Complete the following comparative income statement analysis for Tri-State Data Systems. Round your calculations to the nearest tenth of a percent.

Answers to CYK: *1.* a. $7,785; b. 74.3   *2.* a. (3,490); b. (10.7)   *3.* a. 47,410; b. 43,115; c. 4,295; d. 10   *4.* a. 6,140; b. 800; c. 15   *5.* a. 22,295; b. (5,175); c. 23.2   *6.* a. (4,375); b. 15.8   *7.* a. 24,150; b. $8,670; c. 56.0   *8.* a. 32,460; b. 13.2   *9.* a. 33,200; b. 13.6   *10.* a. 35,400; b. 35.8   *11.* a. (2,200); b. (1.5)   *12.* a. 1,197; b. 1.1   *13.* a. (3,397); b. (10.7)

Tri-State Data Systems, Inc.
Comparative Income Statement
December 31, 1992 and 1993

	1993	Percent	1992	Percent
Net sales	$610,000	_____	$585,000	_____
Cost of goods sold:				
Beginning inventory	$ 30,600	_____	$ 24,500	_____
Net purchases	272,800	_____	260,300	_____
Merchandise available	$303,400	_____	$284,800	_____
Ending inventory	34,300	_____	30,600	_____
Cost of goods sold	$269,100	_____	$254,200	_____
Gross margin	340,900	_____	330,800	_____
Operating expenses:				
Supplies	$ 5,200	_____	$ 4,850	_____
Wages and salaries	125,400	_____	105,200	_____
Utilities	14,800	_____	12,750	_____
Depreciation	8,000	_____	8,000	_____
Insurance	2,800	_____	2,800	_____
Total operating expenses	$156,200	_____	$133,600	_____
Income before taxes	184,700	_____	197,200	_____
Provision for taxes	92,400	_____	99,050	_____
Net income	$ 92,300	_____	$ 98,150	_____

2. Fill in the missing information in Northeast Supply Company's balance sheet. Express your answers to the nearest tenth of a percent or dollar.

Northeast Supply Company
Balance Sheet
December 31, 1993

	Amount	Percent
Assets		
Current Assets:		
Cash	$ 12,500	5.0
Equipment	25,750	10.3
Accounts receivable	31,750	12.7
Merchandise inventory	50,500	20.2
Total current assets	120500	48.2
Fixed assets:		
Land	40,500	16.2
Buildings (Net)	89000	35.6
Total assets	$250,000	

Liabilities

Current liabilities:		
Accounts payable	26,750	10.7
Wages payable	9500	3.8
Total current liabilities	$ 36,250	14.5
Long-term liabilities:		
Mortgages payable	85,250	34.1
Total liabilities	121500	48.6

Owner's Equity

Owner's capital	128500	51.4
Total liabilities and equity	$250,000	100.0

3. Complete the following comparative balance sheet analysis. Round your calculations to the nearest tenth of a percent.

Tri-State Data Systems, Inc.
Comparative Balance Sheet
December 31, 1992 and 1993

	1993	1992	Increase/Decrease Amount	Increase/Decrease Percent
Assets				
Current assets:				
Cash	$ 12,000	$ 10,500	1500	14.3
Accounts receivable	24,500	22,400	2100	9.4
Notes receivable	4,800	8,200	(3400)	(41.5)
Merchandise inventory	30,600	34,300	(3700)	(10.8)
Total current assets	$ 71,900	$ 75,400	(3500)	(4.6)
Fixed assets:				
Land	60,000	60,000	0	0
Building (net)	77,250	80,750	(3500)	(4.3)
Equipment (net)	45,650	42,500	3150	7.4
Total fixed assets	$182,900	$183,250	(350)	(.2)
Total assets	$254,800	$258,650	(3850)	(1.5)
Liabilities				
Current liabilities:				
Accounts payable	$ 28,500	$ 25,000	3500	14.0
Taxes payable	9,200	12,250	(-3050)	(24.9)
Wages payable	7,600	9,500	1900	(20.)
Total current liabilities	$ 45,300	$ 46,750	(1450)	(3.1)

Long-term liabilities:				
Mortgage payable	69,400	65,850	3550	5.4
Total liabilities	$114,700	$112,600	2100	1.9
Stockholder's equity				
Common stock	85,000	85,000	0	0
Retained earnings	55,100	61,050	(5950)	(9.7)
Total equity	$140,100	$146,050	(5950)	(4.1)
Total liabilities and equity	$254,800	$258,650	(3850)	(1.5)

4. Complete the required analysis of Excellent Autoservice Center's condensed comparative income statement.

Excellent Autoservice Center
Comparative Income Statement (condensed)
December 31, 1992 and 1993

	1993	1992	Increase/Decrease Amount	Increase/Decrease Percent	Percent of net sales 1993	Percent of net sales 1992
Net sales	$240,600	$236,800	3800	1.6	100.00	100.00
Cost of goods sold	179,900	181,400	(1500)	(.8)	74.8	76.6
Gross margin	$ 60,700	$ 55,400	5300	9.6	25.2	23.4
Total operating expenses	30,500	24,250	6250	25.8	12.7	10.2
Income before taxes	$ 30,200	$ 31,150	(950)	(3.0)	12.6	13.2
Provision for taxes	13,525	13,925	(400)	(2.3)	5.6	5.9
Net income	$ 16,675	$ 17,225	(550)	(3.2)	6.9	7.0

5.4   RATIO ANALYSIS OF FINANCIAL STATEMENTS

A **ratio** is a comparison of one number to another. The comparison can be of a part to the whole, or of one part to another part. A ratio shows how large/small one number is relative to another number. Ratios are expressed as fractions such as 6/3, or they are expressed horizontally using a colon such as 6:3; they are read as "a ratio of 6 to 3." We can use the techniques of Chapter 1 to simplify the fraction and express the ratio in different but equivalent terms; for example,

$$\frac{6}{3} = \frac{2}{1} \times \frac{3}{3} = \frac{2}{1}$$

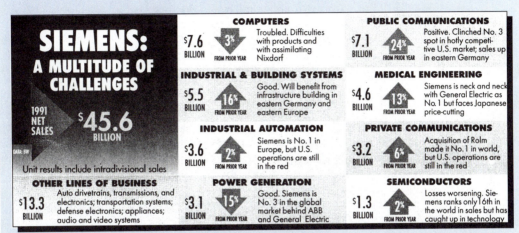

F o r   Y o u r   I n f o r m a t i o n

Financial analysis at a glance

Siemans is a German conglomerate specializing in high-tech industries. In 1990, the company launched a reorganization designed to strengthen its competitive position by investing billions of dollars in acquisitions, new technologies, and structural changes. The following year (1991), Siemans reported $1.1 billion in profits on net sales of $45.6 billion. In an attempt to improve the 2.4% sales margin ratio ($1.1/$45.6 = .0241), management ranked marketing muscle and increased sales as its top priorities for the next few years. A financial analysis of the firm's various divisions generated the information for these decisions and the information shown in the illustration.

In the illustration, the amounts of money (in billions of dollars) represent each division's contribution to Siemans's 1991 net sales of $45.6 billion (vertical analysis), and the percentages inside the arrows represent the rate of change (horizontal analysis) in each division's contributions to Siemans's net sales between 1990 and 1991.

Source: Business Week, March 9, 1992, chart by Arthur Eves. Used with permission.

which is a 2:1 ratio. A 6:3 ratio is equal to a 2:1 ratio. In other words, there are two parts of the first variable to every one part of the second variable.

Example 9

The data processing department of Allied Industries has 50 microprocessors of which 10 are Zeniths, 25 are IBMs, and the remainder are Apple IIs.

What is the ratio of (a) IBMs to total microprocessors, and (b) Apple IIs to Zeniths?

Solution

a. $\text{ratio} = \dfrac{\text{number of IBMs}}{\text{total number micros}} = \dfrac{25}{50} = \dfrac{1}{2}$,   or $1:2$

b. $\text{ratio} = \dfrac{\text{number of Apple IIs}}{\text{number of Zeniths}} = \dfrac{15}{10} = \dfrac{3}{2}$,   or $3:2$

Quite often in business applications, we like the second number of the ratio (the denominator of the ratio when written as a fraction) to be a 1. Especially with financial ratios, we like to compare the number of dollars to *one* dollar. We can express a ratio in an equivalent form with the second number a 1 by dividing both the numerator and denominator by the value in the denominator, for example,

$$\frac{3}{2} = \frac{3/2}{2/2} = \frac{1.5}{1},   \text{or}   1.5:1$$

Example 10

Jeb Wilcox made a $7,000 purchase with $2,000 cash and the remainder on credit. What is the ratio of credit to cash used for Jeb's purchase?

Solution

$$\text{ratio} = \frac{\text{amount of credit}}{\text{amount of cash}} = \frac{\$5,000}{\$2,000} = \frac{5}{2} = \frac{2.5}{1},   \text{or}   2.5:1$$

We could then say that Jeb used $2.50 of credit for every $1 of cash to make the purchase.

We must always be careful about the quantities being compared in a ratio. We generally want to compare quantities that are expressed in the same units so that we have a clear understanding of the magnitude of the ratio. For example, if we were comparing $4.50 to 30 cents we would compare *cents* to *cents*, that is,

$$\frac{450 \text{ cents}}{30 \text{ cents}} = \frac{15}{1},   \text{or}   15:1.$$

If we were comparing $3\frac{1}{3}$ hours to 45 minutes, we would use minutes for the comparison:

$$\frac{3\frac{1}{3} \text{ hours}}{45 \text{ minutes}} = \frac{3\frac{1}{3} \text{ hours} \times 60 \text{ minutes/hours}}{45 \text{ minutes}}$$

$$= \frac{200}{45} = \frac{40}{9}, \quad \text{or} \quad 40:9$$

Most of the problems involving ratios require the calculation of the ratio itself. However, you should be prepared to determine variable quantities when the relationship between variables is expressed as a ratio. Example 11 illustrates the solution to this type of problem.

Example 11

If a firm had total sales for the week of $12,000 with a 5:3 ratio of cash sales to credit sales, what is the amount of cash sales and credit sales for the week?

Solution

Since the sum of the parts equals the whole, we can note that total sales are divided into 8 parts (5 + 3), of which 5 parts are cash sales and 3 parts are credit sales. Next, we can express the ratios as fractions, or their decimal equivalents, to determine what amount of the total each part represents. Therefore, total sales are divided into 8 parts, of which 5 parts ($\frac{5}{8}$) are cash and 3 parts ($\frac{3}{8}$) are credit sales.

$$\frac{5}{8}, \quad \text{or} \quad .625 \times \$12,000 = \$7,500 \text{ cash sales}$$

$$\frac{3}{8}, \quad \text{or} \quad .375 \times \$12,000 = \$4,500 \text{ credit sales}$$

This analysis of parts that make up the whole can be used to solve problems in which the whole is made up of more than two parts.

Example 12

Martin, Browne, Seubert, and Rigal invested a total of $256,000 in a new business venture. The ratio of each investor's share is 7:4:3:2, respectively. How much did each invest?

Solution

The whole is broken into 16 parts (7 + 4 + 3 + 2)

7 of those 16 ($\frac{7}{16}$) represents Martin's share

$$\frac{7}{16} \times \$256,000 = \$112,000$$

4 of those 16 ($\frac{4}{16}$) represents Browne's share

$$\frac{4}{16} \times \$256,000 = \$64,000$$

Similarly 3 of the 16 ($\frac{3}{16}$) and 2 of the 16 ($\frac{2}{16}$) represent Seubert's and Rigal's share, respectively; Seubert invested $48,000 and Rigal invested $32,000.

CHECK YOUR KNOWLEDGE

Ratios

Write a ratio for each phrase. Express each ratio as a part to 1 in problems 1–3.

1. 60 wins to 15 losses
2. 150 rejected units to 2,500 total units produced
3. 45 minutes to 3 hours
4. A university received 5,425 applications for admissions last year. If the admissions office accepted 3,000 of those who applied and 1,800 students enrolled in the freshman class, what is the ratio of freshman enrollment to acceptances?
5. If a firm employs 2,750 people and has a labor-to-management ratio of 20:5, how many workers are there in each category?
6. Barclay, Smithers, and Rice are partners in a business. They agreed to divide profits annually in the ratio 5:3:2, respectively. Find Barclay's and Rice's share of the $93,750 profit reported this past year.

FINANCIAL STATEMENT RATIOS

Ratio analysis of financial statements provides the managers, creditors, and potential investors of a company with information specific to the type of decisions each must make. Ratios provide an assessment of the performance of a company. This assessment is accomplished by comparing a company's current performance either with its own past performance or with the performance of other companies. Ratios expand the vertical and horizontal analysis of financial statements.

Answers to CYK: *1.*   4:1   *2.*   .06:1   *3.*   .25:1   *4.*   .6:1   *5.*   2,200 laborers; 550 managers
6.   a. $46,875; b. $18,750

Ratios are generally classified as liquidity, leverage, activity, or profit ratios. The most significant and commonly used ratios in each category will be discussed in this section. The examples use information contained in the comparative financial statements presented in Figures 5.7 and 5.8.

LIQUIDITY RATIOS

The term *liquidity* refers to the ability of a firm to convert its assets into cash to meet its current debts (liabilities). Liquidity ratios are calculated from information contained in the balance sheet and include the current ratio and the acid test ratio. The **current ratio**, sometimes referred to as the *working capital ratio*, is computed by dividing the total of current assets by the total of current liabilities.

$$\text{current ratio} = \frac{\text{current assets}}{\text{current liabilities}}$$

Example 13

Find the current ratio for Norton Satellite Systems. (Data taken from Figure 5.8.)

Solution

1993
$$\text{current ratio} = \frac{33,980}{16,180} = 2.1, \quad \text{or} \quad 2.1:1$$

1992
$$\text{current ratio} = \frac{30,195}{18,485} = 1.6, \quad \text{or} \quad 1.6:1$$

The above ratios indicate that Norton Satellite Systems' ability to pay its debts has improved (the higher the ratio, the more favorable the position). In 1993, the value of current assets is two times the value of current liabilities, or the company has $2.10 in current assets for every $1.00 that it owes in current liabilities.

The **acid test ratio**, or *quick ratio*, measures the *immediate* debt-paying ability of a company. *Quick assets* (cash, receivables, and marketable securities) are compared to current liabilities. Inventories are omitted from the calculation because it could take a considerable amount of time to convert those assets into cash. Supplies and prepaid insurance are also omitted because those assets are used in operations and will not be sold for cash to resolve a firm's debts.

$$\text{acid test ratio} = \frac{\text{quick assets}}{\text{current liabilities}}$$

Example 14

Find the acid test ratio for Norton Satellite Systems. (Data taken from Figure 5.8.)

Solution

1993

$$\text{acid test ratio} = \frac{6{,}700 + 2{,}980}{16{,}180} = .60, \quad \text{or} \quad .60 : 1$$

1992

$$\text{acid test ratio} = \frac{4{,}250 + 3{,}470}{18{,}485} = .42, \quad \text{or} \quad .42 : 1$$

Norton's creditors may place a greater emphasis on these results than they would on the results of the current ratio. The basis of their concern is the fact that there are only $.60 of liquid assets for every $1.00 of current liabilities. This ratio is below the recommended $1:1$ standard used by many creditors when making decisions regarding credit.

LEVERAGE RATIOS

Most every business borrows money to finance its activity. **Leverage** is a term used to describe an investor's ability to use credit to finance investments. The ability to borrow money is based on the current debt position of the company. *Leverage ratios* provide managers and investors with the information they need to determine the way a business is financed. The information required to calculate the **debt-to-equity ratio** and the *debt-to-total-assets ratio* is found in the balance sheet.

$$\text{debt-to-equity ratio} = \frac{\text{total liabilities}}{\text{total owner's equity}}$$

Example 15

Find the debt-to-equity ratio for Norton Satellite Systems. (Data taken from Figure 5.8.)

Solution

$$\text{debt-to-equity ratio} = \frac{\overset{\textbf{1993}}{\$59,800}}{\$30,550} = 1.96, \quad \text{or} \quad 1.96:1$$

$$\text{debt-to-equity ratio} = \frac{\overset{\textbf{1992}}{\$70,685}}{\$18,535} = 3.81, \quad \text{or} \quad 3.81:1$$

Because this ratio has improved between 1992 (3.81:1) and 1993 (1.96:1), it may be within the recommended guidelines of creditors. The smaller the ratio the more favorable the margin of safety of the creditors. In 1993, for every $1.00 of ownership, there is almost $2.00 in liabilities. In other words, creditors have a claim on ⅔ of the company's assets. Such a position is not always viewed negatively. There are those who believe a firm's operations should be financed to the extent possible through external sources; therefore, companies will continue to borrow funds provided the earnings generated from the investment of borrowed money is sufficient to meet interest payments.

The relationship between the claim on assets of the owners and creditors is further defined by the *debt-to-assets ratio*, which compares total liabilities to total assets.

$$\text{debt-to-assets ratio} = \frac{\text{total liabilities}}{\text{total assets}}$$

Example 16

Find the debt-to-assets ratio for Norton Satellite Systems. (Data taken from Figure 5.8.)

Solution

$$\text{debt-to-assets ratio} = \frac{\overset{\textbf{1993}}{59,980}}{90,530} = .66, \quad \text{or} \quad .66:1$$

$$\text{debt-to-assets ratio} = \frac{\overset{\textbf{1992}}{70,685}}{89,220} = .79, \quad \text{or} \quad .79:1$$

These results can be interpreted in two different but related ways. First, for each $1.00 of assets, the company owes $.66 to its creditors. Second, the relationship can be converted to a percentage indicating that the creditors have claim to 66% of the company compared to the 34% claim held by Norton's owners. A company that uses leverage will have a higher debt-to-assets ratio than one that does not.

Liquidity and leverage ratios

The balance sheet for the ICU Corporation on July 31, 199X contained the following information: cash $25,000, marketable securities $15,000, accounts receivable $85,500, merchandise inventory $130,500, total current assets $256,000, total assets $420,500, total current liabilities $110,250, total liabilities $180,500, and total owner's equity $240,000. From this information, determine: (a) the current ratio, (b) the acid test ratio, (c) the debt-to-equity ratio, and (d) the debt-to-assets ratio. (Express each ratio as a part to 1 and round to the nearest hundredth.)

ACTIVITY RATIOS

Activity ratios analyze the use of assets by a firm. These ratios draw information from both the income statement and the balance sheet because they measure the turnover of assets being utilized to generate sales. Activity ratios are stated in terms of time, which expresses a degree of efficiency. A company that uses its assets efficiently will generate more interest from investors than a company that does not. The **asset turnover ratio** measures the effectiveness with which managers are using assets to produce sales. Assets used to compute the ratio may be the total at the end of the year, the average of the monthly total assets for the year, or the average of the beginning and ending totals of the year. Example 17 is based on total assets reported in Figure 5.7 and net sales reported in Figure 5.8.

$$\text{asset turnover} = \frac{\text{net sales}}{\text{total assets}}$$

Example 17

Find the asset turnover ratio for Norton Satellite Systems. (Data taken from Figures 5.7 and 5.8.)

Answers to CYK: (a) 2.32 : 1 (b) 1.14 : 1 (c) .75 : 1 (d) .43 : 1

Solution

$$\textbf{1993}$$

$$\text{asset turnover} = \frac{84{,}245}{90{,}530} = .93 \text{ times}$$

$$\textbf{1992}$$

$$\text{asset turnover} = \frac{74{,}707}{89{,}220} = .84 \text{ times}$$

The increase in the asset turnover indicates that the assets are being used more efficiently in 1993 than in 1992. Higher ratios suggest better management of assets when compared to activity of other years or other companies within the industry. The ratio also tells us that for each $1.00 invested in assets by management, it returns $.93 in net sales.

The *inventory turnover ratio* analyzes the number of times during the period the inventory has been sold. Since the analysis usually spans a period of time, the average balance of the asset (merchandise inventory) should be used in calculating the ratio. The inventory figures required to calculate the ratio are obtained from the cost of goods sold section of the income statement and from the balance sheet.

$$\text{inventory turnover} = \frac{\text{cost of goods sold}}{\text{average inventory}}$$

Example 18

Find the inventory turnover ratio for Norton Satellite Systems. (Data taken from Figure 5.7.)

Solution

$$\textbf{1993}$$

$$\text{inventory turnover} = \frac{28{,}490}{\dfrac{12{,}650 + 22{,}400}{2}} = \frac{28{,}490}{17{,}525} = 1.63 \text{ times}$$

$$\textbf{1992}$$

$$\text{inventory turnover} = \frac{26{,}725}{\dfrac{14{,}425 + 20{,}200}{2}} = \frac{26{,}725}{17{,}313} = 1.54 \text{ times}$$

CALCULATOR SOLUTION

Keyed entry	Display
* AC 12650 + 22400 =	35050
÷ 2 =	17525
Min	17525
28490 ÷ MR =	1.6256776

* Calculate the denominator as the first step and enter in memory.

Note: Average inventory was obtained by dividing the sum of beginning inventory plus ending inventory by 2.

The increase in inventory turnover suggests Norton Satellite Systems may have used its inventories better in 1993 than it did in 1992. However, when comparing the ratio with that of the industry it may be considered too low. A low ratio indicates Norton may be carrying too much inventory, which increases costs such as insurance, handling, pilferage, and spoilage and obligates amounts of money that could be more effectively utilized. For these reasons many companies have implemented just-in-time (JIT) inventory control systems, which by design can increase the inventory turnover ratio. If Norton takes steps to further increase its inventory turnover ratio, the company must be sure it has enough inventory to meet customer demand, as higher ratios usually result in lower inventory levels.

The relationship between credit sales and accounts receivable is referred to as the *receivables turnover ratio*. This ratio indicates the time required by a business to collect money for merchandise sold on credit to its customers. To determine the number of days accounts receivable have been outstanding, we divide the net sales on credit by the average net accounts receivable. The average accounts receivable may be based on the average monthly balances, or the average of the balances at the beginning and the end of the year. In Example 19, we will assume that all sales reported by Norton Satellite Systems in their income statement (Figure 5.7) were credit sales. Otherwise, we would have to identify what percentage of net sales were credit sales versus cash sales.

$$\text{accounts receivable turnover} = \frac{\text{net credit sales}}{\text{average accounts receivable}}$$

Example 19

Find the accounts receivable turnover for Norton Satellite Systems. (Data taken from Figures 5.7 and 5.8.)

Solution

$$1993$$

$$\text{accounts receivable turnover} = \frac{84,245}{\dfrac{2,980 + 3,470}{2}}$$

$$= \frac{84,245}{3,225} = 26.1 \text{ times}$$

Note: The average accounts receivable figure was found by taking the 1993 account balance ($2,980) and adding to this figure the 1992 account balance ($3,470) and dividing the result by 2. The 1992 balance is, for example purposes, the beginning balance for 1993. The ratio can now be expressed in terms of time by dividing a 360- or 365-day year by the ratio (360 ÷ 26.5 = 13.6). For Norton Satellite Systems, a receivables turnover ratio of 26.5 means that the average credit customer is taking about 14 days to pay its account, as shown below. A comparison with the credit terms offered by Norton (net payment in 30 days) indicates this average collection period is quite favorable.

$$\text{average collection period} = \frac{\text{number of days in year}}{\text{accounts receivable turnover}} = \frac{360}{26.1}$$

$$= 13.8 \text{ days}$$

PROFIT RATIOS

The focus of attention of most individuals associated with an enterprise is its profitability. If a business is not profitable, it will have difficulty attracting the interest of investors; it will encounter problems buying on credit and borrowing; and most importantly, it will eventually become extinct. *Profit ratios* are a measure of earnings and are developed from information found in both the income statement and the balance sheet.

The **return on net sales ratio** is a measure of earnings that identifies the amount of profit derived for each sales dollar. This ratio involves a vertical analysis of information found in the income statement and can be expressed in amounts or percentages.

$$\text{return on net sales} = \frac{\text{net income after taxes}}{\text{net sales}}$$

Example 20

Find the return on net sales ratio for Norton Satellite Systems. (Data taken from Figure 5.7.)

Solution

1993

$$\text{return on net sales} = \frac{\$19,744}{\$84,245} = .2344$$

1992

$$\text{return on net sales} = \frac{\$16,082}{\$74,707} = .2153$$

In 1993, Norton Satellite Systems made 23.4 cents in profit for each $1.00 of sales. The ratio expressed as a percentage (.2343 = 23.4%) can now be compared to company profit goals and industry averages to measure the degree of achievement.

The actual amount of income is not as clear a measure of earnings as is the relationship between the amount of income earned and the owner's investment. To analyze this more important relationship, we would use the **return on investment ratio**, which is obtained by dividing net income by the average owner's equity. The average owner's equity can be found by adding monthly statement figures or by using equity at the beginning and end of the year.

$$\text{return on investment} = \frac{\text{net income after taxes}}{\text{average owner's equity}}$$

We discussed earlier in this chapter how equity is reported in the balance sheet for both proprietorships and corporations. Example 21 is a presentation for a proprietorship. If you were to prepare a return on investment ratio for a corporation, equity would consist of the sum of common stock, preferred stock, and retained earnings.

Example 21

Find the return on investment for Norton Satellite Systems. (Data taken from Figures 5.7 and 5.8.) For this example, assume owner's equity on January 1, 1993 was $15,750.

Solution

1993

$$\text{return on investment} = \frac{\$19,744}{\dfrac{\$30,550 + 18,535}{2}}$$

$$= .8044, \quad \text{or} \quad 80.4\%$$

1992

$$\text{return on investment} = \frac{\$16,082}{\dfrac{18,535 + 15,750}{2}}$$

$$= .9381, \quad \text{or} \quad 93.8\%$$

The return on investment for Norton Satellite Systems is quite high. For each dollar invested by its owner, a return of 93.8 cents (1992) and 80.4 cents (1993) results or a return of 93.8% and 80.4% is realized. The high return on the investment of the owner can be partially explained by the leverage of the firm. Norton has been able to generate good profits by borrowing and purchasing its resale merchandise on credit.

The financial ratios discussed in this section are valuable analytical devices and provide the information necessary to assess an organization's performance and financial position. Careful consideration should be given, however, to the results obtained from these measures; they are not intended to provide their users with specific courses of action. When used with good judgment, industry trends and standards, and other economic indexes, they help to analyze present conditions and interpret future directions of an organization. A summarization of the ratios is presented in Table 5.1 for your convenience when studying or reviewing this chapter.

Table 5.1

Financial ratios

Ratio	Formula	Interpretation
A. Liquidity ratios		
1. Current ratio	$\dfrac{\text{current assets}}{\text{current liabilities}}$	Identifies the amount of current assets available to pay off each \$1 of current debt. A 2:1 is favorable.
2. Acid test ratio	$\dfrac{\text{quick assets}}{\text{current liabilities}}$ (Inventories are omitted from current assets to arrive at quick asset figure.)	Identifies the amount of assets that can be quickly liquidated into cash to cover each \$1 of current liabilities. A 1:1 is favorable.
B. Leverage ratios		
3. Debt-to-equity ratio	$\dfrac{\text{total liabilities}}{\text{total owner's equity}}$	Identifies the amount of total debt the owners have incurred for each \$1 of equity. Determines the claim on assets by owners. A 1:1 is favorable.
		continues

Table 5.1

(Continued)

Ratio	Formula	Interpretation
B. Leverage ratios (cont'd)		
4. Debt-to-assets ratio	$\dfrac{\text{total liabilities}}{\text{total assets}}$	Identifies the amount of total debt that can be covered by each $1 of assets. Determines the claim on assets by the creditors.
C. Activity ratios		
5. Asset turnover ratio	$\dfrac{\text{net sales}}{\text{total assets}}$	Identifies the amount of sales generated from each $1 of assets and the number of times assets have turned over.
6. Inventory turnover ratio	$\dfrac{\text{cost of goods sold}}{\text{average inventory}}$	Identifies the number of times during the period the merchandise inventory has been sold. Higher ratios may be considered more favorable.
7. Accounts receivable ratio	$\dfrac{\text{net credit sales}}{\text{average accounts receivable}}$	Indicates the number of times accounts receivable have turned over into sales.
8. Average collection ratio	$\dfrac{\text{number of days in year}}{\text{average accounts receivable turnover}}$	Identifies the average number of days required to collect accounts receivable.
D. Profit ratios		
9. Return on net sales ratio	$\dfrac{\text{net income after taxes}}{\text{net sales}}$	Identifies the amount of profit derived from each sales $1. Can also be expressed as a percent.
10. Return on investment ratio	$\dfrac{\text{net income after taxes}}{\text{average owner's equity}}$	Identifies the amount of profit realized from each $1 invested by the owners. Can also be expressed as a percent.

CHECK YOUR KNOWLEDGE

Activity and profit ratios

Use the data obtained from the financial statements of Walsh Industries to prepare the required activity and profit ratios. Round your answers to the nearest hundredth.

1. What is the asset turnover if sales are $1,650,000, sales returns and allowances are $20,500, and assets total $875,000?

2. If beginning inventory was $305,200, and ending inventory was $275,400, what was the inventory turnover on the cost of goods sold amounting to $1,059,500?

3. Eighty percent of the net sales of $1,629,500 are credit sales. What is the average time required to collect accounts from customers if January accounts receivable were $105,250, and December's accounts receivable totaled $110,350?

4. What is the rate of return on net sales if net income after taxes is $120,800 and net sales are reported at $1,629,500?

5. Owner's equity on January 1 was $1,320,500 and $1,400,500 on December 31. What is the return on investment if net income after taxes is $120,800?

5.4 EXERCISES

Express exercises 1 through 10 as fractions in lowest terms and also as ratios; for example,

$$25 \text{ cents to } \$1.00 = \frac{25}{100} = \frac{1}{4} = .25:1$$

Where possible, express the quantities in the same unit of measure.

1. Three sales to every 15 customers contacted
2. 45 cents gross profit to every 1 dollar of gross sales
3. 36 hits to 108 times at bat
4. 5 yards to 3 feet
5. 120 passing grades in business mathematics to every 15 failing grades
6. .52 quarts to 1 gallon
7. 3 days to 12 hours

8. 1,272 units produced to every 24 workers
9. 7 cents tax for each 1 dollar of net sales
10. 24 parts syrup to 64 parts water
11. OK Construction Company is planning to build an apartment complex that will include 72 two-bedroom units and 48 one-bedroom units. What will be the ratio of each type of unit to the total number of units to be built?
12. Margaret Sachs, a buyer for Top-Shelf Apparel, purchased 2,400 assorted color handbags from a manufacturer. If the order contained 1,200 black, 800 blue, and 400 brown handbags, determine the following ratios: (a) black to blue handbags, (b) brown to black handbags, and (c) brown to total handbags purchased.
13. A domed stadium has 60,000 seats consisting

Answers to CYK: **1.** 1.86 **2.** 3.65 **3.** 12.09 **4.** 7.4% **5.** 8.88%

of boxed seats, reserved seats, and general admission seats. If the seating ratio is $3:4:5$, respectively, how many seats of each type are there in the stadium?

14. Quality Printing reported assets totaling $120,000. If the company has a total debt to total assets ratio of .65:1, what is the amount of the company debt?

15. The Farnsworth Corporation balance sheet shows total current assets of $185,700. Determine the amount of cash and accounts receivable reported with a .15:1 ratio of cash to total current assets, and a .25:1 ratio of accounts receivable to total current assets.

For the ratios in exercises 16–25, use the comparative financial statements of Tri-State Systems presented in exercises 1 and 3 on pages 170–172. Round answers to hundredths.

16. Current ratio: 1992 _____
                                1993 _____

17. Acid test ratio   1992 _____
     (quick):   1993 _____

18. Debt-to-equity   1992 _____
     ratio: 1993 _____

19. Debt-to-assets ratio: 1992 _____
                                 1993 _____

20. Asset turnover ratio: 1992 _____
                                 1993 _____

21. Inventory turnover   1992 _____
     ratio: 1993 _____

22. Accounts receiv-   1992 _____
     able turnover (60%   1993 _____
     of net sales are
     credit sales and
     1991 accounts re-
     ceivable were
     $21,800):

23. Average collection   1992 _____
     period (365-day   1993 _____
     year):

24. Return on net sales: 1992 _____
                                 1993 _____

25. Return on invest-   1992 _____
     ment ratio (assume   1993 _____
     owner's equity on
     January 1, 1992 of
     $130,600):

26. The current ratio of Hamm Music is 2.8:1 based on total current liabilities of $125,000. What is the amount of Hamm's total current assets?

27. Yesterday's Treasures turned over its inventory 5.7 times this past year. If the antique business had an average inventory of $50,000, how much did it cost to purchase the goods that were sold to generate net sales of $475,000?

28. The accounts receivable turnover ratio of the Di-Tung Oriental Supply Co. is 12.5. If average accounts receivable for the period were $30,000, what percent of the $575,000 net sales were credit sales?

29. If Sample Foods's gross margin decreased 12.5% this year to $95,250, what was the gross margin reported on last year's income statement?

30. Rojon Enterprises reported after tax income of $125,000, which represented a 15.7% return on equity. What was the amount of stockholders' equity listed in the firm's balance sheet?

EXPRESS YOUR THOUGHTS

Compose one or two well-written sentences to express the requested information.

1. Identify and define the three types of accounts found on a balance sheet.

2. Explain how the ownership section of a balance sheet will vary depending on how a business is organized.

3. Identify the main sections of an income statement and illustrate the relationship between the various sections.

4. Discuss the procedure required to determine the cost of merchandise sold at a given amount of net sales.

5. Describe how you would prepare a vertical analysis of an income statement.

6. Explain the mathematical procedure required to complete a horizontal analysis of a balance sheet.

7. Describe how you would interpret the following mathematical expression:

   5:4:3

8. Discuss the primary distinction between the current ratio and the acid-test-ratio.

9. What does the term **leverage** mean and how does a firm evaluate its leverage?

10. Explain the function of profit ratios and discuss how the ROI is determined.

Case exercise *Sherwood Appliance Company*

On September 30 of the current year, the account balances of Sherwood Appliance Co. were reported as follows:

Accounts receivable	$22,200
Accounts payable	28,750
Accumulated depreciation—store equipment	10,400
Advertising expense	2,480
Cash	15,780
Merchandise inventory 9/1	49,560
Depreciation expense—store equipment	2,600
Insurance expense	1,500
Interest expense	225
Merchandise inventory 9/30	65,460
Notes payable	12,500
Prepaid insurance	3,150
Purchases	47,650
Sales	73,440
Sales discounts	1,280

Store equipment	26,800
Supplies	2,640
Supplies expense	1,250
Salaries expense	12,125
Salaries payable	875
Sherwood capital	83,505
Taxes expense	3,390

Quentin Hornsby, the bookkeeper, prepared the balance sheet given below and has brought it to you for your evaluation.

Sherwood Appliance Company
Balance Sheet
September 30, 199X

Assets

Current assets:		
Sales	$73,440	
Accounts receivable	22,200	
Prepaid insurance	3,150	
Supplies	2,640	
Total current assets		101,430
Fixed assets:		
Store equipment	$26,800	
Less depreciation expense	2,600	
Total fixed assets		24,200
Total assets		$125,630

Liabilities

Current liabilities:		
Accounts payable	$28,750	
Salaries expense	12,125	
Supplies expense	1,250	
Total liabilities		$ 42,125

Owner's Equity

Sherwood capital		83,505
Total liabilities and owner's equity		$125,630

A. Do you consider the balance sheet prepared by the bookkeeper to be an accurate assessment of the financial position of Sherwood Appliance Co. on September 30, 199X? Explain your answer.

B. If necessary, prepare your own version of the balance sheet.

C. Prepare a related income statement for Sherwood Appliance Co. using the account balances provided.

D. Using the data in the financial statements, prepare (a) a current ratio, (b) an acid test ratio, (c) a debt-to-equity ratio, and (d) a return on net sales ratio.

SELF-TEST

A. Terminology

Complete the following items using the key terms presented at the beginning of the chapter. Check your responses against the answer key at the end of the test.

1. The _balance_ details the financial position of a business at a specific point in time.

2. The balance sheet equation states, _asset_ must always equal _Liab_ plus _owner_.

3. A claim against the assets of a business by its creditors is called _Liab_.

4. In a sole proprietorship or a partnership, owner's equity is identified as _Cap._.

5. The _income st._ reflects the results of operations in terms of profits.

6. The total of sales returns, allowances, and sales discounts is deducted from _net Sale_ to determine _Gross Sale_.

7. The cost of goods sold is determined by adding to beginning inventory _net purch._ and deducting _endinven_ from merchandise available for sale.

8. When the cost of goods sold is deducted from the value of net sales, the result is _profit_.

9. The percentage analysis of changes in corresponding items in comparative financial statements is referred to as _horizonal analysis_.

10. An analyst will use _vertical_ when the information needed concerns the percentage relationship of the component parts of the financial statement to the total in a single period.

11. A _ratio_ is the comparison of one number to another.

12. The current ratio is found by dividing _Curr Ass_ by the _Curr Liab._.

B. Calculation review

The following concepts and short problems are designed to test your understanding of the objectives identified at the beginning of the chapter. Answers are provided at the end of the test.

13. If a company's assets total $68,975, and liabilities amount to $24,870, what is the claim against the assets by the owners?

14. The following account balances appeared in the records of the Goodtime Amusement Co. on December 30, 199X: cash $12,265, accounts receivable $18,950, accounts payable $4,290, supplies $1,340, salaries expense $10,240, equipment $67,500, depreciation expense—equipment $2,450, and accumulated depreciation—equipment $18,600. Determine the amount of total assets to be reported on the December 30 balance sheet.

15. From the following—sales $87,260, inventory Jan 1 $17,490, purchases $32,840, purchase returns $4,800, purchase discounts $1,260, inventory Jan 30 $16,820—determine (a) cost of goods sold and (b) gross profit.

16. If sales are $65,000 and operating expenses are 45% of sales, what is the net income if the cost of goods sold is $26,500?

17.   Complete the analysis indicated in the partial balance sheet below.

	1993	1992	Increase/Decrease Amount	Increase/Decrease Percent	Percent 1993
Assets					
Current assets:					
Cash	$ 5,000	$ 3,500	a. _____	_____	_____
Accounts receivable	8,750	6,800	b. _____	_____	_____
Prepaid insurance	1,500	2,400	c. _____	_____	_____
Merchandise inventory	27,350	30,250	d. _____	_____	_____
Total current assets	$ 42,600	$ 42,950	e. _____	_____	_____
Fixed assets:					
Equipment (net)	12,800	7,375	f. _____	_____	_____
Building (net)	80,000	85,600	g. _____	_____	_____
Total assets	$135,400	$135,925	h. _____	_____	_____

18.   Charles Lee and Carl Ginter are considering a partnership that requires an investment of $75,000. If Lee invested $25,000 and Ginter invested $50,000, what is the ratio of Lee's investment to (a) the total investment? (b) Ginter's investment?

19.   The asset turnover ratio of Smith Supply Company is 5.8:1. If Smith Supply Company's net sales for the period are $464,000, what is the value of Smith's total assets?

20.   The following data were abstracted from the financial statements of We-Got-It-All Rental Company.

Current assets	$36,000
Average accounts receivable	8,500
Current liabilities	15,500
Total assets	78,500
Inventory	12,000
Net sales	96,250
Net income after taxes	20,800
Owner's equity (January 1)	40,000
Owner's equity (December 31)	52,500
Total liabilities	38,500

From the data, prepare (a) a current ratio, (b) an acid test ratio, (c) a debt-to-equity ratio, and (d) a return on investment ratio.

Answers to self-test: **1.** balance sheet   **2.** assets, liabilities, owner's equity   **3.** liabilities   **4.** capital   **5.** income statement   **6.** gross sales, net sales   **7.** net purchases, ending inventory   **8.** gross profit   **9.** horizontal analysis   **10.** vertical analysis   **11.** ratio   **12.** current assets, current liabilities   **13.** $44,105   **14.** $81,445   **15.** a. $27,450; b. $59,810   **16.** $9,250   **17.** a. $1,500, 42.9%, 3.7%; b. $1,950, 28.7%, 6.5%; c. ($900), (37.5)%, 1.1%; d. ($2,900), (9.6)%, 20.2%; e. $350, .8%, 31.5%; f. $5,425, 73.6%, 9.5%; g. ($5,600), (6.5)%, 59.1%; h. $475, .4%, 100.0%   **18.** a. 1:3; b. 1:2   **19.** $80,000   **20.** a. 2.3:1; b. 1.54:1; c. .96:1; d. 45.0%

6

PURCHASE DISCOUNTS AND RECORDS

Learning objectives

1. Understand the extent of merchandising distribution networks.

2. Differentiate buying and selling terms and processes.

3. Read and prepare invoices.

4. Compute net price based on single and chain trade discounts.

5. Use the complement method to calculate trade discounts.

6. Find the single-equivalent rate for chain or series discounts.

7. Calculate cash discounts using common terms of payment.

continues

Learning Objectives (*continued*)

8. Compute adjustment for returned goods and allowances when discounts are offered.

9. Determine freight charges and net amount due on an invoice.

10. Understand the function of commission agents and how to calculate commissions.

11. Calculate the cash discount and the amount of credit when a partial payment is remitted.

12. Define the key terms.

INTRODUCTION

Learning objective
Understand the extent of merchandising distribution networks.

Every business engaged in merchandising buys and sells goods for a profit. A business must purchase goods at the lowest possible cost and sell them for a price that will recover all costs and business expenses, and generate an acceptable profit (see Chapter 5). In addition, every business must become part of a distribution network designed to market and transport the goods from the manufacturer to the consumer. Figure 6.1 shows examples of some distribution channels used by manufacturers to market their goods.

The longest channel involves the **manufacturer** who buys raw materials or parts and produces or assembles them into finished goods that are then sold to wholesalers. The **wholesaler** or **distributor** then stores and promotes the sale of goods to the **retailer**, who then sells the goods

Figure 6.1

Product distribution channels

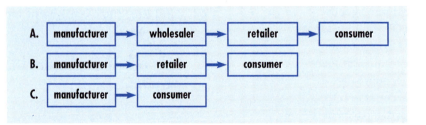

Figure 6.2

Distribution channel: cost versus price analysis

to the consumer. The **consumer** is the part of the channel that will use or consume the product.

Notice that the other channels eliminate (to various degrees) the **middlepersons** between the manufacturer and the consumer. These latter channels have become increasingly popular because they reduce the cost of goods, which in turn lowers the price charged at each step in the channel. This process is generally referred to as *discounting*; the retailers that participate in these channels, such as K mart, Hills, and Ames, are called *discount stores*.

Learning objective
Differentiate buying and selling terms and processes.

Because each business in a distribution channel buys and sells goods, it is important that you, the student, understand that the term *cost* refers to *buying* and the term *price* refers to *selling*. These terms are often used interchangeably because the seller's price is the buyer's cost as the product moves through the distribution channel (Figure 6.2).

Now that you understand these important basic merchandising concepts, we are ready to discuss the focus of this chapter, purchase discounts and records—the process of buying.

6.1   PREPARING INVOICES

An **invoice** is the official record of a business transaction between the seller and the buyer. The buyer prepares a *purchase invoice* that verifies an order has been placed with a specific seller. The seller in turn issues a *sales invoice* when the items ordered have been sold and arrangements for delivery are completed. While invoices vary in appearance, a typical sales invoice will contain the following information:

Learning objective
Read and prepare
invoices.

1. the names and addresses of both the seller and the buyer

2. the invoice number, date, and order reference number

3. a description of the items purchased with quantity, unit price, and extension amount

4. how and who will deliver the merchandise

5. the type and amount of discounts offered

6. the terms of payment

7. shipping and insurance charges

8. the invoice total (sum of all charges associated with sale).

Figure 6.3 is an example of an invoice. Study the example carefully as you will be required to prepare invoices for various problems in this chapter. The section of the invoice that identifies the *quantity* (the number of units sold), the *description* (the identification of the item, the stock number, etc.), the **unit price** (the price per measure of unit), and the **extension amount** (the quantity value of items sold under each description and unit price) provides the data necessary to determine the total amount of the invoice. The *invoice total* is the sum of the extension amounts. The quantitative procedure used to compute each extension amount in Figure 6.3 is:

The extension amount

quantity × unit price = extension amount

This adaptation of the basic *business equation* (quantity × price = revenue) requires the quantity and price to be stated in the same weight or measure. For example, in Figure 6.3, all quantities are stated in the same weight or measure as the unit price of the item. The unit price defines how the item is sold and cannot be changed. To simplify the preparation of the invoice, sellers generally require the buyer to purchase merchandise in quantities consistent with the unit price measure. When the quantity ordered is not consistent with the unit price measure, the quantity must be adjusted as shown in the following example.

Example 1

Find the total amount of an invoice if a customer purchased six two-pole switches at $10.25 each; 350 feet of #14 wire at $.035 per foot; and 1 gross of #6 connectors at $1.27 per dozen.

Figure 6.3

Sample invoice

					Invoice 554	

CAPITAL ELECTRICAL SUPPLY INC.
1269 Industrial Drive
Silver Spring MD 20903
(202) 555-4792

Sold to: Midstate Electric Co.
458 Center Street
Mapleview, N.Y. 13107

Ship to: Same

Shipped via Roadway Express Inc.

Customer's Order XXXXXX	Our Order Number	Salesman Martin	Terms 2/10, n/30	Date Shipped 1/4/93	F.O.B. Destination	Date 1/12/93

Quantity Ordered	Quantity Shipped	Description	Unit Price	Amount
6	6	two-pole switches	$ 10 | 25	$ 61 | 50
350 ft	350 ft	# 14 wire	035	12 | 25
12 doz	12 doz	# 6 connectors	1 | 27	15 | 24
		Subtotals		$ 88 | 99

Misc. Information:	returned merchandise subject to a 10 percent restocking fee	**Trade Discount**
		5% of list $ 4 | 45
Cash discount ▶	**Deduct:** $ _1.69_ **If paid by:** _1/22/93_	**Shipping Charge** $ 18 | 20
		Invoice Total ▶ $ 102 | 74

Notification of shortages or damages and requests for proof of delivery must be made in writing within 30 days of invoice date	**Interest of 2 percent per month assessed on all past due accounts**

Solution

The quantity of both the switches and wire is multiplied by the unit price to determine the extended amount as they are quoted in like terms (6 × $10.25 = $61.50 and 350 × .035 = $12.25). The connectors, however, are sold by the dozen. Therefore, one gross must be converted to dozen (12 dozen in one gross), requiring us to adjust the quantity ordered to 12 dozen for calculation (12 × $1.27 = $15.24). We can now sum the extension amounts to find the invoice total.

Quantity	Description	Unit price	Extension amount
6	Two-Pole Switches	$10.25 ea.	$61.50
350 ft.	#14 Wire	$ 0.035/ft.	$12.25
12 doz.	#6 Connectors	$ 1.27/doz.	$15.24
		Invoice Total	$88.99

Table 6.1 contains standard abbreviations used on invoices, and Figure 6.4 contains the weights and measures. Refer to these tables when you prepare your assignments. When sellers use special abbreviations, the no-

Table 6.1

Invoice abbreviations

Abbreviation	Term	Abbreviation	Term
ea	each	doz	dozen
drm	drum	gro	gross
cs	case	bx	box
ctn	carton	sk	sack
bbl	barrel	qt.	quart
pr	pair	gal.	gallon
C	per hundred (100)	oz.	ounce
M	per thousand (1000)	lb.	pound
cwt.	per hundred weight	ct.	crate
cpm	cost per thousand	ml	milliliter
@	at	cl	centiliter
FOB	free on board	l	liter
COD	cash on delivery	mm	millimeter
ROG	receipt of goods	cm	centimeter
EOM	end of month	m	meter
ex.	extra dating	km	kilometer
FAS	free alongside ship	g	gram
in.	inch	kg	kilogram
ft.	foot	sq. ft.	square feet
yd.	yard	sq. yd.	square yard

Figure 6.4

Units of measure

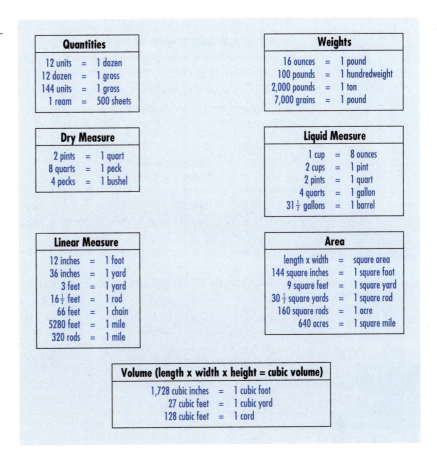

Quantities		
12 units	=	1 dozen
12 dozen	=	1 gross
144 units	=	1 gross
1 ream	=	500 sheets

Weights		
16 ounces	=	1 pound
100 pounds	=	1 hundredweight
2,000 pounds	=	1 ton
7,000 grains	=	1 pound

Dry Measure		
2 pints	=	1 quart
8 quarts	=	1 peck
4 pecks	=	1 bushel

Liquid Measure		
1 cup	=	8 ounces
2 cups	=	1 pint
2 pints	=	1 quart
4 quarts	=	1 gallon
$31\frac{1}{2}$ gallons	=	1 barrel

Linear Measure		
12 inches	=	1 foot
36 inches	=	1 yard
3 feet	=	1 yard
$16\frac{1}{2}$ feet	=	1 rod
66 feet	=	1 chain
5280 feet	=	1 mile
320 rods	=	1 mile

Area		
length x width	=	square area
144 square inches	=	1 square foot
9 square feet	=	1 square yard
$30\frac{1}{4}$ square yards	=	1 square rod
160 square rods	=	1 acre
640 acres	=	1 square mile

Volume (length x width x height = cubic volume)		
1,728 cubic inches	=	1 cubic foot
27 cubic feet	=	1 cubic yard
128 cubic feet	=	1 cord

tation of their meaning is usually printed on the invoice. (An example of a special abbreviation could be a number code used to identify a choice of color.)

CHECK YOUR KNOWLEDGE

Calculating cost, invoice extension amounts, and totals

Solve each of the following problems. Round dollar amounts to the nearest cent.

1. How much did it cost Sarah Bennett to purchase a gallon of vinegar at a unit price of 29 cents a pint?

2.   The Men's Shop purchased 27 shirts for $495.45. What was the unit price if the shirts are sold by the dozen?

3.   General Tire Distributors purchased the following tires from a manufacturer: 135, P165/14 for $22.43; 65, P240/15 for $37.25; and 250, 2185/13 for $48.57. What was the total cost of the order?

4.   Complete the following invoice calculations:

Quan-tity	Description	Unit price	Extension amount
10	Helmets, football Model 60, 5 size 6⅞, 5 size 7¼	$62.95 ea	_____
5 doz.	Socks, Athletic, Tube, Style 137	$29.40/doz	_____
12 bx.	Golf Balls Hy-Fly 50's	$18.50/bx	_____
16 doz.	Sweat Shirts, Athletic; 4 doz ea S, M, L, XL; Color Code Z	$87.50/doz	_____
		Invoice Total	_____

5.   Identify the following invoice abbreviations:

a. cs   *f.* cpm
b. yd   *g.* bbl
c. cwt   *h.* km
d. gr   *i.* lb
e. l   *j.* ctn

6.1 EXERCISES

Complete the following invoice calculation:

	Quantity	Description	Unit price	Extension price
1.	15 gal.	milk	$2.19/gal.	_____
2.	30 lb.	butter	$4.75/5 lb.	_____
3.	10 bottles	syrup	$3.25/bottle	_____
4.	50 lb.	pancake mix	$4.55/5-lb bag	_____
5.	300	paper plates	$2.75/package of 50	_____
6.	500	paper napkins	$3.00/package of 100	_____
7.			Total	_____

Complete the following invoice calculation:

	Quantity	Description	Unit price	Extension price
8.	1,000	notepads 4" × 5" blue	$20/hundred	_____
9.	13 gross	#2 lead pencils	$47.50/gross	_____
10.	1,000	convention folders w/assoc. logo	$130/carton (250 folders/ctn)	_____
11.			Total	_____

Complete the following invoice calculation:

	Quantity	Description	Unit price	Extension price
12.	10 doz.	Adjustable baseball caps—2 doz ea. of red, blue, green, yellow, and orange	$ 3.50/cap	_____
13.	10 doz.	t-shirts with team logo, 2 doz. ea. of red, blue, green, yellow, orange	$3.25/ea.	_____
14.	30	Wood baseball bats, 10 ea. of lengths 26", 28", 30"	$12.50 ea.	_____
15.	5	Catcher's chest protector	$27.50 ea.	_____
16.	5	Catcher's mask	$32.25 ea.	_____
17.	5	Catcher's mitt, model S-1138	$43.25 ea.	_____
18.	6 doz.	Little League approved baseballs	$42/doz.	_____
19.			Total	_____

Complete the following invoice calculation:

	Quantity	Description	Unit price	Extension price
20.	5 doz.	yellow canary legal pads	$9.00/doz	_____
21.	7 bottles	white-out correction	$1.04/bottle	_____
22.	5 boxes	3½" computer disks	$15.00/box	_____
23.	3	desk top staplers	$14.50 ea.	_____
24.	3 boxes	staples	$2.25/box	_____
25.	1	staple remover	$3.50	_____
26.			Total	_____

Solve the following problems. Round dollar amounts to the nearest cent and rates to the nearest tenth of a percent.

27. Sid Jones purchased 8 six-packs of cola at a unit price of $2.58 per six-pack. What was his total cost?

28. Bob Haskins purchased 1 case of motor oil for $15. If a case contains 12 one-quart cans of motor oil, how much did Bob pay for each quart?

29. While shopping for blank video tapes, Gina Sardino discovered that she could purchase a single tape for $3.99 or she could purchase a pack of four video tapes for $14.50. What was the unit price per tape for the four-pack? How much would she save per tape by purchasing the four-pack if she intended to purchase four tapes anyway?

30. Juan Ramirez priced a 10-pack of 5¼″ computer disks to be $13.90, and a 50-pack to be $59.50. What is the unit price per disk of the 10-pack? What is the unit price per disk of the 50-pack? If Juan needed to purchase 100 disks, how much would he save by purchasing the 50-packs rather than the 10-packs?

31. Sally Sanchez discovered that during a holiday sale at a local mall, she could purchase one pullover sweater for $22.50, or two of the same style sweater for $35.00. How much would she save per sweater by buying two sweaters?

32. Rachel Mudhamgha purchased 4 boxes of chocolate candy bars at $10.95 per box; 7 boxes of chewing gum at $7.39 per box; 3 canisters of hard candy at $8.49 per canister; and 9 boxes of licorice sticks at $6.79 per box for her high school store. What was the total of Rachel's order?

6.2   TRADE DISCOUNTS

Manufacturers and wholesalers promote the sale of their products through *catalogs* which contain photos, illustrations, specifications, and descriptions of every product they sell. Catalogs also include the **list price** of each item, which is the suggested selling price the buyers should charge their customers. Sellers may offer buyers trade discounts to encourage buyers to purchase their products. A **trade discount** is a reduction in the list price. The price paid by the buyer after the trade discount is subtracted from the list price is called the **net price** from the seller's perspective, or the **net cost** from the buyer's perspective.

The list price of items listed in catalogs may change and items may be added or deleted before new catalogs can be published. To keep the buyer informed of all changes, the seller will issue a price supplement to the catalog that identifies current trade discounts applicable to the list prices in the catalogs. The price supplement also allows the seller to vary the amount of the trade discount offered to different buyer categories (wholesalers, retailers). If buyers wish to optimize net income, they must be aware of price changes and discount offers of their suppliers so they can purchase the desired quantity of merchandise at the lowest price available.

Trade discounts can be expressed as percentages or as amounts. The size of a discount can vary according to the type of buyer; for example, a wholesaler may receive a 25% discount on an item and a retailer may receive only 15% on the same item. Sellers may also base the amount of the trade discount on the quantity purchased, competitive prices, and product classification. Trade discounts are applied strictly to the list price of an item. Let's see how a trade discount is calculated when a single discount is offered.

CALCULATING SINGLE TRADE DISCOUNTS AND NET PRICE

Learning objective
Compute net price based on single and chain trade discounts.

To find the amount of the trade discount and net price when a single discount is offered, we use the two-step procedure shown in Example 2.

Example 2

A refrigerator lists for $1,200 with a trade discount of 20%. Find the amount of trade discount and the net price.

Solution

Step 1: Find the amount of trade discount.

$$\text{trade discount amount} = \text{list price} \times \text{trade discount rate}$$
$$= \$1,200 \quad \times \ .20$$
$$= \$240$$

Step 2: Find the net price.

$$\text{net price} = \text{list price} - \text{trade discount amount}$$
$$= \$1,200 \quad - \$240$$
$$= \$960$$

As you read the steps, did you recognize the procedure as an application of the percentage formula presented in Chapter 3? The terms would be redefined as follows:

list price × trade discount % = trade discount amount
base   ×   rate   =   part

list price − trade discount amount =   net price
base   −   part   = complement part
$1,200   − $240   = $960

The net price is the **complement** of the trade discount amount (part) because the discount amount is subtracted from the list price (base). In other words, both the net price and trade discount amounts are a part of the base (list price).

The net price for Example 2 can also be found using the *complement method*. The complement of the trade discount expressed as a percent would be 100% − 20% = 80%. A more complete expression of the complement calculation would be:

List price	$1,200	100%
Trade discount	240	20%
Net price	$ 960	80% (complement of the trade discount)

The complement of the trade discount is used as the rate to determine the net price as shown below.

$$\text{net price} = \text{list price} \times \text{trade discount complement rate}$$
$$= \$1,200 \quad \times \ .80$$
$$= \$960$$

CALCULATING CHAIN DISCOUNTS AND NET PRICE

It is quite common for manufacturers and wholesalers to offer retailers additional discounts on merchandise to increase sales, to change prices, to adjust to seasonal trends, and for different types of customers. For example, to increase sales and reduce current inventory, a wholesaler who usually offers a 20% trade discount might offer an additional 15% discount on selected merchandise. The discount would be quoted "20% less 15%" or simply 20/15. This type of discount is called a **chain discount** or *series discount*.

When chain discounts are given, each discount is applied separately. It is important to note that the discounts can never be added together, the reason being, each discount is applied to a different base. There are two methods used to calculate chain discounts and net price. Example 3 illustrates the *declining net price method*, and the *complement method* is explained in Example 4.

Example 3

Leisure-Time Distributors lists a sailboard for $1,500 and offers a trade discount of 25% and 20%. Use the declining net price method to determine the net price of the sailboard.

Solution

Step 1:   Multiply list price by first discount rate to find discount.

$1,500 × .25 = $375

Step 2:   Subtract discount from list price to find net amount.

$1,500 − 375 = $1,125

Step 3:   Multiply net amount by second discount rate to find discount.

$1,125 × .20 = $225

Step 4:   Subtract second discount from the net amount found in Step 2. This is the net price.

$1,125 − 225 = $900

If we want to find the amount of the trade discount, we simply subtract the net price from the list price. ($1,500 − 900 = $600)

trade discount = list price − net price
$$= \$1,500 \quad - \$900$$
$$= \$600$$

The net price can also be found by multiplying the list price by the complements of each single discount in a chain.

Example 4

Learning objective
Use the complement method to calculate trade discounts.

The list price of a lawnmower is $525. Use the complement method to determine the net price to the buyer if the seller offers a trade discount of 10/5/10.

Solution

Step 1:   Find the complement of each trade discount.

100% − 10% = 90%

100% − 5% = 95%

100% − 10% = 90%

Step 2:   Convert each percent in step 1 to a decimal and multiply (do not round off). This is the net price equivalent rate.

.90 × .95 × .90 = .7695

Step 3:   Multiply the list price by the net price equivalent rate found in step 2.

net price = list price × net price equivalent rate
= $525.00 ×   .7695
= $403.99

The trade discount amount is found using the same procedure shown in Example 3.

trade discount = list price − net price
= $525.00 − $403.99
= $121.01

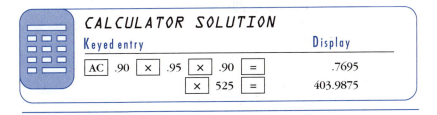

CALCULATOR SOLUTION

Keyed entry	Display
AC .90 × .95 × .90 =	.7695
× 525 =	403.9875

Learning objective
Find the single-equivalent rate for chain or series discounts.

CALCULATING THE SINGLE-EQUIVALENT TRADE DISCOUNT RATE

The most convenient way to find the **single-equivalent trade discount rate** is to again use the complement method. To calculate the single-

Table 6.2

Single-equivalent
rates of chain
discounts

	5%	10%	15%	20%
5	.0975	.145	.1925	.24
10	.145	.19	.235	.28
10/5	.18775	.2305	.27325	.316
10/10	.2305	.271	.3115	.352
15	.1925	.235	.2775	.32
15/10	.27325	.3115	.3475	.388
20	.24	.28	.32	.36
20/15	.354	.388	.422	.456

equivalent discount rate for Example 4, we would simply subtract the net price equivalent rate from 1, which gives us its complement—the equivalent discount rate.

$$\text{single-equivalent discount rate} = 1 - (\text{net price equivalent rate})$$
$$= 1.0000 - .7695$$
$$= .2305$$

The .2305 is the single-equivalent discount rate for a chain discount of 10/5/10. We can also calculate the amount of the trade discount with this rate. Notice that we get the same amount of trade discount shown in Example 4.

$$\text{amount of trade discount} = \text{list price} \times \text{single-equivalent discount rate}$$
$$= \$525.00 \times .2305$$
$$= \$121.01$$

Note: The single-equivalent can also be calculated with the percentage equation $R = P/B$; where P is the amount of discount and B is the list price ($.2305 = \$121.01/\$525$).

Merchants conducting numerous transactions daily will often use single-equivalent discount tables to simplify the process of preparing or interpreting sales invoices. Example 5 shows how the rates in Table 6.2 are determined.

Example 5

Find the single-equivalent discount rate for a chain discount of 20/15/10.

Solution

Step 1:   Calculate the complement of the trade discount.

$$100\% - 20\% = 80\%$$
$$100\% - 15\% = 85\%$$
$$100\% - 10\% = 90\%$$

Step 2: Convert percents to decimals and calculate the net price equivalent rate.

.80 $\times$ .85 $\times$ .90 = .612 net price equivalent

Step 3: Calculate the single equivalent discount rate.

single equivalent rate = 1 $-$ (net price equivalent rate)
= 1 $-$ .612
= .388, or 38.8%

CALCULATOR SOLUTION

Keyed entry	Display
AC .80 $\times$ .85 $\times$ .90 =	.612
Min	.612
1 $-$ MR =	.388

CHECK YOUR KNOWLEDGE

Calculating trade discounts

Solve each of the following problems. Round dollar amounts to the nearest cent and rates to the nearest one hundredth of a percent.

1. What is the amount of trade discount and net price of a ten-pound box of high grade hot dogs that lists for $1.95 per pound and carries a 20% discount per box?

2. Find the net price of a skill saw that lists for $59 with a discount of 35%. (Use the complement method.)

3. The suggested retail price of a 12 foot $\times$ 18 foot above-ground pool with filter, ladder, and cover is $2,400. If the dealer offers a trade discount of 30%, 5%, and 10%, what is the retailer's net price?

4. What is the single-equivalent trade discount rate and amount in problem 3?

5. Find the single-equivalent trade discount rate for a chain (series) discount of 40/25/15.

Answers to CYK: *1.* $3.90, $15.60   *2.* $38.35   *3.* $1,436.40   *4.* .4015   *5.* .6175

6.2 EXERCISES

Solve the following problems. Round dollar amounts to the nearest cent and rates to the nearest tenth of a percent.

Calculate the following *trade discounts* and *net prices:*

	List price	Trade discount rate	Trade discount amount	Net price
1.	$1,500	15%	_____	_____
2.	$2,500	20%	_____	_____
3.	$1,300	22%	_____	_____
4.	$5,000	24%	_____	_____
5.	$7,400	19%	_____	_____

Calculate the *trade discount rate* from the given information. Express the discount rate as a percentage (%).

	List price	Trade discount amount	Trade discount rate
6.	$1,600	400	_____
7.	$750	250	_____
8.	$2,800	560	_____
9.	$12,000	1,200	_____
10.	$850	170	_____

Determine the *complement percentages* for each of the following percentages, and express them in decimal form.

	Percentage	Complement %	Complement % (decimal form)
11.	15%	_____	_____
12.	45%	_____	_____
13.	22%	_____	_____
14.	37%	_____	_____
15.	17%	_____	_____

Determine the *net price* using the complement method.

	List price	Trade discount rate	Complement trade discount rate	Net price
16.	$2,000	.25	_____	_____
17.	$3,500	.20	_____	_____
18.	$5,400	.15	_____	_____
19.	$720	.30	_____	_____
20.	$85	.10	_____	_____

Calculate the trade discount by the *declining net price* method.

	List price	1st discount rate (%)	1st discount amount	1st net amount
21.	$2,000	15	_____	_____
22.	$3,000	25	_____	_____
23.	$350	20	_____	_____
24.	$90	15	_____	_____
25.	$550	30	_____	_____

	2nd discount rate (%)	2nd discount amount	2nd net amount	Trade discount
	10	_____	_____	_____
	10	_____	_____	_____
	15	_____	_____	_____
	12	_____	_____	_____
	5	_____	_____	_____

Determine the *net price equivalent rate* for each of the following.

	Discount rate	Complement of discount	Net price discount rate
26.	20/20	_____	_____
27.	15/10	_____	_____
28.	30/10/5	_____	_____
29.	40/15/10	_____	_____
30.	18/12/7	_____	_____

Calculate the trade discount by the *net price equivalent rate* method.

	List price	Discount rate (%)	Net price equivalent rate	Net price	Trade discount
31.	$3,000	20/15	_____	_____	_____
32.	$5,000	15/10	_____	_____	_____
33.	$900	25/15/10	_____	_____	_____
34.	$15,500	18/12/6	_____	_____	_____
35.	$9,000	12/8/5	_____	_____	_____

Calculate the *single equivalent trade discount rate* for each of the following.

	Discount rate	Net price equivalent rate	Single equivalent trade discount rate
36.	10/20/5	_____	_____
37.	15/10/5	_____	_____
38.	25/12	_____	_____

Discount rate	Net price equivalent rate	Single equivalent trade discount rate
39. 20/10/5/3	_____	_____
40. 30/15/10	_____	_____

41. What is the amount of the trade discount and net price of a portable color television set that lists for $675 if the dealer offers a 25% discount on the set?

42. Eberhart's Mills offered a 30% trade discount to buyers on all bedding purchased during December. How much will a customer pay for 8 cartons of assorted sheet and pillow case sets that list for $49.50 a carton?

43. Julio Santo, a buyer for Hometowne Markets, can purchase a crate of melons from one supplier for $18.75. Another supplier offers a list price of $22 per crate. If Julio accepts the lower price, how much will he save if he buys 12 crates?

44. What is the net price for five dozen t-shirts if the list price is $108 per dozen and the seller offers a trade discount of 12% and 8%?

45. Upstate Distributors provides a chain discount of 25/10/5 to retailers on all appliances. Find the amount of trade discount allowed on the sale of three electric ranges that list for $675 each, and 2 refrigerators listed at $1,025 each to City-Wide Appliance Center.

46. Lefkowicz Carpeting purchased a 400-square-yard roll of carpet from a manufacturer at a list price of $6,000. Find the net cost per square yard if the manufacturer offered Lefkowicz Carpeting a series discount of 25/20/15.

47. A manufacturer lists a snowmobile for $3,500. If the manufacturer offers a chain discount 15/10/15 to wholesalers and a 20/15 chain discount to retailers, find the net cost of the snowmobile for (a) the wholesaler and (b) the retailer.

48. Calculate the single equivalent discount rate in problem 47 for (a) the wholesaler and (b) the retailer.

49. If a merchant offers a chain discount of 12/8/3, what is the single equivalent rate of the chain discount?

50. Quality Crafters lists a line of kitchen cabinets at $1,250. If a customer paid a net price of $893.75, what single rate of trade discount was offered?

6.3   CASH DISCOUNTS

Learning objective
Calculate cash discounts using common terms of payment.

A major percent of sales recorded by manufacturers and wholesalers are credit sales. A *credit sale* (sale on account) allows the buyer to pay for the purchased merchandise at a future date agreed upon at the time of the sale. In Chapter 5, we briefly discussed this procedure when we explained why an account receivable is considered a current asset and appears in the balance sheet. The seller who has agreed to sell merchandise on credit has, in essence, agreed to finance that part of the buyer's inventory. This process allows the buyer to (1) carry a larger selection of merchandise, (2) increase sales potential and profits, and (3) have time to sell the merchandise before the payment date. A credit sale can, however, create a *cash flow* problem for the seller because of the time period between the date of the sale and receipt of payment. To encourage buyers to pay invoices before the required date, many sellers offer a **cash discount**. A cash discount is usually expressed as a percent and is always based on the net price of the sales invoice, excluding other charges such as shipping, insurance, trade discounts, and sales tax. The procedure used to calculate the cash discount is another application of the percentage equation.

Calculating cash discount

cash discount = net price × cash discount rate

part = base × rate

The **terms** of the cash discount are listed on the invoice in the section labeled "terms" or "terms of sale." The terms identify the percent of the cash discount and the time period for which it applies. There are many variations in the terms granted by sellers to buyers. In this section, we will look at the most commonly used expressions of cash discounts.

ORDINARY DATING METHOD

The **ordinary dating method** terms on an invoice would be expressed as 2/10, *n*/30. The "2/10" means the buyer may deduct 2% from the net price noted on the invoice if payment is made within 10 days from the invoice date. The "*n*/30" means the buyer must pay the full amount of the invoice within 30 days. After 30 days, payment is considered "overdue" and the buyer may be required to pay a late charge. Figure 6.5 illustrates the cash discount time line for this situation.

As you can see, dates are an integral part of the cash discount process. The buyer must be aware of the **discount dates** and the **net payment date** to take advantage of the opportunity to reduce the cost of goods. Both the discount date and the net payment date are counted from the invoice date. Two methods are presented to help you calculate these important dates.

Figure 6.5

Cash discount time line

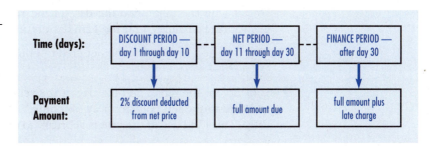

Days-in-a-month-method　　Thirty days has September, April, June, and November; all the rest have 31 except February, which has 28, and 29 during leap year (1992 and 1996 are leap years).

Example 6

An invoice is dated January 12, 1991, with terms 3/10, *n*/30. (a) Find the discount date; (b) find the net payment date.

Solution

a. January 12 plus 10 days brings us to January 22, which is the last date to take the cash discount.

b.　　31　days in January
　　− 12　invoice date

　　19　days remaining in January
　　19　days in January
　+ 11　days in February net amount due

　　30　days to pay net

or

$$N + 19 = 30$$
$$N = 30 - 19$$
$$N = 11$$

We first subtract the invoice date from the number of days in the month. Then, we find what number when added to the days remaining in the month equals the net period (30 days). This number is the net payment date (February 11, 1991).

Days-in-a-year method　　The exact days-in-a-year method requires the use of Table 6.3 to calculate the dates. If we use the information given in Example 3, the invoice due date would be found as follows.

Step 1:　In the table, find the date of the year represented by the invoice date. (January 12 is the 12th day of the year.)

Step 2:　Add to this date the net credit period given on the invoice. (12 + 30 = 42)

Step 3:　In the table, find the day of the year determined in step 2 and read to the left column "Day of month." This is the invoice due date. (The 42nd day of the year is February 11th.)

Do 8.4 Homework

Do Test

Well Shit when you're
got All Day to
figure it out.

Table 6.3

Exact days-of-the-year calendar

Day of month	31 Jan.	28 Feb.	31 Mar.	30 Apr.	31 May	30 June	31 July	31 Aug.	30 Sept.	31 Oct.	30 Nov.	31 Dec.
1	1	32	60	91	121	152	182	213	244	274	305	335
2	2	33	61	92	122	153	183	214	245	275	306	336
3	3	34	62	93	123	154	184	215	246	276	307	337
4	4	35	63	94	124	155	185	216	247	277	308	338
5	5	36	64	95	125	156	186	217	248	278	309	339
6	6	37	65	96	126	157	187	218	249	279	310	340
7	7	38	66	97	127	158	188	219	250	280	311	341
8	8	39	67	98	128	159	189	220	251	281	312	342
9	9	40	68	99	129	160	190	221	252	282	313	343
10	10	41	69	100	130	161	191	222	253	283	314	344
11	11	42	70	101	131	162	192	223	254	284	315	345
12	12	43	71	102	132	163	193	224	255	285	316	346
13	13	44	72	103	133	164	194	225	256	286	317	347
14	14	45	73	104	134	165	195	226	257	287	318	348
15	15	46	74	105	135	166	196	227	258	288	319	349
16	16	47	75	106	136	167	197	228	259	289	320	350
17	17	48	76	107	137	168	198	229	260	290	321	351
18	18	49	77	108	138	169	199	230	261	291	322	352
19	19	50	78	109	139	170	200	231	262	292	323	353
20	20	51	79	110	140	171	201	232	263	293	324	354
21	21	52	80	111	141	172	202	233	264	294	325	355
22	22	53	81	112	142	173	203	234	265	295	326	356
23	23	54	82	113	143	174	204	235	266	296	327	357
24	24	55	83	114	144	175	205	236	267	297	328	358
25	25	56	84	115	145	176	206	237	268	298	329	359
26	26	57	85	116	146	177	207	238	269	299	330	360
27	27	58	86	117	147	178	208	239	270	300	331	361
28	28	59	87	118	148	179	209	240	271	301	332	362
29	29	—	88	119	149	180	210	241	272	302	333	363
30	30	—	89	120	150	181	211	242	273	303	334	364
31	31	—	90	—	151	—	212	243	—	304	—	365

This method can also be used when the credit period begins in one year and ends in the following year by subtracting the invoice date from 365 to give the number of days used in the current year. This figure would then be subtracted from the number of days in the credit period, which would give the day of the following year when the invoice payment is due.

Example 7

What date is 60 days after November 20?

Solution

Step 1:   365   days in year
              −324   calendar date of November 20
              ‾‾‾‾‾
              41   days used in current year

Step 2:   60   credit period
              −41   days used in current year
              ‾‾‾‾
              19   days of following year, or January 19th

Ordinary cash discount terms can be extended to give the buyer more time to take advantage of the discount and make payment. For example, a clothing manufacturer may offer a distributor discount terms of 3/30, 2/60, *n*/90 to purchase its full line in May. The distributor would be able to deduct a 3% discount from the net price if full payment was made within 30 days, a 2% discount if full payment was made between the 31st and the 60th day. The net or full amount of the invoice would be due 90 days from the date of the invoice. Example 8 illustrates how to apply this discount.

Example 8

If payment was made on July 8, how much money would Reynolds Wholesale receive from the Winton Shop for merchandise invoiced on May 10 that listed for $2,750 with a trade discount of 15% and terms of 4/30, 2/60, *n*/90?

Solution

Step 1:   The invoice was paid 59 days from the date of invoice; therefore, the 2% cash discount can be deducted from the net price of the invoice.

31   21 May
−10   30 June
‾‾‾   8 July (payment date)
21 days in May   ‾‾‾‾‾
                           59 days

Step 2:   The cash discount is based on the net price, therefore, the trade discount must be deducted from the list price to determine the net price.

$2,750.00 list price
−412.50 less trade discount (2,750 × .15)
‾‾‾‾‾‾‾‾
$2,337.50 net price

Step 3:   Calculate the amount of the cash discount on the net price.

$$\text{cash discount amount} = \text{net price} \times \text{cash discount rate}$$
$$= \$2{,}337.50 \times .02$$
$$= \$46.75$$

Step 4:   Subtract the cash discount from the net invoice amount to determine the amount due on July 8.

$2,337.50 net invoice amount
$\underline{\quad -46.75}$ less cash discount
$2,290.75 amount due

When merchants use the terms **eom** (*end-of-month*) or *prox* **(Proximo)** on invoices, they are extending their customer's cash discount and periods. For example, when 3/10 eom appears on an invoice, it means the buyer can deduct a 3% cash discount if payment is made 10 days after the end of the month. In other words, the discount period and the credit period do not begin until the first day of the following month. Sellers who use this method will frequently add on an extra month when the date of the invoice is the 26th of the month or later. To illustrate, an invoice dated September 28 with a cash discount of 2/10 eom or 2/10 prox extends the discount period to November 10.

Example 9

Find (a) the discount date and (b) the net payment date for an invoice dated March 12 with terms of 2/15, *n*/30 eom.

Solution

a. The discount period begins on April 1 and ends on April 15, the discount date.
b. The net payment date is 15 days after the discount date (April 30) or 30 days after the end of the month.

Example 10

Art's Crafts and Hobby Shoppe received an invoice on June 29 for $290.50 for purchases. How much must the accounts payable clerk remit if payment is made on August 19 and the terms of the invoice are 3/20, *n*/60 prox?

Solution

Step 1:   Determine if the bill is being paid during the discount period. The discount period begins on August 1 and ends on August 20 (end of July plus 20 days comes to August 20). The discount period begins August 1 because the invoice is dated after the 25th of the month.

Step 2:   Calculate the amount of the cash discount.

$$\text{discount amount} = \text{net price} \times \text{discount rate}$$
$$= \$290.50 \ \times .03$$
$$= \$8.72$$

Step 3:   Find the amount due.

$\$290.50$ net invoice amount
$\underline{\quad 8.72}$ less cash discount
$\$281.78$ amount due

Manufacturers and wholesalers who produce and distribute seasonal goods to retailers will often extend cash discount periods by using the **extra dating method**. For example, when offering terms of 2/10-90X (or 2/10-90 ex), the seller is allowing the buyer an extra 90 days, or a total of 100 days from the date of the invoice, to take advantage of the cash discount. The net payment date would then be 20 days after the discount date. For the seller, these terms could induce sales, reduce inventory storage costs, and provide a more manageable shipping period. For the buyers, such terms allow them to purchase goods in the off season and still take the cash discount. The buyers may also be able to sell the goods before the cash discount period expires, which enhances their cash flow position.

Example 11

If an invoice is dated April 5 with terms 3/15-30X, what is (a) the discount date and (b) the net payment date?

Solution

a.   30 days in April
   $\underline{-5}$ date of invoice
       25 days remaining in April
   $\underline{+20}$ days in May (discount date, May 15)
       45 days in discount period (15 + 30 = 45)

b.   May 20 + 15 days after discount date is June 4, net payment date.

Example 12

An invoice for the purchase of "weed-eaters" totals $945.60 and is dated January 4, 1992 with terms 2/10–60X. If the invoice is paid on March 12, what is the amount of the net payment?

Solution

Step 1:   Determine if payment is made by the discount date.

$$
\begin{array}{rl}
31 & \text{days in January} \\
-4 & \text{date of invoice} \\
\hline
27 & \text{days remaining in January} \\
+29 & \text{days in February (a leap year)} \\
+14 & \text{days in March (discount date)} \\
\hline
70 & \text{days in discount period } (10 + 60 = 70)
\end{array}
$$

The net payment date is April 3 (March 14 plus 20 days). The discount date is March 14 (January 4 plus 70 days comes to March 14).

Step 2:   Calculate amount of cash discount.

$$
\begin{aligned}
\text{discount amount} &= \text{net price} \times \text{discount rate} \\
&= \$945.60 \ \times .02 \\
&= \$18.91
\end{aligned}
$$

Step 3:   Find the amount due.

$$
\begin{array}{rl}
\$945.60 & \text{net invoice amount} \\
\underline{18.91} & \text{less cash discount} \\
\$926.69 & \text{amount due}
\end{array}
$$

Notice that in both Example 11 (15 + 15 = 30) and Example 12 (10 + 20 = 30) the net payment period is adjusted to total 30 days based on the number of days in the discount period.

Some merchants may **postdate** invoices to extend the cash discount and net payment periods. A postdated invoice will show the terms of the invoice in the section reserved for terms (2/10, *n*/30) and the extension of the terms is shown in the date section of the invoice (Date: April 10, *as of* May 15). This postdate means the discount period and the net payment period start on May 15. Therefore, the discount date is May 25 and the net payment date is June 15 (May 15 + 30 days = June 14).

The terms presented thus far are all based on the date of the invoice. However, when it is difficult to determine the shipping or transportation period for merchandise, the seller can use the receipt-of-goods (**ROG**) dating method. This method gives the buyer the opportunity to receive and inspect the goods before the terms of the sale go into effect.

Example 13

Far East Imports ordered merchandise from Orient Export with a net value of $3,500. The invoice for the transaction was dated October 3 with terms of 3/10, *n*/30 ROG. The order arrived at Far East Imports on November 17. What was the amount of the net payment if payment was made on November 30?

Solution

Step 1: Determine if the payment is made during the discount period.

November   17 date goods received
    +10 cash discount terms in days
November   27 cash discount date

Step 2: Calculate the amount of cash discount. A cash discount cannot be taken because the invoice was paid on November 30, 3 days after the discount date (November 27).

Step 3: Find the net amount due.

$3,500 net invoice amount
    0 cash discount amount
$3,500 amount due

Notice that, with this method, the discount period and the credit period begin when the goods are received. The seller will be able to validate this date because the shipping company responsible for delivering the order provides the seller with a shipping invoice that notes the date of delivery.

CHECK YOUR KNOWLEDGE

Calculating cash discounts

Solve each of the following problems. Round dollar amounts to the nearest cent.

1. What is (a) the discount date and (b) the net payment date for an invoice dated June 5 with terms 2/20, *n*/45? (Use Table 6.3.)

2. What would be the net payment of an invoice dated August 22 for $1,800 with terms 3/10, 2/30, *n*/60, if payment was made on: (a) September 1? (b) September 23?

3. What are the discount dates for invoices dated (a) April 10 and (b) September 26 if both invoices offer terms of 1/15 eom?

4. General Fasteners purchased merchandise worth $12,500 on May 14 under terms of 3/10 - 90X. What is (a) the amount of the net payment if the invoice was paid on August 20 and (b) the net payment date?

5. If an invoice is dated June 5, *as of* August 31 with terms of 2/10, *n*/30, what is (a) the discount date and (b) the net payment date?

6. Find the net payment for an invoice dated January 15 for $975.60 with terms 2.5/10 ROG if the order was received on March 20 and payment was made on March 29.

6.3 EXERCISES

Solve the following problems. Round dollar amounts to the nearest cent and rates to the nearest tenth of a percent.

An invoice has the stated terms 4/10, *n*/30 eom. Determine the discount date, and the net payment date.

	Invoice date	Discount date	Net payment date
1.	May 19	_____	_____
2.	Dec. 21	_____	_____
3.	Feb. 26	_____	_____
4.	Oct. 30	_____	_____
5.	Nov. 20	_____	_____

An invoice has the stated terms 3/15, *n*/60 eom. Determine the discount date and the net payment date.

	Invoice date	Discount date	Net payment date	
6.	Jan. 20, 1992	Feb 15	April 1	60 − 15 − 45 để tính
7.	March 28, 1991	April 15	May 30	
8.	May 19, 1990	June 15	July 30	
9.	Dec. 27, 1991	Jan 15	March 1	
10.	June 28, 1993	July 15	Aug. 29	

Answers to CYK: *1.* a. June 25; b. July 20   *2.* a. $1,746; b. $1,800   *3.* a. May 15; b. November 15 (additional month granted because invoice date is after 25th day of month)   *4.* a. $12,125.00; b. September 11   *5.* a. September 10; b. September 30   *6.* $951.21

Khi nào có + thứ +

Determine the discount date and net payment date for an invoice with the terms 4/10-60X if the invoice date is:

	Invoice date	Discount date	Net payment date
11.	Jan. 20, 1991	March 21	April 20
12.	Sept. 23, 1992	Dec 2	Dec. 22
13.	Aug. 11, 1993	Oct 20	Nov. 9
14.	Feb. 3, 1992		
15.	April 28, 1991		

Determine the discount date and the net payment date if the terms of an invoice are 3/15, *n*/60 ROG if the "receipt of goods" dates are:

count 60 days.

	ROG date	Discount date	Net payment date
16.	Sept. 21	Oct 6	Nov 21
17.	March 19	April 3	May 18
18.	May 13		
19.	Aug. 15		
20.	June 23		

Determine the discount date and net payment date for an invoice with the terms 4/10, *n*/30 with the dates:

	Invoice date	Discount date	Net payment date
21.	March 20 *as of* April 10	Ap. 20	May 10
22.	Feb. 13 *as of* March 14	March 24	Ap. 13
23.	Sept. 16 *as of* Oct. 15	Oct. 25	Nov. 14
24.	July 23 *as of* Aug. 25	Sep. 5	Nov. 25
25.	Nov. 28 *as of* Dec. 15	Dec. 25	Jan. 14

An invoice is dated March 23, 1990 and the buyer received the goods on April 15, 1990. Determine the discount date and net payment date if the following terms prevailed:

	Terms	Discount date	Net payment date
26.	4/10, *n*/60		
27.	4/10-90X		
28.	4/10, *n*/60 eom		
29.	4/10, *n*/60 prox.		
30.	4/10, *n*/60 ROG		
31.	4/10, *n*/60 *as of* May 15		

32. An invoice is dated Feb. 12, 1991, with terms 4/10, *n*/30. Find: (a) the discount date and (b) the net payment date.

33. An invoice is dated September 12 with the terms of payment 4/30, 3/60, *n*/90. Determine (a) the 4% discount date, (b) the 3% discount date, and (c) the net payment date.

34. If payment is made on June 5 on an invoice with payment terms of 5/15, 4/30, 3/45, *n*/60 and dated April 25, is the buyer entitled to any of the stated discounts? If so, which?

35. Hernandez Landscaping purchased merchandise worth $8,500 on June 12 under terms of 5/10, 3/20, *n*/60. What is the amount of the payment if the invoice was paid on (a) June 28? (b) July 29?

36. Melanie's Cards and Gifts made a purchase worth $350 on May 28 with the terms 5/20 ROG. If the goods were received on June 15 and the invoice was paid on July 2, how much did Melanie's have to pay?

37. Oscar's Drive-in Beverage Outlet purchased 1,000 shipping cartons for $975 with the terms 6/15, 4/25, *n*/60, eom. The invoice was dated November 20, the cartons were received on December 10; the invoice was paid on December 12th. How much did Oscar's owe when they paid off the bill?

38. How much should Stevens Electrical Service pay for a $1,345 purchase made on February 14, 1991, with the terms 5/10, 2/20, *n*/30 prox if they receive the goods on February 28 and pay the invoice on March 15?

39. What would Bart's Haberdasherie be required to pay for a purchase of $789 made on January 19, 1992, under the terms of 5/15, 3/25, *n*/40 as of January 25, if the invoice is paid on February 18?

40. Arlene's Beauty Salon purchased $1,234 worth of hair and skin care products on September 28 with the terms of 6/10–60X, and made payment on November 27. What would have been the amount of Arlene's net payment?

41. Marlene's Ice Cream Parlor purchased ice cream, toppings, and supplies on March 29 worth $3,350 with the terms 6/10, 2/20, *n*/45 and paid off the invoice on May 20. What was the net payment due on the 20th?

42. Celebreses' Variety Store purchased assorted merchandise for $1,975 with the terms 5/15, 3/25, *n*/90 eom. The invoice was dated October 17 and was paid on December 12. How much did Celebreses' owe on the invoice when they paid off the bill?

43. How much should Caryl's Plumbing and Sewer Service pay for a $2,568 purchase made on February 24, 1992, with the terms 4/10, 2/20, *n*/30 if it receives the goods on February 28 and pays the invoice on March 6?

44. Guthrie's Pizzeria purchased food and soft drink supplies on October 6 for $567 with the terms 4/10, 2/20, *n*/30 ROG and received the order on November 6. If the invoice was paid on November 15, how much was due on that date?

45. Chevon's Sports Shop purchased $4,500 of baseball uniforms on May 23 with the terms 5/20, 4/30 *as of* June 15 and received the goods on June 6. What was the net payment if it paid the invoice on July 13?

6.4 OTHER CHARGES AND ADJUSTMENTS ON THE INVOICE

In Section 6.1, we explained the invoice in terms of its contents and preparation. In this section, we will increase our understanding of invoices as we learn how discounts and other charges such as transportation and commissions are presented on an invoice. We will also learn how to make adjustments in the amount required to pay invoices that result from partial payments and merchandise being returned for credit or refund by the buyer.

Because the invoice is the official record of the sales transaction, it generally lists the seller's policies regarding methods of payment, price changes, and procedures for returning merchandise for credit or refund. This information is used by the buyer to make important financial decisions after the merchandise has been received.

RETURNED GOODS

Learning objective
Compute adjustment for returned goods and allowances when discounts are offered.

The invoice is either sent to the buyer through the mail or shipped with the merchandise. When the merchandise is received, the buyer checks the merchandise to verify that the quantity listed on the invoice agrees with the quantity delivered. The buyer also checks to make sure the merchandise delivered meets specifications, and that it has not been damaged in transit. Merchandise that does not meet specifications or that is damaged in transit is called **returned goods** when it is sent back to the seller for credit. The seller may offer the buyer an *allowance*, which reduces the cost of the goods if the buyer is willing to keep the merchandise.

Trade and cash discounts are based on the merchandise actually purchased. Therefore, merchandise that has been returned is not subject to any discounts offered and must be deducted before discounts are calculated. Example 14 illustrates how to calculate the adjustment for returned goods when trade and cash discounts are offered by the seller.

Example 14

What is the amount required to pay an invoice for $1,200 with a trade discount of 20%, 10%, 5%, and terms of 2/10 ROG, if the buyer returned $400 worth of merchandise and paid the invoice before the discount date?

Solution

Step 1:   Deduct the amount of returned goods from the invoice list price total.

$1,200 list price
$\underline{-400}$ less returned goods
$ 800 adjusted list price

Step 2:   Calculate the net price.

.80 × .90 × .95 = .684 net price equivalent
$800 × .684 = $547.20 net price amount

Step 3:   Calculate the cash discount.

$547.20 net price
  ×.02 cash discount rate

$ 10.94 cash discount amount

Step 4:   Determine the amount due.

$547.20 net price
− 10.94 less cash discount amount

$536.26 amount due

The following calculation summary for Example 14 will help you to better understand the order and basis of the calculations.

$1,200.00 invoice list price total
 − 400.00 less returned goods

$ 800.00 adjusted list price
 − 252.80 less trade discount (800 × .316)

$ 547.20 net price
  − 10.94 less cash discount (547.20 × .02)

$ 536.26 amount due

FREIGHT CHARGES

Learning objective
Determine freight charges and net amount due on an invoice.

The cost of transporting goods has increased considerably over the past decade due to the scarcity of natural resources required to produce the fuels needed by the transportation industry. Consequently, manufacturers and wholesalers have had to develop transportation systems that will move shipments in and out of their organizations in a timely manner, at a competitive price, and that accommodate their customers' requirements. Sellers may elect to transport their own merchandise or employ truck, rail, steamship, or airline companies.

When transportation companies are used to ship merchandise, the *freight charges* may be paid by either the seller or the buyer depending on the shipping terms. For example, the term **FOB** (free on board) **shipping point** means that the buyer pays the freight charges and that ownership of the merchandise transfers to the buyer before shipment. If the term **FOB destination** is used, the seller prepays the freight charges and retains title to the merchandise until it is delivered. The title distinction is important if the merchandise is lost or damaged in transit.

As a matter of practice, the buyer always pays the cost of transportation either directly or indirectly. The buyer pays directly when the goods

For Your Information
Freight rates made easy

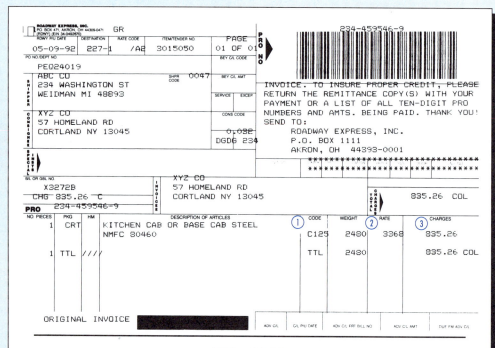

E-Z Rate Schedule

ORIGIN MI 48893   DESTINATION NY 13045   MINIMUM CHARGE
                                         L1C: 68.37   1C: 68.37

Tariff 507-C   Effective 1/1/92

CLASS	L5C	M5C	M1M ②	M2M	M5M	M10M	M20M	M30M	M40M
50	23.94	20.21	16.84	14.95	12.01	11.00	7.53	6.42	5.62
55	26.12	22.05	18.37	16.31	13.10	12.08	8.28	7.05	6.18
60	27.39	23.12	19.26	17.10	13.73	12.55	8.59	7.32	6.42
65	29.56	24.96	20.79	18.46	14.82	13.63	9.34	7.96	6.97
70	31.27	26.40	21.99	19.52	15.68	14.41	9.87	8.41	7.37
775	33.44	28.23	23.52	20.88	16.77	15.49	10.61	9.04	7.92
85	36.68	30.97	25.80	22.91	18.40	16.88	11.56	9.85	8.63
925	39.93	33.71	28.08	24.93	20.02	18.43	12.63	10.76	9.42
100	43.14	36.42	30.34	26.94	21.63	19.98	13.69	11.66	10.22
110	47.45	40.06	33.37	29.63	23.80	21.84	14.96	12.75	11.17
① 125	53.94	45.53	37.94	33.68	27.05	24.94	17.08	14.55	12.75
150	64.71	54.63	45.51	40.40	32.45	29.90	20.48	17.45	15.29
175	75.51	63.74	53.11	47.15	37.87	34.85	23.87	20.34	17.82
200	86.31	72.86	60.71	53.89	43.28	39.96	27.37	23.32	20.43
250	107.88	91.07	75.88	67.36	54.10	49.88	34.16	29.11	25.50
300	129.45	109.28	91.05	80.83	64.92	59.95	41.06	34.98	30.65
400	172.58	145.70	121.39	107.76	86.55	79.93	54.75	46.65	40.87
500	215.75	182.14	151.75	134.72	108.20	99.91	68.43	58.31	51.08

Freight rates made easy (continued)

Many sellers transport their goods to buyers by motor freight. The process of determining a freight cost is complex because the rates charged by carriers depend on the classification of the goods being shipped, the weight of the goods, and the distance between point of origin and point of destination. For years, individuals known as "raters" calculated freight charges using a library of rate manuals and a calculator. In 1983, Roadway Express, Inc., introduced "E-Z Rate" the shipping industry's first simplified nationwide, zip-zone computerized freight rating system. The E-Z rate system reduces the older, complex method to a simple procedure. The freight charges shown in the accompanying Roadway Express invoice were determined from the data given and the rate table (shown) as follows:

1. Determine the National Motor Freight Classification class of the freight. Class of freight is C–125.

2. Determine the applicable base rate for the weight bracket and destination postal or zip zone from the rate table. Base rate is $33.68. Shipment weight is 2,480 pounds. Look down column M2M (more than 2,000 pounds but less than 5,000 pounds) and across row C–125.

3. Divide the weight by 100 and multiply the result by the base rate.

$$\frac{2,480 \text{ lbs.}}{100 \text{ lbs.}} \times \$33.68 = \$835.26$$

The rate table includes all classification codes, weight columns ranging from less than 500 pounds to more than 40,000 pounds, applicable base rates for all classes of freight and their respective weights, and the minimum charge for freight shipped between origin zip 48893 and destination zip 13045. A rate table similar to the one shown would be used to calculate freight charges between every zip zone in the U.S.

Source: Roadway Express, Inc., Akron, Ohio. Used with permission.

are shipped F.O.B. shipping point or when the seller prepays freight charges and includes the freight charges on the invoice. The buyer is paying freight charges indirectly when they are included as part of the unit price charged for the merchandise. This procedure is not as popular today because of the constant fluctuation of transportation rates.

Freight charges are based on a number of factors including weight of the shipment, destination, type of transportation, and the rate charged. The *rate* is the price charged by a transportation company to transport merchandise and is usually quoted per hundred weight (CWT). Rates can also be quoted per thousand pounds (M), or per ton (T). The freight charge is found by multiplying the rate times the number of weight units, as shown in the following example.

Example 15

What is the freight charge for shipping 3,480 pounds if the rate is $.80 per CWT?

Solution

Step 1: Determine the number of weight units (CWT) in the shipment.

3,480 ÷ 100 = 34.8 weight units

Step 2: Calculate the freight charge.

freight charge = weight units × unit rate
= 34.8   × $.80
= $27.84

Rate schedules like the one shown in Table 6.4 are used to determine freight charges and often contain minimum weight requirements. If this rate schedule were used to calculate the freight charge in Example 15, we would have to pay for 5,000 pounds at the $1.10 rate (5,000 lb ÷ 100 lb = 50 CWT, 50 × $1.10 = $55) or $55 CWT. Since the 3,480 pounds is less than the lowest minimum weight listed in the rate schedule, we must either ship or pay for 5,000 pounds. When the actual weight shipped is greater than the minimum weight, we multiply the actual weight by the unit rate in that minimum weight class. For example, if we are shipping 12,500 pounds, the freight charge is $137.50 (125 × $1.10).

Notice that the rates in the schedule decrease as the minimum weights increase. This inverse relationship creates a break-even point at which it costs less to pay for the greater minimum weight at the lower unit rate price. You will not be required to calculate this break-even point; however, you should understand that it is important to plan shipments so that the greatest amount of merchandise can be shipped at the lowest possible cost whenever possible.

Table 6.4

Rate schedule

Minimum weight	Unit rate
5,000	$1.10
15,000	.95
30,000	.54
35,000	.48
40,000	.42

Figure 6.6

Account sale

Account Sale

Neuser's Produce Inc.   Date ___October 2_ 19 _92_
1376 Commerce Blvd.
Syracuse, NY 13215

Sales For Account of Farmers Cooperative
                        Baldwinsville, N.Y. 13027

Date	Description	Price	Amount	Totals
9/10	100 cartons tomatoes	$ 6.50	$650.00	
9/18	50 8-quart boxes plums	8.00	400.00	
9/27	200 50 lb. bags potatoes	4.00	800.00	
				$1,850.00
	Trade Discount 15%			277.50
	Gross Proceeds			$1,572.50
	Charges:			
	Freight		$152.50	
	Storage		65.00	
	Commission 5%		78.63	296.13
	Net Proceeds			$1,276.37

COMMISSIONS

Learning objective
Understand the function of commission agents and how to calculate commissions.

Manufacturers and wholesalers may use *brokers* or **commission agents** to buy or sell merchandise. Commission agents never take title of the merchandise; they simply represent the seller when arranging a sale (**account sale**) or the buyer when arranging a purchase (**account purchase**). Commission agents charge a fee for their services based on the net price of the invoice or the *gross proceeds* of the account sale (see Figure 6.6). A commission agent may be identified on a sales invoice, but the commission charges do not appear on the invoice because the buyer is not responsible for sales commissions. The seller pays the commission agent's commissions earned on sales at the end of the month. Example 16 illustrates how a commission is calculated for an account sale.

Example 16

John Neuser, a commission agent, sold merchandise for Farmers Cooperative worth $1,850, with a trade discount of 15%, freight charges of $152.50, and a storage charge of $65.00. If the agent charged a 5% commission, determine (a) the commission earned on the transaction and (b) the net proceeds remitted by the commission agent to Farmers Cooperative.

Solution

   a. $1,850.00 list price
           − 277.50 less trade discount (1,850 × .15)
        $1,572.50 gross proceeds
           ×   .05 commission rate
        $ 78.63 commission amount

   b. $1,572.50 gross proceeds
                     less total charges (freight $152.50, storage $65, and
         − 296.13   commission $78.63)
        $1,276.37 net proceeds

Now let's consider a transaction involving a sales invoice and the payment of a commission.

Example 17

A bottling company ships 800 cases of soda to a distributor at a price of $3.75 per carton, with a 20% trade discount and freight charges of $240. How much will the distributor have to pay for the merchandise if a broker is paid a 3% commission for services? The terms of the sale are 2/10, *n*/30, and the goods are sent FOB shipping point. Assume the invoice was paid in full before the discount date.

Solution

  $3,000 list price (800 × 3.75)
  − 600 less trade discount (3,000 × .20)
  $2,400 net price
  − 48 less cash discount ($2,400 × .02)
  $2,352
  +240 plus freight charge
  $2,592 amount due

Notice that the commission is not included in the calculation. The commission is paid by the bottling company (seller) directly to the commission agent and is not shown on the invoice. The commission received by the broker would be $72.00 ($2,400 net price × .03 commission rate). Commissions are paid on the net amount of the invoice and exclude freight charges.

PARTIAL PAYMENT OF INVOICE

Every example involving trade and cash discounts thus far has assumed that the buyer made full payment of the invoice. There are, however, times when the buyer's cash flow position does not permit full payment of the amount due within the discount period. The buyer may instead make a series of **partial payments** on the amount due during the discount period to take advantage of the cash discount.

If it is the seller's policy to grant cash discounts on partial payments, the buyer will receive a discount on the proportionate amount paid. When the full amount due is paid, the buyer deducts the discount and remits a lesser amount that is accepted as full payment by the seller. Conversely, when a partial payment is made during the discount period, the seller must credit the buyer's account with an amount that is greater than the amount of the partial payment.

To determine the amount of the credit, we must first find the percent paid, which is the complement of the discount (1.00 − discount rate = percent paid). This percent is then used to calculate the amount of the credit that is the actual value of the partial payment. The credit can be found using either the equation or formula method.

Equation method for determining credit amount

percent paid × amount of credit = amount of partial payment

$$(1 - \text{discount rate}) \times (X) = \text{amount of partial payment}$$

Now we must divide each side by (1 − discount rate).

$$\frac{(1 - \text{discount rate}) \times (X)}{1 - \text{discount rate}} = \frac{\text{amount of partial payment}}{1 - \text{discount rate}}$$

$$\text{amount of credit} = X = \frac{\text{amount of partial payment}}{1 - \text{discount rate}}$$

Formula method for determining credit amount

$$\frac{\text{amount of partial payment}}{1 - \text{cash discount rate}} = \text{amount of credit}$$

To determine the balance due, we have to subtract the amount of the credit from the balance of the account prior to the partial payment (prior balance − amount of credit = balance due) or (invoice amount − amount of credit = balance due).

Example 18

An invoice of $1,250 dated May 18 offers terms of 3/10 eom. A partial payment of $800 is made on June 9. Find (a) the balance due on the invoice and (b) the amount of the cash discount.

Solution

a. $100\% - 3\% = 97\%$ percent paid
$$.97X = \$800$$
$$X = \$800/.97$$
$$X = \$824.74 \text{ amount of credit}$$
$$\$1,250 - \$824.74 = \$425.26 \text{ balance due}$$

b. amount of credit − partial payment = amount of cash discount
$$\$824.74 - \$800.00 \qquad = \$24.74$$

The partial payment is made during the discount period so the buyer is entitled to a cash discount on the proportionate amount paid. In essence, the buyer is able to reduce $1 of the invoice amount for each $.97 that is paid during the discount period ($800 ÷ .97 = $824.74).

CHECK YOUR KNOWLEDGE

Invoice charges and adjustments

Solve each of the following problems. Round dollar amounts to the nearest cent.

1. On August 8, a merchant purchased goods totaling $865.40 with terms 2/10–50X and a trade discount of 5%. The buyer returned goods worth $124.60 and paid the invoice on October 7. How much money did the merchant remit as full payment of the invoice?

2. In problem 1, what is the net payment date of the invoice?

3. A retailer purchased 1,500 cases of canned goods from a food processing company. If each case weighed 24 pounds and the goods were shipped FOB shipping point, what was the freight charge paid by the retailer? (Use the rate schedule in Table 6.4.)

4. Find the amount due on an invoice dated October 27 for $2,840.50 if terms are 3/10 prox, and the invoice is paid on December 10. Freight charges for the shipment amount to $215.40 and the goods were shipped FOB destination.

5. A broker sells merchandise totaling $7,800 on July 14 with a trade discount of 25/10 and freight charges of $462.35 prepaid by the manufacturer. How much will the buyer pay for the order if the terms of the sale are 2/10, 1/20, *n*/30 and payment is made on July 25?

6. If the broker in problem 5 charges a 4% commission, (a) what is the amount of the commission and (b) who will pay the commission?

7. What is the balance due on a $950 invoice dated May 23 with terms 3/20, *n*/60, if a $500 partial payment is made on June 10?

8. If a partial payment of $200 is remitted on September 15 for a $600 invoice dated August 27 with terms 2/10 ROG, what is the balance due? The merchandise was delivered on September 3.

6.4 EXERCISES

Solve the following problems. Round dollar amounts to the nearest cent and rates to the nearest tenth of a percent.

Use Table 6.4 to determine the freight charges for the following weights:

1. 2,857 pounds

2. 8,350 pounds

3. 22,640 pounds

4. 34,980 pounds

5. 46,200 pounds

6. What is the cost of freight for 4,890 pounds of goods if the rate is $.75 per CWT?

7. What is the amount required to pay an invoice for $1,700 with a trade discount of 15%, 10%, 5%, and terms of 3/15 ROG if the buyer returned $500 worth of merchandise and paid the invoice in full before the discount date?

8. How much should a buyer pay on an invoice dated August 12 for $980 with a trade discount of 10%, 5%, and terms of 4/10 eom if she returned $270 of the goods and paid the invoice in full on September 9?

9. Slurry Pump Division of Hackmore Pumps purchased merchandise worth $15,500 with a 15% trade discount, $1,800 shipping charges, and $375 storage charges. If the agent charges a commission of 8%, determine (a) the commission earned on the transaction and (b) the net proceeds remitted by the commission agent to B'ville Pump.

10. A petroleum company ships 500 cases of one-quart containers of motor oil (12 quarts per case) to a distributor at a price of $9.60/case with a 30% trade discount and freight charges of $175. How much will the distributor have to pay for the merchandise if a broker is paid a 4% commission for services, and the terms of the sale are 3/10, *n*/30 FOB shipping point, and the invoice was paid in full before the discount date?

11. An independent grocer orders 200 cases of tomato sauce (12 1-quart jars per case) at $36 per case; 300 cases of vegetables (24 17-oz. cans per case) at $12.00 per case; and 100 cases of canned soup (24 10-oz. cans per case) at $9.00 per case. The grocer is given a trade discount of 20/10/5 and terms of 4/10,

Answers to CYK: *1.* $689.68   *2.* October 27   *3.* $172.80   *4.* $2,970.69   *5.* $5,212.35
6. a. $210.60; b. seller pays commission   *7.* $434.54   *8.* $400.00

2/20, *n*/30 eom and freight charges of $43.00 FOB destination point. The invoice is dated July 23 and will be paid in full on August 15. How much will the grocer have to pay?

12. An invoice of $1,800 dated December 5 offers terms of 4/20 eom. A partial payment of $1,200 is made on December 15. Assuming that the seller does provide cash discounts on partial payments, find (a) the balance due on the invoice and (b) the amount of the cash discount.

13. An invoice of $2,300 dated January 15, 1991, offers terms of 5/15 ROG. The shipment was received on February 1, and a partial payment of $1,500 was made on February 12. Assuming that the seller does provide cash discounts on partial payments, find (a) the balance due on the invoice and (b) the amount of the cash discount.

14. A discount store makes a direct purchase of 500 portable television sets from a manufacturer at a price of $250 per set with a trade discount of 30% and terms of 6/20, 4/30, *n*/60 as of March 15. Shipping charges are $7.00 per set FOB shipping point. The discount store makes a payment of $50,000 on the invoice on March 30, and pays the remaining amount owed on the invoice on April 10. The manufacturer will pay the agent who arranged the sale a commission of 5%. Determine (a) the total amount of money the manufacturer will receive from the discount store, (b) the total amount the transaction will cost the discount store, and (c) the commission to be paid to the sales agent.

15. A national department store chain purchased 1,000 refrigerators directly from a manufacturer for $650 each with a 20%, 15%, 5% trade discount and terms of 5/15, 2/30 ROG, and FOB shipping point of $35 per refrigerator. The store took delivery of the refrigerators at their central warehouse on April 20 and returned 45 of the refrigerators as damaged goods. The store chain paid $300,000 on April 30, and the remainder of the cost on May 15. Determine (a) the total amount of money the manufacturer will receive from the store and (b) the total amount the transaction will cost the store.

EXPRESS YOUR THOUGHTS

Compose one or two well-written sentences to express the requested information in your own words.

1. Identify each type of business involved in the longest distribution channel. Describe why each business is considered both a buyer and a seller.

2. Explain the difference between cost and price. Give an example that supports your explanation.

3. Identify the variables found in the basic business equation. If you have sold 150 items for $3.50 a dozen, what adjustments to the data are necessary to use the equation?

4. Explain how to find the net price when the list price and trade discounts of 10% and 15% are given.

5. Develop a step-by-step description of how you would find the single equivalent trade discount when given a chain discount of 55%, 10%, and 5%.

6. Explain how the terms $2/10$, $1/15$, and $n/30$ are applied to determine the amount of cash discount.

7. Describe how you would determine the exact number of days between March 10th and July 18th.

Case exercise   Dillon's Hardware

Dillon's Hardware is an independently owned and operated business located in a small rural community. The store's owner, Hank Dillon, built the business on a simple but effective policy: to sell quality merchandise at reasonable prices. Hank and his assistant, Mike McFarland, are responsible for all decisions involving the purchase of merchandise stocked by the store. During a recent week, Mike met with a number of salespersons who represent distributors that sell fasteners. Mike has narrowed his choice of possible suppliers down to two companies that both offer the quality and assortment of products he is interested in purchasing. He asked each sales representative to give him pertinent information regarding their company's pricing structure and terms of sale.

Midstate Fasteners quoted the price of assorted machine bolts and nuts at $10.50 per box (2 pounds net weight); assorted wood screws at $14.70 per box (3.5 pounds net weight); ¼-inch threaded steel rod at $.75 per foot; ⅜-inch threaded steel rod at $1.10 per foot; and 3-inch brass plated hinges at $25.20 a case (24 units per case). Midstate offers a 10%, 5%, and 5% trade discount on purchase orders over $500, and terms of 3/10, n/30 ROG. The company ships all merchandise by truck FOB shipping point.

Industrial Supply sells assorted machine bolts and nuts at $5.40 per lb, assorted wood screws at $4.05 per pound, ¼-inch threaded steel rod at $2.20 per piece (3 foot sections), ⅜-inch threaded steel rod at $3.40 per piece (3 foot sections), and 3-inch brass plated hinges at $.95 each. Industrial Supply offers its customers a trade discount of 10% on all purchases, and terms of 2/10 eom. All merchandise is shipped to customers via truck FOB destination.

Using the terms provided by the two suppliers, Mike must decide which company offers him the best opportunity to achieve his store's policy. Mike plans to place an order for the following quantities of merchandise:

40 pounds	assorted machine bolts and nuts
28 pounds	assorted wood screws
42 feet	¼-inch threaded steel rod
57 feet	⅜-inch threaded steel rod
96	3-inch brass plated hinges

Dillon's Hardware remits payment for all merchandise purchased on credit within the terms offered by their suppliers to reduce the cost of their purchases. If the merchandise is of equal quality and the location of the two suppliers results in similar transportation costs and delivery times, with which supplier should Mike place his fastener order?

SELF-TEST

A. Terminology review

Complete the following items using the key terms presented at the beginning of the chapter. Check your responses against the answer key at the end of the test.

1. The distribution channel of getting goods to a consumer begins with the _manufacture_ who buys raw materials or parts and produces and assembles them into finished goods, which are then sold to middlepersons known as wholesalers (or _distributor_) who promote the sale of them to _retailer_ who will sell them to consumers.

2. Store chains that eliminate some or all of the middlepersons in the distribution channel are referred to as _discount_ store chains.

3. The official record of a business transaction is called an _invoice_. This is called a _purchinvoice_ when the buyer prepares it, and a _sale invoice_ when the seller prepares it.

4. The suggested selling price to the consumer is called the _list_ price. A reduction in this price to a buyer is called a _trade_ discount. The _net_ price or cost is determined by subtracting the second of these from the first.

5. The complement of a 17% trade discount is _____.

6. A multiple discount expressed as "15%

less 10% less 5%" is called a _____ or _____ discount.

7. To determine the net price of an item with the multiple discount listed in problem 6 above by the _____ method, one would multiply the list price by $.85 \times .90 \times .95$.

8. The discount rate obtained in problem 7 (i.e., $.85 \times .90 \times .95$) is called the "_____ rate."

9. Sellers often encourage buyers to pay invoices before the required date by offering _cash discount_ which are indicated under terms of the sale using the ordinary dating method such as 2/10, n/30.

10. Proximo and _eom_ are ways of indicating that the terms of payment of an invoice begin with the first day of the next month, and _ROG_ means that the terms begin when the buyer actually receives the merchandise.

11. Extensions of terms may also be arranged by the _____ dating method (e.g., 3/20 – 60X) or by the _____ method using the "*as of*" phrase.

12. FOB _____ point means that the buyer pays shipping costs, whereas FOB _____ point means that the seller pays the shipping costs.

13. A _____ is a percentage amount of the net price of a sale paid to the salesperson or agent who arranged for the sale of the goods.

B. Calculation review

The following concepts and short problems are designed to test your understanding of the objectives identified at the beginning of the chapter. Answers are provided at the end of the test. Round dollar amounts to the nearest cent and rates to the nearest tenth of a percent.

14. Complete the following invoice calculation:

Quantity	Description	Unit price	Extension price
5 gal.	vanilla ice cream	$2.49/gal.	_____
3 pints	fruit flavored ice cream toppings (1 ea. choc., strawb., blueb.)	$3.25/pint	_____
4 pkg.	4″ plastic sauce dishes (10/pkg)	$1.19/pkg.	_____
1 pkg.	plasticware spoons, 50 spoons/pkg.	$3.00/pkg.	_____
		Total	_____

15. Carmen Juarez was offered a chain discount of 15/20/5 to entice her to purchase a new line of swimwear for her retail outlet store early. The list price of her total purchase was $1,850. Determine: (a) the net invoice price of Carmen's purchase, (b) the amount of the trade discount, and (c) the single equivalent discount rate offered to Carmen.

16. Carmen was also offered an incentive to pay her bill for a purchase of women's blouses and sweaters from another seller early with terms of 6/15, 3/25, *n*/60 ROG. The cost of the merchandise was $850 and she paid the entire bill on March 20 after having received her order on March 1. How much cash discount did she receive?

17. How much should Jaoquim's Landscaping Service pay for a $2,175 purchase made on February 10, 1992, with the terms 5/10, 2/20, *n*/30 prox if they receive the goods on February 28 and pay the invoice on March 8?

18. What is the amount required to pay an invoice for $2,700 with a trade discount of 20%, 10%, 5%, and terms of 2/10, *n*/30 ROG if the buyer returned $300 worth of merchandise and paid the invoice in full before the discount date?

19. A sales broker sold $3,900 worth of plumbing fixtures for Blackmore Fixtures with a 15% trade discount and $120 in shipping charges. If the sales agent charges a commission of 7%, determine (a) the commission earned on the transaction and (b) the net proceeds realized by Blackmore.

20. An invoice of $7,500 dated January 25, 1992, offers terms of 4/20 ROG. The shipment was received on February 16, and a partial payment of $4,000 was made on March 5. Assuming that the seller does provide cash discounts on partial payments, find (a) the balance due on the invoice and (b) the amount of the cash discount.

Answers to self-test: *1.* manufacturer, distributors, retailers *2.* discount *3.* invoice, purchase invoice, sales invoice *4.* list, trade, net *5.* 83% *6.* chain, series *7.* complement *8.* net price equivalent *9.* cash discount *10.* eom, ROG *11.* extra, postdating *12.* shipping, destination *13.* commission *14.* $29.96 *15.* a. $1,195.10; b. $654.90; c. 35.4% *16.* $25.50 *17.* $2,066.25 *18.* $1,608.77 *19.* a. $232.05; b. $2,962.95 *20.* a. $3,333.33; b. $166.67

7

MARKUP, MARKDOWN, AND SALES TAX

Learning objectives

1. Explain the financial analysis required to price merchandise.

2. Compute the selling price given cost and the markup based on cost.

3. Find the cost when the selling price and markup rate on cost are known.

4. Calculate the amount and percent of markup based on cost.

5. Compute the selling price given the cost and markup based on selling price.

6. Find the cost when selling price and markup rate on price are known.

7. Calculate the amount and percent of markup based on selling price.

8. Convert the markup rate to the opposite base.

(continued)

Learning Objectives (continued)

9. Compute the markdown amount given the selling price and markdown rate.

10. Determine the selling price required to cover estimated spoilage on perishable merchandise.

11. Calculate the profit or loss from operations and the absolute loss when a markdown is granted.

12. Compute the sales tax and excise tax on goods sold when discounts and other charges are involved.

13. Define the key terms.

INTRODUCTION

Learning objective
Explain the financial analysis required to price merchandise.

In Chapter 6, we examined the basic elements of purchasing goods from the buyer's perspective. An overview of the merchandising process was provided to help you understand the processes and terminology related to both buying and selling. For instance, Figure 6.2 helped explain the relationship between cost and price by showing you how the seller's price becomes the buyer's cost as goods move through various marketing channels. We learned how manufacturers, wholesalers, and retailers purchase merchandise that they intend to sell to their customers for a profit.

To produce a profit, merchants must price their goods so that a profit is possible. *Profit*, as you recall from our discussion of business operations in Chapter 5, is the amount that remains after the cost of goods and all operating expenses have been recovered. (If you do not clearly understand the analysis below, you should review Chapter 5 before proceeding.)

Formula for computing profit or loss

revenue (price per unit × units sold)
− cost of goods sold (cost of units sold)

= gross margin (markup)
− operating expenses*

= net profit or loss

*taxes, supplies, selling expenses, wages, rent, utilities, insurance, etc.

As you can see, the price a merchant charges for goods or services is an economic reflection of cost. A firm must generate sufficient revenue to produce a profit if it is to survive. On the other hand, price is also used by many merchants as a technique to market their products. For example, to stimulate demand, a price lower than the market price may be selected. A price higher than the market price might be used if the price is consistent with the buyer's expectations.

Regardless of the pricing strategy selected, a **markup** will be added to an item's cost to cover operating expenses and profit. To illustrate, if a retailer purchases a personal computer for $850 and sells it for $1,500, the markup is $650. The **markup equation** below summarizes the markup calculation.

$$\text{cost } + \text{ markup} = \text{ selling price}$$
$$\$850 + \quad \$650 \quad = \quad \$1,500$$

As with any equation, if any two variables are known, the third variable can be found by substituting the given variables into the equation and solving for the unknown variable. Therefore, the following two formulas can be derived from the markup equation.

$$\text{selling price } - \text{ markup} = \text{ cost}$$
$$\$1,500 \quad - \quad \$650 \quad = \$850$$

or

$$\text{selling price } - \text{ cost } = \text{ markup}$$
$$\$1,500 \quad - \$850 = \quad \$650$$

Markup can be based on the cost of an item or on its selling price. Regardless of which base is used, the markup equation remains as stated: Cost plus markup equals selling price. Markup is also referred to as the **gross margin** or *margin*, and can be expressed as an amount or as a percent.

In this chapter, you will learn the methods used by merchants to mark up goods, to convert markups to opposite bases, to apply markdowns, and to calculate sales and excise taxes.

7.1 MARKUP BASED ON COST

Many manufacturers, wholesalers, and retailers use cost systems to analyze the unit costs of their products because the cost approach is more appropriate for their organization. When the **markup on cost** method is used, the cost of the item is considered the base (100%); the operating expenses, selling price, and net profit or loss are considered a part of the product cost. The **markup rate** is expressed as a percent of cost and includes the prorated operating expense rate and the target net profit rate. The amount of the markup, prorated operating expense, and net profit can be found easily through the use of the percent equation ($B \times R = P$) presented in Chapter 3. Let's look at an example that illustrates this important point before we calculate the selling price when the markup is based on cost.

Example 1

An appliance store purchased a television set for $125 and sold it for $200. If the store's operating expenses are 40% of cost, (a) how much markup did the store receive on the sale, (b) what were the store's prorated operating expenses, and (c) what was the amount of net profit on the sale?

Solution

a.   Use the markup equation to calculate the amount of markup.

$$C + M = S$$
$$\$125 + M = \$200$$
$$M = \$200 - \$125$$
$$M = \$75$$

Or by formula,

$$S - C = M$$
$$\$200 - \$125 = \$75$$

The markup (gross margin, or margin) on the sale was $75.

b.   Use the percent equation to calculate the prorated operating expense amount.

$$B \times R = P, \text{ where } B = \text{cost}$$
$$\$125 \times .40 = \$50 \qquad R = \text{operating expense rate}$$
$$P = \text{operating expense amount}$$

The store's prorated operating expenses on this sale were $50.

c.   The markup includes operating expenses and net profit; therefore:

$$\text{operating expenses} + \text{net profit} = \text{markup}$$
$$\$50 + P = \$75$$
$$P = \$75 - \$50$$
$$P = \$25$$

A net profit of $25 was realized on the sale of the television. Figure 7.1 diagrams the calculations for Example 1.

Note that a profit is not always realized when the price of an item is greater than its cost. Merchants must price their merchandise to cover all

Figure 7.1

Diagram of calculations in Example 1

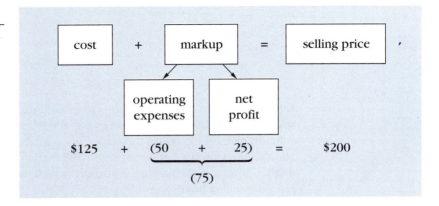

associated expenses and intended profit when they establish markup rates. We will discuss this concept further in Section 7.3 when we focus on markdowns.

CALCULATING SELLING PRICE GIVEN COST AND PERCENT MARKUP BASED ON COST

Learning objective
Compute the selling price given cost and the markup based on cost.

When the cost of an item is known and the rate of markup is based on cost, the selling price is expressed as a percentage of cost as follows:

cost   +   markup   = selling price
100% of cost + 25% of cost = 125% of cost

Remember, the markup can be expressed as an amount or as a percent. In either case, when the markup is based on cost, it is added to the cost to determine the selling price.

Example 2

J and B Supply marks up its plumbing supplies 60% of cost. What is the selling price of a bathroom vanity that costs the company $75?

Solution

In the markup equation, express the markup as a percent of cost, convert the percent to a decimal equivalent, and solve.

$$C + M = S$$
$$100\% \text{ of cost} + 60\% \text{ of cost} = 160\% \text{ of cost}$$
$$1.60C = S$$
$$1.60(\$75) = S$$
$$\$120 = S$$

or

$$C + M = S$$
$$\$75 + .60(\$75) = S$$
$$\$75 + \$45 = \$120$$

Did you notice in the two solutions presented that the markup (portion) was found by multiplying the cost (base) times the markup rate? The first solution method expresses the selling price as a percent of cost (160%), and does not produce the amount of the markup. The second solution method produces the amount of markup which, when added to the cost, gives the selling price.

CALCULATING COST GIVEN SELLING PRICE AND MARKUP BASED ON COST

Learning objective
Find the cost when the selling price and markup rate on cost are known.

Merchants often find that the cost they are able to pay for merchandise is determined by current market prices of the products they intend to sell as well as their markup policies. For example, if a wholesaler selects a pricing strategy to compete with other wholesalers, the price of his product is determined in part by their prices and in part by a markup on cost sufficient to cover operating expenses and required profit. Example 3 shows how to calculate cost when the selling price is known and the markup is based on cost.

Formula for cost

$$\text{cost} = \frac{\text{price}}{1 + \text{markup rate}}$$

Example 3

The buyer for Hanson Shoes wishes to purchase a line of men's walking shoes to sell for $69.95 a pair. How much can the buyer pay for the shoes if she must realize a 45% markup on cost?

Solution

$$\text{cost} + \text{markup} = \text{selling price}$$
$$100\%C + 45\%C = \$69.95$$
$$145C = \$69.95$$
$$C = \$69.95 \div 1.45$$
$$C = \$48.24$$

or $$\text{Cost} = \frac{\text{price}}{1 + \text{markup rate}} = \frac{\$69.95}{1 + .45}$$
$$C = \$48.24$$

The cost of the shoes is \$48.24; the markup is \$21.71 (\$48.24 × .45) or as follows:

$$\text{cost} + \text{markup} = \text{selling price}$$
$$\$48.24 + \$21.71 = \$69.95$$

CALCULATING AMOUNT AND RATE OF MARKUP BASED ON COST

Learning objective
Calculate the amount and percent of markup based on cost.

While retailers know the cost of an item and the price they intend to charge for the item when it is sold, they also need to know the percent of markup relative to their cost and price data. The markup percent is important because costs and expenses are constantly changing. In addition, business may have to reduce the price of items to stimulate sales, or to reduce inventory costs. The financial impact of such changes can be measured somewhat by the markup percent. When an item's cost is used as the base, the percent (rate) of markup is found by dividing the markup amount by the cost. Because we are calculating a percent, we can once again use the percentage equation.

Example 4

Karat Jewelers reduced the selling price on an 18-inch solid gold chain from \$285 to \$225. If the jewelry store paid \$130 for the gold chain, what is the percent markup of cost?

Solution

First, find the amount of markup using the markup equation.

$$\text{cost} + \text{markup} = \text{selling price}$$
$$\$130 + M = \$225$$
$$M = \$225 - 130$$
$$M = \$95$$

or

$$\text{selling price} - \text{cost} = \text{markup}$$
$$\$225 - \$130 = \$95$$

Then, find the markup percent using the percent equation.

$$\text{base} \times \text{rate} = \text{part}$$
$$\$130 \times R = \$95$$
$$130R = \$95$$
$$R = .7307, \text{or } 73.1\%$$

or

$$\begin{aligned}
\text{rate of markup} &= \frac{\text{markup}}{\text{cost}} \quad \left(\text{rate} = \frac{\text{part}}{\text{base}}\right) \\
&= \frac{\$95}{\$130} \\
&= .7307, \text{ or } 73.1\%
\end{aligned}$$

CHECK YOUR KNOWLEDGE

Markup based on cost

1. A retailer purchased a microwave for $136 and sells it for $189.95. What is the amount of markup on the sale?

2. Find the cost of an item that sells for $57 and includes a markup of $20.

3. A dealer purchased an above ground 12-×-24-foot pool for $1,500 and sold it for $2,300. If the company's operating expenses run 30% of cost, what were the expenses related to the sale?

4. In problem 3, what was the amount of (a) markup and (b) net profit on the sale?

5. If a calculator that cost $15 has a markup of 20% of cost, what is the selling price?

6. How much should a wholesaler charge for a mattress that costs $45 if the company's operating expense rate is 50% and the dealer wants a 12% net profit on cost?

7. A clothing store sells a line of jackets for $89.99. What is the maximum price the store can pay for each jacket if its markup on cost is 75%?

8. Find the percent of markup on cost for a radio that costs $18 and sells for $24.30.

Answers to CYK: *1.* $53.95   *2.* $37.00   *3.* $450.00   *4.* a. $800; b. $350   *5.* $18
6. $72.90   *7.* $51.42   *8.* 35%

7.1   EXERCISES

Fill in the missing amounts.

	Selling price	Cost	Gross margin	Operating expenses	Profit/loss
1.	$85	$52	33	$28	5
2.		$35	$13		$3.00
3.	$575		$65	$74	
4.		$340		$115	$24
5.	$1,200	$1,500		$325	

Calculate the missing numbers. Round dollar amounts to the nearest cent and rates to the nearest tenth of a percent.

	Cost	Markup	% Markup on cost	Selling price
6.	$5.00	1.50	30%	6.50
7.		$12.50		$25.00
8.	$65.00	$39.00	60%	
9.	$350.25			$475.50
10.		$82.35	45%	

Solve each of the following problems. Round dollar amounts to the nearest cent, and rates to the nearest tenth of a percent.

11. Upstate Copy Products purchased a desktop copier for 1,200 and sold it for $1,800. If operating expenses run 30% of cost, find (a) the amount of markup, (b) the operating expenses related to the sale, and (c) the amount of profit realized.

12. Family Drugs sells an 8-ounce bottle of cough medicine for $3.69, which includes a markup of $1.05. Find the unit cost of the product.

13. Clark's Men's Shoppe purchased a group of men's topcoats for $89.00 each. If its operating expenses are 20% of cost and the net profit is 15% of cost, find the selling price.

14. Wilkins Jewelers buys a certain style gold bracelet for $450. If the store desires a 150% markup based on cost, determine the selling price of the bracelet.

15. Thornton Bookstore purchases paperback bestsellers from a distributor for $3.40. How much does the bookstore charge customers for the books if it uses a 40% markup on cost?

16. Determine the selling price for a pair of sneakers that cost the retailer $40 if its operating expenses are 30% of its cost, and its net profit margin is 12% of its cost.

17. Sally Steinberg must order 50 fishing rod and reel sets, which her sportshop will sell for $12.50, as part of a promotion for opening day of fishing season. How much can she pay for each set if her markup based on cost is 60%?

18. Find the selling price for an item that costs $149.50 if the seller uses a 50% markup on cost.

19. Raymond Lock Co. sells a door lock for $49 that costs the company $32. What is the percent markup on cost? (Round to the nearest tenth of a percent.)

20. Turnbull Electronics sells a 486 computer system for $2,450. How much does Turnbull pay for each computer system if its markup on cost is 25%?

21. Plainfield Farms Inn offers a complete turkey dinner for $9.95. Find the cost of the dinner if operating expenses are 100% of cost and net profit is 20% of cost.

22. Centervale Hardware purchases interior house paint for $4.25 a gallon, which it sells for $12.95. Find the percent of markup based on cost.

23. A-1 Convenience Store sells a brand of soda pop for $2.59 a six-pack. How much does the store pay for each six-pack if its markup based on cost is 48%?

24. An electrical manufacturer charges distributors $15.25 for switch boxes, which includes a $3.75 markup. Find (a) the cost of the switch boxes and (b) the markup as a percent of cost.

25. A & D Cooling and Heating received an invoice for six hot water heaters with a total list price of $1,275. If the supplier provided a 15% trade discount and charged $20 for delivery, what unit selling price is required to realize a 30% markup on cost?

7.2   MARKUP BASED ON SELLING PRICE

Most retail firms use the **markup on selling price** method to price merchandise because the net sales figure reported in the income statement is the basis for analyzing the efficiency of operations. For example, a firm's cost of goods sold, all operating expenses, and its net profit are all computed as a percent of net sales. (This comparison is referred to as a vertical analysis and was discussed fully in Chapter 5.) In addition, businesses often base payroll commissions, certain taxes, distribution of profit and expenses, and the value of inventory on net sales. These topics will be presented in detail in subsequent chapters.

When a merchant chooses to mark up his merchandise based on selling price, he is able to determine from the daily sales records the estimated gross profit from operations. To illustrate, assume a business reports sales for a given day at $15,000 and uses a markup based on selling price sufficient to produce a 60% gross margin rate. The merchant is able to determine his daily gross profit as follows:

$$\text{base sales} \times \text{rate of gross margin} = \text{gross margin}$$
$$\$15,000 \quad \times \qquad .60 \qquad = \qquad \$9,000$$

If the gross margin is $9,000, then the cost of goods sold is $6,000, or 40% of gross sales. The amount and percent relationships can be expressed as an abbreviated income statement.

Net sales revenue	$15,000	100%
Less cost of goods sold	6,000	40%
Gross margin	$ 9,000	60%
Less operating expenses	7,500	50%
Net profit	$ 1,500	10%

As explained at the beginning of the chapter, gross margin is also referred to as markup. Therefore, in the preceding analysis, a 60% markup on selling price is used to determine the price of items to cover the operating expenses (50%) and profit (10%). In terms of the markup equation, the example would be presented as follows:

cost   +   markup   =   selling price
40% of selling price + 60% of selling price = 100% of selling price

Now, let's look back at various situations involving calculating markup based on selling price.

CALCULATING SELLING PRICE GIVEN COST AND PERCENT MARKUP BASED ON SELLING PRICE

Learning objective
Compute the selling price given cost and markup based on selling price.

When the markup is based on the selling price, and the cost is known, the cost is expressed as a percentage of the selling price (as explained in the preceding section). However, in this situation, we do not know the price (base) so we must use either algebra to find the price charged or a formula derived from the algebraic procedure. The algebraic approach utilizes the markup equation as shown in Example 5.

Formula for selling price

$$\text{selling price} = \frac{\text{cost}}{1 - \text{markup rate}}$$

Example 5

Casual Furniture purchased a patio set for $120. What is the selling price of the patio set if the company expects to earn a 25% markup based on price?

Solution

Algebra:

$$\text{cost} + \text{markup} = \text{selling price}$$
$$\$120 + .25S = S$$
$$120 = S - .25S$$
$$120 = .75S$$
$$\$160 = S$$

Formula:

$$\frac{\text{cost}}{1 \ - \ \text{markup rate}} = \text{selling price}$$

$$\frac{\$120}{1 \ - \ .25} = \frac{\$120}{.75} = \$160$$

In the equation, price (S) is the unknown. Since we know that the markup is 25% of the price, we label it as 25% of the unknown price ($.25S$). Then we gather terms, subtract like terms as required, and solve for the unknown price by dividing the markup complement into the cost as shown in the example.

The formula requires memorization of the algebraic procedure. When you divide the cost by 1 minus the markup percentage, you are performing the last two steps of solving the equation ($120 = S - .25S$ and $120 = .75S$, $S = \$160$).

CALCULATING COST GIVEN SELLING PRICE AND PERCENT MARKUP ON SELLING PRICE

Learning objective
Find the cost when selling price and markup rate on price are known.

Retailers often stock multiple price lines of each item of merchandise they sell because consumer purchases are in part determined by price. For example, a retailer may offer an economy, standard, and deluxe line of merchandise to buyers. When retailers decide to restock a given price line, they must purchase merchandise that will yield the required markup on the target selling price. In other words, the retailers must know the highest price they can afford to pay for the item and realize the required markup.

Example 6

How much can a retailer pay for a product line that will be sold for $40 if a markup of 35% of the selling price is required to cover operating expense and profit?

Solution

Formula:

Step 1:   Calculate the cost percent.

| selling price | − | markup | = | cost |

100% of selling price − 35% of selling price = 65% of selling price

Step 2:   Calculate the cost.

selling price × cost rate = cost

$40   ×   .65   = $26

Algebra:

$$\text{cost} + \text{markup} = \text{selling price}$$
$$C + (.35)(\$40) = \$40$$
$$C + 14 = \$40$$
$$C = \$40 - 14$$
$$C = \$26$$

CALCULATING AMOUNT AND RATE OF MARKUP BASED ON SELLING PRICE

Learning objective
Calculate the amount and percent of markup based on selling price.

In Section 7.1, we explained how to calculate the amount and rate of markup when the markup is based on cost. The same procedure is used to calculate the amount and rate of markup when the markup is based on selling price, except the base is now the selling price. When an item's selling price is used as the base, the percent (rate) of markup is found by dividing the amount of markup by the selling price.

Finding percent of markup

$$\text{percent, or rate, of markup} = \frac{\text{markup}}{\text{selling price}} \quad \left(\text{rate} = \frac{\text{part}}{\text{base}}\right)$$

Example 7

An article that costs $225 was sold for $375. Find (a) the amount of markup and (b) the markup percent based on selling price.

Solution

a. $$\text{cost} + \text{markup} = \text{selling price}$$
$$\$225 + M = \$375$$
$$M = \$375 - \$225$$
$$M = \$150$$

b. $$\text{base} \times \text{rate} = \text{part}$$
$$\$375 \times R = \$150$$
$$\$375R = \$150$$
$$R = \$150/\$375$$
$$R = .40, \text{ or } 40\%$$

or

$$\text{rate} = \frac{\text{markup}}{\text{selling price}} = \frac{\$150}{\$375} = .40, \text{ or } 40\%$$

CONVERTING MARKUP RATE TO OPPOSITE BASE

Learning objective
Convert the markup
rate to the opposite
base.

In Section 7.1, we explained how to calculate markup based on cost, a method used primarily by manufacturers. In this section, we explain how to calculate markup based on price, a method used primarily by retailers. Because retailers often purchase merchandise directly from manufacturers, a business may wish to convert its markup rate to the opposite base for purposes of comparison.

There are two methods that are used to compare markup percent to the opposite base. The first method requires you simply to compute the markup percent based on cost and then compute the markup percent based on selling price. The second method allows you to convert the markup percent on cost to the markup percent on selling price and vice versa with conversion formulas. Both methods are illustrated below using information provided in Example 8.

Example 8

If an item that costs $12 is sold for $18, what is the percent of markup based on cost and on the selling price?

Solution

Method 1:   Calculate markup percent for each base.

$$\text{cost} + \text{markup} = \text{selling price}$$
$$\$12 + M = \$18$$
$$M = \$18 - \$12$$
$$M = \$6$$

$$\text{rate} = \frac{\text{markup}}{\text{cost}} = \frac{6}{12} = 50\% \text{ markup on cost}$$

$$\text{rate} = \frac{\text{markup}}{\text{selling price}} = \frac{6}{18} = .333, \text{ or } 33\tfrac{1}{3}\% \text{ markup on selling price}$$

Method 2:   Convert to opposite base. To convert percent markup on cost to its equivalent markup percent on selling price, use the following formula:

$$\frac{\text{markup percent on cost}}{1 + \text{markup percent on cost}} = \text{markup percent on selling price}$$

$$\frac{.50}{1 + .50} = \frac{.50}{1.50} = .333, \text{ or } 33\tfrac{1}{3}\%$$

To convert percent markup on price to its equivalent markup percent on cost, use the following formula:

$$\frac{\text{markup percent on selling price}}{1 - \text{markup percent on selling price}} = \text{markup percent on cost}$$

$$\frac{.333}{1 - .333} = \frac{.333}{.667} = .50, \text{ or } 50\%$$

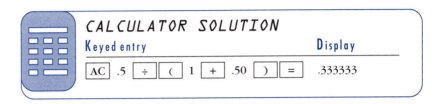

CALCULATOR SOLUTION

Keyed entry	Display
AC .5 ÷ (1 + .50) =	.333333

CHECK YOUR
KNOWLEDGE

Markup based on selling price

1. If a retailer uses an average markup of 45% of the selling price and reports $25,000 in gross sales on October 20, what is (a) the amount of gross margin, (b) the percent of cost of goods sold, and (c) the amount of net profit if operating expenses are estimated at 40% of net sales?

2. If an item costs $45 and carries a markup on the selling price of $17.25, what is the selling price?

3. The markup rate used by Sounds Unlimited is 30% of the selling price. What is the (a) selling price and (b) markup amount of a television set that cost $179?

4. What is the most a buyer for the SportCenter should pay for a snowboard that will be sold for $39.99 if there is to be a 25% markup based on the retail price?

5. The Garden Shop sells a lawnmower for $250. If the shop's operating expenses are 42% of the selling price and the net profit is 6% of the selling price, how much does the lawnmower cost?

6. If an item is purchased for $20 and is sold for $35, what is the markup percent based on price?

7. What markup percent on selling price is equivalent to a 20% markup on cost?

8. If the markup percent on a microcomputer is 37% of the selling price, what is the markup percent based on cost?

Answers to CYK: **1.** a. $11,250; b. 55%; c. $1,250 **2.** $62.25 **3.** a. $255.71; b. $76.71 **4.** $29.99 **5.** $130.00 **6.** 42.9% **7.** 16.7% **8.** 58.7%

7.2 EXERCISES

Calculate the missing numbers. Round dollar amounts to the nearest cent and rates to the nearest tenth of a percent.

	Cost	Markup	% Markup on price	Selling price
1.	_____	_____	20%	$30.00
2.	_____	$50.00	_____	$400.00
3.	$137.00	$27.50	_____	_____
4.	$652.30	_____	_____	$829.50
5.	_____	$94.00	33%	_____

	Cost	Markup	Selling price	% Markup on cost	% Markup on selling price
6.	_____	$20	_____	25%	20%
7.	$12.00	_____	$18.00	_____	_____
8.	_____	$40.65	$135.50	_____	_____
9.	$240.60	174.23	414.83	72.4%	42%
10.	_____	$120.00	_____	60%	_____

Convert each of the following markups to the opposite base. Round to the nearest tenth of a percent.

Markup on cost to price

11.	20%	_____
12.	35.5%	_____
13.	50.25%	_____

Markup on price to cost

14.	15%	_____
15.	40⅓%	_____
16.	28%	_____

Solve the following word problems. Round rates to nearest whole percent and dollar amounts to the nearest cent.

17. Coffee Merchants reported net sales of $50,245 for July. If the firm uses a markup of 55% of the selling price, find (a) the gross margin amount and (b) the amount of net profit for the month if operating expenses are 48% of net sales.

18. Milton's Farm Supply Co. purchased four garden tillers at $312 each. The store's operating expenses average 42% of the selling price and the net profit is 10% of the selling price. What will be the selling price of the tillers?

19. Herman's Department Store purchased three dozen dress shirts at $72 a dozen. If the markup rate is 25% of the selling price, what is the selling price of each shirt?

20. A dealer pays $129.50 for an article that will be sold at a markup of 37½% on the selling price. What is (a) the selling price and (b) the markup amount?

21. The Toy Shack buys video games for $19.50 and sells them for $39. What is the markup rate based on selling price?

22. Clearwater Beverage Co. buys purified water for resale in 45-gallon barrels at $56.25 per barrel. The water is sold in 3 gallon plastic bottles. What is the selling price of each bottle if the company uses a 40% markup based on the selling price?

23. The buyer for Paint-n-Paper wishes to buy a

line of paint brushes to be sold for $8.50 each. If a markup of 28% based on the selling price is required, how much should the buyer pay for the paint brushes?

24. Milton Restaurant Supply Co. bought four pizza ovens at $312 each. The store's operating expenses average 40% of the selling price, and the net profit is 12% of the selling price. What is the selling price of the ovens?

25. The Discount Furniture Mart purchased 250 student desks from a manufacturer at a total list price of $14,750 less a 12% trade discount. If the Mart sold 140 of the desks at $89 each, 80 at $79, and the remainder at $65 each, determine (a) the total amount of sales from the desks, (b) the total gross margin

amount, and (c) the average markup percent on the selling price. (Round to the nearest tenth percent.)

26. The markup rate used by the Village Shop is 20% of the selling price. What is the equivalent markup percent based on cost?

27. A men's clothing store buys ties at $66 per dozen and sells them at $8.75 each. What is the rate of markup (a) based on cost and (b) based on selling price? (Round to the nearest tenth percent.)

28. An item is sold for $59.75, which represents a 27% markup on the cost. What is the equivalent markup percent based on the selling price? (Round to the nearest tenth percent.)

7.3   MARKDOWNS AND PERISHABLES

Retailers often reduce the marked price of their goods for any one of the following reasons:

1. to reduce excessive inventories
2. to adjust for seasonal and fashion changes
3. to move slightly damaged goods
4. to be competitive with prices offered by other merchants
5. to stimulate the sale of unsold merchandise because of size or color
6. to accommodate a reduction in the cost of the merchandise.

Learning objective
Compute the markdown amount given the selling price and markdown rate.

When merchants decide to reduce the **marked price** of their merchandise they usually announce the decision to their market in a promotion referred to as a *sale* in the local media. The reduction in the marked price is called a **markdown** and is expressed as a percent or an amount of the marked price. The price of the item after the markdown has been applied is called the **reduced price**. The markdown equation is, therefore, expressed as follows:

marked price − markdown = reduced price

Because the markdown is expressed as a percent of the marked price, we, once again, have a percent equation application where marked price = base

percent of markdown = rate

markdown amount = part

Now, let's look at a few examples involving markdowns that can be solved with the percent equation.

Example 9

Alter's Shoes reduced the price of its entire stock of shoes 30% for one week. Find the reduced price of a pair of boots with a marked price of $78.99.

Solution

Step 1:   Find the amount of the markdown.

base × rate = part
$78.99 × .30 = $23.70 (markdown amount)

Step 2:   Find the reduced price.

marked price − markdown = reduced price
$78.99   − $23.70   = $55.29

Note: The percent of markdown is always based on the marked price.

Example 10

Center City Auto Parts sells a case of 10-W-40 motor oil for $18. To reduce an overstock of inventory, the motor oil was marked down to a sale price of $13.50 per case. What is the percent of markdown?

Solution

Step 1:   Find the amount of markdown.

marked price − reduced price = markdown
$18.00 − $13.50 = $4.50

Step 2:   Find the percent (rate) of markdown.

$$\text{rate} = \frac{\text{part}}{\text{base}} = \frac{\$4.50}{\$18.00} = .25 \text{ or } 25\%$$

On some occasions, a single markdown may not be sufficient to promote the sale of an item. Consequently, a retailer may decide to continue to reduce the price until the item is sold. When a series of markdowns are applied, each markdown is based on the previous sale price as illustrated in Example 11.

Example 11

Clara's Boutique displayed a sweater for $95 on September 10. The sweater was marked down 15% on October 8 and another 20% on November 12. Find the reduced price if the sweater was sold on November 15.

Solution

Step 1:   Calculate the reduced price on October 8.

$95 × .15 = $14.25 markdown amount
$95 − $14.25 = $80.75 reduced price October 8

Step 2:   Calculate the reduced price on November 12.

$80.75 × .20 = $16.15 markdown amount
$80.75 − $16.15 = $64.60 reduced price November 15

A series markdown can also be calculated with the complement method shown below.

Complement Method

Step 1:   Determine the complement of each markdown.

```
 100%  marked price
− 15%  markdown percent on October 8
  85%  reduced price complement on October 8

 100%  reduced price on October 8
− 20%  markdown percent on November 12
  80%  reduced price complement on November 12
```

Step 2:   Multiply the marked price by the complements determined in step 1.

$95.00 × .85 × .80 = $64.60 reduced price on November 15

(You may have noticed the complement method is the same method we used in Chapter 6 to calculate the net price when a chain trade discount was offered.)

PRICING PERISHABLES

Many businesses purchase merchandise for resale that will spoil if not sold within a short period of time. Such merchandise is referred to as **perishables** and includes dairy products, produce, baked goods, certain canned and packaged goods, and cut flowers. In some cases, merchandise with rapidly changing styles and designs are also considered perishable. Examples that might be considered in this category would be clothing, computers, automobiles, boats, and appliances.

Learning objective
Determine the selling price required to cover estimated spoilage on perishable merchandise.

Merchants are able to estimate from past experience the percent of their perishable inventories that will be sold at the marked price and at a reduced price. In addition, they often determine the portion that may have to be discarded as spoilage. In the introduction of this chapter, we explained that markup (gross profit) must be sufficient to cover operating expenses and target profit. When pricing perishable items, the price of the items that do sell will generate revenues sufficient to also cover the cost of those items that are expected to spoil (will not sell).

Example 12

Michelle Ruggiero, a produce buyer for T and C Food Markets, purchased 500 pounds of grapes for 39 cents per pound. She estimates that approximately 5% of the grapes will spoil before they can be sold. If T and C Markets requires a 60% markup on cost, at what price per pound must the grapes be sold?

Solution

Step 1:   Calculate the total cost of the entire purchase.

quantity $\times$ unit cost = total cost
500   $\times$ $.39   = $195.00

Step 2:   Calculate the total selling price of the entire purchase.

cost + markup = selling price
$C + .6C = S$
$1.6C = S$
$1.6(195) = S$
$\$312 = S$

Step 3:   Calculate the amount of the purchase lot that is expected to sell.

base $\times$ rate = part
500 $\times$ .95 = 475 pounds of grapes are expected to sell

If 5% of the grapes are expected to spoil, then 95% are expected to sell (100% − 5% = 95%).

Step 4:   Calculate the selling price required to cover the estimated spoilage.

$475S = \$312$ (total selling price)
$S = \$.656$, or $.66 per pound (rounded to nearest cent)

To determine the price per pound, we divide the total sales in step 2 by the amount of merchandise that is expected to be sold in step 3.

Note: If T and C Markets sells more than 475 pounds of the 500 pounds of grapes purchased before they spoil, each dollar of sales received will be additional profit.

Now, let's look at an example that involves the appropriate markup to cover a reduction in price of perishable goods.

Example 13

Lakeside Bakery made 250 loaves of Italian bread at a cost of 48 cents each. Experience indicates that 8% of the loaves will be sold the following day at a reduced price of 50 cents. Find the marked price if the bakery wishes to obtain a 125% markup on cost.

Solution

Step 1:   Calculate the total cost and total selling price as we did in steps 1 and 2 for Example 12.

$$\text{cost} + \text{markup} = \text{selling price}$$
$$C + 1.25C = S$$
$$2.25C = S$$
$$2.25(\$120) = S$$
$$\$270 = S$$

The loaves of bread cost the bakery \$120 to bake ($250 \times \$.48$) and the total selling price (\$270) will be 225% of the total cost (\$120).

Step 2:   Calculate the selling price required to cover the estimated reduction in price for "day old" merchandise.

$$\frac{\text{sales from}}{\text{original units sold}} + \frac{\text{sales from}}{\text{reduced units sold}} = \text{total sales}$$
$$(250 - 20)S + (20 \times \$.50) = \$270$$
$$230S + \$10 = \$270$$
$$230S = \$270 - 10$$
$$230S = \$260$$
$$S = \$1.13/\text{loaf (rounded to nearest cent)}$$

The per-unit marked price (selling price) is determined by the total sales required to cover cost and markup (gross margin). Therefore, total sales (revenue) is the number of units sold at the reduced price (250 × .08 = 20; 20 × $.50 = $10) plus the number of units sold at the marked price (250 − 20 = 230 units × *S*, the unknown selling price).

When merchants reduce the prices of their goods, the selected markdowns should be sufficient to promote the sale of the merchandise and provide profits. Under extreme circumstances, merchants may mark down goods to cost and below cost. Obviously, markdowns of this nature must be implemented with a clear understanding of their impact on the financial condition of the business. Figures 7.2 through 7.5 illustrate the various financial effects of markdowns. A **reduced net profit** results when the reduced price is sufficient to cover cost and operating expenses yet provide some profit (Figure 7.2). The **break-even point** occurs when the reduced price is sufficient to cover only cost and operating expenses (Figure 7.3). An **operating loss** results when the reduced price is sufficient to cover cost but not all of the operating expenses (Figure 7.4). The amount of loss is the difference between the break-even point and the sales price. An **absolute loss** occurs when the reduced price is below the actual cost of the merchandise (Figure 7.5). The amount of the absolute or gross loss is the difference between the reduced price and the cost.

Let's look at a couple of examples that will help you gain a better understanding of these financial concepts.

Figure 7.2

Reduced net profit

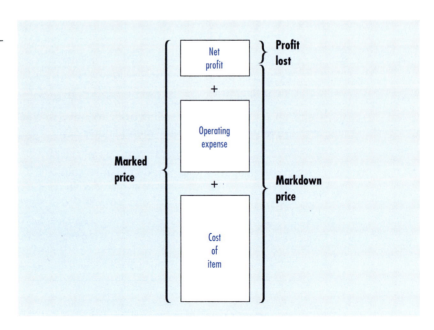

Figure 7.3

Break-even point

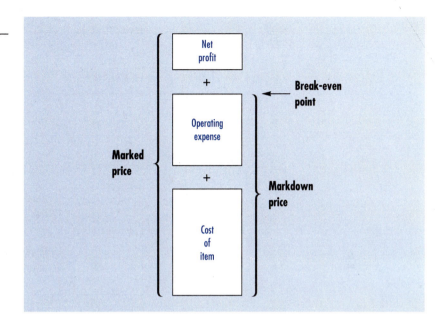

Figure 7.4

Operating loss

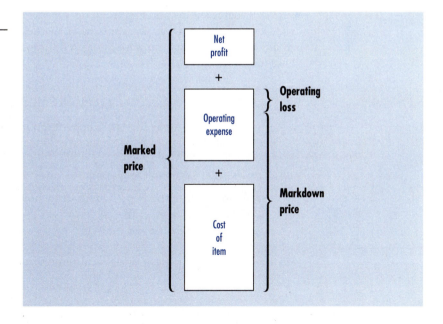

Figure 7.5

Absolute loss

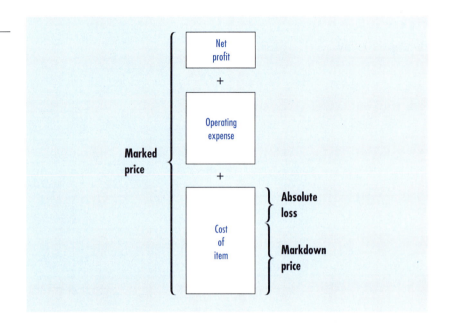

Example 14

Yvette's Bridal Fashions purchased a gown for $295. The store's operating expenses run 40% of cost. The dress has a marked price of $649, but is marked down 35%. Find the amount of profit or loss if the dress is sold at the reduced price.

Solution   *Step 1:*   Calculate the markdown selling price (sale price).

$$\$649 \times .35 = \$227.15 \text{ markdown amount}$$
$$\$649 - \$227.15 = \$421.85 \text{ reduced selling price}$$

Step 2:   Calculate the break-even point.

$$\text{cost} + \text{operating expenses} = \text{break-even point}$$
$$\$295 + (\$295 \times .40) = BEP$$
$$\$295 + \$118 = \$413$$

Step 3:   Determine if a profit or a loss resulted from the transaction.

$$\text{reduced selling price} - \text{break-even point} = \text{profit/loss}$$
$$\$421.85 - \$413.00 = \$8.85 \text{ profit}$$

F or **Y** our **I** nformation
M a r k d o w n s : a w i n o r l o s e s t r a t e g y

"With bankruptcy lurking outside the revolving doors during the holidays, Macy's tried desperately to raise cash by selling its wares at a miniscule profit.

"About $220 million in extra price markdowns on merchandise were made in the quarter as the retailer adjusted prices to try for more sales. It didn't work, and now the retailer has tallied the dire results of that last-ditch effort.

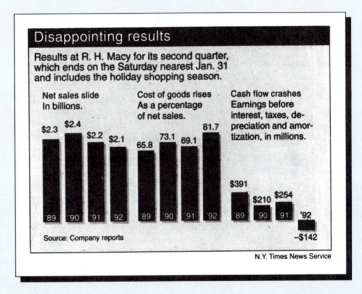

"... Although the quarter included the holiday season, when retailers typically post the strongest revenues and earnings, sales in Macy-owned department and specialty stores dropped 6.4 percent, to $2.1 billion, from $2.2 billion in the quarter a year earlier.

"... The heavily indebted Macy, which operates the Macy's, Bullock's, and I. Magnin chains, filed for Chapter 11 bankruptcy court protection from creditors on Jan. 27, 1992. It has been making use of the protection by writing off bloated inventories, closing stores, and taking other charges to put its balance sheet in order. ..."

Source: Stephanie Strom, "Markdowns at Macy's Add to Losses," New York Times News Service, as it appeared in the Syracuse *Herald-Journal*, March 18, 1992. Used with permission.

E x a m p l e 1 5

The Convenience Food Shop sells a gallon of 2% milk on sale for $1.49. If the cost of the milk is $1.55 a gallon and the Shop's operating expenses are 30% of the cost, find (a) the amount of the operating loss and (b) the amount of the absolute loss.

Solution

Step 1:   Calculate the break-even point.

cost + operating expenses = *BE*
$1.55 + (1.55 × .30) = *BE*
$1.55 + .47 = $2.02

Step 2:   Calculate the amount of the operating loss and the absolute loss.

a.   reduced selling price − break-even point = operating profit/loss
$1.49 − 2.02 = ($.53) operating
loss/gallon

b.   reduced selling price − cost = absolute loss
$1.55 − $1.49 = $.06 absolute loss/gallon

CHECK YOUR KNOWLEDGE

Markdowns and perishables

Calculate the markdown and the sale price.

Marked price	Markdown percent	Markdown amount	Sale price
1. $55	12%	_____	_____
2. $480	8%	_____	_____
3. $6,590	24.5%	_____	_____

Calculate the markdown amount and the percent of markdown.

Marked price	Sale price	Markdown amount	Markdown percent
4. $4.50	$3.75	_____	_____
5. $239.99	$167.99	_____	_____
6. $3,785	$2,865	_____	_____

Solve each of the following word problems. Round dollar amounts to the nearest cent and rates to the nearest tenth of a percent.

7.   A clothing store sells a men's overcoat for $225. The coat was marked down 20% on February 7 and an additional 25% on February 21. Find the sale price if the coat was sold on February 25. (Use the complement method.)

8.   Using the information in problem 7, calculate the percent of markdown.

9.   Mother Nature's Basket purchased 125 quarts of strawberries from a local farm at 60 cents per quart. The store estimates 4% of the berries will spoil before they can be sold. If the store uses a 60% markup on cost, what price should it charge per quart?

10. The Skate-n-Ski Shop bought 50 pairs of cross-country skis at a cost of $30 a pair. If the shop expects 10% of the skis to be sold on sale at $35 a pair, what price should the skis be marked to make a 40% gross profit on cost?

11. Harding Furniture Annex plans to sell a certain style of bedroom set at its inventory clearance sale for $995. If the cost of the set was $800 and the operating expenses were 30% of the cost, find the amount of profit or loss on the sale of each set.

12. A stereo system cost a retailer $750. The retailer's regular marked price was $1,250, but the system was marked down 40% to reduce inventory. If operating expenses are 32% of cost, find (a) the operating loss and (b) the absolute loss.

7.3   EXERCISES

Fill in the blanks with the correct amount. Round amounts to the nearest whole cent.

	Marked price	% Markdown	Markdown amount	Sale price
1.	$19.50	✗ 30%	5.85	13.65 _19.5-5.85_
2.	_100_	15%	15.00	$85.00 ÷ 85 = 1.00 = 100 - 15
3.	$.80	_25%_	= _.20÷80_	$.60 _.80-60_
4.	$1,250		$62.50	
5.		33⅓%	$3.16	
6.	$367.80	20%		
7.	$24.00			$14.40

Complete each calculation using the information provided. If there is no operating loss or absolute loss, place a 0 in the blank space.

	Cost	Operating expense	Break-even amount	Sale price	Operating loss	Absolute loss
8.	$12.00	$4.00	_8_	$14.00	_6_	_2_
9.	$65.00		$80.00	$62.50		
10.	$135.70	$60.40		$189.25		
11.	$8.50	$3.40		$8.65	$3.25	
12.	$525		$705	$510		

Answers to CYK: **1.**   a. $6.60; b. $48.40   **2.**   a. $38.40; b. $441.60   **3.**   a. $1,614.55; b. $4,975.45   **4.**   a. $.75; b. 16.7%   **5.**   a. $72; b. 30%   **6.**   a. $920; b. 24.3%   **7.** $135   **8.**   40%   **9.** $100   **10.** $42.78   **11.** $45 loss   **12.**   a. $240 loss; b. $0 loss

Solve each of the following word problems. Round dollar amounts to the nearest cent, and rates to the nearest tenth of a percent.

13. Heritage Spas marked down its standard outdoor hot tub 40% to be competitive with other area retailers. Find the reduced price if the marked price of the tub was $3,500.

14. The Vision Center sells wire-rimmed eyeglass frames for $139. If the marked price is reduced to $95, what is the percent of markdown?

15. Sal's Hobby Supply sells a radio-controlled car for $420. The cars were marked down 25% on March 15 and another 15% on April 7. What was the reduced price on April 7?

16. Pattello Fruit and Floral Designs purchased 75 dozen long-stem roses at $18 per dozen. Pattello estimates 8% of the roses will not be sold for various reasons. At what price per dozen should the roses be marked to realize a 100% markup on cost?

17. Silver Mountain Ski Shop bought 60 pairs of downhill skis at a cost of $150 each. Past experience suggests 25% of the skis purchased will have to be sold on sale at $175 each. What marked price is required to provide an 80% markup on the cost of the skis?

18. Wilbur's Market bought 120 pounds of bananas at 20 cents per pound. If 5% of the purchase will spoil, what price per pound must be charged to generate a margin of 40% on cost?

19. Fischer Interiors purchased stain resistant nylon carpeting for $10 per square yard. The store's operating expenses are 30% of cost, and the carpet is sold at 25% off the marked price of $18 per square yard. Find the amount of profit or loss if the store sold 3,000 square yards of carpeting during the month.

20. A gas-powered chain saw selling for $225 is marked down 40%. If the cost of the chain saw is $140 and the operating expenses are 20% of the cost, find (a) the amount of the operating loss and (b) the amount of the absolute loss.

7.4   SALES AND EXCISE TAXES

Many sellers (manufacturers, wholesalers, and retailers) are required to collect sales and/or excise taxes on the sale of merchandise. In this section, we will discuss these two taxes and the procedures used in their calculations.

SALES TAX

A **sales tax** is a tax that is charged on the sale of particular goods and services sold by retail merchants. The tax is expressed as a percent of the net sales price and is collected by the seller. As required by regulation, the sales taxes are then remitted to the state, county, or city government in which the goods are sold.

Learning objective
Compute the sales tax and excise tax on goods sold when discounts and other charges are involved.

Sales taxes are an important source of revenue for governmental agencies. Consequently, many states and cities are increasing their sales tax rates as well as expanding the list of taxable goods and services. In addition, some states and municipalities are beginning to collect sales taxes on goods sold outside the jurisdiction of the taxing agency. This departure from the practice of collecting taxes only on goods sold within the tax district is designed to recover the amount of sales tax that is lost on tax-exempt sales that result from mail-order and telemarketing sales.

Sales tax rates vary from state to state and city to city. State tax rates range between 2% and 8%; city and county taxes are usually lower, 1% to 4%. To assist the sales clerk in situations where the cash register does not automatically calculate the sales tax, charts are available. Sales tax charts, such as shown in Figure 7.6, identify the tax to be collected for each consecutive price interval. The price intervals in sales tax charts can be based on a fixed amount or as a percentage determined by the tax rate.

When a merchant reduces the marked price or list price of merchandise by applying a markdown or a trade discount, the sales tax is computed on the marked down selling price or the net price, respectively. If a cash discount is applicable, the discount would be calculated on the net price. The sales tax is also calculated on the net price but added to the net price before the cash discount is deducted to determine the amount to be paid. Other charges such as freight, handling, and late charges are exempt from sales tax and would not be included in the taxable amount of a sale. The examples that follow will explain how to calculate sales tax on regular sales and on sales when discounts and other charges are involved. To calculate the sales tax without a tax chart, we multiply the total amount of the sale that is taxable by the tax rate. The sales tax is then added to the marked price to determine the total price.

Sales tax equations

> taxable sales × sales tax rate = sales tax
>
> marked price + sales tax = total price

Example 16

Lisa Reynolds, a sales clerk for the Cycle Emporium, sold a bicycle for $249.99, the sales slip for which is shown in Figure 7.7 (see p. 271). The store must collect a 5% state sales tax and a 2% city tax. Determine (a) how much sales tax she charged and (b) how much she charged the customer for the bicycle.

Solution

a. marked price × combined sales tax rate =   sales tax
    $249.99   ×   (.05 + .02)   = $17.499, or $17.50

b. marked price + sales tax = total price
    $249.99   + $17.50 = $267.49

Figure 7.6

Sales and use tax bracket schedule for state and local tax purposes

4% Sales and Use Tax Collection Chart

Amount of sale	Tax to be collected	Amount of sale	Tax to be collected	Amount of sale	Tax to be collected	Amount of sale	Tax to be collected
$0.01 to $0.12	$.00	2.63 to 2.87	.11	5.13 to 5.37	.21	7.63 to 7.87	.31
.13 to .33	.01	2.88 to 3.12	.12	5.38 to 5.62	.22	7.88 to 8.12	.32
.34 to .58	.02	3.13 to 3.37	.13	5.63 to 5.87	.23	8.13 to 8.37	.33
.59 to .83	.03	3.38 to 3.62	.14	5.88 to 6.12	.24	8.38 to 8.62	.34
.84 to 1.12	.04	3.63 to 3.87	.15	6.13 to 6.37	.25	8.63 to 8.87	.35
1.13 to 1.37	.05	3.88 to 4.12	.16	6.38 to 6.62	.26	8.88 to 9.12	.36
1.38 to 1.62	.06	4.13 to 4.37	.17	6.63 to 6.87	.27	9.13 to 9.37	.37
1.63 to 1.87	.07	4.38 to 4.62	.18	6.88 to 7.12	.28	9.38 to 9.62	.38
1.88 to 2.12	.08	4.63 to 4.87	.19	7.13 to 7.37	.29	9.63 to 9.87	.39
2.13 to 2.37	.09	4.88 to 5.12	.20	7.38 to 7.62	.30	9.88 to 10.00	.40
2.38 to 2.62	.10						

5% Combined Sales and Use Tax Collection Chart

Amount of sale	Tax to be collected	Amount of sale	Tax to be collected	Amount of sale	Tax to be collected	Amount of sale	Tax to be collected
$0.01 to $0.10	$.00	3.10 to 3.29	.16	6.10 to 6.29	.31	9.10 to 9.29	.46
.11 to .27	.01	3.30 to 3.49	.17	6.30 to 6.49	.32	9.30 to 9.49	.47
.28 to .47	.02	3.50 to 3.69	.18	6.50 to 6.69	.33	9.50 to 9.69	.48
.48 to .67	.03	3.70 to 3.89	.19	6.70 to 6.89	.34	9.70 to 9.89	.49
.68 to .87	.04	3.90 to 4.09	.20	6.90 to 7.09	.35	9.90 to 10.00	.50
.88 to 1.09	.05	4.10 to 4.29	.21	7.10 to 7.29	.36		
1.10 to 1.29	.06	4.30 to 4.49	.22	7.30 to 7.49	.37		
1.30 to 1.49	.07	4.50 to 4.69	.23	7.50 to 7.69	.38		
1.50 to 1.69	.08	4.70 to 4.89	.24	7.70 to 7.89	.39		
1.70 to 1.89	.09	4.90 to 5.09	.25	7.90 to 8.09	.40		
1.90 to 2.09	.10	5.10 to 5.29	.26	8.10 to 8.29	.41		
2.10 to 2.29	.11	5.30 to 5.49	.27	8.30 to 8.49	.42		
2.30 to 2.49	.12	5.50 to 5.69	.28	8.50 to 8.69	.43		
2.50 to 2.69	.13	5.70 to 5.89	.29	8.70 to 8.89	.44		
2.70 to 2.89	.14	5.90 to 6.09	.30	8.90 to 9.09	.45		
2.90 to 3.09	.15						

Figure 7.6

(Continued)

6% Combined Sales and Use Tax Collection Chart

Amount of sale	Tax to be collected	Amount of sale	Tax to be collected	Amount of sale	Tax to be collected	Amount of sale	Tax to be collected
$0.01 to $0.10	$.00	2.59 to 2.74	.16	5.09 to 5.24	.31	7.59 to 7.74	.46
.11 to .22	.01	2.75 to 2.91	.17	5.25 to 5.41	.32	7.75 to 7.91	.47
.23 to .38	.02	2.92 to 3.08	.18	5.42 to 5.58	.33	7.92 to 8.08	.48
.39 to .56	.03	3.09 to 3.24	.19	5.59 to 5.74	.34	8.09 to 8.24	.49
.57 to .72	.04	3.25 to 3.41	.20	5.75 to 5.91	.35	8.25 to 8.41	.50
.73 to .88	.05	3.42 to 3.58	.21	5.92 to 6.08	.36	8.42 to 8.58	.51
.89 to 1.08	.06	3.59 to 3.74	.22	6.09 to 6.24	.37	8.59 to 8.74	.52
1.09 to 1.24	.07	3.75 to 3.91	.23	6.25 to 6.41	.38	8.75 to 8.91	.53
1.25 to 1.41	.08	3.92 to 4.08	.24	6.42 to 6.58	.39	8.92 to 9.08	.54
1.42 to 1.58	.09	4.09 to 4.24	.25	6.59 to 6.74	.40	9.09 to 9.24	.55
1.59 to 1.74	.10	4.25 to 4.41	.26	6.75 to 6.91	.41	9.25 to 9.41	.56
1.75 to 1.91	.11	4.42 to 4.58	.27	6.92 to 7.08	.42	9.42 to 9.58	.57
1.92 to 2.08	.12	4.59 to 4.74	.28	7.09 to 7.24	.43	9.59 to 9.74	.58
2.09 to 2.24	.13	4.75 to 4.91	.29	7.25 to 7.41	.44	9.75 to 9.91	.59
2.25 to 2.41	.14	4.92 to 5.08	.30	7.42 to 7.58	.45	9.92 to 10.00	.60
2.42 to 2.58	.15						

7% Combined Sales and Use Tax Collection Chart

Amount of sale	Tax to be collected	Amount of sale	Tax to be collected	Amount of sale	Tax to be collected	Amount of sale	Tax to be collected
$0.01 to $0.10	$.00	2.93 to 3.07	.21	5.79 to 5.92	.41	8.65 to 8.78	.61
.11 to .20	.01	3.08 to 3.21	.22	5.93 to 6.07	.42	8.79 to 8.92	.62
.21 to .33	.02	3.22 to 3.35	.23	6.08 to 6.21	.43	8.93 to 9.07	.63
.34 to .47	.03	3.36 to 3.49	.24	6.22 to 6.35	.44	9.08 to 9.21	.64
.48 to .62	.04	3.50 to 3.64	.25	6.36 to 6.49	.45	9.22 to 9.35	.65
.63 to .76	.05	3.65 to 3.78	.26	6.50 to 6.64	.46	9.36 to 9.49	.66
.77 to .91	.06	3.79 to 3.92	.27	6.65 to 6.78	.47	9.50 to 9.64	.67
.92 to 1.07	.07	3.93 to 4.07	.28	6.79 to 6.92	.48	9.65 to 9.78	.68
1.08 to 1.21	.08	4.08 to 4.21	.29	6.93 to 7.07	.49	9.79 to 9.92	.69
1.22 to 1.35	.09	4.22 to 4.35	.30	7.08 to 7.21	.50	9.93 to 10.00	.70
1.36 to 1.49	.10	4.36 to 4.49	.31	7.22 to 7.35	.51		
1.50 to 1.64	.11	4.50 to 4.64	.32	7.36 to 7.49	.52		
1.65 to 1.78	.12	4.65 to 4.78	.33	7.50 to 7.64	.53		
1.79 to 1.92	.13	4.79 to 4.92	.34	7.65 to 7.78	.54		
1.93 to 2.07	.14	4.93 to 5.07	.35	7.79 to 7.92	.55		
2.08 to 2.21	.15	5.08 to 5.21	.36	7.93 to 8.07	.56		
2.22 to 2.35	.16	5.22 to 5.35	.37	8.08 to 8.21	.57		
2.36 to 2.49	.17	5.36 to 5.49	.38	8.22 to 8.35	.58		
2.50 to 2.64	.18	5.50 to 5.64	.39	8.36 to 8.49	.59		
2.65 to 2.78	.19	5.65 to 5.78	.40	8.50 to 8.64	.60		
2.79 to 2.92	.20						

(continued)

Figure 7.6

(Continued)

8% Combined Sales and Use Tax Collection Chart

Amount of sale	Tax to be collected	Amount of sale	Tax to be collected	Amount of sale	Tax to be collected	Amount of sale	Tax to be collected
$ .01 to $0.10	$.00	2.57 to 2.68	.21	5.07 to 5.18	.41	7.57 to 7.68	.61
.11 to .17	.01	2.69 to 2.81	.22	5.19 to 5.31	.42	7.69 to 7.81	.62
.18 to .29	.02	2.82 to 2.93	.23	5.32 to 5.43	.43	7.82 to 7.93	.63
.30 to .42	.03	2.94 to 3.06	.24	5.44 to 5.56	.44	7.94 to 8.06	.64
.43 to .54	.04	3.07 to 3.18	.25	5.57 to 5.68	.45	8.07 to 8.18	.65
.55 to .67	.05	3.19 to 3.31	.26	5.69 to 5.81	.46	8.19 to 8.31	.66
.68 to .79	.06	3.32 to 3.43	.27	5.82 to 5.93	.47	8.32 to 8.43	.67
.80 to .92	.07	3.44 to 3.56	.28	5.94 to 6.06	.48	8.44 to 8.56	.68
.93 to 1.06	.08	3.57 to 3.68	.29	6.07 to 6.18	.49	8.57 to 8.68	.69
1.07 to 1.18	.09	3.69 to 3.81	.30	6.19 to 6.31	.50	8.69 to 8.81	.70
1.19 to 1.31	.10	3.82 to 3.93	.31	6.32 to 6.43	.51	8.82 to 8.93	.71
1.32 to 1.43	.11	3.94 to 4.06	.32	6.44 to 6.56	.52	8.94 to 9.06	.72
1.44 to 1.56	.12	4.07 to 4.18	.33	6.57 to 6.68	.53	9.07 to 9.18	.73
1.57 to 1.68	.13	4.19 to 4.31	.34	6.69 to 6.81	.54	9.19 to 9.31	.74
1.69 to 1.81	.14	4.32 to 4.43	.35	6.82 to 6.93	.55	9.32 to 9.43	.75
1.82 to 1.93	.15	4.44 to 4.56	.36	6.94 to 7.06	.56	9.44 to 9.56	.76
1.94 to 2.06	.16	4.57 to 4.68	.37	7.07 to 7.18	.57	9.57 to 9.68	.77
2.07 to 2.18	.17	4.69 to 4.81	.38	7.19 to 7.31	.58	9.69 to 9.81	.78
2.19 to 2.31	.18	4.82 to 4.93	.39	7.32 to 7.43	.59	9.82 to 9.93	.79
2.32 to 2.43	.19	4.94 to 5.06	.40	7.44 to 7.56	.60	9.94 to 10.00	.80
2.44 to 2.56	.20						

Example 17

George Pakova, owner of the Deli-Box luncheonette, purchased a meat slicer for $650. He was granted a trade discount of 15% and terms of 2%, 10 days. If the sales tax was 7% and he remitted payment during the discount period, how much did he pay for the meat slicer?

Solution

$650.00   list price
− 97.50   less trade discount (650 × .15)

$552.50   net price (taxable amount)
+38.68   plus sales tax ($552.50 × .07)

$591.18   total price
− 11.05   less cash discount (552.50 × .02)

$580.13   amount paid

SALES SLIP

Customer's Order No. _____ Phone No. _____ Date 4/12 19 91

Sold To _Mrs Elizabeth Ryan_

Address _127 Bryant Ave._

SOLD BY	CASH	C.O.D.	CHARGE	ON ACCT.	MDSE. RETD.	PAID OUT

QUANTITY	DESCRIPTION	PRICE	AMOUNT
1	Model #127X BMX Bicycle		249 99
	ck# 1263		
		7% TAX	17 50
		TOTAL	267 49

All claims and returned goods MUST be accompanied by this bill.

12299

Rec'd by _____

Note: The sales tax and the cash discount are both calculated on the net price. However, the sales tax is added to the net price where the cash discount is subtracted from the net price.

Example 18

A sales clerk in a drug store charged a customer a total of $16.12 for an item that included 4% sales tax. Find the marked price of the item.

Solution

Algebra:

marked price + sales tax = total price

$$P + .04P = \$16.12$$
$$1.04P = \$16.12$$
$$P = \$15.50 \text{ marked price}$$

Formula:

$$\text{marked price} = \frac{\text{total price}}{1 + \text{sales tax rate}}$$
$$= \frac{\$16.12}{1 + .04}$$
$$= \frac{\$16.12}{1.04}$$
$$= \$15.50$$

EXCISE TAX

Another tax levied on the sale or manufacture of specific goods and services by governmental agencies is the **excise tax**. Governmental agencies may charge an excise tax on the sale of gasoline, tobacco, alcoholic beverages, jewelry, recreational and sporting goods, firearms, entertainment, motor vehicles, luggage, fur, cosmetics, telephone service, tires, and licenses. Excise taxes are paid in addition to sales taxes, and like sales taxes, excise taxes are usually expressed as a percent. However, in some cases, excise taxes are expressed as a fixed amount based on the quantity sold. For example, notice in Table 7.1 the federal excise tax on the sale of gasoline is 14.1 cents per gallon. Excise taxes collected on the sale of goods by sellers are often included in the markup percentage and are passed on to the buyer through the unit selling price. When the excise tax is not included in the price of an item, it must be added to the selling price to determine the taxable amount of the sale before the sales tax can be computed. Examine Examples 19 and 20 carefully so that you thoroughly understand this distinction.

Example 19

On September 15, Alice Littlejohn purchased a set of steelbelted radial tires at $89.95 each from Goodman's Tire and Service Center. How much did the tire center charge Alice for the tires if the excise tax on each tire was $4.29 and the sales tax rate was 6%?

Table 7.1

Federal excise tax schedule

Tax / item	Rate / amount
Air transportation	10%
Coal (underground mined)	$1.10 per ton or 4.4% of sales price, whichever is lower
Ship passenger tax	$3 per person
Communication service	3%
Firearms (pistols, revolvers)	10%
Fishing equipment	10%
Liquor	$12.50 per gallon
Gasoline	14.1 cents per gallon
Diesel fuel	20.1 cents per gallon
Aviation fuel	17.6 cents per gallon
Tires	
40 pounds to 70 pounds	15 cents per pound
70 pounds to 90 pounds	$4.50 plus 30 cents a pound in excess of 70 pounds
over 90 pounds	$10.50 plus 50 cents a pound in excess of 90 pounds
Tractors and trailers over 26,000 pounds gross weight	12% of sales price
Luxury tax	10% of sales price amount over:
Passenger vehicles	$30,000
Boats	$100,000
Aircraft	$250,000
Furs and jewelry (excluding watches)	$10,000
Gas guzzler tax (4-wheel vehicles gross weight 6,000 pounds or less)	
Estimated miles per gallon	
21.5 to 22.4	$1,000 per vehicle
20.5 to 21.4	$1,300
19.5 to 20.4	$1,700
18.5 to 19.4	$2,100
17.5 to 18.4	$2,600
16.5 to 17.4	$3,000
15.5 to 16.4	$3,500
14.5 to 15.4	$4,500
13.5 to 14.4	$5,400
12.5 to 13.4	$6,400
less than 12.5	$7,700

Solution

$359.80   sales price ($89.95 × 4)
+17.16   plus excise tax ($4.29 × 4)

$376.96   total sales price (taxable amount)
+22.62   plus sales tax ($376.96 × .06)

$399.58   total price of sale

Note: The amount of the sale subject to sales tax includes the excise tax when the excise tax is not expressed as part of the unit price.

Example 20

Millie's Service Station sold 10,675 gallons of unleaded gasoline during the month of October at $1.159 a gallon. If the price per gallon included a federal excise tax of 14.1 cents and a state excise tax of 12 cents, find (a) the total revenue from sales of unleaded gasoline during the month, (b) the federal excise tax to be paid for the month, and (c) the state excise tax to be paid for the month.

Solution

a. $10,675 × \$1.159 = \$12,372.33$ total revenue from sales
b. $10,675 × \$.141 = \$1,505.18$ federal excise tax
c. $10,675 × \$.12 = \$1,281.00$ state excise tax

CHECK YOUR KNOWLEDGE

Sales and excise taxes

1. Calculate the sales tax and the total amount on each of the following transactions using a sales tax rate of 3%.
    a. $1.49
    b. $125.99
    c. $4,750

2. Find the sales tax on each of these transactions using the chart for 7.6% in Figure 7.6:
    a.   19 cents
    b.   68 cents
    c. $1.49
    d. $6.05
    e. $9.95

3. Before leaving the grocery store, Marvin Emmons checked his receipt to make sure he was charged properly for his purchases. If all food items are exempt from sales tax and the sales tax rate is 7%, is

the amount shown on the receipt correct? Recalculate the receipt if necessary.

1/11Store #77

Reg. 10   OPR 32

Italian bread	.89
cookies	1.79
dish detergent	1.49 tax
2% milk	2.15
peanut butter	1.89
6 pak Cola	2.59 tax
grapes	.99
nacho chips	2.39 tax
margarine	.59
deodorant	2.39 tax
sub total	$17.16
tax paid	.62
total	$17.78

4. Louis Cirillo purchased a sportcoat at the Gentlemen's Store that had been marked down 30%. If the coat's marked price was $95 and he was charged a sales tax of 6%, how much did he pay for the sportcoat?

5. Mel's Custombile Service Center purchased a brake rotor from Upstate Distributors for $35. How much did Mel pay Upstate Distributors for the rotor if he received a cash discount of 3%, was charged $2.50 to have the part delivered, and paid a 5% sales tax?

6. The records of the Hot Rock Music Company indicate sales of $13,330.60 for the month, including a 7% sales tax. What was the amount of (a) taxable sales for the month and (b) sales tax.

7. Mark Keller purchased a diamond necklace from Wilmont Jewelers for $15,000 plus taxes. How much did the jewelry store receive for the necklace if the excise tax was 10% and the sales tax was 5%?

8. General Petroleum sells 20,000 gallons of diesel fuel to All-State Trucking at $.985 per gallon. If the price includes a federal excise tax of 20.1 cents and a state tax of 6.5 cents, find (a) the amount of federal excise tax collected and (b) the amount of state tax collected on the sale of diesel fuel.

Answers to CYK: *1.* a. $.04; b. $3.78; c. $142.50   *2.* a. $.01; b. $.05; c. $.10; d. $.42; e. $.70   *3.* total incorrect; $17.61 is correct total   *4.* $70.49   *5.* $38.20   *6.* a. $12,458.50; b. $872.10   *7.* $17,325.00   *8.* a. $4,020; b. $1,300

7.4   EXERCISES

Fill in the blanks with the correct amounts. Round amounts to the nearest whole cent.

	Marked price	Mark- down percent	Sale price	Sales tax rate	Sales tax amount	Total sale amount
1.	$34	10%	_____	3%	_____	_____
2.	$282.50	25%	_____	5%	_____	_____
3.	$7.99	8%	_____	7%	_____	_____
4.	$1,450	30%	_____	4%	_____	_____
5.	$168	42%	_____	6%	_____	_____

Find the missing amounts. Use the complement method to calculate your answers.

	List price	Trade discount	Net price	Excise tax	Total sales price	Sales tax	Total amount of sale
6.	$25	5%	_____	2%	_____	4%	_____
7.	$380	10%	_____	1%	_____	2%	_____
8.	$659	25%	_____	3%	_____	3%	_____
9.	$1,850	37%	_____	1½%	_____	5%	_____
10.	$74.60	12%	_____	4%	_____	6%	_____

Solve each of the following problems. Round dollar amounts to the nearest cent, and rates to the nearest tenth of a percent.

11. An automobile stereo cassette system costs the dealer $159. If the system is sold for $230, and the dealer collects a state sales tax of 5% and a city sales tax of 3%, find the amount the customer paid for the system.

12. Jack Karpinski purchased a sportcoat that sold for $139 plus a sales tax of 6%. How much sales tax did Jack pay on the coat?

13. A clerk for Hanson's Department Store sells an expandable watch band to a customer for $8.99. How much should she charge the customer for the band if she uses the sales tax schedule in Figure 7.6?

14. All-Sports Distributors sold merchandise to Jenson's Sport Shop listed at $4,250 with terms of 2/10, *n*/30, and a trade discount of 10%. A sales tax of 5% is required. If Jenson's pays for the merchandise within the discount period, how much must be remitted?

15. The R. D. Jones Company made a purchase of $12,750. The company received a trade discount of 20% and paid a sales tax of 5%. What was the total amount paid for the purchase?

16. Julie Mendoza bought a pair of shoes for $69.54 that included a 7% sales tax. Find (a) the marked price and (b) the sales tax paid.

17. A manufacturer of electric outboard motors sold a distributor 150 motors at $75 each. The manufacturer is required to collect a 3% federal excise tax. How much will the manufacturer charge the distributor for the motors?

18. Amanda Jefferson pays a commercial airline $278 for a round-trip flight from Boston to Orlando excluding taxes. How much will

Amanda's ticket cost if she has to pay an 8% federal excise tax and a 4% state sales tax?

19. Panther Lake Marina sold 7,500 gallons of fuel for motor boats during the month of June at $1.259 a gallon. If the price per gallon included a federal excise tax of 9.1 cents and a state tax of 12.5 cents, find (a) the federal excise tax collected during the month, (b) state tax collected during the month, and (c) the amount of sales from fuel excluding taxes.

20. The billing clerk for Upstate Telephone Co. is preparing a customer's bill for monthly service. Local charges are $15.75, and toll charges total $23.50. If the telephone company must collect a federal excise tax of 3% and a local tax of 4%, find (a) the amount of each tax and (b) the total amount the customer must pay for the month.

EXPRESS YOUR THOUGHTS

Compose one or two well-written sentences to express the requested information in your own words.

1. Describe the effect markup has on an organization's ability to generate profits.

2. Identify the variables of the markup equation. Create an example to illustrate the relationship between each variable.

3. Describe in detail the two methods used to mark up merchandise.

4. Explain how you would determine the selling price of an item that was purchased for $5.00 and is marked up 30% on cost.

5. Describe how you would find the cost of an item that is sold for $29.95 and carries a markup of 50% on cost.

6. Explain how to determine the rate of markup based on cost if both the cost and selling price are known.

7. How would you find the cost of an item if you were given both the markup percent based on selling price and the selling price?

8. If you know the markup percent based on cost, how would you find the equivalent markup percent based on selling price?

9. Explain how a business would price an item when a portion of the items purchased is expected to spoil and a specified markup on cost must be realized.

10. Describe the financial impact of a reduced price that results in an absolute loss.

Case exercise   What price — what profit?

Shawn Kelly manages a retail store in the Village Mall. The store sells a limited assortment of athletic merchandise and over the last two years it has expanded the athletic footwear department to respond to changing market conditions. Three months ago, Shawn purchased 300 pairs of cross-trainer sneakers from a supplier at a cost of $48.30/pair. Shawn decided that he would use a 50% markup on the price to sell this particular line of merchandise. Inventory records at the end of this first month indicated the sneakers were not selling as quickly as expected. The store had sold only 125 pairs at the original price. Shawn marked the remaining inventory down 20% to stimulate sales. At the end of the second month, the store had sold an additional 100 pairs at the sale price. The remaining 75 pairs were marked down an additional 25% at that time to deplete the inventory. By the end of the third month, the entire stock of this purchase order had been sold.

Recently, a shipment of 100 pairs of soccer shoes of various sizes arrived at the store. Shawn wants to price the shoes and place them on display in the store immediately as the soccer season is less than 1 month away.

Shawn has asked you (the store's bookkeeper) to analyze these situations and provide him with the following information:

A.   the amount of profit or loss realized from the sale of the sneaker order over the 3-month period

B.   the actual percent of markup after all markdowns were applied

C.   the marked price per pair of soccer shoes

if they cost $35.00 per pair; 20% of the order is expected to sell at a reduced price of $42.00 per pair and the markup required is 60% on cost. (Round the sales price to the nearest cent.)

You are to base your analysis of the sneaker order strictly on the cost and sales data provided for the 300 pairs of sneakers. Also the store estimates its operating expenses at 40% of sales.

SELF-TEST

A. Terminology review

Complete the following items using the key terms presented at the beginning of the chapter. Check your responses against the answer key at the end of the test.

1.   A _markup_ is added to an item's cost to cover operating expenses and profit.

2.   Markup is also referred to as _gross margin_ ~~can do~~ and can be expressed as an amount or a percent.

3.   When the markup amount is added to the cost, the result is referred to as the _selling price_.

4.   The rate of markup based on cost is found by dividing the _markup am't_ by the _cost_.

5.   When we divide the percent markup on cost by 1 plus the markup percent on cost, we are converting the percent markup on _cost_ to its equivalent markup percent on _selling price_.

6.   A reduction in the marked price is called a _markdown_

7.   _perishable_ are merchandise that will spoil if not sold within a short period of time.

8.   The _break even point_ occurs when the reduced price is sufficient to cover cost and operating expenses.

9.   If the reduced price is below the actual cost of the merchandise, _absolute loss_ will occur.

10.   Governmental agencies often require merchants to collect a _sales tax_ on the sale of particular goods and services.

B. Calculation review

The following concepts and short problems are designed to test your understanding of the objectives identified at the beginning of the chapter. Answers are provided at the end of the test.

11.   Plaza Photo and Camera Shop buys a camera for $85 that it sells for $123.25. If the shop's operating expenses are 35% of cost, find

(a) the amount of the markup and (b) profit from the sale of a camera.

12. Charles Simari, International Rug Merchant, purchased four oriental rugs of the same value for a total cost of $4,800. Find the selling price per rug if the merchant is to realize a 40% markup based on cost.

13. Country Pride Pizza must reprice a two-topping pizza because of recent price changes. Per unit costs are as follows: 1 pound of dough $.85; 1 cup of sauce $.40; 8 ounces of cheese $1.25; toppings $.75 each. If the shop's operating expenses are estimated at 60% of the cost, and the required profit is 15% of the cost, what is the selling price of each pizza?

14. What is the most a retailer should pay for an item that will be sold for $350 if a markup rate of 60% on cost is required?

15. The Lighting Gallery reported net sales of $40,580 for June. If the store averaged a 30% markup on the selling price, what was (a) the gross margin amount and (b) the amount of net profit if operating expenses were 24% of net sales?

16. A department store buys men's dress shirts at $96 a dozen. If the store's markup rate is 20% based on selling price, what is the selling price of each shirt?

17. The Triangle Shoe Store wants to sell a line of boys' shoes for $54. How much should the store pay for the shoes if its operating expenses are 32% of the selling price and the profit is 8% of the selling price?

18. Raymond's Discount Store carries a line of ladies' watches that cost $35 each. The price tag on the watch case lists two different prices, a manufacturer suggested retail price of $85 and a discount price of $60. What is the markup percent based on (a) the manufacturer suggested retail price and (b) the discount price?

19. The markup percent on a gallon of interior latex paint is 20% of the selling price. What is the equivalent markup percent based on cost?

20. During a clearance sale, Hartin's Furniture Store marked down its entire inventory 30%. Find the reduced price of a traditional living room set if the marked price was $1,499.

21. A & B Markets bought six flats of blueberries at $7.60 per flat. If each flat contains 10-quart baskets of berries and approximately 5% of the purchase will spoil before it can be sold, what price should be marked on each quart to realize a markup of 50% on the cost?

22. The Teen Scene purchased six dozen Rugby shirts of assorted sizes at a cost of $264 per dozen. The store expects 25% of the total shirts purchased will be sold on sale for $28 each. What marked price should be placed on the shirt in order to make a 65% markup on total cost?

23. A camcorder with a marked price of $1,000 is marked down 40%. If the cost of the camcorder is $650, and the operating expenses are 28% of the cost, find (a) the operating loss and (b) the absolute loss.

24. Bradford Office Interiors purchased six conference tables with eight matching chairs at $1,250 per set. Bradford was allowed a trade discount of 12% and terms of 3/10, *n*/30. The company is required to pay a 5% sales tax. How much must be remitted if Bradford makes payment during the discount period?

25. Jed Clapton purchased a hunting rifle from Northwest Sport Equipment for $425. What was the total amount of the purchase if the store collected a 10% excise tax and a 7% sales tax on the sale?

Answers to self-test: *1.* markup *2.* gross margin *3.* selling price *4.* markup amount, cost *5.* cost, selling price *6.* markdown *7.* perishables *8.* break-even point *9.* absolute loss *10.* sales tax *11.* a. $38.25; b. $8.50 *12.* $1,680 *13.* $7.00 *14.* $218.75 *15.* a. $12,174; b. $2,434.80 *16.* $10.00 *17.* $32.40 *18.* a. 58.8%; b. 41.7% *19.* 25% *20.* $1,049.30 *21.* $1.20 *22.* $39.07 *23.* a. $232.00; b. $50.00 *24.* $6,732.00 *25.* $500.23

8

SIMPLE INTEREST AND SIMPLE DISCOUNTS

Learning objectives

1. Calculate the dollar amount of interest using the simple interest formula.

2. Calculate the principal, rate, time, or interest when the other three quantities are known.

3. Understand the difference between computing ordinary interest and exact interest, and be able to calculate both.

4. Calculate the amount of the proceeds, bank discount, and maturity value using the simple discount formula.

5. Find the true interest rate for a loan that has been discounted.

6. Determine the face value, interest, and maturity value of a simple interest note.

(continued)

INTRODUCTION

It is unlikely that you will go through life without having either to borrow money or to lend it. Perhaps you have already borrowed money in order to go to college or to buy a car. As the owner of a retail business, you may have needed to borrow money in order to make improvements or to expand your business. When you borrow money from a bank or lending institution, the bank charges you a sum of money (this is called *interest* or a *finance charge*) for the *use* of the money for the length of time that you use it.

Interest may be either an income item or an expense item. If a business borrows money and *pays* interest for the use of it, then the interest paid is an *expense*. If the business loans money for use by someone else and *receives* interest, then, as we learned in Chapter 5, that interest is an *income* item.

There are two basic types of interest: simple interest and compound interest. In this chapter, we will study *simple interest*, which is interest earned on only the original principal invested. *Compound interest*, which is interest earned on principal and past interest, we will study in Chapter 9. Chapter 10 will familiarize you with some day-to-day situations in which individuals and businesses must involve themselves with interest.

8.1   SIMPLE INTEREST

Learning objective
Calculate the dollar amount of interest using the simple interest formula.

Interest is a sum of money paid or charged for the use of money; that is, for borrowing someone else's money. Simple interest is usually calculated for short-term loans rather than for long-term investments and loans. Simple interest is calculated using an expanded form of the "base, rate, and part" formula ($P = B \times R$). The formula for simple interest is shown below.

Formula for simple interest

interest = principal × rate × time

$I = P \times R \times T$
I = interest, the amount charged for the use of money
P = **principal**, the initial amount of money invested or borrowed
R = annual (yearly) rate, expressed as a percent
T = length of time the principal is invested or borrowed, expressed in terms of years or a fraction of 1 year

Example 1

Kevin Robinson borrowed $1,200 for 1 year at a simple interest rate of 11.3%. How much interest did he pay?

Solution

P = amount borrowed = $1,200
R = rate = 11.3%, or .113 (decimal form)
T = time in years = 1 year

$I = P \times R \times T$
$I = \$1,200 \times .113 \times 1$
$I = \$135.60$

At the end of the year, Kevin was required to pay $135.60 interest.

Example 2

Sorensen's Bargain Books borrowed $50,000 from its banker at 12.5% simple interest for 3 years. How much interest will Sorensen's pay at the end of 3 years?

Solution

$P = \text{principal} = \$50,000$
$R = \text{rate} = .125$
$T = \text{time in terms of years} = 3$

$I = P \times R \times T$
$I = \$50,000 \times .125 \times 3$
$I = \$18,750$

$18,750 interest is due at the end of 3 years.

Each of the examples above has time intervals that are expressed in full years. Terms of loans also occur in fractional parts of 1 year. Terms may be expressed in terms of years, months, weeks, etc. To determine the fractional part of a year, T is divided by 1 for years, 12 for months, and 52 for weeks ($T = \text{number of months}/12$, $T = \text{number of weeks}/52$, etc.).

Example 3

The Social Services Department of Minnehaha County has received funding for a special project 9 months prior to when they need to expend the monies. They decide to invest the funds, $130,000, in a short-term investment for 8 months at 12% simple interest. How much will the department earn on the investment?

Solution

$P = \$130,000$

$R = 12\%, \text{ or } .12$

$T = \dfrac{8 \text{ months}}{12 \text{ months}} = \dfrac{8}{12} \leftarrow \text{fractional part of one year}$

$I = P \times R \times T$

$I = \$130,000 \times .12 \times \dfrac{8}{12}$

$I = \dfrac{\$130,000}{1} \times \dfrac{.12}{1} \times \dfrac{8}{12}$

$I = \dfrac{\$130,000 \times .12 \times 8}{12}$

$I = \$10,400$

The interest earned is $10,400.

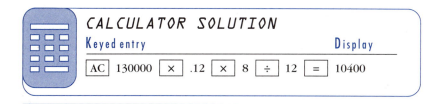

At the end of the term (time period) for a simple interest invest-ment or loan, the total amount to be paid to the lender is the original principal *plus* interest. The **maturity value** of a simple interest invest-ment or loan is the sum of the principal and interest as depicted in Fig-ure 8.1. This maturity value is also referred to as the *future value* of the investment or loan.

Maturity value of a loan

Maturity value = principal + interest

$$M = P + I$$
$$M = P + (PRT)$$
$$M = P(1 + RT)$$

You may also see this formula written as $FV = PV(1 + RT)$, where FV represents the *future value* (or maturity value) of the investment or loan, and PV represents the *present value* (or principal) of the future value. The

Figure 8.1

Maturity value of a loan

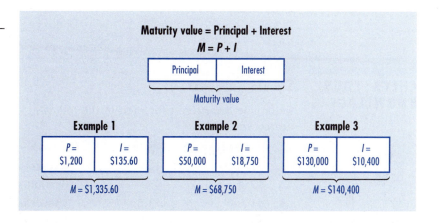

present value of money invested is its value at the time it is invested, and with time it grows to a future value, or maturity value. These are all terms that are commonly used in financial transactions.

Example 4

Jones and Johnson, Attorneys at Law, have received a $100,000 retainer fee to represent R & J Plumbing Supplies in any litigation that might develop in the next 3 years. Jones and Johnson invest the $100,000 at 11% simple interest for 1½ years. What will be the total value of the investment at the end of 1½ years?

Solution

total value = maturity value
maturity value = $P + (P \times R \times T)$

$$P = \$100,000$$
$$R = .11$$
$$T = 1.5 \text{ years}$$

$$M = P + (P \times R \times T)$$
$$M = \$100,000 + (\$100,000 \times .11 \times 1.5)$$
$$M = \$100,000 + \$16,500$$
$$M = \$116,500$$

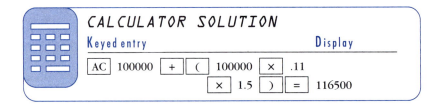

CHECK YOUR KNOWLEDGE

Simple interest

Determine the interest for each of the following (round answers to the nearest cent).

	Principal	Rate	Time	Interest
1.	$10,000	12%	5 years	_____
2.	$750	9%	6 months	_____
3.	$1,300	11.5%	13 weeks	_____
4.	$2,500	7¾%	78 weeks	_____

Determine the maturity value of each of the following:

	Principal	Rate	Time	Maturity value
5.	$7,500	10¼%	2 years	_____
6.	$3,000	8.75%	9 months	_____
7.	$4,000	12.68%	26 weeks	_____

Solve the following word problems. Round dollar amounts to the nearest cent and rates to the nearest hundredth of a percent.

8. Santiago Rubbish Removal borrowed $75,000 at 16% simple interest for 10 months. (a) How much interest will Santiago owe at the end of the term of the loan? (b) Find the total amount Santiago will have to pay at the end of the loan term.

9. Marla Bryant purchased a $7,000 certificate of deposit that paid 9% simple interest for 3 years. What will the value of the CD be at the end of the 3-year period?

10. J. M. Merrill invested $30,000 in a 5-month simple interest investment paying 13% per annum (per year). At the end of the 5-month term, she invested the entire maturity value in an account paying 10% simple interest for 7 months. What was the total value of her investments at the end of the 12-month period?

8.1   EXERCISES

Find the simple interest (round to the nearest cent).

	Principal	Rate	Time	Interest
1.	$12,000	12%	8 months	_____
2.	$8,000	10.5%	10 months	_____
3.	$2,000	12.75%	1½ years	_____
4.	$4,500	11.5%	1 year	_____
5.	$10,000	13%	6 months	_____
6.	$2,350	7%	5 months	_____
7.	$7,750	9.5%	15 months	_____
8.	$12,450	7.75%	26 weeks	_____
9.	$3,345	8.75%	39 weeks	_____
10.	$17,875	13.8%	4 years	_____

Answers to CYK: **1.** $6,000   **2.** $33.75   **3.** $37.38   **4.** $290.63   **5.** $9,037.50   **6.** $3,196.88   **7.** $4,253.60   **8.**   a. $10,000; b. $85,000   **9.** $8,890   **10.** $33,469.79

Find the maturity value.

	Principal	Rate	Time	Maturity value
11.	$12,000	12%	8 months	_____
12.	$8,000	10.5%	13 weeks	_____
13.	$2,000	12.75%	2½ years	_____
14.	$4,500	11.5%	5 years	_____
15.	$10,000	13%	15 months	_____

Solve the following word problems. Round dollar amounts to the nearest cent and rate values to the nearest hundredth percent.

16. Cecilie Morganstein invested $5,000 in a simple interest account paying 9% per year. How much interest will she earn if she leaves her money in the account for 2½ years?

17. Jerry Moss wishes to take out a $7,500 loan at 14% simple interest for 7 months. (a) What is the interest that Jerry must pay at the end of 7 months? (b) What is the total amount that Jerry must repay to the bank at the end of 7 months?

18. Karen Arch wishes to take out a $17,200 loan at 7.9% simple interest for 1½ years. (a) What is the interest that Karen must pay at the end of the term of the loan? (b) What is the total amount that Karen must pay at the end of the term of the loan?

19. Jacksonville Technical College received $3,445,553 in state aid on September 15 for the fall academic semester. The vice-president for finance decided to invest $2,000,000 in a 2-month investment that pays 11.5% simple interest. How much interest will the college earn on the investment?

20. Serendipity County's Planning and Development Office received a $1.5 million grant for urban development. Realizing they would expend the funds somewhat uniformly throughout the year, the agency set aside 50% of the funds for the first 6 months' expenditures. The remainder of the funds were invested in short-term investments paying 15% simple interest per year. One half of these funds were invested for 4 months, and the remainder were invested for 8 months. (a) How much was set aside for the 8-month investment? (b) How much interest was earned on the 8-month investment? (c) What was the maturity value of the 4-month investment? (d) What was the total amount of interest earned on the two investments?

8.2   SOLVING FOR PRINCIPAL, RATE, AND TIME IN THE SIMPLE INTEREST FORMULA

Learning objective
Calculate the principal, rate, time, or interest when the other three quantities are known.

In Section 8.1, we used the simple interest formula to solve for the variable I, interest. We can use algebra to solve for the principal, rate, and time variables as well.

Example 5

If Sumi Komoto paid $42 in interest for a 7-month loan at a rate of 12%, what principal was borrowed?

Solution

$$I = P \times R \times T$$

$$\$42 = P \times .12 \times \frac{7 \text{ months}}{12 \text{ months}}$$

$$\$42 = .07P$$

$$\$\frac{42}{.07} = \frac{.07P}{.07}$$

$$\$600 = P$$

$$\text{principal} = \$600$$

If we solve for P in the formula for simple interest, we can develop a formula for principal too. Since the variable P is multiplied by $(R \times T)$ we will use division, the opposite operation of multiplication, to isolate P on one side of the equal sign.

Formula for principal

$$I = PRT$$

$$\frac{I}{RT} = \frac{P\cancel{R}\cancel{T}}{\cancel{R}\cancel{T}}$$

$$\frac{I}{RT} = P$$

or

$$P = \frac{I}{RT}$$

Principal equals interest divided by the product of rate and time; this formula supplied with the information in Example 5 would give us the same result:

$$P = \frac{I}{RT} = \frac{42}{(.12)\left(\dfrac{7}{12}\right)} = \$600$$

Example 6

Harrison Supply Co. invested $10,000 in a 3-month simple interest account that paid $400. What was the simple interest rate?

Solution

$$I = PRT$$

$$\$400 = \$10,000(R)\frac{3 \text{ months}}{12 \text{ months}}$$

$$\$400 = \$2,500\,R$$

$$\frac{\$400}{\$2,500} = \frac{\$2,500\,R}{\$2,500}$$

$$.16 = R$$

$$\text{rate} = 16\%$$

We can develop the formula for R (rate) the same way we developed the formula for P:

Formula for rate

$$I = PRT$$

$$\frac{I}{PT} = \frac{PRT}{PT}$$

$$\frac{I}{PT} = R$$

or

$$R = \frac{I}{PT}$$

Rate is equal to the interest divided by the product of principal and time. In Example 6, our solution by the rate formula would then be:

$$R = \frac{I}{PT} = \frac{\$400}{\$10,000(3/12)} = \frac{\$400}{\$2,500} = .16$$

Example 7

Jody Richardson paid $76.32 on an $1,100 loan at 9¼% simple interest. What was the length of the loan?

Solution

$$I = PRT$$
$$\$76.32 = \$1{,}100(.0925)T$$
$$\$76.32 = \$101.75T$$
$$\frac{\$76.32}{\$101.75} = \frac{\$101.75T}{\$101.75}$$
$$.75 = T$$
$$\text{Time} = \tfrac{3}{4} \text{ of 1 year}$$

We develop the formula for T (time) as follows:

Formula for term

$$I = PRT$$

$$\frac{I}{PR} = \frac{PRT}{PR}$$

$$\frac{I}{PR} = T$$

or

$$T = \frac{I}{PR}$$

The solution to Example 7 using the term formula then would be:

$$T = \frac{I}{PR} = \frac{\$76.32}{\$1{,}100(.0925)} = \frac{\$76.32}{\$101.75} = .75$$

Solving for P, R, or T can be accomplished most easily by memorizing one formula, $I = PRT$, and then using algebra. However, you can also memorize all four formulas and simply choose the proper one for the task at hand.

$$I = PRT \qquad P = \frac{I}{RT} \qquad R = \frac{I}{PT} \qquad T = \frac{I}{PR}$$

The triangular figures are a pictorial device that can help you to remember these formulas. The quantity shaded is equal to the remaining products and quotients.

CHECK YOUR KNOWLEDGE

Solving for principal, rate, and time

Solve for the remaining quantity in each (round dollar amounts to the nearest cent and rates to the nearest hundredth of a percent).

	Interest	Principal	Rate	Time
1.	_____	$1,500	13%	5 months
2.	$1010.63	_____	11%	15 months
3.	$200	$625	_____	4 years
4.	$262.50	$8,750	12%	_____

5. What percent simple interest is the borrower paying on a 2-year loan of $5,000 of which $990 interest is paid?

6. Martha's Flower Shoppe invested $2,000 in a simple interest investment paying 12½% and received $1,000 in interest. How long was the Shoppe's money invested?

7. Frank Farkwilder is retired and receives $4,950 every 6 months from an investment paying 11% simple interest. Frank receives all the interest generated by the account each 6 months and never takes any of the principal. What is the principal Frank has invested?

8.2 EXERCISES

Fill in the missing entries (round dollar amounts to the nearest cent and rates to the nearest hundredth percent).

	Principal	Rate	Time	Interest
1.	_____	13.1%	6 months	$393.00
2.	_____	14.0%	1 year	$2,478
3.	_____	4.8%	2 years	$216
4.	_____	9.5%	1½ years	$712.50
5.	_____	8.6%	9 months	$838.50
6.	$4,800	_____	11 months	$440.00
7.	$5,200	_____	1¼ years	$487.50
8.	$9,750	_____	12 months	$565.50
9.	$11,000	_____	13 months	$1,251.25

Answers to CYK: **1.** $81.25   **2.** $7,350.00   **3.** 8%   **4.** .25 year, or 3 months   **5.** 9.9%
6. 4 years   **7.** $90,000

	Principal	Rate	Time	Interest
10.	$20,000	_____	1 year	$2,240.00
11.	$30,000	12%	_____	$7,200.00
12.	$33,000	14.1%	_____	$2,326.50
13.	$4,400	13.5%	_____	$594.00
14.	$7,800	11.7%	_____	$608.40
15.	$10,000	6.9%	_____	$1,035.00
16.	$4,000	5.6%	3 months	_____
17.	$6,750	7.8%	14 months	_____
18.	$3,000	10%	2 years	_____
19.	$5,500	11%	4 months	_____
20.	$9,000	7.0%	1 year	_____

Solve the following word problems. Round dollar amounts to the nearest cent and rates to the nearest hundredth of a percent.

21. If the simple interest on $15,000 was $555 for 6 months, what rate of interest was charged?

22. Ray Grey needs to borrow $10,000. The simple interest rate is 12.15%. If Ray can't afford to pay any more than $1,200 for interest, what is the length of time that Ray can borrow the money?

23. Ricardo Rivera loaned his brother Carlos some money at 13% simple interest per year. At the end of 5 months, Ricardo had earned $1,110 in interest from the loan. How much did Carlos borrow from Ricardo?

24. Barney Casey borrowed $40,000 from his parents for 2 years. He paid them a total of $45,000 at the end of the 2-year term of the simple interest loan. What rate of interest did he pay his folks?

25. Carla Swerzik confided in a friend that she had invested some money in an investment paying 7.5% simple interest per year, and that she had earned $200 interest in just 1 year. The friend wanted to know how much was invested, but Carla would not reveal the amount. How much did Carla invest?

8.3   EXACT AND ORDINARY INTEREST

Up until now, time (T) in our simple interest formula has been represented in years, months, or weeks, which means that the denominator in the fraction used to determine T as a part of 1 year has been 1, 12, or 52. When time (T) is given in days, the denominator is either 365 or 360. **Exact interest** is the simple interest determined by dividing the number of days by 365. Exact interest using exact time is:

$$T = \frac{\text{number of days}}{365}$$

Ordinary interest is the simple interest determined by dividing the number of days by 360. Ordinary interest using ordinary time is:

$$T = \frac{\text{number of days}}{360}$$

Use of 360 as the denominator is often referred to as the "banker's rule," because each month is considered to have 30 days (30 x 12 = 360). Let's look at specific examples of each.

Example 8

Find the exact interest for a loan whose length is 120 days; the amount borrowed is $18,000; and the rate of simple interest is 8%.

Solution

$$I = PRT$$

$$I = \$18,000 \times .08 \times \frac{120 \text{ days}}{365 \text{ days}}$$

$$I = \frac{\$18,000 \times .08 \times 120}{365}$$

$$I = \$473.42$$

Note: Be careful in these calculations to multiply the numerator values together, then multiply the denominator values together, and last complete the division. If you choose to first find the decimal equivalent for 120/365 and substitute it into the equation, do not round the decimal or any other part of the calculation until the final step. Here, the decimal equivalent for the time fraction would be expressed in the following calculation:

$$I = \$18,000 \times .08 \times (120/365)$$
$$I = \$18,000 \times .08 \times (.3287671\ldots)$$
$$I = \$473.42466\ldots = \$473.42$$

Example 9

Find the ordinary interest for a loan whose length is 120 days; the amount borrowed is $18,000; and the rate of simple interest is 8%.

Solution

$$I = P \times R \times T$$

$$I = \$18,000 \times .08 \times \frac{120 \text{ days}}{360 \text{ days}}$$

$$I = \$480$$

When we compare Examples 8 and 9, we can see that the dollar amount of interest is higher for ordinary interest than it is for exact interest. Unless a problem specifically states that exact interest is to be used, you should calculate ordinary interest.

CALCULATING THE NUMBER OF DAYS AND DUE DATE

In the previous examples, the number of days of the loan always was given. In some instances, the *dates* of a loan are given and then you have to calculate the number of days of the loan. Either of the two methods we discussed in Section 6.3, the days-of-the-month method or the days-in-a-year method, can be used to determine the exact number of days.

Example 10

If a loan is issued on March 4 and is due on July 15, find the length of this loan.

Solution

First let's use the days-of-the-month method:

March	27 days of loan in March (31 − 4 = 27)
April	30 days of loan in April
May	31 days of loan in May
June	30 days of loan in June
July	15 days of loan in July
total days of loan	133 days

Second, we will use Table 6.3 on page 215, which tells the numerical day of each date of the year. For this example, we see that July 15 is the 196th day of the year and that March 4 is the 63rd day of the year. The difference, 196 − 63, is 133 days. When using Table 6.4, be sure to note whether the calculation includes the month of February during a leap year; this would require 1 additional day to be added to the calculation.

*F*or *Y*our *I*nformation
What lower rates add to the economy

When interest rates on loans decrease, there is more money in the pockets of consumers, businesses, and the government to be spent in the commercial marketplace. Consequently, the economy in general is stimulated by those lower rates by buying. The accompanying diagram projected that lower loan interest rates would send $42 billion of cash into the economy. However, the lower rates also would mean lower rates on savings as well. Lower interest on savings would mean a decrease of $15 billion in cash flow into the economy. The net result was still predicted to be an additional $27 billion in cash in the economy.

Source: Michael J. Mandel, "Economic Trends," *Business Week*, February 3, 1992. Used with permission.

WHAT LOWER RATES ADD TO THE ECONOMY

Effects in 1992*

Billions of dollars

CONSUMER RATES	
MORTGAGE COST	$22
OTHER DEBT Credit cards, home equity and auto loans	2
INTEREST INCOME Certificates of deposit and other savings	−15

BUSINESS BORROWING COSTS	
CORPORATE DEBT	10

GOVERNMENT BORROWING COSTS	
FEDERAL	7
STATE AND LOCAL	1
TOTAL	**$27**

* ASSUMING INTEREST RATES STAY AT CURRENT LEVELS

DATA: MORTGAGE BANKERS ASSN.; DONALDSON, LUFKIN & JENRETTE; BW

Example 11

Calculate the due date using exact time for a 90-day loan made on February 10, 1992.

Solution

Since 4 divides into 1992 evenly with no remainder, 1992/4 = 498, it follows that 1992 is a leap year and that February 1992 has 29 days.

Days-of-the-Month Method:

February	19 days (29 − 10 = 19)
March	31 days (50 days to March 31)
April	30 days (80 days to April 30)
May	10 days (we need 10 days in May)
total	90 days

Therefore, May 10 is the due date.

Days-of-a-Year Method:

February 10 is the 41st day.

Add 90 to 41 to arrive at the 131st day.

Note that February has 29 days in this leap year so we subtract 1 more day, to give us the 130th day of the year.

The 130th day in Table 6.4 is May 10, the due date.

CHECK YOUR KNOWLEDGE

Exact and ordinary interest

Solve the following problems. Round dollar amounts to the nearest cent and rates to the nearest hundredth of a percent.

	Principal	Rate	Time	Exact interest	Ordinary interest
1.	$2,500	12%	90 days	_____	_____
2.	$13,000	9%	250 days	_____	_____
3.	$48,000	10%	400 days	_____	_____

	Date issued	Date due	Number of days
4.	June 7, 1991	November 19, 1991	_____
5.	January 23, 1992	March 30, 1992	_____
6.	February 6, 1993	April 6, 1993	_____

	Date issued	Number of days	Due date (exact time)
7.	November 12, 1992	60	_____
8.	July 23, 1993	120	_____
9.	January 17, 1994	240	_____

10. A loan of $4,400 was issued at a simple interest rate of 11½% on June 14 and is due on September 2. Determine (a) the ordinary interest, (b) the exact interest, and (c) the difference of the ordinary minus the exact interest.

Answers to CYK:
1. $73.97; $75   *2.* $801.37; $812.50   *3.* $5,260.27; $5,333.33   *4.* 165
5. 67   *6.* 59   *7.* Jan. 11, 1993   *8.* Nov. 20, 1993   *9.* Sept. 14, 1995
10. a. $112.44; b. $110.90; c. $1.54

8.3   EXERCISES

Find the exact interest (round answers to the nearest cent).

	Principal	Rate	Time	Exact interest
1.	$12,500	10.4%	120 days	_____
2.	$1,200	11.6%	45 days	_____
3.	$4,700	8.8%	360 days	_____
4.	$6,600	14.5%	365 days	_____
5.	$800	16.0%	280 days	_____

Find the ordinary interest (round answers to the nearest cent).

	Principal	Rate	Time	Ordinary interest
6.	$6,600	14.5%	365 days	_____
7.	$800	16.0%	280 days	_____
8.	$2,000	9.9%	70 days	_____
9.	$8,000	10.5%	100 days	_____
10.	$11,750	12.7%	60 days	_____

Determine the length of the loan that is issued on each given date and due on the date indicated.

	Date issued	Date due	Number of days
11.	January 12, 1991	April 12, 1991	_____
12.	August 23, 1991	November 15, 1991	_____
13.	March 30, 1992	September 30, 1992	_____
14.	December 15, 1991	April 15, 1992	_____
15.	January 25, 1992	May 1, 1992	_____

Calculate the due date using exact time for the following loan dates and terms.

	Date issued	Number of days	Due date
16.	January 22, 1991	60	_____
17.	August 25, 1992	120	_____
18.	May 10, 1992	240	_____
19.	November 15, 1991	30	_____
20.	February 5, 1992	45	_____

Determine the exact interest. (Assume the year is *not* a leap year. Round answers to the nearest hundredth of a percent.)

	Principal	Rate	Dates of loan	Interest
21.	$100,000	8.9%	Jan. 1 to May 1	_____
22.	$1,500	12.3%	June 11 to Aug. 2	_____
23.	$20,000	14.0%	Feb. 15 to July 31	_____
24.	$7,500	14.7%	Apr. 4 to Nov. 3	_____
25.	$15,000	11.0%	May 16 to Dec. 27	_____

Solve the following word problems. Round dollar amounts to the nearest cent and rates to a hundredth of a percent.

26. Sarai Sherman agreed to deposit $4,450 in an account paying 16% simple interest per year for 60 days. If she made the deposit on February 25, determine (a) the date of the end of the term of the investment and (b) the ordinary interest Sarai will earn.

27. Marshall Peters borrowed $3,000 at 20% simple interest per year for 90 days. If he borrowed the money on June 1, determine (a) the due date of his loan based on exact interest and (b) the amount he must repay.

28. Elvis Jones has $10,000 he wishes to invest for 18 months (548 days). He could invest the money in Alpha Bank for 13% exact simple interest or in Beta Bank for 13.5% ordinary interest. (a) Determine how much interest he would earn at Alpha Bank. (b) Determine how much interest he would earn at Beta Bank.

8.4   SIMPLE DISCOUNT

Learning objective
Calculate the amount of the proceeds, bank discount, and maturity value using the simple discount formula.

Thus far in Chapter 8, we have learned that when you take out a loan the initial amount borrowed is called the principal and the amount due is called the maturity value, which is the principal plus interest. The concept of simple discount is very similar to the concept of simple interest except that the terminology is different. We will look at a list of definitions before exploring the formula for discounting.

> ***Proceeds:*** The actual dollar amount of money that the borrower receives or takes home from the lender.
>
> ***Bank discount:*** The interest that is collected at the *beginning* of the loan.
>
> ***Maturity value:*** The proceeds plus the bank discount.

Sometimes banks or other lending institutions collect the interest from a loan at the beginning of the loan rather than at the end of the loan. Taking or deducting interest at the beginning of a loan is called **discounting**.

Formula for simple discount

bank discount = maturity value × discount rate × time
$$D = M \times R \times T$$

where

M = maturity value
R = simple discount rate
T = time, or length of loan in terms of years
D = bank discount or interest

proceeds = maturity value − discount
$$P = M - D$$
$$P = M - (MRT)$$
$$P = M(1 - RT)$$

Example 12

Lynette Cushing needed a loan before she could go to college. Lynette went into the bank and asked to borrow $7,000. The rate was 11% and the length of the loan was for 1 year. Assuming the bank discounted the loan, how much money will Lynette actually receive from the bank?

Solution

Lynette has asked for $7,000, which will be the maturity value. We calculate the simple discount on $7,000 to be

$D = MRT = \$7,000 \times .11 \times 1$ (which is the same form as the simple interest formula)
$D = MRT = \$770$

Now this discount (interest) is *subtracted* from the maturity value to give us the proceeds.

$$P = M - (MRT) = \$7,000 - \$770 = \$6,230$$

The maturity date is 1 year after Lynette borrowed the money. At that time, Lynette must pay the bank $7,000 (proceeds plus discount).

Notice the similarity between Figure 8.2 and Figure 8.1. Since a bank discount is simple interest deducted from the maturity value to arrive at the proceeds, $M = P + I$ and $M = P + D$ are very similar.

TRUE INTEREST RATE

When working with simple discount, we need to be careful not to confuse the discount rate with the simple interest rate. In Example 12, the bank

Figure 8.2

Maturity value—
simple discount

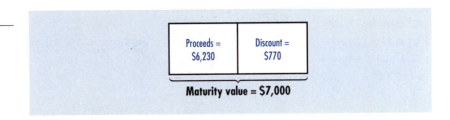

| Proceeds = $6,230 | Discount = $770 |

Maturity value = $7,000

discount of $770 was based on $7,000 maturity value multiplied by the rate of 11%. However, we must remember that Lynette did not have the use of $7,000 but, rather, $6,230. So, to find the *true rate of interest* we must compare the proceeds ($6,230, the actual amount of money borrowed) with the dollar amount of the bank discount ($770). We can compute the simple interest rate that this discount of $770 represents of the actual amount borrowed (proceeds) by using the simple interest formula:

$$I = PRT$$
$$I = \text{interest} = \text{discount amount} = \$770$$
$$P = \text{principal} = \text{proceeds} = \$6{,}230$$
$$T = \text{time} = 1 \text{ year}$$

$$\$770 = (\$6{,}230)R(1)$$

$$\frac{\$770}{\$6{,}230} = R$$

or

$$R = \frac{\$770}{\$6{,}230} = .1235955 \ldots = .1236 \text{ or } 12.36\%$$

This rate of interest is called the true rate of interest of a simple discount loan. We can develop the formula for a true rate of interest as follows: $I = PRT$; for a discount loan,

$$I = \text{discount interest} = D$$
$$P = \text{proceeds}$$
$$T = \text{time}$$
$$R = \text{true interest rate}$$
$$D = PRT$$
$$\frac{D}{PT} = \frac{\cancel{P}R\cancel{T}}{\cancel{P}\cancel{T}}$$
$$R = \frac{D}{PT}$$

Formula for true rate of interest

$$\text{true rate of interest} = \frac{\text{discount interest}}{\text{proceeds} \times \text{time}}$$

To solve Example 12 using the formula, we would start with the formula for true rate of interest and end with the same answer.

$$R = \frac{D}{PT}$$

$$R = \frac{\$770}{(\$6{,}230)(1)} = .1236$$

It is not uncommon to think of the "simple discount rate" as the "simple interest rate" of the loan. However, we must note that they are not the same, even though they are used in a similar way. Remember the base for the simple discount rate is the *maturity value* of the loan, whereas the base of the simple interest rate is the *principal* of the loan.

COMPARING SIMPLE INTEREST AND SIMPLE DISCOUNT LOANS

We can now compare the two types of loans we have studied thus far. The following illustration compares two loans from two different banks and provides a means of analyzing the better offer.

Let's consider Jake Monroe, a beauty shop owner who needs a $5,000 loan for 1 year. Jake asks two different banks, Ace Bank and Barnaby Bank, to consider loaning him money.

Ace Bank's Offer: Ace Bank offers Jake a simple interest loan of $5,000 at 12% per annum for 1 year. The interest would be $I = \$5{,}000 \times .12 \times 1 = \$600$, and the maturity value would be $M = P + I = \$5{,}600$.

Barnaby Bank's Offer: Barnaby Bank offers Jake a discount loan with maturity value of $5,000, discount rate of 12%, and a time period of 1 year. The discount $D = MRT = \$5{,}000 \times .12 \times 1 = \$600$ and the proceeds would be $P = M - D = \$4{,}400$.

In each case, Jake asks for a $5,000 loan, but in the discount case, he receives less than requested.

Example 13

What if Jake needs the full $5,000 he asked for? How much should he request from Barnaby Bank to have proceeds of $5,000?

Solution

We can use algebra to answer this question.

$$\text{proceeds} = M - D = M - (MRT)$$
$$\text{proceeds} = M(1 - RT)$$
$$\$5,000 = M(1 - .12 \times 1) = .88M$$

or

$$.88M = \$5,000$$
$$M = \frac{\$5,000}{.88} = \$5,681.82$$

Consequently, Jake should ask for a $5,681.82 loan at a discount rate of 12% in order to receive the needed $5,000. Notice that the maturity value to be paid back is greater than the maturity value in the simple interest loan above. The reason is that the true interest for the discounted loan is 13.64%.

$$\left(R = \frac{D}{PT} = \frac{600}{(4,400)(1)} = .1364 \right)$$

Clearly a discounted loan would not be what Jake would want in this case.

CHECK YOUR KNOWLEDGE

Simple discounts and true interest rate

Determine the discount for the following simple discount loans (round rates to the nearest hundredth of a percent):

	Maturity value	Rate	Time	Discount
1.	$10,000	12%	1 year	1200
2.	$3,850	11.5%	8 months	295.17
3.	$17,500	13.25%	40 weeks	1783.65

Determine the proceeds for the following simple discount loans:

	Maturity value	Rate	Time	Proceeds
4.	$6,700	9%	2 years	_____
5.	$21,500	10.5%	78 weeks	_____
6.	$73,450	12%	2.5 months	_____

Determine the true interest for each of the following simple discount loans.

Maturity value	Rate	Time	Discount	Proceeds	True interest rate
7. $2,350	15%	1 year	$352.50	$1,997.50	_____
8. $875	11.5%	8 months	$75.47	$799.53	_____
9. $3,940	13%	18 months	$768.30	$3,171.70	_____

Solve the following problems. Round dollar amounts to the nearest cent and rates to the nearest hundredth of a percent.

10. Sammy Phong borrowed $14,000 at 10% for 10 months. Assuming the bank discounted the loan, determine: (a) the dollar amount of the discount, (b) the dollar amount of the proceeds, and (c) the dollar amount of the maturity value.

11. Brenda Lemke borrowed $6,700 on January 7, 1991, at a simple discount rate of 11.5% for 6 months. Assuming the loan was a simple discount loan, determine: (a) the dollar amount of the discount, (b) the dollar amount of the proceeds, (c) the maturity value, (d) the maturity date, and (e) the true interest rate.

12. Anna Garcia needed to borrow $8,000 for 15 months. She approached two banks inquiring about loans. Aldo National Bank offered her a simple interest loan at a rate of 13%. Bonzai International Bank offered her a simple discount loan with a 12% simple discount rate. (a) Determine the interest and maturity value of the Aldo Bank offer. (b) Determine the discount amount and proceeds of the Bonzai offer assuming a maturity value of $8,000. (c) Determine how much Anna would have to borrow from Bonzai in order to have $8,000 in proceeds.

8.4 EXERCISES

Determine the dollar amount of the discount and the proceeds (round answers to the nearest cent).

Maturity value	Discount rate	Time	Discount amount	Proceeds
1. $11,000	15.9%	9 months	_____	_____
2. $15,000	13.9%	15 months	_____	_____
3. $900	12.0%	4 months	_____	_____
4. $7,600	8.0%	11 months	_____	_____

Maturity value	Discount rate	Time	Discount amount	Proceeds
5. $12,000	7.7%	2 years	_____	_____
6. $4,100	4.8%	2.5 years	_____	_____
7. $2,200	10.0%	30 months	_____	_____
8. $1,300	9.9%	48 weeks	_____	_____
9. $6,300	9.0%	39 weeks	_____	_____
10. $10,900	10.0%	15 months	_____	_____

Determine the maturity value that will produce the proceeds as shown (round to the nearest cent).

Maturity value	Discount rate	Time	Discount amount
11. _____	10.0%	15 months	$10,000
12. _____	13.0%	20 months	$40,000
13. _____	14.0%	24 months	$5,000
14. _____	15.0%	11 months	$20,000
15. _____	16.0%	1.25 years	$7,000
16. _____	16.0%	1.5 years	$40,000
17. _____	12.0%	5 months	$33,000
18. _____	13.0%	40 weeks	$16,800

Find the proceeds and the true rate of interest. Round dollar amounts to the nearest cent, and rates to the nearest hundredth of a percent.

Maturity value	Discount rate	Time	Proceeds	True rate
19. $40,000	16.0%	36 months	_____	_____
20. $35,000	11.1%	25 months	_____	_____
21. $28,000	12.2%	8 months	_____	_____
22. $25,000	18.0%	2 years	_____	_____
23. $22,000	14.4%	7 months	_____	_____
24. $19,000	13.3%	10 months	_____	_____
25. $17,000	15.5%	4 months	_____	_____
26. $5,650	9.5%	2.25 years	_____	_____

Answers to CYK: **1.** $1,200   **2.** $295.17   **3.** $1,783.65   **4.** $5,494   **5.** $18,113.75   **6.** $71,613.75   **7.** 17.65%   **8.** 14.16%   **9.** 16.15%   **10.** a. $1,166.67; b. $12,833.33; c. $14,000   **11.** a. $385.25; b. $6,314.75; c. $6,700; d. July 7, 1992; e. 12.20%   **12.** a. $1,300; $9,300; b. $1,200; $6,800; c. $9,411.76

Solve the following word problems. Round dollar amounts to the nearest cent and rates to the nearest hundredth of a percent.

27. Carrie Lewis borrowed $23,500 at 13% for 9 months. Assuming the bank discounted the loan, determine: (a) the amount of the discount, (b) the amount of the proceeds, and (c) the maturity value of the loan.

28. Penny Jenkins borrowed $34,765 on January 30, 1992, at a simple discount rate of 15% for 18 months. For the loan determine: (a) the proceeds, (b) the maturity date, and (c) the true interest rate of the loan.

29. Samuel Smart wants to borrow $3,800 for 10 months. First National Bank offers him a 12% simple interest loan. Second International Bank offers him an 11% simple discount loan. Determine each of the following: (a) the maturity value of the loan at First National, (b) the proceeds of the loan at Sec-

ond International, and (c) the true interest rate of the loan at Second International.

30. Consider Samuel Smart's situation (exercise 29) again. What amount must Samuel request to borrow from Second International Bank in order to actually receive $3,800 in proceeds? What will be the true rate of interest for this loan?

31. Mountain Road Auto Parts needs $50,000 to redesign its store front and showroom. If Mountain Road's bank offers a simple discount loan at a 13% discount for 2 years, how much must Mountain Road borrow in order to actually receive $50,000?

32. New York Trade Shows needs to borrow $15,000 for 6 months in order to set up its next trade show. How much must the company ask to borrow from a bank that offers a simple discount loan at 14% in order to actually receive $15,000?

8.5   PROMISSORY NOTES

A **promissory note** is a written promise by a borrower (*maker*) to pay a sum of money (*face value*) to a designated person or bearer (*payee*) of the note, at a set time or *on demand*. A promissory note is similar to a personal check. When a person—let's call him Abe—writes a personal check to a second person—let's call her Barb—the following transactions occur. First, Abe deposits cash in his bank (called Abe's bank) where he has a checking account. Abe then writes a check to Barb on an- official check supplied by his bank for part or all of the money he deposited. Barb takes the check, which she accepted instead of cash, to her bank which gives her the designated amount of cash on the check. Barb's bank now sends the check to Abe's bank and receives the cash from that bank. Figure 8.3 depicts this transaction. A promissory note is a *negotiable instrument* similar to a check, except that it cannot be cashed until the designated date on the note, and it usually earns interest.

Learning objective
Determine the face value, interest, and maturity value of a simple interest note.

SIMPLE INTEREST NOTE

A promissory note that includes interest added to the face value is called a **simple interest note**. Figure 8.4 shows a typical format for a simple interest note.

Figure 8.3

Two-party check transaction

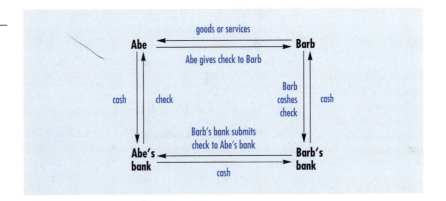

Figure 8.4

A simple interest note

$4,050.00

60 days

Brocksburg, OR 97215   Oct. 1, 1993

AFTER DATE ___I___ PROMISE TO PAY TO

THE ORDER OF _____ E. R. Hawley Construction Co. _____

_____ Four thousand fifty and 00/100 _____ DOLLARS

PAYABLE AT   Brocksburg First National Bank

VALUE RECEIVED WITH INTEREST AT __10.5%__ per annum.

No. 35   Signed *Arn Suedman*

Example 14

With the information given on the note in Figure 8.4, calculate (a) the due date, (b) the ordinary interest, and (c) the maturity value at the due date.

Solution

a. The term of the note is 60 days. From October 2 through October 31 is 30 days; from November 1 through November 30 is 30 days; therefore, November 30 is the due date. By the *days of the year method*, October 1 is the 274th day plus 60 days is the 334th day, which is November 30.

b. $I = PRT$
$I = \$4,050 \times .105 \times 60/360$
$I = \$70.88$

c. $M = P + I$
$M = \$4,050 + \$70.88 = \$4,120.88$

The *face value* of this note is its present value of $4,050, the interest is $70.88, and the *maturity value* or future value of this note is $4,120.88. Notice that the maturity value of a simple interest note is *not* the same as the face value. Maturity value equals face value plus interest.

Learning objective
Determine the face value, discount, proceeds, and maturity value of a simple discount note.

SIMPLE DISCOUNT NOTE

Next, let's consider a **simple discount note** in which the face value and maturity value are the same.

Example 15

Tom Anderson received a discounted loan from Solvay Bank for $9,000 at a 13% discount for 8 months. He agreed to sign a simple discount note for a face value of $9,000 due in 8 months (Figure 8.5). Determine (a) the proceeds Tom received and (b) the due date of the note.

Solution

a.   The face value of the simple discount note is also the maturity value.

Step 1:   Determine the discount amount.

$$\text{discount} = MRT$$
$$= 9{,}000 \times .13 \times 8/12$$
$$= \$780$$

Step 2:   Determine the proceeds.

$$\text{proceeds} = \text{maturity value} - \text{discount}$$
$$= \quad \$9{,}000 \quad - \quad \$780$$
$$= \quad \$8{,}220$$

Figure 8.5

A simple discount note

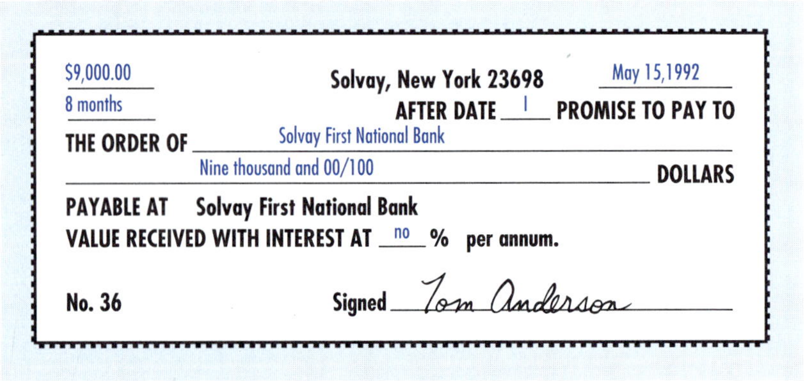

b. The due date of the note will be 8 months after May 1, 1992. Since May is the fifth month of the year, and $5 + 8 = 13$, the due date will be in the first month of 1993. The due date will be January 15, 1993.

We refer to notes that have interest added (such as the simple interest note in Example 14) as *interest bearing notes*. The maturity value of an interest bearing note is the face value plus interest. Notes like the simple discount note in Example 15 are called *non-interest bearing notes*. The maturity value of a non-interest bearing note is the same as the face value of the note. Non-interest bearing notes may have been issued as simple discount notes, or they may have been issued for the full principal with no interest charged either in the form of simple interest or a simple discount.

DISCOUNTING A NOTE

Promissory notes are negotiable instruments that have a specific monetary value at a specified future date. When a note is sold or traded prior to its maturity date, the note's value is usually discounted. Consider the following illustration.

E. T. Steele Wholesalers sold $10,000 worth of school supplies to Norton's Notions and Books with a cash discount of 5/10, *n*/30. After 20 days, Norton realizes that he cannot pay the invoice within the 30-day limit, and he asks Steele for an extension. Steele considers Norton to be a preferred customer and wants to continue to do business with him, but is concerned about his inability to pay on time. Rather than offer Norton a simple extension, Steele askes Norton for a promissory note due in 90 days for the full $10,000. To show good faith, Steele offers to charge no interest for this short-term loan. Norton goes to his bank and obtains a promissory note for $10,000 at 0% interest that is due in 90 days, and presents it to Steele. (See Figure 8.6.)

After 30 days have passed, Steele discovers that she is short of cash and needs to liquidate some of her assets. Steele takes the promissory note to her bank and asks the bank to purchase the note, which has a $10,000 face value. Since the bank wants to make money on the transaction, it negotiates with Steele to buy the note from Steele at a 15% discounted rate; that is, Steele's bank offers to buy the note from her for:

Learning objective
Determine the proceeds of a discounted simple interest note.

$$\text{proceeds} = M - MRT = \$10,000 - \$10,000 \times .15 \times 60/360$$
$$P = \$10,000 - \$250 = \$9,750$$

Notice that the discount time here is 60 days, as shown in Figure 8.7. Steele's bank has now purchased a note that will be worth $10,000 for $9,750. This transaction is shown in Figure 8.8.

Steele's bank will receive $10,000 from Norton 60 days later, at the

Figure 8.6

A promissory note

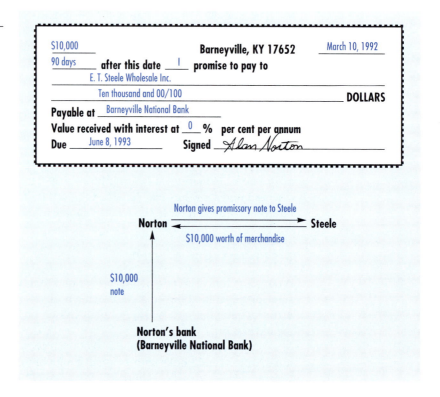

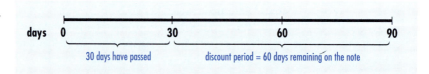

Figure 8.7

Discount period
time line

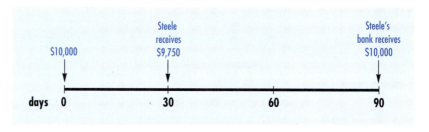

Figure 8.8

Note value time line

end of the original 90-day period; her bank will earn $250 on the transaction, which is a true interest rate of

$$R = \frac{250}{9,750 \times 60/360} = .1538, \text{ or } 15.38\%$$

Figures 8.9 and 8.10 show diagrammatically what has transpired.

Finally, Norton makes sure at the end of 90 days that there are sufficient funds in his bank to cover the note, and Steele's bank cashes in the note with Norton's bank and receives $10,000.

The use of the discount method here provides the bank and Steele with a definite method for negotiation of the sale and purchase of the note. Steele could approach other financial institutions, or other individuals, and offer the note to them, especially if their discount rates are lower. The two banks mentioned in this illustration need not have been involved at all in the exchange of money. Once the promissory note was obtained from the

Figure 8.9

Transaction between Steele and his bank

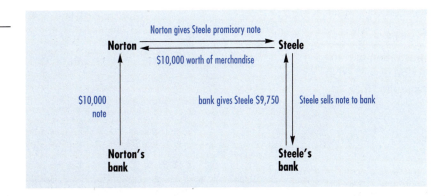

Figure 8.10

Transaction between Steele's bank and Norton's bank

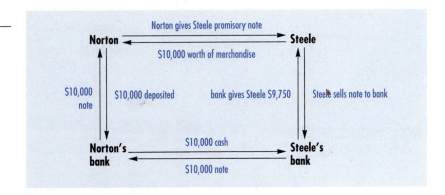

bank, the remaining transactions could have involved only the two parties, Norton and Steele.

Now let's look at an example of discounting a simple interest note.

Example 16

Emilio Johnson borrowed $50,000 from Ben Simpson. Emilio gave Ben a promissory note stating that he would pay Ben $50,000 plus 13% simple interest 9 months from the date of the note. After holding the note for 5 months, Ben sold the note to Janet Whitaker at a 16% discount. Determine: (a) the discounted amount Ben received for the note, (b) Ben's net gain or loss, (c) the amount Janet received for the note, (d) Janet's net gain or loss, (e) the true interest rate Ben earned, (f) the true interest rate Janet earned, (g) the amount Emilio paid, and (h) the value of the note at the time Janet bought it. Refer to Figure 8.11, which illustrates these transactions.

Figure 8.11

Illustration of transaction described in Example 16

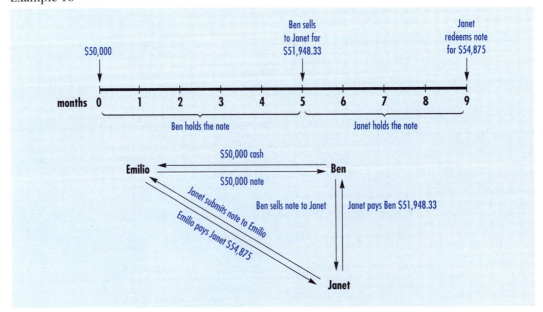

Solution

a. To determine the discounted amount (proceeds), we must complete two steps:

1. determine the maturity value of the note
2. discount the total maturity value to determine the proceeds.

Step 1: The maturity value of the simple interest note is:

$$\text{maturity value} = P + I$$
$$= P + PRT$$
$$= \$50,000 + (\$50,000)(.13)(9/12)$$
$$= \$54,875$$

Step 2: Ben received the proceeds when the note was discounted on the maturity value of $54,875. Since Ben has held the note for 5 months, there are 4 months remaining in the term of the loan. Hence, the discount period is 4 months, and $T = 4/12$.

$$\text{proceeds} = M - D$$
$$= \$54,875 - (\$54,875)(.16)(4/12)$$
$$= \$51,948.33$$

CALCULATOR SOLUTION

Keyed entry								Display
AC	50000	+	50000	×	.13	×		
			9	÷	12	=		54875
		−	54875	×	.16	×		
			4	÷	12	=		51948.3333

b. Ben's net gain is the difference between the amount Janet paid him for the note ($51,948.33), and the amount he loaned Emilio ($50,000). The net gain for Ben is $1,948.33.

c. Janet received the face value of $54,875.

d. Janet's net gain is the difference between what she received from Emilio and what she paid Ben.

$$\text{Janet's net gain} = \$54,875 - \$51,948.33 = \$2,926.67$$

e.   Ben's true interest rate $= \dfrac{\$1,948.33}{\$50,000\ (5/12)} = .0935198$ or 9.35%

f.   Janet's true interest rate $= \dfrac{\$2,926.67}{\$51,948.33\ (4/12)} = .1690143$

or 16.90%

g.   Emilio paid $54,875.

h.   The value of the note when Janet bought it would be the original principal ($50,000) plus 5 months' interest earned on that principal at 13% per annum.

$$
\begin{aligned}
\text{value after 5 months} = M &= P + I \\
&= \$50,000 + (\$50,000)(.13)(5/12) \\
&= \$52,708.33
\end{aligned}
$$

Both Ben and Janet should know this value before they enter into negotiations. Ben wants to receive an amount as close as possible to this figure. Janet wants to pay something less than this figure. They would negotiate the discount rate to be used in the sale of the note to Janet. Since Ben received less than $52,708.33, Janet was more successful in the negotiations.

The Steele illustration and the Johnson example (Example 16) are but two of the many complex business transactions that could occur with negotiable business instruments.

CHECK YOUR KNOWLEDGE

Promissory notes

Solve the following word problems.

1.   Susan Humphreys received a loan from First National Bank. She signed a promissory note with a face value of $9,500 agreeing to pay off the loan in 6 months with interest at 11.5% per annum. Determine the maturity value of the note.

2.   Harry Hanson signed a 120-day simple discount note with a face value of $23,500 on March 3, 1991, with a discount rate of 12%. Determine the proceeds Harry actually received. (Assume 360 days per year.)

3.   Sharon Tasker borrowed $40,000 from Jackson Finance Company. She signed a promissory note on June 2, 1992, with a face value of $40,000 plus 10% interest due in 18 months from the date of the note. Determine the maturity value of the note.

4. Refer to problem 3. Jackson Finance Co. sold Sharon's note (after holding it for 6 months) to Ferguson Funding Corp. at a 15% discount. Determine the proceeds received by Jackson from Ferguson.

5. Now refer to your results in problems 3 and 4 and determine (a) Jackson's net gain or loss and (b) Ferguson's net gain or loss.

Problems 6 through 8 refer to the promissory note below.

$28,750	Hobtown, La. 32457	Feb. 5, 1992

120 days **after this date** ___|___ **promise to pay to**
Haskins Quick Loan Co.

Twenty-eight thousand seven hundred fifty and 00/100 **DOLLARS**

Payable at First State Bank of Hobtown
Value received with interest at 13% per cent per annum

Signed _Silvia Younes_

6. Determine the due date of the note.

7. Determine the maturity value of the note (1 year = 360 days).

8. Assuming that Haskins Loan Co. sells the note to Quick Dollar Funding Corp. at a 17% discount on May 26, 1992, determine the proceeds received by Haskins from Dollar Funding.

8.5 EXERCISES

Solve the following word problems. Round dollar amounts to the nearest cent and rates to the nearest hundredth of a percent.

1. Arnold Jensen received a loan from Chemung Savings and Loan. He signed a promissory note with a face value of $11,500 agreeing to pay off the loan in 15 months with simple interest at 13% per annum. Determine the maturity value of the note.

Answers to CYK: 1. $9,500 + $546.25 = $10,046.25 2. P = $23,500 − $940 = $22,560 3. $40,000 + $6,000 = $46,000 4. $39,100 5. $900; $6,900 6. June 4, 1992 7. $28,750 + $1,245.83 = $29,995.83 8. $29,868.35

Pg 215

2. Consider the following promissory note:

$4,750	Harrowville, Va. 58349	March 12, 1991

240 days _____ **after this date ___I___ promise to pay to**
Signet Loan Co.

Four thousand seven hundred fifty and 00/100 _____ **DOLLARS**

Payable at ___First Bank of Harrowville___

Value received with interest at __14.5%__ **per cent per annum**

Signed _Marla Key_

Determine the date that the loan is due, and the maturity value of the loan.

3. Consider the following promissory note:

$23,450	Lodi, New York 58349	April 15, 1991

300 days _____ **after this date ___I___ promise to pay to**
Kermet Loan Co. Inc.

Twenty-three thousand four hundred fifty and 00/100 _____ **DOLLARS**

Payable at ___Lodi First National Bank___

Value received with interest at __0__ **per cent per annum**

Signed _Janet Hamlin_

Assume that this loan was discounted at 12% and determine (a) the proceeds and (b) the true interest rate of the loan.

4. Consider the following promissory note signed by Rooney Construction Co. for money to purchase a new backhoe:

$38,500	Valoise, New York 14980	September 1, 1992

18 months _____ **after this date ___I___ promise to pay to**
Valois Savings and Loan Co.

Thirty-eight thousand five hundred and 00/100 _____ **DOLLARS**

Payable at ___Valois Savings and Loan___

Value received with interest at __10.5__ **per cent per annum**

Signed _John R. Rooney_

Determine the due date of the loan, and the maturity value of the loan.

5. Refer to the promissory note in exercise 4. Assume that the Valois Savings and Loan sold the note to Nelson Funding Group on September 1, 1993, at a discount rate of 15%. What amount did the Valois Savings and Loan receive from Nelson Funding?

Proceeds

6. Consider the following promissory note signed by Barnes Construction Co. for money to purchase a new utility truck.

$72,500	Elmira, New York 14901	August 15, 1992
15 months **after this date** __I__ **promise to pay to**		
Elmira Savings and Loan Co.		
Seventy-two thousand five hundred and 00/100		**DOLLARS**
Payable at _Elmira First Savings and Loan_		
Value received with interest at _12_ per cent per annum		
Signed _Phyllis Barnes_		

Determine the due date of the loan, and the maturity value of the loan.

7. Refer to the promissory note in exercise 6. Assume that the Elmira First Savings and Loan sold the note to Johnson Funding Group on January 15, 1993, at a discount rate of 17%. What amount did the Elmira First Savings and Loan receive from Johnson Funding?

8. Refer to exercise 7 and determine Elmira First Saving's net gain.

9. Refer to exercise 7. Assume that the Johnson Funding Group also sells the promissory note. They sell it to Fast Funds on June 15, 1993, at a 20% discount. Determine the proceeds Johnson received for the note.

10. Refer to exercise 9 and determine the net gain or loss (a) for Johnson and (b) for Fast Funds.

8.6 PARTIAL PAYMENTS ON A SIMPLE INTEREST LOAN

At the beginning of this chapter, we stated that interest is a sum of money charged for the use of the principal or proceeds of the loan. The longer the borrower has the principal, the greater the interest cost for the loan. If all or part of the principal could be paid off early, the borrower could save on interest costs. When the borrower pays part of the principal prior to the maturity date, the payment is referred to as the **partial payment of a loan**. The U.S. rule, and the merchants rule provide guidelines for partial payments made on loans prior to their due dates.

THE U.S. RULE

Learning objective
Use the U.S. rule to calculate the balance of the principal of a loan when a partial payment is made.

The United States rule (U.S. rule) states that a partial payment must be divided into two parts, principal and interest, just as the loan is made up of those two parts. First, the partial payment must pay any interest accrued to date on the loan, then the remainder of the partial payment is subtracted from the principal to reduce it. The U.S. rule is so named because a U.S. Supreme Court ruling in the 19th century ruled that this procedure is a valid method of applying partial payments to a loan and its interest.

Example 17

Bill Lewkowicz borrowed $3,000 at 12% simple interest for 2 years on March 10, 1991. On March 10, 1992, he made a partial payment of $1,000. Bill made a second partial payment of $500 on June 10, 1992. How much does Bill still owe on the loan after each partial payment?

Solution

First, let's look at a time line on this loan (Figure 8.12).

Step 1:   Determine the amount of interest to be paid on the principal from the beginning of the loan until the first partial payment; that is, for 1 year. This is the simple interest earned at 12% on $3,000 for 1 year.

$$I = PRT$$
$$I = \$3,000 \times .12 \times 1 = \$360$$

Step 2:   We must first pay off all of this accrued interest before any of the principal can be reduced. Subtract the interest, $360, from the partial payment to determine the remaining amount to be credited to the principal.

$$\text{partial payment} - \text{interest} = \text{balance of partial payment}$$
$$\$1,000 \qquad - \quad \$360 \quad = \qquad \$640$$

Step 3:   Subtract the amount to be used to reduce the principal from the principal to determine the unpaid principal, or balance, at the end of 1 year.

$$\text{principal} - \text{balance of partial payment} = \text{unpaid principal}$$
$$\$3,000 \quad - \qquad\qquad \$640 \qquad\qquad = \quad \$2,360$$

Let's update our time line now (Figure 8.13).

Now let's look at the second partial payment of $500, which is made ¼ year after the first partial payment. We apply the same steps to determine the new (reduced principal) balance.

Figure 8.12

Partial payment time line for Example 17

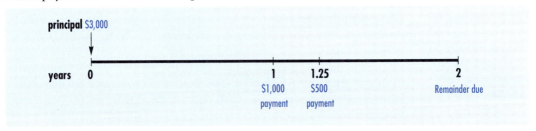

Figure 8.13

First partial payment calculation for Example 17, U.S. rule

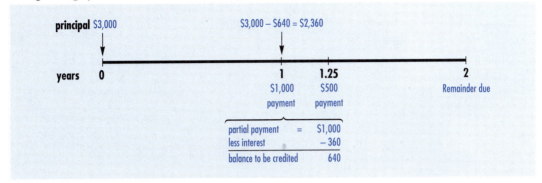

Step 4:   Determine the interest from the 1-year to the 1¼-year time periods.

$$I = PRT$$

$$P = \text{current balance (\$2,360)}$$

$$R = .12$$

$$T = \text{¼ year from 1 year to 1¼ year}$$

$$I = \$2,360 \times .12 \times \text{¼} = \$70.80$$

Step 5:   Subtract the interest from the partial payment.

amount to reduce principal = $500 − $70.80 = $429.20

Step 6:   Determine the balance of the principal and update the time line again, as shown in Figure 8.14.

balance = $2,360 − $429.20 = $1,930.80

Figure 8.14

Second partial payment calculation for Example 17, U.S. rule

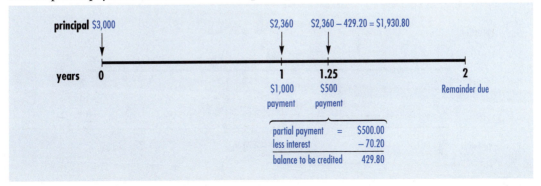

Figure 8.15

Final partial payment calculation for Example 17, U.S. rule

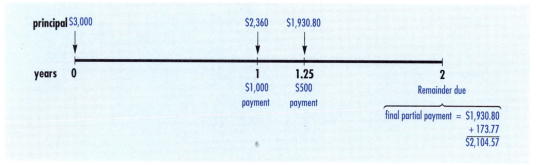

The interest for the remaining ¾ of a year will be calculated on the principal of $1,930.80, and will equal:

$$I = PRT = \$1,930.80 \times .12 \times \tfrac{3}{4} = \$173.77$$

The amount of the last payment will be $1,930.80 (unpaid principal) plus $173.77 (interest for the last ¾ year) = $2,104.57. (See Figure 8.15.)

Assuming Bill makes no more partial payments, and pays off the loan when it is due, he will have paid a total interest of $604.57. (See Figure 8.16.)

$$\text{total interest paid} = \$360 + \$70.80 + \$173.77 = \$604.57$$

If Bill had made no partial payments, and had simply paid off the principal and interest at the end of the 2-year period, he would have paid:

$$I = PRT = \$3,000 \times .12 \times 2 = \$720.00$$

Figure 8.16

Interest with partial payments

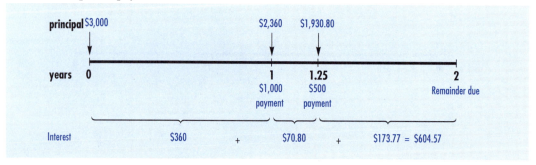

So, the partial payments saved him $115.43 in interest ($720 − $604.57 = $115.43).

THE MERCHANTS RULE

Learning objective
Use the merchants rule to calculate the adjusted maturity value of a loan when a partial payment is made.

The **merchants rule** differs from the U.S. rule in that the entire partial payment is used to reduce the principal of the loan for the remainder of the loan term. Let's use the previous example to compare the difference in the application of the partial payments between the U.S. rule and the merchants rule.

Example 18

Bill Lewkowicz borrowed $3,000 at 12% simple interest for 2 years on March 10, 1991. On March 10, 1992, he made a partial payment of $1,000. Bill made a second partial payment of $500 on June 10, 1992. How much does Bill still owe on the loan after each partial payment?

Solution

First, let's again look at a time line on this loan, Figure 8.17. Notice that in this time line we will focus on the *maturity value* of the loan.

Step 1: Determine the maturity value of the original loan.

maturity value = $P + (PRT)$
maturity value = $3,000 + ($3,000 × .12 × 2)
maturity value = $3,000 + $720 = $3,720

Step 2: Determine the interest the $1,000 partial payment would have earned from the time it was made until the end of the term of the loan (1 year).

$$I = PRT = \$1,000 \times .12 \times 1 = \$120$$

Figure 8.17

Partial payment time line for Example 18

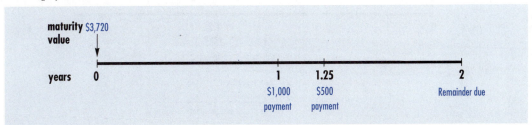

Figure 8.18

First partial payment calculation for Example 18, merchants rule

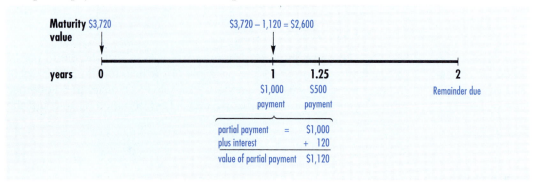

Step 3: Subtract the $1,000 partial payment plus the interest it would have earned from the maturity value of the loan. (See Figure 8.18.)

$$\begin{array}{ll} \text{adjusted maturity} & = \text{current} & - \text{value of} \\ \text{value of loan} & \quad \text{maturity value} & \quad \text{partial payment} \end{array}$$
$$= \$3,720 - \$1,120$$
$$= \$2,600$$

Now repeat steps 2 and 3 above for the $500 partial payment applied to the current $2,600 maturity value.

Step 4: Determine the interest the $500 partial payment would have earned from the time it was made until the end of the term of the loan (¾ year).

$$I = PRT = \$500 \times .12 \times ¾ = \$45$$

Figure 8.19

Second partial payment calculation for Example 18, merchants rule

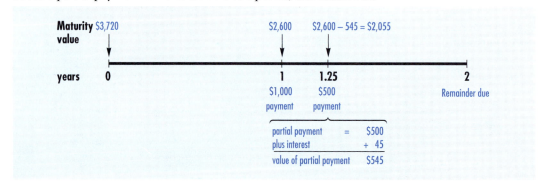

Step 5:   Subtract the $500 partial payment plus the interest it would have earned from the maturity value of the loan (Figure 8.19).

adjusted maturity value = $2,600 − $545
= $2,055

The total due at the end of the term of the loan is $2,055, which means the borrower would have paid a total of $3,555 ($1,000 + $500 + $2,055) for the $3,000 loan. In other words, he paid $555 in interest ($3,555 − $3,000 = $555). The partial payments saved him $165 in interest ($3,720 − $3,555 = $165).

The interest paid using the merchants rule ($555) is less than the interest paid using the U.S. rule ($604.57) since the entire partial payment was used to reduce the principal, rather than the interest being deducted first from the partial payment.

CHECK YOUR KNOWLEDGE

Partial payments of simple interest loans

Solve the following problems. Round dollar amounts to the nearest cent and rates to the nearest hundredth of a percent.

Mary Meston borrowed $8,000 at 10% simple interest for 1½ years on April 15, 1990. Mary made a $4,000 partial payment on April 15, 1991. Use this information to answer problems 1 through 4.

1. Use the U.S. rule to determine the principal balance on the loan after the partial payment.

2. Using the U.S. rule, determine the total amount of interest Mary will pay if no further partial payments are made except for the final payment to pay off the loan on October 15, 1991.

3. Use the merchants rule to determine the adjusted maturity value of Mary's loan as of April 15, 1991.

4. Use the merchants rule to determine Mary's total interest costs if she pays the remainder of the loan on the due date.

Jeff Jones borrowed $14,300 at 12.5% simple interest for 3 years. Jeff made partial payments of $8,500 at the end of 1 year, and $5,000 at the end of 1½ years, and then paid off the loan at the end of the term. Use this information to answer problems 5 through 8.

5. Use the U.S. rule to determine the principal balance on the loan after the first partial payment.

6. Use the U.S. rule to determine the principal balance on the loan after the second partial payment.

7.   Use the merchants rule to determine the adjusted maturity value of Jeff's loan after the first partial payment.

8.   Use the merchants rule to determine the adjusted maturity value of Jeff's loan after the second partial payment.

8.6   EXERCISES

Solve each of the following problems. Round dollar amounts to the nearest cent.

Bart Barlow borrowed $15,000 at 12% simple interest for 2 years on June 15, 1990. He made a partial payment of $9,000 on June 15, 1991. Use this information to answer exercises 1 through 4.

1.   Use the U.S. rule to determine the principal balance on the loan after the partial payment.

2.   Using the U.S. rule, determine the total amount of interest Bart will pay if no further partial payments are made except for the final payment to pay off the loan on June 15, 1992.

3.   Use the merchants rule to determine the adjusted maturity value of Bart's loan as of June 15, 1991.

4.   Use the merchants rule to determine Bart's total interest costs if he pays the remainder of the loan on June 15, 1992.

Lou's Martville Car Care service station borrowed $15,000 to purchase a new hoist for his tow truck. Lou borrowed the money on January 15 at 11.5% simple interest for 9 months. After 6 months, Lou made a partial payment of $9,000. Use this information to answer exercises 5 through 8.

5.   Use the U.S. rule to determine the principal balance on the loan after the partial payment.

6.   Using the U.S. rule, determine the total amount of interest Lou will pay if no further partial payments are made except for the final payment.

7.   Use the merchants rule to determine the adjusted maturity value of Lou's loan after the partial payment.

8.   Use the merchants rule to determine Lou's total interest costs if he pays the remainder of the loan at the end of the 9-month term of the loan.

Dr. Janice Marlow, DDS, borrowed $9,600 at 13.25% simple interest on March 20, 1991, for 18 months to purchase a new x-ray machine for her dental practice. She made a partial payment of $3,000 on June 20, 1991, and a second partial payment of $5,000 on April 20, 1992. Use this information to answer exercises 9 through 14.

9.   Use the U.S. rule to determine the principal balance on the loan after the first partial payment.

10.   Use the U.S. rule to determine the principal balance on the loan after the second partial payment.

11.   Using the U.S. rule, determine the total amount of interest Dr. Marlow will pay if no further partial payments are made except for the final payment to pay off the loan.

12.   Use the merchants rule to determine the adjusted maturity value of Dr. Barlow's loan as of the first partial payment.

13.   Use the merchants rule to determine the adjusted maturity value of Dr. Barlow's loan as of the second partial payment.

14.   Use the merchants rule to determine Dr. Barlow's total interest costs if she pays the re-

Answers to CYK: **1.** $4,800.00   **2.** $1,040.00   **3.** $5,000.00   **4.** $1,000.00   **5.** $7,587.50   **6.** $3,061.72   **7.** $17,537.50   **8.** $3,100.00

mainder of the loan at the end of the term of the loan.

Edwardson's Hog Farm needed to borrow $6,500 to purchase corn seed to plant for use as feed for its livestock. The owners signed a 6-month promissory note with 10% simple interest added, due August 15. Edwardson's made a partial payment of $1,500 after having the loan for 2 months. It made a second partial payment of $3,500 after having the loan for 4 months, and it paid off the loan early with a final partial payment at the end of 5 months. Use this information to answer exercises 15 through 20.

15. Use the U.S. rule to determine the principal balance on the loan after the first partial payment.

16. Use the U.S. rule to determine the principal balance on the loan after the second partial payment.

17. Using the U.S. rule, determine the total amount of interest Edwardson's will pay as of the final payment to pay off the loan.

18. Use the merchants rule to determine the adjusted maturity value of Edwardson's loan as of the first partial payment.

19. Use the merchants rule to determine the adjusted maturity value of Edwardson's loan as of the second partial payment.

20. Use the merchants rule to determine Edwardson's total interest costs if it pays the remainder of the loan at the end of the fifth month of the loan.

EXPRESS YOUR THOUGHTS

Compose one or two well-written sentences to express the requested information in your own words.

1. Explain how you would determine the interest rate in a simple interest problem wherein $168.75 was earned on a principal of $2500 in nine months.

2. Explain what is meant by the future value in a simple interest problem.

3. Describe the most important difference between ordinary interest and exact interest.

4. Describe the steps necessary to determine the exact number of days from January 15, 199x to March 1, 199x, inclusive.

5. Explain how a simple discount loan is different from a simple interest loan.

6. Explain why it is important to know the true interest rate of a simple discount loan.

7. In what way does the true interest rate differ from the discount rate of a discount loan?

8. What is a promissory note?

9. Who is the payee of a promissory note?

10. Who is the maker of a promissory note?

C a s e e x e r c i s e   The effects of inflation on an investment

We discussed the effects of inflation in our economy on our buying power. Inflation also affects the true value of our investment of money when we consider the buying power of the money our investment earns.

During 1991, the rate of inflation in the United States was approximately 3%, which means that we needed $1.03 at the end of 1991 to purchase the same goods that $1.00 would purchase at the beginning of 1991. The simple interest formula can help us with this calculation.

$A = P(1 + rt)$

  $P = \$1.00$
  $r = .03$ (3% rate of inflation)
  $t = 1$ year

$A = \$1[1 + (.03)(1 \text{ year})] = \$1.03$

Now let's assume that we had loaned $1.00 to a friend for 1 year at a simple interest rate of 12% during 1991. The $1.00 investment would have grown by 12% to be worth $1.12.

$A = P(1 + rt)$
$A = \$1[1 + (.12)(1 \text{ year})] = \$1.12$

But the true net gain in "buying power" would have been only $.09.

  Investment net gain = $1.12 − $1.03 = $.09

So, in effect, instead of having a 12% increase on our investment we have only a 9% gain.

Obviously, inflation detracts from our investment and should always be taken into account when considering different ways to invest money either short or long term. The technique described above can be applied to several consecutive years as well.

Alair Cash loaned John Q. Borrowman $10,000 at 11% simple interest for 3 years on January 1, 1989 (which meant it was due to be paid off on December 31, 1991). If the inflation rate was 5% for 1989, 6% for 1990, and 3% for 1991, calculate the following:

A. The amount of interest Alair received on her $10,000 investment.

B. The effect of inflation on each year and the total inflation of all 3 years on the $10,000 investment. Determine the inflated value of the investment.

C. The *net gain* of Alair's investment for the 3-year period when inflation is taken into account.

D. The actual rate of gain of Alair's investment when inflation is taken into account.

SELF-TEST

A.   T e r m i n o l o g y   r e v i e w

Complete the following items using the key terms presented at the beginning of the chapter. Check your responses against the answer key at the end of the test.

1.   The amount of money initially invested or borrowed is called the principle

2.   Money charged for the use of money is called interest.

3. Principal plus interest is the _maturity value_ .

4. Using a 360-day calendar year when calculating interest is called _ordinary_ interest.

5. Using a 365-day calendar year for the calculation of interest results in _exact_ interest.

6. The amount of money a borrower <u>actually</u> receives on a discount loan is called the _proceed_

7. The rate of interest calculated using simple interest methods on a <u>discount loan</u> is called the _true_ rate of interest.

8. _discounting_ a promissory <u>note means</u> that the interest is deducted in advance.

9. When a <u>partial</u> payment is made on a loan and the payment is used to <u>pay interest</u> accrued first, and then to decrease the principal, the _U.S. rule_ is being applied.

10. When a <u>partial payment</u> is made and the entire amount is applied to <u>the principal</u> of the loan, the _merchants rule_ is being applied.

B. Calculation review

Solve each of the following problems. Round dollar amounts to the nearest cent and rates to the nearest hundredth of a percent. Answers are provided at the end of the test.

11. What is the exact interest for a $1,000 loan from January 14 to June 28, 1991, at a 9¾% rate of simple interest?

12. What is the principal of an investment if the interest received on a 6-month 8% simple interest loan is $89?

13. What percent interest is the investor earning on a 2-year loan of $5,000 if $990 is the interest earned? (Round to the nearest tenth of a percent.)

14. When a business borrows $30,000 from a bank for 4 years at a 12.5% simple discount rate, what are the <u>proceeds</u> of the discounted loan?

15. What is the <u>true rate</u> of interest on a simple discount loan of $1,200 for 9 months at a 15% simple discount rate?

Use the following information to complete problems 16 through 18. Eberhard's Card Shoppe signed a promissory note with a face value of $8,000 for 18 months agreeing to pay the face value plus 10% simple interest to Bronxtown Citizens' Bank.

16. Determine the <u>maturity value</u> of the note.

17. Assume Citizens' Bank sells the note to Hometown Investors at a 14% discount rate after Citizens' had held the <u>note 8 months</u>. How much did Citizens' receive for the note?

Use the following information to solve problems 18 and 19. Martha Miller's Home Aids borrowed $4,500 for 6 months at 9% simple interest. A partial payment of $2,500 was made after 4 months.

18. Use the U.S. rule to determine the principal balance after the partial payment.

19. Use the merchants rule to determine the adjusted maturity value of the loan after the partial payment.

COMPOUND INTEREST AND ANNUITIES

Key terms

compound interest
compound amount
future value of a
    compound amount
periodic interest rate
present value of a
    compound amount
effective rate
nominal rate
annuity
future value of an
    ordinary annuity
present value annuity
sinking fund
amortization

Learning objectives

1. Explain the difference between simple interest and compound interest.

2. Calculate the compound interest and compound amount using the multistep method, formula, and compound interest tables.

3. Calculate the present value of a compound amount by using a formula and/or a table.

4. Identify *nominal rate* and *effective rate* and be able to distinguish between them.

5. Determine the effective rate by using a formula and/or a table.

6. Explain the difference between a compound amount and an annuity.

7. Calculate the future value of an ordinary annuity by using a formula and/or a table.

(continued)

8. Calculate the amount necessary to establish a present value annuity by using a formula and/or a table.

9. Calculate the regular payment necessary for establishing a sinking fund by using a formula and/or a table.

10. Calculate the equal regular payments that will amortize a specific sum of money over a set period of time.

11. Define the key terms.

INTRODUCTION

As we mentioned earlier in the text, there are different methods used for calculating interest. In Chapter 8, you learned the simple interest and bank discount methods. In this chapter, we will introduce the compound interest and annuities methods.

The calculations for compound interest and annuities are used to determine interest for savings accounts, and for setting up insurance schedules and pension plan benefit schedules. These calculations are also used to determine bond values, mortgage payments for a house, and monthly payments for a car.

In this chapter, we will discuss in detail the concept of compound interest as interest on original principal plus past interest earned. This discussion will extend from principal (as a single lump-sum deposit) to the concept of regular deposits that periodically add to the principal (that is, the total investment will grow in size by regular additions to the principal *as well as* by interest added per period). Finally, we will consider an investment made in the form of a single lump sum deposit that pays out of the fund a set amount periodically (regular payments) until the fund cancels itself out to zero dollars (i.e., liquidates itself). We refer to these last two concepts involving regular (periodic) payments as *annuities*.

9.1 COMPOUND INTEREST

Compound interest differs from simple interest in the following way. The principal amount in a *simple interest* calculation always remains the same,

Figure 9.1

Future value of a
compound amount

Learning objective
Explain the differ-
ence between simple
interest and com-
pound interest.

no matter how many days, years, or months are in the term of the investment or loan. The principal amount in a *compound interest* calculation is
increased periodically by adding the past interest earned to the previous
principal. **Compound interest** is calculated using the interest formula,
$I = PRT$, which multiplies the principal, *P*, times the rate, *R*, times the
time, *T* (where the principal includes previous interest already earned).
Figure 9.1 illustrates how the compound interest, when added to the principal (present value), accumulates up to the future value.

 P here is the principal that will grow to be the compound amount, *A*,
also called the future value.

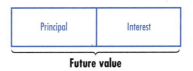

Principal   Interest

Future value

 In order to better understand the difference between simple interest and compound interest, let us examine the following two examples,
$P = \$1,000$; $R = 6\frac{1}{2}\%$, and $T = 3$ years.

Example 1

Ian Simon deposited $1,000 in a savings account that offered $6\frac{1}{2}\%$ simple
interest for 3 years. How much interest did Ian earn in the 3 years, and
what was the total value of his account at the end of 3 years?

Solution

At the end of 3 years, Ian had earned in interest

$$I = PRT = \$1,000 \times .065 \times 3 = \$195$$

The total value of Ian's account would be the maturity value of the simple
interest account:

$$M = P + I = \$1,000 + \$195 = \$1,195$$

Example 2

Ian Simon deposited $1,000 in a savings account that offered $6\frac{1}{2}\%$ interest
compounded (or calculated) *yearly*. Ian left the original principal plus all

of the accumulated interest in his savings account for 3 years. What was the total value of his account at the end of 3 years? How much interest did the account earn in the 3-year period?

Solution

Step 1:   Calculate the maturity value for the first year.

$$M = P + (PRT)$$
$$M = \$1,000 + (\$1,000 \times .065 \times 1) = \$1,065$$

The total amount at the end of the first year is $1,065

Step 2:   Calculate the maturity value for the second year. The principal here is the *sum* of the previous principal and the interest earned during the first year.

$$M = P + (PRT) = \$1,065 + (\$1,065 \times .065 \times 1)$$
$$M = \$1,065 + 69.23 = \$1,134.23$$

The total amount at the end of the second year is $1,134.23

Step 3:   Calculate the maturity value for the third year. The principal here is the *sum* of the previous principal and the interest earned during the first and second years.

$$M = P + (PRT) = \$1,134.23 + (\$1,134.23 \times .065 \times 1)$$
$$M = \$1,134.23 + 73.73 = \$1,207.96$$

The total amount at the end of the third year is $1,207.96. The total interest earned in the 3-year term is:

total interest $= \$1,207.96 - \$1,000 = \$207.96$

Let us now examine the solution to Example 2. The **compound amount** is the principal plus interest, where the principal includes previous interest already earned. Notice that the compound amount at the end of the first year ($1,065) is substituted into the formula as *P* at the beginning of the second year. This principal amount of $1,065 includes the previous interest of $65 earned during the first year. The principal amount of $1,065 at the beginning of the second year will now be earning interest throughout the second year. This process continues and the compound amount of $1,134.23 at the end of the second year is the principal amount of $1,134.23 at the beginning of the third year. Figure 9.2 illustrates the comparison of compound versus simple interest from Examples 1 and 2.

Notice that Examples 1 and 2 are virtually the same *except* that in Example 1 interest was calculated only on the original principal of $1,000 each year, and for Example 2 interest was calculated on the principal plus interest accumulated at the end of the first and second years. The simple

Figure 9.2

Time line comparison of simple interest and compound interest

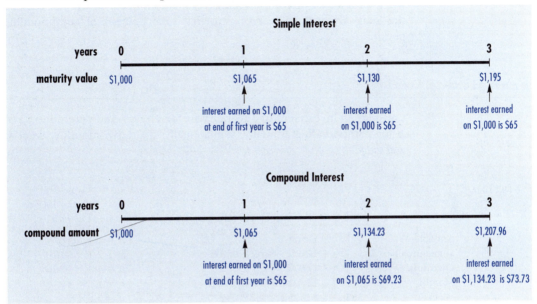

interest produced $195 ($65 each year) interest, whereas interest compounded yearly produced the greater amount of interest, $207.96 ($65 + $69.23 + $73.73 = $207.96).

Let's step back for a moment to remind ourselves what we are trying to accomplish here. We know the exact amount of money that we are investing *today*. What we are trying to find is an accumulated *future value*. The **future value of a compound amount** includes the original principal plus the interest.

MULTISTEP METHOD

Whenever interest is compounded more than once a year (e.g., semi-annually, quarterly, monthly, daily), the formula $I = PRT$ must be calculated for each *period* that interest is compounded during the length of the loan. If interest is compounded annually, then we calculate the interest for 1 period per year. If interest is compounded semiannually, quarterly, monthly, or weekly, there are 2, 4, 12, and 52 periods per year, respectively.

When the interest rate is given, it is given as an annual rate. Whenever interest is compounded more than once a year, the rate R must be adjusted for the number of times interest is compounded. We will let i represent the **periodic interest rate**, which is the annual interest rate divided by the total number of compounding periods in 1 year. We will need to know the total number of compounding periods that occur in the full term of the loan. We will let n represent that total number of compounding periods.

Example 3

Consider an investment of 12% per year for 5 years, and determine i and n for compounding annually, semiannually, quarterly, monthly, weekly, and daily.

Solution

Compounding	Periods per year	$i = \%$ /periods per year	$n =$ (periods per year /years)
Annually	1	12%/1 = 12%, or .12	$n = 1 \times 5 = 5$
Semiannually	2	12%/2 = 6%, or .06	$n = 2 \times 5 = 10$
Quarterly	4	12%/4 = 3%, or .03	$n = 4 \times 5 = 20$
Monthly	12	12%/12 = 1%, or .01	$n = 12 \times 5 = 60$
Weekly	52	12%/52 = .23%, or .0023	$n = 52 \times 5 = 260$
Daily	365	12%/365 = .03288%, or .0003288	$n = 365 \times 5 = 1{,}825$

Example 4

Joe Schulle deposited $100 into a savings account that offered 8% interest compounded semiannually. Joe kept the original deposit plus the accumulated interest in the savings account for 3 years. What was the accumulated amount at the end of 3 years?

Solution

The method we are using here is called the *multistep method* since we calculate the compound amount for each period, one step at a time, until we have the future amount. The first step is to calculate the interest for the first period, which is for the first half-year. Recall the yearly rate is 8% and this is compounded semiannually (2 times per year), so the periodic rate is:

$$i = \frac{R}{2} = \frac{.08}{2} = .04$$

Also note that T for compound interest will always equal 1, meaning "one" period.

Figure 9.3

Compound interest
time line

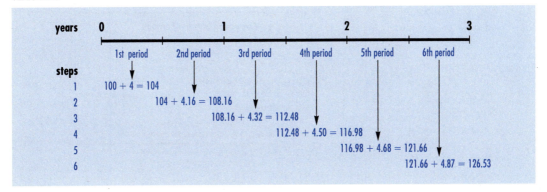

	P	**+**	**(P**	**×**	**i**	**×**	**T) =**	**Compound amount**
End of 1st period	100	+ (100		× .04 × 1)				
	100	+ 4					=	$104
End of 2nd period	104	+ (104		× .04 × 1)				
	104	+ 4.16					=	$108.16
End of 3rd period	108.16	+ (108.16 × .04 × 1)						
	108.16	+ 4.33					=	$112.49
End of 4th period	112.49	+ (112.49 × .04 × 1)						
	112.49	+ 4.50					=	$116.99
End of 5th period	116.99	+ (116.99 × .04 × 1)						
	116.99	+ 4.68					=	$121.67
End of 6th period	121.67	+ (121.67 × .04 × 1)						
	121.67	+ 4.87					=	$126.54

Figure 9.3 illustrates how the periodic interest amount is added to the previous principal to determine the new principal at the end of each period.

The compound amount at the end of three years is $126.53.

CALCULATING COMPOUND INTEREST USING A FORMULA

You can see from the previous examples how long and tedious the multi-step process of calculating compound interest can be. This can be avoided by using the formula in Figure 9.4. Let's use the formula to calculate the compound amount from Example 4.

Figure 9.4

Compound interest formula

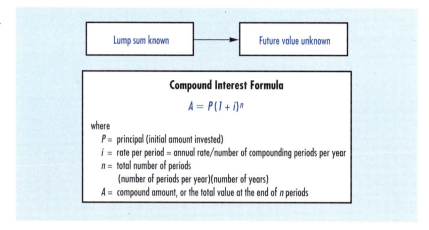

Example 5

Joe Schulle deposited $100 into a savings account that offered 8% interest compounded semiannually. Joe kept the original deposit plus the accumulated interest in the savings account for 3 years. What was the accumulated amount at the end of 3 years?

Solution

Refer to Figure 9.4. The lump sum (known) is $100. We are trying to determine the unknown future value.

$$A = P(1 + i)^n$$
$$P = \$100$$
$$i = \frac{R}{\text{periods per year}} = \frac{R}{2} = \frac{.08}{2} = .04$$
$$n = (\text{periods per year})(\text{years}) = 2 \times 3 = 6$$
$$A = \$100(1 + .04)^6$$
$$A = \$100(1.04)^6$$
$$A = \$100 \times 1.265319018 = \$126.53 \text{ (rounded to nearest cent)}$$

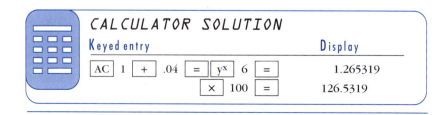

CALCULATING COMPOUND
INTEREST USING TABLES

Another method for computing compound interest is to use *compound interest tables*. A sample of these tables can be found in Table 9.1 and in the Appendix of this text. Column A in the tables in this text is titled "Future Value." In other sources, it may be referred to as "$1 at compound interest," or "future value of a present amount." The tables will act in lieu of the $\boxed{y^x}$ key on your calculator. Let us rework Example 4 to demonstrate how the tables work for us.

Example 6

Joe Schulle deposited $100 into a savings account that offered 8% interest compounded semiannually. Joe kept the original deposit plus the accumulated interest in the savings account for 3 years. What was the accumulated amount at the end of 3 years?

Solution

Refer to Figure 9.4. The lump sum (known) is $100. We are trying to determine the unknown future value.

Step 1:   Determine i in terms of %, and n.

$$i = \frac{\%}{\text{compounding periods per year}} = \frac{8\%}{2} = 4\%$$
$$n = (\text{compounding periods per year})(\text{years}) = (2)(3) = 6$$

Step 2:   Look in the future value for compound interest table in the column for 4% and the row for $n = 6$. Go to the table for rate = 4%. Now go to the compound amount table column A. Next, go down the n column until you reach the number 6, then move to the right until you reach the compound amount column. The number at the intersection of these two columns is 1.265319.

Step 3:   Multiply the principal ($100) times this table number.

$A = 100 \times$ (table value for $i = 4\%$ and $n = 6$)
$A = \$100 \times (1.265319) = \$126.5319$, or $126.53 (rounded)

We are still working with our formula for compound amount.

$A = P(1 + i)^n$
$A = 100(1.04)^6$. The compound interest tables will give us the value
    of $(1.04)^6$; that is $(1.04)^6 = 1.265319$
$A = 100(1.265319) = \$126.53$ (rounded)

Table 9.1

Sample compound interest table at 4%

N	A Future Value	B Present Value	C Ordinary Annuity	D Sinking Fund	E Present Annuity	F Amortization
	Rate = 4 %					
1	1.040000	0.961539	0.999999	1.000001	0.961538	1.040001
2	1.081600	0.924556	2.039999	0.490196	1.886094	0.530196
3	1.124864	0.888997	3.121597	0.320349	2.775088	0.360349
4	1.169859	0.854804	4.246462	0.235490	3.629893	0.275490
5	1.216653	0.821927	5.416319	0.184627	4.451821	0.224627
6	1.265319	0.790315	6.632972	0.150762	5.242135	0.190762
7	1.315932	0.759918	7.898289	0.126610	6.002053	0.166610
8	1.368569	0.730690	9.214220	0.108528	6.732742	0.148528
9	1.423312	0.702587	10.582790	0.094493	7.435328	0.134493
10	1.480244	0.675564	12.006100	0.083291	8.110891	0.123291
11	1.539454	0.649581	13.486340	0.074149	8.760472	0.114149
12	1.601032	0.624597	15.025800	0.066552	9.385071	0.106552
13	1.665073	0.600574	16.626820	0.060144	9.985642	0.100144
14	1.731676	0.577475	18.291900	0.054669	10.563120	0.094669
15	1.800943	0.555265	20.023570	0.049941	11.118380	0.089941
16	1.872981	0.533908	21.824510	0.045820	11.652290	0.085820
17	1.947900	0.513374	23.697490	0.042199	12.165660	0.082199
18	2.025816	0.493628	25.645390	0.038993	12.659290	0.078993
19	2.106848	0.474643	27.671200	0.036139	13.133930	0.076139

Table 9.2

Sample compound interest table at 1.5%

N	A Future Value	B Present Value	C Ordinary Annuity	D Sinking Fund	E Present Annuity	F Amortization
	Rate = 1.5 %					
1	1.015000	0.985222	0.999999	1.000001	0.985221	1.015001
2	1.030225	0.970662	2.014995	0.496279	1.955879	0.511279
3	1.045678	0.956317	3.045217	0.328384	2.912192	0.343384
4	1.061363	0.942184	4.090890	0.244446	3.854374	0.259446
5	1.077284	0.928261	5.152250	0.194090	4.782629	0.209090
6	1.093443	0.914543	6.229528	0.160526	5.697167	0.175526
7	1.109845	0.901027	7.322972	0.136557	6.598195	0.151557
8	1.126492	0.887711	8.432810	0.118584	7.485903	0.133584
9	1.143390	0.874593	9.559298	0.104610	8.360494	0.119610
10	1.160540	0.861668	10.702680	0.093435	9.222154	0.108435
11	1.177948	0.848934	11.863220	0.084294	10.071090	0.099294
12	1.195617	0.836388	13.041160	0.076680	10.907470	0.091680
13	1.213552	0.824028	14.236780	0.070241	11.731500	0.085241
14	1.231755	0.811850	15.450320	0.064724	12.543340	0.079724
15	1.250231	0.799852	16.682080	0.059945	13.343200	0.074945
16	1.268985	0.788032	17.932310	0.055765	14.131230	0.070765
17	1.288019	0.776386	19.201290	0.052080	14.907610	0.067080
18	1.307340	0.764912	20.489300	0.048806	15.672520	0.063806
19	1.326950	0.753608	21.796640	0.045879	16.426130	0.060879

Joe's compound amount is $126.53, and he has earned $26.53 in interest during the 3 years he invested it. Notice that multiplying the number in the table (1.265319) by the principal ($100) was exactly what we did when using the formula in Example 5.

At this time, it is important to understand exactly what the numbers in the table are telling us. Let's refer to the number that we just looked up, 1.265319. What exactly is this number telling us? Essentially, it indicates that if we had invested $1 at 8% interest compounded semiannually, at the end of 3 years we would have a compound amount of $1.27 (this amount was obtained by rounding 1.265319). However, we did not invest $1, but rather we invested $100, which is why we multiplied the $100 principal by the number in the table to obtain the compound amount of $126.53.

CHECK YOUR KNOWLEDGE

Compound interest

Solve the following problems. Round dollar amounts to the nearest cent and rates to the nearest hundredth of a percent.

Use the multistep method for problems 1 and 2.

1. Determine the compound amount at the end of 4 years for $20,000 deposited at 10% interest compounded annually.

2. If $2,500 is deposited for 3 months into an account paying 18% interest compounded monthly, determine: (a) the compound amount at the end of 3 months and (b) the amount of interest earned during this time.

3. Identify i and n for each of the following: (a) 6% compounded quarterly for 4 years, (b) 10.5% compounded semiannually for 5 years, (c) 12% compounded monthly for 6 years, (d) 10% compounded weekly for 3 years, and (e) 15% compounded daily for 5 years. (Use 360 days per year.)

Use the compound interest formula to complete problems 4 through 6.

4. Determine the compound amount of $30,000 invested at 6% compounded semiannually for 4 years.

5. Find the compound interest for a $13,500 investment at 12% compounded quarterly for 2 years.

6. If $7,000 is invested at 18% compounded monthly for 1 year, determine (a) the compound amount and (b) the total interest earned.

Use the compound interest tables to complete problems 7 through 8.

7. Fred Rooney invested $25,000 in a compound interest account paying 6% compounded monthly for 5 years. Determine the value of (a) Fred's investment at the end of 5 years and (b) the interest earned.

8. Emily Broadbent has a certificate of deposit that pays 12% compounded quarterly. If Emily's initial investment was $17,500 and it is a 6-year certificate, what will the value of the certificate be at the end of the 6-year term?

9.1 EXERCISES

Solve the following exercises. Round dollar amounts to the nearest cent and rates to the nearest hundredth of a percent.

Determine i and n.

Rate/ year	Compounding	Number of years	i	n
1. 8%	semiannually	9	_____	_____
2. 21%	quarterly	6	_____	_____
3. 6%	monthly	10	_____	_____
4. 9½%	yearly	30	_____	_____
5. 10%	quarterly	15	_____	_____

Find (a) the compound amount and (b) the compound interest using the multistep method for each of the following.

6. $3,000 at 6% compounded quarterly for 1 year.

7. $7,000 at 11% compounded semiannually for 2 years.

8. $300,000 at 9½% compounded yearly for 3 years.

9. $1,000 at 11.5% compounded semiannually for 2 years.

10. $10,000 at 4% compounded quarterly for 1 year.

11. $10,000 at 5% compounded quarterly for 12 months.

Determine the compound amount (future value) using the compound interest formula.

12. $5,000 at 6% compounded monthly for 10 years.

13. $5,000 at 6% compounded quarterly for 10 years.

Answers to CYK: **1.** $29,282   **2.** a. $2,614.20; b. $114.20   **3.** a. i = .015; n = 16; b. i = .0525; n = 10; c. i = .01; n = 72; d. i = .001923; n = 156; e. i = .0004166...; n = 1,800   **4.** $38,003.10   **5.** $3,601.40   **6.** a. $8,369.33; b. $1,369.33 **7.** a. $33,721.28; b. $8,721.28   **8.** $35,573.90

14. $5,000 at 6% compounded semiannually for 10 years.

15. $5,000 at 6% compounded annually for 10 years.

16. $35,000 at 12% compounded monthly for 9 years.

In problems 17–23, determine the compound amount using the compound interest tables found in Appendix A.

17. $5,000 at 6% compounded monthly for 10 years

18. $5,000 at 6% compounded quarterly for 10 years

19. $5,000 at 6% compounded semiannually for 10 years

20. $5,000 at 6% compounded annually for 10 years

21. $10,000 at 7% compounded semiannually for 8 years

22. $35,000 at 12% compounded monthly for 7 years

23. $11,000 at 9% compounded semiannually for 4 years

Solve the following exercises using either the compound interest formula or the compound interest tables.

24. Connors Realty Corp. enjoyed a fruitful month of income last month and found that it had $30,000 that it could invest in a compound interest investment paying 12% compounded monthly. If the firm leaves the money in the account for 2½ years, what will be the value of the account at that time?

25. Bianco Big "B" Markets made a $13,000 investment in a compound interest account paying 18% compounded monthly. What was the value of its investment at the end of 8 months?

26. Hazelmyer Heirloom Plastic Furniture borrowed $125,000 from a bank to make improvements in its showroom. If it borrowed the money at 10% compounded quarterly for

3 years, how much will it owe at the end of the 3-year period?

27. Sally Betson invested $300 at 6% compounded monthly for a total of 3 years. Sally took the total value of her investment at the end of 3 years, and added $500 to it and invested the total at 8% compounded quarterly for 4 years. What was her total investment worth at the end of the 7-year period?

Use the following information to complete problems 28 through 30. Rita Menkins recently inherited $43,500. She has chosen to invest it in an insurance policy that guarantees to pay 10% compounded quarterly for the first 5 years, and a minimum of 6% compounded quarterly for the remaining 3 years of the policy.

28. Determine the value of Rita's investment at the end of the first 5-year period.

29. Determine the value of Rita's investment at the end of the last 3-year period, assuming she only receives the minimum rate and that she leaves all her money in the investment account.

30. Determine the total interest Rita will earn over the 8-year term of the policy assuming she receives only the minimum rate for the last 3 years.

31. Jack LaMonti borrowed $10,000 and agreed to pay interest at 8% compounded quarterly. How much will Jake have to pay at the end of the term of the loan if he keeps the loan for 2 years?

32. Herbert Farnsley deposited $7,850 into an account paying 10% compounded twice yearly. Determine (a) the compound amount and (b) the interest earned if he leaves all of the money in the account for 8 years.

33. Charlene Jenkins borrowed $40,000 to purchase new equipment for her Copies-Plus Shoppe. If she agreed to pay 12% compounded monthly for the use of the money for 2 years, how much will she have to have to pay off the loan at the end of the 2-year period?

9.2   PRESENT VALUE OF A COMPOUND AMOUNT

Learning objective
Calculate the present value of a compound amount by using a formula and/or a table.

In Section 9.1, we learned how to find a compound amount (future value) when given the amount of the principal plus the terms of interest. In this section, the problems presented will be just the opposite; that is, we will be given the compound amount that we need to attain in the future and our unknown variable will be the principal, which we will call the present value. The **present value of a compound amount** is the amount of principal that we need to invest *today* to attain our desired future value, as depicted in Figure 9.5.

P here is the principal, which will grow to be the compound amount, A, also called the future value. P in this case is also called the present value of the compound amount.

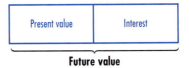

Future value

Example 7

Cheryl Terry wishes to have $12,000 2 years from now in order to buy the car she has her eye on. What amount of money does she need to invest in her savings account today at an interest rate of 6% compounded quarterly in order to attain her goal?

Solution

This is a compound interest problem in which we know the future value, A ($12,000), and we need to determine P (present value) if it is to grow at an interest rate of 6% compounded quarterly for 2 years. Using the compound interest formula,

$$A = P(1 + i)^n$$
$$A = P(\text{table value for } i = 1.5\% \text{ and } n = 8)$$
$$A = \$12,000$$
$$i = \frac{6\%}{4} = 1.5\%$$
$$n = 2 \text{ years} \times 4 \text{ quarters per year} = 8$$
$$\$12,000 = P(1.126492)$$

Figure 9.5

Present value of a compound amount

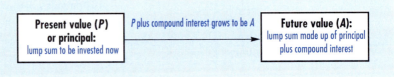

Next, solve for *P* by dividing both sides by 1.126492.

$$P = \frac{\$12,000}{1.126492} = \$10,652.533 = \$10,652.53 \text{ (rounded)}$$

The above calculation for *P* is the same as

$$P = \$12,000 \times \frac{1}{1.126492}$$

This fraction, 1/1.126492, is the same as .8877111 and the calculation is the same as:

$$P = \$12,000 \times \frac{1}{1.126492} = \$12,000 \times (.8877111)$$

This value can be found in the present value tables.

Refer back to Table 9.2 (page 338), which has a sample of the present value tables for a compound amount at the 1.5% rate. Looking down column B, present value, to where the *n* column equals 8, the intersection of that row and column is the value .8877111.

We can check our solution by solving the compound interest formula for *A*, using *P* = $10,652.53, *i* = .015, and *n* = 8. If *A* is the desired $12,000, then we have correctly found the present value.

$$A = \$10,652.53 \times (1.015)^8 = \$11,999.96$$

The slight discrepancy here is due to the rounding of $10,652.533 to $10,652.53.

What does our answer of $10,652.53 mean to us? It means that at 6% interest compounded quarterly, Cheryl Terry must deposit or invest $10,652.53 *today* so that this amount plus interest will accumulate to $12,000 in 2 years time and Cheryl may buy her car. The $12,000 amount is the *future value* of her account. The *present value* is the amount that must be in the account *at the present time* to generate the necessary interest to achieve that future value in 2 years.

Once again, it is important to understand exactly what the numbers in the table are telling us. Let us refer to the number .8877111 that we obtained from the present value table. If Cheryl Terry had wished to have $1 two years from now, at 6% interest compounded quarterly, she would have had to invest approximately $.89 today. (The $.89 came from rounding .88771112.) However, Cheryl wished to have $12,000, not $1, so we needed to multiply .88771112 by $12,000.

It is also important to understand that the present value of a compound amount uses the same compound interest formula, $A = P(1 + i)^n$, that we used in Section 9.1. The difference is that we solve the formula for P, called our principal or present value.

$$A = P(1 + i)^n$$

$$\frac{A}{(1 + i)^n} = P\frac{\cancel{(1 + i)^n}}{\cancel{(1 + i)^n}}$$

$$P = A\frac{1}{(1 + i)^n} \qquad \text{present value formula}$$

$$P = \$12{,}000 \times \frac{1}{(1 + .06/4)^8}$$

$$= \$12{,}000 \times .88771112$$

$$P = \$10{,}652.53 \text{ (rounded)}$$

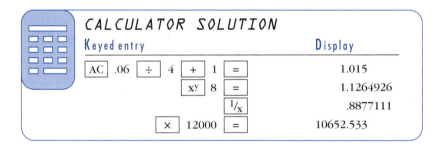

CALCULATOR SOLUTION

Keyed entry	Display
AC .06 ÷ 4 + 1 =	1.015
x^y 8 =	1.1264926
1/x	.8877111
× 12000 =	10652.533

Let's look at another problem in which we use only the tables to solve the problem. Please note that although tables are a helpful tool in making our work a bit easier, tables are not available for all situations. Consequently, you should be familiar with the formula and be able to use it if necessary.

Example 8

H. R. Jason anticipates the need to replace an office copier in 5 years. How much should the company invest in a compound interest account paying 18% compounded monthly so that it will have the $5,000 in 5 years?

Solution

Refer to Figure 9.6 (page 346). The future value (known) is $5,000. We are trying to determine the lump sum.

For Your Information

IRAs can earn you more money

Individual retirement accounts (IRAs) became very popular in 1981 when they could be used by just about everyone as a tax deferred investment. That meant that each year a person could designate $2,000 of savings as a contribution to an IRA and not pay taxes on that money until withdrawing it from the account. In 1986, certain restrictions (as indicated in the diagram) were instituted by the government that made IRAs less accessible to the general public. A taxpayer in the 28% tax bracket who invested $2,000 in an IRA at 7% each year for 25 years could accrue over $130,000. If the investor paid income taxes on the $2,000 instead of investing in the IRA, the effect of the dollars lost to taxes would be to reduce the rate from 7% to 5%, and the resulting future value would be a bit less than $100,000 ($30,000 less).

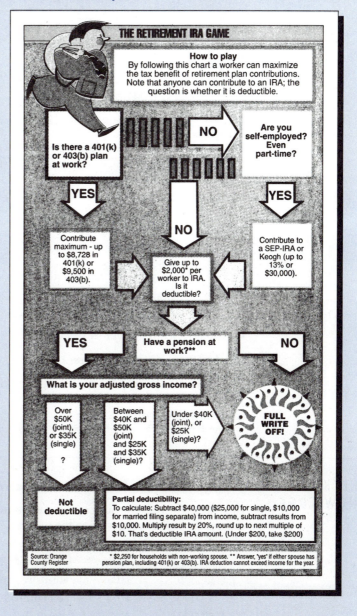

THE RETIREMENT IRA GAME

How to play
By following this chart a worker can maximize the tax benefit of retirement plan contributions. Note that anyone can contribute to an IRA; the question is whether it is deductible.

Is there a 401(k) or 403(b) plan at work?

NO → Are you self-employed? Even part-time?

YES → Contribute maximum - up to $8,728 in 401(k) or $9,500 in 403(b).

NO

YES → Contribute to a SEP-IRA or Keogh (up to 13% or $30,000).

Give up to $2,000* per worker to IRA. Is it deductible?

YES

Have a pension at work?**

NO

What is your adjusted gross income?

Over $50K (joint), or $35K (single) ?

Between $40K and $50K (joint) and $25K and $35K (single)?

Under $40K (joint), or $25K (single)?

FULL WRITE OFF!

Not deductible

Partial deductibility:
To calculate: Subtract $40,000 ($25,000 for single, $10,000 for married filing separate) from income, subtract results from $10,000. Multiply result by 20%, round up to next multiple of $10. That's deductible IRA amount. (Under $200, take $200)

Source: Orange County Register

* $2,250 for households with non-working spouse. ** Answer, 'yes' if either spouse has pension plan, including 401(k) or 403(b). IRA deduction cannot exceed income for the year.

Source: The *Orange County Register*, April 20, 1992, as it appeared in the Syracuse *Herald-Journal*, April 20, 1992. Reprinted with permission of The *Orange County Register*, copyright 1992.

Figure 9.6

Present value
formula

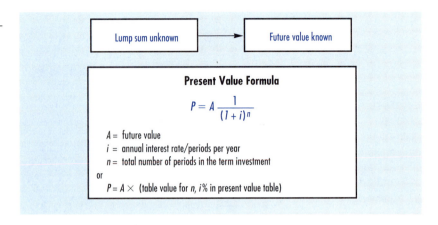

$P = A \times$ (present value table value for n, i)

$A = \$5,000$

$i = \dfrac{18\%}{12} = 1.5\%$

$n = 5$ years $\times$ 12 periods per year $= 60$

$P = (\$5,000)(.409296)$ (see Table 9.2, page 338)

$ = \$2,046.4798$, or $\$2,046.48$

We can check our answer by calculating

$A = P(1 + i)^n = \$2,046.48(2.4432198) = \$5,000$

If H. R. Jason invests $2,046.48 in a compound interest account paying 18% compounded monthly and leaves it there untouched for 5 years, the account will be worth $5,000.

CHECK YOUR KNOWLEDGE

Present value of a compound amount

Determine the present value of the compound amount for each set of conditions. Round your answers to the nearest cent.

	Future value	Rate per year	Compounded	Number of years	Present value
1.	$7,000	10%	annually	5	_____
2.	$7,000	10%	semiannually	5	_____
3.	$7,000	10%	quarterly	5	_____
4.	$8,000	6%	monthly	3	_____
5.	$3,750	8%	semiannually	8	_____
6.	$14,900	12%	monthly	7	_____

Solve the following word problems. Round dollar amounts to the nearest cent and rates to the nearest hundredth of a percent.

7. Your company needs to have $40,465 five years from now. If the interest rate at your bank is 6% compounded monthly, how much will you need to deposit into your account today in order to have the desired amount in 5 years?

8. If a compound amount in 1 year is $575,000, what is the present value of this amount if the interest terms are 8% compounded quarterly?

9. The interest rate at your bank is 12% compounded quarterly. If someone gave you a choice of either receiving $27,443 six years from now or receiving a lesser amount today that you could deposit in your bank, what is the least amount you could accept for payment today and still have the $27,443 value in 6 years?

10. Nancy Wilkinson won a contest that will pay her $100,000 3 years from now. How much must the contest organizers deposit today into a compound interest account paying 10% compounded quarterly in order to have the required payoff amount for Nancy in 3 years?

9.2   EXERCISES

Solve the following exercises. Round each dollar amount to the nearest cent and each rate to the nearest hundredth of a percent.

In exercises 1 through 8, determine the present value of the compound amount.

	Future value	Rate	Compounded	Time	Present value
1.	$1,000	7.5%	annually	3 years	_____
2.	$10,500	9%	semiannually	2 years	_____
3.	$6,300	6%	monthly	$1\frac{1}{2}$ years	_____
4.	$23,450	14%	quarterly	4 years	_____
5.	$81,540	8%	annually	24 months	_____

6. Determine the principal that must be deposited at 10% compounded annually to have an amount of $5,000 in 5 years.

7. MacGregor Sports Shoppe in Kermittown agrees to pay a $5,000 scholarship to the outstanding junior high school athletes, one male and one female, at the end of successful completion of their first year of college (i.e., 5 years after they receive the award). How much must MacGregor invest in a com-

Answers to CYK: **1.** $4,346.45   **2.** $4,297.40   **3.** $4,271.90   **4.** $6,685.16   **5.** $2,002.16
  6. $6,459.39   **7.** $29,999.62   **8.** $531,211.45   **9.** $13,500.14
  10. $74,355.60

pound interest account paying 12% compounded quarterly in each winner's name in order to have the correct amount to award them at the end of 5 years?

8. Bob Farley wants to have $11,500 to purchase a new auto 2 years from now. How much must he invest in a compound interest account paying 8% compounded semiannually in order to achieve his goal?

Use the following information to solve exercises 9 through 12. Mary Walton's parents know that Mary is going to attend a state college where the tuition, room and board, and other costs for each year for the next 4 years will be approximately $6,000. Mary's parents have saved for her education and they decide to invest money in four separate certificates of deposit (compound interest accounts) each of which will mature at the beginning of a new academic year (i.e., the first will mature at the beginning of her freshman year, the second at the beginning of her sophomore year, and so on). Mary will begin college one year from now. Each certificate of deposit will earn 10% compounded quarterly.

9. How much must be invested in the first CD in order for Mary to have $5,800 at the beginning of her freshman year?

10. How much must be invested in the second CD in order for Mary to have $5,800 at the beginning of her sophomore year?

11. How much must be invested in the third CD

in order for Mary to have $5,800 at the beginning of her junior year?

12. How much must be invested in the fourth CD in order for Mary to have $5,800 at the beginning of her senior year?

Use the following information to solve exercises 13 through 17. Marcia Jankowski worked for 5 years after graduation from college and saved her money in order to pay for 3 years of law school, which she will begin 1 year from now. Edinborough Bank will offer Marcia the following rates on certificates of deposit:

1 year	8% compounded quarterly
2 year	10% compounded quarterly
3 year	12% compounded quarterly

13. How much must Marcia deposit in the 1-year CD in order to have $15,000 for her first year costs?

14. How much must she deposit in a 2-year CD in order to have $15,750 for her second year costs?

15. How much must she deposit in a 3-year certificate in order to have $16,500 for her third year costs?

16. Assuming Marcia does follow this plan, how much will she have invested for her law degree?

17. How much interest will she have earned if she follows this plan?

Solve the following problems. Round each dollar amount to the nearest cent and each rate to the nearest hundredth of a percent.

	Principal	R	Period	Total time	Future value
18.	$19,300	12%	quarterly	5 years	_____
19.	_____	18%	monthly	20 months	$450
20.	$3,250	10%	semiannually	6 years	_____
21.	_____	8%	quarterly	10 quarters	$2,780
22.	$6,500	15%	daily	2 years	_____
23.	$19,300	12%	quarterly	5 years	_____
24.	_____	18%	monthly	20 months	$1,000
25.	$3,250	10%	semiannually	6 years	_____
26.	$2,870	8%	quarterly	10 quarters	_____
27.	_____	15%	daily	2 years	$6,550

28. Hartnett Heating and Air Conditioning borrowed $75,000 at 12% interest compounded monthly for 1 year. At the end of the loan term, the company paid off its total debt (principal and interest). How much did Hartnett pay back totally, and how much interest did it pay?

29. Happy Hideaway Campground anticipates that an expenditure of $16,500 will be necessary to renovate the lavatory and laundromat areas of the campground. The management wishes to set aside the money now for the renovation project, which will begin in one year. If they can invest the money they set aside at 14% interest compounded quarterly, what is the minimum they should invest in order to meet their goals?

30. Anslow Furniture Company deposited $53,000 into an account paying 12% interest compounded monthly and left it there for 8 months. How much interest did the company earn on the investment?

31. Hamilton Warehousing must replace two forklift trucks 5 years from now. If each truck will cost $19,500, what is the present value of the trucks if money can be invested at 12% interest compounded monthly?

32. The interest rate at your bank is 14%, compounded quarterly. If someone gave you a choice of either receiving $15,500 eight years from now or receiving a lesser amount today that you could deposit in your bank, what is the least amount you could accept for payment today and still have the $15,500 value in 8 years?

9.3   EFFECTIVE RATE

Learning objective
Identify *nominal rate* and *effective rate* and be able to distinguish between them.

Savings institutions today offer a wide variety of opportunities for people to safely invest money in compound interest accounts. Such accounts offer a variety of annual interest rates and compounding periods. Investors need a means by which these different forms of compound interest opportunities can be compared so that they can make choices wisely. Effective rate is a tool we can use to make comparisons between different compound interest opportunities.

Effective rate is the rate of simple interest you would need to receive from a bank so that the simple interest account will earn the same amount of interest in 1 year as a specific compound interest account would earn in 1 year. **Nominal rate** is the compound interest rate for 1 year.

Example 9

The Whimsical National Bank of Condolenceville offers a compound interest account with a nominal (yearly) rate of 8% compounded quarterly. What annual simple interest rate (effective rate) would yield the same earnings?

Solution

simple interest:

$$A = P + (PRT)$$
$$A = P(1 + RT), \quad T = 1 \text{ year}$$
$$A = P(1 + R)$$

compound interest:

$$A = P(1 + i)^n$$

where

$$i = \frac{\text{nominal (yearly rate)}}{\text{number of compounding periods in 1 year}}$$

In this case,

$$A = P\left(1 + \frac{.08}{4}\right)^4$$

Let's let our principal P be \$1, then each dollar we invest ($P = \$1$) in the compound account will accumulate to a future value of $A = 1(1 + .02)^4 = 1.0824322$. Each \$1 we invest in the simple interest account will accumulate to $A = 1(1 + R)$.

simple interest:

$$A = P(1 + PR), \qquad P = \$1$$
$$A = 1(1 + 1R)$$
$$A = 1 + R \qquad \text{(This } R \text{ will be our effective rate, so we will label it } R_{\text{eff}}.)$$
$$A = 1 + R_{\text{eff}}$$

compound interest:

$$A = P(1 + i)^n$$
$$P = \$1$$
$$i = \frac{.08}{4} = .02$$
$$n = 4 \text{ periods in 1 year}$$
$$A = 1(1 + .02)^4$$
$$A = 1.0824322$$

Now the "A" value for simple interest must *equal* the "A" value of compound interest, so let's set them equal to each other.

$$\text{simple interest} = \text{compound interest}$$
$$1 + R_{\text{eff}} = 1.0824322$$
$$R_{\text{eff}} = 1.0824322 - 1$$
$$R_{\text{eff}} = .0824322$$

or

$$R_{\text{eff}} = 8.24\% \text{ (rounded)}$$

Effective rate formula

$$R_{\text{eff}} = (1 + i)^m - 1$$

$$i = \frac{(\text{nominal rate})}{m}$$

m = number of compounding periods in 1 year

Learning objective
Determine the effective rate by using a formula and/or a table.

We can determine effective rate either by using a calculator alone, or by using compound interest tables.

Three-step method for finding effective rate using compound interest tables

Step 1:   Look up table value for m and i% in compound interest table.

Step 2:   Subtract 1 from this table value. This is the effective rate in decimal form.

Step 3:   Multiply the result of step 2 by 100 to give effective rate in % form.

Example 10

Determine the effective rate of a compound interest account paying 6% interest compounded monthly.

Solution

First we will use the three-step method:

Step 1: Determine m and i% and look up the table value $m = 12$ compounding periods in one year:

$$i\% = \frac{6\%}{12} = .5\% \text{ per month.}$$

The table value for $m = 12$; $i\% = .5\% = 1.061678$.

Step 2: Subtract 1 from table value:

$$R_{\text{eff}} = 1.061678 - 1 = .0616787 \text{ (decimal form).}$$

Step 3: Multiply by 100 to put in % form:

$$R_{\text{eff}} = .061678 \times 100 = 6.17\% \text{ (rounded).}$$

Second, let's look at the calculator solution for this problem:

$$R_{\text{eff}} = (1 + i)^m - 1$$

$$= \left(1 + \frac{.06}{12}\right)^{12} - 1$$

$= 1.06168 - 1$ (value from compound interest table)

$= .06168$, or 6.17% (rounded)

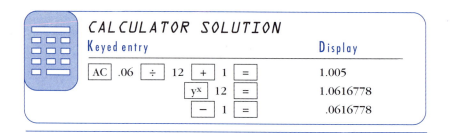

CALCULATOR SOLUTION

Keyed entry	Display
AC .06 ÷ 12 + 1 =	1.005
yˣ 12 =	1.0616778
− 1 =	.0616778

Example 11

Emilio Fernandez has an opportunity to invest his money in an account paying 12% compounded quarterly or into a second account paying 12% compounded monthly. Which account has the better yield?

Solution

To determine the better yield, we compare the effective rates of the two opportunities. The higher effective rate will be the better yield. (The *yield* on an investment is the same as the *effective rate* of the investment: the two expressions are used interchangeably.) First we use the three-step method. Determine the effective rate for the 12% quarterly:

Step 1: $m = 4$, $i\% = 3\%$ table value $= 1.125509$
Step 2: $R_{\text{eff}} = .125509$
Step 3:   or 12.55%

Determine the effective rate for 12% monthly:

Step 1: $m = 12$, $i\% = 1\%$ table value $= 1.126825$
Step 2: $R_{\text{eff}} = .126825$
Step 3:   or 12.68%

The second rate has a better yield, so Emilio would earn .13% more interest by investing at 12% monthly.

If you were to use a calculator the solution for this problem would be as follows:

12% interest compounded quarterly

$$R_{\text{eff}} = \left(1 + \frac{.12}{4}\right)^4 - 1 = .1255, \text{ or } 12.55\%$$

12% interest compounded monthly

$$R_{\text{eff}} = \left(1 + \frac{.12}{12}\right)^{12} - 1 = .1268, \text{ or } 12.68\%$$

Again, we can see that the first rate has a better yield, so Emilio would earn .13% more interest by investing at 12% monthly.

CHECK YOUR KNOWLEDGE

Effective rate

Solve the following problems. Round rates to a hundredth of a percent.

A credit union offers 12.0% compounded quarterly. Use this information to answer the following.

1. What is the nominal rate? *Base amount*
2. What is the periodic rate? *little "i" .3%*
3. What is the compounding period? *4*
4. Determine the effective rate for deposits made in this credit union.

Compute the effective rate (R_{eff}) for each of the following:

Nominal rate (yearly rate)	Compounding periods	Number of compounding periods per year	R_{eff}
5. 12%	semiannually	_____	_____
6. 10%	quarterly	_____	_____
7. 6%	monthly	_____	_____

Tara Buffa can earn 8% compounded quarterly at Blarneyville Bank, or she can earn 9% compounded semiannually at Morristown First National Bank. Use this information to answer the following.

8. Determine the effective yield at Blarneyville Bank. *8.24%*
9. Determine the effective yield at Morristown First National. *9.2%*
10. Which bank has the higher yield, and what is the difference? *.96%*

Answers to CYK: *1.* 12%   *2.* 3%   *3.* quarter   *4.* 12.55%   *5.* 12.36%   *6.* 10.38%
7. 6.17%   *8.* 8.24%   *9.* 9.20%   *10.* Morristown First Nat'l; .96% difference

9.3   EXERCISES

Solve the following exercises (round rates to the nearest hundredth of a percent).

Compute the effective rate (R_{eff}) for each of the following. *Note:* You will need a scientific calculator to complete exercises 7 and 8.

Nominal rate (yearly rate)	Compounding periods	Number of compounding periods per year	R_{eff}
1. 18%	semiannually	_____	_____
2. 18%	quarterly	_____	_____
3. 18%	monthly	_____	_____
4. 15%	semiannually	_____	_____
5. 15%	quarterly	_____	_____
6. 12%	monthly	_____	_____
7. 18%	weekly	_____	_____
8. 18%	daily (360 days)	_____	_____

9. Chemung Bank and Trust offered a compound interest account paying 10% compounded quarterly. What should it advertise as their effective yield on the account?

Use the following information to answer exercises 10 through 12. Juan Carlos is wondering whether it would be wiser to invest in a compound interest investment paying 10% compounded quarterly or one paying 11% semiannually.

10. What is the effective rate of the 10% investment?

11. What is the effective rate of the 11% investment?

12. Determine the difference of the two yields (higher yield − lower yield), and determine

how much more interest would be earned in 1 year on a $1,000 investment.

13. Merchants State Bank advertises that its regular savings account pays 6% interest compounded monthly for an annual yield of 6.2%. Is its claim correct?

14. First Trust and Deposit advertises that its effective yield on 10% interest compounded quarterly is 10.5%. Determine the magnitude of the error in this claim.

15. (Scientific calculator required) Jackson Investment offers a money market account for 8% compounded daily (365 days). If you invested $10,000 with Jackson for exactly 1 year, (a) what would be the effective rate of the account and (b) how much interest would you earn?

9.4   FUTURE VALUE ANNUITIES

An annuity is a special type of compound interest account. The concept of compound interest thus far presented establishes a principal with one lump sum that remains in the account and earns interest. The principal increases only as the interest earned is added to it.

An **annuity** provides a series of periodic deposits into the account or periodic payments out of the account, which add to or subtract from the

Figure 9.7

Future value of an annuity

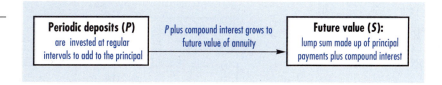

principal. Here we will examine future value (deposit into account) annuities, as depicted in Figure 9.7; present value (payment out of account) annuities will be discussed in Section 9.5.

p here is the regular equal payments that will each earn interest and accumulate to be a lump sum amount we will denote as S, also called the future value.

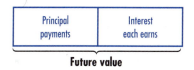

Suppose we agree to pay $100 per year, at the end of each year, into an account paying 8% compounded annually for 4 years. This type of account is called an *ordinary annuity*, which means that the payments are made at the end of each period. Consider the diagram in Figure 9.8, which illustrates the activity in this account.

Figure 9.8

Time line for the future value of an ordinary annuity

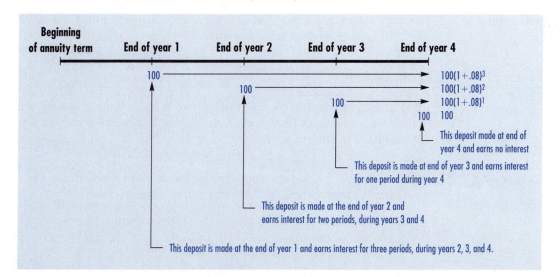

Figure 9.9

Formula for the future value of an ordinary annuity

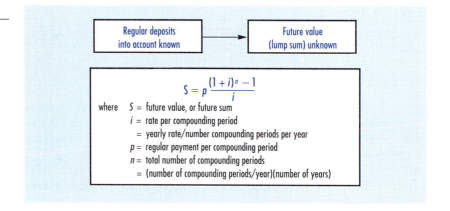

The first $100 deposit grows to be $125.97; the second $100 grows to be $116.64; the third $100 grows to be $108; and the last $100 deposit earns no interest. The total value of the annuity (future value) is the sum of these parts.

$$\text{future value} = 100(1.08)^3 + 100(1.08)^2 + 100(1.08)^1 + 100$$
$$= 125.97 + 116.64 + 108 + 100$$
$$= 450.61$$

Notice that the value of the annuity increased as a result of regular deposits, which increased the principal and earned interest on that changing principal.

Learning objective
Calculate the future value of an ordinary annuity by using a formula and/or a table.

The formula diagrammed in Figure 9.9 allows us to compute the **future value** or future sum **of an ordinary annuity.**

The Appendix at the end of the book provides us with *amount of annuity* values in column E, which we can use instead of the formula to find the value of a future value annuity.

Example 12

Joel Bragg deposited $100 per year into an ordinary annuity paying 8% compounded annually for 4 years. What was the total value of the annuity at the end of the fourth year?

Solution

Refer to Figure 9.9. Regular deposits into the account (known) are $100 per year. We must determine the future value of the account.

$$p = \$100$$
$$i = 8\%, \text{ or } .08$$
$$n = 4$$

Table: **Formula:**

Table value for 8% page,
$n = 4$ in column C $= 4.506114$

$$S = p\,\frac{(1 + i)^n - 1}{i}$$

$S = (\text{payment})(\text{table value})$

$$S = 100\,\frac{[(1 + .08)^4 - 1]}{.08}$$

$S = 100 \times (4.506114)^*$

$S = 100(4.506114)$

$S = \$450.61$

$S = \$450.61$

*This value can be calculated on a calculator, or it can be found in the table in the Appendix (back of the book). In order to use the table you need only know that $n = 4$, $r = 8\%$, and that we are working with an annuity. Column C, entitled *Ordinary Annuity*, will provide the value to be multiplied by the regular payment to determine the future value. Find the page for the 8% rate, move down column C to the row opposite $n = 4$ and read 4.506112, which is the entire value of

$$\frac{(1 + .08)^4 - 1}{.08}$$

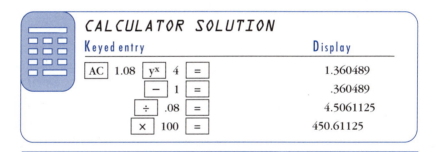

The regular deposits made to an ordinary annuity are, by convention, made at the end of each period. If deposits are made at the beginning of a period the annuity is called an *annuity due* and the formula is different. (We will work only with ordinary annuities.)

Example 13

Sophia Warner decides she will deposit \$2,000 a year into her savings account, which pays 6½% compounded annually. What amount of money will Sophia have in her savings account at the end of 5 years?

Solution

Refer to Figure 9.9. Regular deposits into the account (known) are \$2,000 per year. We must determine the future value of the account.

$p = \$2,000$

$i = .065$ or $6\frac{1}{2}\%$

$n = 5$

Table:

Table value = 5.69364098*

S = (payment)(table value)

$S = \$2,000 \times 5.69364098$

$S = \$11,387.28$

Formula:

$$S = p\,\frac{(1 + i)^n - 1}{i}$$

$$S = \$2,000\,\frac{(1 + .065)^5 - 1}{.065}$$

$$S = \$2,000 \times 5.69364098$$

$$S = \$11,387.28$$

*Turn to the Appendix for $i = 6.5\%$, column C, and look up the number where $n = 5$. This number is 5.69364098, which is then multiplied by $2,000 to give us

$$S = 2,000(5.69364098) = \$11,387.28 \text{ (rounded)}$$

Example 14

Raenel Jones decides to deposit $50 per month into an annuity paying 12% compounded monthly for 3 years. What will the annuity be worth at the end of 3 years? How much interest will be earned?

Solution

Refer to Figure 9.9. Regular deposits into the account (known) are $50 per month. We must determine the future value of the account.

$p = \$50$

$$i = \frac{.12}{12} = .01 \text{ or } 1\%$$

$$n = \frac{12 \text{ periods}}{\text{year}} \times 3 \text{ years} = 36 \text{ periods}$$

Table:

Table value for $i = 1\%$, column C, and $n = 36$ is 43.076878

S = payment $\times$ table value

$S = 50 \times 43.076878$

$S = \$2,153.84$

Formula:

$$S = p\,\frac{(1 + i)^n - 1}{i}$$

$$S = \$50\,\frac{(1 + .01)^{36} - 1}{.01}$$

$$S = 50(43.076878)$$

$$S = \$2,153.84$$

Raenel's deposits total $50 × 36 payments = $1,800.00. The difference, $2,153.84 − $1,800.00 = $353.84, is the interest she earned.

CHECK YOUR KNOWLEDGE

Ordinary **annuities**

Solve the following problems. Round dollar amounts to the nearest cent and rates to the nearest hundredth of a percent.

For each of the compounding periods and time spans listed in problems 1 through 5, determine *i* and *n*:

	Compounded	Yearly rate	Number of years	*i*	*n*
1.	annually	7.25%	5	_____	_____
2.	quarterly	12%	3	_____	_____
3.	semiannually	10%	4	_____	_____
4.	monthly	6%	7	_____	_____
5.	daily (365 days)	15%	10	_____	_____

6. Determine the future value of an ordinary annuity paying 12% interest compounded monthly for 5 years if a regular deposit of $100 is made monthly.

7. Sally Martin's parents began a savings program in which they deposited $200 quarterly into an annuity paying 8% interest compounded quarterly. They began this program when she was born and gave her the total 15 years later. How much was the annuity worth when she assumed ownership of it?

8. Molly Rainsford, attorney, has established a retirement account into which she will deposit $3,000 semiannually until she is 65 years old. How much will Molly accrue in the account if she establishes it at age 29 and the account earns 11% interest compounded semiannually?

9. In problem 8, calculate the total amount of the payments Molly will have deposited.

10. Use the results of problems 8 and 9 to determine the total interest Molly's retirement account will earn.

Answers to CYK: *1.* $i = .0725; n = 5$ *2.* $i = .03; n = 12$ *3.* $i = .05; n = 8$ *4.* $i = .005; n = 84$
5. $i = .00041; n = 3,650$ *6.* $8,166.96   *7.* $22,810.20   *8.* $2,521,377.90
9. $216,000   *10.* $2,305,377.90

9.4 EXERCISES

Solve the following exercises. Round dollar amounts to the nearest cent and rates to the nearest hundredth of a percent.

Complete problems 1 through 5 by determining the value of the ordinary annuity at the end of the specified term.

	Regular payment	Rate per year	Payments made	Number of years	Future value
1.	$200	9%	annually	10	_____
2.	$300	10%	semiannually	20	_____
3.	$600	8%	quarterly	5	_____
4.	$1,000	12%	quarterly	7	_____
5.	$150	6%	monthly	3	_____

6. Determine the amount of an ordinary annuity for annual deposits of $1,000 at 9% compounded annually at the end of the fourth deposit.

7. What is the accumulated amount for annual deposits of $1,000 invested in an account paying 11% compounded semiannually following the eighth deposit?

8. Three years ago, Marley Symanski's parents began putting $75 each month into a savings account. If the terms of the interest were 12% compounded monthly, how much money has been accumulated?

9. What is the value at the end of 15 years of quarterly deposits of $2,000 with terms of 8% compounded quarterly?

10. Jason M. Goldman established his own retirement account ten years ago by making semi-annual deposits of $6,000 into an ordinary annuity that pays 10% compounded semi-annually. (a) What is the value of his retirement account today? (b) How much interest has been earned?

11. Jason Goldman has discovered that he can obtain a better rate for the next 10 years at 11% interest compounded semiannually. Consequently, Jason established a new ordinary annuity account (beginning amount $0) and he will contribute $7,000 semiannually into it for the next 10 years. (a) What will the value of this account be at the end of the 10-year period? (b) How much interest will the account earn?

12. Jennifer Jones is an Army reservist as well as an accountant for a local auditing firm. Jennifer regards the salary she earns from her reserve activities as extra income that she can invest at this time. If Jennifer invests $500 every 3 months into an ordinary annuity paying 8% interest compounded quarterly, how much will she have accumulated at the end of 5½ years?

13. Arnie Mankewicz owns five video rental stores in the Springfield area, and they are realizing a good profit. Arnie decides to invest part of the profits in an annuity offered by United Life Insurance. United Life will guarantee Arnie 10% interest compounded quarterly for up to 5 years as long as he deposits $10,000 every quarter of the term of the guaranteed rate. Assuming that Arnie does fulfill the obligations of the investment, (a) what will be the value of his investment at the end of the 5-year term? (b) how much interest will he earn?

14. Everette Aldo receives $330 in dividends every quarter from a stock investment he holds. If Everette deposits his dividend into an ordinary annuity paying 14% interest compounded quarterly, how much will he earn in interest in an 11-year period?

15. Estelle Fareweathers plays drums in a dance band on weekends in addition to her full-time job at the Marcyville Savings and Loan. Estelle decided on her 35th birthday to establish her own retirement savings account by investing $400 of her weekend earnings every month into an ordinary annuity paying 12% interest compounded monthly. If Estelle makes these regular deposits until her 65th birthday, how much will this retirement account be worth?

16. Art and Janey Longly's son Jim has a disability that will likely prevent him from earning a full-time income as an adult. Art and Janey want to assure that Jim will be able to financially support himself after reaching the age of 21 years. Art and Janey have invested $1,000 monthly into an ordinary annuity earning 12% interest compounded monthly ever since Jim's first birthday. How much will they have accumulated for Jim on his 21st birthday?

17. Frank Hofstedder was injured while employed at Martin Industries and will receive disability pay since he will not be able to return to work. Martin has agreed to establish an education fund for Frank's 14-year-old son Ryan. For the next 4 years, Martin will deposit $2,000 per quarter into an ordinary annuity paying 8% interest compounded quarterly. If Martin fulfills its commitment for 4 years, how much will be available for Ryan's education when he goes to college in 4 years?

Use the following information to answer problems 18 through 20. Jan Greeley has deposited $250 per month in Fastgrowth Investments monthly for the last 10 years. Fastgrowth is an ordinary annuity investment that has offered 12% interest compounded monthly. At the end of the 10-year term, Jan withdrew her total investment and deposited it into a compound interest account paying 9% interest compounded yearly. Jan began a new annuity savings program with Fastgrowth but due to changing economic conditions, the company could only guarantee her 10% compounded semiannually for the next 5 years. Jan will now deposit $1,500 semiannually into this new annuity.

18. What was the value of Jan's 10-year investment with Fastgrowth at the end of the 10-year term?

19. Recall that at the end of the 10-year plan, Jan put her accumulated savings in a straight compound interest account. If Jan leaves her investment in the compound account and allows it to grow in interest only for the next 5 years, what will its value be at the end of the 5-year term?

20. If Jan fulfills her commitment to the new annuity, what will its value be at the end of the 5-year period?

9.5   PRESENT VALUE ANNUITIES

A **present value annuity** is a form of a compound interest account that is established with a single lump sum, which periodically pays out of the account a specified number of equal payments that liquidate the account, as shown in Figure 9.10.

Figure 9.10

Present value annuity

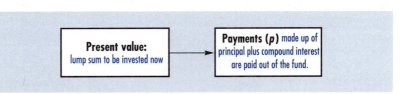

Example 15

Sherry Moss' grandfather wants to provide her with $5,000 at the end of each of her four college years to help her pay off any extraneous expenses and to help her have a pleasant summer. Grandpa Moss intends to deposit a lump sum of money into a present value annuity, which pays 10% interest compounded annually and which will pay Sherry $5,000 at the end of each year from principal and accumulated interest, and which will liquidate itself with the last payment (that is, after the last payment the account will have exactly $0.00 in it). How much must Grandpa Moss invest in the present value annuity to accomplish his stated goals?

Solution

Figure 9.11 shows diagrammatically what action is taking place in the account. Note that the original principal continues to earn interest throughout the 4 years, but that each payment contains part of the principal and part of the interest earned. Altogether, the principal and interest total $20,000, which Sherry will receive. More principal will be needed in the first year, when less interest will have been earned, than in the fourth year when four years' interest has been earned.

Learning objective

Calculate the amount necessary to establish a present value annuity by using a formula and/or by using a table.

Figure 9.12 gives us a formula that allows us to compute the present value of an annuity. It is not always necessary to use this formula since there are tables for compound interest and ordinary annuities that make our work easier. These tables are found in Appendix A on pages 662 through 680.

Referring to Figure 9.12, the regular payments out of the account (known) are $5,000 per year. We must determine the lump sum amount (unknown).

Figure 9.11

Time line for a present value annuity

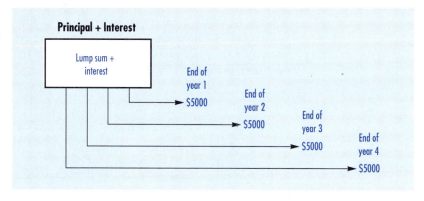

Figure 9.12

Formula for a present value annuity

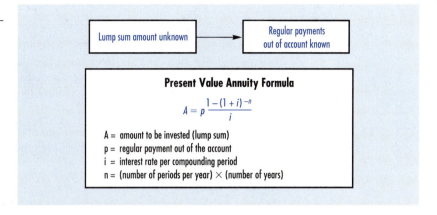

Note that Sherry will receive $20,000 but her grandfather only invested $15,849.33; so the interest the annuity earned is:

interest = $20,000.00 − $15,849.33 = $4,150.67

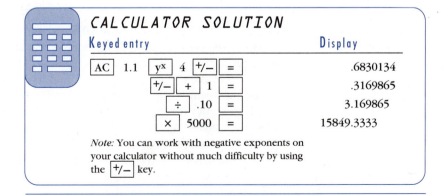

$p = \$5,000$

$i = 10\%, \text{ or } .10$

$n = 4$

Table:

table value for 10%, N = 4, column E is 3.1698655

$A = (\text{payment})(\text{value from the Appendix, column E})$

$A = (\$5,000)(3.1698655)$

$A = \$15,849.33$

Formula:

$$A = p \, \frac{1 - (1 + i)^{-n}}{i}$$

$$A = \$5,000 \, \frac{1 - (1 + .10)^{-4}}{.10}$$

$A = (\$5,000)(3.1698655)$

$A = \$15,849.33$

Example 16

Suppose you had to pay your ex-spouse $10,000 per ½-year in alimony payments over the next 5 years. How much would you need to put into a savings account paying 8% interest compounded semiannually so that you would have enough money to cover each alimony payment?

Solution

Refer to Figure 9.12. The regular payments out of the account (known) are $10,000 per ½-year. We must determine the lump sum amount (unknown).

$$p = \$10,000$$

$$i = \frac{.08}{2} = .04 \text{ or } 4\%$$

$$n = \left(\frac{2 \text{ periods}}{\text{year}}\right)(5 \text{ years}) = 10$$

Table:

Table value for 4% page, $n = 10$ in column E = 8.11089578

$A = (\text{payment})(\text{table value})$

$A = (\$10,000)(8.11089578)$

$A = \$81,108.96$

Formula:

$$A = p\,\frac{1 - (1 + i)^{-n}}{i}$$

$$A = \$10,000\,\frac{1 - (1 + .04)^{-10}}{.04}$$

$A = (\$10,000)(8.11089578)$

$A = \$81,108.96$

CHECK YOUR KNOWLEDGE

Present value annuities

Solve the following problems. Round dollar values to the nearest cent and rates to the nearest hundredth of a percent.

1. Mari and Lou Hencle intend to retire next year and they want to establish a present value annuity that will pay out $8,000 each year to cover the costs of their real estate taxes, home insurance costs, and other incidental home costs for the next 3 years while they travel. How much must they invest at 7% interest compounded annually to accomplish their goals?

2. Farley Davidson has decided to take a year off from work without pay to sail around the world on a cruise ship. He wants to establish a present value annuity that will pay him $2,000 per month for one year. How much must he invest at 12% interest compounded monthly to meet his needs?

3. Home Owner's Digest is running a $1,000,000 lottery as a sales promotion. The winner will receive $50,000 per year for the next 20 years (i.e., a total of $1,000,000). What is the minimum amount the Digest must invest in an account paying 8% interest compounded annually in order to meet the commitment to the winner?

4. Faraday Construction Co. was judged to have been liable for the death of Ben Arnold in one of its construction projects. Ben's relatives sued Faraday for negligence and settled out of court for $130,000 per year for 15 years. The family agreed to accept payment in the form of four quarterly payments of $32,500 each year. The court ordered Faraday to establish a present value fund that would guarantee the family received their award. How much must Faraday deposit into the fund if it pays 10% interest compounded quarterly in order to settle the judgment and satisfy the requirements of the court?

9.5 EXERCISES

Solve the following problems. Round dollar amounts to the nearest cent and rates to the nearest hundredth of a percent.

Complete exercises 1 through 5 by determining the present value amount.

Regular payment	Rate per year	Payments made	Number of years	Present value
1. $200	9%	annually	5	_____
2. $300	10%	semiannually	11	_____
3. $600	8%	quarterly	6	_____
4. $1,000	12%	quarterly	7	_____
5. $150	6%	monthly	4	_____

6. Determine the present value of an annuity for which the fund pays out $10,000 per year at 9% interest compounded annually for 30 years.

7. Jackson and Parkins Greenhouses needs to have $25,000 from investments each year to make improvements in its business. How much must the company invest at 7½% interest compounded annually in order to achieve its goal for the next 5 years?

8. What is the minimum amount of money you could accept today in place of receiving quarterly payments of $4,000 each at 8% interest compounded quarterly for the next 12 years?

9. What is the present value of semiannual payments of $15,500 at 11% interest compounded semiannually over the next 9 years?

10. What is the current value of $999 semiannual payments made over the next 9 years if the interest rate is 9% interest compounded semiannually?

11. Linda Kowalski will begin attending Barry Town College 1 year from now and will attend for the next 4 years; her annual costs

Answers to CYK: *1.* $20,994.54 *2.* $22,510.14 *3.* $490,907.45 *4.* $1,004,531.10

will be $14,000 which her parents have agreed to pay. Linda's parents have saved enough money to meet Linda's needs. How much must they invest in an account paying 10% interest compounded annually in order to receive $14,000 at the end of each of the next 4 years, and have nothing left in the account at the end of that time?

12. Ramon's Plumbing and Heating is a very successful business developed by José Ramon over the last 30 years. José will retire this year and has sold his business for $1,250,000. José will invest part of this money in an account paying 12% interest compounded monthly, which will pay him $10,000 per month for the next 20 years. What is the minimum amount he must invest to accomplish his goal?

13. The Super Sweepstakes lottery was won by Barbara Thompson when the winnings were $500,000 to be paid in quarterly payments of $12,500 each over a 10-year period. How much must Super Sweepstakes deposit in an account paying 8% interest quarterly for 10 years in order to meet its commitment to Barbara?

14. Security Life Insurance Co. offers an income disability policy that will pay $2,000 per month to an insured claimant until age 65 if a full disability occurs. Julie Hanson suffered such a disability at age 55 and filed a claim that was approved for her to receive the full benefit of $2,000 per month for $9\frac{1}{2}$ years until her 65th birthday. What is the minimum amount Security Life must invest in an account paying 6% interest compounded monthly in order to meet its commitment to Julie?

15. Mrs. Christianson found it necessary to sell her home and move into a senior citizens housing complex. She agreed to receive a $65,000 down payment, plus the buyers will pay her $500 per month for the next 20 years. If the terms she and the buyers agreed to were at 12% interest compounded monthly for the next 20 years, what is the present value of their agreement? (Note: Figure this out as a present value annuity for $500 per month at 12% interest compounded monthly for 20 years.)

16. Refer to exercise 15. What was the selling price of the house? (Note: Selling price = down payment + present value of financing.)

17. Refer to exercise 15. How much will Mrs. Christianson realize from the sale of her house if we add the down payment and the total amount she will receive in the financing arrangement?

18. Assume you sell a business for $35,000 in cash plus monthly payments of $750 for 3 years. If today's interest terms are 12% compounded monthly, what is the equivalent cash selling price of your business?

19. Li Tung bought a car and financed it with a 4-year loan at a 12% nominal interest rate compounded monthly. Li is to pay off the loan and interest with 48 payments of $200 each. How much did Li borrow? (Hint: This is a present value problem; i.e., what is the current value of $200 monthly for 48 months at 12% interest compounded monthly?)

20. John Cooper purchased a car with a 7-year loan at 18% interest compounded monthly, and is paying $300 per month for 84 months. John recently inherited a large sum of money and wants to pay off his loan early. He has 36 payments left. How much does he still owe? (Hint: What is the current value of $300 monthly for 36 months at 18% interest compounded monthly?)

9.6   SINKING FUNDS

Often in our business and personal lives we are able to anticipate future expenses. A business may anticipate the replacement of a piece of equipment or a parent may anticipate the need for a lump sum of money to assist a child in obtaining a college education. Sometimes it is possible to plan ahead financially for anticipated expenses and either set aside a sum of money immediately to meet later expenditures, or even to plan to set aside smaller sums of money on a regular basis that together with interest will accumulate to the desired amount of money. A **sinking fund** is an ordinary annuity into which regular equal periodic deposits are made so that a specific lump sum of money is accumulated (payments plus interest on them) at the end of a set time.

Example 17

Expresso Printing anticipates the need to replace a printing machine in 5 years. The anticipated cost of the replacement machine is $9,000.00. The company can earn 8% interest compounded quarterly and wishes to invest the funds prior to the need so they will not have to borrow money to replace the machine.

Solution

a.   One option is for Expresso to make a one-time lump sum investment into the compound interest account and allow that sum to accumulate interest until the interest and initial principal total the $9,000 needed. How much should be invested?

$$A = P(1 + i)^n \qquad \text{compound interest formula}$$

$$\$9{,}000 = P\left(1 + \frac{.08}{4}\right)^{20}$$

$$P = \frac{\$9{,}000}{\left(1 + \dfrac{.08}{4}\right)^{20}}$$

$$P = \frac{\$9{,}000}{1.485946} \qquad \text{value from column A in the Appendix}$$

$$P = \$6{,}056.74$$

This is the present value of a compound interest problem with $i = .02$ and $n = 20$. A single lump sum investment of $6,056.74 at 8% interest compounded quarterly will yield the $9,000 in 5 years.

b.   But what if Expresso cannot spare $6,056.74 to be set aside immediately? A second option would be to make regular payments into a sinking fund, which will accumulate, with interest, to $9,000 at the end of 5 years. Since regular payments are made into a compound interest fund, we are working with an ordinary annuity,

$$S = p \frac{(1 + i)^n - 1}{i}$$

in which we know S = \$9,000, n = 20, i = .08/4 = .02, and we need to determine the regular payment p.

$$\$9,000 = p \frac{(1 + .08/4)^{20} - 1}{.02}$$

$$\$9,000 = p(24.29737)$$

$$p = \frac{\$9,000}{24.29737}$$

$$= \$370.41$$

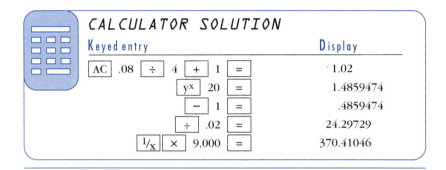

Either of the options in Example 17 may be thought of as a sinking fund, which is a fund accumulated to pay off a long-term expenditure. However, the second option, which uses the future sum of an ordinary annuity, is formally regarded as a sinking fund. The formula for a sinking fund is depicted in Figure 9.13.

We can use the tables in Appendix A to determine the regular payment for the sinking fund. Column D, labeled "sinking fund" provides us with a simple means of determining p.

In Example 17, we would look to column D on the page for i = 2% and n = 20. Moving down the column and across the row for n = 20 we would find .041157. If we multiplied this factor by \$9,000 we would obtain the regular payment of \$370.41.

Learning objective
Calculate the regular payment necessary for establishing a sinking fund by using a formula and/or a table.

Example 18

Sara Delmore plans to vacation in Europe 3 years from now. She wants to have \$6,000 available for the trip, and plans to make regular semiannual

Figure 9.13

Formula for a sinking fund

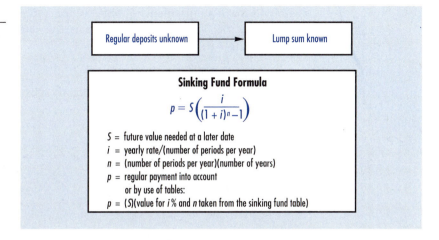

Regular deposits unknown ⟶ Lump sum known

Sinking Fund Formula

$$p = S\left(\frac{i}{(1+i)^n - 1}\right)$$

S = future value needed at a later date
i = yearly rate/(number of periods per year)
n = (number of periods per year)(number of years)
p = regular payment into account
  or by use of tables:
p = (S)(value for i% and n taken from the sinking fund table)

payments into an account paying 10% interest compounded semiannually. How much should her semiannual deposits be to achieve her goal?

Solution

Since regular deposits are being made into the fund, we have a future sum annuity; and since we know the future sum of the annuity ($6,000) but not the size of the regular payments, it is a sinking fund.

Refer to Figure 9.13. The lump sum (known) is $6,000. We must determine the regular deposit to be made.

$$S = \$6,000$$

$$i = \frac{10\%}{2} = 5\%$$

$$n = (3 \text{ years})(2 \text{ periods per year}) = 6$$

Table:

table value for 5%, N = 6, column D is .1470174

p = (lump sum)(table value)

p = ($6,000)(.1470174)

p = $882.10

Formula:

$$S = p\,\frac{(1+i)^n - 1}{i}$$

$$\$6,000 = p\,\frac{(1 + .10/2)^6 - 1}{.05}$$

$6,000 = p(6.801912)$ value from the future value annuity column C, $i = 5\%$, $n = 6$

$$p = \frac{\$6,000}{6.801912} = \$882.10$$

Sara will make six payments of $882.10 for a total of $5,292.60, which means that the interest she will earn is the difference of $6,000 and $5,292.60; that is,

> interest = $6,000 − $5,292.60 = $707.40.

Remember that we can check our solution by substituting the information into the ordinary annuity formula.

Check: Ordinary annuity formula

$S = p \times$ (future annuity table value for $i = 5\%$, $n = 6$)
$= \$882.10 \times (6.801912)$
$= \$5,999.96$

Or with a calculator,

$$S = p \, \frac{(1 + i)^n - 1}{i}$$

$$= \$882.10 \times \frac{(1 + .05)^6 - 1}{.05}$$

$$= \$882.10 \times (6.801912)$$
$$= \$5,999.96$$

(The 4 cent discrepancy is due to rounding error.)

CHECK YOUR KNOWLEDGE

Sinking funds

Solve the following problems. Round dollar amounts to the nearest cent.

For each of the following sinking fund annuities in problems 1 through 5, determine the regular payments.

	Future value	Rate/year	Compounded	Number of years	Regular payment
1.	$10,000	9%	annually	5	_____
2.	$22,500	10%	semiannually	3	_____
3.	$8,750	16%	quarterly	4	_____
4.	$43,250	18%	monthly	4	_____
5.	$875	8%	quarterly	6	_____

6. Sureway Machine Shop will need to replace a drill press 3 years from now. The projected cost of a new press is $10,000. How much should be deposited quarterly into an annuity paying 8% interest compounded quarterly so that SMS will have $10,000 in 3 years?

7. Acme Vending Co. needs to purchase a new van to be used in servicing its machines every 4 years. With the purchase of each new van, Acme establishes a sinking fund to save for the next purchase. Acme anticipates the cost in 4 years to be $17,500. How much should Acme invest monthly into an account paying 12% interest compounded monthly so they will have $17,500 at the end of 4 years?

8. Refer to problem 7 and determine the following for Acme: (a) the total in payments Acme will make and (b) the total interest that will be earned by the sinking fund.

9. Matt Brewster Oil Distributors decides to purchase a motor home to transport company personnel to business meetings, and to use for a variety of sales promotions. Brewster decides to establish a sinking fund paying 10% interest compounded quarterly to accrue a total of $50,000 in 5 years to make the purchase. How much must Matt Brewster deposit into the fund each quarter to achieve his goal?

10. Refer to problem 9 and determine for Brewster: (a) the total amount that will be deposited into the account and (b) the total interest the sinking fund will earn.

9.6 EXERCISES

Solve the following exercises. Round dollar amounts to the nearest cent and rates to the nearest hundredth of a percent.

For each of the sinking fund annuities in exercises 1 through 5, determine the regular payments.

	Future value	Rate/year	Compounded	Number of years	Regular payment
1.	$5,000	8%	quarterly	8	_____
2.	$13,000	9%	semiannually	11	_____
3.	$7,000	10%	annually	12	_____
4.	$28,000	12%	monthly	4	_____
5.	$4,350	14%	quarterly	5	_____
6.	$3,275	11%	semiannually	3.5	_____

Answers to CYK: *1.* $1,670.92 *2.* $3,307.91 *3.* $400.93 *4.* $621.72 *5.* $28.76 *6.* $745.60 *7.* $285.85 *8.* a. $13,720.80; b. $3,779.20 *9.* $1,957.35 *10.* a. $39,147; b. $10,853

7. You wish to establish a sinking fund that will be worth $3,000 in 4 years. If you establish such a fund in an account paying 8% interest compounded quarterly, how much must you deposit quarterly to meet your goal?

8. Jack Smythe will need $6,000 accumulated in 8 years in order to replace an office copy machine for his business. How much must he deposit semiannually into a sinking fund paying 7% interest compounded semiannually in order to have the required amount?

9. E. Z. Fixit is a small repair business run by its owner Ed Zambino. Ed's main asset is his own ability and a good truck. He needs to replace his truck every 4 years, and saves ahead so that he can pay cash for the new vehicle. Ed just bought a new truck for $19,500. He believes inflation will be about 4% per year for the next 4 years and using the compound interest formula he has calculated that the same truck will cost $22,812.24 then. How much will Ed need to deposit monthly into a sinking fund paying 12% interest compounded quarterly in order to have the desired amount?

10. Tim and Sally Fredette gave birth to a baby girl this year and want to establish a college fund for her higher education. They estimate that even a public education will cost at least $10,000 per year when she attends college.

How much must they invest quarterly into a fund paying 8% interest quarterly in order to have $40,000 in 18 years.

11. Sharon Barrister is a professor at a small college who likes to travel. She has decided to take a leave of absence 3 years from now and travel throughout Eastern Europe for a semester and the summer that follows it. She will need $12,000 to accomplish her goal. How much must she deposit annually into an annuity paying 9% interest compounded annually in order to meet her needs?

Use the following situation to answer exercises 12 through 15. Art Barrett has signed a promissory note that will be due in 30 months, at which time he will have to pay a total of $9,000. Since the note was a discounted note, $2,025 is interest.

12. If Art establishes a sinking fund paying 12% interest compounded monthly, how much must he invest monthly in order to have the $9,000 in 30 months' time?

13. How much did Art actually deposit in the fund?

14. How much interest did the fund earn him?

15. In effect, Art's plan retrieved some of the interest cost on the original promissory note. What was the net cost of the original note if we credit this interest earned against that interest paid?

9.7   AMORTIZATION OF AN AMOUNT OF MONEY

Amortization of a lump sum of money is an application of the present value annuity. When we worked with the present value annuity, we asked the question, *How large a sum of money must be invested* in an account paying R% interest per year compounded m times per year in order to receive n equal payments of $\$p$? We knew p, R, i, and n, and we were looking for A.

With an "amortization," we start out with a known lump sum of $\$A$ and we ask, *How large will our equal payments be* if we invest $\$A$ in an account paying R% per year compounded m times per year for a total of n payments? Here we know A, R, i, and n, and we are looking for p.

Amortization is used whenever we have an account with a lump sum of money that is earning interest and that we wish to liquidate (decrease the value of principal + interest to $0.00) with n equal payments. Typical examples of amortizations are retirement funds and loans (such as auto loans and mortgages on property).

Amortization is a present value annuity in which we are trying to determine the value of the regular payment, p. Consequently, if we begin with our present value annuity formula and solve for p, we can develop a formula for amortization. (See Figure 9.14.)

Present value annuity formula

$$A = p \left[\frac{1 - (1 + i)^{-n}}{i} \right]$$

Learning objective
Calculate the equal regular payments that will amortize a specific sum of money over a set period of time.

If we solve this equation for p, we will have

$$p = A \frac{1'}{\left[\dfrac{1 - (1 + i)^{-n}}{i} \right]}$$

The value of the entire quantity that is multiplied by A is given to us in the Appendix column F, which will assist us in our work.

Figure 9.14

Amortization formula

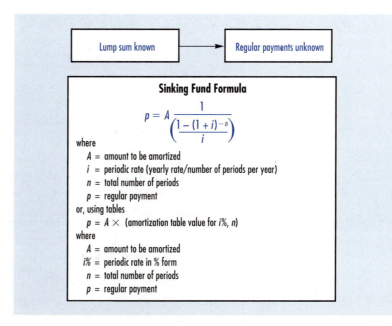

Lump sum known → Regular payments unknown

Sinking Fund Formula

$$p = A \frac{1}{\left(\dfrac{1 - (1 + i)^{-n}}{i} \right)}$$

where
  A = amount to be amortized
  i = periodic rate (yearly rate/number of periods per year)
  n = total number of periods
  p = regular payment
or, using tables
  $p = A \times$ (amortization table value for $i\%$, n)
where
  A = amount to be amortized
  $i\%$ = periodic rate in % form
  n = total number of periods
  p = regular payment

Example 19

Solution

Martha McGrath, a sculptor of miniature wildlife scenes, has worked as an independent craftswoman for 15 years. She created an independent retirement account and has saved a total of $200,000 from the sales of her work. She will retire this month and wishes to establish a fund with her savings ($200,000), which will make equal monthly payments to her for the next 20 years. If she sets up the retirement fund with an institution paying 12% compounded monthly, how much will she receive monthly?

Martha is establishing a present value annuity since regular payments will be made out of the fund to her. Since we know the amount of money with which she will establish the fund, and we need to determine p, this is an amortization problem. Refer to Figure 9.14. The lump sum (known) is $200,000; we are trying to determine the regular payments (unknown). First, let's solve this problem by using the tables:

$$p = A \times (\text{amortization value for } i\%, n)$$
$$A = \$200,000$$

$$i\% = \frac{.12}{12} = .01 \text{ or } 1\%$$

$$n = (12 \text{ periods per year})(20 \text{ years}) = 240$$
table value for 1%, N = 240, column F is .0110109

$$p = \$200,000 \times (.0110109) = \$2,202.17 \text{ per month.}$$

Second, let's solve by using the present value formula:

$$A = p \, \frac{1 - (1 + i)^{-n}}{i}$$

$$A = \$200,000$$

$$i = \frac{.12}{12} = .01$$

$$n = 12 \times 20 = 240$$

$$\$200,000 = p \, \frac{1 - (1.01)^{-240}}{.01}$$

$$\$200,000 = p(90.819410)$$

$$p = \frac{\$200,000}{90.819410} = \$2,202.17 \text{ per month}$$

Notice that the actual amount Martha will receive is

$$\text{total} = 240 \times \$2,202.17 = \$528,520.80$$

which means that the account will earn $328,520.80 in interest as it liquidates itself.

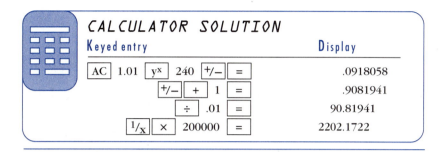

CALCULATOR SOLUTION

Keyed entry	Display
AC 1.01 y^x 240 +/− =	.0918058
+/− + 1 =	.9081941
÷ .01 =	90.81941
1/x × 200000 =	2202.1722

Loans that are amortized work in this same way; that is, they earn interest as they liquidate themselves. The interest they earn is the finance charge the borrower pays for the use of the money.

Example 20

Faith MacArthur bought a new car and financed $17,000 at 18%. The loan was amortized monthly for 5 years. Determine Faith's monthly payment and the total interest she will pay for the loan.

Solution

Refer to Figure 9.14. The lump sum (known) is $17,000. We are trying to determine the regular payments (unknown).

The amount, A, to be amortized here is the $17,000 she borrowed. The periodic rate is $i = .18/12 = .015$ per month. The loan is for 5 years, so there will be 60 periods in the loan.

$$p = A(\text{amortization table value for } i\% = 1.5\%, n = 60)$$
$$= \$17,000(.025393) = \$431.688, \text{ or } \$431.69 \text{ per month.}$$

The total of Faith's payments will be:

$$\text{total} = 60 \text{ payments} \times \$431.69 = \$25,901.40$$

The interest Faith will pay will be:

$$\text{interest} = \text{total payments} - \text{amount borrowed}$$
$$= \$25,901.40 - \$17,000$$
$$= \$8,901.40$$

Amortized loans provide the benefits of equal payments while truly charging interest on the unpaid balance only of the loan.

Amortization of an amount of money

Solve each of the following problems. Round dollar amounts to the nearest cent.

Determine the regular payment p in the amortization of the amount in problems 1 through 5.

	Amount	Rate/year	Compounding	Number of years	Payment
1.	$4,000	8%	semiannually	6	_____
2.	$12,500	10%	quarterly	5	_____
3.	$3,250	6%	monthly	3	_____
4.	$22,250	9%	annually	13	_____
5.	$50,000	14%	quarterly	8	_____

6. Jake McDougald won a $500,000 lottery prize in his state's lottery. His winnings were reduced to $400,000 after taxes were deducted and he decided to amortize the winnings by investing them in a fund that would make quarterly payments to him for 15 years. If the fund pays 10% compounded quarterly, how much will he receive each quarter?

7. Refer to problem 6. Determine the total amount that Jake will receive from the fund. Also determine the total interest the fund will earn.

9.7 EXERCISES

Solve the following problems. Round dollar amounts to the nearest cent and rates to the nearest hundredth of a percent.

Determine the regular payment for the amortization of the given amount of money at the given rate for the stated time in exercises 1 through 5.

Answers to CYK: *1.* $426.21   *2.* $801.84   *3.* $98.87   *4.* $2,971.87   *5.* $2,622.10
    6. $12,941.20   *7.* a. $776,472; b. $376,472

	Amount	Rate/year	Compounding	Number of years	Payment
1.	$20,000	5%	annually	10	_____
2.	$12,000	6%	monthly	5	_____
3.	$200,000	8%	quarterly	15	_____
4.	$75,000	10%	semiannually	7	_____
5.	$17,000	12%	monthly	5	_____

6. Jean LaFleur recently inherited $100,000 and wants to receive regular quarterly payments from this sum to supplement her income for the next 10 years. If she invests the money in an account paying 10% compounded quarterly that will liquidate itself at the end of 10 years, how much will she receive each quarter?

7. Mark Green bought a new power boat for $75,000. He paid a $30,000 down payment and financed the remainder with an amortized loan at 12% compounded monthly for 5 years. What will be his monthly payment?

8. Sally Markham has saved $180,000 over the last 15 years to supplement her income during retirement. Now that she has retired, Sally wants to amortize this amount so that she will receive regular payments over the next 30 years and liquidate the account. She arranges to do this with an investment that pays 10% compounded quarterly. How much will she receive each quarter?

Use the following information to complete problems 9 through 11. Janet Ordway won the Pennsyl-vania lottery and was given a prize of $500,000. She decided to invest this amount in an account that would amortize it over a 10-year period at 12% interest compounded monthly.

9. How much will she receive each month?

10. What will be the total amount of the payments that she will have received as of the end of the 10-year period.

11. How much interest will the account have earned?

Use the following information to answer problems 12 through 15. Jack and Marge Janson purchased a home for $170,000 and put a 20% down payment on the purchase. They financed the remainder with a loan that was amortized at 12% interest compounded monthly for 20 years.

12. How much did Jack and Marge finance?

13. What will be Jack and Marge's monthly payment?

14. How much will their total payment be to pay off the loan?

15. How much interest will they pay for the loan?

EXPRESS YOUR THOUGHTS

Compose one or two well-written sentences to express the requested information in your own words.

1. Describe the difference between compound interest and simple interest.

2. Explain how the future value in a compound interest problem differs from the future value in a simple interest problem.

3. Which would yield a higher interest in one year: $1,000 compounded weekly at 12% or $1,000 compounded daily at 12%? Why?

4. Describe the steps you would use to calculate the future value of $1,000 at 12% compounded monthly for three years.

5. Explain the difference between present value and future value in a compound interest problem.

6. Explain what is meant by the effective rate of a compound interest rate.

7. Describe the difference between an annuity and a basic compound interest problem.

8. How is an ordinary annuity related to a sinking fund?

9. What does it mean to say that the present value of an annuity of six monthly payments of $100 is $3,000?

10. How is amortization related to present value annuity?

Case exercise   Build a retirement plan

Nancy Karstic is a self-employed attorney who has a successful law practice in her hometown of Curleyville. Nancy will be 35 years old on her next birthday. She has entered into a contract with Legal Professionals Annuity Investments for a retirement program into which she will make quarterly payments of $1,000 each. She will be guaranteed 8% interest compounded quarterly for the duration of her contract.

She will begin the ordinary annuity part of her program at the end of the first quarter after her 35th birthday and she will stop payments on her 65th birthday. The retirement plan will then make equal quarterly payments out of the fund (which is still earning 8% compounded quarterly) to Nancy for 21 years, at which point the fund will have liquidated itself.

A. Determine the total value of Nancy's annuity on her 65th birthday.

B. Determine the amount of interest earned by Nancy's annuity as of her 65th birthday.

C. Determine the amount of the equal quarterly payments Nancy will receive from age 65 until age 86.

D. Determine the amount of interest earned in part C.

E. Determine the total interest earned over the life of the investment.

Compound interest and annuities — a summary

When we first read a problem, how do we know if it is an annuity or a basic compound interest problem? If periodic deposits or payments are involved then it is an annuity. If it is an annuity, how do we know if it is an ordinary annuity or a present value annuity? If regular deposits are made into an account that will grow to a lump sum, it is an ordinary annuity. If regular payments are made from the account with the goal of liquidating the account, then it is a present value annuity.

Using this information, we can diagram a means of analyzing a problem after we first read it, as follows.

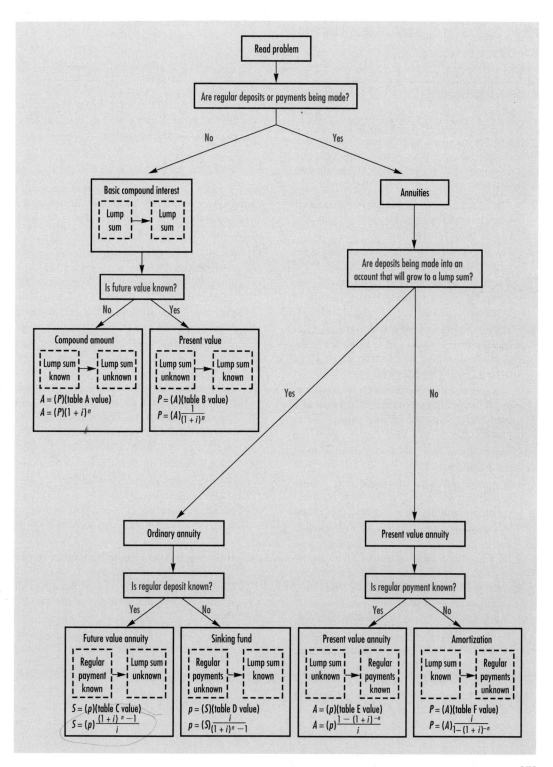

SELF-TEST

A. Terminology review

Complete the following items using the key terms presented at the beginning of the chapter. Check your responses against the answer key at the end of the test.

1. _Compound interest_ is produced when interest is earned on principal plus previously earned interest.

2. The future value of the principal plus compound interest is called _compound Amt_.

3. A series of equal periodic payments into or out of a compound interest paying account is called an _annuity. tiền góp hàng năm_.

4. The amount of money you would accept today (or the principal) instead of a known compound amount is called the _present value_ of a compound amount.

5. The simple interest rate necessary to generate the same amount of interest in 1 year as a particular compound interest rate is called _effective rate_.

6. The yearly interest rate is also referred to as the _nominal_ rate.

7. If regular payments are made into a compound interest account, the total of these payments and the interest they earn is called the _FV_ _____ of an annuity.

8. The _PV_ _____ annuity tells us what lump sum of money must be invested at a given rate in order to receive equal periodic payments from the fund for a certain number of years.

9. A compound interest fund into which payments are made so that those payments plus interest will meet a certain future financial need is sometimes referred to as a _sinking_ fund.

10. When a lump sum is invested in a compound interest paying fund in such a way that the fund will make equal periodic payments un-

til it liquidates itself, we say that we have _amortize_ the lump sum.
trả dần

B. Calculation review

The following concepts and short problems are designed to test your understanding of the objectives identified at the beginning of the chapter. Answers are provided at the end of the test.

11. Jason Roberts deposited $3,000 into an account paying 9% interest compounded semi-annually. If he makes no deposits or withdrawals from the account, (a) what will be the value of the account at the end of seven years? (b) how much interest will the account have earned at that time?

12. You wish to make a one-time deposit into a compound interest account paying 14% interest compounded quarterly and you wish to have the value of the account be $2,000 at the end of 4 years. (a) How much must you deposit now to meet your goal? (b) How much interest will the account earn?

13. What is the effective yield of an account paying 11% compounded semiannually?

14. If Ann Williams deposited $500 quarterly into an account paying 16% compounded quarterly, how much would her account be worth at the end of 7 years?

15. How much must Emelde Hernandez put in a present value annuity paying 8% interest compounded quarterly so that her son will receive $2,500 per quarter for the next 5 years?

16. How much would you need to deposit monthly in an investment paying 18% interest for the account to be worth $875 at the end of 30 months?

Use the following information to answer questions 17 through 20. Joe Armani purchased a new car for $18,000 and made a down payment of $8,000. Joe financed the remaining amount with an amortized loan at 12% interest compounded monthly for 5 years.

17. How much did Joe finance?

18. What are Joe's regular payments?

19. How much will Joe pay back in total for the loan?

20. How much interest will Joe pay for the loan?

Answers to self-test: **1.** compound interest **2.** compound amount **3.** annuity **4.** present value **5.** effective rate **6.** nominal **7.** future value **8.** present value **9.** sinking **10.** amortized **11.** a. $5,555.84; b. $2,555.84 **12.** a. $1,153.41; b. $846.59 **13.** 11.30% **14.** $24,983.77 **15.** $40,878.50 **16.** $23.31 **17.** $10,000 **18.** $222.44 **19.** $13,346.40 **20.** $3,346.40

10

BUSINESS AND CONSUMER CREDIT

Learning objectives

1. Determine the daily balance for a revolving credit account.

2. Calculate the average daily balance for a revolving credit account.

3. Calculate the amount of the regular payments of an installment contract.

4. Calculate, using tables, the equal regular payments of an amortized loan.

5. Create loan repayment tables for amortized loans.

6. Calculate the outstanding principal of an amortized loan.

7. Calculate the interest rebate for a loan paid off early.

(continued)

Learning Objectives (continued)

8. Calculate the approximate interest rebate using the sum of digits and rule of 78s methods.

9. Calculate the regular payment, outstanding principal, and interest rebate for a mortgage.

10. Determine the true annual percentage rate for a loan.

11. Define the key terms.

INTRODUCTION

Whenever a person or a company purchases goods or services they must decide whether to pay cash or buy on credit (i.e., purchase now and pay later). If the only choice possible were to pay cash, our economy as we know it would not exist. The economies of countries and of the world depend on the ability of individuals and companies to buy now and pay later. Our goal in this chapter will be to explore the basics of consumer credit.

A merchant's goal is to sell merchandise to a customer. If the customer has the cash to buy the merchandise, the merchant may need only a quality product and a competitive price to make the sale. If the customer does not have the cash available to buy, then the merchant may need to provide the customer with one more incentive, *financing*.

Whenever a merchant offers financing to a customer, that merchant assumes increased responsibilities, risks, and costs. Merchants may choose to finance the customer's purchase themselves, or they may seek out financing to offer the customer from an additional source. Merchant-financed loans are those the seller makes directly to the buyer; for example, the short-term loan, such as when a furniture store offers "90 days is the same as cash." In this instance, the seller agrees to give the buyer up to 90 days to pay for merchandise without a finance charge. If the buyer holds the item during this 90-day period, the seller has effectively loaned the value of that merchandise to the buyer for 90 days, interest free.

The merchant may also finance a loan by offering an installment contract over a period of time with a finance charge included. Revolving credit accounts and charge cards offered by local department stores or national chain stores—such as Sears, Radio Shack, or K mart—are another form of merchant financing.

A merchant may prefer to provide financing through a third party. For example, an automobile dealer may initiate an installment contract for a customer to buy a car, but the contract is really between the customer and a financial institution, such as a bank. The car dealer may receive a commission for completing the initial paperwork; however, he or she may be required to pay the institution a fee for the lower annual percentage rate meant to entice the customer.

Many merchants, especially those with small businesses, prefer to use the services of national or international credit cards such as MasterCard, VISA, American Express, or Discover, which reduce the responsibilities and risks. Whenever the borrower requests to use such credit, the merchant obtains an electronic verification from the lender and extends the credit accordingly. The merchant does incur costs of 3% to 5% of the average ticket value for the benefit of using national credit card services. We will discuss this process in detail in Chapter 11.

A lender may reduce the risk of making a loan by requiring some form of security in the form of collateral from the borrower. **Collateral** is simply something of value that is used as security for a loan. If the borrower cannot pay off the loan, he agrees to give up all or part of the ownership of the item used as collateral to the lender. **Unsecured loans** are loans that have no specific collateral provided to the lender; the lender is relying upon the borrower's ability and willingness to pay. **Secured loans** provide lower interest rates than unsecured loans because they represent less risk to the lender.

We will consider two basic categories of consumer credit: **open-ended credit,** which includes various types of charge accounts and credit cards, and **closed-ended credit,** which includes installment buying and mortgages. We will also briefly consider consumer credit from the seller's (merchant's) point of view.

Perhaps the following illustration will help explain the basis on which open-ended credit is offered.

> Arlene Slater has lived in the village of Johnsville for most of her life and she has purchased her groceries at Sigsbee's Market for the last 30 years. Each week she shops, and the owner, Jay Sigsbee, keeps a record of how much Arlene owes. At the end of each month, after Arlene receives her retirement check, she pays Jay the entire amount that she owes for the month.

Arlene's arrangement with Jay Sigsbee is, perhaps, one of the simplest forms of open-ended credit. Her credit arrangement is based on "trust." Jay trusts that Arlene will pay her bill in an honest and timely manner. Arlene may or may not be required to pay a finance charge for the privilege of doing her grocery shopping in this way. A **finance charge** is interest paid for using someone else's money for a period of time. The finance charge is usually based on the amount of money used, principal, P; a percentage rate, r; and the time, t, the money is used (finance charge = interest = $P \times r \times t$). With this model, all credit advanced to either an individual or to an organization is based on *trust* that the loan, plus interest, will be paid back fully and in proper time.

Today's highly mobile and transient society has resulted in fewer financial arrangements like the small town grocery arrangement of Arlene Slater. However, credit accounts offered by local department stores or national store chains such as Sears or JC Penney are very similar. These stores accept our application for a credit line, evaluate our ability and willingness to pay our debts (trust), and issue us a line of credit that is open ended up to some upper limit such as $500, $1,000, or $2,500. We, then, are able to purchase goods and services openly up to our upper limit just by saying, "Charge it."

10.1   REVOLVING CREDIT

Revolving credit is the most common type of open credit. Revolving credit as we know it is really a form of two types of charge accounts. With a *regular charge account*, we take the goods and agree to pay for them fully within a set time period, say 30, 60, or 90 days. Furniture stores often offer this type of credit with no finance charge as an inducement to convince a customer to buy now. A **revolving charge account** is an open account in which we are allowed to charge up to a certain limit and we agree to pay at least a percentage, say 10%, 15%, or 20%, of our outstanding balance at the end of a set time period (called a *billing period* or *billing cycle*), which is often set at 25 or 30 days. A finance charge is assessed on the outstanding balance of the account each month.

Revolving credit is credit automatically available up to a specified limit while payments are periodically made. If the entire balance due at the end of a billing period is paid, then no finance charge is assessed. If only the minimum amount due, or some amount less than the entire balance, is paid, then the finance charge will be assessed on the amount *carried over* into the next billing period. Typically, a statement describing the customer's purchases and payments is sent to the customer each month, as shown in Figure 10.1. If a customer pays the balance in full each month, then there is no finance charge added to the balance. If, however, the customer pays less than the balance in full, then a finance charge must be paid each month a balance is left. The finance charge is calculated as a percentage of either the *adjusted balance* or the *average daily balance*. We will demonstrate both of these methods of calculation in this section.

In the adjusted balance method, the finance charge is calculated as a percentage of the unpaid balance as of the end of the previous month.

Figure 10.1

Billing statement

Anita's Department Stores
Statement of Account

The Customer Is Always Our First Concern

ACCOUNT NUMBER **000-00-00000**

CURRENT BILLING DATE **02-27-XX**

PAGE 01 OF 01

To Avoid Additional Finance Charge, Pay New Balance By ▶ **03-24-XX**

Date	Store/Reference Number	Balance Type	Item Description	Charges	Payments and Credits
02-13	6501-0025375	R	PYMT -THANK YOU		60.00
			THANK YOU!		

BALANCE SUMMARY	PREVIOUS BALANCE	− PAYMENTS AND CREDITS	+ FINANCE CHARGE	+ CHARGES	= NEW BALANCE	MINIMUM PAYMENT
REG	136.36	60.00	1.91	.00	78.27	20.00

Your finance charge rates are: (See reverse side for important information and explanation of your finance charge method)

BAL TYPE	ON BALANCE OF	AS OF	ON BALANCE THRU $	MONTHLY PERIODIC RATE(S) %	ANNUAL PERCENTAGE RATE(S) %	ON BALANCE OVER $	MONTHLY PERIODIC RATE(S) %	ANNUAL PERCENTAGE RATE(S) %
R	A 109.08	02-92	ALL	1.75	21.0			

△ Your Finance Charge Method is (see reverse)

MINIMUM *FINANCE CHARGE* $ .50

Example 1

José Chingo has a revolving charge account for which the terms of payment are as follows: "The customer must pay a minimum of $25 and a finance charge of 1½% per month. To avoid paying a finance charge, the customer must pay the entire balance amount." Assume that José pays the minimum payment of $25 each month for the next 3 months and that his previous balance was $654. Find (a) his new balance and (b) the total amount in finance charges he has paid during these 3 months.

Solution

truoc (old)

Month	Previous balance	+	Finance charge	+	Current pur- chases	− Payments	=	New balance
1	$654.00		$9.81 (654 × .015)		0	$25.00		$638.81
2	$638.81		$9.58 (638.81 × .015)		0	$25.00		$623.39
3	$623.39		$9.35 (623.39 × .015)		0	$25.00		$607.74

a. The new balance is $607.74.

b. The total amount of finance charges is $28.74 (9.81 + 9.58 + 9.35 = 28.74).

Example 2

Stacy's previous balance on her charge account is $780.21. This month she has purchased goods worth $35 and has made a payment of $40. What is the new balance in her account if the finance charge is 1.75%?

Solution

Month	Previous balance	+	Finance charge	+	Pur- chases	− Payments	=	New balance
1	$780.21		$13.65 (780.21 × .0175)		$35	$40.00		$788.86

Learning objective
Determine the daily balance for a revolving credit account.

Although the methods for calculating finance charges vary for different institutions that issue credit cards, many use the average daily balance method. The **average daily balance** is the sum of daily balances divided by the number of days in a billing cycle. The **daily balance** is equal to the previous balance plus new purchases and cash advances, minus payments and credits.

Calculating daily balance	daily balance = previous balance + new purchases + cash advances − payment − credits

Example 3

The following information represents the monthly statement for Joan Gansk's credit card account.

6/17	previous balance	$420
6/28	purchase	$ 50
7/2	payment	$100
7/9	purchase	$ 30

Find the daily balance for Joan's account on (a) June 28, (b) July 2, (c) July 7, and (d) July 12.

Solution

a.   previous balance − payments + purchase = daily balance on 6/28

          $420   + $50   = $470   *4 days*

b.   previous balance − payments + purchases = daily balance on 7/2

          $470   − $100   = $370   *8 days*

c.   previous balance − payments + purchases = daily balance on 7/7

          $370   = $370

d.   previous balance − payments + purchases = daily balance on 7/12

          $370   + $30   = $400

Example 4

Learning objective
Calculate the average daily balance for a revolving credit account.

The following information represents the monthly statement for Kerry Milhouse's credit card account:

3/25	previous balance	$580	*660*
3/31	purchase	$ 80	*610*
4/4	payment	$ 50	*635*
4/17	purchase	$ 25	

Find the daily balance for Kerry's account as of (a) March 31, (b) April 4, and (c) April 25. (d) Find the average daily balance as of April 25. (e) Find the finance charge as of April 25 if it's 1½% of the daily average balance.

Solution

3/25   P = 586

3/31   pur = 80

4/4   pay = 50

4/17   pur = 25

a.   previous balance − payments + purchases = daily balance on 3/31

   $580   + $80   = $660

b.   previous balance − payments + purchases = daily balance on 4/4

   $660   − $50   = $610

c.   previous balance − payments + purchases =   daily balance 4/25

   $610   +   25   = $635

d.   daily balance × number of days

$$\$580 \times \quad 5 \quad (3/26 - 3/30) = \$ \ 2{,}900$$
$$660 \times \quad 4 \quad (3/31 - 4/3) \ \ = \quad 2{,}640$$
$$610 \times 13 \quad (4/4 - 4/16) \ \ = \quad 7{,}930$$
$$635 \times \underline{\quad 9 \quad} (4/17 - 4/25) = \underline{\quad 5{,}715}$$
$$\qquad\qquad 31 \qquad\qquad\qquad\qquad \$19{,}185$$

$$\frac{\$19{,}185}{31} = \$618.87 \text{ average daily balance}$$

e.   .015 × $618.87 = $9.28 amount of finance charge

CHECK YOUR KNOWLEDGE

Revolving credit

Refer to the following monthly statement for Randall Stewart's revolving charge account:

11/23	previous balance	$890
11/30	payment	100
12/5	purchase	210
12/12	purchase	75

1. Find the daily balance for Randall's account as of (a) November 30, (b) December 5, and (c) December 15.

2. Find the average daily balance for the period November ~~30~~ through December 23.

3. What is the amount of the finance charge as of December 23 if it is 1.75% of the average daily balance?

Refer to the following monthly statement for Shannon Rossi's revolving charge account:

1/28	previous balance	$570
2/10	payment	150
2/15	purchase	120
2/17	cash advance	250
2/20	credit for returned merchandise	325

4. Find the daily balance for Shannon's account as of (a) February 10, (b) February 15, (c) February 17, and (d) February 20.

5. Find the average daily balance for the period January 29 through February 28.

6. What is the amount of the finance charge as of February 28 if it is 1.25% of the average daily balance?

10.1   EXERCISES

Solve the following problems. Round dollar amounts to the nearest cent.

Refer to the following monthly statement for Leah Johnson's revolving charge account.

Aug. 3	previous balance	$326.70
Aug. 10	payment	125.00
Aug. 24	purchase	73.20
Aug. 30	purchase	89.60

1. Find the daily balance for Leah's account as of (a) August 10, (b) August 24, and (c) August 30.

2. Find the average daily balance as of August 30.

3. What is the finance charge as of August 30 if it is 1.5% of the average daily balance?

Refer to the following monthly statement for Sean Humphry's revolving charge account.

May 12	previous balance	$435.67
May 15	purchase	143.50
May 23	payment	213.45
May 30	payment	67.00

4. Find the daily balance for Sean's account as of (a) May 15, (b) May 23, and (c) May 30.

5. Find the average daily balance as of May 30.

6. What is the finance charge as of May 30 if it is 1.5% of the average daily balance?

Answers to CYK: **1.** a. $790.00; b. $1,000.00; c. $1,075.00   **2.** $973   **3.** $17.03   **4.** a. $420; b. $540; c. $790; d. $465   **5.** $534.68   **6.** $6.68

Refer to the following monthly statement for Karen Sweet's revolving charge account.

July 1	previous balance	$745.98
July 12	payment	145.00
July 17	purchase	111.65
July 22	purchase	47.34
July 31	purchase	223.54

7. Find the daily balance for Karen's account as of: (a) July 12, (b) July 17, and (c) July 31.

8. Find the average daily balance as of July 31.

9. What is the finance charge as of July 31 if it is 1.75% of the average daily balance?

Refer to the following monthly statement for Andy Frederick's revolving charge account.

March 2	previous balance	$543.24
March 8	payment	543.24
March 15	purchase	258.96
March 27	purchase	87.43
March 30	purchase	275.87

10. Find the daily balance for Andy's account as of (a) March 8, (b) March 27, and (c) March 30.

11. Find the average daily balance as of March 27.

12. What is the finance charge as of March 30 if it is 1.85% of the average daily balance?

10.2   INSTALLMENT CREDIT

Closed-ended credit differs from open-ended credit in that the fixed principal borrowed in closed-ended credit is set at the time of the loan. Two types of closed-ended credit that we will consider are installment loans and mortgages.

Installment loans are generally used when purchasing items that can be paid off with monthly income on a short-term basis. Automobiles, boats, motorhomes, motorcycles, and appliances are often purchased on an installment plan. **Mortgage loans** are generally used for long-term loans of large principals. Homes, summer cottages, and businesses are purchased with mortgage loans.

Example 5

Jake Shuron is about to purchase a new car for $10,300. Jake will put $3,000 down and finance the remainder at 12% interest for 48 months with monthly payments of $192.24 per month. (a) How much is Jake actually financing, assuming that all other fees and charges (license fee, tax, preparation charges, etc.) will be paid for separately? (b) How much will he actually pay back if he completes the terms of the loan as stated? (c) How much will the finance charge for this loan be?

Solution

a. amount to be financed = (cost of car) − (down payment)
$$= \$10,300 - \$3,000$$
$$= \$7,300$$

b.   actually paid = (number of payments) $\times$ (amount each payment)
$$= 48 \times \$192.24$$
$$= \$9,227.52$$

c.   amount of finance charge = amount paid $-$ amount financed
$$= \$9,227.52 - \$7,300$$
$$= \$1,927.52$$

Example 6

Barney Buff and his wife have just purchased an entirely new kitchen for their home for $13,000. They made a down payment of $4,000 and agreed to finance the remainder at an annual percentage rate of 18% interest for 36 months. The finance charge for their installment plan is $2,713.32. (a) How much did Barney actually finance? (b) How much will they pay back totally? (c) How much will each of the 36 equals payments be?

Solution

a.   amount financed = (total cost) $-$ (down payment)
$$= \$13,000 - \$4,000$$
$$= \$9,000$$

b.   total paid back = (amount financed) + (finance charge)
$$= \$9,000 + \$2,713.32$$
$$= \$11,713.32$$

c.   amount of each payment $= \dfrac{\text{total paid back}}{\text{number of payments}}$
$$= \frac{\$11,713.32}{36}$$
$$= \$325.37$$

Example 7

Jethro and Kay Sullivan have agreed to buy a home for $115,000 with a down payment of $45,000 and a $70,000 mortgage at an annual percentage rate of 9% interest for 30 years. Their monthly payments will be $563.24. Assuming Jethro and Kay pay off their mortgage in 30 years, (a) how much will they pay back totally? (b) how much will their interest costs total?

Solution

a.   There are 360 months in 30 years, so

total paid back = 360 $\times$ $563.24 = $202,766.40.

          b.   total interest paid = total paid back − amount financed
$$= \$202,766.40 - \$70,000$$
$$= \$132,766.40$$

DETERMINATION OF REGULAR PAYMENT AMOUNT

Learning objective
Calculate the amount of the regular payments of an installment contract.

How do we determine the amount of each regular payment? Although there are several ways to determine payment, we will consider three simple examples.

    First, consider an example in which simple interest is added to the principal.

Example 8

Tom Evans borrowed $1,200 at 9% simple interest for 1 year. Thrifty Finance Company, Tom's lender, and Tom agreed that the simple interest would be calculated for 1 year and added to the principal. Tom's payment each month would be $\frac{1}{12}$th of the total. Determine (a) the simple interest, (b) the total Tom will owe, and (c) Tom's monthly payment.

Solution

a.   Thrifty Finance Company calculated the interest using the simple interest formula:

$$I = Prt = \$1,200 \times .09 \times 1 = \$108$$

b.   Thrifty then added the interest to the principal for a total of $1,308.
c.   Thrifty and Tom agreed that he would pay the total in 12 monthly installments of $1,308/12 = $109 each.

Now we will consider a simple discount loan handled in a similar way.

Example 9

Alyssa Meyers borrowed $1,200 from Thrifty Finance Company as well. If her loan was discounted at 9%, determine the amount she actually received and the amount she must pay back.

Solution

proceeds $= M - Mrt$
$$= \$1,200 - 1,200 \times .09 \times 1$$
$$= \$1,200 - 108$$
$$= \$1,092$$

So Alyssa actually received $1,092 in proceeds but agreed to pay back the full $1,200 since it was a discount loan. She paid Thrifty $100 each month for 1 year to pay off her loan.

We shall show later, in Section 10.7, that although Tom and Alyssa may believe they have obtained 9% interest loans, their true percentage rates as determined by federal standards are actually higher.

A third example of regular payment determination leaves the borrower with regular but unequal payments.

Example 10

Nancy Green borrowed $1,200 from Integrity Finance and agreed to pay $\frac{1}{12}$th of the principal plus 1% interest on the unpaid principal balance each month for 1 year. What will Nancy's payments be for the year?

Solution

Nancy's payments will be as follows:

Month	Principal balance	Interest on unpaid balance	Payment
1	$1,200	$1,200 \times .01 = 12$	$100 + 12 = \$112$
2	1,100	$1,100 \times .01 = 11$	$100 + 11 = \ 111$
3	1,000	$1,000 \times .01 = 10$	$100 + 10 = \ 110$
4	900	$900 \times .01 = 9$	$100 + \ 9 = \ 109$
5	800	$800 \times .01 = 8$	$100 + \ 8 = \ 108$
6	700	$700 \times .01 = 7$	$100 + \ 7 = \ 107$
7	600	$600 \times .01 = 6$	$100 + \ 6 = \ 106$
8	500	$500 \times .01 = 5$	$100 + \ 5 = \ 105$
9	400	$400 \times .01 = 4$	$100 + \ 4 = \ 104$
10	300	$300 \times .01 = 3$	$100 + \ 3 = \ 103$
11	200	$200 \times .01 = 2$	$100 + \ 2 = \ 102$
12	100	$100 \times .01 = 1$	$100 + \ 1 = \ 101$

Nancy's loan at 1% per month would be considered a 12% per year rate of interest. Tom and Alyssa's loans provide the benefit of equal regular payments but they have been led to believe that their loan rates are lower than Nancy's. This occurs because the simple interest computed on Tom's and Alyssa's loans assumes that they have the entire principal amount for the full year, which is not true. After each payment they have less of the principal in their possession. In truth, their interest rates are considerably higher than Thrifty Finance has suggested. Federal laws on "Truth in Lending" require that Thrifty inform its borrowers of the true annual percentage rate. The **annual percentage rate** is the yearly rate of interest that is being charged on the *unpaid balance* after each payment.

In the next section, we will examine *amortization of a loan*, which provides us with both the benefits of equal regular periodic payments and interest on the unpaid balance after each payment.

CHECK YOUR KNOWLEDGE

Installment credit

1. For each of the following, determine the amount to be financed.

	Total cost	Down payment	Amount to be financed
a.	$8,000	$2,500	_____
b.	$3,000	$700	_____
c.	$6,000	$1,500	_____
d.	$750	10% down	_____

2. For each of the following, determine the amount of the finance charge.

	Amount to be financed	Monthly payments	Interest rate	Total number of months	Finance charge
a.	$10,000	$332.14	12%	36	_____
b.	$10,000	$263.14	12%	48	_____
c.	$10,000	$222.44	12%	60	_____
d.	$10,000	$195.50	12%	72	_____
e.	$10,000	$176.53	12%	84	_____

3. Determine for each of the following the total amount to be paid and the amount of each equal installment.

	Amount to be financed	Finance charge	Total amount to be paid	Number of months	Amount of each payment
a.	$8,000	$80	_____	12	_____
b.	$10,000	$1,297	_____	24	_____
c.	$6,000	$435.29	_____	6	_____
d.	$15,000	$3,960.48	_____	48	_____

4. Debby Ross purchased a $3,000 piano and borrowed $2,000 at 8% simple interest add-on for 3 years. (a) Determine the interest (finance charge) Debby agreed to pay. (b) Determine the amount of the equal payments if Debby agreed to pay off the principal and interest in 12 equal quarterly payments.

5. Kevin Mark borrowed $200 from his father and agreed to repay the loan in four quarterly payments of $50 each plus 2% interest on the unpaid portion of the loan for that quarter. Construct a payback table for Kevin's loan. (See Example 10.)

	Number	Principal	Interest	Payment
a.	1	200	4	54
b.	2	150	3	53
c.	3	100	2	52
d.	4	50	1	51

10.2 EXERCISES

Determine the finance charge in each of the following problem sets. Round dollar amounts to the nearest cent.

	Amount to be financed	Monthly payment	Total number of payments	Finance charge
1.	$11,000	$325	36	_____
2.	$3,000	$130	24	_____
3.	$780	$75	12	_____
4.	$1,500	$35	48	_____
5.	$23,450	$1,200	20	_____

	Amount to be financed	Monthly payment	Total number of payments	Finance charge
6.	$15,000	$450.00	36	_____
7.	$8,000	$350.00	24	_____
8.	$2,467	$210.50	12	_____
9.	$7,500	$165.00	48	_____
10.	$3,450	$120.00	30	_____

Answers to CYK: **1.** a. $5,500; b. $2,300; c. $4,500; d. $675 **2.** a. $1,957.05; b. $2,630.72; c. $3,346.40; d. $4,076.00; e. $4,828.52 **3.** a. $8,080; $673.33; b. $11,297; $470.71; c. $6,435.29; $1,072.55; d. $18,960.48; $395.01 **4.** a. $I = $2,000(.08)(3) = $480.00; b. $206.67 **5.** a. $200; 4; 54; b. $150; 3; 53; c. $100; 2; 52; d. $50; 1; 51

Amount to be financed	Monthly payment	Total number of payments	Finance charge
11. $17,650	$600.00	30	_____
12. $2,675	$71.00	40	_____
13. $750	$192.00	8	_____
14. $3,700	$74.50	52	_____
15. $7,985	$141.00	60	_____

Determine the total amount to be paid and the amount of each equal installment in each of the following problem sets. Round dollar amounts to the nearest cent.

Amount to be financed	Finance charge	Total amount to be paid	Number of months	Amount of each payment
16. $7,000	$84	_____	12	_____
17. $3,900	$780	_____	24	_____
18. $16,500	$32,000	_____	360	_____
19. $4,700	$1,380	_____	36	_____
20. $9,500	$3,040	_____	48	_____

Amount to be financed	Finance charge	Total amount to be paid	Number of months	Amount of each payment
21. $8,000	$74.00	_____	12	_____
22. $2,770	$332.00	_____	24	_____
23. $34,245	$40,000	_____	360	_____
24. $5,757	$2,100.00	_____	36	_____
25. $7,450	$1,337.00	_____	48	_____

Amount to be financed	Finance charge	Total amount to be paid	Number of months	Amount of each payment
26. $1,300	$13	_____	15	_____
27. $900	$162	_____	30	_____
28. $6,500	$15,000	_____	360	_____
29. $10,000	$3,116	_____	48	_____
30. $9,500	$3,762	_____	60	_____

31. Erin Cole purchased a new refrigerator for $990 and after making a 10% down payment on her purchase, financed the remainder at a 10% add-on simple interest for 1 year. (a) How much did Erin finance? (b) How much interest will Erin pay? (c) If Erin agreed to pay the total (principal + interest) that she owed in four equal quarterly installments, how much will each installment be?

32. Lynette Harvey purchased a new computer for $1,650 and financed the total cost with a 12% per year add-on simple interest for 2

years. (a) How much interest will Lynette pay? (b) If Lynette agreed to pay the total (principal + interest) with eight equal quarterly installments, how much will each installment be?

33. Carl Fignon purchased a mountain bike for $650. He made a 15% down payment and financed the remainder at 12% yearly interest rate for 36 months. If Carl's monthly payments are $18.35, how much finance charge will he pay?

34. Carry Marshall purchased a new large-screen television set for $5,500. After making a 20% down payment, she financed the remainder at 10% interest per year to be paid in quarterly installments for 3 years. Her finance charge was $747.31. How much will she pay in each of her equal quarterly installments?

35. Don Browne borrowed $4,000 to make some improvements to his home. Don agreed to repay the loan in four quarterly payments of $1,000 per quarter plus 3% interest on the unpaid portion of the loan for that quarter.

Construct a payback table for Don's loan. How much interest will Don pay for the loan?

36. Jan Barrett borrowed $8,000 to pay for a trip to Europe for her family. Jan agreed to repay the loan in eight semiannual payments of $1,000 each plus 4% interest on the unpaid portion of the loan for that period. Construct a payback table for Jan's loan. How much interest will Jan pay for the loan?

37. Jeff Jones borrowed $9,000 to add a small room to his summer cottage on the lake. Jeff agreed to repay the loan in six quarterly payments of $1,500 per quarter plus 2.5% interest on the unpaid portion of the loan for that quarter. Construct a payback table for Jeff's loan. How much interest will Jeff pay for the loan?

38. Betty Brunno borrowed $3,600 to repair her motorhome. She agreed to repay the loan in twelve quarterly payments of $300 per quarter plus 3% interest on the unpaid portion of the loan for that quarter. Construct a payback table for Betty's loan. How much interest will Betty pay for the loan?

10.3 **AMORTIZATION OF A LOAN**

Learning objective
Using tables, calculate the equal regular payments of an amortized loan.

The most common method to determine the regular monthly payment for a loan is called **amortization**. Generally, to amortize a debt is to liquidate the debt with a series of regular payments or installments. In the case of a loan, we will liquidate the total of the principal and finance charge of the loan with regular equal payments. How do we determine the amount of each payment? We use the *present value of an annuity*. Recall that present value annuity problems asked the question, "How much (lump sum) must we deposit into a fund so that the fund will pay out regular payments of a certain amount to us?"

Example 11

How much must be invested in a fund paying 12% compounded monthly to receive $100 per month for 48 months?

Solution

$$A = p \frac{1 - (1 + i)^{-n}}{i} \qquad = p \quad \times \text{(value for } n, r \text{ in present value}$$
$$\text{table, Appendix A, column E)}$$

$$A = 100 \frac{1 - (1.01)^{-48}}{.01} \qquad = 100 \times (37.97395)$$

$$= 3,797.395, \text{ or } \$3,797.40$$

From the individual consumer's point of view, a deposit of $3,797.40 into the fund will generate $100 per month (principal and interest) for 48 months and the fund will liquidate itself to $0.

We use this same concept with a small modification for loans. Picture the role of the bank and the consumer reversed. The bank invests a lump sum of money (the loan principal) in the consumer at a rate of interest. The consumer will pay back to the bank the principal plus interest with regular equal payments. The consumer now becomes the fund generating regular payments, which are in part repayment of the principal and in part payment of the interest. The difference is that we know the size of the lump sum (loan principal) and we need to determine the size of the regular payment.

Present value annuity formula

$$A = p \frac{1 - (1 + i)^{-n}}{i}$$

A = loan amount

p = regular payment

$$p = A \frac{1}{\dfrac{1 - (1 + i)^{-n}}{i}} \qquad \text{Solve for } p.$$

or

$$p = A \frac{i}{1 - (1 + i)^{-n}}$$

Fortunately, we have *amortization tables* in Appendix A, column F that assist us in this process.

Example 12

Determine the regular monthly payment for a loan of $4,800 borrowed at a 12% annual percentage interest rate for 48 months.

Solution

By tables and calculator:

$A = \$4,800$

$n = 48$

$i = \dfrac{.12}{12} = .01$ or 1%

$p = A$(table value in column F for 1%, $n = 48$)

$p = \$4,800(.026334)$

$p = \$126.40$

By formula and calculator:

$A = \$4,800$

$n = 48$

$i = \dfrac{.12}{12} = .01$

$p = A \dfrac{1}{\dfrac{1 - (1 + i)^{-n}}{i}}$

$p = A \dfrac{i}{1 - (1 + i)^{-n}}$

$p = \$4,800 \dfrac{.01}{1 - (1.01)^{-48}}$

$p = \$4,800 \dfrac{.01}{.3797396}$

$p = \$4,800 \, (.026334)$

$p = \$126.40$

Now let's consider a car buying situation in which the same interest rate is applied monthly over two different time spans, 4 years and 5 years. We can observe the effect of the time periods on the monthly payments, as well as on the total finance charge.

Example 13

Everett Michels has decided to purchase a new car for $17,000. The dealer will give him a trade-in allowance of $5,000 on his old car and Everett will put an additional $3,000 down on the car. He can finance the remaining $9,000 at an annual percentage interest rate of 18% for either 48 months or 60 months. (a) How much will his monthly payments be in each of the two plans? (b) How much finance charge will he pay in each of the two plans?

For Your Information
Should you buy or should you lease?

Historically, consumers have generally purchased their automobiles for personal and business use. Over the past few years, however, dealers have actively marketed the lease option to their customers. The advertisement shown here is a typical presentation of these options. To determine which option is most appropriate, a potential buyer would have to consider a number of factors, many of which are mathematical in nature. The primary distinction between the two options is ownership. If the buyer elects the lease option, title will not transfer to the leasee (customer) at the end of the lease. The monthly payments made by the leasee include interest and the declining value of the vehicle during the lease period. For this reason, the monthly lease payment is always less than the monthly payment under the purchase option for the same time period. In addition, the lease option usually requires the leasee

EXTENDED FOR A LIMITED TIME!

JUST TRY TO BEAT THIS LEASE

$264.⁷⁷ per mo. *

3 years/45,000 miles

WHILE SUPPLIES LAST!

1992 VOLVO 240 DL SEDAN

Air conditioning, power windows, stereo, driver's side airbag. ABS brakes, 3 year/50,000 mile Warranty and more! (Metallic Paint Extra).

OR PURCHASE FOR
$19,738
Plus tax, title & tags
Finance rate 7.95% APR available through VFNA for up to 60 months.

* 36 month lease at $264.77/month for a total of $9531.72 plus tax. $1000 cap reduction required. Documentary fee (gap insurance included) of $450. First payment of $264.77 plus taxes of $686.22 due at lease inception. No security deposit. Title & reg. extra. 15¢ per mile over 15,000 miles per year. Option to purchase at lease end at price equal to fair wholesale market value based on NADA used car guide. Lessee responsible for maintenance and repair not covered by warranty, as well as abnormal wear & tear. Subject to credit approval by Volvo Finance of North America.

Source: Alan Buyer Auto Sales, Syracuse, NY. Used with permission.

to pay special fees and a mileage penalty if the vehicle is driven more than a certain number of miles per year. Both options require the buyer to pay taxes, registration, insurance, and all service and repair costs. A mathematical analysis of the accompanying ad is given on the next page.

(continued)

*F*or *Y*our *I*nformation
*S*hould *y*ou *b*uy *o*r *s*hould *y*ou *l*ease? *(*continued*)*

Buy option		Lease option	
$19,738	Cost of car or lease	$7,738	($19,738 − $12,000)
−1,000	Down payment	1,000	
18,738	Amount to be financed	6,738	
1,382	Sales tax	+686	
20,120		7,424	
+2,561	Finance charge (7.95%)	+1,771	(lease charge)
22,681		9,195	
+1,000	Add $1,000 back in for total investment	1,450	($1,000 + document fee)
23,681		10,645	
$12,000	Value of investment at end	0	
$630.03	Monthly payment for 36 months	$264.77	

Solution

48 Months:

$A = \$9,000$

$n = 48$

$i = \dfrac{.18}{12} = .015$ or 1.5%

(a) $p = A$(table value in column F for 1.5%, $n = 48$)

$p = 9,000(.029375)$

$p = \$264.38$

(b) Total payments:

$48 \times 264.38 = \$12,690.24$

Finance charge

$\$12,690.24 − 9,000 = \$3,690.24$

60 Months:

$A = \$9,000$

$n = 60$

$i = \dfrac{.18}{12} = .015$ or 1.5%

(a) $p = A \times$ (table value in column F for 1.5%, $n = 60$)

$p = 9,000(.0253934)$

$p = \$228.54$

(b) Total payments:

$60 \times 228.54 = \$13,712.40$

Finance charge

$\$13,712.40 − 9,000 = \$4,712.40$

Notice that Everett can reduce his monthly payment by $35.84 ($264.38 − $228.54) per month by electing the 60-month plan; however, it will cost him an additional $1,022.16 ($4,712.40 − $3,690.24) in finance charges.

<table>
<tr><td>**CHECK YOUR KNOWLEDGE**</td><td>

Amortization of a loan

For problems 1 through 5, use the tables in column F of Appendix A to determine the monthly payment.

</td></tr>
</table>

	Loan principal (A)	i	n	p
1.	$1,000	1.5%	36	_____
2.	$4,000	.5%	24	_____
3.	$8,000	1.0%	48	_____
4.	$20,000	1.5%	30	_____
5.	$100,000	1.0%	360	_____

6. Determine the quarterly payments of a loan of $40,000 taken for 5 years at an annual percentage interest rate of 12%.

7. Marcia Wilkins has obtained an auto loan for $15,000 for 5 years at 12% annual percentage interest rate per year. (a) Determine Marcia's monthly payments. (b) Determine the total of the payments Marcia will make if she makes all scheduled payments. (c) Determine the finance charge.

10.3 EXERCISES

Solve the following problems. Round dollar amounts to the nearest cent.

For problems 1 through 4, use the tables in column F of Appendix A to determine the monthly payment.

	Loan (A) principal	i	n	p
1.	$3,000	1.0%	36	_____
2.	$5,000	1.5%	24	_____
3.	$1,000	2.0%	30	_____
4.	$2,000	0.5%	48	_____

Answers to CYK: **1.** $36.15   **2.** $177.28   **3.** $210.67   **4.** $832.78   **5.** $1,028.60
   6. $2,688.64   **7.** a. $333.66; b. $20,019.60; c. $5,019.60

For problems 5 through 8, use the tables in column F of Appendix A to determine the quarterly payment.

	Loan (A) principal	i	Number of years	p
5.	$5,200	2.0%	3	_____
6.	$6,400	2.5%	2	_____
7.	$8,000	4.0%	5	_____
8.	$4,500	6.0%	4	_____

For problems 9 through 12, use the tables in column F of Appendix A to determine the periodic payment.

	Loan (A) principal	i	Compounding	Number of years	p
9.	$4,200	3.0%	quarterly	4	_____
10.	$15,000	3.5%	semiannually	10	_____
11.	$2,500	9.0%	annually	5	_____
12.	$6,850	0.5%	monthly	3	_____

13. Bruce Bodkin recently borrowed $10,000 to purchase a new motorcycle. The loan is to be amortized monthly over a 5-year term and 12% interest per year. Determine: (a) the monthly payment and (b) the total finance charge for the loan.

14. Francine Martin borrowed $7,500 to invest in a small business venture. Her loan is to be amortized on a quarterly basis for 6 years at 10% interest per year. Determine: (a) Francine's quarterly payments, (b) the total amount she will pay on the loan, and (c) the total finance charge for her loan.

15. Marla Kex purchased a new audio–video entertainment center for her home for $4,200. She made a down payment of $1,200 and borrowed the remainder, which will be amortized monthly over a 2-year period at 18% interest. Determine: (a) the monthly payment and (b) the finance charge.

16. Bruce and Nancy Hanson purchased a new van. They wanted to finance the van with a loan of $10,000 so they shopped around for

financing. Fultown Trust offered them 12% amortized monthly for 4 years. What will be the amount of their monthly payments, and what will be their total finance charge?

Use the following information to answer questions 17 through 21. Jonathan Marx recently purchased a home and sought a mortgage for $50,000. Solvay Trust & Deposit offered to amortize the loan monthly at 12% interest per year for either 20 or 30 years. Determine:

17. Jonathan's monthly payments on the 20-year loan.

18. The total interest Jonathan would pay on the 20-year loan.

19. Jonathan's monthly payments on the 30-year loan.

20. The total interest Jonathan would pay on the 30-year loan.

21. The interest savings of the 20-year loan over the 30-year loan.

22. Marcie Metzler purchased a summer home for $65,000. She had a choice of either a 10-,

20-, or 30-year mortgage amortized monthly at 12% interest per year. Determine the monthly mortgage for each of the different terms and the total interest that would be paid under each of the terms.

10.4   LOAN REPAYMENT TABLES AND EARLY LIQUIDATION OF A LOAN

Amortization as explained in Section 10.4 is a fair and honest form of consumer loan, for both lender and borrower. By "fair" we mean simply that in the borrowing and repayment process the borrower pays the greatest amount of interest when he or she is holding the most amount of the loan principal, and the least amount of interest when holding the least amount of the loan principal.

Example 14

Learning objective
Create loan repayment tables for amortized loans.

Consider a loan of $1,000 borrowed at a 12% annual percentage interest rate (APR), which will be paid back in 1 year with equal monthly payments. Determine (a) the monthly payments and (b) construct a loan repayment table.

Solution

a. Using amortization, we can determine the monthly payments and finance charge ($n = 12$, $i = .12/12 = .01$ or 1%).

$$p = A\left(\frac{i}{1 - (1 + i)^{-n}}\right) = 1,000(.088848)^* = \$88.85$$

*Appendix A, column F, $i = 1\%$, $n = 12$

Note that the finance charge is:

$$12(88.85) - 1,000 = \$66.20$$

b. We will build our table by (1) computing the interest (1%) on each month's outstanding principal balance, (2) subtracting that interest from that month's regular payment to determine how much of the payment will be used to reduce the principal, and (3) determining the next month's principal by subtracting that principal part of the payment from that month's original principal. (See table on page 407.)

Month	Principal	Payment number	Interest on unpaid balance	Regular payment	Amount of payment of principal	New principal
1	$1,000.00	1	$1,000 × .01 = $10.00	$88.85	$88.85 − 10 = $78.85	$1,000 − 78.85 = $921.15
2	921.15	2	921.15 × .01 = 9.21	88.85	88.85 − 9.21 = 79.64	921.15 − 79.64 = 841.51
3	841.51	3	841.51 × .01 = 8.42	88.85	88.85 − 8.42 = 80.43	841.51 − 80.43 = 761.08
4	761.08	4	7.61	88.85	81.24	679.84
5	679.84	5	6.80	88.85	82.05	597.79
6	597.79	6	5.98	88.85	82.87	514.92
7	514.92	7	5.15	88.85	83.70	431.22
8	431.22	8	4.31	88.85	84.54	346.68
9	346.68	9	3.47	88.85	85.38	261.30
10	261.30	10	2.61	88.85	86.24	175.06
11	175.07	11	1.75	88.85	87.10	87.96
12	87.97	12	.88;	88.85	87.97	0*

*Occasionally this final balance is *not exactly* $0. Rounding numbers may result in small errors that cause the discrepancy in the final balance.

Notice that the largest amount of interest ($10) is paid when the borrower possesses the largest amount of the lender's money ($1,000). The least amount of interest ($.88) is paid when the borrower holds the least amount of the lender's money ($87.95). Notice also that, after six payments, the outstanding principal is $514.92, and more than half ($1,000/2 = $500) of the loan is still outstanding.

Example 15

Construct a loan repayment table for a loan of $5,000 borrowed at 8% interest per year to be paid off quarterly over a 2-year period.

Solution

$A = \$5,000$

$i = .8/4 = .02$ or 2% per quarter

$$n = 2 \text{ years} \times \frac{4 \text{ quarters}}{\text{year}} = 8 \text{ quarters}$$

regular payment = $5,000 × (column F value for $n = 8$, $i = 2$)

$p = \$5,000(.136510) = \$682.55$

Quar-ter	Principal	Interest on unpaid balance	p	Principal part	New principal
1	$5,000.00	$5,000 × .02 = $100.00	$682.55	$582.55	$4,417.45
2	4,417.45	4,417.45 × .02 = 88.35	682.55	594.20	3,823.25
3	3,823.25	3,823.25 × .02 = 76.46	682.55	606.09	3,217.16
4	3,217.16	64.34	682.55	618.21	2,598.96
5	2,598.96	51.98	682.55	630.57	1,968.39
6	1,968.39	39.37	682.55	643.18	1,325.20
7	1,325.20	26.50	682.55	656.05	669.16
8	669.16	13.38	682.55	669.16	0.00

CALCULATOR SOLUTION

Keyed entry	Display
AC 5000 Min × .02 =	100
− 682.55 =	−582.55
M+ MR	4417.45

First quarter principal balance

× .02 =	88.349
− 682.55 =	−594.201
M+ MR	3823.249

Second quarter principal balance

DETERMINING OUTSTANDING PRINCIPAL OF A LOAN

Learning objective
Calculate the outstanding principal of an amortized loan.

Recall that the present value annuity formula was used to establish the amortization formula.

Amortization formula

present value *Annuity* $A = p \dfrac{1 - (1 + i)^{-n}}{i}$

amortization $p = A \dfrac{1}{\dfrac{1 - (1 + i)^{-n}}{i}}$

$\qquad\qquad = A \dfrac{i}{1 - (1 + i)^{-n}}$

The present value annuity can be used to determine the outstanding principal of a loan at any stage in the loan.

Example 16

Determine the amount of outstanding loan principal for a loan of $1,000 at 12% interest per year to be amortized monthly over 1 year after (a) six payments, (b) three payments, and (c) nine payments have been made. (Note: Please consult the loan repayment table of Example 14.)

Solution

a.   If we had the loan repayment table available, we could see that the outstanding principal is $514.93. If we did not have the loan repayment table, we could use the present value annuity.

$$A = p \frac{1 - (1 + i)^{-m}}{i} \qquad \text{(Appendix, column E)}$$

for $p = \$88.85$, $i = 1\%$, and $m = 6$ payments yet to be made. The present value formula tells us what lump sum of money would be necessary to generate six more payments of $88.85 each at 1% interest per month. That same amount is also the amount of the unpaid principal of the loan.

$$A = \$88.85(5.795473)$$
$$= \$514.93$$

Note: we are replacing n with m in the formula simply to point out that the power in the formula for computing the outstanding principal is:

m = the number of *remaining payments* in the loan

b.   After three payments, there will be $12 - 3 = 9$ payments left, so

$m = 9$
$i = .01$ or 1%
$p = 88.85$

$$A = p \, \frac{1 - (1 + i)^{-m}}{i} = \$88.85(8.566011) = \$761.09$$

Checking the repayment table, we can see that this is correct with a minor rounding error.

c.   After eight payments, there will be $12 - 8 = 4$ payments left so,

$m = 4$
$i = .01$ or 1%
$p = 88.85$

$$A = p \, \frac{1 - (1 + i)^{-m}}{i} = 88.85 \, \frac{1 - (1.01)^{-4}}{.01}$$

$$= 88.85(3.90165) = 346.69$$

This form of consumer loan is very common because it provides the borrower with the convenience of equal regular payments, and because it distributes the interest portion of the payments fairly.

CHECK YOUR KNOWLEDGE

Loan repayment and early liquidation of a loan

Solve the following problems. Round dollar amounts to the nearest cent.

1.   Construct an amortized loan repayment table for a principal of $1,000 borrowed at 12% interest per year and repaid quarterly over 2 years. (*Note:* $p = 1,000(.142456) = \$142.46$ per quarter.)

$i = .03$

$n = 8$

n	Principal	Interest	Payment	Principal payment	New principal
1	$1,000.00	30	$142.46	$112.46	$887.54
2	887.54	26.63	142.46	115.83	771.71
3	771.71	23.15	142.46	119.31	652.40
4	652.40	19.57	142.46	122.89	529.51

n	Principal	Interest	Payment	Principal payment	New principal
5	_____	_____	142.46	_____	_____
6	_____	_____	142.46	_____	_____
7	_____	_____	142.46	_____	_____
8	_____	_____	142.46	_____	_____

2.   Construct an amortized loan repayment table for the first four payments of a $600 loan at 18% interest to be paid monthly for 1 year. (*Note:* $p = 600(.091680) = \$55.01$ with rounding.)

n	Principal	Interest	Payment	Principal payment	New principal
1	$600	_____	$55	_____	_____
2	_____	_____	55	_____	_____
3	_____	_____	55	_____	_____
4	_____	_____	55	_____	_____

3.   Use the present value annuity formula to determine the outstanding principal amounts in problem 1 after (a) three payments, (b) five payments, and (c) seven payments. (Check your answers with the table you developed in problem 1.)

4.   Use the present value annuity formula to determine the outstanding principal amounts in problem 2 after (a) two payments, (b) five payments, and (c) nine payments.

5.   Brian Paul bought a new car for $13,000. After paying all incidental costs and putting a down payment on the car, Brian agreed to finance the remaining costs with an $11,000 loan at 12% APR to be paid monthly for 4 years. After 3 years of payments (36 months), Brian wants to see if he can afford to pay off the remaining principal of the loan. How much does Brian owe on the principal? (Note: You must first determine Brian's regular payment, and then determine his outstanding principal.)

Answers to CYK: **1.**   principal: 771.71, 652.40, 529.51, 402.94, 272.57, 138.29; interest: 26.63, 23.15, 19.57, 15.89, 12.09, 8.18, 4.15; principal payment: 115.83, 119.31, 122.89, 126.57, 130.37, 134.28, 138.31; new principal: 771.71, 652.40, 529.51, 402.93, 272.56, 138.28, 0   **2.**   principal: 554.00, 507.31, 459.92; interest: 9.00, 8.31, 7.61, 6.90; principal payment: 46.00, 46.69, 47.39, 48.10; new principal: 554.00, 507.31, 459.92, 411.82   **3.**   a. $652.42; b. $402.96; c. $138.31   **4.**   a. $507.22; b. $362.90; c. $160.17   **5.**   payment = $289.67, remaining after 36 months = $3,260.26

(10.4) EXERCISES

1. Construct a loan repayment table for a loan of $4,500 borrowed at 8% interest per year amortized quarterly for 2 years.

n	Principal	Interest	Payment	Principal payment	New principal
①	$4,500	90	$614.30	$524.30	$3,975.70
2	3,975.70		614.30		
3			614.30		
④			614.30		
5			614.30		
⑥			614.30		
7			614.30		
8			614.30		

2. Construct a loan repayment table for a loan of $8,000 borrowed at 12% interest per year amortized monthly for 1 year.

n	Principal	Interest	Payment	Principal payment	New principal
1	$8,000		$710.79		
2			710.79		
3			710.79		
4			710.79		
5			710.79		
6			710.79		
7			710.79		
8			710.79		
9			710.79		
10			710.79		
11			710.79		
12			710.79		

3. Construct a loan repayment table for a loan of $2,400 borrowed at 10% interest per year amortized semiannually for 3 years.

4. Construct a loan repayment table for a loan of $3,000 borrowed at 18% interest per year amortized monthly for 1 year.

5. Construct a loan repayment table for a loan of $12,000 borrowed at 8% interest per year amortized quarterly for 2 years.

6. Consider a $9,000 loan amortized monthly at 12% interest per year for 4 years. If the monthly payments are $237, determine the outstanding principal on this loan after (a) 12 payments, (b) 24 payments, (c) 36 payments, and (d) 44 payments.

7. Consider a $12,000 loan amortized at 12% interest per year for 4 years. If the monthly payments are $316, determine the outstanding principal on this loan after (a) 15 payments, (b) 24 payments, (c) 36 payments, and (d) 40 payments.

8. Consider a $19,000 loan amortized monthly at 12% interest per year for 5 years. If the monthly payments are $422.64, determine the outstanding principal on this loan after (a) 12 payments, (b) 24 payments, (c) 36 payments, and (d) 48 payments.

9. Consider a $15,000 loan amortized monthly at 12% interest per year for 3 years. If the monthly payments are $498.21, determine the outstanding principal on this loan after (a) 12 payments, (b) 24 payments, and (c) 36 payments.

10. Consider a $2,000 loan amortized monthly at 18% interest per year for 2 years. If the monthly payments are $99.85, determine the outstanding principal on this loan after (a) 6 payments, (b) 12 payments, (c) 18 payments, and (d) 20 payments.

11. Consider a $3,000 loan amortized quarterly at 12% interest per year for 4 years. If the quarterly payments are $238.33, determine the outstanding principal on this loan after (a) 4 payments, (b) 8 payments, (c) 12 payments, and (d) 15 payments.

12. Consider a $9,000 loan amortized quarterly at 8% per year for 5 years. If the quarterly payments are $550.41, determine the outstanding principal on this loan after (a) 5 payments, (b) 10 payments, (c) 12 payments, and (d) 15 payments.

13. Consider a $6,000 loan amortized semiannually at 12% interest per year for 4 years. If the semiannual payments are $966.22, determine the outstanding principal on this loan after (a) 2 payments, (b) 4 payments, (c) 6 payments, and (d) 7 payments.

14. Sherry Lynne purchased new appliances for her kitchen with $4,500 she borrowed to be amortized monthly for 2 years at 12% interest per year. She has made 18 payments on the installment contract and now wishes to pay off the loan. How much does Sherry still owe on the original principal?

15. Maryanne Leo purchased a new silver tea set for her parents' 50th wedding anniversary for $1,800. Maryanne agreed to an installment contract for the entire $1,800 to be amortized monthly for 2 years at 12% interest per year. She has made 12 payments on the installment contract and now wishes to pay off the loan. How much does Maryanne still owe on the original principal?

16. Jack Rogers purchased a new boat for $6,700 and borrowed $5,000 to be amortized quarterly for 4 years at 10% interest per year. He has made 12 payments on the installment contract and now wishes to pay off the loan. How much does Jack still owe on the original principal?

17. Jerry Schurfun purchased a new jetski and borrowed $4,100 to be amortized monthly for 2 years at 6% interest per year. He has made 15 payments on the installment contract and now wishes to pay off the loan. How much does Jerry still owe on the original principal?

18. Lloyd and Sue Darryl purchased matching snowmobiles last winter. The snow machines cost $11,000, $7,500 of which was amortized monthly for 2½ years at 12% interest per year. They have made 24 payments on the installment contract and now want to pay off the loan. How much do they still owe?

19. Aaron and Megan Earl purchased a home 20 years ago with a 30-year 6% interest rate mortgage on which they have been paying $98 monthly. They have recently inherited some money and would like to pay off their mortgage. What is their outstanding principal after 240 payments?

10.5   REBATE OF INTEREST ON A LOAN PAID OFF EARLY

Learning objective
Calculate the interest rebate for a loan paid off early.

Whenever a borrower pays off a loan principal sooner than the loan contract requires, the borrower expects to save on interest costs. The amount of interest saved is called an **interest rebate**. After all, if the borrower is no longer holding the loan principal, no interest should be charged.

Determining the outstanding principal on either an *amortized loan* (equal regular payments) or a *principal plus interest on the unpaid balance loan* can be accomplished either by a loan repayment table or the techniques we discussed in Section 10.4. Consequently, if a borrower chooses to liquidate a loan early, either the individual or the lending institution can determine the outstanding principal that will then be paid to the lender and the contract will be brought to closure. Some lending institutions prefer that the repayment terms of the contract be met fully, and then they offer a rebate of interest to the borrower.

Next we will use some of the methods and examples developed earlier in this chapter to determine the amount of rebate a borrower might receive on a loan paid off early.

PRESENT VALUE METHOD FOR DETERMINING INTEREST REBATE

Example 17 is based on the information we developed earlier in Example 14. The table in the solution of Example 14 should be helpful.

Example 17

Craig Barrett borrowed $1,000 at 12% annual percentage interest rate to be amortized monthly over a 1-year period. Craig's contract stated that he would make 12 monthly payments of $88.85 each and that the finance charge would be $66.20. Craig made six payments as the contract specified and then decided he would pay off the loan. Since Craig had studied business in college, he knew his outstanding balance to be $514.92. Primal Loan Company, Craig's lender, insisted that Craig make the final six payments, after which it would grant him an interest rebate. How much should Craig be rebated?

Solution

Step 1: Determine the amount of the unpaid principal. We also know Craig still owes $514.92 on the principal (Example 16) of the loan, so, thus far, he has paid $1,000 - 514.92 = $485.08 of the principal.

Step 2: Determine the amount of interest paid to date. The difference between the total payments made and the total principal paid is the amount of interest Craig should pay for six months' use of Primal Loan's money.

We know that the monthly payments are $88.85 and that Craig has made six payments for a total of 6 × $88.85 = $533.10.

interest = $533.10 - 485.08 = $48.02

Step 3: Calculate the amount of the rebate. Craig's rebate can be calculated by subtracting this amount from the full finance charge of $66.20.

$$\text{interest rebate} = \text{full finance charge} - 6 \text{ months' interest}$$
$$= (\$66.20 - 48.02)$$
$$= \$18.18$$

The next example will demonstrate quite clearly the benefit of paying off a loan as early as possible. It also reinforces the concept mentioned earlier that less interest is paid when less principal is held by the borrower.

Example 18

Eileen Simpson borrowed $2,000 at a yearly percentage rate of 18% interest amortized monthly for 2 years. The installment contract indicates a finance charge of $396.35 and monthly installments of $99.85. What interest rebate should Eileen receive if she pays off her loan after (a) 18 months, (b) 12 months, or (c) 6 months?

Solution

a. *Step 1:* Determine the outstanding principal after 18 months. Present value formula:

$$A = p \, \frac{1 - (1 + i)^{-m}}{i}$$

$$m = 24 - 18 = 6$$
$$i = .18/12 = .015 \text{ or } 1.5\%$$
$$A = \$99.85(5.697167) = \$568.86$$

Step 2: Determine the amount of interest paid thus far.

$$\text{interest paid} = \text{sum of 18 payments} - \text{principal paid to date}$$
$$= (18)(99.85) - (\$2,000 - 568.86)$$
$$= \$1,797.30 - \$1,431.14$$
$$= \$366.16$$

Step 3: Determine the rebate.

$$\text{rebate of interest} = \text{finance charge} - \text{interest paid}$$
$$= \$396.35 - \$366.16$$
$$= \$30.19$$

b. *Step 1:* Determine the outstanding principal and the principal paid to date.

$$p = \$99.85$$
$$m = 24 - 12 = 12$$
$$i = .015 \text{ or } 1.5\%$$
$$A = \$99.85(10.907470) = \$1,089.11$$

principal paid to date $= \$2,000 - \$1,089.11 = \$910.89$

Step 2: Determine the interest paid to date.

interest paid $= 12(99.85) - \$910.89$
$= \$1,198.20 - \$910.89 = \$287.31$

Step 3: Determine the interest rebate.

interest rebate $=$ finance charge $-$ interest paid to date
$= \$396.35 - \$287.31$
$= \$109.04$

c. *Step 1:* Determine the principal paid to date.

$$p = \$99.85$$
$$m = 24 - 6 = 18$$
$$i = .015 \text{ or } 1.5\%$$
$$A = \$99.85(15.672520) = \$1,564.90$$
principal outstanding $= \$1,564.90$
principal paid to date $= \$2,000 - \$1,564.90 = \$435.10$

Step 2: Determine interest paid to date.

interest paid $= 6(99.85) - \$435.10$
$= \$599.10 - \$435.10$
$= \$164$

Step 3: Determine the interest rebate.

interest rebate $= \$396.35 - \$164 = \$232.35$

SUM OF DIGITS METHOD OF DETERMINING INTEREST REBATE

Another method for computing the amount of interest rebate a borrower is entitled to on an early pay loan is based on a mathematical formula that quickly adds up a sequence of digits from 1 to n that differ from each other by 1. This formula is the **sum of digits** formula.

$$S = \text{sum of digits} = \frac{n(n + 1)}{2}$$

Example 19

Determine the sum of the digits (a) 1 through 10, (b) 1 through 12, (c) 1 through 24, and (d) 1 through 36.

Solution

a. $n = 10$ because there are 10 digits, and

$$\text{sum} = \frac{10(10 + 1)}{2} = \frac{(10)(11)}{2} = 55$$

b. $n = 12$

$$\text{sum} = \frac{12(12 + 1)}{2} = 78$$

c. $n = 24$

$$\text{sum} = \frac{24(25)}{2} = 300$$

d. $n = 36$

$$\text{sum} = \frac{36(37)}{2} = 666$$

Learning objective
Calculate the approximate interest rebate using the sum of digits and rule of 78s methods.

The **rule of 78s** is used to *approximate* the amount of interest contained in each regular payment of a 12-installment loan. The rule of 78s is a very common example of the general sum of digits concept. This method makes use of the fact that the sum of the 12 digits $1 + 2 + 3 + 4 + \cdots + 12 = 78$ and that, if we form the fractions $\frac{1}{78}, \frac{2}{78}, \frac{3}{78}, \cdots, \frac{12}{78}$, the sum of these fractions is 1; that is,

$$\frac{1}{78} + \frac{2}{78} + \frac{3}{78} + \cdots + \frac{12}{78} = \frac{78}{78} = 1$$

Now we take the total finance charge and break it up into parts using these fractions. For the 12 payments of a loan, these fractions represent the amount of the finance charge that corresponds to each payment; that is,

$\frac{12}{78}$ of finance charge is included in payment 1

$\frac{11}{78}$ of finance charge is included in payment 2

$^{10}\!/_{78}$ of finance charge is included in payment 3

$^{9}\!/_{78}$ of finance charge is included in payment 4

$^{8}\!/_{78}$ of finance charge is included in payment 5

$^{7}\!/_{78}$ of finance charge is included in payment 6

$^{6}\!/_{78}$ of finance charge is included in payment 7

$^{5}\!/_{78}$ of finance charge is included in payment 8

$^{4}\!/_{78}$ of finance charge is included in payment 9

$^{3}\!/_{78}$ of finance charge is included in payment 10

$^{2}\!/_{78}$ of finance charge is included in payment 11

$^{1}\!/_{78}$ of finance charge is included in payment 12

Again, note that if you add up the fractions $^{12}\!/_{78} + {}^{11}\!/_{78} + {}^{10}\!/_{78} + \cdots + {}^{1}\!/_{78} = {}^{78}\!/_{78} = 1$, which means that all of the finance charges will be collected over the 12-installment period. If the loan has fewer or more than 12 payment periods, then a different rule must be developed using the sum of digits technique.

Example 20

Consider the loan in Example 17. $A = \$1,000$, $p = \$88.85$, $i = 1\%$, $n = 12$, finance charge = \$66.20, and Craig chose to pay off the loan after 6 months of payments. Determine Craig's interest rebate using the rule of 78s.

Solution

The rule of 78s would distribute the finance charge of \$66.20 over the life of the loan in the following way:

Payment number	Rule of 78s part of finance charge	Amount of finance charge
1	$^{12}\!/_{78}$	$^{12}\!/_{78} \times 66.20 = 10.18$
2	$^{11}\!/_{78}$	$^{11}\!/_{78} \times 66.20 = 9.34$
3	$^{10}\!/_{78}$	$^{10}\!/_{78} \times 66.20 = 8.49$
4	$^{9}\!/_{78}$	$^{9}\!/_{78} \times 66.20 = 7.64$
5	$^{8}\!/_{78}$	$^{8}\!/_{78} \times 66.20 = 6.79$
6	$^{7}\!/_{78}$	$^{7}\!/_{78} \times 66.20 = 5.94$
7	$^{6}\!/_{78}$	$^{6}\!/_{78} \times 66.20 = 5.09$
8	$^{5}\!/_{78}$	$^{5}\!/_{78} \times 66.20 = 4.24$
9	$^{4}\!/_{78}$	$^{4}\!/_{78} \times 66.20 = 3.39$
10	$^{3}\!/_{78}$	$^{3}\!/_{78} \times 66.20 = 2.55$
11	$^{2}\!/_{78}$	$^{2}\!/_{78} \times 66.20 = 1.70$
12	$^{1}\!/_{78}$	$^{1}\!/_{78} \times 66.20 = .85$
	$^{78}\!/_{78} = 1$	66.20

CALCULATOR SOLUTION

Keyed entry	Display
AC 66.20 ÷ 78 =	.8487179
Min. MR × 12 =	10.184615
MR × 11 =	9.3358974
MR × 10 =	8.4871795
MR × 9 =	7.6384615
. . . .	
. . . .	
. . . .	
MR × 1 =	.84871

Now adding the last six interest amounts gives us $17.82 rebate of interest. Our earlier calculation in Example 17 yielded a higher rebate of $18.18 to the borrower. The $17.82 yielded by the rule of 78s is an *approximation* to the correct rebate of $18.16. You might want to compare the table in Example 14 to the table above to see the assignment of interest to each payment and to observe where the differences occur. A shorter and quicker means of computing the approximate interest rebate by the rule of 78s follows:

1. Note that after 6 months of payments on a 12-month loan, 6 payments remain. Use the sum of digits formula to add the digits 1 through 6.

$$\text{sum} = \frac{6(7)}{2} = 21$$

2. Form the ratio 21/78; this is the ratio of the finance charge remaining in those 6 payments, or the approximate interest rebate due the borrower.

$$\frac{21}{78} \times \$66.20 = \$17.82$$

Example 21

Use the rule of 78s to approximate the interest rebate due on a loan amortized over 12 months with a finance charge of $65 if the loan is paid off after the following number of payments: (a) 10, (b) 7, and (c) 4.

Solution

a. $n = 12 - 10 = 2$ $\text{sum} = \dfrac{2(3)}{2} = 3$

approximate interest rebate $= \dfrac{3}{78} \times 65 = \$2.50$

b. $n = 12 - 7 = 5$ $\text{sum} = \dfrac{(5)(6)}{2} = 15$

approximate interest rebate $= \dfrac{15}{78} \times 65 = \$12.50$

c. $n = 12 - 4 = 8$ $\text{sum} = \dfrac{(8)(9)}{2} = 36$

approximate interest rebate $= \dfrac{36}{78} \times 65 = 30$

The sum of digits method described above for the rule of 78s (12 installment payments) also may be applied to loans with different numbers of payments, for example, 24 or 36.

Example 22

Use the sum of digits method to approximate the interest rebate on a loan amortized over 24 months with a finance charge of $120 if the loan still has the remaining number of payments: (a) 18, (b) 12, and (c) 9.

Solution

The denominator of our fraction is determined by the sum of the digits 1 through 24 because there are 24 installments in the entire loan.

$$\text{denominator} = \text{sum} = N \frac{(n + 1)}{2} = \frac{24(25)}{2} = 300$$

a. $n = 18$ payments remain

$\text{sum} = \dfrac{18(19)}{2} = 171$

approximate interest rebate $= \dfrac{171}{300} \times \$120 = \$68.40$

b. $n = 12$ payments remain

$\text{sum} = \dfrac{12(13)}{2} = 78$

approximate interest rebate $= \dfrac{78}{300} \times \$120 = \$31.20$

c. $n = 9$ payments remain

$$\text{sum} = \frac{9(10)}{2} = 45$$

$$\text{approximate interest rebate} = \frac{45}{300} \times \$120 = \$18.00$$

Although the difference in the amount of interest rebate calculated using present value methods and sum of digits methods may have seemed minor in Example 20, in other situations, the differences could be significant.

Example 23

Carin Sward obtained an auto loan for $10,000 at 12% APR that was amortized monthly over a 4-year period (48 months). Carin paid off the loan after 24 monthly payments. Determine (a) Carin's monthly payment, (b) Carin's total finance charge under the original agreement, and (c) Carin's interest rebate after 24 months of payments by: (1) the present value method, and (2) the sum of digits method.

Solution

a. $A = \$10,000$

$n = 48$

$i = .12/12 = .01 \text{ or } 1\%$

Amortization formula:

$$p = A \frac{i}{1 - (1 + i)^{-n}} = 10,000 \times \frac{.01}{1 - (1.01)^{-48}}$$

$p = 10,000 \times (.026334)^* = 263.34 \text{ per month}$

*Appendix A, column F, 1%, N = 48

b.   total payments $= 48 \text{ months} \times 263.34 = \$12,640.32$

finance charge $=$ total payments $-$ loan principal $= \$2,640.32$

c.   Interest rebate:

1.   present value method:

rebate $=$ finance charge $-$ interest paid to date

principal remaining: $A = p \dfrac{1 - (1 + i)^{-m}}{i}$

$$m = 48 - 24 = 24$$
$$i = .01 \text{ or } 1\%$$
$$p = 263.34$$

$$A = \$263.34 \times \frac{1 - (1.01)^{-24}}{.01}$$

$$A = \$263.34 \times (21.24338)^*$$

*Appendix, column E, $n = 24$, $i = 1\%$

principal remaining = $5,594.23

principal paid to date = $10,000 - $5,594.23 = $4,405.77

interest paid to date = total payments to date − principal
                          to date
= 24($263.34) − $4,405.77
= $6,320.16 − $4,405.77
= $1,914.39

interest rebate = $2,640.32 − $1,914.39 = $725.93

2. sum of digits method:
First determine the sum of the digits 1 through 48 (denominator).

$$\text{sum} = \frac{n(n + 1)}{2} = \frac{(48)(49)}{2} = 1,176$$

Second, determine the sum of digits for the remaining payments (numerator). 24 payments remain, so

$$\text{sum} = \frac{(24)(25)}{2} = 300$$

$$\text{interest rebate} = \frac{300}{1,176} \times \$2,640.32 = \$673.55$$

Notice that the sum of digits method would rebate $52.38 less than the borrower should receive. Some states have prohibited the use of the sum of digits method because it does not accurately determine the interest rebate due to the borrower.

CHECK YOUR KNOWLEDGE

Interest rebate

1. Use the present value annuity method to determine the interest rebate on a $20,000 loan at 6% APR amortized monthly ($608.44 per month) over a period of 3 years, if the loan is paid off after (a) 10 payments, (b) 20 payments, and (c) 30 payments.

2. Simon Florcyk borrowed $30,000 for 1 year and agreed to pay a finance charge of $1,200. He agreed to pay back the loan with twelve monthly installments of $2,600 each. Use the rule of 78s to determine the amount of the finance charge assigned to each of the twelve payments.

Payment	Rule of 78s fraction	Amount of finance charge
1	_____	_____
2	_____	_____
3	_____	_____
4	_____	_____
5	_____	_____
6	_____	_____
7	_____	_____
8	_____	_____
9	_____	_____
10	_____	_____
11	_____	_____
12	_____	_____

3. Use the sum of digits method to approximate the interest rebate for a $15,000 loan amortized monthly over a 5-year period with a finance charge of $2,595.00 if the loan is paid off after (a) 50 payments, (b) 30 payments, and (c) 15 payments.

4. Harry Orwell purchased new appliances for his kitchen and signed an installment contract for a loan of $3,000. The loan will be amortized over 24 months at an annual percentage interest rate of 18%. The contract calls for 24 monthly payments of $149.77 each, which means the finance charge is $594.48. If Harry pays off the loan after 18 months, what will his interest rebate be by (a) the present value method? (b) the sum of digits method?

10.5 **EXERCISES**

Solve the following. Round dollar amounts to the nearest cent.

1. Consider a $9,000 loan amortized monthly at 12% interest per year for 4 years. If the monthly payments are $237, and the finance charge is $2,376, determine the interest rebate due if the loan is paid off after (a) 12 payments, (b) 24 payments, and (c) 36 payments.

2. Consider a $12,000 loan amortized at 12% interest per year for 4 years. If the monthly payments are $316, and the finance charge is

Answers to CYK: **1.** a. $1,019.72; b. $401.61; c. $63.03 **2.** $^{12}/_{78}$, $184.62; $^{11}/_{78}$, $169.23; $^{10}/_{78}$, $153.85; $^{9}/_{78}$, $138.46; $^{8}/_{78}$, $123.08; $^{7}/_{78}$, $107.69; $^{6}/_{78}$, $92.31; $^{5}/_{78}$, $76.92; $^{4}/_{78}$, $61.54; $^{3}/_{78}$, $46.15; $^{2}/_{78}$, $30.77; $^{1}/_{78}$, $15.38 **3.** a. $77.99; b. $659.39; c. $1,467.66 **4.** a. $45.41; b. $41.62

$3,168, determine the interest rebate due if this loan is paid off after (a) 15 payments and (b) 24 payments.

3. Consider a $19,000 loan amortized monthly at 12% interest per year for 5 years. If the monthly payments are $422.64 and the finance charge is $6,358.40, determine the interest rebate due if the loan is paid off after (a) 12 payments, (b) 24 payments, (c) 36 payments, and (d) 48 payments.

4. Consider a $15,000 loan amortized monthly at 12% interest per year for 3 years. If the monthly payments are $498.21, and the finance charge is $2,935.56, determine the interest rebate due if the loan is paid off after (a) 12 payments, (b) 24 payments, (c) 36 payments, and (d) 48 payments.

5. Consider a $2,000 loan amortized monthly at 18% interest per year for 2 years. If the monthly payments are $99.85 and the finance charge is $396.40, determine the interest rebate if the loan is paid off after (a) 6 payments, (b) 12 payments, and (c) 18 payments.

6. Consider a $3,000 loan amortized quarterly at 12% interest per year for 4 years. If the quarterly payments are $238.33 and the finance charge is $821.33, determine the interest rebate due if the loan is paid off after (a) 4 payments, (b) 8 payments, and (c) 12 payments.

7. Consider a $9,000 loan amortized quarterly at 8% interest per year for 5 years. If the quarterly payments are $550.41, and the finance charge is $2,008.20, determine the interest rebate if the loan is paid off after (a) 5 payments, (b) 10 payments, (c) 12 payments, and (d) 15 payments.

8. Consider a $6,000 loan amortized semiannually at 12% interest per year for 4 years. If the semiannual payments are $966.22, and the finance charge is $1,729.76, determine the interest rebate if the loan is paid off after (a) 2 payments, (b) 4 payments, and (c) 6 payments.

9. Sherry Lynne purchased new appliances for her kitchen, borrowing $4,500 to be amortized monthly for 2 years at 12% interest per year. She has made 18 payments on the installment contract and now wishes to pay off the loan. How much would Sherry save in interest if she paid off the loan after 18 payments?

10. Marybeth Leo purchased six place settings of flatware for her granddaughter's wedding present for $1,800. Marybeth agreed to an installment contract for the entire $1,800 to be amortized monthly for 2 years at 12% interest per year. She has made 12 payments on the installment contract and now wishes to pay off the loan. How much will Marybeth save in interest if she does pay off the loan?

11. Jack Rogers purchased a new boat for $6,700; he borrowed $5,000 to be amortized quarterly for 4 years at 10% interest per year. He has made 12 payments on the installment contract and now wishes to pay off the loan. How much does Jack expect to save in interest if he does pay off the loan?

12. Jerry Schein purchased a new motor bike and borrowed $4,100 to be amortized monthly for 2 years at 6% per year. He has made 15 payments on the installment contract and now wishes to pay off the loan. How much will Jerry save in interest if he does pay off the principal?

13. The Andersons purchased matching custom saddle sets for horseback riding costing $11,000; $7,500 was amortized monthly for 2½ years at 12% interest per year. They have made 24 payments on the installment contract and now want to pay off the loan. How much interest will they save?

14. Use the formula for the sum of digits to determine the sum of the digits from 1 to (a) 20, (b) 30, (c) 40, (d) 50, (e) 100, and (f) 1,000.

15. Use the rule of 78s to approximate the interest rebate on a 1-year loan paid monthly with a finance charge of $132.38 if the loan is paid off after (a) 4 months, (b) 6 months, (c) 8 months, and (d) 11 months.

16. Use the rule of 78s to approximate the interest rebate on a 1-year loan paid monthly with a finance charge of $198.56 if the loan is paid off after (a) 3 months, (b) 6 months, (c) 9 months, and (d) 10 months.

17. Use the rule of 78s to approximate the interest rebate on a 1-year loan paid monthly with a finance charge of $330.94 if the loan is paid off after (a) 3 months, (b) 6 months, and (c) 9 months.

18. Use the rule of 78s to approximate the interest rebate on a 1-year loan paid monthly with a finance charge of $529.50 if the loan is paid off after (a) 4 months, (b) 6 months, (c) 8 months, and (d) 11 months.

10.6   MORTGAGES

Learning objective
Calculate the regular payment, outstanding principal, and interest rebate for a mortgage.

A **mortgage** is a pledge of property to a creditor for the repayment of a debt. The most common form of a mortgage by consumers is to secure a loan to purchase real estate. Mortgage loans usually involve a larger loan principal and a longer term to maturity, 15 to 30 years, than other types of installment loans. The property pledged provides the lender with security for the loan. If the borrower defaults on the loan, then he or she may be required to forfeit the property to the lender.

Mortgage loans are commonly used by consumers to buy homes and by businesses to finance fixed assets. The simplest type of mortgage loan is called a *fixed-rate mortgage loan*. Fixed-rate mortgages are amortized loans that are calculated in the same manner as the loans presented in Sections 10.3 through 10.5.

Example 24

Bob and Marlene Harvey have purchased a new home for $90,000. Bob and Marlene have been granted a 12% interest rate mortgage for $60,000 to be amortized monthly for 30 years. Determine: (a) Bob and Marlene's monthly payment, (b) the total amount Bob and Marlene will pay the lender if they fulfill the terms of the contract over the 30-year period, (c) the total amount of interest they will pay if they take the entire 30 years to pay, (d) the remaining amount of principal that they will still owe after 20 years of payments, and (e) the interest Bob and Marlene would save if they paid off the loan after 20 years.

Solution

a. Using the amortization table in Appendix A column F, for $i = .12/12 = .01$ or 1%, $n = 360$,

$$p = A \frac{i}{1 - (1 + i)^{-n}}$$

$$= 60,000 \times \frac{.01}{1 - (1.01)^{-360}}$$

$$= 60,000 \times (.010286)^* = \$617.16 \text{ per month}$$

*value in column F for $i = 1\%$, $n = 360$

b. Total repaid = 360 months × $617.16/month = $222,177.60.

c. Total interest = $222,177.60 − $60,000 = $162,177.60.

d. After 20 years, or 240 payments, there are 120 payments remaining in the contract. Using the present value annuity formula,

$$A = p \frac{1 - (1 + i)^{-n}}{i} = p \times \text{(value in column E, } i = 1\%, n = 120)$$

$$= \$617.16 \times (69.700510)$$
$$= \$43,016.37$$

principal remaining = $43,016.37

e. interest paid to date = 240 × ($617.16) − ($60,000 − $43,016.37)
$$= \$148,118.40 - \$16,983.63$$
$$= \$131,134.77$$

interest saved by early payoff = $162,177.60 − $131,134.77
$$= \$31,042.83$$

A loan repayment table can be generated for Bob and Marlene using the techniques in Section 10.5 (and preferably a computer with high speed printer) as well.

Example 25

How much would Bob and Marlene (Example 24) save if they took a 15-year mortgage rather than a 30-year mortgage?

Solution

monthly payment = $p = A \times$ (value in column F for $r = 1\%$,
$$n = 180)$$
$$= \$60,000 \times (.0120017)$$
$$= \$720.10 \text{ per month}$$

total payments = 180 × $720.10
$$= \$129,618$$

total interest = $129,618 − $60,000
$$= \$69,618$$

total interest savings = $162,177.60 − $69,618
$$= \$92,559.60$$

So, if Bob and Marlene can find a way to pay $102.50 more each month for 15 years, they can save $92,559.60 in interest, and that is more than the original cost of their home.

Bob and Marlene could also consider a *biweekly mortgage* plan. Under this plan they would divide their $617.60 monthly payment in half ($617.60/2 = $308.80) and pay $308.80 every 2 weeks, 26 times per year. Since they will be paying part of the principal off 2 weeks earlier each month, this plan results in substantial savings of time and money.

The biweekly plan will result in the shortening of the term of their loan from 30 years to 19 years. The total interest they will pay will be $92,238 rather than $162,178 for the 30-year loan. They pay $69,940 less in interest and they own their home 11 years earlier than expected.

Notice that Bob and Marlene will pay the same amount per month, but since they have accelerated their payments, they have retired the principal faster and saved considerable interest.

INNOVATIVE MORTGAGE FINANCING

Increasing costs of homes and rising interest rates have resulted in lending institutions' creating new variations of conventional mortgage financing. *Adjustable-rate mortgages* (*ARMs*) were introduced to make it possible for first-time homeowners to purchase homes with smaller down payments and/or lower monthly payments in the earlier portion of the term of the mortgage. Adjustable-rate mortgages have variable interest rates that may change every year, or every 3 years. The interest rate is determined by the interest rate of U.S. treasury bonds during the month that the ARM's term ends and a new term begins. The rate is then fixed for the new term. Usually, there is a limit on the amount of change that can occur in the interest rate (e.g., at most 2% increase or decrease) and there is an upper "cap" on the rate (e.g., 15%). Adjustable-rate mortgages usually carry lower interest rates than fixed-rate mortgages, but provide less stability because of the potential for rate fluctuation.

Adjustments during the term of the mortgage loan can be made in interest rates, unpaid balance, and overall length of the term of the loan. As these adjustments are made, there are corresponding changes in the monthly payments and amount of interest (finance charge) paid.

Additionally, there are loans that can be offered by the builders and/or owners of homes to help move both older and new homes on the real estate market. These innovative forms of mortgage loans have become necessary due to higher costs of real estate and of borrowing money. The use of computers has made such innovations possible because the computer can be programmed to perform many tasks very quickly. While we might hesitate to redo the computations necessary to calculate a new mortgage payment, new interest charge, or mortgage repayment table, the computer can complete such tasks in minutes.

CHECK YOUR KNOWLEDGE

Mortgages

Solve the following problems. Round dollar amounts to the nearest cent.

1. Determine the monthly payments for each of the following mortgages paid on a monthly basis.

Amount of principal	Rate	Number of years	Monthly payment
$50,000	12%	20	_____
$50,000	6%	20	_____
$50,000	18%	20	_____
$70,000	12%	10	_____
$70,000	12%	20	_____
$70,000	12%	30	_____

2. Melanie Archer recently purchased a home for $90,000. She made a down payment of $25,000 and financed the remainder with a 12% interest rate mortgage to be paid monthly for 30 years. Determine: (a) how much Melanie mortgaged, (b) Melanie's monthly payment, and (c) the total interest Melanie will have paid if she makes all the payments over the 30-year period.

3. Jack Johnson has been making regular payments of $137.91 per month on his 30-year 6% interest rate home mortgage for 25 years. Jack originally borrowed $23,000. How much principal does he still owe after 25 years?

(10.6) EXERCISES

Determine the monthly payments for the mortgages in problems 1 through 5.

	Amount of principal	Rate	Number of years	Monthly payment
1.	$150,000	12%	20	_____
2.	$200,000	6%	20	_____
3.	$100,000	18%	20	_____
4.	$90,000	12%	15	_____
5.	$120,000	12%	20	_____

Answers to CYK: *1.* $550.55; $358.20; $771.65; $1,004.29; $770.77; $720.02   *2.*   a. $65,000; b. $668.59; c. $175,692.40   *3.* $7,133.48

Handwritten margin notes:
$A = 75000$
$T = 30$ yr
$\%. = 12\%$
$i = .01$
$n = 360$
$p = m/45$
$p = m/45 \rightarrow$

6. Fred and Ann Karpel recently agreed to buy a home for $95,000. After a down payment of $20,000 they financed $75,000 with a 30-year fixed-rate mortgage of 12% interest per year to be paid monthly. (a) Determine the monthly payments of the loan. (b) Determine the total interest charge if the loan is paid off according to the mortgage agreement in 30 years.

7. Mary and Jack Kronnen recently agreed to buy a home for $105,000. After a down payment of $25,000 they financed $80,000 with a 30-year fixed-rate mortgage of 12% interest per year to be paid monthly. (a) Determine the monthly payments of the loan. (b) Determine the total interest charge if the loan is paid off according to the mortgage agreement in 30 years.

8. Arnie McElroy recently agreed to buy a home for $88,000. After a down payment of $20,000 he financed $68,000 with a 20-year fixed-rate mortgage of 12% interest per year to be paid monthly. (a) Determine the monthly payments of the loan. (b) Determine the total interest charge if the loan is paid off according to the mortgage agreement in 20 years.

9. Ingvar Borg recently agreed to buy a cottage for $60,000. After a down payment of $20,000, he financed $40,000 with a 20-year fixed-rate mortgage of 12% interest per year to be paid monthly. (a) Determine the monthly payments of the loan. (b) Determine the total interest charge if the loan is paid off according to the mortgage agreement in 20 years.

10. Sue Marshall purchased a townhouse for $125,000. After a down payment of $30,000, she financed the remainder with a 30-year fixed-rate mortgage of 12% interest per year to be paid monthly. (a) Determine the principal financed. (b) Determine the monthly payments of the loan. (c) Determine the total interest charge if the loan is paid off according to the mortgage agreement in 30 years.

11. Cindy Jacobi purchased a two-family home for $185,000. After a down payment of $55,000, she financed the remainder with a 30-year fixed-rate mortgage of 12% interest per year to be paid monthly. (a) Determine the principal financed. (b) Determine the monthly payments of the loan. (c) Determine the total interest charge if the loan is paid off according to the mortgage agreement in 30 years.

12. Pat Avery purchased a townhouse for $140,000. After a down payment of $30,000, she financed the remainder with a 20-year fixed-rate mortgage of 12% interest per year to be paid monthly. (a) Determine the principal financed. (b) Determine the monthly payments of the loan. (c) Determine the total interest charge if the loan is paid off according to the mortgage agreement in 20 years.

13. Amy and Bob Harkness purchased a small camp for $25,000. After a 20% down payment, they financed the remainder with a 10-year fixed-rate mortgage of 6% interest per year to be paid monthly. (a) Determine the principal financed. (b) Determine the monthly payments of the loan. (c) Determine the total interest charge if the loan is paid off according to the mortgage agreement in 10 years.

14. Kara and Al Jenkins purchased a lakefront cottage for $45,000. After a 10% down payment, they financed the remainder with a 10-year fixed-rate mortgage of 6% interest per year to be paid monthly. (a) Determine the principal financed. (b) Determine the monthly payments of the loan. (c) Determine the total interest charge if the loan is paid off according to the mortgage agreement in 10 years.

15. Sue and Jay Black purchased a small business for $250,000. After a 30% down payment, they financed the remainder with a 30-year fixed-rate mortgage of 6% interest per year to be paid monthly. (a) Determine the principal financed. (b) Determine the monthly payments of the loan. (c) Determine the total interest charge if the loan is paid off according to the mortgage agreement in 30 years.

16. Cheryl Martin purchased her home 20 years ago with a 30-year fixed-rate mortgage of 6% interest to be paid monthly on a $25,000 principal. She has made 240 monthly payments of $150 per month. (a) Determine how much is still owed on the original principal. (b) Determine how much interest will be saved if the loan is paid off at this time.

17. Dave Jansen purchased a home 20 years ago with a 30-year fixed-rate mortgage of 6% interest to be paid monthly on a $35,000 principal. He has made 240 monthly payments of $210 per month. (a) Determine how much is still owed on the original principal. (b) Determine how much interest will be saved if the loan is paid off at this time.

18. Girard Amory purchased his home 22 years ago with a 30-year fixed-rate mortgage of 6% interest to be paid monthly on a $28,000 principal. He has made 264 monthly payments of $168 per month. (a) Determine how much is still owed on the original principal. (b) Determine how much interest will be saved if the loan is paid off at this time.

19. Jeff Hoxie purchased a cottage 25 years ago with a 30-year fixed-rate mortgage of 6% interest to be paid monthly on a $15,000 principal. He has made 300 monthly payments of $90 per month. (a) Determine how much is still owed on the original principal. (b) Determine how much interest will be saved if the loan is paid off at this time.

10.7   ANNUAL PERCENTAGE RATE

Learning objective
Determine the true annual percentage rate for a loan.

The Truth in Lending Act passed by Congress in 1969 is designed to protect consumers against dishonest lenders. It also provides consumers with standardized interest rate terms that must be given to them in writing and that provide them with a means by which they can compare different loan offers.

The *annual percentage rate* (*APR*) is the rate of interest stated on a yearly basis and calculated on the unpaid principal balance of each period of loan payments. For a loan with equal periodic payments, it is the yearly interest stated in the amortized loan methods studied in Section 10.3. For loans like the one in Example 10, with an unequal payment based on a part of the principal plus a percentage of the unpaid balance, APR is that interest multiplied by the number of payments in 1 year.

In this section, we will use the APR tables found in the Appendix to show how APR is determined. The procedure requires that we follow four steps:

Step 1:   Determine the total number of payments, n.

Step 2:   Calculate M:

$$M = \left(\frac{\text{finance charge}}{\text{loan principal}} \right) \times 100$$

Step 3:   Consult the APR table in the Appendix (of this text) and find M in row n.

Step 4: Determine the annual percentage rate by looking to the top of the column in which M appears.

Example 26

Determine the APR for the loan Tom Evans obtained in Example 8. Tom borrowed $1,200 at 9% simple interest add-on for 1 year. The finance charge was $108, and Tom was to pay $109 monthly for 1 year.

Solution

$$n = 12$$

$$M = \frac{\$108}{\$1,200} \times 100 = 9$$

Find M in row n and at the top of the column APR $= 16.25\%$ (nearest value). Notice that the true APR based on interest on the unpaid balance is much greater than the suggested 9%.

Example 27

Reconsider Allyssa Meyers' discounted loan of $1,200 with a $108 (Example 9) finance charge for 1 year to be paid monthly. Determine the true APR charged Allyssa.

Solution

Recall that Allyssa received only $1,092 since she accepted a discounted loan.

loan principal = proceeds = $1,200 − $108 = $1,092

$$n = 12$$

$$M = \frac{\$108}{\$1,092} \times 100 = 9.89$$

APR $= 17.75\%$

Now let's consider the last of our three original examples of installment loans, that of Nancy Green. Nancy borrowed $1,000 and paid back the loan in twelve equal payments plus 1% of the unpaid balance.

Example 28

Determine the APR being charged Nancy Green in Example 10. Nancy borrowed $1,200 for 1 year and paid a finance charge of $78. The terms of her loan were that she would pay 1% interest per month on the unpaid balance as well as $\frac{1}{12}$ of the principal each month. The 1% interest per month suggests a yearly rate of 12%. The terms of her agreement are in the true spirit of APR and thus we should find her APR to be 12%, or at least very close to it.

Solution

$n = 12$

loan principal = $1,200

finance charge = $78

$$M = \frac{\$78}{\$1,200} \times 100 = 6.5$$

APR = 11.75% (nearest value)

Let's look at one last example that will represent a situation we almost all find ourselves in at one time or another, that of buying a vehicle.

Example 29

Andy Jones purchased a motorcycle and borrowed $8,000 for 4 years with a finance charge of $2,687.00. What is the APR charged Andy?

Solution

$n = 48$

$$M = \frac{\$2,687}{\$8,000} \times 100 = 33.59$$

APR = 15%

A formula exists for calculating APR as well, but it provides only an approximation to APR, so we have not included it here.

CHECK YOUR KNOWLEDGE

Annual percentage rate

Solve the following problems. Round dollar amounts to the nearest cent and rates to the nearest one-hundredth of a percent.

1. Determine the annual percentage rate for each of the following loans.

Principal	Interest finance charge	Total number monthly payments	APR
$3,000	$1,649.75	60	_____
$7,000	$1,859.59	36	_____
$9,000	$2,165.23	48	_____
$20,000	$5,496.54	60	_____
$12,000	$3,595.90	48	_____
$15,000	$3,673.23	42	_____

2. Sean Gillis borrowed $3,000 from Sure and Quick Loan Finance Company for 2 years. The finance charge method S&QL used was a 12% simple interest add-on that was calculated to be $2 \times .12 \times \$3,000 = \$720$, with Sean making 24 payments of $155 each. What is the APR that S&QL is charging Sean?

3. Marty Bickoff needed $1,500 in a hurry and borrowed it from his uncle. Marty agreed to pay his uncle $300 interest, and to pay back the loan plus interest in monthly installments over a 24-month period. What APR did Marty agree to?

10.7 EXERCISES

For each of the following problem sets, determine the annual percentage rate for the loans. Round dollar amounts to the nearest cent and rates to the nearest one-hundredth of a percent.

	Principal	Interest	Number of monthly payments	APR
1.	$5,000	$1,465.00	24	_____
2.	$8,000	$3,912.80	36	_____
3.	$3,000	$317.70	12	_____
4.	$6,000	$1,495.20	30	_____
5.	$2,000	$434.80	48	_____

Answers to CYK: *1.* 18.75%; 16%; 11%; 10%; 13.5%; 12.75% *2.* 21.5% *3.* 18.25%

Principal	Interest	Number of monthly payments	APR
6. $7,000	$908.60	24	_____
7. $4,000	$714.40	36	_____
8. $8,000	$2,064.80	48	_____
9. $5,000	$1,930.00	30	_____
10. $3,000	$1,141.80	60	_____

Principal	Interest	Number of monthly payments	APR
11. $10,000	$2,174.00	48	_____
12. $15,000	$2,487.00	36	_____
13. $12,000	$997.20	12	_____
14. $10,500	$2,309.00	30	_____
15. $13,000	$5,167.50	48	_____

Principal	Interest	Number of monthly payments	APR
16. $2,500	$660.00	48	_____
17. $15,000	$5,137.50	36	_____
18. $4,700	$688.00	12	_____
19. $12,400	$2,101.80	30	_____
20. $7,800	$4,354.74	48	_____

Solve the following problems. Round dollar amounts to the nearest cent and rates to the nearest one-hundredth of a percent.

21. Les Jackson borrowed $3,900 from his local E-Z Loan office and agreed to pay a finance charge of $955.89. He also agreed to pay the total $4,855.89 (loan + interest) in 24 monthly installments. Les thought he had a 12.16% (955.89/2 = 477.95, 477.95/3,900 = .1226) interest loan rate. What was Les's APR?

22. Maggie Jenks borrowed $7,000 from her local loan company and agreed to pay a finance charge of $2,754.50 to make a total of $9,754.50 that she would pay back in 36 equal monthly installments of $270.96. What annual percentage rate did Maggie agree to pay?

23. Jake and Joanna Jefferson were a bit short on cash when they needed $2,100 worth of repairs done on their car. They borrowed the $2,100 from a local loan company and agreed to pay off the loan and interest in 15 monthly installments of $167.54 each. How much will they pay back totally? How much finance charge will they pay? What is their true annual percentage rate?

EXPRESS YOUR THOUGHTS

Compose one or two well-written sentences to express the requested information that follows in your own words.

1. What is the daily balance of a revolving credit account?

2. Explain the difference between an installment loan and a mortgage loan.

3. What is interest on the unpaid balance?

4. Explain what it means to amortize a $10,000 loan over a two-year period with monthly payments.

5. Explain how you would determine the outstanding principal of a loan that has twenty more monthly payments of $98 each, if the annual interest rate is 12% compounded monthly.

6. What is the rebate of interest on a loan paid off early?

7. Explain how the rule of 78s distributes a $156 yearly interest over the twelve months of a year.

8. Describe a quick way to determine the sum of the digits in the first four hundred numbers, i.e., $1 + 2 + 3 + \ldots + 400$.

9. Describe the kinds of purchases generally financed by mortgage loans.

10. What is the annual percentage rate (APR) of a loan?

Case exercise   Financial planning

Julio Hernandez, at 35 years of age, has a successful construction business and has a financially comfortable life style. Julio's first marriage ended in divorce and he agreed to pay his former spouse $2,000 per month for 10 years to help her reestablish herself financially. Julio's second marriage has produced his first child, Maria, who is 1 year old. At each stage of his life, Julio has planned for his personal financial future.

A. At the time of his divorce, he decided to deposit a lump sum of money into an account paying 12% interest compounded monthly that would pay his former wife $2,000 per month for 10 years. How much did he need to deposit into the account so that his obligations would be met as he wished?

B. Julio estimates that his daughter's college education, beginning when she is 18 years old, will cost $80,000 total. How much must he deposit semiannually into an account paying 10% interest compounded semiannually in order to have the $80,000 available in 17 years?

C. Julio plans to retire at age 65 (30 years from now) and wants to be able to supplement his monthly retirement income (from social security and a private retirement plan to which he subscribes) with an additional $3,000 per month for 20 years after retiring. Julio's banker offers him a plan that provides an account paying 12% interest compounded monthly into which Julio can make equal monthly deposits until age 65, and which would then make regular equal monthly payments to him of $3,000 per month for 15 years. (a) How much money must Julio accumulate in the account by age 65 in order for the account to pay out to him $3,000 per month for 15 years? (Use the present value annuity equation.) (b) How much must Julio deposit monthly into this 12% interest account compounded monthly in order to accumulate the required sum by age 65? (Use the future value annuity equation.)

SELF-TEST

A. Terminology review

Complete the following items using the key terms presented at the beginning of the chapter. Check your responses against the answer key at the end of the test.

1. The interest paid for using someone else's money for a period of time is called a <u>Finance charge</u>.

2. Two categories of consumer credit are: (1) <u>open end</u> credit, such as credit cards, and (2) <u>Close end</u> credit, such as installment loans and mortgages.

3. The daily balance of a revolving charge account is computed as:

    daily balance = previous balance + <u>Pur.</u>
                   + cash advances − <u>Pay.</u>
                   − credits.

4. The average <u>daily balance</u> is computed by adding together the _____ of each of the days in the billing period and dividing by the number of <u>day</u> in the billing cycle.

5. <u>installment</u> loans are generally used to purchase items such as appliances, cars, and boats, while <u>mortage</u> loans are used for longer term loans to purchase homes.

6. An amortized loan is a loan in which the principal and interest are liquidated with a series of <u>equal regular</u> payments.

7. The <u>annual %</u> rate is the rate of interest calculated on the unpaid principal of each period of the loan payments.

8. Something of value that is used to secure a loan is called <u>Collateral</u>

9. Financial assets that may be converted to cash quickly are called <u>liquid</u> assets.

B. Calculation review

The following concepts and short problems are designed to test your understanding of the objectives identified at the beginning of the chapter. Answers are provided at the end of the test.

10. Consider the following monthly statement for Leah Ficker's revolving charge account:

Date	Activity	Amount
Feb. 28	previous balance	$256.38
March 12	purchase	$128.75
March 23	purchase	$73.18
March 31	payment	$150.00

(a) Find the daily balance for Leah's account as of March 12, March 23, and March 31. (b) Find the average daily balance for the period March 1 through March 31. (c) What is the finance charge as of March 31 if it is 1.5% of the average daily balance?

11. Chanel Maxson purchased a new rack stereo system with CD player for $3,750. After making a 20% down payment she financed the remainder at 10% interest per year to be paid in quarterly installments for 3 years. Her finance charge was $509.53. How much will she pay in each of her equal quarterly installments? How much will she pay in total to complete her financial contract?

12. Use the tables in Appendix column F to determine the periodic payments.

$$p = 1 - (1+i)^{-n}$$
$$\frac{}{i}$$

Loan (A) principal	r	Compounding period	Years	p
$5,300	3.0%	quarterly	5	_____
$16,000	3.5%	semiannually	8	_____
$4,700	9.0%	annually	4	_____
$7,850	0.5%	monthly	6	_____

13. Jeffry Sussex recently bought a video camcorder, VCR, and TV for $3,500.00. He made a down payment of $1,200.00 and borrowed the remainder, which will be amortized monthly over a 3-year period at 18%. Determine (a) the monthly payment and (b) the finance charge.

14. Use the rule of 78s to approximate the interest rebate on a 1-year loan paid monthly with a finance charge of $147.78 if the loan is paid off after: (a) 4 months, (b) 7 months, and (c) 9 months.

15. Use the sum of digits rule to approximate the interest rebate on a 2-year loan paid monthly with a finance charge of $400.00 if the loan is paid off after: (a) 10 months and (b) 18 months.

16. Mark and Sandy Barker agreed to buy a home for $175,000. After a down payment of $50,000, they financed $125,000 with a 30-year fixed-rate mortgage of 12% interest per year to be paid monthly. (a) Determine the monthly payments of the loan. (b) Determine the total interest charge if the loan is paid off according to the mortgage agreement in 30 years.

17. Alvin Johnson borrowed $4,500 from the Quick and Slick Loan Company and agreed to pay a finance charge of $902.70. He also agreed to pay the total $5,402.70 (loan + interest) in 18 monthly installments. Alvin thought he had a 13.37% (902.70/1.5 = 601.80, 601.80/4,500 = .1337) interest loan rate. What was Alvin's APR?

Answers to self-test: **1.** finance charge   **2.** open-ended, closed-ended   **3.** purchase, payments   **4.** daily balances, days   **5.** installment, mortgage   **6.** equal regular   **7.** annual percentage **8.** collateral   **9.** liquid   **10.** a. (1) $385.13 (2) $458.31 (3) $308.31; b. $355.85; c. $5.34   **11.** each payment = $292.46; total repaid = $3,509.53   **12.** $356.24; $1,322.96; $1,450.74; $130.10   **13.** a. $83.15; b. $693.39   **14.** a. $68.21; b. $28.42; c. $11.37   **15.** a. $140; b. $28   **16.** a. $1,285.75; b. $337,870   **17.** 24%

11

BANK SERVICES AND RECORDS

Learning objectives

1. Perform all activities necessary to establish a personal or business checking account.

2. Describe the different types of checks and endorsements.

3. Prepare the required calculations to maintain checking account records.

4. Explain checking account services provided by banks.

5. Complete deposit records of credit card transactions.

6. Reconcile bank statements and check registers by preparing bank reconciliation statements.

7. Define the key terms.

INTRODUCTION

Banking services can be traced as far back as 352 B.C. with the invention of the check by the Romans. However, the earliest printed checks appeared in England in the latter part of the 17th century to allow people to receive checks from different people drawn on different banks. While this service was somewhat limited, its convenience and safety proved to be invaluable.

Today, due to dynamic changes in the marketplace, banks offer customers many services besides checking accounts and a safe place to deposit their savings. For example, in addition to a complete line of long- and short-term loan programs, banks offer financial management, electronic banking, credit cards, investment counseling, and insurance. These services have resulted because of changes in federal banking laws designed to protect and better serve the depositor. To illustrate this point, in 1980, a change in banking regulations allowed savings and loan associations, credit unions, and other similar financial institutions to offer their customers a service comparable to the checking account called a **share account**. This change made these institutions more competitive with full-service banks and, in turn, forced full-service banks to reevaluate their scope of services and associated fee schedules.

This chapter examines bank services associated with checking accounts. It will instruct you on how to maintain both personal and business checking accounts records, deposit credit card transactions, and prepare bank reconciliation statements. All of the other banking services noted above will be presented in later chapters.

11.1   CHECKING ACCOUNTS AND RECORDS

Banks provide many services to individuals and businesses, the most notable being the checking account. This service enables us to conduct all types of business transactions, such as purchasing goods and services or paying debts, without having to use cash. A check is a safe, convenient method of payment. In addition, a check provides an accurate record of the transaction for future reference. It is for these reasons that most individuals and businesses use the checking account service provided by financial institutions including commercial banks, savings and loan associations, and credit unions.

Learning objective
Perform all activities necessary to establish a personal or business checking account.

A **check** is a written order from an individual or a company (drawer) to their banking institution instructing it to pay a designated party (payee) a specified amount of funds kept on deposit. Checks may involve more than two parties, and are often sent great distances. Therefore, it is important to understand how to fill out a check correctly. The various parts of a check are explained in Figure 11.1.

Figure 11.1

How to write
a check

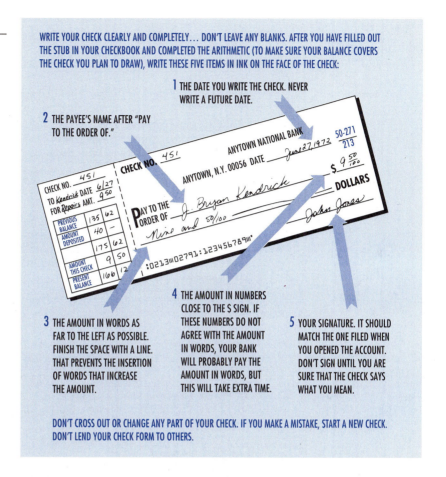

WRITE YOUR CHECK CLEARLY AND COMPLETELY... DON'T LEAVE ANY BLANKS. AFTER YOU HAVE FILLED OUT
THE STUB IN YOUR CHECKBOOK AND COMPLETED THE ARITHMETIC (TO MAKE SURE YOUR BALANCE COVERS
THE CHECK YOU PLAN TO DRAW), WRITE THESE FIVE ITEMS IN INK ON THE FACE OF THE CHECK:

1 THE DATE YOU WRITE THE CHECK. NEVER
WRITE A FUTURE DATE.

2 THE PAYEE'S NAME AFTER "PAY
TO THE ORDER OF."

3 THE AMOUNT IN WORDS AS
FAR TO THE LEFT AS POSSIBLE.
FINISH THE SPACE WITH A LINE.
THAT PREVENTS THE INSERTION
OF WORDS THAT INCREASE
THE AMOUNT.

4 THE AMOUNT IN NUMBERS
CLOSE TO THE S SIGN. IF
THESE NUMBERS DO NOT
AGREE WITH THE AMOUNT
IN WORDS, YOUR BANK
WILL PROBABLY PAY THE
AMOUNT IN WORDS, BUT
THIS WILL TAKE EXTRA TIME.

5 YOUR SIGNATURE. IT SHOULD
MATCH THE ONE FILED WHEN
YOU OPENED THE ACCOUNT.
DON'T SIGN UNTIL YOU ARE
SURE THAT THE CHECK SAYS
WHAT YOU MEAN.

DON'T CROSS OUT OR CHANGE ANY PART OF YOUR CHECK. IF YOU MAKE A MISTAKE, START A NEW CHECK.
DON'T LEND YOUR CHECK FORM TO OTHERS.

When filling out a check, it is important to follow these guidelines so
that the check cannot be altered, and errors can be detected easily.

1. Write legibly in ink. If typewritten, complete all parts but the signature line.

2. Begin the amount to be paid in words at the far left of the line
provided. Express any part of a dollar as a numerator of a fraction with a denominator of 100. Fill any space between the end
of the written amount and the printed word "dollars" with a
solid line as shown in Figure 11.1.

3. Position the numerals of the check amount close to the printed
dollar sign to prevent any adjustment in the amount. (By law,
the bank will honor the check at the amount that is to be paid
in words.)

Figure 11.2

Signature card

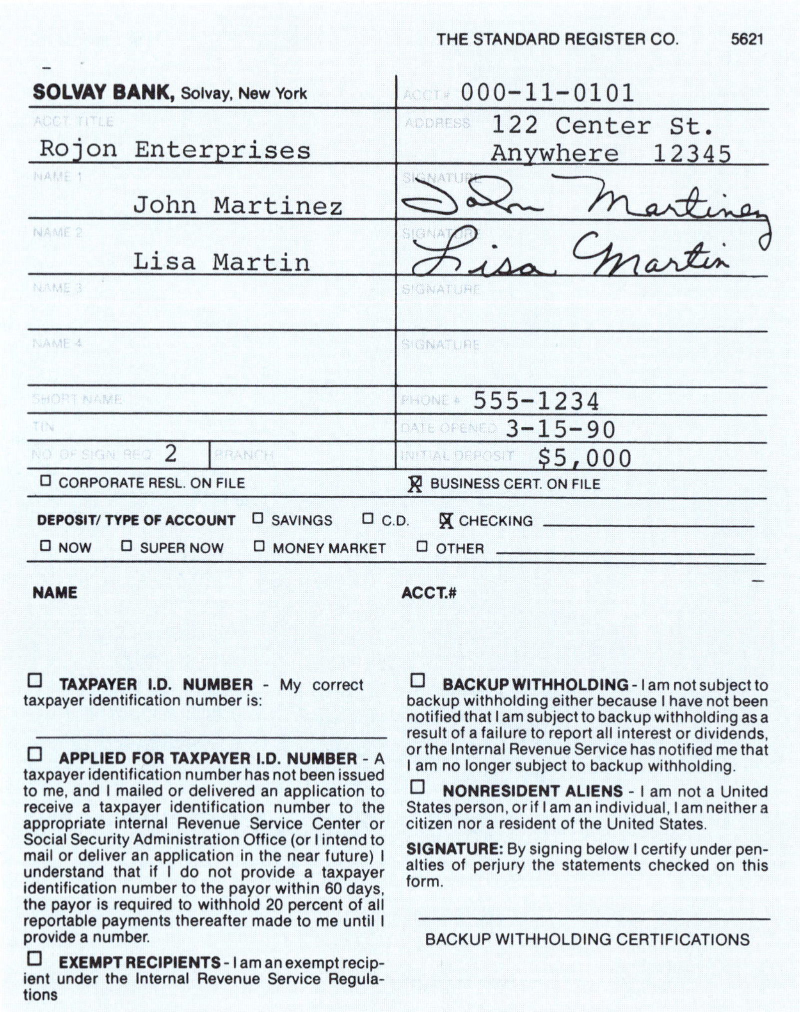

THE STANDARD REGISTER CO.   5621

SOLVAY BANK, Solvay, New York

ACCT # 000-11-0101

ACCT TITLE

Rojon Enterprises

ADDRESS 122 Center St.
Anywhere   12345

NAME 1   John Martinez

SIGNATURE *John Martinez*

NAME 2   Lisa Martin

SIGNATURE *Lisa Martin*

NAME 3

SIGNATURE

NAME 4

SIGNATURE

SHORT NAME

PHONE # 555-1234

TIN

DATE OPENED 3-15-90

NO. OF SIGN. REQ. **2**   BRANCH

INITIAL DEPOSIT $5,000

☐ CORPORATE RESL. ON FILE

☒ BUSINESS CERT. ON FILE

DEPOSIT/ TYPE OF ACCOUNT   ☐ SAVINGS   ☐ C.D.   ☒ CHECKING _____

☐ NOW   ☐ SUPER NOW   ☐ MONEY MARKET   ☐ OTHER _____

NAME   **ACCT.#**

☐ **TAXPAYER I.D. NUMBER** - My correct taxpayer identification number is:

☐ **APPLIED FOR TAXPAYER I.D. NUMBER** - A taxpayer identification number has not been issued to me, and I mailed or delivered an application to receive a taxpayer identification number to the appropriate internal Revenue Service Center or Social Security Administration Office (or I intend to mail or deliver an application in the near future) I understand that if I do not provide a taxpayer identification number to the payor within 60 days, the payor is required to withhold 20 percent of all reportable payments thereafter made to me until I provide a number.

☐ **EXEMPT RECIPIENTS** - I am an exempt recipient under the Internal Revenue Service Regulations

☐ **BACKUP WITHHOLDING** - I am not subject to backup withholding either because I have not been notified that I am subject to backup withholding as a result of a failure to report all interest or dividends, or the Internal Revenue Service has notified me that I am no longer subject to backup withholding.

☐ **NONRESIDENT ALIENS** - I am not a United States person, or if I am an individual, I am neither a citizen nor a resident of the United States.

SIGNATURE: By signing below I certify under penalties of perjury the statements checked on this form.

_____

BACKUP WITHHOLDING CERTIFICATIONS

Source: Solvay Bank, Solvay, NY. Used with permission.

4. Sign all checks with your legal signature as noted on your signature card (Figure 11.2).

Before you open a checking account, you should investigate the scope of service and fees charged for services of various financial institutions in your area. Some of the regulations the federal government has been modifying have induced competition, which has resulted in a variation of fees and services.

All banks require checking account applicants to complete a **signature card** similar to the one shown in Figure 11.2 that lists personal

Table 11.1

Service charge
schedule

Average balance	Monthly charge
$0 – $200	$6.50
$201 – $400	$4.00
$401 – $599	$2.50
$600 or more	free
plus $.20 per check paid	

information and identifies the signature you will use to sign checks. An initial deposit is usually required that opens the account and the bank will provide some blank checks with your account number and a checkbook record.

CALCULATING SERVICE CHARGES ON CHECKING ACCOUNTS

There are two basic types of checking accounts, personal and business. *Personal checking accounts* are used by individuals. The bank provides personalized printed checks for a fee, checkbook cover, and selected checkbook record.

The *regular account plan* requires a monthly service charge to cover the cost of maintaining the account. The **service charge** is usually based on the average balance and the number of checks written during the month. Many banks will eliminate or prorate the monthly service charge based on a required minimum monthly balance. Table 11.1 is a service charge schedule that illustrates how the service charge in Example 1 is determined.

Example 1

Rose Heckla has an average balance of $375 in her account. What is the amount of her service charge if she wrote 34 checks during the month?

Solution

Monthly charge	$ 4.00	($201 – $400)
Checks paid charge	6.80	(34 checks × $.20)
	$10.80	

Most banks will provide *special checking accounts* for individuals who write only a few checks each month and do not want to leave a minimum balance in their account. The service charge may consist of a charge for blank checks, a charge for each check processed, or a monthly maintenance fee.

Example 2

A bank charges a per-check charge of $.30 and a monthly maintenance fee of $2.50. Determine the service charge for a customer who had 12 checks processed this month.

Solution

Check fee	$3.60	(12 checks $\times$ $.30)
Maintenance fee	2.50	
Total service charge	$6.10	

Learning objective
Describe the different types of checks and endorsements.

Many banks offer *flat fee checking accounts*. Under this plan, a fixed charge per month covers the cost of checks, the checking account, bank charge card, and other bank services.

Another type of personal checking account that has become popular in recent years is the *interest-bearing account*. This account pays interest on the average daily balance or on the lowest balance recorded during the month. The interest-bearing account also provides free checking if the required minimum balance is maintained during the month. If the balance drops below the stipulated balance, a monthly fee and a per check fee will be charged. The interest earned on checking accounts is **simple interest** which means the rate of interest paid is applied to the principal (lowest or average account balance) on an annual or per annum basis. Because banks provide bank statements to their customers each month, the time period of the interest equation is adjusted to $\frac{1}{12}$ (one-twelfth) of a year as shown in the solution to Example 3.

Example 3

Community Bank offers interest-bearing checking, which provides free checking based on the schedule shown in Table 11.1. It also pays $5\frac{1}{2}\%$ interest on the lowest monthly balance. A customer's account record indicates an account balance ranging from $457.85 to $1,365.90 with an average balance of $682.50 for the month. What charges (debits) or payments (credits) are there on the customer's account for the period if the bank paid 32 checks?

Solution

P = lowest monthly balance

r = annual rate of interest paid

t = time period based on 1 full year or a part of 1 year

I = interest earned

interest payment: $I = P \times r \times t$ (interest earned on lowest balance)

$$\$2.10 = \$457.85 \times .055 \times \frac{1}{12}$$

There is no service charge because the customer's average balance exceeded the minimum $600 average balance for free checking. The customer will, however, collect $2.10 in interest based on the lowest balance of $457.85 recorded in the account during the month, and pay a $6.40 checks paid fee.

Business checking accounts, sometimes referred to as commercial accounts, have different rate schedules and charges than personal accounts because of the financial services required to control the business cashflow. For example, banks will collect receipts and make payments for a business. A typical rate schedule, as shown in Table 11.2, might include

1. a fee for checks paid on behalf of the business

2. a fee for each deposit made by the business during the month

3. a charge for each check received by the business included with deposits

4. a monthly maintenance fee for maintaining the account

5. an earned credit, which is annual interest based on the average daily balance.

Example 4 illustrates the application of charges and payments to a business checking account.

Table 11.2

Service charge schedule

Service	Charge
1. Maintenance fee	$10.00
2. Checks paid	.09 each
3. Deposit fee	.30 per deposit
4. Checks deposited	.06 each
5. Interest credit	5.25 percent per annum based on average balance

Example 4

Northside Auto Supply made 12 deposits, which included 287 customer checks, had 130 checks paid by its bank, and had an average balance for September of $5,392.60. What are the monthly charges (debits) and payments (credits) to the account? (Use Table 11.2, schedule of charges.)

Solution

Maintenance fee	$10.00	
Checks paid	11.70	(130 × $.09)
Deposit fee	3.60	(12 × $.30)
Checks deposited	17.22	(287 × $.06)
total charges (debit)	$42.52	

Interest payment (credit)   23.59 $\left(\$5{,}392.60 \ \times \ .0525 \ \times \ \dfrac{1}{12} \right)$

MAINTAINING CHECKING ACCOUNT RECORDS

At this point, we have explained the parts of a check, how to calculate service charges on different types of checking accounts, and how to open a checking account. We are now ready to learn how to deposit money in an account and to record various types of transactions in the checkbook register.

A **deposit** increases the amount of money in a checking account and can include checks as well as cash. When checks are deposited in an account, they must be properly endorsed or they will not be accepted by the bank.

An *endorsement* is a signature or instructions with a signature written on the back of the check legally transferring ownership of the check. There are three methods of endorsing a check, each serving a specific purpose. A **restrictive endorsement** limits the ability to cash the check as it includes the words "for deposit only" and the signature of the depositor. Most businesses will use this type of endorsement when depositing customer checks. The **blank endorsement** requires only the signature of the person or firm appearing on the check as the payee. Consequently, if the check is lost or stolen, it could be further endorsed and cashed. The final endorsement is called a **special endorsement**. This method allows the payee to transfer the check amount to a third party (another person or company). However, only the party named in the endorsement can cash the check. Sample endorsements are illustrated in Figure 11.3.

The *deposit slip* is the official record of the transaction and is provided by the bank. The slip contains personalized printed information and space for the amounts to be deposited in cash and checks for both personal and

Learning objective
Prepare the required calculations to maintain checking account records.

Figure 11.3

Check endorsements

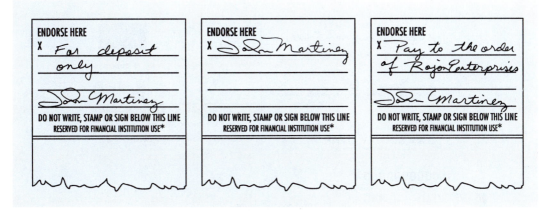

business accounts. In Figure 11.4 are copies of actual deposit slips for personal and business accounts.

Note that when you deposit checks, you must, in addition to the amount, list each check's bank identification number or check serial number. With each deposit, you will receive a copy for your records so that you can verify the transaction. The reconciliation procedure will be explained later in the chapter.

Example 5

Using the following financial data, prepare the daily deposit for the Country Pride Gift Shoppe: Currency: 15 twenty-dollar bills, 20 ten-dollar bills, 12 five-dollar bills, 43 one-dollar bills; coins: 5 rolls of quarters, 3 rolls of dimes, 6 rolls of nickels, 4 rolls of pennies; checks: no. 6735-027 for $68.95, no. 3746-127 for $148.27, no. 7042-098 for $439.62, no. 9062-143 for $15.45, and no. 3546-017 for $38.65.

Solution

Currency	$	603.00	($300 + 200 + 60 + 43)
Coin		79.00	($50 + 15 + 12 + 2)
Checks			
1. 6735-027		68.95	
2. 3746-127		148.27	
3. 7042-098		439.62	
4. 9062-143		15.45	
5. 3546-017		38.65	
total		$1,392.94	

Figure 11.4

Deposit slips

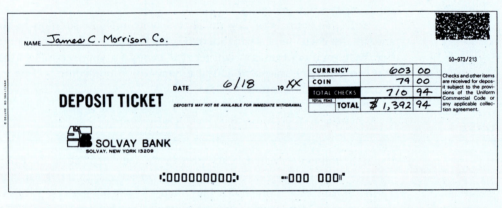

(a) Personal account deposit slip

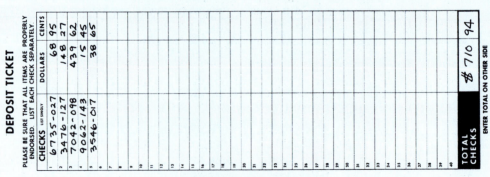

(b) Commercial deposit slip

Source: Solvay Bank, Solvay, NY. Used with permission.

Figure 11.5

Check stub

Source: Solvay Bank, Solvay, NY. Used with permission.

Banks require currency and coins to be separated by denomination and either banded or rolled. Therefore, in the above example, the total currency was found by multiplying the number of bills by their value (15 × $20.00 = $300) plus (20 × $10.00 = $200), and so on. The same procedure was followed to determine the total coin deposit. The coin wrapper for each coin size indicates the required value of each roll: $10 for quarters, $5 for dimes, $2 for nickels, and 50 cents for pennies. In the example, the quarters totaled $50 ($10 × 5 rolls). The completed deposit slip is illustrated in Figure 11.4(b).

Each time a deposit is made or a check is written, the transaction is recorded on a check stub or in a check register. The type of record selected depends upon the preference of the individual or business. The **check stub** is attached to each check and remains as part of the checkbook once the check has been removed. The check stub in Figure 11.5 illustrates the information and procedure necessary to complete the record. Notice that the check number is printed on the check stub. To complete the check stub, start at the top and fill in each line as required. The information shown in Figure 11.5 is developed in Example 6.

Example 6

Amanda Chambers, an accounts payable clerk for County Airport, wrote check no. 991 on October 10 to General Supply in the amount of $386.95 for a file cabinet. If the balance in the account is $4,735.57, and a deposit of $1,320 had been made since the last check was written, what is the balance forward on the check stub?

Solution

Step 1: Complete the date, to whom the check was written, and for what purpose.

Step 2: Record "balance brought forward" $4,735.57.

Step 3: Add deposit to balance brought forward for total ($6,055.57).

Step 4: Enter the amount of this check, no. 1001, and subtract from the total amount ($5,668.62).

Step 5: Record the difference on the balance forward line and on the balance brought forward line of the check stub in no. 1002 (next check stub).

#1001	October 10, 1990	
To: General Office Supply		
For: file cabinet		
Balance brought forward		$4,735.57
Amount deposited	+	1,320.00
Total	=	6,055.57
Amount this check	−	386.95
Balance forward	=	5,668.62

A **check register** may be preferred by some depositors because it is usually in book form and can be separated from the checkbook. The check register also allows depositors to evaluate multiple transactions at one time and provides a column to check off each check as it is returned from the bank. The same information is recorded in the check register that is recorded on the check stub. The process of entering transactions is shown in Figure 11.6. While check registers may vary slightly, all require that you add deposits (credits) and deduct payments (debits) from the balance forward. Whatever method is used to record checkbook transactions, it is important that you record all required information for each check when the check is written.

Example 7

Enter the following transactions in the checkbook register and determine the balance forward: balance brought forward, $689.47; payment on November 25 of $49.75, check no. 172 to Central States Electric Company for monthly electric bill; payment on November 28 of $235.62, check no. 173 to Community Bank for November car payment; deposit Decem-

Figure 11.6

Checkbook register

NUMBER	DATE	DESCRIPTION OF TRANSACTION	PAYMENT/DEBIT (−)	✔ T	FEE (IF ANY) (−)	DEPOSIT/CREDIT (+)	BALANCE
							$ 689 | 47
172	11/25	Central States Electric	49 | 75				639 | 72
173	11/28	Community Bank	235 | 62				404 | 10
	12/2	Deposit				850 | 00	1,254 | 10
174	12/4	Food Center	148 | 27				1,105 | 83

RECORD ALL CHARGES OR CREDITS THAT AFFECT YOUR ACCOUNT

REMEMBER TO RECORD AUTOMATIC PAYMENTS / DEPOSITS ON DATE AUTHORIZED.

ber 2 of $850; payment on December 4 of $148.27, check no. 174 to Food Center for weekly groceries. (Refer to Figure 11.6.)

Solution

Step 1: Enter balance brought forward from preceding check register page ($689.47).

Step 2: Record the first transaction, which is a payment of $49.75 as indicated. This reduces the balance brought forward to $639.72.

Step 3: Enter the second transaction—a payment of $235.62 reducing the balance forward to $404.10.

Step 4: Record the next required transaction—a deposit of $850 on December 2, which is added to the balance forward. The balance forward is now $1,254.10.

Step 5: Enter the final transaction—another payment of $148.27, which reduces the balance forward to $1,105.83.

CHECK YOUR KNOWLEDGE

Checking account records and service charges

1. What is the monthly service charge for Sam's Hobby Shop if the average balance is $527.89 and 64 checks were written during the month? (Use Table 11.1.)

2. Gladys Raymond has a special checking account. She is charged 20 cents for each check, 30 cents for each check paid by her bank, plus a monthly maintenance fee of $4.50. If Gladys wrote nine checks during the month and five were paid by the bank, how much would the bank charge her account for checking service?

3. You have your checking account with a bank that pays 4¾% interest on the lowest monthly balance. The bank also offers free checking under the terms shown in Table 11.1. Your account balance range this month was $289.45 to $726.84, with an average balance of $482.60. If you wrote 28 checks during the month, what would be the net cost (charges minus payments) of your account for the month?

4. Homemaid Cleaning Service had an average balance for January of $3,692.37. During the month, it made 8 deposits, which included a total of 124 checks, and the bank paid 82 checks on the company's behalf. Using the rate schedule in Table 11.2, calculate Homemaid's monthly service charge.

5. Using the following data, complete a sketch of the deposit slip provided: 9 fifty-dollar bills, 25 twenty-dollar bills, 47 ten-dollar bills, 87 one-dollar bills, 19 rolls of quarters, 13 rolls of dimes, 26 rolls of nickels, 6 rolls of pennies; checks: no. 291–32 for $289.22, no. 432–61 for $542.87, no. 1036 for $56.99, no. 148 for $136.45, no. 273–10 for $198.65.

6. Sketch a blank check and check stub like the one shown and complete it. Make the check out to the campus bookstore in the amount of $126.89 for textbooks. Use the current date. The balance brought forward in the account is $267.45 and a deposit of $300 was made prior to writing this check.

Source: Solvay Bank, Solvay, NY. Used with permission.

7. Complete the balance column for each transaction.

NUMBER	DATE	DESCRIPTION OF TRANSACTION	PAYMENT/DEBIT (−)	✓ T	FEE (IF ANY) (−)	DEPOSIT/CREDIT (+)	BALANCE $ 647 80
67	3/8	Adams Cleaners	35 60				
68	3/9	Hillman Dept. Store	49 32				
69	3/12	Central Mortgage	462 50				
	3/15	Deposit				800 00	
70	3/16	Janet Sullivan	45 00				
71	3/20	Food-Mart	79 30				
72	3/22	Mike's Repair	29 80				
74	3/25	Value Hardware	146 28				
75	3/27	The Spent-Shop	387 57				
	3/29	Deposit				950 00	
76	4/2	Bill Charles	65 00				

11.2   CHECKING ACCOUNT SERVICES AND CREDIT CARD TRANSACTIONS

CHECKING ACCOUNT SERVICES

Learning objective
Explain checking account services provided by banks.

Financial institutions are constantly analyzing their markets to improve existing services and/or develop new services. As in any competitive industry, banks must strive to offer the highest quality service at the lowest possible cost within federal and state regulations. To attract depositors, some banks currently offer the following additional checking account services to personal and business accounts; for these services, they may charge a

Answers to CYK: *1.* $15.30   *2.* $7.80   *3.* $6.95   *4.* $11.07   *5.* $3,041.18   *6.* $440.56   *7.* $1,097.43

Figure 11.7

Checking account service charge schedule

Demand Deposit Accounts

Economy
- No minimum balance
- $2.00 monthly maintenance fee
- 15¢ per check paid
- Customer will be charged for check printing costs

Personal
- Must maintain a $400 average available balance for no service charges
- If the average available balance during the statement cycle falls below $400, the service charge for the statement cycle will be $3.00 plus 15¢ per check paid
- Customer will be charge for check printing costs

Business
- $4.00 monthly maintenance fee
- 14¢ per check paid
- 10¢ per check deposited and not drawn on us
- An earnings credit allowance will be applied at 4.8% annually on the minimum monthly balance
- Customer will charged for check printing costs

NOW
- $500 minimum balance
- The NOW Rate will be paid on the available balance
- If the average balance falls below $500 during a statement cycle, a service charge of $5.00 plus 15¢ per check paid will be charged
- Customer will be charged for check printing costs

SuperNOW
- $2,500 minimum balance
- The SuperNOW Rate will be paid each day the available balance in the account is $2,500 or above. The NOW Rate will be paid for each day the available balance falls below $2,500
- If the average balance during the statement cycle falls below $2,500, a service charge of $5.00 plus 15¢ a check will be charged
- Customer will be charged for check printing costs

Money Market Checking
- $2,500 minimum balance
- The Money Market Rate will be paid for each day the available balance in the account is $2,500 or more. For those days the available balance in the account falls below $2,500, no interest will be paid
- The account is limited to an aggregate of six third party transfers and transfers by preauthorized debits per month, of which only three may be by check. There will be a $5.00 charge for EACH transaction in excess of the limit
- If the transaction limitations of this account are violated in excess of 2 times in a rolling 12 month period, we will close the account
- Customer will be charged for check printing costs if checks in excess of the starter kit are requested

Liquid Prime
- $2,500 minimum balance
- The Liquid Prime Rate (70% of the Wall Street Prime) will be paid for each day the available balance in the account is $10,000 or more. For those days the available balance is falls between $2,500 and $10,000, interest will be paid at the Money Market Rate. For those days the available balance in the account is below $2,500, no interest will be paid.
- The account is limited to a aggregate of six third party transfers and transfers by preauthorized debit per month, of which only three may be by check. There will be a $5.00 charge for EACH transaction in excess of the limit.
- If the transaction limitations of this account are violated in excess of 2 times in a rolling 12 month period, we will close the account
- Customer will be charged for check printing costs if checks in excess of the starter kit are requested.

Other Miscellaneous Charges

Certified Checks	
Depositor	$ 3.00
Non-Depositor	5.00
Cashiers Check	2.50
Counter Check	.15
Traveler's Checks per $100	1.00
Money Order	.50
Stop Payment	10.00
Overdraft	15.00
Returned Deposited Check	
Personal	2.00
Business	5.00
Protest Check	10.00
Wire Transfer	
Outgoing	20.00
Incoming	NC
Bond Coupon	
New York City	3.00
All Other	4.50
Bond Coupon Return	20.00
Collection	
Incoming	5.00
Outgoing	10.00
Telephone Transfers	
Less than $200	2.00
$200 or greater	NC
Statement Request	2.00
Research per hour - Minimum charge $5.00	15.00
Microfiche/Microfilm Copy	1.00
Photocopy	.50
Duplicate Passbook	1.00
Safe Deposit Box	10.00 to 50.00
Duplicate Safe Deposit Box Key	10.00
Night Deposit Bag	15.00
Amortization Schedule	5.00
Fax	
Long Distance	4.00
Local	2.00
Coin Counting - per bag	3.00
Non-Proprietary ATM transactions	.75

Source: Solvay Bank, Solvay, NY. Used with permission.

fee that will appear on the bank statement as a *debit memo* (DM). Figure 11.7 illustrates typical charges for the miscellaneous checking account services described in this section. These charges must be deducted from the depositor's checkbook balance at the time of reconciliation. The reconciliation process will be presented in Section 11.3 of this chapter.

A **certified check** is a personal or business check that is certified by the bank that guarantees the payee payment. A certified check eliminates the possibility of having regular checks returned due to nonsufficient funds. The bank will hold a sufficient amount of money in the depositor's account to cover the check amount until the check is paid.

Overdraft protection requires the bank to pay all checks presented for payment even though there may be insufficient funds in the account. Instead of being charged for each overdraft the bank automatically transfers funds from the depositor's savings account or issues a minimum loan. The charge for this service is the current interest charge for the type of loan provided, together with a transfer fee. A fee for a **returned check** is usually charged to a depositor's account for checks deposited and returned to the bank due to nonsufficient funds (NSF) in the account of the party issuing the check.

Commercial banks will perform *collections* of funds for business depositors that usually result from transactions financed with negotiable orders of payment called *notes*. (See Chapter 8, Section 5.) When a note is collected by a bank, the proceeds are added to the depositor's account and appear on the bank statement as a *credit memo* (CM). Such credits are added to the checkbook balance when the account is reconciled.

Many banks offer *NOW* (negotiable orders of withdrawal) *accounts*, which are savings accounts with terms and conditions similar to interest-bearing checking accounts. The depositor prepares an order of withdrawal that works like a check.

Stop payment orders are provided by banks when a depositor requests that the bank not pay a check that has been written.

Banks will provide *duplicate bank statements* and passbooks when requested by the depositor.

Cancelled checks are often needed to verify payments of debts. As most banks no longer return cancelled checks with monthly bank statements, photocopies are made available upon request.

Electronic banking is a service made available to depositors that uses computer technology to transfer funds into and out of checking accounts without the presence of the depositor or without the traditional documents required by the transaction. Funds can be transferred anywhere, for any purpose, wherever the telecommunications

For Your Information
Bank credit cards: understanding the monthly statement

Credit cards can provide a convenient and effective means of paying for goods and services. Some 83 million Americans hold credit cards, for an average of 2.68 cards per person. But many people who use credit cards do not fully understand their monthly statement and therefore end up paying increased costs. Understanding how fees and interest are determined can decrease credit card costs and enable consumers to choose the least costly cards. The explanations and suggestions that follow are keyed numerically to the monthly bank credit card statement shown.

1. **Transaction/posting date:** The transaction date is the date on which the card was used by the cardholder for a purchase or cash advance. A record of the transaction is sent to the cardholder's bank and is entered in the cardholder's account on the posting date. If the cardholder does not pay the balance on time, interest is charged on the average daily balance as of the posting date.

2. **Annual percentage rate:** This is the yearly interest rate used to determine finance charges to the customer for card use. Rates average about 18.6% per year, but may vary from around 11% to around 22%. If a bank charges variable rates, the rates run approximately 6 to 10 percent higher than the current prime lending rate.

3. **Days in the billing cycle:** This is the number of days between one month's payment due date and the next month's payment due date. The more days in the cycle, the higher the finance charge if the card holder carries a balance from month to month.

4. **Payment due date:** This is the date on which the full amount of the account balance or the minimum payment is due. If the cardholder pays nothing, some banks impose a late fee. Such fees are illegal in some states.

5. **Minimum payment due:** This is the smallest amount that the cardholder is required to pay on his or her account. Most banks require a minimum payment of $20 on account balances from $20 to $720. On balances of more than $720, the minimum payments can range from 2.5% to 5% of the average daily balance, plus any amount the cardholder has charged in excess of the credit line.

6. **Finance charge:** This is the interest charged on the average daily balance when the entire balance is not paid within a grace period (which is usually 25 to 30 days). The charge is calculated by multiplying the average daily balance by the daily periodic rate by the number of days in the billing period. It may be calculated as $\frac{1}{12}$ of the bank's annual interest rate if a monthly periodic rate is used. A minimum finance charge may be imposed when the actual charge is less than the minimum.

7. **Debit adjustments:** If a cardholder asks the bank to correct a mistake involving a charge to her or his account, the bank will delete the charge from the cardholder's account while the error is being investigated. The adjustment will appear in this section of the monthly statement. If no error has occurred, the bank will rebill the cardholder's account for the amount and will also add interest for the period.

(continued)

For Your Information

Bank credit cards: understanding the monthly statement (continued)

8. **Cashback bonus:** To encourage use of their card, some financial institutions, such as Discover Card, provide a periodic cash-back bonus based on qualified purchases. This bonus reduces the cost of the card.

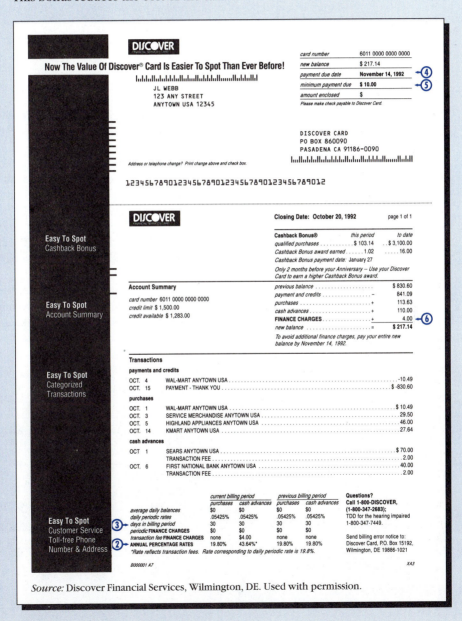

Source: Discover Financial Services, Wilmington, DE. Used with permission.

networks are available. An example of electronic banking offered by financial institutions is the *automatic teller machine* (ATM). These computerized bank machines can be found outside financial institutions and places of business with high traffic patterns. Depositors can conveniently withdraw cash, make deposits, or transfer funds to other accounts any time day or night.

Banks will also provide *account reconcilement* if the depositor is unable to reconcile their own account. The fee will vary depending on the type of account and the number of items involved. Many banks set a minimum fee for this type of service.

CREDIT CARD TRANSACTIONS

A large portion of today's retail transactions are made with credit cards. Have you ever wondered how a business collects payment for merchandise you purchased with either a Visa or MasterCard?

Learning objective
Complete deposit records of credit card transactions.

The process begins when you present your card to the cashier who transfers required information on the card to the credit card sales slip using a stamping machine. The sales slip (Figure 11.8) must be signed by you verifying the purchase information and authorizing payment. The business then deposits the credit card transaction into its checking account using the **merchant's deposit summary** shown in Figure 11.9. Credit card sales and cash sales can be deposited at the same time using separate deposit slips.

Figure 11.8

Credit card
sales slip

The merchant's deposit summary lists both sales slips (charges) and credit slips (refunds). The net deposit (total sales slips recorded minus total credit slips) increases the balance in the check register just like a regular

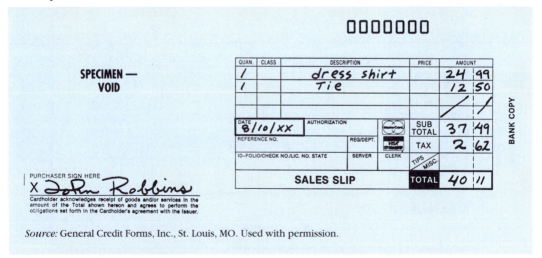

Source: General Credit Forms, Inc., St. Louis, MO. Used with permission.

Figure 11.9

Merchant's deposit ticket

0000000

Northshore Marine Supply
2469 Bayside Drive
Skaneateles, N.Y. 13152

DEPOSIT RECAP	VISA		MasterCard	
DATE 3/10/XX	NO. SLIPS	AMOUNT	NO. SLIPS	AMOUNT
SALES SLIPS	5	495 82		
LESS CREDIT SLIPS	2	86 07		
NET SALES		409 75		
LESS DISCOUNT	4¾%	19 46	%	
DEPOSIT		390 29		

TOTAL VISA AND/OR M C DEPOSITS → $ 390 29

x Ann Snyder
MERCHANT AUTHORIZED SIGNATURE

MERCHANT COPY

MERCHANT DEPOSIT TICKET

Source: General Credit Forms, Inc., St. Louis, MO. Used with permission.

deposit. The bank charges the business a **discount fee** of 2 - 5% of the net amount deposited during the month. The discount fee covers the cost of immediately providing funds to the business while the bank awaits payment from the customer through the interbank fund transfer process. This fee in effect reduces the net deposit as it becomes part of the total bank charges appearing on the monthly bank statement to be reconciled.

Example 8

On March 10, 199X, Northshore Marine Supply had credit card sales of \$29.85, \$162.49, \$8.35, \$57.14, \$237.99, and credit refunds of \$71.45 and \$14.62. (a) Complete the deposit summary. (b) Calculate the discount fee that will appear on Northshore's bank statement if the bank charges 4¾%. (Refer to Figure 11.9.)

Solution

a. **Deposit Summary—March 10, 199X**

	Credit slips		Sales slips
1.	\$71.45	1.	\$ 29.85
2.	14.62	2.	162.49
3.	______	3.	8.35
4.	______	4.	57.14
5.	______	5.	237.99
Total	\$86.07		\$495.82

Total amounts:	Sales slips	\$495.82
	Less credit slip	86.07
	Net deposit	\$409.75

b. \$409.75 × .0475 = \$19.46 discount fee

CHECK YOUR KNOWLEDGE

Checking account services and credit card transactions

The sales records of Carl's Men's Shoppe indicate the following credit card transactions for April 12th. Deposits are made daily.

Sales		Refunds
$139.69	$ 76.49	$ 9.34
10.42	29.87	34.69
49.99	52.12	116.50
259.78	187.06	

1. What are the total credit card sales?
2. What are the total credits (refunds)?
3. What is the net deposit to be recorded on the merchant's deposit summary?
4. If the bank charges a 3½% discount fee, what amount will be charged to Carl's account for credit card transactions?
5. Sketch a deposit slip like the one shown and complete it.

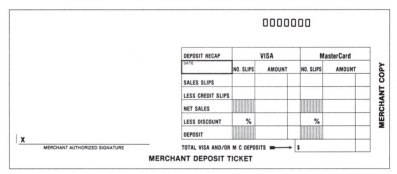

Source: General Credit Forms, Inc., St. Louis, MO. Used with permission.

Answers to CYK: *1.* $805.42   *2.* $160.53   *3.* $644.89   *4.* $22.57

11.2   EXERCISES

Use Table 11.1 to find the monthly service charge for the following personal checking accounts based on the regular account plan.

	Name	Checks written	Average balance	Service charge
1.	Charles Adams	15	$1,451	_____
2.	Cynthia Johnson	28	$4,622	_____
3.	Elizabeth Cruz	62	$2,103	_____
4.	Matthew Koski	46	$7,154	_____
5.	Mavis Tuttle	85	$3,875	_____

Use Table 11.2 to find the monthly service charge for the following business checking accounts.

	Company	Checks paid	Deposits made	Checks deposited	Average balance	Service charge
6.	Pasta Pantry	52	8	12	$874.90	_____
7.	Eastside Sports Center	127	12	293	$5,346.75	_____
8.	Goldman Furniture	243	20	461	$8,790.50	_____

Use the deposit information below to complete each deposit slip on the dates indicated for Perfection Cleaners.

		Bills (quantity)				Coin (rolls)				Checks	
	Date	20s	10s	5s	1s	25	10	5	1	Number	Amount
9.	Nov. 7	15	26	12	43	10	3	8	6	2146–126	$127.10
										5621–287	56.45
										1874–521	365.10
10.	Nov. 15	28	47	54	185	22	12	18	9	7364–432	212.75
										4267–893	62.20
										3642–127	436.82
										2983–622	38.46
										6876–539	123.95

9. **Deposit slip**

currency   _____
coin   _____
checks   _____
_____ _____
_____ _____
_____ _____
_____ _____
_____ _____
Total   _____

10. **Deposit slip**

currency   _____
coin   _____
checks   _____
_____ _____
_____ _____
_____ _____
_____ _____
_____ _____
Total   _____

For exercises 11 – 13, sketch checks like the one shown, and endorse each with your signature as required using the information provided.

11. You want to transfer the amount of this check to Sutter's Hardware to be applied to your account balance.

12. This check has been made out to you and you are about to cash it at your bank.

```
ENDORSE HERE
X
_____
_____
_____
_____
DO NOT WRITE, STAMP OR SIGN BELOW THIS LINE
     RESERVED FOR FINANCIAL INSTITUTION USE*
```

13. You received this check from one of your customers and you want to deposit the amount in your checking account.

```
ENDORSE HERE
X
_____
_____
_____
_____
DO NOT WRITE, STAMP OR SIGN BELOW THIS LINE
     RESERVED FOR FINANCIAL INSTITUTION USE*
```

For exercises 14–16, sketch check stubs like the ones shown, and complete each for We-Fix-It Appliance Repair using the information provided below.

Stub number	Date	To	For	Amount
14. 136	Jan. 6	Adams Electric Company	Electric Motor	$562.15
15. 137	Jan. 8	Spectrum Business Supply	Office Supply	83.28
16. 138	Jan. 9	Millie's Auto Center	Truck Repair	249.50

Balance brought forward on stub #136: $2,892.40

Deposits made: Jan. 7 $135.25
Jan. 9 $379.70

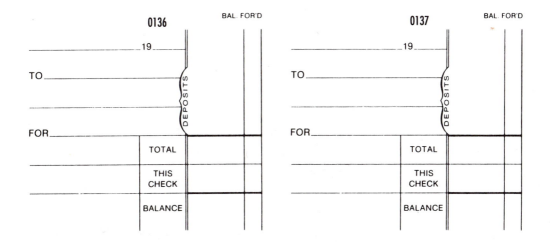

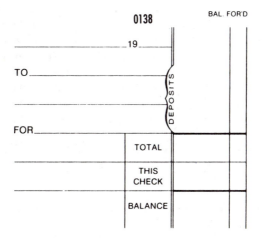

17. Complete the required computations, arranged as in the check register.

RECORD ALL CHARGES OR CREDITS THAT AFFECT YOUR ACCOUNT

NUMBER	DATE	DESCRIPTION OF TRANSACTION	PAYMENT/DEBIT (−)		✔ T	FEE (IF ANY) (−)	DEPOSIT/CREDIT (+)		BALANCE $ 147 60	
124	3/12	Dr. Wilson	$ 35	50		$	$			
	3/15	Deposit					450	00		
125	3/16	Paper Cutter	18	70						
126	3/18	SOLVAY BANK (loan)	146	20						
127	3/20	West End Pharmacy	26	80						
128	3/21	P & C Foods	59	90						
129	3/23	Niagara Mohawk	169	40						
	3/23	Deposit					500	00		
130	3/25	Rent	425	00						
131	3/26	Addis & Dey's	48	72						
132	3/28	Byrne Dairy	8	40						
133	4/2	Deluxe Checks	4	60						
134	4/5	Chuck's Service Center	29	75						
135	4/8	Wegman's Market	47	35						

REMEMBER TO RECORD AUTOMATIC PAYMENTS / DEPOSITS ON DATE AUTHORIZED.

Use the following credit card transactions to answer problems 18–22. Sales codes: (V) Visa; (M) MasterCard.

Sales slips	Credit slips
$ 27.38(V)	$15.95(M)
52.45(V)	38.64(M)
129.36(M)	87.12(V)
82.47(V)	9.45(M)
15.95(M)	
167.32(M)	
48.50(V)	
109.25(M)	
21.89(M)	
64.75(M)	

18. What are the total sales slips for the month?

19. What are the total credit slips for the month?

20. What is the amount of the net deposits?

21. If the bank charges a 3½% discount fee, what is the amount of the discount fee to appear on the customer's bank statement?

22. Complete a sketch of the merchant's deposit summary shown using the calculations from exercises 18–21.

Source: General Credit Forms, Inc., St. Louis, MO. Used with permission.

23. Find the monthly service charge for Lisa Williams if her average balance is $387.50 and 27 checks were written during the month of October. (Use Table 11.1.)

24. Harold Cohen has a special checking account with Community Bank. The bank charges his account 10 cents for each check, 20 cents for each check paid, plus a monthly maintenance fee of $6.25. If Harold wrote 17 checks during the month, how much would Community Bank charge his account for checking service?

25. Christine Plavocus has a checking account with a bank that pays 3¼% interest on the lowest monthly balance. Using Table 11.1, determine the net service charge (charges minus payments) to her account if the bank paid 23 checks during the month and her account balance range was $137.45 to $489.62 with an average balance of $368.15.

26. Determine the charges and payments to a checking account if the bank pays 4¼% interest on the lowest monthly balance. The lowest account balance is $592.65; the average balance for the month is $725.90; and 44 checks were paid by the bank. (Use Table 11.1.)

27. Panther Lake Inn made 15 deposits during July, which included 392 customer checks. A total of 64 checks were paid by the bank and the average balance for the month was $3,689.45. Determine the total debits and credits to the account based on the service charge schedule, Table 11.2.

28. Determine the total amount to be deposited by Frank's Pizzeria based on the following: 10 twenty-dollar bills, 30 ten-dollar bills, 25 five-dollar bills, 87 one-dollar bills; 6 rolls of quarters, 8 rolls of dimes, 5 rolls of nickels, 2 rolls of pennies; checks amounting to $689.50.

29. Alice Newser bought a desk for $329.62 and paid with check no. 108. If the balance prior to the purchase of the desk was $586.48 and she made a deposit of $250.00 since the last check was written, what is her balance forward on check stub number 108?

30. Fred's Cycle Shop had credit card sales that were deposited on December 15 of $79.95, $149.57, $356.92, and $89.75, and credit refunds of $59.95 and $24.69. Determine (a) the amount of the net deposit recorded on the merchant's deposit summary and (b) the discount fee charged to Fred's account if the bank charges 3½%.

11.3   THE RECONCILIATION PROCESS

Learning objective
Reconcile bank statements and check registers by preparing bank reconciliation statements.

Figure 11.10

A sample bank statement

Now that we understand how to maintain the required checking account records and how the bank determines the monthly service charge, we are ready to discuss the reconciliation process. Each month the bank will send depositors a **bank statement** (Figure 11.10) that lists deposits made during the period and checks paid by the bank, as well as a record of other transactions and service charges. Checks listed on the bank statement are referred to as **cancelled checks**. Figure 11.11 shows how a check written by a depositor in New York to a payee in California is processed by the

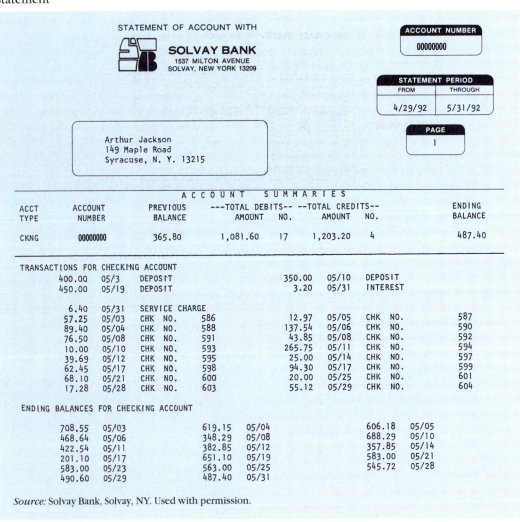

STATEMENT OF ACCOUNT WITH

SOLVAY BANK
1537 MILTON AVENUE
SOLVAY, NEW YORK 13209

ACCOUNT NUMBER
00000000

STATEMENT PERIOD

FROM	THROUGH
4/29/92	5/31/92

PAGE
1

Arthur Jackson
149 Maple Road
Syracuse, N. Y. 13215

A C C O U N T   S U M M A R I E S

ACCT TYPE	ACCOUNT NUMBER	PREVIOUS BALANCE	---TOTAL DEBITS-- AMOUNT	NO.	--TOTAL CREDITS-- AMOUNT	NO.	ENDING BALANCE
CKNG	00000000	365.80	1,081.60	17	1,203.20	4	487.40

TRANSACTIONS FOR CHECKING ACCOUNT

| 400.00 | 05/3 | DEPOSIT | | 350.00 | 05/10 | DEPOSIT | |
| 450.00 | 05/19 | DEPOSIT | | 3.20 | 05/31 | INTEREST | |

6.40	05/31	SERVICE CHARGE					
57.25	05/03	CHK NO.	586	12.97	05/05	CHK NO.	587
89.40	05/04	CHK NO.	588	137.54	05/06	CHK NO.	590
76.50	05/08	CHK NO.	591	43.85	05/08	CHK NO.	592
10.00	05/10	CHK NO.	593	265.75	05/11	CHK NO.	594
39.69	05/12	CHK NO.	595	25.00	05/14	CHK NO.	597
62.45	05/17	CHK NO.	598	94.30	05/17	CHK NO.	599
68.10	05/21	CHK NO.	600	20.00	05/25	CHK NO.	601
17.28	05/28	CHK NO.	603	55.12	05/29	CHK NO.	604

ENDING BALANCES FOR CHECKING ACCOUNT

708.55	05/03	619.15	05/04	606.18	05/05
468.64	05/06	348.29	05/08	688.29	05/10
422.54	05/11	382.85	05/12	357.85	05/14
201.10	05/17	651.10	05/19	583.00	05/21
583.00	05/23	563.00	05/25	545.72	05/28
490.60	05/29	487.40	05/31		

Source: Solvay Bank, Solvay, NY. Used with permission.

Figure 11.11

Check cancellation
process

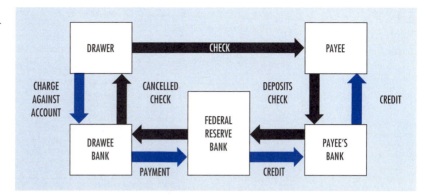

federal reserve system. Notice that the check is physically returned to the
depositor's bank for payment. Some banks still return the cancelled checks
to the depositor with the bank statement.

The ending balance on the bank statement will most likely differ from
the balance on the depositor's checkbook record. The process of analyzing these two records and making the required adjustments to bring the
balances into agreement is called **reconciliation**. The fact that the two
balances do not agree does not mean that either record is in error. What
the difference does suggest is that amounts have been added to or deducted from the balance in one record but not the other. These amounts
and their purposes become clear when the information on the bank statement is compared to the checkbook record. Ordinarily the adjustments to
the records are due to the following reasons:

1. *Deposits in transit*. These are deposits made to the checking
   account that do not appear on the bank statement. These deposits have been included in the checkbook balance but are
   not received by the bank in time to be recorded on the bank
   statement.

2. *Collections*. The bank will often collect funds on the depositor's
   behalf. Such funds are reflected in the bank balance but seldom
   in the checkbook balance.

3. *Outstanding checks*. These are checks that have been written
   and recorded in the checkbook register but have not been paid
   by the bank as of the statement date.

4. *Bank charges*. The bank will deduct from the bank balance all
   charges for the services provided and/or requested during the
   period. These fees may or may not be included in the checkbook balance.

5. *Errors*. Both depositor and bank make errors. Errors must be
   analyzed carefully and corrected. If the error is a bank error, the

Figure 11.12

Bank reconciliation form for Example 9

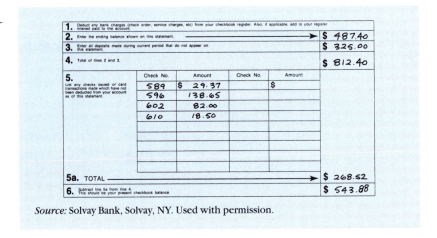

1.	Deduct any bank charges (check order, service charges, etc) from your checkbook register. Also, if applicable, add to your register interest paid to the account.				
2.	Enter the ending balance shown on this statement.				$ 487.40
3.	Enter all deposits made during current period that do not appear on this statement.				$ 325.00
4.	Total of lines 2 and 3.				$ 812.40

5. List any checks issued or card transactions made which have not been deducted from your account as of this statement.	Check No.	Amount	Check No.	Amount	
	589	$ 29.37		$	
	596	138.65			
	602	82.00			
	610	18.50			

5a. TOTAL					$ 268.52
6. Subtract line 5a from line 4. This should be your present checkbook balance.					$ 543.88

Source: Solvay Bank, Solvay, NY. Used with permission.

depositor should notify the bank so that the proper adjustment can be made to the bank record.

The bank statement can be reconciled by using the *bank form* (Figure 11.12) printed on the reverse side of the statement or by preparing the **account form** shown in Figure 11.13. The account form is often preferred by businesses when preparing the monthly bank reconciliation statement.

To illustrate the steps involved in reconciliation, Example 9 uses the information on the bank statement provided in Figure 11.10 to complete

Figure 11.13

Account form bank reconciliation for Example 9

Art Jackson
Bank Reconciliation
May 31, 1993

Bank Balance	$487.40	Book Balance	$547.10
Add:		*Add:*	
Deposit in Transit	325.00	Interest Credit	3.18
Total	$812.40	Total	$550.28
Deduct:		*Deduct:*	$ 6.40
Outstanding Checks		Service Charge	
589 $ 29.37			
596 138.65			
602 82.00			
610 18.50	268.52		
Adjusted Bank Balance	$543.88	Adjusted Book Balance	$543.88

the bank form (Figure 11.12) on the reverse side of the statement and the account form (Figure 11.13).

Example 9

The following checkbook register of Art Jackson shows a checkbook balance of $547.10. After comparing the entries in the checkbook register with the bank statement, we find that check nos. 589 for $29.37, 596 for $138.65, 602 for $82.00, and 610 for $18.50 have not been paid, and that the bank paid $3.20 in interest and charged $6.40 for its services. Also, the register lists a deposit of $325 that was not included in the bank statement balance of $487.40. Use the bank form (Figure 11.13) to reconcile Art Jackson's checking account.

RECORD ALL CHARGES OR CREDITS THAT AFFECT YOUR ACCOUNT

NUMBER	DATE	DESCRIPTION OF TRANSACTION	PAYMENT/DEBIT (−)		✓ T	FEE (IF ANY) (−)	DEPOSIT/CREDIT (+)		BALANCE $	
						$	$		405	32
584	4/18	Telephone Co.	$ 24	50	✓				380	82
585	4/20	CASH	15	00	✓				365	82
586	4/28	Sports Outfit	57	25					308	82
587	4/29	Fred's Drugs	12	97					295	60
588	4/30	P&C Markets	89	40					206	20
	4/30	Deposit					400	00	606	20
589	5/4	Cable TV	29	37					576	83
590	5/4	Niagara Mohawk	137	54					439	29
591	5/5	Raymond's Furniture	76	50					362	79
592	5/6	Northshore Lumber	43	85					318	94
	5/7	Deposit					350	00	668	94
593	5/7	Youth Center	10	00					658	94
594	5/7	Car Payment	265	75					393	19
595	5/9	Chappels	39	69					353	50
596	5/10	Credit Union	138	65					214	85
597	5/11	SEARS	25	00					189	85
598	5/12	Snyder's Autocenter	62	45					127	40
599	5/13	Sibley's	94	30					33	10
	5/16	Deposit					450	00	483	10
600	5/17	Gary's TV Repair	68	10					415	00
601	5/19	Marie's Gifts	20	00					395	00
602	5/22	William's Market	82	00					313	00
603	5/26	Village Water	17	28					295	72
604	5/27	Healthcenter East	55	12					240	60
	5/30	Deposit					325	00	565	60
605	5/30	Bryne Dairy	18	50					547	10

REMEMBER TO RECORD AUTOMATIC PAYMENTS / DEPOSITS ON DATE AUTHORIZED.

RECORD ALL CHARGES OR CREDITS THAT AFFECT YOUR ACCOUNT

NUMBER	DATE	DESCRIPTION OF TRANSACTION	PAYMENT/DEBIT (−)		✓ T	FEE (IF ANY) (−)	DEPOSIT/CREDIT (+)		BALANCE $	
			$			$	$		547	10
	6/3	Service Charge	6	40					540	70
		Interest	(Adjusted	Balance)			3	20	543	90

Solution

Step 1: First, add to the checkbook balance any bank payments (credit memos) such as interest earned on the account. The interest paid by the bank appears in the bank statement. (Checkbook balance, $547.10, plus interest, $3.18, totals $550.28.)

Second, deduct all bank charges (debit memos) from the total obtained above ($550.28 − $6.40 = $543.88). This total is the *adjusted checkbook balance* and should agree with the adjusted bank balance found by completing steps two through six of the bank reconciliation form.

Step 2: Enter statement balance ($487.40) on line 2 of the reconciliation form.

Step 3: List all deposits recorded in the check register that do not appear in the bank statement. (A deposit of $325 is not yet recorded on the bank statement.)

Step 4: Add the total deposits in transit to the bank statement balance ($487.40 + $325 = $812.40).

Step 5: Compare the checks written in the register with the cancelled checks listed in the bank statement. Checks listed in the register and not in the bank statement are outstanding. Record these outstanding checks in the space provided on the form and total.

#589	$ 29.37
596	138.65
602	82.00
610	18.50
total	$268.52

Step 6: Deduct the total outstanding checks ($268.52) from the step 4 total ($812.40). This total ($543.88) is called the *adjusted bank balance*.

If the adjusted balances do not agree, check arithmetic on the reconciliation statement and recheck each step of the process to make sure you did not omit any adjustments. When rechecking, make sure the adjustment is made to the correct record. Other common errors to look for include: recording the amount of the check incorrectly, addition and subtraction errors in the check register, and the omission of transactions by both depositor and bank.

Example 10 shows how to prepare a bank reconciliation statement for a business account using the *account form*.

Example 10

Spenser's Travel Agency has a checkbook balance of $4,396.63. The balance shown on the November bank statement is $3,684.97. A comparison of the checking account records indicates the following checks have not yet been paid by the bank: no. 689 for $237.85, no. 704 for $50.35, no. 712 for $382.72, no. 713 for $129.68, and no. 716 for $672.35. In addition, Spenser's had deposits of $825.50 and $1,345.00, which were recorded in the checkbook register but did not appear in the bank statement. The bank statement also shows a check charge of $12.50, a monthly service charge of $6.40, and an interest payment of $4.79. Prepare a bank reconciliation statement for Spenser's Travel Agency.

Solution

Spenser's Travel Agency
Bank Reconciliation
November 199X

Bank balance	$3,684.97	Checkbook balance	$4,396.63
Add:		*Add:*	
Deposits in transit		Interest credit	4.79
$ 825.50			
1,345.00	2,170.50		
Total	$5,855.47	Total	$4,401.42
Deduct:			
Outstanding checks		Service charge 6.40	
no. 689 $237.85		Check charge 12.50	
no. 704 50.35			18.90
no. 712 382.72			
no. 713 129.68			
no. 716 672.35	1,472.95		
Adjusted bank balance $4,382.52		Adjusted book balance $4,382.52	

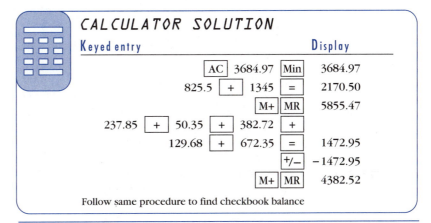

CALCULATOR SOLUTION

Keyed entry					Display
	AC 3684.97	Min			3684.97
825.5	+	1345	=		2170.50
	M+	MR			5855.47
237.85 +	50.35	+	382.72	+	
129.68 +	672.35	=			1472.95
			+/−		−1472.95
	M+	MR			4382.52

Follow same procedure to find checkbook balance

The steps involved in preparing the report form reconciliation statement are the same as those used to prepare the bank form. In both presentations, you are adjusting the records to reflect any increases or decreases to the balances that have not been recorded in the records as of that date.

The reconciliation process

1. Find the adjusted bank balance using the following information. Deposits in transit: $262.50 and $379.62. Checks outstanding: no. 1031 for $60.00, no. 1046 for $187.50, no. 1051 for $42.95, and no. 1056 for $13.50. Bank statement balance: $429.34.

2. Determine the adjusted checkbook balance if the bank statement showed an interest payment to the customer's account of $3.21, an NSF (nonsufficient funds) charge of $15.00, a check printing charge of $6.75, and a monthly service charge of $4.50. The balance in the check register is $279.54.

3. Use the report form to reconcile Bob's Lawn and Garden Store account. The bank statement shows a balance of $3,742.90, a service charge of $4.50, an NSF charge of $20.00, and an interest credit of $5.74. Checks outstanding are: $69.30, $127.48, $642.25, $312.60, and $258.75. The checkbook register balance is $3,926.78, which includes a deposit of $1,575.50 not recorded on the bank statement.

11.3 EXERCISES

Find the adjusted bank balance for each of the following accounts.

	Opening bank balance	Deposits in transit	Outstanding checks	Adjusted bank balance
1.	$648.72	$287.36	24.37	_____
		129.43	186.25	
			62.94	
2.	$7,246.25	$1,436.80	$572.12	_____
			78.52	
			168.97	
3.	$32,568.47	$2,876.25	$12,145.10	_____
		4,165.97	1,215.50	
			861.43	
			79.43	

Answers to CYK: *1.* $767.51   *2.* $256.50   *3.* $3,908.02

Calculate the adjusted checkbook balance for each of the following business accounts.

Opening checkbook balance	Check charges	Service charge	Notes collected	Interest payment	Adjusted checkbook balance
4. $457.90	$9.00	$6.50		$3.45	_____
5. $1,648.32	$18.20	$12.15		$8.97	_____
6. $12,366.15	$54.90		$1,578.40	$29.17	_____

7. From the following information, prepare an account form bank reconciliation for Nu-Wave Coiffures.

		Nu-Wave Coiffures		
Bank balance	$4,246.25	**Bank Reconciliation Statement**		
Checkbook balance	2,831.05	**July 199X**		
Deposits in transit	1,650.00			
Service charge	12.50	Bank balance $_____	Book balance	$_____
Outstanding checks	2,972.50	*Add:*	*Add:*	
Interest credit	14.20	Total _____	Total	_____
Check charge	9.00	*Deduct:*	*Deduct:*	
		Total _____	Total	_____
		Adjusted bank balance _____	Adjusted book balance	_____

8. Use the following information to complete a bank form like the one provided. Verify bank balance against checkbook balance.

Bank balance	$682.40
Deposits in transit	350.00
	175.00
Outstanding checks	
#243	29.62
#247	245.20
#253	119.75
Checkbook balance	$828.43
Service charge	9.00
Interest credit	6.25
Check charge	12.85

1. Deduct any bank charges (check order, service charges, etc) from your checkbook register. Also, if applicable, add to your register interest paid to the account.					
2. Enter the ending balance shown on this statement.					$
3. Enter all deposits made during current period that do not appear on this statement.					$
4. Total of lines 2 and 3.					$
5. List any checks issued or card transactions made which have not been deducted from your account as of this statement.	Check No.	Amount $	Check No.	Amount $	
5a. TOTAL					$
6. Subtract line 5a from line 4. This should be your present checkbook balance.					$

Source: Solvay Bank, Solvay, NY. Used with permission.

9. Janet Green received her bank statement showing a balance of $197.14, a service charge of $12.50, an interest credit of $2.50, and a returned check amounting to $35.25. When Janet compared her checkbook register to the bank statement, she noted a checkbook balance of $465.20, a deposit of $350.00 that was not recorded on the bank statement, and that check no. 136 for $74.65, check no. 138 for $12.55, and check no. 143 for $39.99 had not been processed by her bank for payment. Prepare a bank reconciliation for Janet organized like the account form shown.

Bank balance _____ Checkbook balance _____
Add: _____ *Add:* _____
Deduct: _____ *Deduct:* _____
Adjusted bank balance _____ Adjusted checkbook balance _____

10. Central Trust charges "economy" checking account customers 20 cents for each check written and a monthly maintenance fee of $4.50. Reconcile an "economy" statement showing a balance of $369.42 with twelve checks having been paid by the bank. The customer's register indicates a deposit of $200 is not shown on the statement, a balance of $110.82, and that check no. 78 for $15.50 and check no. 82 for $450 are outstanding. Reconcile the customer's checking account, organizing the information according to the blank bank form shown.

1. Deduct any bank charges (check order, service charges, etc) from your checkbook register. Also, if applicable, add to your register interest paid to the account.					
2. Enter the ending balance shown on this statement.					$
3. Enter all deposits made during current period that do not appear on this statement.					$
4. Total of lines 2 and 3.					$
5. List any checks issued or card transactions made which have not been deducted from your account as of this statement.	Check No.	Amount	Check No.	Amount	
		$		$	
5a. TOTAL					$
6. Subtract line 5a from line 4. This should be your present checkbook balance.					$

Source: Solvay Bank, Solvay, NY. Used with permission.

11. New-Release Video received its November bank statement showing a balance of $1,247.25, check printing charges of $23.40, a service charge of $16.61, and an interest credit of $9.30. The checkbook register balance was $1,509.41. The bank statement indicated deposits in transit of $850, $1,200, and $575, and that checks of $98.50, $470.25, $689.20, and $1,135.60 had not been paid by the bank. Use the account form below to reconcile the accounts.

Bank balance _____ Checkbook balance _____
Add: _____ *Add:* _____
Deduct: _____ *Deduct:* _____
Adjusted bank balance _____ Adjusted checkbook balance _____

12. Reconcile the business checking account for Rojon Enterprises for the month of March. All debits and credits to Rojon's account were computed using rates from Table 11.2. The bank statement shows a balance of $2,194.70, a service charge including all charges of $58.52, a discount fee for credit card sales of $22.50, and an interest credit of $5.58 based on an average balance of $1,275.50. The bank

statement does not show a deposit of $875 or check nos. 246, 252, 257, 263, and 265 for $45.50, $163.20, $239.60, $87.35, and $19.15, respectively, having been paid by the bank. Rojon's checking records indicate a balance of $2,590.34; 20 deposits were made during the month (which included 356 customer checks), 124 checks were paid by the bank, and the checkbook balance is $2,590.34. (Note: Verify all bank charges.)

Bank balance	_____	Checkbook balance	_____
Add:	_____	*Add:*	_____
Deduct:	_____	*Deduct:*	_____
Adjusted bank balance	_____	Adjusted checkbook balance	_____

EXPRESS YOUR THOUGHTS

Compose one or two well-written sentences to express the requested information in your own words.

1. Explain the procedure required to properly write a check. Why should this procedure be followed?

2. How would you endorse a check that you received from a customer which is to be transferred to one of your suppliers as payment for goods purchased? Why would you use this type of endorsement?

3. Describe how you would prepare a commercial deposit if you planned to deposit $500 in bills of various denominations, $125 in coin of various denominations, and 20 checks of various amounts.

4. Identify the types of information required to enter a transaction in a checkbook register.

5. Describe fully how a business collects payment for sold merchandise that was purchased by the buyer with a credit card.

6. Explain how a check written by you for merchandise moves through the cancellation process. Be sure to use appropriate terminology in your explanation.

7. Why is it necessary for a business or an individual to prepare a periodic bank reconciliation?

8. Identify the information on a bank statement that is required to determine the adjusted book balance portion of a reconciliation statement. Explain how the information affects this balance.

9. Explain how information found in both the checkbook register and the bank statement is used to determine the adjusted bank balance portion of the reconciliation statement.

10. What would you do if after completing a bank reconciliation you discovered that the adjusted balances did not agree?

Case exercise The difficult reconciliation

Margaret Green sat down at her desk to prepare the monthly reconciliation of her checking account. She had gone through the process many times, and seldom had difficulty reconciling her checkbook balance with the bank statement balance. This month, however, she could not get the account balance to agree. To resolve her problem, Margaret decided to seek the assistance of the bank's customer service department. She presented the following records to the customer service representative and asked her to explain why she was not able to reconcile her checking account.

Assume the job of the customer service representative of Solvay Bank:

A. Evaluate the records provided and identify the adjustments necessary to complete the bank reconciliation.

B. Identify any errors Margaret may have made and explain how they should be corrected.

C. Prepare an account form bank reconciliation statement. (Assume the bank statement to be *correct* as printed.)

RECORD ALL CHARGES OR CREDITS THAT AFFECT YOUR ACCOUNT

NUMBER	DATE	DESCRIPTION OF TRANSACTION	PAYMENT/DEBIT (−)	✓ T	FEE (IF ANY) (−)	DEPOSIT/CREDIT (+)	BALANCE
							$ 406 90
124	7/20	Ryan's Florist	$ 19 50	✓	$	$	387 40
125	7/25	General Finance	135 20				252 20
126	7/27	Ann Hart	20 00	✓			232 20
127	8/1	Mitzi's Coiffures	47 50				184 70
128	8/3	Goldman's Furniture	65 85				118 85
	8/5	Deposit				600 00	718 85
129	8/7	RENT	550 00				158 85
130	8/10	Health Club	28 40				130 45
131	8/13	Wegman's Grocery	41 70				88 75
	8/15	Deposit				500 00	588 75
132	8/18	Car Payment	236 90				351 85
133	8/21	JC Penney's	73 50				278 35
134	8/23	Central Electronics	92 29				186 06
135	8/26	Liberty Travel	150 00				36 06
	8/28	Deposit				250 00	286 06
136	8/28	Dr. Porter	39 42				246 64
137	8/29	General Finance	135 20				111 44

REMEMBER TO RECORD AUTOMATIC PAYMENTS / DEPOSITS ON DATE AUTHORIZED.

STATEMENT OF ACCOUNT WITH

SOLVAY BANK
1537 MILTON AVENUE
SOLVAY, NEW YORK 13209

ACCOUNT· NUMBER
00000000

STATEMENT PERIOD	
FROM	THROUGH
7/30/92	8/31/92

PAGE
1

Margaret Green
2749 Hillside Drive
Lakeland, N. Y. 13209

ACCOUNT SUMMARIES

ACCT TYPE	ACCOUNT NUMBER	PREVIOUS BALANCE	---TOTAL DEBITS-- AMOUNT	NO.	--TOTAL CREDITS-- AMOUNT	NO.	ENDING BALANCE
CKNG	00000000	367.40	1,311.14	12	1,102.10	3	158.36

TRANSACTIONS FOR CHECKING ACCOUNT

600.00	08/07	DEPOSIT		500.00	08/19	DEPOSIT
2.10	08/31	INTEREST				
5.50	08/31	SERVICE CHARGE		12.50	08/31	CHECK CHARGES
135.20	08/02	CHK NO.	125	47.50	08/03	CHK NO.	127
65.85	08/06	CHK NO.	128	550.00	08/09	CHK NO.	129
20.00	08/10	ATM		28.40	08/13	CHK NO.	130
41.40	08/16	CHK NO.	131	236.90	08/20	CHK NO.	132
75.30	08/23	CHK NO.	133	92.29	08/25	CHK NO.	134

ENDING BALANCES FOR CHECKING ACCOUNT

232.20	08/02	184.70	08/03	118.85	08/06
718.85	08/07	168.85	08/09	148.85	08/10
120.45	08/13	78.75	08/16	578.75	08/19
341.85	08/20	266.55	08/23	174.26	08/25
158.36	08/31				

1. Deduct any bank charges (check order, service charges, etc) from your checkbook register. Also, if applicable, add to your register interest paid to the account.		
2. Enter the ending balance shown on this statement. ⟶		$ 158,36
3. Enter all deposits made during current period that do not appear on this statement.		$ 250.00
4. Total of lines 2 and 3.		$ 408,36

5. List any checks issued or card transactions made which have not been deducted from your account as of this statement.	Check No.	Amount	Check No.	Amount	
	135	$ 150.00		$	
	136	39.42			
	137	135.20			

5a. TOTAL ⟶	$ 324,62
6. Subtract line 5a from line 4. This should be your present checkbook balance.	$ 83.74

Source: Solvay Bank, Solvay, NY. Used with permission.

SELF-TEST

A. Terminology review

Complete the following items using the key terms presented at the beginning of the chapter. Check your response against the answer key at the end of the test.

1. A _Check_ is a written order from an individual or company to their bank instructing it to pay a designated party a specified amount of funds.

2. Banks deduct a _Serve Charge_ to cover the cost of maintaining the customer's account.

3. A _deposit_ increases the amount of money in a checking account and can include checks as well as cash.

4. A _restrictive endorsement_ limits the ability to cash the check as it includes the words "for deposit only" and the signature of the depositor.

5. When a person or business wishes to transfer the amount of a check to a third party they must use a _special endorsement_ .

6. The record maintained by the depositor listing all transactions to their checking account is called a _check_ . _register_

7. Banks charge businesses a _discount fee_ for credit card sales identified on the merchant's deposit summary.

8. A check that is guaranteed by a bank is referred to as a _certified check_ .

9. Checks that have been deposited but not paid by the bank because there was not enough money in the account to cover the check are called _NSF_ .

10. A _cancel check_ is a check that has been paid by the depositor's bank.

11. When a depositor requests the bank not to pay a check, they have the bank issue a _stop payment order_ .

12. _Bank sta_ are provided to depositors by banks and list all charges (debits) and payments (credits) to the checking account during a specified period.

13. The process of analyzing the check register and bank statement to bring their balances into agreement is called _reconciliation_

B. Calculation review

The following concepts and short problems are designed to test your understanding of the objectives identified at the beginning of the chapter. Answers are provided at the end of the test.

14. Centerville Bank's personal checking account carries service charges of 15 cents for each check written; 30 cents for each check paid; and a monthly maintenance fee of $3.50. What is the monthly service charge if a depositor wrote 18 checks, 12 of which were paid by the bank during the month?

15. Oak Corners Grocery had an average balance for May of $2,875.50. During the month, the store made 10 deposits, which included a total of 192 checks, and the bank paid 63 checks. Using the rate schedule provided, calculate the store's monthly service charge.

Service	Charge
$4.00	Maintenance fee
$0.07	Per check paid
$0.10	Per check deposited
$0.50	Per deposit fee

16. Howard Dolan banks with First Federal Savings and Loan, which pays $5\frac{1}{4}\%$ interest on its NOW accounts if the average monthly balance is at least $500. How much interest should be credited to Mr. Dolan's account if his average monthly balance is $892.70?

17. What amount of money would be deposited based on the following: 3 fifty-dollar bills, 18 twenty-dollar bills, 32 ten-dollar bills, 13 five-dollar bills, 108 one-dollar bills; 7 rolls of quarters, 9 rolls of dimes, 12 rolls of nickels; and checks of $115.47, $73.69, $328.62, $39.99, and $12.50?

18. Determine the amount to be brought forward on check stub no. 153 if the amount brought forward on check stub no. 152 was $1,467.29, check no. 152 was written for $215.95, and a deposit of $375.00 was made before check no. 152 was written.

19. Jean's Unlimited had the following credit card transactions during a recent period. Sales: $39.95, $20.42, $69.55, $103.26, $9.67, $54.32, and $71.77. Refunds: $48.52, $20.42, and $19.25. Determine (a) the net deposit for the merchant deposit summary and (b) the amount of the discount fee to be charged to Jean's Unlimited's account if the bank charges a $4\frac{1}{4}\%$ discount fee.

20. On October 8, J. T. Ryan and Sons received a bank statement showing a balance of $1,874.30. The checking account balance was $2,139.18. An inspection of the check

register and bank statement revealed the following: There were deposits in transit of $850 and $525, and outstanding checks of $267.42, $98.25, $143.27, $364.18, and $56.00. There were check printing charges of $12.50, a service charge of $8.40, an inter-est credit of $5.20, a discount fee of $18.30, and a note collected by the bank for $250. A check from Charles Williams for $35 that had been deposited was returned due to nonsufficient funds. Prepare a bank reconciliation for J. T. Ryan and Sons.

12

SECURITIES AND DISTRIBUTION OF INCOME AND EXPENSES

Learning objectives

1. Explain the advantages and disadvantages an investor has in owning stocks and bonds.

2. Explain the advantages and disadvantages a company has in issuing stocks and bonds.

3. Interpret stock and bond quotations.

4. Calculate a capital gain or loss from the sale of stock.

5. Prorate bond interest.

6. Distribute company profits to partners and stockholders.

7. Distribute the expenses of a company on the basis of the number of employees, the square footage, and the amount of sales.

8. Define the key terms.

INTRODUCTION

Perhaps you presently own a business or maybe you'll own a business at some time in the future. As the owner of a business, the day will probably come when you will need a substantial amount of extra money in order to expand or improve your business. This chapter discusses two ways in which a business generates extra cash:

1. by issuing stocks

2. by issuing bonds.

We often hear references made to stocks and bonds, but what are they and how do they affect us? A **stock** is a share or portion of ownership of a particular company or corporation. A **bond** is an interest-bearing loan that the investor makes to a company. Stocks and bonds are referred to as **securities**.

To illustrate, let us suppose you have some extra cash that you would like to invest. You decide that you would like to purchase some shares of American Telephone and Telegraph (AT&T) stock. (At this point, the term *stock* shall refer to common stock rather than preferred stock, each of which will be clearly explained later.) In order to do this, you go to a **stockbroker** (a broker is a person who buys and sells stocks and bonds). The stockbroker in turn contacts the **stock exchange** where your shares of AT&T stock will be purchased, makes the purchase for you, and charges you a fee for the services provided. The stock exchange, sometimes called the **stock market**, is a place where securities that are registered with the exchange are bought and sold. If each share of AT&T stock is selling for $40 per share, and if you had $400 to invest, then you would be able to purchase 10 shares of stock ($400/$40 = 10 shares). After purchasing this stock, you would receive a **stock certificate**, which is a certificate indicating ownership of 10 shares of AT&T stock. Since purchasing this stock means that you would now be part owner of AT&T and would be considered a **stockholder** in its corporation (a stockholder is a holder, or owner, of stock in a corporation), you would be entitled to dividends. **Dividends** are a portion of a company's profits, usually paid to its stockholders in the form of cash. As an illustration, let us suppose that AT&T has $70,000 in profits that it wishes to distribute among 200,000 shareholders. This means that for each share of AT&T stock, you would receive $.35 in dividends ($70,000/200,000 = $.35). Since you have just purchased 10 shares of stock, you would receive $3.50 in dividends ($.35 × 10 shares).

A second way for corporations to acquire cash is by issuing bonds. A bond is an interest-bearing certificate issued by a government or business, redeemable on a specified date. In other words, the investor is lending money to the corporation for a certain length of time. In turn, the corporation must pay the investor a predetermined rate of interest during the life of the bond and it must repay the **principal** (the original amount borrowed) at some future specified date.

Most corporate bonds are in $1,000 denominations, although bonds of $5,000 and $10,000 are also issued. Each bond bears a stated rate of interest, such as 7%, 9⅛%, or 12⅜%. Usually, corporations pay interest to the bondholder semiannually. The life of a bond begins the day the bond is purchased and ends on the **maturity date**, that is, the date on which the principal of the bond is to be repaid. Most bonds have a fairly long life such as 10, 20, or 30 years, although the life of a bond can be as short as 2 years.

From the investor's point of view, there are both advantages and disadvantages to owning securities. The advantages to the investor of owning stocks in a company are:

Learning objective
Explain the advantages and disadvantages an investor has in owning stocks and bonds.

- The dollar value of the stock may increase.
- Dividends may be paid to the stockholder by the issuing company.
- Ownership of stocks can easily be sold or traded.
- The stockholder, as an owner of the corporation, has voting privileges in major company decisions and therefore has some control over business decisions.
- Stocks are negotiable; therefore they can be bought and sold.

Some disadvantages of owning stock are:

- The dollar value of the original shares may decrease.
- The corporation is not required to issue dividends.

The advantages to the investor who purchases bonds are as follows:

- The investor receives regular, semiannual interest payments during the life of the bond.
- Bonds are considered a low-risk investment and therefore a good investment for the risk avoider.
- Bonds are negotiable, which means that the original purchaser of the bond can sell it to someone else.

Disadvantages of owning bonds include:

- The investor has no voting privileges in the issuing corporation and therefore has no input into the operation of the company.
- Bond prices may decrease.

Since we have just looked at some reasons why an investor would want to purchase securities, let us take the opposite perspective and look at the reasons why corporations issue securities.

When a company needs money to expand its business, one way to get that necessary money is to issue shares of stock. To illustrate, let us suppose that 5 years ago, three people started a business. This company now needs $50,000 to expand its business. If the three people could find one person to invest $50,000 then there would be four owners (three original plus one new owner). However, it might be easier to get five people to each invest $10,000. In this case, there would be eight owners (three original plus five new owners). It might even be easier to get 2,000 people to each invest $25. Then, of course, there would be a total of 2,003 owners. Remembering that each stockholder receives one vote for each share of stock held, this company would now have 2,003 people voting rather than just the original three. The original owners would now probably lose some control over the business decisions affecting the company. Loss of control would be one reason why a company might not want to issue stock. On the other hand, an advantage of issuing stocks, rather than issuing bonds, is that the company's capital, or assets, increases. This means that there is no debt to repay as there would be with bonds. Another advantage is that the issuing company does not have to pay out dividends to stockholders on a regular basis. These advantages and disadvantages are listed in Figure 12.1.

Figure 12.1

Advantages and disadvantages to the issuing of securities for a corporation

Learning objective
Explain the advantages and disadvantages a company has in issuing stocks and bonds.

The advantages of issuing stock to the company are:
1. There is an increase in its assets and capital.
2. The principal amount invested does not have to be repaid to the investor as it would be if a bond were issued.
3. There is no requirement that a dividend be paid to the investor.

The disadvantages of issuing stock are:
1. Some loss of control over business decisions.

The advantages to a company of issuing bonds are:
1. The company still maintains control over business decisions since bondholders have no voting privileges.

The disadvantages to the company are:
1. The company must repay the principal amount to the bondholders at some future date.
2. The company must pay interest to bondholders during the life of the bond.

If you have neither the desire nor the opportunity to own a business, this chapter will still be of interest to you since we will discuss practical calculations such as calculating profits and losses from the sale of securities (stocks and bonds) and distributing income and expense amounts in a business. Each of these topics will help you with your financial investments and your future success in the business world.

12.1   STOCK QUOTATIONS AND CAPITAL GAINS

People who wish to invest their money in stocks need information about the value, performance, and costs of the stocks available for purchase. Such information is provided in a format called a *stock quotation*. When investors want to sell stocks, they need to know the profit or loss that they have realized with their investments. This profit or loss is referred to as a *capital gain* or *capital loss*.

STOCK QUOTATIONS

Learning objective
Interpret stock and bond quotations.

As an investor, it is important that you understand how to read stock and bond quotations. Stock and bond quotations are printed in local, daily papers as well as in financial publications such as the *Wall Street Journal*. Figure 12.2 represents a stock quotation and the following paragraphs explain this figure.

The first two columns of numbers in Figure 12.2 labeled "52 Weeks High–Low" represent the highest price and lowest price, respectively, that this stock sold for within the past year. To convert these mixed numbers to dollar and cents amounts, simply convert the fractions to their decimal equivalents. Therefore, 130⅞ becomes $130.875 (⅞ = .875) and 106¼ becomes $106.25. The heading "Stock" refers to the name of the corpo-

Figure 12.2

Sample stock quotation

| 52 Weeks | | Stock | Div. | Yld % | P–E Ratio | Sales 100s | High | Low | Close | Net Change |
High	Low									
130 7/8	106 1/4	XYZ	4.84	4.2	12	96543	119 3/8	114 7/8	115 1/2	−1/4
highest and lowest prices over the last 52 weeks		company name	annual dividend	% yield	price–earnings ratio	number of shares sold at current price	highest and lowest trading prices on this day		closing price on this day	change in the closing price from previous day

ration that is issuing the stock. Usually, it is necessary to abbreviate the name of the company. The fourth column, "Div.," approximates the annual dividends per share paid to the stockholders. In this case, $4.84 were paid in annual dividends. The next column, "Yld %," shows that 4.2% is the percent of dividends you would receive if you bought this stock at the current closing price. In other words, divide the dividend by the closing price (4.84/115.50 = .0419, or 4.2%).

The "P–E Ratio" column is the price–earnings ratio. This ratio compares the *closing price* with the corporation's *earnings per share* for the past year. In this case, the current selling price is 12 times the earnings per share. Usually, a 10 in this column means that the selling price is a fair price; therefore, we might assume that 12 means that the current selling price is slightly overpriced in relation to the company's earnings. Notice that the company's earnings are not stated on a stock quotation. The next column, "Sales 100s," shows the number of shares (in hundreds) traded on this 1 day. Therefore, 9,654,300 shares of XYZ stock were traded on this day. The eighth, ninth, and tenth columns, labeled "High," "Low," and "Close," represent the highest price the stock traded for on this day, the lowest price the stock traded for on this day, and the closing price for the day. In this case, the high price was $119.375, the low price was $114.875, and the closing price at the end of the day was $115.50.

The last column, "Net Change," shows the net change in closing price from the previous day with that of today's closing price. In other words, today's closing price is −¼, or $0.25, less than yesterday's closing price. Therefore, yesterday's closing price was $115.75.

CAPITAL GAINS

As an investor, when you determine that it is time to sell your shares of stock, you need to know how to calculate capital gains. A **capital gain** is the profit earned from the sale of assets, such as securities or real estate.

Learning objective
Calculate a capital gain or loss from the sale of stock.

It is important for you to know that each time you buy or sell securities, you must pay the broker a commission. Calculating the broker's commission is confusing because each brokerage house (e.g., Merrill Lynch, Prudential-Bache, Dean Witter Reynolds) has its own set of rules for calculating commissions. Adding to the confusion is the fact that there is a different commission structure for the over-the-counter market (where lesser-known stocks that are not registered with a stock market are traded) than there is for the stock exchange, such as the New York Stock Exchange (where larger, well-known stocks are traded). The phrase "over-the-counter market" is used to describe a variety of ways that stocks and bonds not registered with a stock exchange—and therefore not traded through a stock exchange—can be bought and sold. Usually, you will pay a larger commission for a smaller stock. In order to simplify this process, we will assume in our examples that a broker's commission is 3% of the selling price of the stock.

When it comes time to sell your stock, you will need to compute your *capital gain*, or profit, from the sale. There are three steps in computing the capital gain. Step 1 is to determine the total cost of buying the shares. This includes the purchase price plus broker's commission. Step 2 determines the total amount received from the sale of stock. The total amount received equals the selling price minus the broker's commission. Step 3 is the difference between Step 1 and Step 2. Example 1 illustrates how to calculate a capital gain.

Example 1

If you buy ten shares of a stock at $40 each and then later sell them at $57, what is your capital gain? Assume the commission is 3% of the market price.

Solution

Step 1: Determine the cost to buy shares.

10 shares at $40 per share	$400.00
+ commission (.03 × 400)	12.00
total cost	$412.00

Step 2: Determine the amount received from sale of the stock.

10 shares at $57 per share	$570.00
− commission (.03 × $570)	17.10
total received	$552.90

Step 3: Determine the difference.

total received	$552.90
− total cost	412.00
capital gain	$140.90

Note: If the total cost is greater than the total received, then this would be a capital loss rather than a capital gain.

Not too long ago **long-term capital gains** (a gain on an asset that has been held longer than 6 months) received tax-favored treatment. Instead of paying taxes on 100% of the capital gain, taxes were paid on only 40%

of the capital gain. The tax reforms initiated in 1986 have changed this so that long-term capital gains no longer receive the favored treatment.

CHECK YOUR KNOWLEDGE

Stocks, bonds, stock quotations, and capital gains

1. If XYZ Corporation wishes to distribute $110,000 in dividends among its 400,000 shareholders, how much will you receive in dividends if you own 10 shares of XYZ?

2. From the investor's point of view, list one advantage of owning bonds.

3. From the corporation's point of view, list one advantage of issuing stocks.

Refer to the following stock quotation when answering questions 4 through 7.

52 Weeks		Stock	Div.	Yld %	P–E Ratio	Sales 100s	High	Low	Close	Net Change
High	Low									
30 3/4	24 5/8	ABC	.88	3.2	9	112	28	27 3/4	27 7/8	+1/4

4. What was the low trading price for the day?

5. What was the low price for the year?

6. How many shares of stock were traded on this day?

7. Did the stock increase or decrease in price from the previous day, and by how much did it change?

8. If you bought 300 shares at 108½, and the broker received 3% commission, what would have been the total cost to you?

9. If you sold 300 shares at 105¾, and the broker received a 3% commission, what would have been the total amount you received?

10. Compute the gain or loss using the information from problems 8 and 9, assuming that it was the same stock traded in each case.

Answers to CYK: *1.* $2.75   *2.* steady (periodic) interest income   *3.* not a debt, therefore, nothing to repay   *4.* $27.75   *5.* $24.625   *6.* 11,200   *7.* increased by ¼, or $.25   *8.* $33,526.50   *9.* $30,773.25   *10.* $2,753.25 capital loss

12.1 EXERCISES

Find the dividends per share and total dividends received.

	Profits to distribute	Number of shareholders	Dividends per share	Number of shares owned	Total dividend
Example	$60,000	100,000	$.60	25	$15.00
1.	$250,000	100,000	_____	25	_____
2.	$500,000	554,900	_____	500	_____
3.	$400,000	998,000	_____	100	_____
4.	$300,000	400,000	_____	250	_____
5.	$200,000	50,000	_____	20	_____

Refer to the following stock quotation to complete the missing information below. Convert all fractions to decimals.

52 Weeks		Stock	Div.	Yld %	P–E Ratio	Sales 100s	High	Low	Close	Net Change
High	Low									
37 7/8	31	BBD	2.56	7.0	11	12955	37 3/4	36 3/8	36 1/2	−1
10 1/2	6 7/8	IBN	20	2.0	7	2803	10 1/2	8 3/8	10 1/8	+1 3/8
117	106 7/8	ATD	15.25	13.3	—	3080	115 1/2	114	114 1/2	−5
99 3/8	87 1/3	GMK	9.25	9.7	—	420	98	98	98	−1 3/8
35 1/4	22 7/8	BMZ	1.00	3.0	6	4112	35 1/4	33 3/8	33 5/8	−1/2
60 1/8	41 1/2	NBO	1.20	2.2	22	1173	59 1/4	51 1/4	55 3/4	+4 3/4
23 7/8	14 3/4	TRL	.60	2.6	8	2871	23 7/8	22 1/8	23 1/2	+1 1/2
73 1/4	52 1/2	BVD2	.04	2.8	19	22934	73 1/2	64 1/8	72 5/8	+8
25 3/4	21 3/8	PGE	1.07	4.2	14	15788	25 5/8	24 1/2	25 3/8	+1/8
17 1/4	12 7/8	GTS	.32	1.9	18	58431	17 1/4	15 7/8	16 1/2	+1/2

		52-week high	Yearly dividend	Number of shares sold	Close	Net change
6.	BBD	_____	_____	_____	_____	_____
7.	IBN	_____	_____	_____	_____	_____
8.	ATD	_____	_____	_____	_____	_____
9.	GMK	_____	_____	_____	_____	_____
10.	BMZ	_____	_____	_____	_____	_____
11.	NBO	_____	_____	_____	_____	_____
12.	TRL	_____	_____	_____	_____	_____
13.	BVD2	_____	_____	_____	_____	_____
14.	PGE	_____	_____	_____	_____	_____
15.	GTS	_____	_____	_____	_____	_____

Calculate the total cost to the buyer. Assume the broker's commission is 3% of the market price per share.

		Stock cost	Commission	Total cost
16.	100 shares at 63	_____	_____	_____
17.	100 shares at 24⅞	_____	_____	_____
18.	500 shares at 78	_____	_____	_____
19.	200 shares at 182¾	_____	_____	_____
20.	250 shares at 33¼	_____	_____	_____

Calculate the total amount received if the shares were sold at the prices listed below. Assume the broker's commission is 3% of the total market price.

		Stock revenue	Commission	Total received
21.	100 shares at 63	_____	_____	_____
22.	500 shares at 101⅞	_____	_____	_____
23.	250 shares at 88⅛	_____	_____	_____
24.	200 shares at 11⅝	_____	_____	_____
25.	400 shares at 36¾	_____	_____	_____

Find the capital gain or loss. Assume a broker's commission of 3%.

26. Bought 100 shares at 14¼; sold 100 shares at 15¼.

27. Bought 200 shares at 21¼; sold 200 shares at 22.

28. Bought 200 shares at 21¼; sold 100 shares at 22.

29. Bought 500 shares at 108; sold 500 shares at 138.

30. Bought 500 shares at 76⅝; sold 350 shares at 80⅜.

31. Bought 400 shares at 26¼; sold 400 shares at 22⅛.

32. Bought 150 shares at 120⅞; sold 150 shares at 80⅞.

33. Bought 60 shares at 52; sold 60 shares at 36⅞.

34. Bought 800 shares at 8⅜; sold 800 shares at 64⅞.

35. Bought 360 shares at 11⅜; sold 360 shares at 7⅝.

Refer to the stock quotation provided for problems 6 through 15.

36. Yesterday you bought 100 shares of BVD2 stock at the quoted price; you sold all 100 shares at today's quoted price and paid a broker's fee of 2% for each transaction. (a) What was the total selling price of the stock when you bought it? (b) What was the total you paid for the stock, including broker's fees? (c) What was the total selling price of the stock when you sold it? (d) What was the total you received for the stock? (e) What were the capital gains or losses?

37. Yesterday you bought 2,100 shares of NBO stock at the quoted price; you sold all 2,100 shares at today's quoted price and paid a broker's fee of 1% for each transaction. (a) What was the total selling price of the stock when you bought it? (b) What was the total you paid for the stock, including broker's fees? (c) What was the total selling price of the stock when you sold it? (d) What was the total you received for the stock? (e) What were the capital gains or losses?

38. Yesterday you bought 500 shares of GMK stock at the quoted price; you sold all 500 shares at today's quoted price and paid a broker's fee of 3% for each transaction.

(a) What was the total selling price of the stock when you bought it? (b) What was the total you paid for the stock, including broker's fees? (c) What was the total selling price of the stock when you sold it? (d) What was the total you received for the stock? (e) What were the capital gains or losses?

39.   Jack Mangan bought 250 shares of ATD stock

yesterday and must sell some of it today. He has decided to sell 100 shares. The broker's fees were 3% in both transactions. What is Jack's capital loss?

40.   Bob Burnet bought 1,000 shares of GTS stock yesterday; he sold it at today's high price, with broker's fees of 2%. What is his capital loss or gain?

12.2   BOND QUOTATIONS AND ACCRUED INTEREST

When investing in bonds, information about value, performance, and costs of bonds is contained in a *bond quotation*. The interest earned while an investor owns a bond is called *accrued interest*.

BOND QUOTATIONS

Learning objective
Interpret stock and bond quotations.

As demonstrated earlier, bonds are issued as a way for corporations to borrow money. The denomination of a bond is referred to as the **face value of a bond**. In this chapter, we will assume that each bond has a face value of $1,000. If you were interested in buying or selling bonds, you would go to a stockbroker just as you would if you were buying or selling stocks. Bonds are traded at a stock exchange or on the over-the-counter market.

Even though a bond has a face value of $1,000, it can be purchased at a price higher or lower than $1,000. When the market price (or selling price) of a bond is lower than its face value, the price is called a **discount price** and the bond is said to be selling at a *discount*. When the market price is higher than its face value, the price is called a **premium price** and the bond is said to be selling at a *premium*. The market price of a bond fluctuates from day to day to reflect the current state of the economy. This fluctuation allows bonds to compete with the current interest rates of other investments. The market price of a bond can also reflect the current status of the issuing corporation (e.g., whether it's growing, stable, innovative, and so on).

The market price of a bond is stated as a percent of its face value. To illustrate, suppose a bond is listed as 99. This means that the current market price is 99% of the $1,000 face value or $990 (.99 × $1,000). Suppose a second bond is listed as 105. Then the current market price is 105% of $1,000, or $1,050 (1.05 × $1,000).

Figure 12.3

Sample bond
quotation

Bond			Cur. Yld.	Vol.	High	Low	Close	Net Chg.
Btmm Corp	7 5/8	**09**	8.0	20	95	95	95	−1 5/8
name of company issuing the bond	interest rate	year bond matures (2009)	current yield	volume of bonds sold on this day	highest and lowest prices bond sold for on this day		closing price on this day	net change from previous day

The current market price of a bond can be found in a bond quotation. As with stock quotations, bond quotations can be found in daily newspapers or in financial periodicals. Figure 12.3 represents a bond quotation and the following paragraphs explain this figure.

Under the heading of "bonds," first the abbreviated name of the company is listed; next, the 7⅝ represents the 7⅝% stated interest rate on the bond. The large "09" stands for 2009, the year in which the bond matures. If, instead of "09" the number was "95," it would mean that the maturity date was in 1995.

The data in the column labeled "Cur. Yld." means the bond has a current yield of 8.0%. Current yield is determined by dividing the dollar amount of interest you expect to make on the $1,000 bond by today's closing price of $950; your return on investment would be 8% here.

$$\text{expected interest} = 7\tfrac{5}{8} \times 1{,}000 = \$76.25$$

$$\text{current yield} = \frac{76.25}{950} = .0802 = 8\%$$

The "Vol." heading stands for the volume of bonds that were traded on this 1 trading day. In this case, 20 bonds were traded. The column labeled "High" represents the highest price that one of these bonds traded for on this day. Notice that the market price is stated as a percent of the face value of the bond. That is, the current market price is $950 (.95 × $1,000).

The next two columns represent the lowest price that one of these bonds traded for on this day and the closing price, respectively.

The last column is the net change from the previous day's closing price compared with the closing price of today. The number listed in this column is stated as a percent of the face value. Therefore, a net change of $-1\frac{5}{8}$ means that today's closing price is lower than yesterday's closing price by $16.25.

$$-1\tfrac{5}{8}\% = -1.625\% \qquad -.01625 \times \$1,000 = -\$16.25$$

ACCRUED INTEREST ON A BOND

Learning objective
Prorate bond interest.

Two important points were mentioned earlier that bear repeating at this time. First, bonds are negotiable, which means that the original purchaser of the bond can sell it to someone else. Second, interest is paid to the bondholder semiannually. In this chapter, we will assume that interest is paid to the bondholder on January 1 and July 1. If bondholders decide to sell their bonds on a date other than January 1 or July 1, then they must know how to prorate (to divide proportionately) bond interest. Example 2 illustrates this concept and procedure.

Example 2

Alice currently owns a $1,000 bond with a stated interest rate of 10%. On June 1, she will sell it to Benny. The commission is $20. On July 1, the issuing corporation will send the interest payment, for the past 6 months, to Benny, who will be the current bondholder. In order for Alice to receive interest payments for the 5 months during which she held the bond, the buyer must pay the seller for any interest that has accrued since the last interest payment. Determine how much Alice should receive from Benny.

Solution

The formula for determining how much the buyer pays, and the seller receives, is:

buyer pays = market price + accrued interest + commission

seller receives = market price + accrued interest − commission

Determine the accrued interest amount. The interest for 5 months, or 150 days of 360 days in a year, is 150/360 of the total interest.

$$I = prt$$
$$= 1,000 \times .10 \times \frac{150}{360}$$
$$= \$41.67$$

For **Y**our **I**nformation
What causes variation in bond prices?

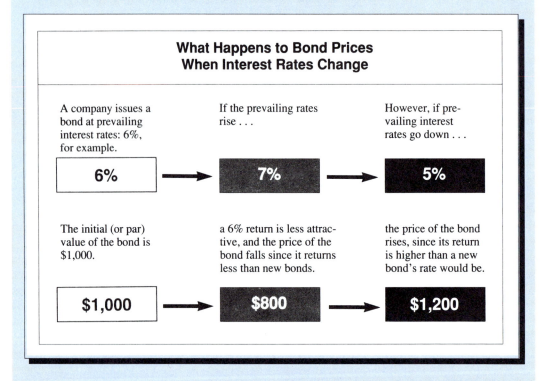

What Happens to Bond Prices When Interest Rates Change

A company issues a bond at prevailing interest rates: 6%, for example.

If the prevailing rates rise . . .

However, if prevailing interest rates go down . . .

| 6% | → | 7% | → | 5% |

The initial (or par) value of the bond is $1,000.

a 6% return is less attractive, and the price of the bond falls since it returns less than new bonds.

the price of the bond rises, since its return is higher than a new bond's rate would be.

| $1,000 | → | $800 | → | $1,200 |

When a company issues a bond, say a 20-year $1,000 face value bond at 6% interest per year, the bond will pay $60 per year and return the $1,000 face value at its maturity. Bonds are negotiable instruments that may be bought and sold, and their market value changes daily. If the prevailing interest rate on other investments jumps to 7%, then investors will not want to buy the 6% bond, so the selling price of the bond will fall, perhaps to $800. On the other hand, if the prevailing interest rates on other investments drop, say to 5%, then the 6% bond will be more attractive to investors and the price of the bond will rise, perhaps to $1,200. Remember, the bond promises to pay $60 per year for 20 years, for a total of $1,200 in interest.

Source: Teachers Insurance and Annuity Association; College Retirement and Equities Fund. Used with permission.

$$\begin{aligned}
\text{Benny pays} &= \text{market price} + \text{accrued interest} + \text{commission} \\
&= \quad \$1{,}000 \quad + \quad\quad \$41.67 \quad\quad + \quad \$20 \\
&= \$1{,}061.67
\end{aligned}$$

$$\begin{aligned}
\text{Alice receives} &= \text{market price} + \text{accrued interest} - \text{commission} \\
&= \quad \$1{,}000 \quad + \quad\quad \$41.67 \quad\quad - \quad \$20 \\
&= \$1{,}021.67
\end{aligned}$$

Let's look at a similar transaction except, this time, the market price will not be exactly $1,000 and more than one bond will be purchased.

Example 3

Mark Van Kuren owned five bonds with face values of $1,000 each when he purchased them. He sold all five bonds on May 1 to Sharon Martin. The bond quotation for May 1 was 11½ quoted at 96, and the commission for each bond was $8. Find (a) the amount that the buyer paid and (b) the amount the seller received.

Solution

January 1 to May 1 is 4 months, or 120 days/360.

$$I = prt$$
$$= 1{,}000 \times .115 \times \frac{120}{360}$$
$$= \$38.33$$

a.   buyer pays = market price + accrued interest + commission

$$= \$960 + \$38.33 + \$8$$
$$= \$1{,}006.33 \text{ for one bond}$$

buyer pays $5,031.65 total for five bonds (1,006.33 × 5)

b.   seller receives = market price + accrued interest − commission
$$= \$960 + \$38.33 - \$8$$
$$= \$990.33 \text{ for one bond}$$

Seller receives $4,951.65 total for five bonds (990.33 × 5)

CHECK YOUR KNOWLEDGE

Bond quotations and accrued interest

Refer to the following bond quotation when answering questions 1 through 4.

Bond			Cur. Yld.	Vol.	High	Low	Close	Net Chg
Woody Corp	8 1/4	01	7.8	30	105	103	105	+1/4

1. What is the year of maturity?

2. What is the rate of return?

3. What is the stated rate of interest?

4. How much would you pay for this bond if you bought it at the closing price?

5. Today is August 1, and on this date, Shelley decides to sell her bond. The stated rate of interest is 9¼%, while the bond is quoted at 106. The commission is $20. How much interest has accrued since July 1?

6. If Edna buys the bond from Shelley under the conditions stated in problem 5, what is the total amount that Edna will pay?

7. What is the total amount that Shelley will receive?

12.2 EXERCISES

Refer to the following bond quotation when answering questions 1 through 20.

Bond			Vol.	Close	Net Chg
Lavender C	9 3/8	93	10	103	+6
Teal Corp	8 3/4	01	200	94	−3/4
Lime C	9 3/8	09	13	105	−3/8
Pink Pw	7 1/8	95	20	97	+1/4
Blue Ed	7 1/4	05	14	62 1/2	−5/8
Green Pw	14	00	32	117 1/2	−3 1/2
Yellow Mills	5 3/4	11	12	85	+2 1/8
Orange Ed	11	09	8	99	−1
Red Dyn	12 1/8	91	24	101	+1 7/8
Peach Cp	8 1/4	97	26	124 1/2	−2 1/4

Answers to CYK: *1.* 2001¹⁄₁₂   *2.* 7.8%   *3.* 8.25%   *4.* $1,050.00   *5.* $I = prt = \$1,000 \times$ .0925 × $7.71   *6.* $1,087.71   *7.* $1,047.71

For each bond, list the year of maturity and calculate the annual interest income.

Corporation	Year of maturity	Interest income
1. Lavender C	_____	_____
2. Teal Corp	_____	_____
3. Lime C	_____	_____
4. Pink Pw	_____	_____
5. Blue Ed	_____	_____
6. Green Pw	_____	_____
7. Yellow Mills	_____	_____
8. Orange Ed	_____	_____
9. Red Dyn	_____	_____
10. Peach Cp	_____	_____

For each bond, calculate the current yield. Remember that the current yield is the relationship between the interest income (already calculated in exercises 1 – 10) and the closing market price.

Company	Interest income	Closing market price	Current yield
11. Lavender C	_____	_____	_____
12. Teal Corp.	_____	_____	_____
13. Lime C	_____	_____	_____
14. Pink Pw	_____	_____	_____
15. Blue Ed	_____	_____	_____
16. Green Pw	_____	_____	_____
17. Yellow Mills	_____	_____	_____
18. Orange Ed	_____	_____	_____
19. Red Dyn	_____	_____	_____
20. Peach Cp	_____	_____	_____

For problems 21 through 30, calculate (a) the accrued interest, (b) the amount the buyer pays, and (c) the amount the seller receives. Assume that each bond is of $1,000 denomination, the commission is $20 per bond, and that interest is paid to the bondholder on January 1 and July 1.

21. One ABE 8¼, closing at 98, date of sale is February 1.

22. Two XYZ 9⅝, closing at 100, date of sale is March 1.

23. Five BCD 6¼, closing at 102, date of sale is October 1.

24. Four LMN 7⅜, closing at 92, date of sale is November 1.

25. Eight STU 11½, closing at 101, date of sale is May 1.

26. Ten QRS 10, closing at 99, date of sale is April 1.

27. Twelve TUV 7⅞, closing at 105, date of sale is February 1.

28. One CDE 8⅜, closing at 88, date of sale is December 1.

29. One FGH 8⅜, closing at 100, date of sale is December 1.

30. Five NOP 9¾, closing at 106, date of sale is March 1.

Solve the following word problems.

31. Sara Johnson owned ten bonds whose face value was $1,000 each when she purchased them. She sold all ten bonds on April 1 to Joyce Birch. The bond quotation for April 1

was 9½ quoted at 98, and the commission for each bond is $10. Find (a) the amount that the buyer paid and (b) the amount the seller received.

32. Alan Swarde purchased 20 bonds with a face value of $1,000 each. When he purchased them, they were being sold at a discount quoted at 97. He sold all 20 bonds on June 1 to Carole Harvey at a premium of 103. The interest rate on the bonds was 10⅜ and the broker's fee was $15 per bond. Find (a) the amount that the buyer paid and (b) the amount the seller received.

33. J. C. Roppel purchased 40 bonds with a face value of $1,000 each. When she purchased them, they were being sold at a premium quoted at 102. She sold all 40 bonds on March 1 to Sharon Dall at a premium of 105. The interest rate on the bonds was 9⅝ and the broker's fee was $13 per bond. Find (a) the amount that the buyer paid and (b) the amount the seller received.

34. Harmon Ziminski purchased 100 bonds with a face value of $1,000 each. When he pur-chased them they were being sold at a pre-mium quoted at 102. He sold all 100 bonds on March 1 to Steve Malii at a discount of 95. The interest rate on the bonds was 12⅞ and the broker's fee was 4% of the face value per bond. Find (a) the amount that the buyer paid and (b) the amount the seller received. (c) If Steve had held the bonds for 4 years and re-ceived eight interest payments prior to this sale, how much interest income did Steve realize in this investment?

35. Ann Warwick purchased five bonds with a face value of $1,000 each. When she pur-chased them they were being sold at a pre-mium quoted at 105. She then sold all of the bonds on Feb. 1 to Stan James at a premium of 107. The interest rate on the bonds was 14⅞ and the broker's fees were 3% of the face value per bond. Find (a) the amount that the buyer paid and (b) the amount the seller received. (c) If Ann had held the bonds for 2 years and received four interest payments prior to this sale, how much interest income did she realize in this investment?

12.3   DISTRIBUTION OF INCOME AND EXPENSES

There are three basic types of ownership of a business: sole proprietor-ship, a partnership, and a corporation. The sole proprietor of a business receives all of the income from the business and also is responsible for all expenses. Because a partnership and a corporation have more than one owner, a procedure for distribution of income and expenses is necessary.

DISTRIBUTION OF PROFITS TO PARTNERS OF A BUSINESS

First, let's consider a business that is owned by four partners who have made equal investments in the company and, therefore, who own an equal part of the business. Whenever the business makes a profit, the partners must decide how to divide this income. There are two usual ways of doing this. The first is simply to divide the profit equally among all partners. Table 12.1 demonstrates the equal distribution of income assuming the

Learning objective
Distribute company profits to partners and stockholders.

Table 12.1

Example of equal
distribution of
income in a
partnership

Partner	Income		Fraction		Portion of income
Abbey	$100,000	×	1/4	=	$25,000
Burt	100,000	×	1/4	=	25,000
Caroline	100,000	×	1/4	=	25,000
Darla	100,000	×	1/4	=	25,000
					$100,000

company has a profit of $100,000. Since there are four partners, each re-
ceives one-fourth of the income.

An alternative method of dividing income is to divide it according to a
predetermined ratio. For instance, suppose a group of partners did not
make equal investments in a business and they decide to divide future profits by the percent of their individual investments in the business. Income
or profit would then be multiplied by this percent to determine the
amount of money each partner would receive.

Example 4

Three years ago, the following partners invested money in a business:
Abbey, $35,000; Burt, $15,000; Caroline, $40,000; and Darla, $60,000.
They now have a total of $142,000 profit, which they want to divide ac-
cording to the percent that each initially invested. What amount will each
partner receive?

Solution

Partner	Initial investment
Abbey	$ 35,000
Burt	15,000
Caroline	40,000
Darla	60,000
total investment	$150,000

Partner	$\dfrac{\text{Initial investment}}{\text{total investment}}$ =	Rate each invested
Abbey	35,000/150,000	.233
Burt	15,000/150,000	.100
Caroline	40,000/150,000	.267
Darla	60,000/150,000	.400
		1.000

Partner	Rate invested	×	Income	=	Portion of income
Abbey	.233		142,000	=	$ 33,086
Burt	.100		142,000	=	14,200
Caroline	.267		142,000	=	37,914
Darla	.400		142,000	=	56,800
					$142,000

CALCULATOR SOLUTION

Keyed entry	Display
AC 35000 ÷ 150000 =	.2333
× 142000 =	33086
Abbey's share of income	
AC 15000 ÷ 150000 =	.10
× 142000 =	14200
Burt's share of income	

Use the same procedure to find other partners' shares.

The partners of a company share in the assets of their business, and they share in any liabilities that the company may incur. They are personally responsible for the company. A corporation on the other hand is a legal entity that is set up in such a way that the stockholders own the business and are responsible for it rather than the people who work for the company and operate it.

DISTRIBUTION OF PROFIT TO STOCKHOLDERS OF A CORPORATION

Earlier we mentioned two types of stock that could be purchased in a corporation, preferred stock and common stock. An investor who purchases **preferred stock** is entitled to some preferential treatment in terms of receiving dividends (a share of company profits) and of having an early claim on any assets the company may have if it is dissolved as a company. An investor who purchases **common stock** receives his/her share of the dividends and company assets after the preferred stockholder. Neither the preferred nor the common stockholder has a guarantee that the company will ever pay a dividend on the stock, but if it does, the preferred stockholders receive their share first. Both types of investors hope that their stock will increase in value before they sell it, and that the company will make a profit that will be shared with the investors in the form of dividends.

Investors who purchase preferred stock do not receive a guarantee that their stock will appreciate in value, but they are guaranteed a yearly dividend at a fixed rate of interest based on the purchase value of the stock, if the company pays a dividend that particular year. *Cumulative preferred stockholders* also enjoy the privilege that while the company may defer payment of these dividends, the company is responsible for paying them whether or not it makes a profit during a given year. Whenever the company does declare its intent to pay a dividend to its investors, cumulative preferred stockholders receive their share of the profits *first* and the remainder of the profits are then distributed to the common stockholders.

Example 5

Furbush Electric Components Company has 10,000 stockholders of which 4,000 hold preferred stock and 6,000 hold common stock. The preferred stock was sold for $100.00 per share (called the *face value* or *par value* of the stock) with a guaranteed yearly dividend of 5%. Each share of common stock was sold for $50.00. The company has made a profit of $40,000. Determine the amount of dividend per share that will be paid for preferred stock (a) and for common stock (b), and the common dividend rate (c).

Solution

(a) *Step 1:*   Determine the amount to be paid per share for the preferred stock. Each share of preferred stock must receive 5% of the $100 cost of the stock.

$$\text{dividend for preferred stock} = .05 \times \$100 = \$5.00/\text{share}$$

Step 2:   Determine the total to be paid to preferred stockholders.

$$\text{total} = \text{dividend per share} \times \text{number of shares}$$
$$= \$5.00 \times 4,000 = \$20,000$$

(b) *Step 3:*   Determine the amount of dividends to be distributed to common stockholders.

$$\frac{\text{amount to common}}{\text{stockholders}} = \text{total dividends} - \frac{\text{amount to preferred}}{\text{stockholders}}$$
$$= \$40,000 - \$20,000$$
$$= \$20,000$$

Step 4:   Determine the amount of dividends to be distributed to each share of common stock.

$$\frac{\text{dividend/share}}{\text{common stock}} = \frac{\text{Amount to be distributed to common stock}}{\text{Number of common stockholders}}$$

$$= \$20,000 \div 6,000$$

$$= \$3.33/\text{share}$$

(c) *Step 5:*   Determine the percentage dividend to each common stockholder.

$$\text{percentage dividend} = \frac{\text{dividend per share}}{\text{cost per share}} \times 100$$

$$= \frac{\$3.33}{\$50} \times 100$$

$$= 6.66\%$$

In Example 5, the preferred stockholders received a larger dividend in dollars per share of stock they owned than the common stockholders; however, the common stockholders received a greater percentage return on their investment.

Finally, let's consider a situation in which the company does not declare a dividend during a given year, and defers payment of its cumulative preferred stock dividend as well.

Example 6

Furbush Electric had a bad year during 1991 and chose not to pay any dividends to its investors. During 1992, the company declared a profit of $100,000 to be distributed to its stockholders. The cumulative preferred stock was purchased at $100 per share and pays 5% per share. There are 6,000 shares of common stock and 4,000 shares of cumulative preferred stock that will receive dividends in 1992.

Solution

As determined in Example 5, the company owes $20,000 in dividends to its cumulative preferred stockholders each year.

amount due cumulative preferred stockholders, 1991	$20,000
amount due cumulative preferred stockholders, 1992	$20,000
total to be paid to cumulative preferred stockholders	$40,000

amount to be distributed to common
   stockholders = $100,000 − $40,000 = $60,000

amount per share of common stock = $60,000 ÷ 6,000 = $10/share

In these past examples, we assumed that the preferred stockholders were entitled only to their 5% of the dividends, which classifies them as *nonparticipating preferred stockholders. Participating preferred stockholders* also are entitled to a share of the dividends left over after they have received their normal distribution. Consequently they receive not only their guaranteed dividend amount, but also an additional share of the remaining dividends.

DISTRIBUTION OF EXPENSES

Learning objective
Distribute the expenses of a company on the basis of the number of employees, the square footage, and the amount of sales.

Just as it is important to understand how to divide income, it is equally important to be able to divide costs and expenses. For instance, if your business has two departments, the accounting department and the sales department, how will you divide overhead expenses (such as gas and electric, rent, or garbage pickup)? There are three common ways to divide expenses. One is according to the number of employees in each department, another is according to the square footage of each department, and a third is determined by the proportion of sales made by each department. First, let's consider the distribution of expenses by the proportion of employees working in each department.

Example 7

The accounting department of a small department store has 3 employees and the sales department has 12 employees. Divide a $500 utility bill according to the percentage of employees in each department.

Solution

Department	Number of employees	÷ Total employees	= Rate
Accounting	3	15	20%
Sales	12	15	80%
	15		100%

Department	Rate	× Expense	= Department expense
Accounting	.20	$500	$100
Sales	.80	$500	$400
			$500

Next, consider the distribution of these same expenses by the number of square feet of space each occupies within the company.

Example 8

The accounting department, with all of its computer equipment, uses 1,680 square feet of office space, whereas the sales department uses only 720 square feet. Distribute a $500 utility bill according to the percent of square feet used by each department.

Solution

Department	Square feet	÷	Total square feet	=	Rate
Accounting	1,680		2,400		.70
Sales	720		2,400		.30
	2,400				1.00

Department	Rate	×	Expense	=	Department expense
Accounting	.70		$500		$350
Sales	.30		$500		$150
					$500

A third method of distribution of expenses could be used in a business that is primarily involved in sales of different products, such as a department store.

Example 9

Harmon's Department Store reported department sales for October as follows: Housewares, $15,000; Women's Apparel, $26,000; Men's Clothing, $18,000; Children's Clothing, $22,000; Jewelry, $11,000; and Footware, $8,000. The store's overhead expenses for the month totaled $80,000. Distribute the expenses on the bases of sales per department.

Solution

Step 1: Determine total sales for the month.

$$\text{Total sales} = \$15,000 + \$26,000 + \$18,000 + \$22,000$$
$$+ \ \$11,000 + \$8,000$$
$$= \$100,000$$

Step 2: Determine each department's rate of total sales.

$$\text{rate of total sales} = \frac{\text{sales amount for department}}{\text{total sales}}$$

Department	Sales amount	Total sales	Rate
Housewares	$15,000	$100,000	.15
Women's Apparel	$26,000	$100,000	.26
Men's Clothing	$18,000	$100,000	.18
Children's	$22,000	$100,000	.22
Jewelry	$11,000	$100,000	.11
Footware	$ 8,000	$100,000	.08

Step 3: Determine the amount of the expenses to be distributed to each department.

amount = rate × total expenses

Department	Rate	×	Total expenses	=	Department share
Housewares	.15		$80,000		$12,000
Women's Apparel	.26		$80,000		$20,800
Men's Clothing	.18		$80,000		$14,400
Children's	.22		$80,000		$17,600
Jewelry	.11		$80,000		$ 8,800
Footware	.08		$80,000		$ 6,400
					$80,000

These are three basic ways that expenses could be distributed, but obviously they cannot be applied to every business. Variations on these basic concepts are often used to find the most appropriate way to distribute expenses fairly within any particular business operation.

CHECK YOUR KNOWLEDGE

Distributing income and expense

1. Three people start a business together. Divide a $90,000 income equally among all partners.

2. Three partners invest the following amounts of money when they initially began their business: Robinson, $80,000; Cripe, $110,000; and Short, $130,000. Distribute a profit of $60,000 among them according to the percent that each initially invested.

3. Thompson Office Supplies has 7,000 shares of stock. 3,000 are preferred stock and 4,000 are common stock. The preferred stock was sold for $100.00 per share with a guaranteed yearly dividend of 6%. If the company declared $60,000 for the year's profits for dividends, determine the amount of dividend per share that will be paid for preferred stock and for common stock.

4. A company has 35 employees located on the first floor and 50 employees on the second. Distribute a $27,000 installation charge between the two departments according to the number of employees in each department.

12.3 EXERCISES

Solve the following word problems. Round answers to the nearest cent and interest rates to the nearest tenth of a percent.

1. Three years ago, the following partners invested money in a business as follows: Abner, $60,000; Twila, $75,000; and Karl, $40,000. They now have a total of $600,000 profit that they will divide according to the percent that each initially invested. What amount of profit does each partner receive?

Partner	Amount invested	Rate of total	Share of profit
Abner	_____	_____	_____
Twila	_____	_____	_____
Karl	_____	_____	_____

2. Four partners invest the following amounts of money when they start their business: Larry, $200,000; Bobby, $8,000; Johnny, $50,000; and Colleen, $150,000. Distribute a profit of $500,000 among them according to the percent that each initially invested.

Partner	Amount invested	Rate of total	Share of profit
Larry	_____	_____	_____
Bobby	_____	_____	_____
Johnny	_____	_____	_____
Colleen	_____	_____	_____

3. Distribute a $15,000 dividend among 300 preferred stockholders and 700 common stockholders if the preferred stockholders are guaranteed 6% on each share of stock whose per value is $200.

Amount of dividend for each share of preferred stock   _____
total amount to be paid preferred stockholders   _____
total to be distributed to common stockholders
($15,000 − _____)   _____
amount of dividend per share of common stock   _____

4. Distribute a $215,000 dividend among 5,000 preferred stockholders and 15,000 common stockholders if the preferred stockholders are guaranteed 7% on each share of stock whose per value is $300.

Amount of dividend for each share of preferred stock   _____
total amount to be paid preferred stockholders   _____
total to be distributed to common stockholders
($215,000 − _____)   _____
amount of dividend per share of common stock   _____

Answers to CYK: *1.* $30,000 each   *2.* Robinson's share = 15,000; Cripe's share = $20,625.00; Short's share = $24,375   *3.* preferred stock = $6.00 per share; common stock = $10.50   *4.* first floor = $11,117.65; second floor = $15,882.35

5. Distribute an expense of $2,500 to four departments by percent of employees if each department has the following number of employees:

Department	Number of employees	Rate of total	Amount of expense share
A	5	_____	_____
B	2	_____	_____
C	3	_____	_____
D	10	_____	_____

6. Distribute an expense of $4,000 to five departments by percent of employees if each department has the following number of employees:

Department	Number of employees	Rate of total	Amount of expense share
E	4	_____	_____
F	3	_____	_____
G	2	_____	_____
H	6	_____	_____
I	5	_____	_____

7. Distribute an expense of $8,000 to four departments by amount of floor space each department occupies:

Department	Floor space	Rate of total	Amount of expense share
J	300	_____	_____
K	200	_____	_____
L	100	_____	_____
M	400	_____	_____

8. Distribute an expense of $7,000 to five departments by amount of floor space each department occupies:

Department	Floor space	Rate of total	Amount of expense share
N	700	_____	_____
O	550	_____	_____
P	320	_____	_____
Q	610	_____	_____
R	120	_____	_____

9. Distribute an expense of $10,000 to four departments by amount of sales that each department made for a set period of time.

Department	Floor space	Rate of total	Amount of expense share
S	$50,000	_____	_____
T	$25,000	_____	_____
U	$15,000	_____	_____
V	$20,000	_____	_____

10. Distribute an expense of $3,500 to five departments by amount of sales for each department.

Department	Sales	Rate of total	Amount of expense share
W	$2,300	_____	_____
X	$4,300	_____	_____
Y	$6,500	_____	_____
Z	$1,100	_____	_____
A	$ 900	_____	_____

11. Five sorority sisters start a dating service. Each invested the following amounts: Felicia, $2,000; Muriel, $3,000; Aubrey, $4,400; Ingrid, $3,078; and Guinevere, $2,050. Divide their $500,000 profits from their first-quarter earnings according to the percent that each initially invested.

12. The O'Malley Brothers opened a tune-up garage. Each brother contributed the following amount: Hank, $15,000; Henry, $1,000; Harold, $2,000; Harvey, $2,300; and Homer, $1,700. Distribute their $50,000 loss according to the percent that each invested.

13. Three business math instructors quit their jobs in order to start a dairy farm. Each invested the following amounts: Turner, $8,000; Babcock, $5,000; Connor, $6,000. Distribute the $22,000 loss among the three ex-instructors according to the percent that each initially invested.

14. Levinson and Esposito Company has 10,000 stockholders of which 2,000 hold preferred stock and 6,000 hold common stock. The preferred stock was sold for $100.00 per share with a guaranteed yearly dividend of 7%. Each share of common stock was sold for $50.00. The company has made a profit of $40,000. Determine the amount of dividend per share that will be paid for preferred stock and for common stock.

15. Delorme and Schurman Real Estate Corporation has 1,000 preferred stockholders and 8,000 common stockholders. The preferred stock was sold for $150.00 per share with a guaranteed yearly dividend of 5.5%. Each share of common stock was sold for

$75.00. The corporation has made a profit of $80,000. Determine the amount of dividend per share that will be paid for preferred stock and for common stock.

16. The Popsicle Recording Company has three departments. Divide the $980 utility bill among the departments according to the percentage of employees in each department. The legal department has 43 employees, the accounting department has 5 employees, and the music department has 30 employees.

17. The Bee-Bop Art Supply Store wishes to divide a $500 bonus between its two departments according to the percentage of employees in each department. The paint department has two employees while the brush department has one.

18. Wings is a pet store in Gotham City. Management wishes to divide a $4,100 maintenance bill among the three departments on the basis of the number of birds (or flying mammals) in each department. There are 23 parrots, 41 canaries, and 198 bats.

19. Han's Department Store needs to distribute a $555 lighting bill between its departments according to the percent of employees in each department. The furniture department has 5 people, and the housewares department has 6.

20. The largest musical instrument store in Grant City needs to divide a $1,001 utility bill among its departments according to the percent of employees in each department. The string instrument department has 404 employees, the wind instrument department has

606 employees, the percussion instrument department has 808 employees, and the brass instrument department has 909 employees.

21. The largest musical instrument store in Grant City has received another bill—this one is for cleaning services that were rendered last month. This time the store wishes to divide the $1,150 bill among its departments according to the square footage in each department. The strings have 1,700 square feet, the winds have 800 square feet, the percussions have 990 square feet, and the brass have 1,000 square feet.

22. Cunningham's plumbing store wishes to divide a $67 bill between its two departments according to the square footage in each department. The chrome department has 2,300 square feet, while the copper department has 300 square feet.

23. The Red Balloon Toy Shop wishes to divide a $600 remodeling bill among three groups of toys according to the square footage used by each group. The PeeWee Herman dolls use 50 square feet, the Cowboy Curtis dolls use 25 square feet, and the Miss Yvonne dolls use 30 square feet.

24. The Mahatma Jewelry Store needs to divide a $7,000 bill between its two departments based on the square footage used by each. The yellow gold department has 30 square feet, and the white gold department has 20 square feet.

25. Hail-Ye-Good-Fellow car dealership needs to distribute a $3,000 water bill among its departments according to the square footage used by each. The new car department has 4,000 square feet, the used car department has 2,800 square feet, and the maintenance department has 6,200 square feet.

26. Addis's Department Store reported department sales for October as follows: Housewares, $5,000; Women's Apparel, $15,000; Men's Clothing, $8,000; Children's Clothing, $12,000; Jewelry, $1,000; and Footware, $700. The store's overhead expenses for the

month totaled $21,000. Distribute the expenses on the basis of sales per department.

27. Hail-Ye-Good-Fellow car dealership decides to distribute the $3,000 water bill among its departments according to the amount of sales made by each. The new car department had $400,000; the used car department had $28,000; and the maintenance department had $16,200 in total sales each. How much should each department pay of the water bill?

28. Bee Town Mini Mall has four shops within it that have agreed to share any real estate tax bills the building may have each year. Distribute this year's tax bill of $16,000 by sales if each shop had the following sales: Jan's Maternity Shoppe, $120,000; Fredd's Hobby and Crafts, $80,000; Sally's Cafe, $75,000; and Marti's Music Box Shoppe, $90,000.

29. Tom Green rents a vacant storefront each weekend of the summer and sets up a flea market with five booths, each of equal size. His rental cost of the storefront is $700. The sales of each booth this last weekend were: booth 1, $520; booth 2, $670; booth 3, $750; booth 4, $330; and booth 5, $900. Distribute the rental fee by (a) the amount of space used by each booth, and (b) the amount of sales of each booth.

30. The Germantown Oktoberfest Committee rents large tents to house several nonprofit community groups that sell food and other items, as well as provide game concessions for the weekend festivities. The committee distributes its costs for rental, electric, plumbing, etc. by the amount of sales reported by the groups. Distribute an expense of $2,200 to the following groups: Grace Church, $3,500; St. Luke's Church, $1,400; Optimist Club, $890; Rotary, $1,300; Boy Scout Troop #119, $1,700; Pop Warner Football Club, $1,200; Lacross Support Group, $2,300; Project Children, $450; Marching Band Support Group, $1,700; and Theater Guild, $1,300.

EXPRESS YOUR THOUGHTS

Compose one or two well-written sentences to express the requested information in your own words.

1. Why might an investor select an investment in bonds versus an investment in stock?

2. Explain why a business would issue stock instead of bonds as a means of increasing the availability of money for operations.

3. In a stock quotation, what does the "yld" column represent? How is the figure presented in this column determined?

4. Describe the procedure you would use to determine the capital gains or capital loss on a sale of stock.

5. In a bond quotation, what does the column "cur. yld" represent? How is the amount shown determined for a bond with a face value of $1,000?

6. Explain how accrued interest on a $1,000-bond is determined. Create an example that illustrates the procedure.

7. What does the phrase "8½ quoted at 98" mean when applied to a bond with a $10,000 face value?

8. Describe the steps necessary to distribute $80,000 in profits among three partners if profits are divided according to each partner's investment and the investments were $20,000, $50,000, and $30,000 respectively.

9. Explain how to calculate the amount of dividend to be paid to a common stockholder who owns stock in a company that does not have any preferred stock outstanding.

10. Describe the procedure necessary to determine the total dividend to be paid to preferred stockholders.

Case exercise   The stock portfolio

Different people invest in stocks for different reasons. Your job is to read the following descriptions of why these two individuals want to invest in stocks. Then, read and interpret the stocks listed in the following stock quotation. Finally, decide which stock each person should buy.

Person 1:   wants a stock that pays a steady dividend to the stockholder each quarter.

Person 2:   is a speculator; he likes to gamble and take risks. He is always looking for ways to make a "fast buck."

A. Which stock should each person buy? Explain how your choice of stock fulfills their objectives.

B. How many shares of this stock will each be able to purchase at the closing price of the day? Assume that each person has $10,000 to spend.

52 Weeks					P–E	Sales				
High	Low	Stock	Div.	Yld %	Ratio	100s	High	Low	Close	Net Change
124	107	LEP	2.50	7.6	10	23004	116	112	114	+1/4
119	112	JCN	3.20	7.6	10	22906	116	113	115 1/4	− 1/4
179	39	KDO	1.80	7.6	10	21896	128	112	120 1/2	+4

SELF-TEST

A. Terminology review

Complete the following items using the key terms presented at the beginning of the chapter. Check your responses against the answer key at the end of the test.

1. A _____ is a share or portion of a corporation.

2. _____ are a portion of the issuing company's profits, usually paid to the stockholder in the form of cash.

3. The life of a bond begins the day the bond is purchased and ends on the _____.

4. A _____ is the profit from the sale of assets such as securities or real estate.

5. A _____ is an interest-bearing certificate issued by a government or corporation, redeemable on a specified date.

6. A person who buys and sells securities is known as a _____.

7. Stocks and other securities are traded at a place called the stock exchange or sometimes called the _____.

8. The denomination of a bond is referred to as the _____ of a bond.

9. When the market price of a bond is lower than its face value, it is called a _____.

10. When the market price of a bond is higher than its face value, it is called a _____.

B. Calculation review

The following concepts and short problems are designed to test your understanding of the objectives identified at the beginning of the chapter. Answers are provided at the end of the test.

11. List one advantage a company has in issuing bonds rather than stocks.

12. List two advantages a company has in issuing stocks rather than bonds.

13. IF FGH Corporation wishes to distribute $400,000 in dividends among its 580,000 shareholders, how much will you receive in dividends if you own 200 shares of FGH?

Refer to the following stock quotation for problems 14–18.

52 Weeks					P–E	Sales				Net
High	Low	Stock	Div.	Yld %	Ratio	100s	High	Low	Close	Change
61 1/4	49 1/4	ZERG	6.01	7.2	10	224	56	54	54 1/2	+1/2

14. What was the high trading price for the day?

15. What was the high trading price for the year?

16. How many shares of stock were traded on this day?

17. What was yesterday's closing price?

18. Ahmad Dieg bought 200 shares of ZERG stock at yesterday's price and must sell some of it today. He has decided to sell 100 shares. The broker's fees were 3% in both transactions. What is Ahmad's capital gain or loss?

Refer to the following bond quotation for problems 19–21.

Cur. Bonds	Net Yld.	Vol.	High	Low	Close	Change
Wills Cp	8 3/8	910	86	85	85	− 5/8

19. How much would you pay for this bond if you bought it at the closing price?

20. How much interest would you receive from the issuing company if you held this bond for one year?

21. Calculate the current yield. Be sure to show your work.

22. Kevin Harvey owned five bonds whose face value was $1,000 each when he purchased them. He sold all five bonds on April 1 to Janet Green. The bond quotation for April 1 was 7½ quoted at 99, and the commission for each bond is $10. Find (a) the amount that the buyer paid and (b) the amount the seller received.

23. Jackson's Floor and Tile Company has three departments. Divide an $875 utility bill among the departments according to the percent of employees in each department. The sales department has 13 employees, the billing and accounting department has 5 employees, and the manufacturing and shipping department has 30 employees.

24. The Bonwit Clothing Store wants to divide a $9,500 bill among its three departments based on the square footage used by each. The coats and outer apparel department has 230 square feet, the dress department occupies 520 square feet, and the intimate apparel department uses 250 square feet. How much should each department be charged?

25. The Thousand Islands Mini Mart has three shops within it. Distribute a one-month $2,500 utility bill by sales if each shop recorded the following sales: Big Mac's Gun Shop $12,000; Carm's Breakfast Nook $17,000; and Mario's Shoe Repair Shop $9,000.

Answers to self-test: *1.* stock   *2.* Dividends   *3.* maturity date   *4.* capital gain   *5.* bond   *6.* stockbroker   *7.* market   *8.* face value   *9.* discount   *10.* premium   *11.* any of those listed in Figure 12.1   *12.* any of those listed in Figure 12.1   *13.* $137.93   *14.* 56   *15.* 61¼   *16.* 22,400   *17.* 54   *18.* − $275.50   *19.* $850   *20.* $83.75   *21.* 9.85%   *22.* a. $5,093.75; b. $4,993.25   *23.* sales, $236.98; billing, $91.15; manufacturing, $546.88   *24.* apparel, $2,185; dress, $4,940; intimate, $2,375   *25.* gun shop, $789.47; breakfast nook, $1,118.42; shoe repair, $592.11

13

DEPRECIATION

Learning objectives

1. Explain why businesses depreciate assets.

2. Understand the conceptual difference between depreciation and cost recovery.

3. Prepare a depreciation schedule using the straight-line method.

4. Use the declining-balance method to develop a depreciation schedule.

5. Calculate depreciation using the units-of-production method.

6. Use the accelerated cost-recovery system (ACRS) to recover an asset's cost.

7. Recover an asset's cost using the modified accelerated cost recovery system (MACRS) guidelines.

8. Define the key terms.

INTRODUCTION

Businesses purchase assets such as production machinery, vehicles, buildings, land, and equipment for use in their daily operations to produce goods and provide services. As we learned in Chapter 5, revenue generated from the sale of these goods and services is reduced by the cost of the goods sold and by the operating expenses reported in the period to determine the net income from operations. Because business assets are used to produce revenue, their cost is periodically deducted from revenue as an expense. **Depreciation** is the process of charging the cost of an asset to the revenues earned over the useful life of the asset. The amount of the periodic deduction is reported as **depreciation expense** in the income statement and as an increase in the **accumulated depreciation** of the asset on the balance sheet. The **book value** of an asset is the net value reported on the balance sheet after deducting the accumulated depreciation from the total cost of the asset recorded at the time the asset was placed in service.

Learning objective
Explain why businesses depreciate assets.

Assets are depreciated to reflect the usage of the asset over time. Therefore, we must be able to predict the useful life of the asset. An asset's **useful life** is the period of time the asset is used to generate revenue. An automobile can be depreciated because its useful life can be determined by considering such factors as its mileage, repair costs, and model year. Land, on the other hand, is not depreciated because its useful life is indefinite. Property can be depreciated if it meets the following requirements:

1. It is used in a business or held for the production of income.
2. It has a determinable life and that life is longer than one year.
3. It is something that wears out, decays, is used up, becomes obsolete, or loses value from natural causes.

Depreciable assets are defined by categories, which serve in part to identify the method of depreciation used to determine the periodic depreciation expense. **Tangible property**, for example, is property that can be seen or touched, such as machinery, equipment, and vehicles. *Intangible assets* include copyrights, franchise fees, designs, patents, and customer lists. *Personal property* is property, such as equipment and machinery, that is not real estate. **Real property** is land and generally anything that is erected on, growing on, or attached to land.

Learning objective
Understand the conceptual difference between depreciation and cost recovery.

Depreciation as reported on a company's income statement (books) may not agree with the amount of depreciation claimed on the company's tax return. This discrepancy results from the use of traditional depreciation methods (straight-line, declining-balance, and units-of-production) for book purposes, and IRS prescribed methods for tax purposes (traditional methods, ACRS, and MACRS).

There are many different methods allowed by the IRS to determine depreciation. Businesses may use any acceptable method as long as they apply the method consistently. In general, a business must use for tax purposes the appropriate methods defined by changes in the depreciation guidelines reported in Publication 534, which is published by the IRS. A company can select different methods to depreciate different assets; however, once a method has been selected, it must be used throughout the useful life of the asset. (Under certain circumstances, a company may acquire permission from the IRS to change from one method to another.)

In this chapter, we will examine the concepts and procedures of the following systems used to calculate depreciation and cost recovery for *tax purposes*.

1.   *Traditional Methods*   These methods are used to compute depreciation on assets that were placed in service before 1981, or that are excluded under MACRS. They include straight-line, declining-balance, and units-of-production methods. These methods are also required under *Generally Accepted Accounting Principles* guidelines.

2.   *ACRS Method*   This method of computing cost recovery applies to all assets placed in service between 1981 and 1986.

3.   *MACRS Method*   This method is used to calculate cost recovery on all assets placed in service after 1986.

13.1   TRADITIONAL METHOD: STRAIGHT-LINE DEPRECIATION

Learning objective
Prepare a depreciation schedule using the straight-line method.

The traditional methods discussed in Sections 13.1, 13.2, and 13.3 are presented because they were the accepted methods of calculating depreciation before the ACRS or MACRS methods were enacted. Businesses that either placed assets into service before 1981 or that are depreciating assets placed in service after 1981, which are covered by the "excluded property rules" contained in IRS Publication 534, must use these methods for tax purposes.

As you work through the examples presented, you will see that each method varies in focus and procedure. The **straight-line method**, for example, allows a business to evenly distribute the cost of an asset over its useful life. The **declining-balance method**, on the other hand, is considered an accelerated method of depreciating assets because the amount of depreciation will be greater in the earlier years and less in the latter years. The **units-of-production method** is used to depreciate assets when the actual service rendered by the asset is a more appropriate base for depreciation than its years of service.

Now, let's work through examples of each of these traditional methods so that we clearly understand how to calculate the periodic depreciation expense, and prepare a useful life–depreciation schedule. The *straight-line method* allows a business to depreciate an average amount of an asset's depreciable amount during each year of the asset's useful life. Before we analyze an example, let's familiarize ourselves with a few terms that apply to most of the depreciation methods discussed in this chapter.

Total cost: The purchase cost plus freight and/or installation charges required to place the asset into service.

Salvage value: The estimated value of an asset at the end of its useful life; sometimes referred to as residual value.

Useful life: The number of years the asset is expected to be in service. The useful life may be based on industry standards or on the experience of an individual company for book purposes. The useful life is mandated by the IRS for tax purposes.

Depreciable amount: The amount of the asset to be depreciated. (Total cost − salvage value = depreciable amount.)

To calculate the straight-line periodic depreciation expense, we divide the depreciable amount by the useful life of the asset. This process is expressed in the following formula:

$$\text{periodic depreciation expense} = \frac{\text{total cost} - \text{salvage value}}{\text{useful life (years)}}$$

Example 1

Let us assume that Wilfred's Window and Glass Company has just purchased an asset for use in its business that falls under the excluded property rules. The cost of the asset is $250,000; it cost $4,000 to have it installed; the estimated salvage value is $25,875; and the estimated useful life is 4 years. Find (a) the annual amount of depreciation and (b) the book value at the end of the first year if the asset was purchased on January 5, 1991.

Solution

a.   Calculate the first year depreciation amount (expenses).

$$\text{depreciation amount} = \frac{\text{total cost} - \text{salvage value}}{\text{useful life}}$$

$$= \frac{\$254,000 - \$25,875}{4}$$

$$= \frac{\$228,125}{4}$$

$$= \$57,031.25$$

b.   The book value at the end of the first year is:

$$\text{book value} = \text{total cost} - \text{accumulated depreciation}$$
$$= \$254{,}000 - \$57{,}031.25$$
$$= \$196{,}968.75$$

A business will often summarize the depreciation of an asset in a table called a **depreciation schedule**. The table shows the annual depreciation expense, accumulated depreciation, and the book value of the asset each year of its useful life. Table 13.1 is a straight-line depreciation schedule for the asset listed in Example 1.

The accumulated depreciation increases as the current year's depreciation amount is added to the previous year's balance ($57,031.25 + 57,031.25 = \$114,062.50$). The current year-end book value is found by subtracting the accumulated depreciation from the total cost at the time the asset was placed in service ($254,000.00 − \$114,062.50 = \$139,937.50$). The book value at the end of an asset's useful life should always be equal to its **salvage value**. Neither GAAP nor IRS guidelines allow an asset to be depreciated below its estimated salvage value.

If an asset is estimated to have no salvage value at the end of its useful life or if its salvage value is estimated to be less than 10% of its total cost, the total cost of the asset can be depreciated for tax purposes. To illustrate, if the equipment in Example 1 had been estimated to have a salvage value of $20,000, the annual amount of depreciation would have been $63,500 ($254,000 ÷ 4 = \$63,500$). We depreciate the total cost of the asset because the estimated salvage value ($20,000) is less than 10% of the asset's total cost ($254,000 × .10 = \$25,400$).

The problems encountered thus far in this section have all had purchase dates before January 10. It is unlikely that a business would purchase all of its tangible assets on the first day of the year. Therefore, it is necessary to calculate depreciation for part of a fiscal year.

When an asset is placed in service during any month other than January, the annual depreciation expense is prorated based on the number of months the asset was in service. If the asset is placed in service on or before the 15th of the month, that month is included in the calculation of the

Table 13.1

Straight-line depreciation schedule

Year	Depreciation amount	Accumulated depreciation	Book value
			$254,000.00
1	$57,031.25	$ 57,031.25	196,968.75
2	57,031.25	114,062.50	139,937.50
3	57,031.25	171,093.75	82,906.25
4	57,031.25	228,125.00	25,875.00

first year's depreciation expense. The procedure explained in Example 2 is applied only to those assets being depreciated under the straight-line, declining-balance, and units-of-production methods.

Example 2

On April 10, 1991, Brown Industries placed in service an asset that qualifies as excluded property. The company selected the straight-line method to depreciate the asset, which cost $15,800. Find the book value of the asset at the end of the first year if freight charges were $200, installation costs totaled $1,500, and the salvage value is estimated to be $2,700. The asset has an expected useful life of 4 years.

Solution

Step 1: Determine the annual depreciation expense.

$$\text{depreciation expense} = \frac{\text{total cost} - \text{salvage value}}{\text{useful life (years)}}$$

Amount

$$= \frac{(\$15,800 + \$200 + \$1,500) - \$2,700}{4}$$

$$= \frac{\$14,800}{4}$$

$$= \$3,700$$

Step 2: Calculate the prorated amount of depreciation for the 9 months the asset was in service during the first year.

$$\text{prorated depreciation expense} = \text{annual depreciation expense} \times \text{prorated time factor}$$
$$= \$3,700 \times 9/12$$
$$= \$2,775$$

Step 3: Determine the book value at the end of the first year.

$$\text{book value} = \text{total cost} - \text{accumulated depreciation}$$
$$= \$17,500 - \$2,775$$
$$= \$14,725$$

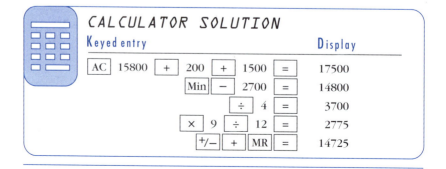

```
CALCULATOR  SOLUTION
Keyed entry                                    Display

AC  15800  +   200   +   1500   =              17500
           Min    −   2700   =                 14800
                        ÷   4   =              3700
           ×   9   ÷   12   =                  2775
           +/−   +   MR   =                    14725
```

Table 13.2

Prorated straight-line depreciation schedule

Year	Depreciation expense	Accumulated depreciation	Book value
			$17,500
1991	$2,775 (9/12 of annual)	$ 2,775	14,725
1992	3,700	6,475	11,025
1993	3,700	10,175	7,325
1994	3,700	13,875	3,625
1995	925 (3/12 of annual)	14,800	2,700

The useful life depreciation schedule for this asset would be extended into the fifth calendar year to completely depreciate the asset's total cost to its salvage value. The 3 months of depreciation not claimed during the first year would be claimed during the fifth year ($925 = $3,700 × 3/12) resulting in a book value equal to the salvage value as shown in Table 13.2.

CHECK YOUR KNOWLEDGE

Straight-line depreciation

1. On January 12, 1980, John Brown, a farmer from Gary, Indiana, purchased a small airplane to be used for crop dusting. The original cost of the airplane was $85,000, the estimated salvage value is $12,250, and the useful life is 15 years. Calculate (a) the annual depreciation expense and (b) the book value at the end of the first year using the straight-line method.

2. Find the book value at the end of the second year for an asset costing $28,000 and having a useful life of 4 years. The company paid $625 to have the asset shipped and an additional $1,800 to have it installed. The asset has an estimated salvage value of $6,425, was placed in service on January 4, and is depreciated under the straight-line method.

3. If the asset in problem 2 is placed in service on August 8, what is the book value at the end of (a) year 1 and (b) year 2?

4. A construction company purchased an asset costing $35,000 on January 10 with a salvage value of $2,800 and an estimated useful life of 7 years. Find (a) the first-year depreciation amount and (b) the book value at the end of the first year using the straight-line method.

5. An asset was purchased by Rojon Enterprises on March 10 for $8,600. Freight and installation costs totaled $1,200. The asset's life expec-

tancy is 5 years and its salvage value is estimated to be $2,300. Prepare a straight-line depreciation schedule using these headings:

Year	Depreciation amount	Accumulated depreciation	Book value

13.1 EXERCISES

Find the annual depreciation expense for the following assets using the straight-line method. Round answers to nearest cent.

	Cost	Freight charge	Installation cost	Salvage value	Estimated life	Depreciation expense
1.	$15,000	$0	$0	$3,000	4 years	_____
2.	$20,300	$0	$1,200	$1,800	10 years	_____
3.	$50,000	$840	$2,160	$11,000	7 years	_____
4.	$120,000	$1,800	$5,750	$10,500	20 years	_____
5.	$250,800	$0	$12,250	$33,000	12 years	_____

Complete the following straight-line depreciation schedule. The asset's salvage value is $4,800.

Year	Depreciation expense	Accumulated depreciation	Year-end book value
			$31,000
6. 1	$5,240	_____	_____
7. 2	_____	_____	_____
8. 3	_____	_____	_____
9. 4	_____	_____	_____
10. 5	_____	_____	_____

11. Tyson Zinc has just purchased equipment for his business that falls under the excluded property rules. The original cost is $10,000, plus an installation cost of $300. The salvage value is $1,300 and the estimated useful life is 6 years. Find (a) the amount of depreciation expense and (b) the book value at the end of the first year.

12. Community Hospital uses the straight-line method of depreciation to depreciate an asset costing $30,500. If the asset is estimated to have a useful life of 10 years and a salvage value of $1,200, what is (a) the annual amount of depreciation expense and (b) the book value at the end of the first year?

Answers to CYK: *1.* a. $4,850; b. $80,150   *2.* $6,000   *3.* a. $27,925; b. $21,925   *4.* a. $5,000 (10% rule); b. $30,000   *5.* $1,500 annual depreciation expense; year 1, $8,550 book value; year 3, $5,550 book value; year 6, $2,300 book value

13. The Sterne Construction Company purchased a backhoe on July 8, 1980, that cost $375,000. The company estimated the asset would have a useful life of 15 years and a salvage value of $45,000. What was (a) the amount of depreciation expense claimed in 1980 and (b) the book value at the end of 1981?

14. An asset is purchased for $65,000 on January 10, 1980. The owner paid $425 for freight charges and $575 to have the asset installed.

The asset has an estimated life of 8 years and a salvage value of $4,500. Prepare a depreciation schedule for the asset using the straight-line method of depreciation.

15. Pilgrim Packaging placed an asset in service on September 12, 1992, that qualifies as excluded property. The company selected the straight-line method to depreciate the asset, which cost $6,300 and has a 5-year useful life with an estimated salvage value of $900. Prepare a depreciation schedule for the asset.

13.2   TRADITIONAL METHOD: DECLINING-BALANCE DEPRECIATION

Learning objective
Use the declining-balance method to develop a depreciation schedule.

The declining-balance method is an accelerated method of depreciation because it results in larger amounts of depreciation expense in the beginning years of the depreciation schedule compared to the straight-line method. A company might select the declining-balance method for a number of reasons. First, the book value of the asset may compare more favorably with the fair market value of the asset. Second, since the business reports a greater amount of depreciation expense, the taxable income will be lower in the earlier years, giving the company the use of those tax dollars. This method could also be attractive to companies that use high-technology machinery and equipment; such companies often depreciate their assets as rapidly as possible because of frequent technological change.

The declining-balance method allows a business to use a rate of depreciation equal to 150% of the straight-line rate to depreciate tangible personal property with a useful life of 3 years or more, and 125% of the straight-line rate for real property with a useful life of 20 years or more. When using this method, you must first determine the rate of depreciation. The rate of depreciation is determined by dividing the number 1 by the asset's useful life. For example, if the asset has a useful life of 5 years, its straight-line rate would be 20% (1/5 = .20). The straight-line rate is then multiplied by 150% to determine the declining-balance rate (.20 × 1.50 = .30). The rate of depreciation can also be found by dividing the 150% by the asset's useful life (1.50/5 = .30). To further accelerate the depreciation, we do not subtract the salvage value when calculating the yearly depreciation expense. We adjust the amount of depreciation expense in the last year of the depreciation schedule to equal the salvage value. IRS guidelines prohibit depreciating an asset below its salvage value. Use the same rules discussed under the straight-line method, including the 10% rule, to determine salvage value.

Example 3

On January 12, 1992, Fast-Roll Bearings purchased and placed in service an asset for $35,000. If the asset is depreciated under the 150% declining-balance method using a 5-year useful life and a salvage value of $8,000, find the depreciation expense and the book value of the asset at the end of the first year.

Solution

Step 1: Calculate the declining-balance rate.

$$\text{declining-balance rate} = \frac{1}{\text{useful life}} \times 1.5$$

$$= \frac{1}{5} \times 1.5$$

$$= .20 \times 1.5$$

$$= .30, \text{ or } 30\%$$

Step 2: Calculate the depreciation expense using the asset's total cost and the declining-balance rate found in step 1. (Remember, we do not subtract the salvage value.)

$$\text{1st year's depreciation expense} = \text{total cost} \times \text{declining-balance rate}$$
$$= 35,000 \times .30$$
$$= \$10,500$$

Step 3: Calculate the book value at the end of the first year.

$$\text{1st year book value} = \text{total cost} - \text{accumulated depreciation}$$
$$= \$35,000 - \$10,500$$
$$= \$24,500$$

This procedure would be repeated for each of the remaining four years to fully depreciate the asset, as shown in Table 13.3. After the first year, the book value is found by adding the current year's depreciation expense to the previous year's accumulated depreciation ($7,350 + 10,500 = $17,850). The accumulated depreciation is then subtracted from

Table 13.3

Declining-balance depreciation schedule

	Beginning book value	× Rate	= Depreciation expense	Accumulated depreciation	Book value
					$35,000.00
1992	35,000.00	.30	$10,500.00	$10,500.00	24,500.00
1993	24,500.00	.30	7,350.00	17,850.00	17,150.00
1994	17,150.00	.30	5,145.00	22,995.00	12,005.00
1995	12,005.00	.30	3,601.50	26,596.50	8,403.50
1996	8,403.50	.30	403.50	27,000.00	8,000.00

the asset's total cost ($35,000 − 17,850 = $17,150) to give us the 1993 book value.

CALCULATOR SOLUTION

Keyed entry	Display
AC 35000 Min	35000
1 ÷ 5 × 1.5 =	.3
× MR =	10500
+/− M+ MR	24500
First year calculation	
× .3 =	7350
+/− M+ MR	17150
Second year calculation	
× .3 =	5145
+/− M+ MR	12005
Third year calculation	

In the final year (1996), we can claim a depreciation expense of only 403.50, since that is the amount that would reduce the previous year's book value to equal the salvage value ($8,403.50 − $8,000 = $403.50). If we claimed the full 30% of the 1995 book value as the 1996 depreciation expense ($8,403.50 × .30 = $2,521.05), we would be depreciating the asset below the salvage value ($35,000 − $29,117.55 = $5,882.45), which is not allowed under IRS rules.

The depreciation schedule shown in Table 13.3 for Example 3 is based on a purchase date of January 12, 1992. Consequently, a full year's depreciation was claimed the first year. Let us now analyze Example 4, which is the same asset used in Example 3, except the asset was placed in service on November 5, 1992. The depreciation expense must be prorated in the first year for the number of months the asset was in use. However, because larger amounts of depreciation are allowed in the early years and smaller or no depreciation is allowed in the later years, the unclaimed portion of the first year's depreciation is claimed in the second year. This procedure is continued until the asset is depreciated to the salvage value.

Example 4

On November 5, 1992, Fast-Roll Bearings purchased and placed in service an asset that cost $35,000. If the asset is depreciated under the 150% declining-balance method using a 5-year useful life and a salvage value of $8,000, find the depreciation expense and the book value for (a) 1992 and (b) 1993.

Solution

a.

Step 1: Calculate the declining balance rate.

$$.30 = 1/5 \times 1.5, \quad \text{or} \quad .30 = 1.5/5$$

Step 2: Calculate the first year's depreciation expense

$$\$10,500 = \$35,000 \times .30$$

Note: The amounts calculated in the first two steps presented in Example 3 are the same for this example.

Step 3: Calculate the prorated amount of depreciation for the 2 months the asset was in service during the first year.

$$\text{prorated depreciation expense} = (\text{annual depreciation}) \times (\text{prorated time factor})$$
$$= \$10,500 \times 2/12$$
$$= \$1,750$$

Step 4: Determine the book value at the end of the first year.

$$\text{book value} = \text{total cost} - \text{accumulated depreciation}$$
$$= \$35,000 - \$1,750$$
$$= \$33,250$$

b.

Step 1: Calculate the second year's annual depreciation expense using a book value based on a full year's depreciation the first year ($35,000 − 10,500 = $24,500). Refer to Table 13.3 for the book value amounts.

$$\text{annual depreciation expense} = \text{book value} \times \text{declining-balance rate}$$
$$= \$24,500 \times .30$$
$$= \$7,350$$

Step 2: Determine the prorated depreciation expense for the second year (1993).

$8,750.00 = 10,500 × 10/12	(10 months of 1992)
$1,225.00 = 7,350 × 2/12	(2 months of 1993)

$9,975.00 depreciation expense

Step 3: Determine the book value at the end of the second year.

$$\text{book value} = \text{total cost} - \text{accumulated depreciation}$$
$$= \$35,000 - (\$1,750 + \$9,975.00)$$
$$= \$35,000 - \$11,725$$
$$= \$23,275$$

Table 13.4

Prorated declining-balance depreciation schedule

Prorated declining-balance depreciation expense			Accumulated depreciation	Book value
				$35,000.00
1992	35,000.00 × .30 =	$10,500.00 × 2/12 = $1,750.00	$1,750.00	$33,250.00
1993	35,000.00 × .30 =	10,500.00 × 10/12 = 8,750.00		
	24,500.00 × .30 =	7,350.00 × 2/12 = 1,225.00	$11,725.00	$23,275.00
		$9,975.00		
1994	24,500.00 × .30 =	7,350.00 × 10/12 = 6,125.00		
	17,150.00 × .30 =	5,145.00 × 2/12 = 857.50	$18,707.50	$16,292.50
		$6,982.50		
1995	17,150.00 × .30 =	5,145.00 × 10/12 = 4,287.50		
	12,005.00 × .30 =	3,601.50 × 2/12 = 600.25	$23,595.25	$11,404.75
		$4,887.75		
1996	12,005.00 × .30 =	3,601.50 × 10/12 = 3,001.25		
	8,403.50 × .30 =	403.50 × 2/12 = 67.25	$26,663.75	$8,336.25
		$3,068.50		
1997		403.50 × 10/12 = 336.25	$27,000.00	$8,000.00

Table 13.4 shows the calculations required to complete a depreciation schedule for this asset. Notice in year 5 (1996) the depreciation expense of the asset ($11,404.75 − $3,001.25 = $8,403.50) is $8,403.50. We are not allowed to depreciate the asset below $8,000; therefore we must prorate the last year's depreciation expense ($8,403.50 − $8,000 = $403.50) by claiming 2/12 of the $403.50 in 1996 ($403.50 × 2/12 = $67.25) and 10/12 of the $403.50 in 1997 ($403.50 × 10/12 = $336.25) to completely depreciate the asset.

CHECK YOUR KNOWLEDGE

Declining-balance method

1. The original cost of an asset is $75,000, the estimated salvage value is $15,000, and the asset's useful life is 10 years. If the asset is depreciated at the 150% rate, what is (a) the depreciation expense and (b) the book value for the first year?

2. Using the information provided in problem 1, determine the book value for (a) the second and (b) the third year.

3. A construction company purchased an asset on January 5 that cost $60,000 with a salvage value of $12,500 and an estimated useful life of 5 years. The asset falls under the excluded property rules and is depreciated at the 150% declining-balance rate. Prepare a depreciation schedule using the form provided below.

Year	Depreciation amount	Accumulated depreciation	Book value
			$60,000.00
1	_____	_____	_____
2	_____	_____	_____
3	_____	_____	_____
4	_____	_____	_____
5	_____	_____	_____

4. Ultra-Tech placed in service on April 10 equipment that cost $9,600. It is estimated that the equipment will have a useful life of 4 years and a salvage value of $500. If the equipment is depreciated under the 150% declining-balance rate, what is the depreciation expense and book value at the end of (a) the first year and (b) the second year?

13.2 EXERCISES

Find the first-year depreciation expense for each of the following assets using the declining-balance method. Round answers to the nearest cent.

	Cost	Freight charge	Installa- tion charge	Salvage value	Declin- ing- balance rate	Estimated life	Depreciation expense
1.	$8,000	$500	$0	$3,200	150%	3 years	_____
2.	$17,500	$250	$1,350	$1,500	200%	5 years	_____
3.	$64,750	$0	$2,400	$8,000	125%	20 years	_____
4.	$47,800	$650	$0	$9,500	150%	12 years	_____
5.	$175,000	$1,200	$4,300	$15,000	125%	25 years	_____

Answers to CYK: 1.   a. $11,250; b. $63,750   2.   a. $54,187.50; b. $46,059.37   3.   .30 rate; book value year 1, $42,000, book value year 3, $20,580, year 5, $12,500   4.   a. $6,900; b. $4,059.37

Complete the following declining-balance depreciation schedule. The asset's salvage value is $2,000.

Year	Beginning book value	Declining rate	Depreciation expense	Accumulated depreciation	Year-end book value
6. 1	$12,000.00	.30	$_____	$_____	$_____
7. 2	_____	.30	_____	_____	_____
8. 3	_____	.30	_____	_____	_____
9. 4	_____	.30	_____	_____	_____
10. 5	_____	.30	_____	_____	_____

11. Marble Farms placed an asset in service on January 4, which can be depreciated under the 150% declining-balance rate. The asset cost $12,000 and has a useful life of 5 years and an expected salvage value of $3,000. Find (a) the amount of depreciation expense and (b) the book value at the end of the first year.

12. Inland Supply erected a warehouse on its property at a total cost of $1,500,000, which is classified as excluded recovery property. If the building has a useful life of 25 years and a salvage value of $250,000, what was the book value at the end of the second year? The asset was placed in service on January 7, 1978, and is depreciated at the 125% declining-balance rate.

13. On April 2, Healthcare purchased and placed in service an asset that cost $80,000. If the asset is depreciated under the 150% declining-balance method with a 10-year useful life and a salvage value of $5,000, find (a) the book value at the end of the first year and (b) the book value at the end of the second year.

14. Prepare a declining-balance depreciation schedule for exercise 11.

15. Niki's Body Shop purchased equipment for her business, which was placed in service on October 8. The equipment cost $8,000, has a useful life of 4 years, and a possible trade-in value of $2,000. Prepare a 150% declining-balance depreciation schedule.

13.3 TRADITIONAL METHOD: UNITS-OF-PRODUCTION DEPRECIATION

Learning objective
Calculate depreciation using the units-of-production method.

The units-of-production method is another traditional method used by businesses. An asset whose useful life is more accurately defined by the units produced, hours utilized, or miles driven could be depreciated by the *units-of-production method*. This method is also used to depreciate assets that are used seasonally. For example, construction, farm, and recreational equipment are often used quite heavily during some months of the year and not at all during other months of the year.

The amount of depreciation under the units-of-production method is based on a constant amount per unit of use as opposed to the time base of both the straight-line and declining-balance methods. To calculate the annual depreciation amount, we must first determine the per-unit depreciation factor and then multiply the factor by the number of units produced, hours utilized, or miles driven. The following equation is used to calculate the depreciation amount:

Units-of-production depreciation method equation

$$\text{annual depreciation amount} = \frac{(\text{total cost} - \text{salvage value})}{\text{units of life}} \times \text{units or hours, miles produced}$$

Example 5

Santos Machine Works installed a stamping machine at a cost of $50,000 and expects the machine will produce 1,000,000 units of product before it must be replaced. If the salvage value of the machine is estimated to be $10,000 and the machine produced 80,000 units during the year, find (a) the first year's depreciation amount and (b) the book value at the end of the first year.

Solution

Step 1:   Determine the annual depreciation amount for the stamping machine using the equation,

$$\text{depreciation amount} = \frac{(\text{total cost} - \text{salvage value})}{\text{units of life}} \times$$

$$\text{units produced}$$

$$= \frac{(\$50,000 - \$10,000)}{1,000,000} \times 80,000$$

$$= \frac{(\$40,000)}{1,000,000} \times 80,000$$

$$= (\$.04)80,000$$

$$= \$3,200 \text{ annual depreciation expense}$$

Step 2:   Calculate the book value at the end of the first year.

$$\text{book value} = \text{total cost} - \text{accumulated depreciation}$$
$$= \$50,000 - \$3,200$$
$$= \$46,800$$

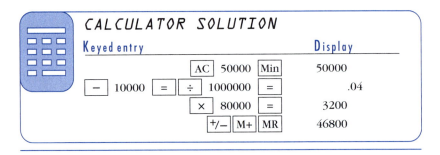

CALCULATOR SOLUTION

Keyed entry					Display
		AC 50000 Min			50000
− 10000 =	÷	1000000 =			.04
	×	80000 =			3200
	+/− M+ MR				46800

It should be noted that when an asset is depreciated under the units-of-production method, the date the asset is placed in service will not affect the amount of depreciation claimed during the year; only the usage of the asset will change its depreciation amount.

Let us now analyze an example that is based on the number of hours of operation and that requires the preparation of a useful-life depreciation schedule.

Example 6

Silver Mountain Ski Center purchased a double chair lift in 1980 for $60,000 and paid $20,000 to place the lift in service. The center estimates the lift will have a useful life of 25,000 hours and a salvage value of $15,000. Prepare a depreciation schedule using the units-of-production method if the asset was operated a total of 1,850 hours during the year.

Solution

Step 1: Determine the depreciation factor (per-hour rate of depreciation) of the asset.

$$\text{unit depreciation factor} = \frac{\text{total cost } - \text{ salvage value}}{\text{units of life}}$$

$$= \frac{60,000 + 20,000 - 15,000}{25,000 \text{ (hours)}}$$

$$= \$2.60 \text{ per hour unit}$$

Step 2: Calculate the depreciation amount for the first year.

$$\text{depreciation amount} = \text{unit depreciation factor} \times \text{hours}$$
$$= \$2.60 \times 1,850$$
$$= \$4,810$$

Step 3: Calculate book value for the first year.

$$\text{book value} = \text{total cost } - \text{ accumulated depreciation}$$
$$= \$80,000 - \$4,810$$
$$= \$75,190$$

Step 4: Complete the depreciation schedule using the procedure shown in steps 2 and 3 for each year in the depreciation schedule shown in Table 13.5.

Table 13.5

Units-of-production
depreciation
schedule

Year	Hours utilized	Depreciation expense	Accumulated depreciation	Book value
0				$80,000
1	1,850	$4,810	$ 4,810	75,190
2	1,975	5,135	9,945	70,055
3	2,325	6,045	15,990	64,010
4	1,940	5,044	21,034	58,966
5	2,320	6,032	27,066	52,934
6	2,050	5,330	32,396	47,604
7	1,875	4,875	37,271	42,729
8	2,260	5,876	43,147	36,853
9	2,080	5,408	48,555	31,445
10	2,360	6,136	54,691	25,309
11	1,950	5,070	59,761	20,239
12	2,015	5,239	65,000	15,000

CALCULATOR SOLUTION

Keyed entry	Display
AC 80000 Min	80000
1850 × 2.6 =	4810
+/− M+ MR	75190

First year calculation

| 1975 × 2.6 = | 5135 |
| +/− M+ MR | 70055 |

Second year calculation—use this same
procedure to complete the depreciation
schedule.

Notice in Table 13.5 that a column is designated for the unit measure of production (in this case, hours) and that the number of hours the equipment was utilized varies from year to year. When preparing a depreciation schedule using the units-of-production method, the schedule must contain information indicating the pattern of use for each year the asset is being depreciated.

COMPARISON OF TRADITIONAL METHODS

If the traditional methods of depreciation presented in this section were to be applied to the same asset, the total amount of depreciation expense

Table 13.6

Comparison of depreciation using traditional methods

Year	Straight-line	150% declining-balance	Units-of-production
1	$ 36,000	$ 69,000	$ 40,000
2	36,000	48,300	100,000
3	36,000	33,810	5,000
4	36,000	14,445	25,000
5	36,000	14,445	10,000
Total	$180,000	$180,000	$180,000

claimed and the asset's book value at the end of its useful life would be the same. However, the annual depreciation expense will vary in any given year. Let's consider a $200,000 machine placed in service on January 1 that cost $30,000 to install, has a useful life of 5 years, and an estimated salvage value of $50,000. If the machine is estimated to produce 90,000 units and actually produced 20,000 units the first year, 50,000 units the second year, 2,500 units the third year, 12,500 units the fourth year, and 5,000 units the fifth year, the three methods of depreciation would result in the annual depreciation expenses shown in Table 13.6.

The depreciation expenses shown in Table 13.6 are based on the amount of the asset's value being depreciated ($180,000) over the 5-year period. (This procedure was explained earlier in this section.)

$$\text{amount to be depreciated} = \text{total cost} - \text{salvage value}$$
$$= (\$200,000 + \$30,000) - \$50,000$$
$$= \$180,000$$

The annual depreciation expense in the first and subsequent years is determined by the three depreciation methods. The first year's depreciation expense for each of the three methods is calculated as follows:

Straight-line method:

$$\text{depreciation expense} = \frac{\text{total cost} - \text{salvage value}}{\text{useful life}}$$
$$= \frac{\$230,000 - \$50,000}{5}$$
$$= \$36,000$$

Declining-balance method:

$$\text{depreciation expense} = \text{book value} \times \text{declining-balance rate}$$
$$= \$230,000 \times .30 \quad (1.50/5 = .30)$$
$$= \$69,000$$

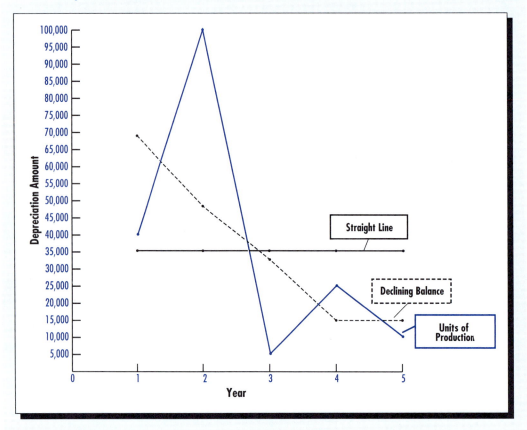

The method of depreciation chosen by a business for tax purposes is defined by the Internal Revenue Service. However, the method selected by a business to depreciate assets for "book" purposes within the business is determined by the firm's management. Therefore, managers must decide which of the traditional methods best achieves their financial objectives. The process of selecting which method of depreciation is most preferable is difficult, but, in most cases, the managers will consider the following factors in their search for the answer:

1. obsolescence
2. projected market values of the asset
3. Internal Revenue Service requirements
4. impact on earnings per share.

The three traditional methods of depreciation are compared visually on the accompanying graph. The graph is developed from the data presented in Table 13.6. Each depreciation method generates a different depreciation expense and book value each year. The slope of the curve defines the degree of acceleration for comparison purposes.

Units-of-production method:

$$\text{depreciation expense} = \frac{(\text{total cost} - \text{salvage value})}{\text{units of life}} \times$$
$$\text{units produced}$$

$$= \frac{(\$230,000 - \$50,000)}{90,000} \times 20,000$$

$$= \$40,000$$

As you can see, each method of depreciation produces a different depreciation expense for the first year. The declining-balance method accelerates the depreciation process, the units-of-production method depreciates the asset according to its use, while the straight-line method depreciates the asset in equal amounts each year. Managers must decide which of these methods best accommodates their financial strategies. This is not a simple decision and the factors that affect their choice are complex and go beyond the scope of this text.

These traditional methods are used to record depreciation for bookkeeping purposes, regardless of the acquisition date, but they will only be used for tax purposes on assets acquired prior to 1981.

CHECK YOUR KNOWLEDGE

Units-of-production method

Find the unit depreciation factor and the annual depreciation amount for each of the following:

	Cost	Salvage value	Useful life	Units produced / utilized	Unit depreciation	Annual depreciation amount
1.	$8,500	$1,000	50,000 units	3,500	$_____	$_____
2.	$32,000	$6,000	80,000 hours	6,250	_____	_____
3.	$75,000	$15,000	120,000 miles	18,720	_____	_____

4. A machine costs $89,500, has an estimated salvage value of $12,500, and has an estimated useful life of 275,000 units. If the machine produced 8,743 units the first year, find (a) the first year's depreciation amount and (b) the book value of the machine at the end of the first year.

5. National Transportation purchased a tractor, which qualifies under the excluded property rules, at a cost of $95,000. The company estimates the tractor will be driven 200,000 miles and will have a salvage value of $35,000. Prepare a useful-life depreciation schedule using the units-of-production method and the mileage given in the schedule (.30 unit expense).

Year	Annual mileage	Depreciation amount	Accumulated depreciation	Book value
				$95,000
1	20,540	$_____	$_____	_____
2	65,780	_____	_____	_____
3	72,165	_____	_____	_____
4	41,515	_____	_____	_____

13.3 EXERCISES

Find the unit and yearly depreciation expense for each of the following assets using the units-of-production method. Round answers to the nearest cent.

	Cost	Installa-tion charge	Salvage value	Useful life	Units pro-duced/ utilized	Unit depreciation factor	Depreciation expense
1.	$10,000	$350	$1,400	100,000 units	3,250	_____	_____
2.	$27,500	$0	$2,000	50,000 miles	15,000	_____	_____
3.	$130,800	$4,200	$25,000	128,400 hours	6,420	_____	_____
4.	$3,400	$125	$500	75,000 units	12,500	_____	_____
5.	$80,450	$875	$9,200	250,000 units	16,840	_____	_____

Complete the following units-of-production depreciation schedule. The asset's salvage value is $5,400, and its useful life is estimated to be 50,000 units.

	Year	Miles driven	Depreciation factor	Depreciation expense	Accumulated depreciation	Book value
						$22,850
6.	1	4,340	_____	$_____	$_____	$_____
7.	2	13,965	_____	_____	_____	_____
8.	3	15,250	_____	_____	_____	_____
9.	4	12,472	_____	_____	_____	_____
10.	5	3,973	_____	_____	_____	_____

Answers to CYK: *1.* .15; $525   *2.* .325; $2,031.25   *3.* .50; $9,360.00   *4.* a. $2,448.04; b. $87,051.96   *5.* $.30 depreciation rate/mile; $35,000 book value end of year 4

11. In 1979, Rojon Enterprises installed a grinding machine in its production department. The company paid $52,500 for the machine and $3,250 to have it installed. Find the annual depreciation amount if the machine has a salvage value of $5,500, was operated 4,160 hours, and has an estimated life of 75,000 hours.

12. Using the information given in exercise 11, calculate the book value at the end of the third year the machine was operated when it was operated 6,280 hours the second year and 5,915 hours the third year.

13. A vehicle that qualifies as excluded property costs $78,500, has a trade-in value of $8,000, and has an estimated useful life of 150,000 miles. Find the book value at the end of the first year if the vehicle was driven 24,635 miles.

14. American Foods purchased a labeling machine to be used in its packing plant at a cost of $135,000. The machine is expected to produce 1,500,000 units during its useful life, at which time it will have a salvage value of $15,000. Find the book value of the machine at the end of the second year if the machine labeled 80,250 units the first year and 132,745 units the second year.

15. Johanson's Ice Cream Company purchased a delivery truck at a cost of $34,000, which is classified as excluded recovery property. The company estimates the truck will have a trade-in value of $6,000, and company policy is to replace delivery vehicles every 100,000 miles. Prepare a depreciation schedule using the units-of-production method based on the following mileage:

first year	18,250 miles
second year	27,920 miles
third year	31,490 miles
fourth year	22,340 miles

13.4 ACCELERATED COST-RECOVERY SYSTEM (ACRS)

The **accelerated cost-recovery system (ACRS)** was enacted by the Internal Revenue Service (IRS) as part of the Economic Recovery Act of 1981. As a tax method of determining depreciation, ACRS allows businesses to write off the cost of most tangible depreciable assets placed in service after 1980 and before 1987.

Learning objective
Use the accelerated cost-recovery system (ACRS) to recover an asset's cost.

Under ACRS, the **unadjusted basis** (salvage value is not used to reduce the asset's original cost) of the asset is recovered over a specified recovery period. The recovery period is determined by the class life of the asset and defines the time period over which the asset's total cost will be recovered. The recovery period may be longer or shorter than the useful life of the asset because it is based on law instead of actual utilization. The type of recovery property being depreciated determines which **class life** will be used to calculate the recovery amount. Each item of recovery property is assigned to a class of property. The class to which an item is assigned is determined by its use and is therefore categorized as either tangible personal property or real property. Table 13.7 lists the asset classifications and their respective recovery periods under the accelerated cost-recovery system.

Class-life period	Types of recovery property (assets)
3-year property	Automobiles, light-duty trucks, tractor units for use over the road, race horses over 2 years old, and any house over 12 years old.
5-year property	Computers, copiers, office furniture and fixtures, single-purpose agricultural or horticultural structures, petroleum storage facilities excluding buildings.
10-year property	Theme-park structures, certain public utility property, mobile homes, railroad tank cars.
15-year property	Any real property placed in service before March 16, 1984, that cannot be designated as 5-year or 10-year property.
18-year real property	Real property placed in service after March 15, 1984, and before May 9, 1985, that cannot be designated as 5-, 10-, or 15-year real property.
19-year real property	Any real property placed in service after May 8, 1985, and before January 1, 1987, that cannot be designated as 5-, 10-, 15-, or 18-year real property.

CALCULATING 3-, 5-, 10-YEAR COST RECOVERY

When an asset has a class life of 3, 5, or 10 years, the depreciation deduction is determined using percentage tables provided by the IRS. Remember, under ACRS we are allowed to depreciate the *unadjusted basis* (total cost) of the asset. Therefore, the percentages shown in Table 13.8 repre-

Table 13.8

ACRS cost-recovery
periods and rates

Recovery period	Asset class		
	3-year	5-year	10-year
1	25%	15%	8%
2	38	22	14
3	37	21	12
4		21	10
5		21	10
6			10
7			9
8			9
9			9
10			9
	100%	100%	100%

sent the percent of the asset's value recovered in each year of the asset's class life.

Example 7

On April 10, 1986, Kline's Insurance Company placed in service an $80,000 mini-computer system for office use. Determine the ACRS deduction for 1986 and the book value at the end of 1986.

Solution

Step 1: Determine the class life of the asset using Table 13.7. The asset is classified as 5-year property, which means the asset's total cost will be recovered in 5 years.

Step 2: Calculate the ACRS deduction (depreciation) for 1986 (use Table 13.8, 15% found under 5-year class).

$$\text{cost recovery amount} = \text{original cost} \times \text{recovery rate}$$
$$= \$80,000 \times .15$$
$$= \$12,000$$

Step 3: Determine the asset's year-end book value.

$$\text{book value} = \text{original cost} - \text{accumulated depreciation}$$
$$= \$80,000 - \$12,000$$
$$= \$68,000$$

Note: Under ACRS, a full year of depreciation ($80,000 $\times$ .15 = $12,000) is claimed regardless of the month the asset is placed in service. This procedure applies to all assets with 3-, 5-, or 10-year recovery periods.

Example 8

Prepare a cost recovery schedule for the mini-computer system in Example 7.

Solution

5-year cost recovery schedule

Year	Original cost	Cost-recovery rate	Cost-recovery amount	Accumulated cost recovery	Book value
					$80,000
1	$80,000	.15	$12,000	$12,000	68,000
2	80,000	.22	17,600	29,600	50,400
3	80,000	.21	16,800	46,400	33,600
4	80,000	.21	16,800	63,200	16,800
5	80,000	.21	16,800	80,000	0

CALCULATING COST RECOVERY FOR REAL PROPERTY

Assets classified as real property, which are not designated as 3-, 5-, or 10-year property, are depreciated using IRS percentage tables specific to each time category. Consequently, we have to use a different table to recover the cost of an asset covered under 15-, 18-, and 19-year recovery periods. However, the method of calculating the cost-recovery amount is identical for each class life. For this reason, the example presented in this section will be based on percentages found in Table 13.9, 19-year real property. Unlike personal property, real property cost-recovery rates are based on the month of the tax year the asset is placed in service. Let's look at a 19-year real property example.

Example 9

Sun Properties purchased a parcel of land for $30,000 and erected a six-unit apartment building that cost $275,000. The building was placed in service on May 21, 1985. Find the cost-recovery amount and the year-end book value for 1985.

Solution

Step 1: To determine the class life of the asset, we use Table 13.7, since the asset is real property placed in service after May 8, 1985.

Step 2: Calculate the ACRS deduction for 1985. The asset was placed in service during the fifth month of the year. From Table 13.9, the cost-recovery rate is 5.8% for the first year.

Table 13.9

19-year real property percentage rates

Year	\multicolumn{12}{c}{Month placed in service}
	1	2	3	4	5	6	7	8	9	10	11	12
1	8.8	8.1	7.3	6.5	5.8	5.0	4.2	3.5	2.7	1.9	1.1	0.4
2	8.4	8.5	8.5	8.6	8.7	8.8	8.8	8.9	9.0	9.0	9.1	9.2
3	7.6	7.7	7.7	7.8	7.9	7.9	8.0	8.1	8.1	8.2	8.3	8.3
4	6.9	7.0	7.0	7.1	7.1	7.2	7.3	7.3	7.4	7.4	7.5	7.6
5	6.3	6.3	6.4	6.4	6.5	6.5	6.6	6.6	6.7	6.8	6.8	6.9
6	5.7	5.7	5.8	5.9	5.9	5.9	6.0	6.0	6.1	6.1	6.2	6.2
7	5.2	5.2	5.3	5.3	5.3	5.4	5.4	5.5	5.5	5.6	5.6	5.6
8	4.7	4.7	4.8	4.8	4.8	4.9	4.9	5.0	5.0	5.1	5.1	5.1
9	4.2	4.3	4.3	4.4	4.4	4.5	4.5	4.5	4.5	4.6	4.6	4.6
10–19	4.2	4.2	4.2	4.2	4.2	4.2	4.2	4.2	4.2	4.2	4.2	4.2
20	0.2	0.5	0.9	1.2	1.6	1.9	2.3	2.6	3.0	3.3	3.7	4.0

$$\text{cost-recovery amount} = \text{original cost} \times \text{cost-recovery rate}$$
$$= \$275,000 \times .058$$
$$= \$15,950$$

Note: The land is excluded in the calculation of the cost-recovery amount.

Step 3: Determine the asset's year-end book value.

$$\text{book value} = \text{original cost} - \text{accumulated depreciation}$$
$$= \$275,000 - \$15,950$$
$$= \$259,050$$

We develop a cost-recovery schedule for real property by using the steps shown above for each year of the recovery period. A complete recovery schedule for Example 9 is shown below in Table 13.10.

Table 13.10

19-year cost-recovery schedule

Year	Original cost	Cost-recovery rate	Cost-recovery amount	Accumulated cost recovery	Book value
					$275,000
1	$275,000	.058	$15,950	$ 15,950	259,050
2	275,000	.087	23,925	39,875	235,125
3	275,000	.079	21,725	61,600	213,400
4	275,000	.071	19,525	81,125	193,875
5	275,000	.065	17,875	99,000	176,000
6	275,000	.059	16,225	115,225	159,775
7	275,000	.053	14,575	129,800	145,200
8	275,000	.048	13,200	143,000	132,000
9	275,000	.044	12,100	155,100	119,900
10	275,000	.042	11,550	166,650	108,350
11	275,000	.042	11,550	178,200	96,800
12	275,000	.042	11,550	189,750	85,250
13	275,000	.042	11,550	201,300	73,700
14	275,000	.042	11,550	212,850	62,150
15	275,000	.042	11,550	224,400	50,600
16	275,000	.042	11,550	235,950	39,050
17	275,000	.042	11,550	247,500	27,500
18	275,000	.042	11,550	259,050	15,950
19	275,000	.042	11,550	270,600	4,400
20	275,000	.016	4,400	275,000	0

CHECK YOUR KNOWLEDGE

Accelerated cost recovery (ACRS)

Use Table 13.8 to find the cost-recovery period and the cost-recovery rate given the following:

Recovery year	Type of recovery property	Class-life period	Recovery rate
1. 3	office copier	_____	_____
2. 1	automobile	_____	_____
3. 4	railroad tank car	_____	_____

4. Rolling-Acres Homes placed a $24,000 mobile home in service on June 12, 1985, to be used as rental property. What was the ACRS deduction for (a) year 1 and (b) year 3?

5. Amodio's Florists purchased a truck for $18,500 to deliver flowers. Prepare a recovery schedule using the ACRS method of depreciation.

6. On February 10, 1986, John and Elizabeth Roberts placed in service a rental property. The total cost of the house was $148,500, including the land, which was valued at $35,000. What was the ACRS deduction for 1986?

7. Using the information in problem 6, find the book value at the end of the fourth year.

13.4 EXERCISES

Use Table 13.7 to complete the following.

	Date placed in service	Recovery year	Type of recovery property	Class-life period
1.	March 10, 1980	2	3-year-old race horse	_____
2.	April 3, 1984	5	public utility	_____
3.	October 22, 1982	10	warehouse structure	_____
4.	July 17, 1986	8	office building	_____
5.	May 26, 1981	4	petroleum storage tank	_____
6.	June 1, 1984	7	apartment building	_____

Answers to CYK: *1.* 5-year; 21%   *2.* 3-year; 25%   *3.* 10-year; 10%   *4.* a. $1,920; b. $2,880
5. book value year 1 $13,875; book value year 2 $6,845; book value year 3 $0
6. $9,193.50   *7.* $77,974.50

Use Tables 13.8 and 13.9 to complete the following.

	Date placed in service	Class-life period	Original cost	Recovery year	Recovery rate	Recovery amount
7.	2/7/83	3	$5,000	2	_____	_____
8.	7/21/87	10	$32,800	6	_____	_____
9.	9/8/85	19	$245,000	8	_____	_____
10.	5/1/84	5	$18,400	3	_____	_____
11.	11/25/82	10	$72,500	9	_____	_____
12.	1/10/86	19	$120,000	12	_____	_____

Use the appropriate tables presented in Section 13.4 to solve the following word problems.

13. A&E Rentals purchased an automobile for rental purposes for $26,970. The automobile was placed in service under the ACRS method of depreciation. Find the ACRS depreciation for each year of the recovery period.

14. Given the information in exercise 13, find the book value at the end of the second year.

15. Medical Associates purchased new furniture for its office that cost $15,000. Prepare a cost-recovery schedule using the ACRS method of depreciation.

16. Fun City Amusement Park erected a new arcade at a cost of $180,500, including land acquired for $60,000. Find the book value at the end of the fifth year using the ACRS method of depreciation.

17. Northeast Oil Company purchased a 10,000-gallon bulk storage tank to store fuel oil. The tank was placed in service on March 12, 1985, at a total cost of $92,500. Prepare a cost-recovery schedule using the accelerated cost-recovery system.

18. General Supply Company built a new retail sales facility that cost $520,000, excluding a land cost of $40,000. The store was placed in service on August 18, 1985. Find the ACRS depreciation for each of the first 5 years of the recovery period.

19. Given the information in exercise 18, find the book value at the end of the twelfth year using the ACRS method of cost recovery.

13.5 MODIFIED ACCELERATED COST-RECOVERY SYSTEM (MACRS)

Learning objective
Recover an asset's cost using the modified accelerated cost-recovery system (MACRS) guidelines.

The **modified accelerated cost-recovery system (MACRS),** also known as the "general depreciation system," or "GDS," applies to all tangible property placed in service after 1986. As the name implies, MACRS is a modification of the accelerated cost-recovery system discussed in Section 13.4 of this chapter. The changes were enacted as part of the Tax Reform Act of 1986 and included the creation of two new classes of property, the reclassification of some property, and changes in the depreciation procedures and rates. Under MACRS, the depreciation deduction can be calculated in one of two ways. The depreciation can be computed using (1) a depreciation method and convention over the recovery period or

Recovery period/ (class life)	Asset description
3-year property (0–4 yrs)	Tractor units for use over-the-road, any race horse over 2 years old, and any horse that is over 12 years old.
5-year property (5–10 yrs)	Taxis, buses, heavy general-purpose trucks, computers and peripheral equipment, office machinery (typewriters, calculators), automobiles, and research equipment.
7-year property (10–16 yrs)	Office furniture and fixtures (desks, files) and any property that does not have a class life and that has not been designated by law as being in any other class.
10-year property (16–20 yrs)	Vessels, barges, tugs, similar water transportation equipment, any single-purpose agricultural or horticultural structure, and any tree or vine bearing fruits or nuts.
15-year property (20–25 yrs)	Roads, shrubbery, wharves, and any municipal wastewater treatment plant.
20-year property (25 yrs or more)	Farm buildings and municipal sewers.
27.5-year property	Residental rental real property such as rental houses, apartments, and mobile homes.
31.5-year property	Any nonresidental rental real property (office buildings, stores, warehouses, etc.)

(2) MACRS percentage tables. The depreciation deduction is the same under both methods.

All property depreciated under MACRS is assigned to a property class in the same manner as ACRS. The class to which property is assigned is determined by its class life. The class life of an asset is the basis of its recovery period and the method of depreciation that can be used to recover the asset's cost. Table 13.11 shows the class life and recovery period for property depreciated under MACRS.

Under MACRS, we are allowed to recover the asset's total original cost. Therefore, we do not have to estimate its salvage value. Also, as mentioned earlier, we can elect to compute the depreciation deduction using a depreciation method and convention over the recovery period, or by using percentage tables. We will use the same example to illustrate both methods because they both result in the same depreciation deduction.

Table 13.12

Declining-balance
methods and rates

Recovery class	Declining-balance method	Depreciation rate
3	200%	66.67%
5	200	40.00
7	200	28.57
10	200	20.00
15	150	10.00
20	150	7.50

DECLINING-BALANCE METHOD

The declining-balance method can be used to depreciate all tangible assets. However, the class life of the asset determines the percentage method used to calculate the depreciation rate. Table 13.12 shows the applicable declining-balance method for each class of property and the corresponding depreciation rate.

The depreciation rates in Table 13.12 are determined by dividing the specified declining-balance percent (200% or 150%) by the recovery period. For example, for 5-year property, we divide 2.00 by 5 = .4, or 40%. For 20-year property, we divide 1.50 by 20 = .075, or 7.5%.

Under MACRS, the month of the year the asset is placed in service is not a factor in calculating the first year's depreciation expense. This is because the *half-year convention* treats all assets as placed in service on the midpoint of the first year. Consequently, the number of recovery years is always 1 year greater than the class life of the asset. If, however, over 40% of a company's assets in any tax year are placed in service during the last 3 months of that year, then a *midquarter convention* must be used. To calculate the MACRS deduction for an asset subject to the midquarter convention, we first compute the depreciation for the full year and then multiply the appropriate percentages for the quarter of the tax year the asset is placed in service. Let's develop an example step-by-step using the declining-balance method and appropriate convention.

Example 10

Central Farm Supply purchased a full-color copier for $15,000. The copy machine was placed in service on April 20, 1991. Find the amount of depreciation and the book value at the end of the first year using the declining-balance method.

Solution

Step 1: Determine the class life of the property using Table 13.11. The asset is classified as a 5-year property and will be depreciated using the 200% declining-balance method (Table 13.12).

Step 2: Calculate the yearly depreciation deduction.

$$\text{depreciation deduction} = \text{original cost} \times \text{depreciation rate}$$
$$= \$15,000 \times .40$$
$$= \$6,000$$

Step 3: Determine the depreciation deduction for the first year using the half-year convention.

$$\text{1st year depreciation amount} = \text{annual depreciation} \times \text{half-year}$$
$$\text{depreciation rate}$$
$$= \$6,000 \times .5$$
$$= \$3,000$$

Step 4: Find the book value at the end of the first year.

$$\text{book value} = \text{original cost} - \text{accumulated depreciation}$$
$$= \$15,000 - \$3,000$$
$$= \$12,000$$

Notice in step 3 that the first year's depreciation amount ($3,000) is one-half the annual amount ($6,000). This is because the half-year convention allows us to claim only half of the annual depreciation amount the first year, regardless of when the asset is placed in service. The remaining half-year will be recovered during the sixth calendar year of the recovery schedule. The entire cost recovery calculations for this example are summarized in Table 13.13.

If we were to continue multiplying the adjusted basis of the property (book value) by the declining-balance rate, we would never be able to

Table 13.13

200% declining-balance cost recovery schedule

Year	Depreciation calculations	Depreciation expense	Accumulated depreciation	Book value
0				$15,000.00
1	$15,000 × .40 × .5	$3,000.00	$ 3,000.00	12,000.00
2	12,000 × .40	4,800.00	7,800.00	7,200.00
3	7,200 × .40	2,880.00	10,680.00	4,320.00
4	4,320 × .40	1,728.00	12,408.00	2,592.00
5	2,592 × .6667	1,728.09	14,136.09	863.91
6		863.91	15,000.00	0.00

depreciate the asset's value to 0. Therefore, we apply the straight-line method for the last 2 years (4th and 5th) and claim the balance as the depreciation amount for the carry over year (6th). In the fourth year, the straight-line rate is 40% (1 divided by 2.5 remaining years), which in this case just happens to be the same as the declining-balance rate. In the fifth year, the straight-line rate is 66.67% (1 divided by 1.5 remaining years). For the sixth year, the depreciation expense is the fifth-year book value, since the remaining recovery period (a half-year) is less than one year and the asset's original value must be fully recovered.

Table 13.14

MACRS percentage table: 200% or 150% declining-balance depreciation switching to straight-line for 3, 5, 7, 10, 15, and 20 years using half-year convention

PERCENTAGE TABLE METHOD

The Internal Revenue Service provides tables that can be used to figure depreciation under MACRS. The tables may be used for any property placed in service in a tax year and they are based on the appropriate depreciation method, recovery period, and convention. If the table method is elected, the percentage from the table must be used to figure depreciation deductions for the entire recovery period of the property. The rates shown in Table 13.14 are based on the 200% or 150% declining-balance

Recovery year	Recovery period					
	3 years	5 years	7 years	10 years	15 years	20 years
1	33.33	20.00	14.29	10.00	5.00	3.750
2	44.45	32.00	24.49	18.00	9.50	7.219
3	14.81	19.20	17.49	14.40	8.55	6.677
4	7.41	11.52	12.49	11.52	7.70	6.177
5		11.52	8.93	9.22	6.93	5.713
6		5.76	8.92	7.37	6.23	5.285
7			8.93	6.55	5.90	4.888
8			4.46	6.55	5.90	4.522
9				6.56	5.91	4.462
10				6.55	5.90	4.461
11				3.28	5.91	4.462
12					5.90	4.461
13					5.91	4.462
14					5.90	4.461
15					5.91	4.462
16					2.95	4.461
17						4.462
18						4.461
19						4.462
20						4.461
21						2.231

method applying the half-year convention to each recovery period. To determine the rate of depreciation for any year, we find the recovery year in the left-hand column, and read across to the appropriate recovery period. For example, the depreciation rate for property with a 10-year recovery period in the sixth year of life is 7.37%.

Example 11

Let's assume the same facts as in Example 10 except that we will use the percentage table method to determine the depreciation deduction.

Solution   *Step 1:*   Determine the class life of the property using Table 13.11. The asset is classified as a 5-year property.

Step 2:   Find the depreciation rate in Table 13.14 for a 5-year property in the first year of life (.20) and multiply this rate by the original cost of the property to determine the amount of depreciation.

$$\text{depreciation amount} = \text{original cost} \times \text{depreciation rate}$$
$$= \$15{,}000 \times .20$$
$$= \$3{,}000$$

Step 3:   Find the book value at the end of the first year.

$$\text{book value} = \text{original cost} - \text{accumulated depreciation}$$
$$= \$15{,}000 - \$3{,}000$$
$$= \$12{,}000$$

Notice that the depreciation amount and the book value for the first year are the same for both methods.

STRAIGHT-LINE METHOD

A business can elect to depreciate tangible property using the straight-line method instead of the declining-balance method. To figure the MACRS deduction under the straight-line method, divide the number 1 by the years remaining in the recovery period at the beginning of the tax year. This procedure produces a different depreciation rate for each year of the recovery period. The rate is then applied to the previous year's book value to determine the current year's depreciation deduction. The half-year convention also applies to the straight-line method; therefore, a half-year of depreciation is deducted the first year the property is placed in service and the unrecovered value of the property at the end of the recovery period is claimed in the carry over year.

Example 12

Management Consulting Group purchased $40,000 of office furniture for its new facility in Chicago, which was placed in service on September 20, 1991. Prepare a cost recovery schedule using the MACRS straight-line method.

Solution

Step 1: Determine the class life and recovery period of the property. The property would be considered a 7-year property.

Step 2: Find the depreciation rate for a 7-year property in the first year of life (1/7 = .1429) and multiply this rate by the original cost of the property to determine the annual amount of depreciation.

$$\begin{aligned}
\text{annual depreciation amount} &= \text{original cost} \times \text{depreciation rate} \\
&= \$40,000 \times .1429 \\
&= \$5,716
\end{aligned}$$

Step 3: Determine the depreciation deduction using the half-year convention.

$$\begin{aligned}
\text{1st year depreciation amount} &= \text{annual depreciation} \times \text{half-year} \\
&\qquad\qquad \text{depreciation rate} \\
&= \$5,716 \times .5 \\
&= \$2,858
\end{aligned}$$

Step 4: Find the book value at the end of the first year.

$$\begin{aligned}
\text{book value} &= \text{original cost} - \text{accumulated depreciation} \\
&= \$40,000 - \$2,858 \\
&= \$37,142
\end{aligned}$$

Table 13.15

Straight-line cost recovery schedule

These steps would be completed for each year of the recovery period as shown in Table 13.15.

Year	Depreciation calculations		Depreciation expense	Accumulated depreciation	Book value
					$40,000.00
1	$40,000.00 × .1429	× .5	$2,858.00	$ 2,858.00	37,142.00
2	37,142.00 × .1538		5,712.44	8,570.44	31,429.56
3	31,429.56 × .1818		5,713.89	14,284.33	25,715.67
4	25,715.67 × .2222		5,714.02	19,998.35	20,001.65
5	20,001.65 × .2857		5,714.47	25,712.82	14,287.18
6	14,287.18 × .4		5,714.87	31,427.69	8,572.31
7	8,572.31 × .6667		5,715.16	37,142.85	2,857.15
8			2,857.15	40,000.00	0

Examine the depreciation calculation column carefully and notice how the unrecovered basis (previous year's book value) and the depreciation rate changes each year of the recovery period. The second year's depreciation rate (.1538) is found by dividing 1 by the 6.5 remaining years in the recovery period and the third year's depreciation rate (.1818) is found by dividing 1 by the 5.5 remaining years and so forth. The carryover year's (8th year) depreciation expense is the unrecovered value of the property at the end of the seventh year.

REAL PROPERTY

Real property, or real estate, is land and generally anything that is erected on, growing on, or attached to land. The land itself, however, is not depreciable property.

For depreciation purposes, real property is classified as either *residential rental property* or *nonresidential rental property*. Table 13.11 gives a description of property that qualifies under each class in the last two recovery periods. The IRS tax guidelines require that businesses use the straight-line method to depreciate real property. The method is applied exactly as explained in the preceding section. There is, however, one modification involving the date the property is placed in service. For all depreciable real property, we use a *midmonth* convention. Under the midmonth convention, property is treated as placed in service on the midpoint of the month regardless of the day of purchase. Therefore, to determine the first year's depreciation deduction, we include one-half of the first month and each of the months that follow. Each year thereafter, we are allowed a full year's depreciation deduction based on the unrecovered value of the property and the depreciation rate for that year. Because of the number of years (27.5 and 31.5) and since these calculations are repetitive, we will use the percentage table method discussed earlier to determine the depreciation deduction for real property. The depreciation rates can be found in Tables 13.16 and 13.17.

Example 13

Cedarvale Development Corporation purchased a ten-unit apartment complex for $800,000, which included land valued at $100,000. The property was placed in service on August 15, 1991. Prepare a depreciation schedule using the MACRS method of calculating depreciation.

Solution

Step 1:   Determine the class life and the recovery period of the property. The property is considered residential rental real property and has a recovery period of 27.5 years.

Table 13.16

MACRS percentage table: Straight-line depreciation over 27.5 years using midmonth convention

Recovery year	Month in the first recovery year the property is placed in service											
	1	2	3	4	5	6	7	8	9	10	11	12
1	3.485	3.182	2.879	2.576	2.273	1.970	1.667	1.364	1.061	0.758	0.455	0.152
2	3.636	3.636	3.636	3.636	3.636	3.636	3.636	3.636	3.636	3.636	3.636	3.636
3	3.636	3.636	3.636	3.636	3.636	3.636	3.636	3.636	3.636	3.636	3.636	3.636
4	3.636	3.636	3.636	3.636	3.636	3.636	3.636	3.636	3.636	3.636	3.636	3.636
5	3.636	3.636	3.636	3.636	3.636	3.636	3.636	3.636	3.636	3.636	3.636	3.636
6	3.636	3.636	3.636	3.636	3.636	3.636	3.636	3.636	3.636	3.636	3.636	3.636
7	3.636	3.636	3.636	3.636	3.636	3.636	3.636	3.636	3.636	3.636	3.636	3.636
8	3.636	3.636	3.636	3.636	3.636	3.636	3.636	3.636	3.636	3.636	3.636	3.636
9	3.636	3.636	3.636	3.636	3.636	3.636	3.636	3.636	3.636	3.636	3.636	3.636
10	3.637	3.637	3.637	3.637	3.637	3.636	3.636	3.636	3.636	3.636	3.636	3.636
11	3.636	3.636	3.636	3.636	3.636	3.637	3.637	3.637	3.637	3.637	3.637	3.637
12	3.637	3.637	3.637	3.637	3.637	3.636	3.636	3.636	3.636	3.636	3.636	3.636
13	3.636	3.636	3.636	3.636	3.636	3.637	3.637	3.637	3.637	3.637	3.637	3.637
14	3.637	3.637	3.637	3.637	3.637	3.636	3.636	3.636	3.636	3.636	3.636	3.636
15	3.636	3.636	3.636	3.636	3.636	3.637	3.637	3.637	3.637	3.637	3.637	3.637
16	3.637	3.637	3.637	3.637	3.637	3.636	3.636	3.636	3.636	3.636	3.636	3.636
17	3.636	3.636	3.636	3.636	3.636	3.637	3.637	3.637	3.637	3.637	3.637	3.637
18	3.637	3.637	3.637	3.637	3.637	3.636	3.636	3.636	3.636	3.636	3.636	3.636
19	3.636	3.636	3.636	3.636	3.636	3.637	3.637	3.637	3.637	3.637	3.637	3.637
20	3.637	3.637	3.637	3.637	3.637	3.636	3.636	3.636	3.636	3.636	3.636	3.636
21	3.636	3.636	3.636	3.636	3.636	3.637	3.637	3.637	3.637	3.637	3.637	3.637
22	3.637	3.637	3.637	3.637	3.637	3.636	3.636	3.636	3.636	3.636	3.636	3.636
23	3.636	3.636	3.636	3.636	3.636	3.637	3.637	3.637	3.637	3.637	3.637	3.637
24	3.637	3.637	3.637	3.637	3.637	3.636	3.636	3.636	3.636	3.636	3.636	3.636
25	3.636	3.636	3.636	3.636	3.636	3.637	3.637	3.637	3.637	3.637	3.637	3.637
26	3.637	3.637	3.637	3.637	3.637	3.636	3.636	3.636	3.636	3.636	3.636	3.636
27	3.636	3.636	3.636	3.636	3.636	3.637	3.637	3.637	3.637	3.637	3.637	3.637
28	1.970	2.273	2.576	2.879	3.182	3.485	3.636	3.636	3.636	3.636	3.636	3.636
29	0.000	0.000	0.000	0.000	0.000	0.000	0.152	0.455	0.758	1.061	1.364	1.667

Table 13.17

MACRS percentage table: Straight-line depreciation over 31.5 years using midmonth convention

Recovery year	Month in the first recovery year the property is placed in service											
	1	2	3	4	5	6	7	8	9	10	11	12
1	3.042	2.778	2.513	2.249	1.984	1.720	1.455	1.190	0.926	0.661	0.397	0.132
2	3.175	3.175	3.175	3.175	3.175	3.175	3.175	3.175	3.175	3.175	3.175	3.175
3	3.175	3.175	3.175	3.175	3.175	3.175	3.175	3.175	3.175	3.175	3.175	3.175
4	3.175	3.175	3.175	3.175	3.175	3.175	3.175	3.175	3.175	3.175	3.175	3.175
5	3.175	3.175	3.175	3.175	3.175	3.175	3.175	3.175	3.175	3.175	3.175	3.175
6	3.175	3.175	3.175	3.175	3.175	3.175	3.175	3.175	3.175	3.175	3.175	3.175
7	3.175	3.175	3.175	3.175	3.175	3.175	3.175	3.175	3.175	3.175	3.175	3.175
8	3.175	3.175	3.175	3.175	3.175	3.175	3.175	3.175	3.175	3.175	3.175	3.175
9	3.174	3.174	3.174	3.174	3.174	3.174	3.174	3.175	3.174	3.175	3.174	3.175
10	3.175	3.175	3.175	3.175	3.175	3.175	3.175	3.174	3.175	3.174	3.175	3.174
11	3.174	3.174	3.174	3.174	3.174	3.174	3.174	3.175	3.174	3.175	3.174	3.175
12	3.175	3.175	3.175	3.175	3.175	3.175	3.175	3.174	3.175	3.174	3.175	3.174
13	3.174	3.174	3.174	3.174	3.174	3.174	3.174	3.175	3.174	3.175	3.174	3.175
14	3.175	3.175	3.175	3.175	3.175	3.175	3.175	3.174	3.175	3.174	3.175	3.174
15	3.174	3.174	3.174	3.174	3.174	3.174	3.174	3.175	3.174	3.175	3.174	3.175
16	3.175	3.175	3.175	3.175	3.175	3.175	3.175	3.174	3.175	3.174	3.175	3.174
17	3.174	3.174	3.174	3.174	3.174	3.174	3.174	3.175	3.174	3.175	3.174	3.175
18	3.175	3.175	3.175	3.175	3.175	3.175	3.175	3.174	3.175	3.174	3.175	3.174
19	3.174	3.174	3.174	3.174	3.174	3.174	3.174	3.175	3.174	3.175	3.174	3.175
20	3.175	3.175	3.175	3.175	3.175	3.175	3.175	3.174	3.175	3.174	3.175	3.174
21	3.174	3.174	3.174	3.174	3.174	3.174	3.174	3.175	3.174	3.175	3.174	3.175
22	3.175	3.175	3.175	3.175	3.175	3.175	3.175	3.174	3.175	3.174	3.175	3.174
23	3.174	3.174	3.174	3.174	3.174	3.174	3.174	3.175	3.174	3.175	3.174	3.175
24	3.175	3.175	3.175	3.175	3.175	3.175	3.175	3.174	3.175	3.174	3.175	3.174
25	3.174	3.174	3.174	3.174	3.174	3.174	3.174	3.175	3.174	3.175	3.174	3.175
26	3.175	3.175	3.175	3.175	3.175	3.175	3.175	3.174	3.175	3.174	3.175	3.174
27	3.174	3.174	3.174	3.174	3.174	3.174	3.174	3.175	3.174	3.175	3.174	3.175
28	3.175	3.175	3.175	3.175	3.175	3.175	3.175	3.174	3.175	3.174	3.175	3.174
29	3.174	3.174	3.174	3.174	3.174	3.174	3.174	3.175	3.174	3.175	3.174	3.175
30	3.175	3.175	3.175	3.175	3.175	3.175	3.175	3.174	3.175	3.174	3.175	3.174
31	3.174	3.175	3.174	3.175	3.174	3.175	3.174	3.175	3.174	3.175	3.174	3.175
32	1.720	1.984	2.249	2.513	2.778	3.042	3.175	3.174	3.175	3.174	3.175	3.174
33	0.000	0.000	0.000	0.000	0.000	0.000	0.132	0.397	0.661	0.926	1.190	1.455

Step 2:   Find the depreciation rate for a 27.5-year real property using the midmonth convention placed in service in August (see Table 13.16). Multiply this rate times the unadjusted basis of the property ($800,000 − 100,000 = $700,000) to determine the annual amount of depreciation for the first year.

$$\text{annual depreciation} = \text{unadjusted basis} \times \text{depreciation rate}$$
$$= \$700,000 \times .01364$$
$$= \$9,548$$

Step 3:   Calculate the book value at the end of the first year.

$$\text{book value} = \text{original cost} - \text{accumulated depreciation}$$
$$= \$700,000 - 9,548$$
$$= \$690,452$$

Since the property was placed in service during the eighth month of the tax year, we must multiply the previous year's book value of the property each year by the percentages for the eighth month in Table 13.16 to determine the annual depreciation. The rates in the table reflect the midmonth convention and require no further calculations. However, if we wanted to determine the monthly depreciation expense for financial purposes, we would divide the first year's depreciation amount by 4.5 ($9,548 ÷ 4.5 = $2,121.78). Under the midmonth convention, we are allowed to claim only one-half of the monthly depreciation amount the month the property is placed in service ($2,121.78 × .5 = $1,060.89), and a full month's depreciation for the remaining 4 months ($2,121.78 × 4 = $8,487.12) for a total of $9,548.01 ($8,487.12 + 1,060.89 = $9,548.01) for the first year. Each year thereafter, we would divide the annual depreciation amount by 12 to determine the monthly depreciation amount.

The calculations required to complete a depreciation schedule for Example 13 are shown in Table 13.18.

Notice that it takes 29 calendar years to depreciate property with a 27.5-year recovery period. This is because we can only claim part of a year's depreciation in the first and twenty-ninth years as indicated by the reduced percentages for these years shown in Table 13.15.

The MACRS method of calculating the recovery cost of property is less complicated compared to other methods presented in this chapter and provides for an accelerated rate of recovery that can be beneficial to a business and the economy. The tax considerations involving the deprecia-

Table 13.18

Percentage method depreciation schedule

Year	Depreciation calculation	Depreciation amount	Accumulated depreciation	Book value
0				$700,000
1	$700,000 × .01364	$ 9,548	$ 9,548	690,452
2	700,000 × .03636	25,452	35,000	665,000
3	700,000 × .03636	25,452	60,452	639,548
4	700,000 × .03636	25,452	85,904	614,096
5	700,000 × .03636	25,452	111,356	588,644
6	700,000 × .03636	25,452	136,808	563,192
7	700,000 × .03636	25,452	162,260	537,740
8	700,000 × .03636	25,452	187,712	512,288
9	700,000 × .03636	25,452	213,164	486,836
10	700,000 × .03636	25,452	238,616	461,384
11	700,000 × .03637	25,459	264,075	435,925
12	700,000 × .03636	25,452	289,527	410,473
13	700,000 × .03637	25,459	314,986	385,014
14	700,000 × .03636	25,452	340,438	359,562
15	700,000 × .03637	25,459	365,897	334,103
16	700,000 × .03636	25,452	391,349	308,651
17	700,000 × .03637	25,459	416,808	283,192
18	700,000 × .03636	25,452	442,260	257,740
19	700,000 × .03637	25,459	467,719	232,281
20	700,000 × .03636	25,452	493,171	206,829
21	700,000 × .03637	25,459	518,630	181,370
22	700,000 × .03636	25,452	544,082	155,918
23	700,000 × .03637	25,459	569,541	130,459
24	700,000 × .03636	25,452	594,993	105,007
25	700,000 × .03637	25,459	620,452	79,548
26	700,000 × .03636	25,452	645,904	54,096
27	700,000 × .03637	25,459	671,363	28,637
28	700,000 × .03636	25,452	696,815	3,185
29	700,000 × .00455	3,185	700,000	0

tion methods presented in this chapter can be found in the Internal Revenue Service Publication 534.

CHECK YOUR KNOWLEDGE

Modified cost recovery system (MACRS)

Use Tables 13.11 and 13.12 to determine the cost-recovery period and cost-recovery rates for the following property.

	Type of recovery property	Class-life period	Recovery rate
1.	delivery truck	_____	_____
2.	winery grape vineyard	_____	_____
3.	office furniture	_____	_____
4.	dairy building	_____	_____

Use the appropriate tables in Section 13.5 to solve the following word problems.

5. Using the declining-balance method, what is the amount of depreciation and the book value for a $20,000 automobile at the end of the first year. Round to nearest dollar.

6. Southside Press purchased an offset printer for $7,500 that was placed in service on October 15, 1989. Prepare a depreciation schedule for the property using the MACRS percentage table method. Round to the nearest dollar.

7. Powers General Contractors purchased and placed in service a small backhoe that cost $50,000 on May 5, 1991. Prepare a cost-recovery schedule for the machine using the MACRS straight-line method. Round to the nearest dollar.

8. The law firm of Rivera & Ponto built an office building for its practice that was placed in service on June 29, 1990. The facility cost $295,000 including land, which was valued at $70,000. Prepare a partial cost-recovery schedule for the first 5 years using the MACRS percentage table method. Round to the nearest dollar.

13.5 EXERCISES

Use Table 13.14 to complete the following.

	Type of property	Recovery year	Class-life recovery period	Recovery rate
1.	microcomputer	3	_____	_____
2.	apple orchard	5	_____	_____
3.	3-year-old race horse	2	_____	_____
4.	wastewater treatment plant	10	_____	_____
5.	commercial bus	4	_____	_____
6.	office desks/chairs	6	_____	_____
7.	farm equipment storage building	15	_____	_____

Answers to CYK: *1.* 5-year; 40%   *2.* 10-year; 20%   *3.* 7-year; 28.7%   *4.* 10-year; 20%   *5.* $4,000, $16,000   *6.* book value year 1, $6,000, book value year 3, $2,160, book value year 6, $0   *7.* book value year 1, $45,000, book value year 3, $25,000, book value year 6, $0   *8.* book value year 5, $192,555

Use Table 13.14 to compute the first year depreciation for the following. Round to nearest dollar.

	Property cost	Recovery period	Recovery rate	Recovery amount	Book value
8.	$5,000	3	_____	_____	_____
9.	$18,500	5	_____	_____	_____
10.	$32,700	10	_____	_____	_____
11.	$85,250	20	_____	_____	_____
12.	$48,600	7	_____	_____	_____
13.	$125,000	15	_____	_____	_____

Use the appropriate tables presented in Section 13.5 to solve the following word problems.

14. Lockner Cards and Gifts purchased display fixtures for $12,800. Calculate the book value at the end of the first year using the MACRS declining-balance method. Round to the nearest dollar.

15. Prepare a cost recovery schedule using the information given in exercise 12. Round to the nearest dollar.

16. Allied Transport Systems purchased a tractor to haul freight trailers for $80,000. Prepare a depreciation schedule using the MACRS percentage table method (Table 13.14). Round to the nearest dollar.

17. Georgio's Professional Cleaning Services purchased three automobiles for use by its sales personnel at $16,500 each. Prepare a depreciation schedule for the automobiles using the MACRS percentage table method (Table 13.14). Round to the nearest dollar.

18. Springwood Farms erected a horse stable for $175,000. Find the book value at the end of the tenth year using the MACRS percentage table method (Table 13.14). Round to the nearest dollar.

19. Metroplex Transportation purchased a bus for $120,000, which was placed in service on November 12, 1992. Find the book value at the end of the first year using the MACRS straight-line method. Round to the nearest dollar.

20. Prepare a cost recovery schedule using the information given in exercise 18 the first ten years. Round to the nearest dollar.

21. Marine Salvage purchased a tugboat for $350,000. The vessel was placed in service on July 20, 1991. Find the book value at the end of year 1 using the MACRS straight-line method. Round to the nearest dollar.

22. Marcia Perez purchased a three-family house for $145,000 that she intends to use as rental property. The property was placed in service on April 5, 1991. Find the book value at the end of the first year using the MACRS percentage table method. Round to the nearest dollar.

23. Prepare a cost recovery schedule using the information given in exercise 21.

24. Realty Management purchased a six-unit apartment building for $375,000, which included land valued at $50,000. The property was placed in service on May 2, 1990. Find the book value of the property for each of the first 5 years using the MACRS percentage table method.

25. Metropolitan Development built a new retail store complex for $850,000. The rental property was placed in service on September 28, 1991. Find the book value of the property for each of the first 5 years.

EXPRESS YOUR THOUGHTS

Compose one or two well-written sentences to express the requested information in your own words.

1. What is depreciation and why do businesses depreciate their assets?

2. How would you determine the monthly amount of depreciation expense of an asset using the traditional straight-line method, if the asset was purchased on January 10 and is expected to have no value once it is depreciated?

3. Explain how the traditional declining-balance method of depreciating assets differs from the traditional straight-line method.

4. What does the term book value mean and how is an asset's book value determined?

5. Describe how you would determine the annual depreciation expense for an asset using the traditional units-of-production method. How does this method of depreciation differ from the other traditional methods?

6. Describe the steps required to find the annual amount of cost recovery on an asset to write off the cost of the asset under the accelerated cost recovery system.

7. Under ACRS, how is the class life of an asset determined and categorized?

8. Describe how the modified accelerated cost recovery system differs from the accelerated cost recovery system.

9. Describe the steps required to determine an asset's book value at the end of the first year using the MACRS straight-line method of cost recovery. Assume the asset is classified as personal property and is placed in service on October 3 of the first year.

10. Explain how you would determine the book value of an asset at the end of the first year using the MACRS percentage-table method for an asset with a ten-year recovery period.

Case exercise   The Country Loft

Christie Newman is the sole proprietor of an interior decorating business known as The Country Loft. She operates this business out of her home at the present time but hopes to eventually establish a following that will allow her to locate the business in a nearby shopping plaza. Christie has just purchased a new minivan for local business travel to the homes or offices of her clients, to pick up and deliver merchandise, and to meet with various suppliers and subcontractors associated with the business. The van cost $12,300 and was placed in service on April 15, 1992. While the van is used primarily for business use, Christie and other members of her family also use the van for personal purposes. Because the van is used for both business and personal use, Christie has maintained records that contain sufficient information regarding each aspect of every business/investment use. The records of the business during the first year indicate that 60% of the van's use was devoted to business-related activities. At the end of each calendar year, Christie has a public accounting firm prepare her taxes. She has provided the firm with all personal and business records required to prepare her annual income tax report.

As a staff accountant for the firm, you have been assigned the responsibility of preparing the current year's income tax return for The Country Loft. Use the tax information provided and your knowledge of the IRS tax guidelines regarding depreciation presented in this chapter to do the following.

A. Determine the amount of depreciation deduction for 1992.

B. Determine the depreciation deduction at the end of the second year (1993) if the business records adequately support an increase in the use of the van for business purposes to 80%.

SELF-TEST

A. Terminology review

Complete the following items using the key terms presented at the beginning of the chapter. Check your responses against the answer key at the end of the test.

1. The periodic deduction allowed by the Internal Revenue Service to recover the cost of a business asset that is used more than 1 year is called ___depreciation___ *lậm sự kt giá*

2. The amount of the periodic deduction is reported as ___dep e+p___ in the income statement and as an increase in the ___accumulated dep.___ *t ổn lại.* of the asset in the balance sheet.

3. The ___book value___ of an asset is the value reported in the balance sheet after deducting the accumulated depreciation from the total cost of the asset when it is placed in service.

4. The ___straight line___ method of depreciation allows a business to evenly distribute the cost of an asset over its useful life. *increase*

5. A traditional method used to accelerate the depreciation of an asset's cost is called ___declining balance___

6. When the actual service rendered by an asset is a more appropriate base for depreciation than its years of service, a business may use the ___units of production___ method.

7. The _____ allows businesses to write

off the cost of most tangible depreciable assets placed in service after 1980 and before 1987 more quickly than traditional methods.

8. Under ACRS and MACRS, the type of recovery property being depreciated determines which ___class___ will be used to determine the recovery amount.

9. The ___modified accelerated cost___ is also known as the General Depreciation System and applies to all tangible property placed in service after 1986.

10. Under MACRS, the ___half year convention___ treats all property as being placed in service on the midpoint of the year regardless of when the property is actually placed in service.

B. Calculation review

The following concepts and short problems are designed to test your understanding of the objectives identified at the beginning of the chapter. Answers are at the end of the test. Use the appropriate tables presented in this chapter to solve.

11. Jo-Ann's placed in service $8,000 of equipment for use in its business. The equipment falls under the excluded property rules and will be depreciated using the straight-line method. If the equipment is estimated to have a useful life of 5 years and a salvage

value of $1,200, find the book value at the end of the first year.

12. An asset costing $25,000 is depreciated under the 150% declining-balance method. The asset has a useful life of 5 years and a salvage value of $3,500. Find the book value at the end of the first year if the asset was placed in service on October 2, 1991, and the asset qualified as excluded property.

13. In 1980, Poland Casting Company placed in service a stamping machine that cost $80,650. The company paid an additional $2,500 to have the machine installed. Find the amount of depreciation claimed the first year if the machine has a salvage value of $3,200, it was operated 1,640 hours during the year, and has an estimated life of 65,000 hours. Round your answer to the nearest dollar.

14. Hastings Bottling Company purchased a bottle capping machine at a cost of $48,000. The machine is expected to cap 4,000,000 units during its useful life and is estimated to have a salvage value of $2,000. Find the book value of the machine at the end of the second year if the machine capped 60,250 units the first year and 580,470 units the second year. (Round your answer to the nearest dollar.)

15. Ever-Green Landscaping Company purchased a light-duty truck for $28,000 on March 12, 1985. Prepare a cost-recovery schedule using the accelerated cost-recovery

system. Round your answer to the nearest dollar.

16. Determine the book value at the end of the first year of a tractor used to haul trailers over the road using the MACRS declining-balance method. The tractor cost $200,000 and was placed in service on March 15, 1992. Round your answer to the nearest dollar.

17. Nugent Foods purchased a computer for $3,500 that was placed in service on December 6, 1990. What was the book value at the end of the second year if the property is being depreciated by the MACRS straight-line method? Round your answer to the nearest dollar.

18. Trim-N-Fit Conditioners purchased furniture for its office at a cost of $18,200. Find the book value at the end of the third year using the MACRS percentage table method.

19. James Anderson purchased a duplex for rental purposes for $140,000. The property was placed in service on April 8, 1991. Find the book value of the property at the end of the second year using the MACRS percentage tables. Round your answer to the nearest dollar.

20. Three-Star Investment purchased an eight-store mini mall for $750,000 that included land valued at $125,000. The property was placed in service on May 20, 1990. What was the book value of the property at the end of the first year?

Answers to self-test: 1. depreciation   2. depreciation expense, accumulated depreciation   3. book value   4. straight-line   5. declining-balance   6. units-of-production method   7. accelerated cost recovery system   8. class   9. modified accelerated cost recovery system   10. half-year convention   11. $6,640   12. $23,125   13. $2,017.20   14. $40,311   15. second year   16. $133,330   17. $2,450   18. $7,959   19. $131,303   20. $612,600

14

INVENTORY VALUATION

Learning objectives

1. Calculate the value of ending inventory using the average cost method.

2. Calculate the value of ending inventory using the FIFO method.

3. Calculate the value of ending inventory using the LIFO method.

4. Calculate the value of ending inventory using the specific identification method.

5. Calculate the value of ending inventory using the lower-of-cost-or-market method.

6. Estimate the value of ending inventory using the retail method.

7. Estimate the ending inventory by using the gross margin method.

8. Define the key terms.

INTRODUCTION

An **inventory** is a list of items that a company or business has in its possession at any specific time. For a manufacturer, this list may be made up of a variety of items ranging from raw materials to be used in a production process, to finished goods waiting to be shipped to wholesalers and retailers. In a small business, the list might consist primarily of goods, such as sneakers, bicycles, hammers, or rakes, owned by the business and held for resale to customers.

Inventory is recorded as a current asset on a business's balance sheet and since it is very important for businesses to know the value of their assets, they must be able to determine the value of their remaining inventory at any time in the business cycle, such as at the end of a month, quarter, or year.

Initially, this may sound like a simple task, but when businesses have very large inventories of a variety of goods and materials, it is far from a simple task to maintain an accurate inventory. Ideally, a company would like to maintain a *continuous inventory* that would indicate at any instant in the business cycle exactly what items were in the business's possession. The use of computers and scanners is helping businesses to come closer to this ideal. In most cases, this ideal is far from being attained; consequently, a form of *periodic inventory* is used in which the company or business

1. periodically takes a physical count of the inventory to determine how *many* items are presently in the company's possession

2. determines the *dollar value* of those items.

We refer to this as a **periodic inventory system** since inventory is counted periodically rather than continuously.

In this chapter, we will present several different accounting methods used to place a value on *beginning inventory* and *ending inventory*, which are phrases we will use to mean the value of inventory either at the beginning or at the end of some specified period of time. In order to better demonstrate these various methods, we will refer to the following illustration of Big Tex Oil Company.

The Big Tex Oil Company is a refinery. It purchases crude oil from companies that pump oil from the ground and then refines this oil to transform it into gasoline, fuel oil, or petroleum distillants. Immediately following, is a partial income statement for Big Tex showing barrels of crude oil purchased during the year.

Income Statement for Big Tex Oil Company
(this is not a complete income statement)

Cost of goods sold:
  Beginning inventory (carried over
    from last year):   1,000 barrels @ $34 = $ 34,000
  Purchases during the current year:
    January 24   5,000 barrels @ $30 = 150,000
    June 17   5,000 barrels @ $20 = 100,000
    September 11   8,000 barrels @ $17 = 136,000
    December 6   1,000 barrels @ $16 =   16,000

  Total goods available for sale: 20,000 barrels $436,000
  Less value of ending inventory: ?
    units of physical inventory
    remaining = 2,000
    Unit value of inventory = $____?____

Cost of goods sold $____?____

Big Tex must now place a dollar value on the remaining barrels of oil
but at what price? at $34? at $30? or $16? Since many barrels of oil are
placed in a single tank, Big Tex Oil Company cannot distinguish between
the oil purchased at $16 per barrel and that purchased at $34 per barrel.
Sections 15.1 through 15.5 will demonstrate five different methods Big
Tex (and other companies) can use to place a value on ending inventory.

14.1   THE AVERAGE COST METHOD

Learning objective
Calculate the value of
ending inventory us-
ing the average cost
method.

The **average cost method** identifies the average cost per unit of each
item that remains in the inventory at the end of a period. To calculate the
average cost of ending inventory, we use the *quantity times price equals
cost* concept of the basic business transaction. In Example 1 illustrating
Big Tex Oil, the *quantity* column is the number of barrels purchased, the
price column is the dollar amounts for barrels purchased, and the *cost*
column is obtained by multiplying the price times the quantity. Next, we
divide the total of the cost column by the total of the quantity column (in
this case, in barrels). This calculation will always result in the average cost
per unit.

Example 1

Determine the value of Big Tex's ending inventory using the average cost
method.

Solution

Step 1:   Determine the total value of the inventory for the period.

Quantity	Unit × price =	Cost
1,000 barrels	$34	$ 34,000
5,000	30	150,000
5,000	20	100,000
8,000	17	136,000
1,000	16	16,000
20,000 barrels		$436,000

Step 2:   Determine the average cost per unit (i.e., per barrel).

$436,000 ÷ 20,000 barrels = $21.80 average cost per barrel

Step 3:   Determine the value of the ending inventory by multiplying the number of units remaining in inventory by the average cost per unit.

$21.80 × 2,000 barrels = $43,600

CALCULATOR SOLUTION

Keyed entry						Display
AC	1000	×	34	=	Min	34000
	5000	×	30	=	M+	150000
	5000	×	20	=	M+	100000
	8000	×	17	=	M+	136000
	1000	×	16	=	M+	16000
					MR	436000
		÷	20000	=		21.80
		×	2000	=		43600

This will allow Big Tex Oil Company to complete its *Less ending inventory* line of its income statement.

Now that we have the value of the ending inventory, we can complete the cost of goods sold section of the income statement of the Big Tex illustration.

cost of goods sold = total goods available for sale − ending inventory
= $436,000 − $43,600
= $392,400

The ending inventory value is also shown as merchandise inventory in the current assets section of the company's balance sheet.

CHECK YOUR KNOWLEDGE

The average cost method

1. Shirley opened a brand new shoe store during the month of June. Using the following information regarding the purchases for Shirley's Shoe Store, find the value of her ending inventory using the average cost method.

purchases:

June 7	1,000 pair @ $10
August 11	1,500 pair @ $11
October 21	900 pair @ $17
Ending inventory:	1,100 pair

2. Use the following partial income statement for Carmen's Hardware Store to determine (a) the value of his ending inventory using the average cost method and (b) the cost of goods sold.

Beginning inventory (for 4″ carpenter nails):	7,000 @ $0.10
Purchases:	
February 1	15,000 @ $ .07
May 1	20,000 @ $ .04
December 1	5,000 @ $ .02
Ending inventory:	10,000 nails

14.2   THE FIRST-IN, FIRST-OUT (FIFO) METHOD

The **first-in, first-out (FIFO) method** is an accounting procedure that describes the way a company might sell its goods. This method assumes that those purchases made first (earliest in the year) will be sold first. Hence, any goods remaining unsold at the end of the year will be valued at the price paid for the latest or most recent purchases, as shown in Figure 14.1.

When a company uses the FIFO method of inventory valuation it does not mean that the company's actual physical flow of goods is to be sold in this way—this assumption is made for accounting purposes only.

Learning objective
Calculate the value of ending inventory using the FIFO method.

Answers to CYK: *1.* average cost per pair = $12.29; value of inventory = $13,519   *2.* a. average cost per nail = $.06; value of ending inventory = $600.00; b. cost of goods sold = $2,050.00

Figure 14.1

FIFO method of inventory valuation

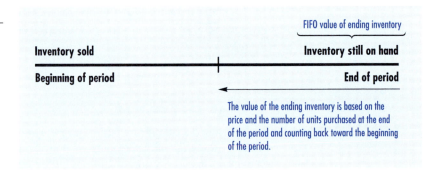

FIFO value of ending inventory

Inventory sold | Inventory still on hand

Beginning of period | End of period

The value of the ending inventory is based on the price and the number of units purchased at the end of the period and counting back toward the beginning of the period.

Example 2

Calculate the value of the ending inventory for Big Tex Oil Company using the FIFO method.

Solution

To calculate the value of the ending inventory using the FIFO method, we must refer to the purchase record of the Big Tex Oil Company.

Beginning inventory:	1,000 barrels @ $34
Purchases:	
January 24	5,000 barrels @ $30
June 17	5,000 barrels @ $20
September 11	8,000 barrels @ $17
December 6	1,000 barrels @ $16
Ending inventory:	2,000 barrels @ ?

Starting with the most recent or latest purchases, we value the remaining 2,000 barrels as follows:

1,000 barrels @ $16 (from Dec. 6 purchases)	= $16,000
+1,000 barrels @ $17 (from Sept. 11 purchases)	= $17,000
2,000 ending inventory	$33,000

CHECK YOUR KNOWLEDGE

First-in, first-out method

Solve the following problems.

1. Use the following information to evaluate the ending inventory of Shirley's Shoe Store by the FIFO method.

Purchases:

June 7	1,000 pair @ $10
August 11	1,500 pair @ $11
October 21	900 pair @ $17
Ending inventory:	1,100 pair

2. Use the following partial income statement for Carmen's Hardware Store to determine the value of his ending inventory by the FIFO method.

Beginning inventory (for *4″* carpenter nails):	7,000 @ $.10
Purchases:	
February 1	15,000 @ $.07
May 1	20,000 @ $.04
December 1	5,000 @ $.02
Ending inventory:	10,000 nails

28000

14.3 THE LAST-IN, FIRST-OUT (LIFO) METHOD

Learning objective
Calculate the value of ending inventory using the LIFO method.

The **last-in, first-out (LIFO)** method for determining the value of ending inventory more closely resembles the way in which a company actually moves its physical inventory. That is, those purchases made during the latter part of the year are sold first. Hence, any goods remaining unsold at the end of the year will be valued at the price paid for the first or earliest purchases as shown in Figure 14.2.

Figure 14.2

LIFO value of ending inventory

LIFO value of ending inventory

Inventory still on hand	Inventory sold
Beginning of period	End of period

The value of the ending inventory is based on the price and the number of units purchased at the beginning of the period and counting to the end of the period.

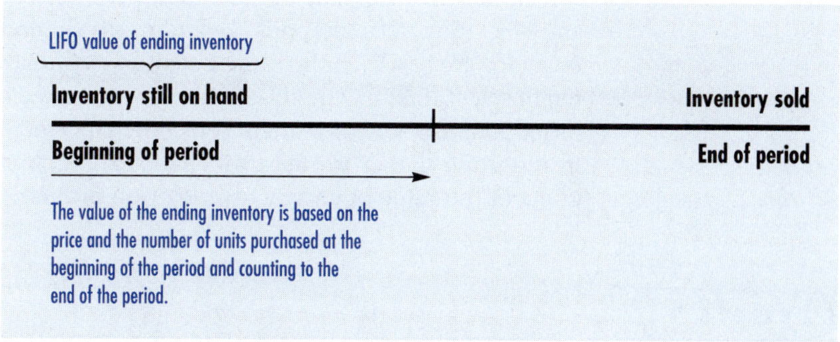

Answers to CYK: *1.* $17,500.00 *2.* $300.00

When a company uses the LIFO method of inventory valuation it does not mean that the company's actual physical flow of goods occurs in this way—this assumption is made for accounting purposes only.

Example 3

Use the LIFO method to calculate the value of the ending inventory for the Big Tex Oil Company.

Solution

To calculate the value of the ending inventory using the LIFO method, we must again refer to the purchase record of the Big Tex Oil Company.

Beginning inventory:	1,000 barrels @ $34
Purchases:	
January 24	5,000 barrels @ $30
June 17	5,000 barrels @ $20
September 11	8,000 barrels @ $17
December 6	1,000 barrels @ $16
Ending inventory:	2,000 barrels @ ?

Starting with the earliest barrels on hand (in this case, beginning inventory), we value the ending inventory of 2,000 barrels as follows:

1,000 barrels @ $34 (from beginning inventory) = $34,000
1,000 barrels @ $30 (from Jan. 24 purchases)   = $30,000
2,000 ending inventory $64,000

Notice that the value of the ending inventory using the FIFO ($33,000) and LIFO ($64,000) methods is significantly different even though the calculations are based on the same inventory information. Therefore, Big Tex might select the FIFO method if it were interested in reporting lower profits for tax purposes, or it might select the LIFO method if it were interested in reporting higher profits to its investors. Example 4 will illustrate the effect of the value of ending inventory on profits.

Example 4

During the current period, Big Tex Oil Company reported revenues of $750,000 and operating expenses of $58,000. Calculate the profit before taxes based on the value of ending inventory determined by the FIFO method in Example 2 and the LIFO method in Example 3.

Solution

FIFO Method:

Revenue:		$750,000
Cost of goods sold:		
Beginning inventory:		
1,000 barrels @ $34 = $ 34,000		
Purchases during the current year:		
Jan. 24 5,000 barrels @ $30 = $150,000		
June 17 5,000 barrels @ $20 100,000		
Sept. 11 8,000 barrels @ $17 136,000		
Dec. 6 1,000 barrels @ $16 16,000		
Total value available for sale:	$436,000	
Less ending inventory:	33,000	
Cost of goods sold		$403,000
Gross profit		$347,000
Less operating expenses		58,000
Profit before taxes		$289,000

LIFO Method:

Revenue:		$750,000
Cost of goods sold:		
Beginning inventory:		
1,000 barrels @ $34 = $ 34,000		
Purchases during the current year:		
Jan. 24 5,000 barrels @ $30 = 150,000		
June 17 5,000 barrels @ $20 = 100,000		
Sept. 11 8,000 barrels @ $17 = 136,000		
Dec. 6 1,000 barrels @ $16 = 16,000		
Total value available for sale:	$436,000	
Less ending inventory:	64,000	
Cost of goods sold		$372,000
Gross profit		$378,000
Less operating expenses		58,000
Profit before taxes		$320,000

CHECK YOUR KNOWLEDGE

Last-in, first-out method

Solve the following problems. Round dollar amounts to the nearest cent.

1. Use the following information to value the ending inventory of Shirley's Shoe Store using the LIFO method.

    Purchases:
June 7	1,000 pair @ $10
August 11	1,500 pair @ $11
October 21	900 pair @ $17
Ending inventory:	1,100 pair

2. Use the following partial balance sheet for Carmen's Hardware Store to determine the value of his ending inventory using the LIFO method.

Beginning inventory (for 4″ carpenter nails):	7,000 @ 10 cents
Purchases:	
February 1	15,000 @ 7 cents
May 1	20,000 @ 4 cents
December 1	5,000 @ 2 cents
Ending inventory:	10,000 nails

14.3 EXERCISES

Solve the following problems. Round dollar amounts to the nearest cent.

1. For the following information, find the value of the ending inventory by the average cost method.

Beginning inventory:	200 units	@ $15	= $_____
Purchases:			
March 10	300 units	@ $20	= $_____
March 19	100 units	@ $17	= $_____
March 24	400 units	@ $24	= $_____
Total cost of goods available for sale:			$_____
Value of ending inventory			$_____
Average unit cost of inventory			= $___?___
Units of physical inventory remaining			= 350

Answers to CYK: *1.* $11,100.00   *2.* $910.00

2. Find the value of the ending inventory by the first-in, first-out (FIFO) method for the following information.

Beginning inventory:	150 units	@ $45	= $_____
Purchases:			
September 4	250 units	@ $55	= $_____
September 12	300 units	@ $40	= $_____
September 20	200 units	@ $47	= $_____
September 30	175 units	@ $50	= $_____

Units of physical inventory remaining at the end of the month = 560

_____units	@ $_____	= $_____
_____units	@ $_____	= $_____
_____units	@ $_____	= $_____
_____units	@ $_____	= $_____
Value of ending inventory		$_____

3. Find the value of the ending inventory by the last-in, first-out (LIFO) method for the following information.

Beginning inventory:	150 units	@ $45	= $_____
Purchases:			
September 4	250 units	@ $55	= $_____
September 12	300 units	@ $40	= $_____
September 20	200 units	@ $47	= $_____
September 30	175 units	@ $50	= $_____

Units of physical inventory remaining at the end of the month = 560

_____ units	@ $_____	= $_____
_____ units	@ $_____	= $_____
_____ units	@ $_____	= $_____
_____ units	@ $_____	= $_____
value of ending inventory		= $_____

4. Find the cost of goods sold using the following information.

Beginning inventory:	3,000	@ $1.45	= $_____
Purchases:			
April 15	2,000	@ $1.50	= $_____
May 12	4,000	@ $1.65	= $_____
June 10	3,500	@ $1.75	= $_____
Total cost of goods available for sale:			$_____
Less ending inventory:	3,800	$1.61	= $_____
Cost of goods sold:			$_____

5. Dexter Ellsworth owns a sporting goods store in Bakersfield, California, where skateboards are a new item in his inventory. Use the following information about skateboards to determine the value of Dexter's ending inventory using (a) the average cost method, (b) the FIFO method, and (c) the LIFO method.

Purchases:
June 21	15 @ $45
August 23	30 @ $55
November 22	20 @ $65
Ending inventory:	17 skateboards

6. Olivia Meredith owns a haircutting salon. Olivia has decided to purchase a new brand of shampoo for her salon. Using the records below, calculate the value of ending inventory using (a) the average cost method, (b) the FIFO method, and (c) the LIFO method.

Purchases:
February 17	10 cases @ $36
April 13	20 cases @ $42
June 14	100 cases @ $40
Ending inventory:	20 cases

7. Maria Vasquez is the accountant for the Peculiar Paint Store. It is Maria's job to determine the value of the cans of Primrose Pink paint remaining in inventory at the year end. Determine the value of ending inventory using (a) the average cost method, (b) the FIFO method, and (c) the LIFO method.

Beginning inventory
(Primrose Pink):	2 gal @ $ 8

Purchases:
January 3	50 gal @ $10
April 3	20 gal @ $20
July 3	10 gal @ $25
Ending inventory:	33 gal

8. Percy Longfellow is the proud owner of a bookstore in Worcester, Massachusetts, that sells only classic novels. Percy received word from the station manager at Channel 10 that, on December 8, *The Scarlet Pimpernel* would be shown on television. Percy knew from past experience that, after a classic film has been aired on TV, scores of people flock to his bookstore to buy copies of the book on which the film was based. At the end of the year, Percy had five copies of *The Scarlet Pimpernel* remaining in inventory. Help Percy determine the value of these five remaining copies using (a) the average cost method, (b) the FIFO method, and (c) the LIFO method.

Beginning inventory (*The*
Scarlet Pimpernel):	1 copy @ $1.00

Purchases:
September 4	50 copies @ $2.00
October 4	60 copies @ $2.25
November 4	70 copies @ $2.95

9. Ophelia Jenkins owns a small nursery where 90% of the plants, trees, and shrubs that are for sale are grown on the premises. The other 10% are purchased from a local farmer. Use the partial balance sheet below to help Ophelia calculate the value of her ending inventory using (a) the average cost method, (b) the FIFO method, and (c) the LIFO method.

Beginning inventory
(for geraniums):	10 plants @ $2

Purchases:
April 1	70 plants @ $5
May 1	100 plants @ $4
June 1	50 plants @ $3
Ending inventory:	40 plants

10. Mary Stewart is the owner, manager, and bookkeeper of the Downtown Diner. At the end of her first year in business, Mary took a physical count of all the items in the warehouse. Mary found that she had an inordinate amount of 32-ounce cans of tomato juice—800,000 cans to be exact. When Mary returned to the office she immediately looked at the records for tomato juice purchases (listed below). Calculate the value of these 800,000 cans using (a) the average cost method, (b) the FIFO method, and (c) the LIFO method.

Purchases:
January	100,000 cans @ $ .38
March	600,000 cans @ $1.00
June	200,000 cans @ $1.75
December	500,000 cans @ $1.95

11. Mark Soffietti was the bookkeeper for Anthony Orsky's liquor store. At year end, Anthony found that he had 250,000 cases of vodka remaining in inventory. Use the following information to determine the value of Anthony's vodka using (a) the average cost method, (b) the FIFO method, and (c) the LIFO method.

Purchases:

February 2	50,000 cases @ $ 75
April 2	50,000 cases @ $ 80
June 2	50,000 cases @ $ 85
August 2	50,000 cases @ $ 90
October 2	50,000 cases @ $ 95
December 2	50,000 cases @ $100

12. Ernest Zorro, owner of the Masquerade Costume Shop, discovered he overestimated the demand for Dracula costumes this year and is therefore left with 100 such costumes. Determine the value of these costumes using (a) the average cost method, (b) the FIFO method, and (c) the LIFO method.

Purchases:

August 30	200 Dracula costumes @ $30
September 30	200 Dracula costumes @ $50

14.4   SPECIFIC IDENTIFICATION METHOD

Learning objective
Calculate the value of ending inventory using the specific identification method.

The **specific identification method** is a method of identifying and labeling each unit with the original cost of the unit. This makes the job of evaluating ending inventory very easy. As you physically count your remaining inventory, you also record the cost identified on the tag or label of each unit.

If Big Tex Oil Company continued to pour all barrels of oil into a single tank, this method of specific identification would be impossible to use. On the other hand, if Big Tex kept each barrel of oil in its own container and labeled each container with the cost it paid for that barrel of oil, then the specific identification method could be used.

Example 5

Big Tex Oil Company stores its oil in individual 55-gallon barrels. Determine the value of the ending inventory using the specific identification method, assuming that at the end of the period there are 300 barrels that cost $34 each, 450 barrels that cost $30, 350 barrels that cost $20, and 900 barrels that cost $17.

Solution

Cost of goods sold:

Beginning inventory:	1,000 barrels @ $34
Purchases:	
January 24	5,000 barrels @ $30
June 17	5,000 barrels @ $20
September 11	8,000 barrels @ $17
December 6	1,000 barrels @ $16
Total goods available for sale:	20,000

Ending inventory:
$$
\begin{array}{rcl}
300 \text{ barrels @ } \$34 &=& \$10,200 \\
450 \text{ barrels @ } \$30 &=& 13,500 \\
350 \text{ barrels @ } \$20 &=& 7,000 \\
\underline{900} \text{ barrels @ } \$17 &=& \underline{15,300} \\
2,000 & & \$46,000
\end{array}
$$

The specific identification method would be very time consuming and impractical for those companies having units with low costs. However, this method is very beneficial for those companies having very expensive units such as works of art or automobiles.

Thus far, we have described four different methods used to place a dollar value on items remaining in ending inventory. A business may elect to use a fifth method, the **lower-of-cost-or-market method**, when calculating the value of ending inventory under the specific identification method. This procedure allows individual units of the inventory to be valued at either the actual cost at the time of purchase or at the current market value, whichever is lower. (The **current market value** is what it would cost to replace the unit.) This procedure could also be applied to the LIFO, FIFO, and average cost methods as well.

Learning objective
Calculate the value of ending inventory using the lower-of-cost-or-market method.

Example 6

In Example 5, the value of the ending inventory for the Big Tex Oil Company using the specific identification method was $46,000. If the current market value is $16 per barrel, calculate the value of ending inventory using the lower-of-cost-or-market procedure.

Solution

The total number of barrels of oil in the inventory at the end of the period is 2,000 barrels. Therefore, the market value of the oil is $32,000 (2,000 @ $16/barrel). According to the procedure of the lower-of-cost-or-market method, the ending inventory would be valued at the lower price of $32,000, rather than the actual cost of $46,000.

CHECK YOUR KNOWLEDGE

Specific identification method

Solve the following problems. Round dollar amounts to the nearest cent.

1. Let us suppose that the Impressionistic Art department at the National Gallery of Art in Washington, D.C., made three purchases during this past year:

July 2	a Monet painting for $100 million
September 3	a Renoir painting for $120 million
November 4	a Seurat painting for $110 million.

If the Impressionistic Art department sold the Renoir, and we make the assumption that the department had no beginning inventory, then what is the value of the ending inventory?

2.   Using the information given in problem 1, determine the value of the Impressionistic Art department's ending inventory by the lower-of-cost-or-market procedure.

Beginning inventory: none
Purchases:

		Cost	Market
July 2	Monet	$100 million	$150 million
Sept. 3	Renoir	$120 million	$120 million
Nov. 4	Seurat	$110 million	$ 90 million
Ending inventory:		Monet and Seurat	

14.4   EXERCISES

1. Determine the value of the ending inventory by the specific identification method.

    300 units @ $28 = _____
    175 units @ $31 = _____
    550 units @ $37 = _____
    875 units @ $26 = _____
    Value of ending
        inventory   _____

2. Determine the value of the ending inventory by the lower-of-cost-or-market method.

Cost	Market	
500 units @ $55	$60	_____
230 units @ $53	$50	_____
630 units @ $57	$54	_____
725 units @ $54	$56	_____
Value of ending inventory		_____

3. The Creepy Critter Pet Store had always had a large supply of insects and spiders, but presently, Craig Croger, the owner of Creepy Critters, has decided to expand into the area of snakes. So during this past month, Craig made the following purchases:

October 12	cobra for $100
October 13	python for $60
October 27	anaconda for $75

    On December 31, Craig counted his inventory and noted that, of the three snakes purchased, he was able to sell only the cobra. Using the specific identification method, value Creepy Critter's ending inventory for snakes.

Answers to CYK: *1.* $210 million   *2.* $190 million

4. Aidan Kelsey inherited the Pirate's Cove Marina from his uncle — the late, great Captain Kelsey. Captain Kelsey had not only been in the business of docking yachts but also of buying and selling sailing vessels. Since the marina now belonged to Aidan, he decided to expand his business to include cabin cruisers. Aidan made the following purchases:

April 22	36' Carver	$100,000
June 29	35' Criss Craft	$120,000
August 26	38' Criss Craft	$169,000
August 31	40' Criss Craft	$189,000
September 3	35' Carver	$110,000

During the year, Aidan sold the 35' and 36' Carvers. Calculate the value of Aidan's ending inventory using the specific identification method.

5. Use the following information to determine the value of the cabin cruisers at the Pirate's Cove Marina. Apply the rule of lower-of-cost-or-market to this situation.

Beginning inventory: none
Purchases:

		Cost	Market
April 22	36' Carver	$100,000	$120,000
June 29	35' Criss Craft	120,000	100,000
August 26	38' Criss Craft	169,000	149,000
August 31	40' Criss Craft	189,000	180,000
September 3	35' Carver	110,000	130,000
Ending inventory:	35' Criss Craft		
	38' Criss Craft		
	40' Criss Craft		

6. Rocko Kaminsky owns a TV repair shop and also sells a handful of new television sets. Use the following information to determine the value of Rocko's new television sets at year end. Apply the rule of lower-of-cost-or-market.

Beginning inventory:

		Cost	Market
	13" Zenith	$300	$200
	19" RCA	$200	$325
Purchases:			
February 13	25" SONY	$700	$900
February 20	19" Zenith	$450	$550
March 4	25" RCA	$699	$899
Ending inventory:	all sets (Rocko sold none of the new TVs)		

14.5   INVENTORY ESTIMATION

Throughout this chapter, we have learned several methods used to value the units remaining in ending inventory. For each of these methods, the units in ending inventory were determined by a physical count. Since taking a physical count is very time consuming and therefore very costly, it is usually done only once a year. During the remainder of the year, ending inventory must be estimated since this information is necessary for the preparation of monthly and quarterly financial statements. This section illustrates two methods, the retail method and the gross margin method, to estimate the cost of ending inventory.

RETAIL METHOD

Learning objective
Estimate the value of ending inventory using the retail method.

Retail merchandise outlets often use the **retail method** to estimate the value of their ending inventory. This method is based on the financial information reported in the income statement and does not require the business to calculate the individual cost of each item. The value of ending inventory is determined by first calculating the cost of goods available for sale at both cost and retail. Next, a *cost ratio* is formed by dividing the *cost of goods available for sale at cost* by the *cost of goods available for sale at retail*.

Formula for
cost ratio

$$\text{cost ratio} = \frac{\text{cost of goods available for sale at cost}}{\text{cost of goods available for sale at retail}}$$

The cost ratio is then used to convert the value of ending inventory at retail to cost by multiplying the cost ratio by the ending inventory at retail. Example 7 illustrates this procedure step by step.

Example 7

Based on the following financial data, estimate the cost of the ending inventory for Solomon Software Company using the retail method.

	Cost	Retail
Beginning inventory for January	$ 58,500	$ 90,000
Purchases during January	$ 52,000	$ 80,000
Goods available for sale	$110,500	$170,000
Net sales during January		$ 70,000

Solution

Step 1: Calculate the value of ending inventory at retail:

Goods available for sale at retail	$170,000
Less net sales during the month	70,000
Ending inventory at retail	$100,000

Step 2:   Compute the cost ratio

$$\text{cost ratio} = \frac{\text{cost of goods available for sale}}{\text{retail value of goods available for sale}}$$
$$= \frac{\$110,500}{\$170,000} = .65$$

Step 3:   Determine the value of ending inventory at cost:

$$\text{ending inventory at cost} = \text{ending inventory at retail} \times \text{cost ratio}$$
$$= \$100,000 \times .65$$
$$= \$65,000$$

GROSS MARGIN METHOD

Learning objective
Estimate the ending
inventory value using
the gross margin
method.

The **gross margin method** is another method used to estimate inventory. In order to use this method, we must show gross margin as a percentage of sales revenues. This percentage is used to determine the cost of goods sold, which provides us with the necessary information to calculate the value of ending inventory.

Example 8

The Acme Company has a beginning inventory of $40,000 for March 1, purchases during March of $52,000, and March sales of $100,000. Gross margin as a percent of sales has been approximately 38% during the past year. Estimate inventory for the end of March assuming the gross margin percentage remains at 38%.

Solution

Step 1:   Calculate the gross margin. We use the gross margin percentage for the past year (38%) to determine the part of sales ($100,000) that is the gross margin.

$$\text{gross margin} = \text{total sales for the period} \times \text{gross margin percent}$$
$$= \$100,000 \times .38$$
$$= \$38,000$$

Step 2:   Recall that

$$\text{gross margin} = \text{sales} - \text{cost of goods sold}$$

For Your Information

Inventory control: economic order quantity

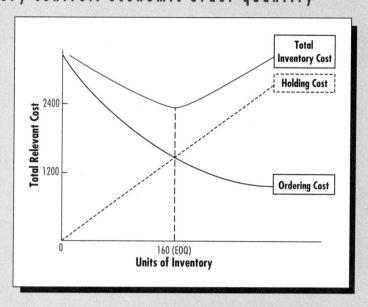

Inventory is an important consideration to business organizations because it represents cost. The aim of inventory control is to minimize the cost of ordering, holding, or running out of stock. Once a firm has determined the demand for its products, it often uses mathematical models to maintain inventories at optimum levels. The economic order quantity (EOQ) is a mathematical inventory control method that identifies the number of units to be ordered each time an order is placed. The equation includes annual demand (D), ordering costs (O), and holding costs (H). For example, assume a manufacturer estimates a total demand of 1,600 units of a part to be used in a manufacturing process, ordering costs amount to $120 per order, and holding costs are $15 per unit per year. Based on these values, the EOQ is 160 units.

$$EOQ = \sqrt{\frac{2DO}{H}} = \sqrt{\frac{2(1600)(120)}{15}} = \sqrt{25,600} = 160 \text{ units}$$

As shown in the accompanying graph, the EOQ (160) is the point where the ordering cost curve intersects the holding cost curve; the total inventory cost is minimized when these costs are equal. The graph also shows that ordering costs decrease as the number of units ordered in each lot increases because fewer orders are placed during the period, and that holding costs (storage) increase proportionally to the number of units ordered in each lot. The EOQ assumes that unit cost and demand are constant. If either of these variables changes, the EOQ must be adjusted accordingly for this method of inventory control to be effective.

Solving this equation for cost of goods sold, we have:

cost of goods sold = sales − gross margin

Using the information in this example, this computation is:

sales	$100,000
− gross margin	− 38,000
= cost of goods sold	$ 62,000

Step 3: Calculate the value of ending inventory. Recall the procedure for calculation of the value of ending inventory is

beginning inventory
+ purchases
= goods available for sale

and

goods available for sale
− cost of goods sold
= ending inventory

The computation is as follows:

beginning inventory	$40,000
+ purchases	+52,000
= goods available for sale	$92,000

and

goods available for sale	$92,000
− cost of goods sold	− 62,000
= ending inventory	$30,000

CHECK YOUR KNOWLEDGE

Inventory estimation

Solve the following problems. Round dollar amounts to the nearest cent and ratios to the nearest ten-thousandth.

1. The Spindler Corporation needs to estimate the value of its ending inventory in order to complete its financial statements for the month of July. (a) Calculate the cost ratio. (b) Use the retail method to estimate the value of ending inventory at the end of July.

	Cost	Retail
Beginning inventory for July	$20,000	$37,735.85
Purchases during July	30,000	66,603.77
Goods available for sale	50,000	104,339.62
Net sales during July		54,000.00

2. The Peabody Corporation needs to estimate the cost of its ending inventory as of the end of June in order to complete its second-quarter financial statements. Sales for the month were $70,000, purchases during June were $30,000, beginning inventory for the month was $20,000, and it is assumed that gross margin is 40% of sales. (a) Find the dollar amount of cost of goods sold. (b) Use the gross margin method to estimate the value of ending inventory for the month of June.

14.5 EXERCISES

Solve the following problems. Round dollar amounts to the nearest cent and ratios to the nearest ten-thousandth.

1. The following information refers to the Mercury Corporation. Calculate the cost ratio using the retail method.

	Cost	Retail
Beginning inventory	$ 58,000	$ 80,000
Purchases during the month	87,000	120,000
Goods available for sale	$145,000	$200,000
Net sales during the month		$140,000

2. Use the retail method to calculate the cost ratio using the following information:

	Cost	Retail
Beginning inventory	$21,000	$ 30,000
Purchases during the month	59,500	85,000
Goods available for sale	$80,500	$115,000
Net sales during the month		$ 60,000

3. The Konar Company needs to estimate the cost of its ending inventory in order to complete its financial statements for the month of April. Find the cost ratio using the retail method.

Answers to CYK: *1.* a. .5033; b. $72,817.06   *2.* a. gross margin = $28,000; cost of goods sold = $42,000;
b. ending inventory = $8,000

	Cost	Retail
Beginning inventory	$168,000	$280,000
Purchases during the month	348,000	580,000
Goods available for sale	$516,000	$860,000
Net sales during the month		$350,000

4. The MacKenzie Company needs to estimate the cost of its ending inventory in order to complete its financial statements for the month of May. Find the cost ratio using the retail method.

	Cost	Retail
Beginning inventory	$15,400	$22,000
Purchases during the month	12,600	18,000
Goods available for sale	$28,000	$40,000
Net sales during the month		$10,000

5. Calculate the estimated inventory from the information in problem 1 using the retail method.

6. Calculate the estimated inventory from the information in problem 2 using the retail method.

7. Calculate the estimated inventory from the information in problem 3 using the retail method.

8. Calculate the estimated inventory from the information in problem 4 using the retail method.

9. The Stonybrook Corporation needs to estimate the cost of its ending inventory as of the end of August. Sales for the month were $140,000, purchases during August were $60,000, beginning inventory for the month was $40,000, and it is assumed that gross margin is 35% of sales. Find the dollar amount of the cost of goods sold using the gross margin method.

10. The Birnbaum Company needs to estimate the cost of its ending inventory as of the end of October in order to complete its financial statements. Sales for the month were $300,000, purchases during October were $100,000, beginning inventory was $80,000, and it is assumed that gross margin is 45% of sales. Find the dollar amount of the cost of

goods sold using the gross margin method.

11. The Harrison Company needs to estimate the cost of its ending inventory as of the end of November. Sales for the month were $200,000, purchases during November were $75,000, beginning inventory was $95,000, and gross margin was 30% of sales. Using the gross margin method find the dollar amount of the cost of goods sold.

12. The El Guapo Company needs to estimate its ending inventory as of the end of February in order to complete its monthly financial statements. Beginning inventory was $20,000, purchases during February were $24,000, sales for the month were $50,000, and gross margin is 36% of sales. Find the dollar amount of the cost of goods sold using the gross margin method.

13. Find the cost of ending inventory using the information from problem 9.

14. Calculate the ending inventory as of the end of October using the information from problem 10.

15. Calculate the cost of ending inventory using the information from problem 11.

16. Find the ending inventory as of the end of February using the information from problem 12.

EXPRESS YOUR THOUGHTS

Compose one or two well-written sentences to express the requested information in your own words.

1. Give a description of the steps necessary to determine the average cost of a unit remaining in ending inventory.

2. How would you describe the difference between the FIFO and LIFO methods of inventory valuation?

3. How would you go about determining the value of ending inventory using the specific identification method?

4. Explain the basis of the "lower of cost or market" approach to determining the value of ending inventory.

5. Describe the procedure required to estimate the value of ending inventory for the retail method.

6. Explain how you would calculate the cost ratio to estimate the value of ending inventory under the retail method.

7. Assuming that a business has a gross margin of 40% of sales, explain how the margin can be used to estimate the value of ending inventory.

8. Why do businesses estimate the value of their ending inventories?

Case exercise   Esther Millicent Murray Shoe Store

Esther Millicent Murray, the famous fashion designer, has a shoe store carrying only one product: shoes (designed by Esther, of course!). Esther physically counts her inventory only once, at the end of the year. As she acquires items from the warehouse she does not tag or label each item with the cost paid for each item. Therefore, she cannot use the specific identification method to value her ending inventory.

Income Statement for Esther Millicent Murray Shoe Store
(This is not a complete income statement.)

Goods available for sale:

Beginning inventory:	200 pair @ $17 =	$ 3,400
Purchases:		
January 5	180 pair @ $18 =	3,240
March 5	300 pair @ $20 =	6,000
May 5	210 pair @ $21 =	4,410
July 5	215 pair @ $22 =	4,730
September 5	205 pair @ $25 =	5,125
November 5	150 pair @ $27 =	4,050
Total goods available for sale:	1,460	$30,955
Value of ending inventory:		$____?____

units of physical inventory remaining = 405 pair
(determined by physical count)

A. If Ms. Murray wants the value of her ending inventory to be as small as possible, which method should she use? The average cost method? FIFO? LIFO? (Support your answer.)

B. If Esther adds a 90% markup based on cost,

calculate the selling price for each group of shoes acquired during the year.

C. If Esther adds a 90% markup based on the selling price, then determine the selling price for each group of shoes acquired during the year.

SELF-TEST

A. Terminology review

Complete the following items using the key terms presented at the beginning of the chapter. Check your responses against the answer key at the end of the test.

1. Goods that are owned by the business and held for resale are called ___inventory___

2. ___LIFO___ is a method used to value inventory that assumes purchases made during the latter part of the year are sold first.

3. ___FIFO___ is a method used to value· inventory that assumes purchases made during the first part of the year will be sold first.

4. Inventory may be valued at either the cost of the unit or at the current market value—whichever is lower. The name of this rule is ___low of cost or market method___

5. ___special identification___ is a method used to value inventory that assumes each item purchased is identified and labeled with the original cost of the unit.

6. Since continuous inventory systems are not common, most businesses use a ___estimation since continuous___ ___method___ system.

7. The ___retail___ method uses the cost ratio to estimate the value of ending inventory.

8. The ___gress margin___ method employs the percentage of sales revenues to determine cost of goods sold and the estimated value of ending inventory.

B. Calculation review

The following concepts and short problems are designed to test your understanding of the objectives

identified at the beginning of the chapter. Answers are provided at the end of the test.

9. The Better Buy Clothing Store sells men's suits. Use the following information to determine the value of ending inventory using the average cost method.

Purchases:	
January 31	30 @ $220
May 22	60 @ $170
September 4	40 @ $100
Ending inventory:	20 suits

10. Value the ending inventory in exercise 6 using the FIFO method.

11. Value the ending inventory in exercise 6 using the LIFO method.

12. A large department store has just started a stereo department. Determine the value of ending inventory using the specific identification method.

Purchases:		Cost	Market
January 2	Hitachi	$400	$450
February 15	RCA	$780	$750
April 30	Samsung	$600	$625
July 31	SONY	$850	$800
August 23	Fisher	$930	$900

Ending inventory: Hitachi, SONY, and Fisher

13. Apply the rule of lower-of-cost-or-market to determine the value of ending inventory in problem 12.

14. Using the retail method, estimate the value of ending inventory for the month of August based on the following financial information:

	Cost	Retail
Beginning inventory August 1	$ 40,000	$ 54,000
Purchases during August	$ 70,000	$ 94,500
Goods available for sale	$110,000	$148,500
Net sales for August		$ 90,500

15. A company wishes to estimate the cost of its ending inventory, as of the end of October, to prepare financial statements. If sales for the month are $80,000, purchases are $40,000, beginning inventory is $30,000, and the firm's gross margin is 40% of sales, what is the estimated value of ending inventory for the month based on the gross margin-method?

15

INTERPRETATION OF BUSINESS DATA

Key terms

measures of central
  tendency
mean
median
mode
measures of dispersion
range
variance
standard deviation
control chart
bar graph
line graph
circle graph

Learning objectives

1. Explain the use of measures of central tendency.

2. Calculate the mean, weighted mean, median, and mode from a set of ungrouped data.

3. Explain the advantages and the disadvantages of using either the mean, the median, or the mode.

4. Calculate the range, variance, and standard deviation for a given set of data.

5. Construct a control chart given a mean and standard deviation for a set of data.

6. Plot points on a control chart and detect outliers and trends in the data.

7. Construct a bar graph, a line graph, and a circle graph from a given set of data.

(continued)

8. Interpret information from bar, line, and circle graphs.

9. Define the key terms.

INTRODUCTION

Every day we are confronted by masses of data, in our personal lives and as managers at work. What exactly are data? Data are news, knowledge, information, facts, figures, and numbers. Numerical data we encounter every day may take the form of profits, expenses, sales, ages, heights, weights, volumes, temperatures, grades, speeds, sports scores and statistics, train schedules, election results, and so on.

What do we do with all of this data? Before large amounts of numerical data can be analyzed, they need to be organized and put into usable, workable form. One way to accomplish this is to summarize the data; the other method is to graph the data. Both of these methods allow users of the data to make comparisons between the data more easily. Once comparisons are made, then conclusions can be stated. Possible conclusions from different industries might include:

This new motion picture is going to be a big hit this season, according to a poll taken of our viewers.

The Ford Probe will be as successful as the Ford Mustang was, in terms of the number of cars sold.

The stock market will bottom out again in 1994 as it did in 1982.

It is likely that Boris Becker will win more tournaments at Wimbledon than any other tennis player in history; at age 19, he had already won it twice.

In this chapter, several methods used to summarize and graph data will be demonstrated.

15.1   MEASURES OF CENTRAL TENDENCY

When analyzing business data, we often like to know whether the data we collected is "typical" of previous findings. If it is not typical, then we usually wish to know how it differs—is our data greater than or less than what we consider typical?

Learning objective
Explain the use of
measures of central
tendency.

Measures of central tendency are statistical measures used to locate the center or the average of a set of data. Measures of central tendency are used to summarize large sets of data. It is much easier to work with a single number that represents a group than to work with the entire group itself. There are three such measures. These are the mean, the median, and the mode.

MEAN

Learning objective
Calculate the mean,
weighted mean, me-
dian, and mode from
a set of ungrouped
data.

The **mean** is the measure of central tendency we usually think of when we mention the word "average." The mean is easily calculated as follows:

$$\text{mean} = \frac{\text{sum of all values}}{\text{number of values}}$$

Let's use the data from Example 1 to calculate the mean.

Example 1

Garbonzo Crouton was an instructor at a community college in Des Moines, Iowa. Garbonzo wanted to know if he was being underpaid at the college where he worked, so he decided to take a very small sample of other instructors' incomes and then analyze the data. Each instructor he chose had a similar background; that is, each was an instructor of business mathematics at a community college with 7 years of experience. He sampled 13 cities from across the country and chose one instructor from each city. His data looked like this:

Greenville, S. Carolina	$32,750
Duluth, Minnesota	$29,900
Cedar Creek, Utah	$32,750
Lubbock, Texas	$34,200
Anchorage, Alaska	$87,000
Casper, Wyoming	$29,900
Great Falls, Montana	$29,900
Seattle, Washington	$34,200
Marquette, Michigan	$31,500
Pittsburgh, Pennsylvania	$32,750
Bangor, Maine	$29,900
Little Rock, Arkansas	$31,500
Syracuse, New York	$29,900

Calculate the mean of Garbonzo's data.

Solution

To calculate the mean of Garbonzo's data, we must first sum all of the incomes; the result will be the numerator of our formula.

$$
\begin{array}{r}
\$\ 32{,}750 \\
29{,}900 \\
32{,}750 \\
34{,}200 \\
87{,}000 \\
29{,}900 \\
29{,}900 \\
34{,}200 \\
31{,}500 \\
32{,}750 \\
29{,}900 \\
31{,}500 \\
\underline{29{,}900} \\
\$466{,}150
\end{array}
$$

Next, we count the number of incomes Garbonzo has in his set of data; there are 13. This is our denominator.

$$
\frac{\text{sum of all values}}{\text{number of values}} = \frac{\$466{,}150}{13} = \$35{,}857.69
$$

The mean of the incomes is $35,857.69.

How do we interpret our answer of $35,857.69? Remember, the mean is meant to be the average, or the typical value, of all the values. Our mean of $35,857.69 is meant to be the one number that represents the entire set of incomes.

When working with data, we usually refer to a quantity as a *variable* and denote it with a letter such as x, y, or z. It is called a variable because it can assume several different values, in this case, the salaries of the individuals in Garbonzo's study. We use the uppercase Greek letter sigma, Σ, to represent the phrase "sum up"; an x with a bar over it, $\bar{x}$, to represent the "mean"; and n to represent the "number of values." Our formula for mean then can be written:

$$
\text{mean} = \bar{x} = \frac{\Sigma\ x}{n} = \frac{\text{sum of all values}}{\text{number of values}}
$$

If we could choose one value of x to represent all the incomes (all the values of x) in Example 1, it would not be $17,396.15. Nor would we likely choose our mean of $35,857.69 because 12 of the 13 incomes are equal to or less than $34,200 (which is approximately $1,600 less than this mean). Our mean turned out to be greater than most of the incomes because the extremely high income of just one salary, $87,000, was included in the numerator of our formula. If instead we were to exclude the largest income of $87,000 and the smallest of $29,900 from our data and then calculate the mean of the remaining 11 values, our new mean would be

$$\frac{\$349,250}{11} = \$31,750.00$$

This mean is called a *trimmed mean* and may be a better representation of the typical income in the set of incomes.

MEDIAN

Another measure of central tendency is the **median**. The median is the middle value of all the values. The steps for calculating a median are as follows:

Step 1: Arrange the values in sequential order from highest to lowest, or from lowest to highest.

Step 2: Count the number of values (n) plus 1 and divide by 2.

$$\frac{n + 1}{2}$$

Step 3: Using the value calculated from step 2, count down (or up) the array of values, that number of values.

Example 2

Find the median of the data in Example 1.

Solution

Step 1: First, we arrange the incomes in order from highest value to lowest value.

$87,000
34,200
34,200
32,750
32,750
32,750
31,500
31,500
29,900
29,900
29,900
29,900
29,900

Step 2:   Since there are thirteen values of the data, $n = 13$.

$$\frac{n + 1}{2} = \frac{13 + 1}{2} = \frac{14}{2} = 7$$

Note: The number 7 is not the median, it is the *location* of the median.

Step 3:

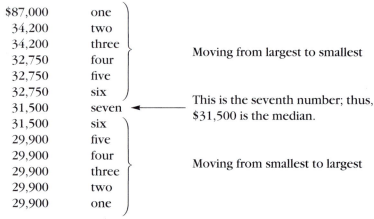

$87,000	one
34,200	two
34,200	three
32,750	four
32,750	five
32,750	six
31,500	seven
31,500	six
29,900	five
29,900	four
29,900	three
29,900	two
29,900	one

Moving from largest to smallest

This is the seventh number; thus, $31,500 is the median.

Moving from smallest to largest

How do we interpret this number? Garbonzo Crouton realizes that half of the incomes are above this number while the other half are below. If Garbonzo's income is above $31,500 then perhaps he is not being underpaid. Generally speaking, $31,500 is a fair or typical number to represent the entire set of incomes.

Suppose we alter Example 1 so that we include Garbonzo's income of $34,200. When we arrange the values and then calculate the median, we find that the median falls between two values.

Step 1:

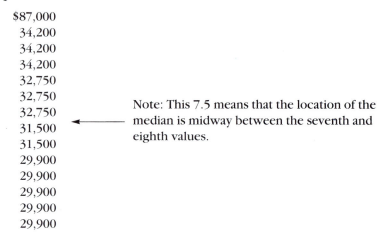

$87,000
34,200
34,200
34,200
32,750
32,750
32,750
31,500
31,500
29,900
29,900
29,900
29,900
29,900

Note: This 7.5 means that the location of the median is midway between the seventh and eighth values.

Step 2:

$$\frac{n + 1}{2} = \frac{14 + 1}{2} = \frac{15}{2} = 7.5$$

Step 3: Since the median falls between two values, we must find the midpoint of these two values as follows:

$$\frac{\$32,750 + \$31,500}{2} = \frac{\$64,250}{2} = \$32,125 = \text{median value}$$

MODE

The **mode** is a third measure of central tendency used to summarize a set of data. The mode is the data value that occurs most frequently. The mode of Example 1 is $29,900. It is possible to have more than one mode or no mode for a set of data. There are two modes in Example 3.

Example 3

Determine the mode of the following set of data: $87,000, $34,200, $34,200, $34,200, $32,750, $32,750, $32,750, $31,500, $31,500.

Solution

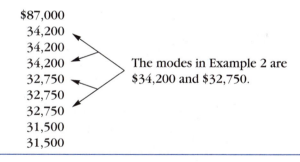

$87,000
34,200
34,200
34,200
32,750
32,750
32,750
31,500
31,500

The modes in Example 2 are
$34,200 and $32,750.

Whenever a set of data has one mode it is called unimodal; two modes is said to be bimodal; and more than two modes is said to be multimodal. The data set in Example 1 is unimodal at $29,900, and in Example 3, is bimodal at $34,200 and $32,750.

Let us review the three measures of central tendency we calculated for the data presented in Example 1:

the mean = $35,857.69
the median = $31,500.00
the mode = $29,900.00

Each of these values has often been referred to as an *average* for the set of incomes. Actually, they each represent a *center* around which the income data is clustered. Notice that even though each is representative of the center of the data, they are quite different from each other. In fact, the overall spread, or range, between the values is $5,957.69.

In the study of any data set, you should look at all three measures, and take care to know what other people mean when they refer to an average.

COMPARISON OF USES OF MEAN, MEDIAN, AND MODE

Learning objective
Explain the advantages and the disadvantages of using either the mean, the median, or the mode.

Under what circumstances would it be best to use the mean, the median, or the mode? The answer lies in what is to be accomplished. For example, suppose the state government created a new policy for personal income taxes where each individual had to pay 40% of the average income among those in their profession. Which average would supply the government with the most money? Referring to the instructors' incomes in Example 1, the mean of $35,857.69 would generate the most money. From the individual taxpayers' point of view, which average would allow them to pay the least? The mode of $29,900 would allow them to pay the least in taxes. Unfortunately, there is no single rule that describes which measure of central tendency is the best to use and when. That is why all three measures are often calculated for a single problem.

WEIGHTED MEAN

At times, large sets of data are broken down into smaller, distinct sets of data. When these smaller sets, or subsets, of data are each a different size or have a different degree of importance, then a *weighted mean* is calculated. Let's use Example 1 to calculate the weighted mean.

We could have summarized the data of Example 1 in a table, called a frequency distribution.

Salary (s)	Frequency (f)
$29,900	5
31,500	2
32,750	3
34,200	2
87,000	1

(*Frequency* merely indicates how often the salary occurs in the data set.) We can calculate the mean, median, and mode from this grouped format as well. To calculate the *mean of a frequency distribution*, we multiply each salary by its corresponding frequency, and then add these subtotals to get a total sum ($466,150) and divide this total by the sum of the frequencies (13).

Example 4

Calculate the mean, median, and mode of the salaries of Example 1 arrayed in a frequency distribution.

Solution

Mean:

Salary (s)	Frequency (f)	Frequency × salary
$29,900	5	$149,500
31,500	2	63,000
32,750	3	98,250
34,200	2	68,400
87,000	1	87,000

$$\Sigma (f \times s) = \$466,150$$

$$\bar{x} = \frac{\Sigma (f \times s)}{n} = \frac{\$466,150}{13} = \$35,857.69$$

Median: The median is obtained by a method similar to our method with the ungrouped data. The number of the median term is $(13 + 1)/2 =$ 7th term. Now count down the frequency column until you reach the seventh term.

Salary (s)	Frequency (f)	
$29,900	5	← 5th term is at $29,900
31,500	2	← 7th term is at $31,500
32,750	3	
34,200	2	
87,000	1	

So the median is $31,500.

Mode: The mode is simply that salary, or salaries, that has the highest frequency. In this example, the mode is $29,900.

CALCULATOR SOLUTION

Keyed entry					Display
AC	29900	×	5	=	Min	149500
	31500	×	2	=	M+	63000
	32750	×	3	=	M+	98250
	34200	×	2	=	M+	68400
	87000	×	1	=	M+	87000
					MR	466150
			÷	13	=	35857.69

The technique for determining the mean in Example 4 is a form of weighted mean. The *weighted mean* is defined to be

$$\text{weighted mean} = \frac{\Sigma \ (\text{value} \times \text{weight})}{\Sigma \ \text{weights}}$$

Example 5

A student's cumulative grade point average at an institution that uses the 4.0 system where quality points are awarded for different grade levels (A = 4.0 quality points, B = 3 quality points, C = 2 quality points, D = 1 quality point and F = 0 quality points) is a weighted mean. Determine the semester cumulative average for Fran Harper if she received the following:

Course	Credits	Grade
Intro to Business	3	A
English Composition	3	B
Physical Science	4	C
Intro to Sociology	3	B
Physical Education	1	A

Solution

The grades carry a numerical value or worth as listed above, but the weighting is based on the number of credits that are assigned to each course.

Course	Credits (weight)	Grade	Quality points (value)	Quality points × credits
Intro to Business	3	A	4	12
English Composition	3	B	3	9
Physical Science	4	C	2	8
Intro to Sociology	3	B	3	9
Physical Education	1	A	4	4
	14			42

$$\text{cumulative average} = \frac{\Sigma \ (\text{quality points} \times \text{credits})}{\Sigma \ \text{credits}} = \frac{42}{14} = 3.0$$

Example 6

An insurance company has different rates for surviving past the age of 70 depending on whether the individual smokes and/or drinks alcoholic beverages. The company's rates indicate an 80% chance of living past age 70 for people who refrain from both drinking alcohol and smoking, a 75% chance for those who refrain from alcohol alone, 55% chance for those who refrain from smoking alone, and a 25% chance for those who both drink alcohol and smoke. The results of interviewing ten individuals follow. Determine the mean, median, and mode.

Solution   *Mean:*

Insurance category	Chance of living past age 70 (value)	Number of people frequency (weight)	Weighted value
Refrain	.80	1	.80
Drink alcohol	.75	2	1.50
Smoke	.55	3	1.65
Smoke and drink alcohol	.25	4	+1.00
		10	4.95

Next, divide the sum of the weighted values by the number of frequencies.

4.95 ÷ 10 = .495, or 49.5% weighted mean

According to the weighted mean, these ten individuals have, on the average, a 49.5% chance of living past the age of 70.

Median: Using the columns we constructed to calculate the weighted mean, the median is calculated as follows:

Step 1:   Arrange the values.

Refrain	.80
Drink alcohol	.75
Smoke	.55
Smoke and drink alcohol	.25

Step 2:

$$\frac{\text{number of frequencies} + 1}{2} = \frac{10 + 1}{2} = 5.5$$

Step 3:   Count down the frequency column until the midpoint of the fifth and sixth values are found.

Category	Values	Frequency	
Refrain	.80	1	These three people are represented by the 5th and 6th values, and since they fall in the category of .55, the median is .55.
Drink alcohol	.75	2	
Smoke	.55	3	
Smoke and drink alcohol	.25	4	

On the average, these ten people have a 55% chance of living past the age of 70.

Mode: To find the mode, look down the frequency column until the highest number of frequencies for any one group of values is found. According to the mode, this group of individuals has a 25% chance of living past the age of 70.

CHECK YOUR KNOWLEDGE

Measures of central tendency

Solve the following problems. Round answers to the nearest tenth.

Ten students received the following test scores on their second business mathematics exam: 10, 10, 27, 33, 27, 22, 27, 33, 99, 22.

1. Determine the mean.
2. Determine the median.
3. Determine the mode.

The accounting manager of Acme Company recorded the number of sick days taken last year by each employee in his department.

Employee	Sick days
Aaron	17
Baker	8
Cohen	9
Delia	6

4. Determine the mean of the sick days.
5. Determine the median of the sick days.
6. Determine the mode of the sick days.
7. A survey was taken asking 12 people how many hours per week they watched television. The following are the results: 5, 7, 8, 30, 7, 5, 5, 7, 7, 7, 30, 5. Find the weighted mean and be sure to show your work.
8. Ten students received the following test scores on their second business mathematics exam: 10, 10, 27, 33, 27, 22, 27, 33, 99, 22. Determine the weighted mean of the scores.

15.1 **EXERCISES**

Solve the following problems. Round answers to the nearest tenth.

1. Each household on Blueberry Lane was asked, How many pets are in your household? The results were: 1, 2, 3, 2, 1, 1, 1, 1, 2, 3, 0, 3, 0, 0, 2, 1, 3. Find the (a) mean number of pets, (b) median number of pets, and (c) mode number of pets.

2. In order to draw up a contract with a leasing company to lease new cars for his sales representatives, Mr. Acme needed to find the average number of miles driven per year. The annual number of miles driven by each sales representative of Acme Company were as follows:

Abrams	18,000
Bartley	21,000
Lions	15,000
Schwinn	20,000
Zikirsky	18,000

Answers to CYK: *1.* 31 *2.* 27 *3.* 27 *4.* 10 *5.* 8.5 *6.* none *7.* 10.3 *8.* 31

Calculate (a) the mean number of miles, (b) the median number of miles, and (c) the mode for the number of miles.

3. The principal of Oakleaf School wished to know the average number of students using the computer lab per day. If the average was greater than 150 students, he would then allocate money to buy more computer terminals. The data for 2 weeks are as follows:

Monday	200	Monday	190
Tuesday	100	Tuesday	130
Wednesday	10	Wednesday	20
Thursday	220	Thursday	210
Friday	200	Friday	220

Calculate (a) the mean number of students who used the lab per day, (b) the median per day, and (c) the mode per day.

4. You are trying to get accepted into the MBA program at Randolph University. Although you are uncertain about the acceptance requirements, last year you knew six seniors from the state college who were accepted into this program. A list of their grade point averages follows:

Joshua	95.0
Gabriel	89.0
David	93.2
Bridgette	99.0
Murray	98.8
Trevor	98.8

You conclude that if your GPA is at least as high as the average GPA of these six individuals, then you are sure to be accepted. Calculate (a) the mean, (b) the median, and (c) the mode, to see if you will be accepted.

5. The president of Sunny Realestate Corporation asks you to sell real estate for him. You will be paid $1,000 per month plus commissions of 5% of the average dollar amount sold per month. While having lunch with one of the employees of Sunny Realestate, you discover the following information:

Employee	Amount sold last month
Rebecca	$10,000,000
Maureen	800,000
Steven	800,000
Leslie	800,000

Calculate (a) the mean, (b) the median, and (c) the mode. (d) Which average (mean, median, or mode) would you like your 5% commission to be based on? Why? (e) Which average would the company president like your 5% commission to be based on? Why?

6. Use the data from exercise 3 to (a) calculate the weighted mean (be sure to show your work!) and (b) find the median using the columns of figures you created.

7. A survey was conducted at State University. All students and faculty were asked how many cups of coffee they drank each day. The results of the survey are as follows:

Number of people	Cups of coffee
600	2
200	1
500	6
400	4
100	5
300	3

Calculate (a) the weighted mean (be sure to show your work!), (b) the median, and (c) the mode. (d) Explain in words your calculation of the weighted mean.

8. Each household on Blueberry Lane was asked, How many pets are in your household? The results are: 1, 2, 3, 2, 1, 1, 1, 1, 2, 3, 0, 3, 0, 0, 2, 1, 3. Calculate (a) the weighted mean and (b) the median using the columns of data you created.

9. Jessie Bell decided to start her own floral shop. Before establishing the prices for her shop, Jessie decided she would look at the prices set by her competitors. Ms. Bell decided she would price a dozen long-stem roses. The following data are the results of her investigation: $60, 70, 75, 60, 45, 60, 70, 70, 45, 75, 75, 75, 45, 45, 60, 60, 60, 70,

70, 70. According to these results, what is the average price of long-stem roses? (Hint: the average price may vary depending on which average is calculated.)

10. Edward Blight wished to open a limousine service in Huntwood, Rhode Island. After having done preliminary research, Edward discovered that a community's average yearly income must be at least $1,000,000 in order to support a limousine service. The following are the incomes of those individuals presently residing at Huntwood:

Annual income	Number of individuals
$2,000,000	400
500,000	600

Should Edward open his limousine service in Huntwood?

15.2 MEASURES OF SPREAD OF DATA

The measures of central tendency indicate where the data are centered. Another concern we have with the interpretation of data is the spread of the data. How are the data grouped around the center, or centers? What is the overall spread of the data? Is it grouped together somewhat tightly around the center of the data, or is it spread out widely from the center? The spread of the data can be very helpful to us when we are trying to maintain some form of control over a variable or process. Knowing the dispersion (spread) of the data is every bit as important as knowing where its centers are located.

Learning objective
Calculate the range, variance, and standard deviation for a given set of data.

RANGE

The simplest measure of spread of data is known as the range. The **range** of a set of data is defined to be the difference between the largest and the smallest values.

Formula for range

range = largest value − smallest value

Example 7

Consider the following data for tips received by a waiter during the 2-hour lunch period at Chez Paris Restaurant in downtown Syracuse: $2.20, 4.75, 1.00, .75, 5.50, 2.40, 3.20, 4.75, 4.75, 6.00, 3.50, 3.50, 5.50. Determine the mean, median, mode, and range of the tip values.

Solution

The mean of this data is $3.68: $47.80 ÷ 13 = 3.6769.

If we rearrange the data in ascending order we can see the maximum tip, the minimum tip, and the median tip:

$.75, 1.00, 2.20, 2.40, 3.20, 3.50, 3.50, 4.75, 4.75, 4.75, 5.50, 5.50, 6.00

We now can see easily that the maximum tip received was $6.00 and the minimum tip was $.75. The median of the tip data is $3.50, and the mode of the data is $4.75. The *range* of the data is:

$$\text{range} = \text{maximum} - \text{minimum}$$
$$= \$6.00 - \$.75$$
$$= \$5.25$$

We can form a graphical arrangement of the data in Example 7 as in Figure 15.1. Notice that the data are spread out from $.75 to $6.00, and that although the data does group around the centers at $3.50, $3.68, and $4.75, it has a wide range of $5.25. We would like to have a measure that would not only describe the overall spread of the data but that would also describe the spread within the distribution. The measures of *variance* and *standard deviation* will provide us with such a description.

VARIANCE AND STANDARD DEVIATION

Variance is a form of an average based on the squared differences of each data value with the distribution's mean:

$$\text{variance} = \frac{\Sigma \, (x - \bar{x})^2}{n - 1}$$

A shorter and easier form of this formula is called the *computational form of variance*:

$$\text{variance} = \frac{\Sigma \, x^2 - \dfrac{(\Sigma \, x)^2}{n}}{n - 1}$$

Figure 15.1

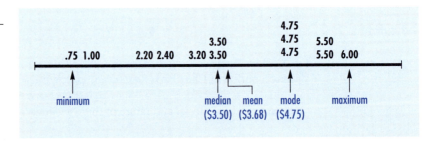

The **standard deviation** is simply the square root of variance.

standard deviation $= \sqrt{\text{variance}}$

Example 8

Solution

Determine the mean, variance, and standard deviation for the following set of data: 3, 5, 6, 7, 9.

Step 1:   List the data in a column, and sum up the column:

$$\begin{array}{r} 3 \\ 5 \\ 6 \\ 7 \\ \underline{9} \\ 30 \end{array} \qquad \bar{x} = \frac{\Sigma x}{n} = \frac{30}{5} = 6$$

Step 2:   Make a second column next to the first, and square each piece of the data:

x	x^2
3	9
5	25
6	36
7	49
9	81

sum of data $(\Sigma\ x) = 30$ sum of squared data $(\Sigma\ x^2) = 200$

Step 3:   Enter the sums above into the formula and calculate the variance:

$$\text{variance} = \frac{\Sigma\ x^2 - \dfrac{(\Sigma\ x)^2}{n}}{n - 1}$$

$$= \frac{200 - (30)^2/5}{4}$$

$$= \frac{200 - (900/5)}{4}$$

$$= \frac{200 - 180}{4}$$

$$= \frac{20}{4}$$

$$= 5$$

standard deviation $= \sqrt{\text{variance}} = \sqrt{5} = 2.236$

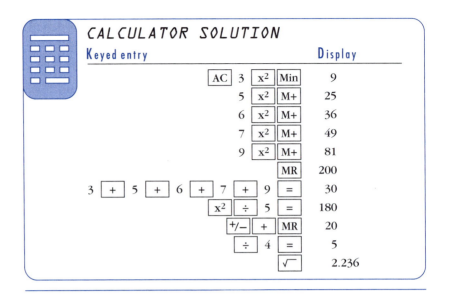

Variance is symbolized s^2, and standard deviation is s. So, in Example 8, $s^2 = 5$ and $s = 2.236$.

Let's consider another example that will show how the standard deviation can be helpful in describing the spread of a distribution.

Example 9

Consider the following three sets of data (values ranging from 1 to 9) with their mean, median, mode, and range.

Data set I:

```
                        5
                  4     5     6
            3     4     5     6     7
      1     2     3     4     5     6     7     8     9
```

mean = 90/18 = 5
median = 5
mode = 5
range = 9 − 1 = 8

Data set II:

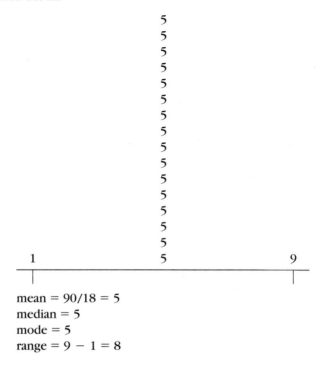

mean = 90/18 = 5
median = 5
mode = 5
range = 9 − 1 = 8

Data set III:

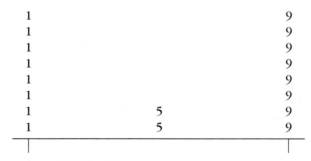

mean = 90/18 = 5
median = 5
mode: bimodal, one at 1 and one at 9
range = 9 − 1 = 8

If we did not have the graphs to look at, and only had the numerical summary measures (mean, median, mode, and range), the first two distributions might seem to be the same, and only the mode would tip us off that the third data set is different from the first two sets. But we can see that all three data sets are significantly different. Determine the variance and standard deviation for each of the data sets:

Solution

Data set I		Data set II		Data set III	
x	x^2	x	x^2	x	x^2
1	1	1	1	1	1
2	4	5	25	1	1
3	9	5	25	1	1
3	9	5	25	1	1
4	16	5	25	1	1
4	16	5	25	1	1
4	16	5	25	1	1
5	25	5	25	1	1
5	25	5	25	5	25
5	25	5	25	5	25
5	25	5	25	9	81
6	36	5	25	9	81
6	36	5	25	9	81
6	36	5	25	9	81
7	49	5	25	9	81
7	49	5	25	9	81
8	64	5	25	9	81
9	81	9	81	9	81
90	522	90	482	90	706
Σx	Σx^2	Σx	Σx^2	Σx	Σx^2

$$s^2 = \text{variance} = \frac{\Sigma x^2 - \dfrac{(\Sigma x)^2}{n}}{n - 1}$$

Data set I:

$$\text{variance of } s^2 = \frac{522 - (90)^2/18}{17} = 4.24$$

$$\text{standard deviation} = s = \sqrt{4.20} = 2.06$$

Data set II:

$$\text{variance of } s^2 = \frac{482 - (90)^2/18}{17} = 1.88$$

$$\text{standard deviation} = s = \sqrt{1.88} = 1.37$$

Data set III:

$$\text{variance of } s^2 = \frac{706 - (90)^2/18}{17} = 15.06$$

$$\text{standard deviation} = s = \sqrt{15.05} = 3.88$$

The largest standard deviation, $s = 3.88$, tells us that the data of the third data set is spread furthest from its center of 5, and the smallest standard deviation, $s = 1.37$, tells us that the data of the second data set is closest to its center of 5.

Quite often, distributions are shaped like data set I, in a mound-like, somewhat symmetrical shape; then we can mentally estimate what our standard deviation should be. Generally, the standard deviation should be equal to about ¼ of the range. So we could expect that the standard deviation for a distribution with a range of 8 to be about 2. When our actual calculation is close to this estimate we would expect our computation to be correct and that the shape of the data would be similar to that of data set I. If our actual calculation is substantially different, such as with data set III, we might want to double check our calculations. If the calculations are correct, then we would want to make a closer inspection of the data and note any special characteristics such as the fact that the data is located at the outer extremities of the distribution as in data set III.

CHECK YOUR KNOWLEDGE

Measures of spread of data

Solve the following problems. Round answers to the nearest hundredth.

1.   Calculate the mean, range, variance, and standard deviation for: 3, 6, 7, 7, 2.

2.   Given the set of data: 2, 6, 8, 9, 11, 12, (a) determine the range, (b) estimate the standard deviation by using ¼ of the range, and (c) compute the standard deviation using the formula for s.

3.   Determine the mean, median, mode, range, and standard deviation for the following set of data: 2, 3, 3, 5, 5, 5, 6, 6, 7, 8.

4.   WBXL radio station decided to investigate the cost of unleaded gasoline in its hometown of Beeville. Staff went to the eight self-serve gas stations in town and priced 87-octane unleaded gas at the pump. Their results follow. Determine the mean, median, maximum, minimum, range, and standard deviation of the cost of 87-octane gas on the day of the survey.

Cost per gallon, c	c^2
1.43	_____
1.28	_____
1.55	_____
1.37	_____
1.35	_____
1.33	_____
1.36	_____
1.33	_____

5. Calculate the variance and standard deviation for the tip data in Example 4.

Tip, t	t^2
$ .75	_____
1.00	_____
2.20	_____
2.40	_____
3.20	_____
3.50	_____
3.50	_____
4.75	_____
4.75	_____
5.50	_____
5.50	_____
5.50	_____
6.00	_____

15.2 EXERCISES

Solve the following exercises. Round answers to the nearest hundredth.

1. Calculate the mean, range, variance, and standard deviation for: 7, 4, 9, 11, 13, 17, 21, 14.

2. Calculate the mean, range, variance, and standard deviation for: −3, 5, −7, 4, −6, 2, 5, 11, 7.

3. Calculate the mean, range, variance, and standard deviation for: 20, 21, 25, 29, 30.

4. Given the set of data: 5, 6, 7, 7, 8, 8, 8, 9, 9, 10, 11, (a) determine the range of the data,

Answers to CYK: **1.** mean = 5; range = 5; variance = 5.50; standard deviation = 2.35   **2.** a. 10; b. 2.5; c. 3.63   **3.** mean = 5; median = 5; mode = 5; range = 6; standard deviation = 1.89   **4.** mean = $1.38; median = $1.36; mode = $1.33; max = $1.55; min = $1.28; range = $.27; standard deviation = $.08   **5.** variance = s^2 = 3.12; standard deviation = $1.77

(b) estimate the standard deviation by using ¼ of the range, (c) compute the standard deviation. (d) Was the estimate close to the standard deviation value? If not, then why not?

5. Given the set of data: 1, 7, 1, 7, 1, 7, 1, 7, 1, 7, 1, 7, (a) determine the range of the data, (b) estimate the standard deviation by using ¼ of the range, (c) compute the standard deviation. (d) Was the estimate close to the standard deviation value? If not, then why not?

6. Given the set of data: 12, 17, 17, 17, 17, 17, 17, 17, 22, (a) determine the range of the data, (b) estimate the standard deviation by using ¼ of the range, (c) compute the standard deviation. (d) Was the estimate close to the standard deviation value? If not, then why not?

Use the following information to complete exercises 7 through 11. Janet Dahl works for a regional power company that employs over 1,000 people. Jan is one of 100 supervisors who perform similar work and whose jobs are classified at the same level for compensation purposes. Jan felt that male supervisors were paid more than female supervisors. To check her suspicions, she took a random sample of five men's salaries and a second sample of five women's salaries.

Men's salaries (1000s of dollars)	Women's salaries (1000s of dollars)
29	30
26	28
31	24
35	22
27	26

7. Determine the mean and median of the men's salaries.

8. Determine the mean and median of the women's salaries.

9. Determine the range and standard deviation of the men's salaries.

10. Determine the range and standard deviation of the women's salaries.

11. Do you believe Jan has a legitimate complaint based on the data?

Use the following data to complete exercises 12 through 14. Speedy's Pizza delivery service has eight delivery persons. The mileage for each driver on a given day is: 32, 50, 24, 45, 56, 71, 100, 30.

12. Determine the mean of the miles driven for that day.

13. Determine the range of the mileages.

14. Determine the variance and standard deviation.

Use the following information to complete exercises 15 through 20. Elbridge Public Library wanted to determine the use of its computer software during weekends in the fall (September through November) and the spring (April through June). The number of times software was checked out for a weekend in either season follows.

Fall checkouts	Spring checkouts
11	13
9	15
6	12
13	16
10	10
8	16
12	9
11	13
12	15
11	8
8	14
12	15

15. Determine the mean use during the fall.

16. Determine the mean use during the spring.

17. Determine the range of use during the fall.

18. Determine the range of use during the spring.

19. Determine the standard deviation of the use in the fall.

20. Determine the standard deviation of the use in the spring.

15.3   CONTROL CHARTS: AN APPLICATION OF MEAN AND STANDARD DEVIATION

Learning objective

Construct a control chart given a mean and standard deviation for a set of data.

Learning objective

Plot points on a control chart and detect outliers and trends in the data.

Control charts are graphs that are constructed from statistical data collected from a business or manufacturing process. As the process goes on, new data is collected and plotted on the graph to determine if the process is *in control*. We will use the following illustration to demonstrate how control charts can be used in business.

JoAnna Jacobi owns and manages five pizza shops (called JoAnna's Pizza Shoppes) in five shopping malls in her metropolitan area. Some of the shops are in urban malls and some are in suburban malls, and the amount of business transacted by each varies. JoAnna has decided through the study of past receipts from the five shops that the average weekly receipts for the five shops is $10,500 per week and that the standard deviation of the receipts is $1,500. JoAnna realizes that the average weekly receipts will vary from week to week depending on the seasons of the year, weather conditions, and so on. She has determined, however, that 95% of the time, the average weekly receipts of the five shops will be within two standard deviations of the mean. JoAnna has made herself a chart similar to the one in Figure 15.2 that she uses to plot the average receipts of the five shops weekly.

JoAnna can analyze the chart and know quite a bit about her five store operations. She expects each plotted value to fall within two standard deviations of the mean value of weekly receipts. That is, the average of the receipts of the five stores each week should fall between $10,500 + (2 × $1,500) = $13,500 and $10,500 − (2 × $1,500) = $7,500. If the weekly average does fall between $7,500 and $13,500, then JoAnna feels that her

Figure 15.2

Control chart

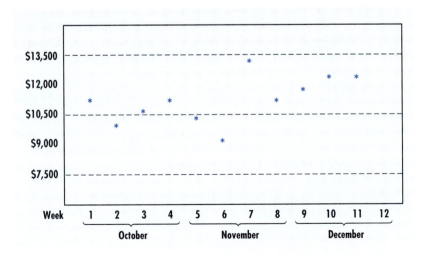

business is *in control*. JoAnna expects the plotted weekly values to randomly fall above or below the mean line as the weeks go by. She is concerned when a particularly high or low value occurs, such as during the third week of November when average receipts went up to $13,000. She might have wondered why such an unusual value occurred, and then have decided that since Thanksgiving occurred during that week there simply were many more shoppers in the malls, which resulted in increased sales of pizza. She also might have taken note of the fact that, during the month of December, each weekly average was above the mean line and got even higher each week of the month. This could have indicated a trend in business that could have affected how she manages the business and plans for the future. However, she also may have decided that receipts were up during those weeks due to the increased number of people in the malls prior to a holiday, and to the fact that, when students are on vacation, they spend more time and money at malls. Control charts such as these can be maintained for other aspects of JoAnna's business as well. They can be kept from year to year to provide visual comparisons that can indicate seasonal trends as well as how well the business is doing in any given year compared to a previous year.

The use of these control charts in business and industry is not a new concept. We have provided you with a very basic introduction to the control chart concept, but there is much more to know to properly set up charts and analyze them. If you are interested in further study you may wish to enroll in a course in statistics and eventually study *statistical process control*.

CHECK YOUR KNOWLEDGE

Control charts

The following are the average miles per gallon computed on a fleet of automobiles owned by a local automobile rental company.

Week	Average miles
1	24
2	22
3	23
4	19
5	30
6	16
7	8
8	15
9	24
10	26
11	28
12	30

1.   Plot the mileages on the control chart below.

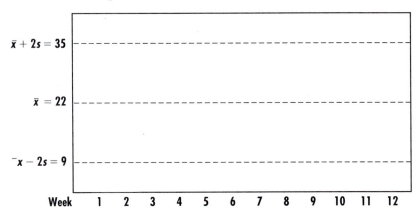

2.   Are any points out of control (that is, outside the lines for $\bar{x} + 2s$ and $\bar{x} - 2s$)?

3.   Which weeks indicate a possible trend?

Answers to CYK: *1.*

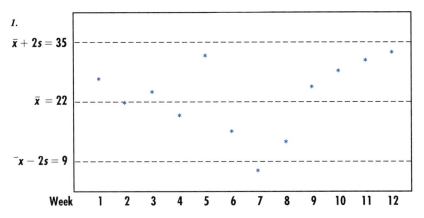

2.   Yes, at week number 7.   *3.*   Weeks 7 through 12 indicate an increasing trend.

15.3   EXERCISES

The following data represent the average daily number of workers absent during the week due to illness.

Week	Average daily absence
1	2
2	1
3	3
4	4
5	5
6	1
7	2
8	3
9	4
10	5

1. Determine the mean.
2. Determine the standard deviation.
3. Draw the mean line and control lines on the chart below.
4. Plot the data on the control chart.
5. Are any points out of control?
6. Are there any trends?

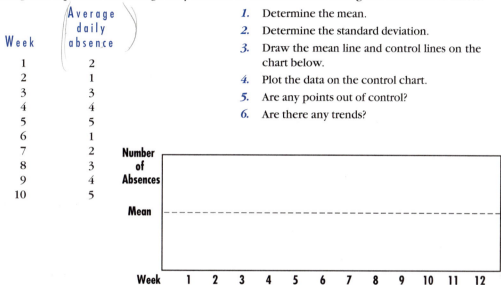

The following data represent the average daily number of students absent during the week due to the flu.

Week	Average daily absence
1	7
2	9
3	8
4	6
5	5
6	12
7	9
8	8
9	7
10	6
11	5
12	8

7. Determine the mean.
8. Determine the standard deviation.
9. Draw the mean line and control lines on the chart on page 614.
10. Plot the data on the control chart on page 614.
11. Are any points out of control?
12. Are there any trends?

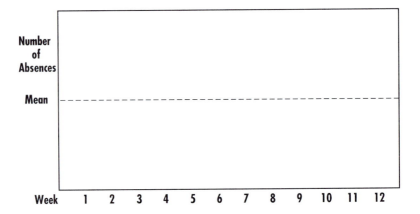

15.4 INTERPRETING BUSINESS DATA THROUGH THE USE OF GRAPHS

You saw in Section 15.1 that the mean, the median, and the mode are useful tools for summarizing data and for finding out if data are *typical* compared with that of the *average*. Graphs are also used for comparison purposes. A single graph can show relationships among dozens of variables. Graphs are pictorial representations of data that help a reader to interpret the data; they may help us visualize, for example, the following:

Profits have risen steadily over the past 10 years.

The rate of inflation has decreased by 2% each year since 1988.

Product Z needs to increase its market share by 11% if it wishes to remain competitive.

In this section, we describe three types of graphs:

1. the bar graph

2. the line graph

3. the circle graph.

Each type of graph will be developed from the data in Table 15.1, which displays the expenses of three different departments in a store for the years 1990 through 1993.

Learning objective
Construct a bar graph, a line graph, and a circle graph from a given set of data.

BAR GRAPHS

Bar graphs are often used to represent data at a single point in time (for example, a day, month, or year). If several time frames are included, the graph could be depicting data for a single company, a single department,

Table 15.1

Data for developing example graphs

Year	Wallpaper department	Paint department	Hardware department	Total expenses
1990	$1,000	$9,000	$7,000	$17,000
1991	2,000	7,000	8,000	17,000
1992	3,000	4,000	3,000	10,000
1993	4,000	2,000	5,000	11,000

or a single product over the course of time. Amounts or units of data are represented by either vertical bars or horizontal bars that correspond in height or length to increments marked on a set of *axes* (see Figure 15.3).

Example 10

Draw a vertical bar graph of the expenses that occurred in 1990 (see Table 15.1).

Solution

Step 1:   Draw a set of axes using graph paper.

Step 2:   Label the dollar increments on the vertical axis, making sure that a uniform amount is represented by a uniform distance (i.e., each $10 increment is represented by one square on the graph paper), and label the horizontal axis with the 3 departments.

Step 3:   For the wallpaper department, draw a vertical bar from the horizontal axis up to the line that represents $1,000. Draw a bar up to the line that represents $9,000 for the paint department and then another bar up to the line that represents $7,000 for the hardware department. (Fig-

Figure 15.3

Setup of a bar or line graph

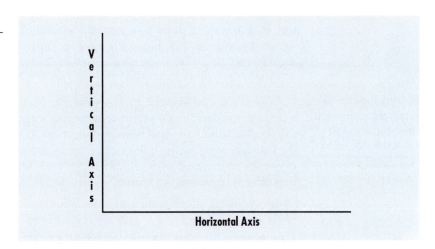

Figure 15.4

Illustration of
Example 10

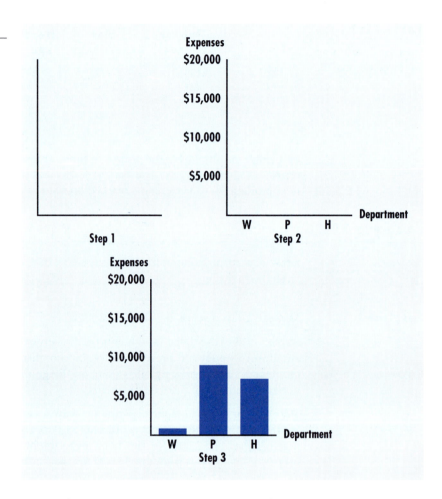

ure 15.4 illustrates steps 1–3.) Now you should be able to see clearly which department is spending the most on expenses and which is spending the least.

Learning objective
Interpret information
from bar, line, and
circle graphs.

Given the data in Table 15.1, it would be useful for a manager to find a trend in the data. If one of the departments' expenses had been increasing steadily while sales had remained the same, it would be important for the manager to be aware of this circumstance and to begin to either reduce expenses or increase sales. Figure 15.5 shows separate graphs for each department (covering the span of 4 years) to see if a trend is apparent.

LINE GRAPHS

Line graphs, like bar graphs, are used for comparison purposes and to detect changes and spot trends easily. Line graphs use the same axis frame-

Figure 15.5

Graphs of department expenses, 1990–1993

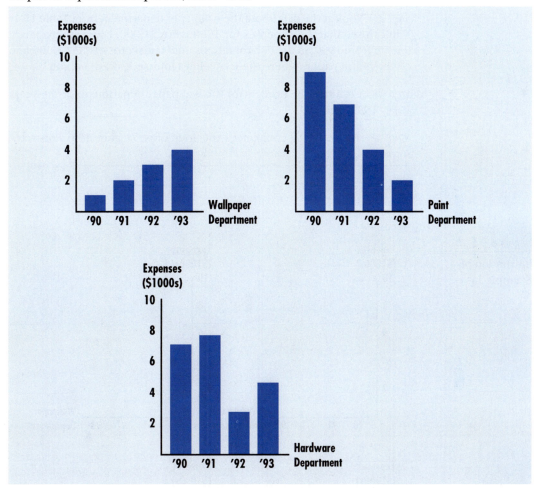

work as bar graphs, but instead of drawing bars, points are plotted corresponding to the increments marked on the axes, and then those points are connected by a line from one to the next.

Example 11

Construct a line graph of the wallpaper department data for the years 1990–1993.

Solution

Step 1: Begin the same way you would for a bar graph, by drawing a set of axes, then labeling both the verticle axis and the horizontal axis.

Step 2: Look at the data about the wallpaper department from Table 15.1. You can see that the expenses for 1990 were $1,000. Draw an imaginary line up from 1990 on the horizontal axis until it just crosses the $1,000 line on the graph paper. Where these two lines intersect, draw a point.

Step 3: Continue the process for the wallpaper department for the years 1991, 1992, and 1993.

Step 4: Draw a line connecting the four dots. (Figure 15.6 illustrates steps 1–4.)

Figure 15.6

Illustration of Example 11

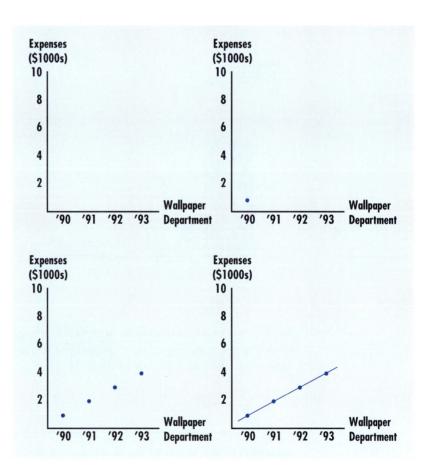

Figure 15.7

Illustration of
Example 12

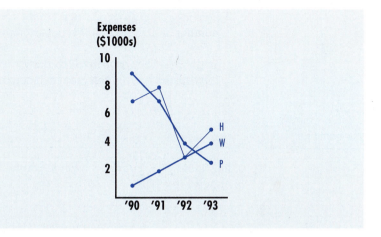

From the Figure 15.6 line graph, you can clearly see the steady increase in expenses for the wallpaper department. But, how do these expenses compare with those in the paint and hardware departments? To
answer this question, we will graph all three departments on one set
of axes.

Example 12

Use line graphs to compare all three departments listed in Table 15.1.

Solution

Figure 15.7 is a composite line graph of the expenses for the three departments. You can see that as the expenses of the wallpaper department have
increased, the expenses of both the paint and hardware departments have
decreased since 1990. Note that the expenses of all three departments are
within $1,000 of each other during 1992. Perhaps the paint department
should be commended for its steady decrease in expenses!

CIRCLE GRAPHS

Circle graphs are used to show the proportion or the percentage of each
part as it relates to the whole. For example, a dime represents 10% of a
dollar; the dime is the portion and the dollar is the whole. Circle graphs
are constructed using a 360° circle rather than a set of axes. The four steps
needed to construct a circle graph are as follows:

Step 1:   Sum the departments' expenses.

Step 2:   Divide each department's expenses by the total expenses.
This will,give you a percentage (in decimal form) of the total expenses
for each department.

Step 3:   Multiply each percentage by 360°. This will give you the number of degrees that this department represents on the circle.

Step 4:   Use a *protractor* to draw the various degrees. The sum of the degrees (in this case, for each department) should total 360°.

Example 13

Using Table 15.1, construct a circle graph of the expenses of all three departments in 1990.

Solution

Steps 1 - 3:   Create a table of the data (Table 15.2).

Step 4:   Using the information in the degrees for department column of Table 15.2, create a circle graph, as shown in Figure 15.8.

Table 15.2

Data table for Example 13

Department	Department expenses	÷	Total expenses	=	Percent	×	Total degrees	=	Degrees for department
Wallpaper	$1,000	÷	$17,000	=	.059	×	360°	=	21°
Paint	9,000		17,000		.529		360°		191°
Hardware	7,000		17,000		.412		360°		148°

Figure 15.8

Circle graph for Example 13

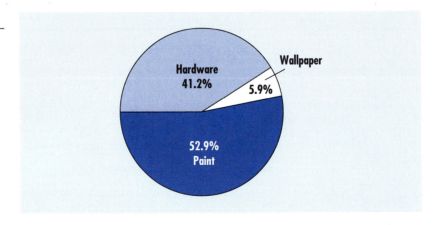

For Your Information

Who stokes the market?

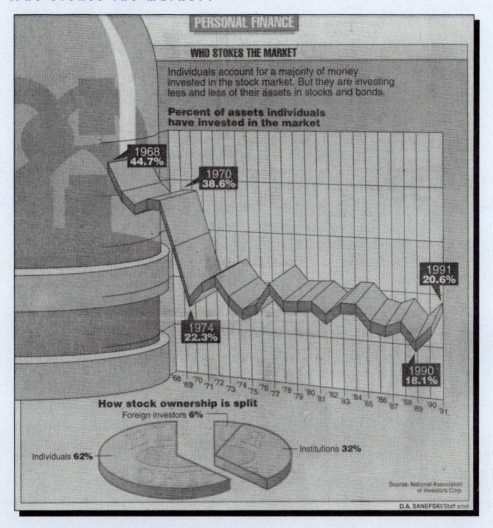

PERSONAL FINANCE

WHO STOKES THE MARKET

Individuals account for a majority of money invested in the stock market. But they are investing less and less of their assets in stocks and bonds.

Percent of assets individuals have invested in the market

1968 44.7%

1970 38.6%

1991 20.6%

1974 22.3%

1990 18.1%

'68 '69 '70 '71 '72 '73 '74 '75 '76 '77 '78 '79 '80 '81 '82 '83 '84 '85 '86 '87 '88 '89 '90 '91

How stock ownership is split

Foreign investors 6%

Individuals 62%

Institutions 32%

Source: National Association of Investors Corp.

D.A. SANEFSKI/Staff artist

The accompanying pictograph shows an enhanced line graph and an enhanced circle graph. These enhancements provide an eye-catching three-dimensional appearance. They also provide a quick means of providing information such as "How stock ownership is split" (circle graph), and "Percent of assets individuals have invested in the market" (line graph). The line graph shows a substantial decrease in percentage between 1970 and 1974, and a slight downward trend from 1974 to 1990. The increase in 1991 could suggest the beginning of an upward trend for the future.

Source: Data from the National Association of Investors Corporation; D. A. Sanefski, Syracuse *Herald Journal* staff artist.

Figure 15.9

Common abuses of graphical representations

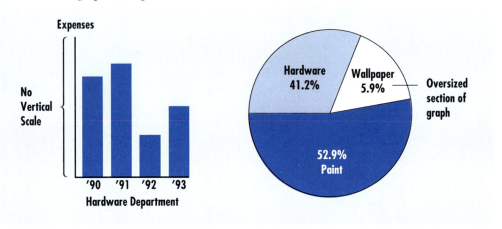

Graphical presentations can provide quick and easy visual analyses of data; however, graphs can also misrepresent data. Common abuses of graphical representations include the failure to label the axes of a graph, or misrepresenting parts of a graph by using improper sizes or proportions (Figure 15.9).

CHECK YOUR KNOWLEDGE

B a r   g r a p h s ,   l i n e   g r a p h s ,   a n d   c i r c l e   g r a p h s

1. Use the data in Table 15.1 to draw a vertical bar graph of all expenses that occurred during 1992.

2. Use the data in Table 15.1 to draw a horizontal bar graph of all expenses that occurred during 1992.

3. Use the data in Table 15.1 to draw a line graph of all three departments' expenses during 1993.

4. Use the data in Table 15.1 to draw a line graph of the total expenses from the years 1990 through 1993.

5. Use the data in Table 15.1 to set up a table for 1992 similar to Table 15.2.

6. Use the information calculated from problem 1 to draw a circle graph.

Answers to CYK: **1.**

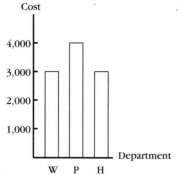

2.

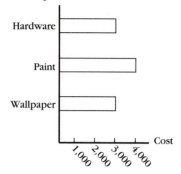

3.

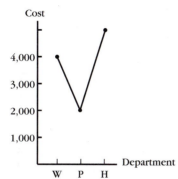

4.

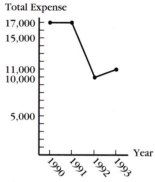

5.

Department	Expenses	Percent	Degree
Wallpaper	$3,000 ÷ $10,000 = .30	× 360°	= 108°
Paint	4,000 ÷ 10,000 = .40	× 360°	= 144°
Hardware	3,000 ÷ 10,000 = .30	× 360°	= 108°

6.

15.4 EXERCISES

Use the information below to complete problems 1 through 10.

JCN Corporation sells three different kinds of products: computers, small office equipment (such as adding machines and typewriters), and office furniture. The president of JCN claims that total profits have decreased by 24% since 1991. He is concerned that he may have to eliminate one of the products in order to maintain profits.

Year	Computers	Office equipment	Furniture	Total profit
1988	$100,000	$600,000	$300,000	$1,000,000
1989	150,000	575,000	500,000	1,225,000
1990	150,000	550,000	800,000	1,500,000
1991	300,000	475,000	800,000	1,575,000
1992	375,000	440,000	500,000	1,315,000
1993	450,000	420,000	300,000	1,170,000
1994	600,000	400,000	200,000	1,200,000

In order to help the president get a clear picture of the situation, complete the following.

1. Draw a vertical bar graph for the company from 1988 through 1994 showing profits on computers.

2. Draw a vertical bar graph for the company from 1988 through 1994 showing profits on equipment.

3. Draw a vertical bar graph for the company from 1988 through 1994 showing profits on furniture.

4. Draw a line graph that indicates the profits from computer products from 1988 to 1994.

5. Draw a line graph that indicates the profits from office equipment from 1988 to 1994.

6. Draw a line graph that indicates the profits from furniture from 1988 to 1994.

7. Draw a composite line graph that shows the profits from all three types of product from 1988 to 1994 on the same set of axes.

8. Draw a circle graph showing each product as a percentage of the total profit for 1988.

9. Draw a circle graph showing each product as a percentage of the total profit for 1990.

10. Draw a circle graph showing each product as a percentage of the total profit for 1992.

EXPRESS YOUR THOUGHTS

Compose one or two well-written sentences to express the requested information in your own words.

1. What does a measure of central tendency describe about a set of data?
2. Describe how you would calculate the mean of a set of data.
3. Explain how you determine the range of a set of data.
4. What is the mode of a set of data?
5. Explain how you determine the range of a set of data.
6. What is the relationship between variance and standard deviation?
7. Explain how you would determine the number of degrees in the three

areas of a circle graph representing 25%, 20%, and 55% of total revenues for a company.

8. Describe how you would build a bar graph representing revenue from departments A, B, and C, and their corresponding percentages of 25%, 20%, and 55% of total revenues.

Case exercise   Analyzing employment test data

R.C. Droid has developed a new computer. He calls it the Droid computer. R.C. has virtually every aspect of his new company well under way except for his sales force; R.C. has not yet hired any salespeople to sell the Droid computer. Mr. Droid believes that any person with a high degree of intelligence (not necessarily high grades) can be trained to sell his computer. Thus, Mr. Droid administered an I.Q. test to three groups of applicants: accounting majors, English literature majors, and electrical engineering majors. The following data are the results of the test:

Number in group	Accounting score	Number in group	English score	Number in group	Engineering score
20	165	30	160	30	160
30	160	90	10	20	150
30	150			30	155
20	155			40	165

A. Which of the groups had the highest mean test score?

B. What is the average test score for the entire group of applicants?

C. Which average (mean. median, or mode) *best* describes this set of applicants? Why?

D. Draw a vertical bar graph showing the mean I.Q. from each major.

SELF-TEST

A. Terminology review

Complete the following items using the key terms presented at the beginning of the chapter. Check your responses against the answer key at the end of the test.

1. Statistical measures used to locate the center or the average of a set of data are called _____.

2. The _____ is a measure of central tendency describing the value that occurs most frequently.

3. The _____ is a measure of central tendency describing the middle value or the midpoint of a group of values.

4. The _____ is a measure of central tendency in which the sum of all values is divided by the number of values.

5. Measures that indicate the spread of data are called measures of _____.

6. The measure that is the square root of the variance is called _____ _____.

B. Calculation review

The following concepts and short problems are designed to test your understanding of the objectives identified at the beginning of the chapter. Answers are provided at the end of the test. Round answers to the nearest hundredth.

7. Calculate the mean for these values: 1,000, 50, 50, 50, 50, 50, 50, 50, 50, 50.

8. Calculate the median for the values in problem 7.

9. What is the mode for the values in problem 7.

10. Look at your answers from problems 7 and 8; which answer best represents the group of values as a whole? Explain why.

11. Determine the range of the data in problem 7.

12. Determine the variance and standard deviation of the data in problem 7.

13. During the month of May, you made 30 phone calls from 8 A.M. to 5 P.M.; you made 50 phone calls from 5 P.M. to 8 A.M.; and you made 15 phone calls during the weekends. Find the average cost of a phone call by calculating the weighted mean. Use the following telephone rates:

8 A.M. to 5 P.M. weekdays: $.60 per phone call

5 P.M. to 8 A.M. weekdays: $.45 per phone call

Weekends: $.15 per phone call

14. Find the average cost of a phone call by calculating the median. Use the telephone rates from problem 13.

15. List the mode cost from problem 13.

16. Monthly revenues for the Paradise Health Club are listed below. Draw a line graph of this information.

April	$6,000
May	$7,300
June	$7,100

17. Draw a vertical bar graph of the revenues from problem 16.

18. Draw a circle graph of the revenues from problem 16.

Answers to self-test: **1.** measures of central tendency **2.** mode **3.** median **4.** mean **5.** dispersion **6.** standard deviation **7.** 145 **8.** 50 **9.** 50 **10.** 50 **11.** 950 **12.** 300.42 **13.** $.45 per call **14.** $.45 **15.** $.45

16.

17.

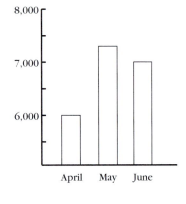

18.

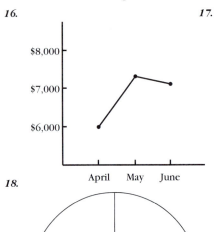

16

RISK MANAGEMENT

Learning objectives

1. Calculate a simple probability.

2. Calculate a probability from a mortality table.

3. Calculate a premium for term, ordinary life, decreasing term, limited pay life, and endowment life insurance.

4. Calculate the cash surrender value of an insurance policy.

5. Calculate the premium for a fire insurance policy.

6. Calculate the amount of claim covered using the coinsurance clause.

7. Calculate liability insurance coverage of an automobile.

8. Define the key terms.

INTRODUCTION

We live in a world of *uncertainty*. As much as we might like to think that we have control of the world around us, that is only true in a very limited sense.

The mathematics of business does provide a mathematical model of **certainty**. Most business transactions have been conceived using pure mathematics. The concepts of simple interest, simple discounts, compound interest, and annuities were all conceived by applying algebra to business concepts in a very logical manner.

We know that if we invest $1,000 at 10% interest compounded quarterly for 8 years, it will have a value of $2,203.76 at the end of the 8-year term. This is one example of many considered in this text that clearly involve certainty.

While it is true that business, unlike the natural sciences, does provide us with a true example of the mathematics of certainty, there are many aspects of the business field that are fraught with uncertainty. How do we deal with the uncertainties that surround us? Is there any way to add some order or control to these uncertainties? Is there an area of mathematics that helps us to deal with uncertainty? How do we confront, control, and cope with the risks that are ever present as a result of that uncertainty?

RISK

Personal risk   Many decisions we make every day involve risk due to uncertainty. The route we choose to travel in an automobile on any given day can result in an accident, or in delays that make us late for an appointment. Decisions we elect can result in damage to our self-image or the images others have of us.

Some decisions we make, however, directly affect our financial condition, both present and future. In this chapter, we will confine our concern for risk management to financial risks.

Business risk   Whenever we are involved in a business venture, the success or failure of that venture is measured in terms of financial gain or loss. Although, in business, we do encounter some degree of personal risk, we clearly regard risk in the business world to mean *risks of financial loss incurred by uncertainty*.

Definition of risk   We shall regard the definition of *risk* for both personal risk and business risk as *the uncertainty of financial loss*.* When we apply

*David Bicklehaupt, *General Insurance* (Homewood, IL: Richard D. Irwin, 1983).

this definition to our personal lives, we can consider risks to our personal earning ability due to death, illness, accident, injury, or age. Other such risks might involve the loss or damage to property we own, such as our homes or automobiles. We might also be held accountable (liable) for any damage or harm we cause to other people and their property.

When we apply the definition to our business lives, financial risks to our business can be caused by uncertainties such as: loss of property or product due to accident or theft; loss of business income due to illness of employees; loss due to employee dishonesty; liability loss due to civil or criminal wrongs to the public or to individuals; or, simply, losses due to unexpected economic changes in our society.

RISK MANAGEMENT

Risk management can be defined as the attempt to minimize loss by (a) controlling risk, and (b) using insurance to compensate for any losses incurred due to accidents. Risk control in our personal lives might include monitoring our health to minimize loss of work time due to illness, injury, or death. We might drive defensively to decrease the chance of an auto accident. We also might monitor our property to decrease the risk of loss or damage due to fire, theft, or vandalism. Such measures might decrease the probability of the risks mentioned above, but they won't eliminate the risks entirely.

Our risk control efforts might be backed up by insurance to cover lost wages due to lost work time caused by illness or injury (disability insurance), or death (life insurance). We also protect our financial losses with health insurance to offset the costs of regaining our health. Other insurance includes auto (liability and collision) and property (fire, theft, and comprehensive).

Similar efforts at control and financial back-up are exercised by businesses. Large companies employ **risk managers** whose primary function is to investigate all aspects of a business with the goal of determining the existence of risk, recommending and implementing plans of action to control risk, and exploring and obtaining programs of economic back-up (such as insurance) to help maintain the fiscal stability of the business should any adversity occur due to uncertainty.

16.1 PROBABILITY: THE BASIC MATHEMATICS OF RISK MANAGEMENT

The mathematics of uncertainty is known as **probability**. Probability in its simplest form is a ratio.

Probability ratio

Learning objective
Calculate a simple probability.

$$\text{probability that an event will occur} = \frac{\text{number of outcomes in which the event occurs}}{\text{total number of outcomes in the experiment}},$$

provided all outcomes are equally likely. Let's explain with two examples.

Example 1

Toss a six-sided die (singular of dice) once and determine the probability that the side showing up will be (a) a 3 or (b) a 1 or a 3.

Solution

There are six different ways the face of the die could turn up; that is, the face showing up could have a 1, 2, 3, 4, 5, or 6 (each of these is called an **outcome**).

a. The probability the die will show a 3?

$$\text{probability of 3} = \frac{\text{number of ways a 3 could occur}}{\text{total number of ways die could turn up}}$$

$$= \frac{1}{6}$$

$$= .167$$

b. probability of a 1 or 3 occurring $= \frac{2}{6} = \frac{1}{3} = .33$

Example 2

Professor Garcia as an accounting class of 8 men and 17 women for a total of 25 students. If Professor Garcia randomly picks 1 student from the class (assuming all students have an equal chance to be chosen), what is the probability she will choose: (a) a man? (b) a woman?

Solution

a. $\dfrac{\text{probability}}{\text{of a man}} = \dfrac{\text{number of men in class}}{\text{total number of students in class}} = \dfrac{8}{25}$ or .32

b. $\dfrac{\text{probability}}{\text{of a woman}} = \dfrac{\text{total of women in class}}{\text{total number of students in class}} = \dfrac{17}{25}$ or .68

How can probability be used in management?

E x a m p l e   3

Easyflow Conduit Company employs 1,000 workers and keeps daily records showing the number of workers absent from work each day due to illness. The company's records for the last 3 years show that, during the month of October, an average of 22 workers have been absent daily due to illness. Interpret this data in terms of what might be expected (a) for daily absences and (b) for the likelihood that a particular worker will be absent on a particular day in future Octobers.

S o l u t i o n

a.   We might expect for October of the coming year that a daily average of 22 people will miss work due to illness.

b.   We might say that the probability of any one worker being absent on a given day is $^{22}/_{1,000} = .022$.

Consider the data in Table 16.1. They indicate for different age groups, from 0 years to 85 years, the number of people in that age group who were alive during 1987, out of every 100,000 people born the same year they were born. For example, 98,989 of 100,000 babies born in 1986 lived through 1987, their first year of age. Similarly, 95,373 40-year-olds were alive in 1987 compared to the original 100,000 of them born during the same year. The table breaks down data for all races, white, black, and all other races, as well as by sex.

E x a m p l e   4

Learning objective
Calculate a probability from a mortality table.

Use Table 16.1 to determine the following probabilities: (a) What was the probability that any one 20-year-old person would survive 1987, that is, live to be 21 years old, for both sexes of all races? (b) What was the probability that any one 50-year-old person would die during 1987?

S o l u t i o n

a.   First we look down the age column to the ages of 20 and 21, and move to the right to the column under "all races" and "both sexes" under that heading. The probability will be the ratio that compares the number of 21-year-olds alive in 1987 with the number of 20-year-olds alive in 1987.

$$\text{probability} = \frac{\text{number of 21-year-olds alive during 1987}}{\text{total number of 20-year-olds alive during 1987}}$$

$$= \frac{98,018}{98,122}$$

$$= .9989 \qquad \text{(continued on page 637)}$$

Table 16.1

Life tables: number of survivors at single years of age, out of 100,000 born alive, by race and sex: United States, 1987

| | All races | | | White | | | All other | | | | | |
| | | | | | | | Total | | | Black | | |
Age	Both sexes	Male	Female	Both sexes	Male	Female	Both sexes	Male	Female	Both sexes	Male	Female
0	100,000	100,000	100,000	100,000	100,000	100,000	100,000	100,000	100,000	100,000	100,000	100,000
1	98,989	98,880	99,104	99,136	99,037	99,241	98,448	98,297	98,604	98,205	98,026	98,389
2	98,919	98,802	99,043	99,072	98,965	99,185	98,355	98,194	98,521	98,101	97,911	98,296
3	98,865	98,742	98,995	99,023	98,911	99,142	98,280	98,112	98,453	98,018	97,820	98,221
4	98,823	98,695	98,957	98,985	98,869	99,109	98,220	98,046	98,399	97,951	97,747	98,161
5	98,788	98,656	98,927	98,954	98,834	99,082	98,171	97,991	98,355	97,897	97,687	98,113
6	98,758	98,621	98,902	98,927	98,802	99,059	98,130	97,945	98,320	97,853	97,637	98,075
7	98,731	98,589	98,880	98,902	98,772	99,039	98,096	97,905	98,292	97,816	97,594	98,045
8	98,707	98,560	98,861	98,879	98,744	99,021	98,067	97,870	98,269	97,785	97,557	98,020
9	98,686	98,534	98,845	98,859	98,719	99,006	98,041	97,839	98,250	97,758	97,524	97,999
10	98,667	98,511	98,831	98,841	98,698	98,993	98,018	97,811	98,232	97,734	97,495	97,980
11	98,650	98,491	98,818	98,826	98,680	98,981	97,996	97,784	98,215	97,710	97,467	97,962
12	98,633	98,471	98,805	98,811	98,662	98,969	97,972	97,755	98,197	97,685	97,436	97,943
13	98,612	98,444	98,789	98,791	98,637	98,954	97,944	97,719	98,177	97,655	97,398	97,922
14	98,581	98,403	98,768	98,761	98,598	98,934	97,907	97,670	98,153	97,616	97,345	97,898
15	98,536	98,342	98,740	98,717	98,539	98,906	97,859	97,602	98,125	97,565	97,273	97,869
16	98,476	98,260	98,703	98,657	98,458	98,869	97,798	97,514	98,092	97,500	97,180	97,835
17	98,402	98,157	98,659	98,583	98,357	98,823	97,724	97,406	98,054	97,421	97,065	97,794
18	98,316	98,036	98,609	98,497	98,238	98,771	97,636	97,277	98,009	97,327	96,926	97,747
19	98,222	97,902	98,556	98,405	98,108	98,718	97,534	97,125	97,958	97,218	96,762	97,692
20	98,122	97,758	98,503	98,309	97,970	98,666	97,417	96,950	97,900	97,093	96,572	97,630
21	98,018	97,604	98,451	98,211	97,825	98,616	97,284	96,750	97,833	96,951	96,354	97,560
22	97,909	97,440	98,398	98,110	97,673	98,568	97,136	96,526	97,759	96,791	96,109	97,481
23	97,796	97,269	98,344	98,007	97,516	98,520	96,976	96,285	97,678	96,618	95,844	97,395
24	97,682	97,096	98,289	97,904	97,359	98,472	96,810	96,034	97,593	96,437	95,567	97,304
25	97,567	96,924	98,232	97,801	97,204	98,422	96,641	95,780	97,505	96,251	95,284	97,209
26	97,453	96,755	98,173	97,698	97,052	98,370	96,470	95,524	97,414	96,062	94,997	97,110

27	97,006	94,704	95,867	97,320	95,263	96,295	98,316	96,903	97,596	98,113	96,588	97,339
28	96,894	94,400	95,663	97,220	94,995	96,114	98,261	96,755	97,493	98,050	96,421	97,223
29	96,771	94,077	95,444	97,112	94,714	95,922	98,204	96,604	97,388	97,984	96,250	97,104
30	96,634	93,730	95,206	96,994	94,416	95,717	98,145	96,448	97,280	97,915	96,073	96,980
31	96,482	93,357	94,948	96,864	94,099	95,497	98,084	96,287	97,168	97,842	95,888	96,851
32	96,315	92,959	94,671	96,722	93,765	95,262	98,021	96,120	97,052	97,765	95,696	96,716
33	96,135	92,534	94,374	96,570	93,410	95,012	97,954	95,947	96,931	97,684	95,496	96,575
34	95,943	92,080	94,057	96,408	93,033	94,747	97,883	95,768	96,805	97,598	95,288	96,427
35	95,741	91,596	93,721	96,238	92,632	94,466	97,807	95,584	96,674	97,506	95,071	96,273
36	95,528	91,080	93,365	96,059	92,204	94,169	97,725	95,392	96,536	97,408	94,845	96,110
37	95,303	90,532	92,989	95,869	91,749	93,854	97,637	95,191	96,391	97,303	94,607	95,938
38	95,065	89,955	92,592	95,668	91,271	93,522	97,542	94,982	96,238	97,191	94,359	95,757
39	94,811	89,353	92,175	95,454	90,774	93,174	97,440	94,765	96,078	97,071	94,102	95,569
40	94,539	88,730	91,738	95,225	90,260	92,811	97,331	94,539	95,910	96,944	93,837	95,373
41	94,247	88,084	91,280	94,979	89,728	92,431	97,214	94,302	95,732	96,808	93,562	95,167
42	93,033	87,414	90,799	94,715	89,176	92,031	97,087	94,052	95,543	96,662	93,273	94,950
43	93,597	86,718	90,294	94,431	88,602	91,610	96,948	93,785	95,340	96,503	92,968	94,718
44	93,240	85,996	89,765	94,128	88,003	91,167	96,794	93,498	95,119	96,328	92,641	94,468
45	92,860	85,245	89,211	93,804	87,376	90,699	96,622	93,187	94,877	96,134	92,289	94,195
46	92,456	84,466	88,631	93,458	86,721	90,206	96,431	92,848	94,612	95,920	91,908	93,898
47	92,026	83,656	88,021	93,086	86,033	89,684	96,219	92,479	94,321	95,684	91,495	93,574
48	91,562	82,802	87,373	92,683	85,303	89,125	95,983	92,074	94,000	95,423	91,045	93,218
49	91,056	81,890	86,675	92,242	84,519	88,520	95,722	91,628	93,646	95,134	90,552	92,827
50	90,502	80,909	85,919	91,756	83,672	87,861	95,433	91,136	93,255	94,815	90,011	92,397
51	89,894	79,850	85,097	91,221	82,755	87,143	95,113	90,593	92,823	94,462	89,416	91,924
52	89,231	78,716	84,210	90,635	81,768	86,365	94,760	89,996	92,347	94,074	88,765	91,404
53	88,518	77,518	83,265	90,002	80,717	85,532	94,372	89,340	91,824	93,650	88,054	90,837
54	87,761	76,275	82,274	89,328	79,611	84,651	93,949	88,621	91,252	93,190	87,282	90,222
55	86,965	74,997	81,242	88,615	78,457	83,725	93,489	87,834	90,629	92,693	86,446	89,556
56	86,131	73,690	80,173	87,865	77,257	82,757	92,990	86,977	89,951	92,158	85,544	88,839
57	85,253	72,346	79,061	87,072	76,004	81,741	92,448	86,046	89,215	91,581	84,571	88,065
58	84,314	70,943	77,886	86,223	74,685	80,662	91,856	85,031	88,412	90,955	83,518	87,226
59	83,289	69,452	76,623	85,298	73,279	79,502	91,207	83,922	87,534	90,270	82,373	86,312

(continued)

Table 16.1 (continued)

Life tables: number of survivors at single years of age, out of 100,000 born alive, by race and sex: United States, 1987

| | All races | | | White | | | All other | | | | | |
| | | | | | | | Total | | | Black | | |
Age	Both sexes	Male	Female	Both sexes	Male	Female	Both sexes	Male	Female	Both sexes	Male	Female
60	85,316	81,126	89,519	86,574	82,710	90,494	78,247	71,774	84,285	75,254	67,853	82,163
61	84,230	79,771	88,696	85,526	81,389	89,712	76,890	70,164	83,175	73,771	66,138	80,926
62	83,055	78,308	87,799	84,389	79,959	88,858	75,435	68,454	81,972	72,181	64,316	79,584
63	81,794	76,746	86,830	83,165	78,426	87,933	73,895	66,657	80,688	70,501	62,404	78,153
64	80,454	75,096	85,793	81,860	76,802	86,937	72,287	64,790	79,340	68,755	60,426	76,659
65	79,040	73,366	84,688	80,477	75,095	85,871	70,623	62,868	77,940	66,961	58,401	75,119
66	77,553	71,562	83,513	79,017	73,309	84,732	68,909	60,897	76,494	65,126	56,338	73,540
67	75,986	69,677	82,263	77,474	71,437	83,513	67,140	58,876	74,994	63,246	54,234	71,913
68	74,327	67,634	80,927	75,834	69,461	82,206	65,307	56,798	73,425	61,311	52,085	70,224
69	72,560	65,589	79,493	74,080	67,355	80,798	63,396	54,652	71,767	59,306	49,880	68,450
70	70,672	63,346	77,951	72,200	65,101	79,281	61,397	52,433	70,005	57,222	47,615	66,577
71	68,659	60,963	76,294	70,189	62,697	77,648	59,305	50,140	68,130	55,056	45,291	64,595
72	66,524	58,450	74,521	68,052	60,153	75,896	57,128	47,782	66,148	52,816	42,918	62,512
73	64,274	55,822	72,630	65,793	57,484	74,021	54,881	45,377	64,074	50,517	40,514	60,342
74	61,920	53,098	70,621	63,421	54,708	72,021	52,587	42,947	61,932	48,182	38,100	58,110
75	59,469	50,295	68,493	60,943	51,843	69,894	50,261	40,510	59,738	45,825	35,694	55,830
76	56,925	47,427	66,243	58,363	48,903	67,634	47,908	38,074	57,493	43,453	33,306	53,504
77	54,290	44,502	63,864	55,684	45,897	65,237	45,523	35,640	55,185	41,062	30,939	51,122
78	51,564	41,527	61,350	52,906	42,835	62,697	43,095	33,205	52,796	38,644	28,591	48,668
79	48,746	38,511	58,694	50,031	39,727	60,009	40,611	30,765	50,303	36,188	26,260	46,123
80	45,839	35,465	55,889	47,063	36,587	57,167	38,062	28,316	47,687	33,688	23,947	43,470
81	42,847	32,406	52,929	44,007	33,433	54,166	35,440	25,860	44,934	31,138	21,654	40,697
82	39,777	29,353	49,810	40,873	30,288	51,003	32,743	23,401	42,032	28,538	19,387	37,795
83	36,640	26,332	46,529	37,672	27,179	47,675	29,972	20,947	38,977	25,892	17,157	34,762
84	33,449	23,374	43,083	34,418	24,140	44,179	27,133	18,511	35,769	23,206	14,977	31,600
85	30,220	20,513	39,473	31,127	21,208	40,514	24,236	16,109	32,414	20,492	12,865	28,317

Source: Vital Statistics of the United States, 1987, National Center for Health Statistics, U.S. Department of Health and Human Services. Used with permission.

b. What was the probability that any one 50-year-old person would die during 1987?

$$\text{probability} = \frac{\text{number of 50-year-olds who died}}{\text{total number of 50-year-olds living in 1987}}$$

$$= \frac{(\text{number of 50-year-olds alive in 1987}) - (\text{number of 51-year-olds alive})}{\text{number of 50-year-olds alive during 1987}}$$

$$= \frac{92,397 - 91,924}{92,397}$$

$$= \frac{473}{92,397}$$

$$= .0051$$

Example 5

Assume that an insurance company sold life insurance policies with a face value of $1,000 to each 20-year-old person alive during 1987. (a) How much would the insurance company have had to pay to the beneficiaries by the end of the year? (b) How much would the insurance company have had to collect from each of the insured in order to have collected enough money in premiums to cover the cost in benefits paid out?

Solution

a. benefits paid = (number who died) × ($1,000)
= (number of 20-year-olds − number of 21-year-olds) × $1,000
= (98,122 − 98,018) × $1,000 = 104 × $1,000
= $104,000

b. premium per $1,000 policy = $\dfrac{\text{total benefits paid}}{\text{total number insured}}$

$$= \frac{\$104,000}{98,122}$$

$$= \$1.06 \text{ per } \$1,000$$

If each of the 98,122 20-year-olds alive at the beginning of their 20th year purchased a $1,000 life insurance policy in 1987, each would have had to pay $1.06 for the policy to cover the cost of benefits (claims) paid out to the families of those 104 who died in 1987.

In Example 5, the insurance company would have added additional charges to this premium to help cover the cost of running its business, and to provide for profit.

total premium = costs to cover claims
+ expenses of doing business + profit

Mathematicians known as **actuaries** work with this type of data and even more sophisticated mathematical principles to assist insurance companies to cope with *uncertainty* and make the best possible decisions to minimize risk and maximize profits while staying competitive in the open market.

CHECK YOUR KNOWLEDGE

Probability: the basic mathematics of risk management

Solve the following problems. Round dollar amounts to the nearest cent, and probabilities to the nearest ten-thousandth.

1. A twelve-sided die (each face having a single number from 1 through 12 on it) is tossed once. What is the probability that the side showing up is: (a) the side with a 7 on it? (b) the side with a 4 on it? (c) a side with an even number on it? (d) a side with a number less than 4 on it? (e) a side with a number evenly divisible by three on it?

2. The B'ville Optimist Club has a drawing at each of its regular meetings. If the club has three members whose first names are all Dave, four Mikes, two Bobs, one Bruce, one Jerry, two Bills, one Carmen, and one Ed at its next meeting, and they all participate in the drawing of one of their names from a hat, what is the probability the winner will have a first name of: (a) Bob? (b) Dave? (c) Jack? (d) Jerry?

3. Use Table 16.1 to determine the probability that a person in each of the following age categories would have survived the year 1987: (a) a 15-year-old, (b) a 23-year-old, (c) a 37-year-old, (d) a 45-year-old, (e) a 56-year-old, and (f) a 68-year-old.

4. Use Table 16.1 to determine the probability that a person in each of the following age categories would have died during 1987: (a) a 15-year-old, (b) a 23-year-old, (c) a 37-year-old, (d) a 45-year-old, (e) a 56-year-old, and (f) a 68-year-old.

5. Subtract each of the probabilities you determined in problem 3 from the number 1, and compare the result with the probabilities you found in problem 4. That is, compare (1 − probability found in problem 3a) with the probability found in problem 4a. Notice that the probability a person will die during 1987 equals 1 minus the probability he/she will live through 1987.

6. Assume that each 30-year-old person represented in Table 16.1 purchased a $5,000 life insurance policy. (a) How many 30-year-olds would have died by the end of 1987? (b) How much would the insur-

ance company have had to pay out in claims to beneficiaries by the end of the year? (c) How much would the insurance company have had to collect from each insured to have collected enough money in premiums to cover the costs of benefits paid out? (d) What was the probability that a 30-year-old would die during 1987? (e) Multiply your answer in part (d) by $5,000 and compare the result with your answer in part (c). This is another way to determine the premium amount to be paid.

premium = (probability of dying) × (face value of policy)

16.1 EXERCISES

Solve the following problems. Round dollar amounts to the nearest cent, and probabilities to the nearest ten-thousandth.

1. A four-sided die (each face having a single number from 1 to 4 on it) is tossed once. What is the probability that the face that lands down has a number satisfying the following conditions: (a) the number 3 on it, (b) the number 1 on it, (c) either the number 2 or the number 4 on it, (d) an even number (divisible by 2) on it, (e) a number greater than 3 on it?

2. An eight-sided die (each face having a single number from 1 to 8 on it) is tossed once. What is the probability that the face that lands down has a number satisfying the following conditions: (a) the number 5 on it, (b) the number 7 on it, (c) either the number 5 or the number 7 on it, (d) a number divisible by 3 on it, (e) a number greater than 3 on it?

3. The "Thespians," a college drama club, has 13 men and 17 women members. Each member's name is to be put in a hat and one name will be drawn; the person whose name is drawn will receive free tickets to a performance of "Les Miserables." What is the probability that the name drawn will be that of (a) a man? (b) a woman?

4. A group of card players who frequent the college snack bar includes two men named Bob, three women named Diane, and one man each named Jack, John, Arnie, and Jose. There are also two women named Michelle and one woman each named Rita, Lynette, and Susan. All the card players agree to meet at the snack bar at 8:00 P.M. on Friday for an evening of cards. If they all have an equal chance of arriving on time for the game, what is the probability that the first person to arrive will be (a) a woman? (b) a man? (c) a woman named Michelle? (d) a man named Bob? (e) a man whose name starts with a J? (f) a woman whose name is either Diane or Michelle?

Answers to CYK: 1.   a. $\frac{1}{12}$; b. $\frac{1}{12}$; c. $\frac{6}{12} = \frac{1}{2}$; d. $\frac{3}{12} = \frac{1}{4}$; e. $\frac{4}{12} = \frac{1}{3}$ 2.   a. $\frac{2}{15}$; b. $\frac{3}{15} = \frac{1}{5}$; c. 0; d. $\frac{1}{15}$
3.   a. .9994; b. .9988; c. .9981; d. .9968; e. .9913; f. .9762   4.   a. .0006; b. .0012; c. .0019; d. .0032; e. .0087; f. .0238   5.   answers are the same as problem 4   6.   a. 129; b. claims to pay total = $645,000.00; c. $6.65; d. .0013; e. .0013 × $5,000 = $6.5

5. A five-dollar bill, a one-dollar bill, a ten-dollar bill, and a twenty-dollar bill are put into a hat, and one is drawn out randomly. What is the probability that the value of the bill drawn is (a) $10? (b) $20? (c) $5 or $10 or $20? (d) $50?

6. A one-dollar bill, a five-dollar bill, a ten-dollar bill, a twenty-dollar bill, and a fifty-dollar bill are put into a hat, and one bill is drawn out randomly. What is the probability that the value of the bill drawn is (a) $10 or 20? (b) less than $50? (c) $10 or $20 or $50? (d) $50?

7. The "Commuters Club" membership at Good Times College has 7 members who are in their 20s, 10 in their 30s, 5 in their 40s, and 2 in their teens. If one person is chosen at random from the group, what is the probability the person's age is in (a) the 20s? (b) the 40s? (c) the teens? (d) the 50s?

8. Use Table 16.1 to determine the probability that a person in each of the following age categories would have died in 1989: (a) a 13-year-old, (b) a 28-year-old, (c) a 33-year-old, (d) a 48-year-old, (e) a 53-year-old, (f) a person between 42-years- and 47-years-old inclusive.

9. Use Table 16.1 to determine the probability that a person in each of the following age categories would have died in 1987: (a) a 17-year-old, (b) 9-year-old, (c) 50-year-old, (d) a 23-year-old.

10. Assume that each 45-year-old person represented in Table 16.1 purchased a $3,000 life insurance policy. (a) How many 45-year-olds would have died by the end of 1987? (b) How much would the insurance company have had to pay out in claims to beneficiaries by the end of the year? (c) How much would the insurance company have had to collect from each insured to have collected enough money in premiums to cover the cost of benefits paid out? (d) What was the probability that a 45-five-year-old would die during 1987? (e) Multiply your answer in part (d) by $3,000 and compare your answer with the answer in part (c).

11. Assume that each 65-year-old person represented in Table 16.1 purchased an $8,000 life insurance policy. (a) How many 65-year-olds would have died by the end of 1987? (b) How much would the insurance company have had to pay out in claims to beneficiaries by the end of the year? (c) How much would the insurance company have had to collect from each insured to have collected enough money in premiums to cover the cost of benefits paid out? (d) What was the probability that a 65-year-old would die during 1987? (e) Multiply your answer in part (d) by $8,000 and compare your answer with the answer in part (c).

16.2   LIFE INSURANCE

The insurance industry is a business that provides financial protection to offset economic losses due to uncertainty. Just as probability is the area of mathematics that deals with uncertainty, **insurance** is the area of business that deals with uncertainty.

Probability provides us with a means of assessing the likelihood that a person will die in a given year. Expressed differently, *probability gives us a means of estimating how many people we expect will die in a group of people in a given year*. Life insurance provides us with a means of assessing and offsetting the economic losses due to the death of a person.

Insurance in a broader sense provides economic protection in situations that cause economic loss such as loss of life; loss of health; loss of employment; loss of, or damage to, property due to fire, theft, or vandalism, and so on.

Probability combined with statistical data helps us to know what to expect in many situations of uncertainty. What is the likelihood of economic loss due to loss of health from an accident or illness? transportation losses, such as automobile or marine accidents? property losses, such as damage to our home, business, or other property?

Life insurance provides compensation for economic loss due to the death of the insured. The basic types of life insurance include: term, decreasing term, ordinary (whole or straight) life, limited pay, endowment, and universal life. Each of these types of insurance has a **face value**, which is the amount of money paid to a *beneficiary* upon the death of the insured person. The **beneficiary** is the person designated to receive the insurance award (money). The **premium** is the amount of money paid to the insurance company to purchase the insurance.

- **Term life insurance** pays the face value of the policy to the beneficiary if the insured dies within the specified time period (term) of coverage. Term life insurance generally provides a higher amount of coverage per premium dollar than other forms of life insurance. On the other hand, term life insurance usually requires that the insured requalify for coverage at the end of each term.

- **Whole life insurance** provides protection for the insured's entire life, so long as the premiums are paid.

- **Limited pay life** provides protection for the insured's entire life, but is paid up with a limited number of premium payments.

- **Endowment life insurance** provides life insurance coverage that pays the face value of the policy upon the death of the insured, or pays an amount of money to the insured at the end of a specified period of time if the insured is still living at that time.

- **Annuity life insurance** provides life insurance that pays a specified amount upon the death of the insured, or if the insured lives past a specified age, pays a regular periodic payment to the insured for the remainder of his/her life (or for a predetermined time period).

- **Universal life insurance** is a flexible form of insurance that incorporates many of the features of the above policies and tailors them to the needs of the insurance customer. This form of insurance provides protection, savings, and annuity benefits that can be adapted to the changing needs of the insured.

Learning objective

Calculate a premium for term, ordinary life, decreasing term, limited pay life, and endowment life insurance.

Table 16.2

Typical annual premiums for $1,000 face value life insurance

Age	5-year renewable	Whole life	20-year limited pay	20-year endowment
20	$1.10	$17.50	$27.30	$48.30
25	1.10	19.30	29.80	48.70
30	1.16	21.90	33.10	49.60
35	1.40	25.10	36.60	50.10
40	1.94	29.60	40.20	51.80
45	2.90	35.10	46.10	52.30
50	5.00	43.10	54.30	56.50

Table 16.2 lists some typical premiums for life insurance with a $1,000 face value.

Example 6

Arnie Johnson is 25 years old and wishes to purchase $10,000 of life insurance. Determine the annual premium payments he would be required to pay for (a) 5-year renewable term life, (b) whole life, (c) 20-year limited pay life, and (d) 20-year endowment life.

Solution

Step 1: First, we determine the number of $1,000 units of face value of life insurance Arnie wants to purchase:

$$\text{number of } \$1,000 \text{ units} = \frac{\text{face value}}{\$1,000} = \frac{\$10,000}{\$1,000} = 10$$

Step 2: Next, we multiply the number of $1,000 units by the appropriate premium per $1,000 indicated in Table 16.2 for Arnie's age (25 years) and the type of insurance desired.

a. 5-year term premium = number of units × table value
= 10 × table value of 5-year term and age 25
= 10 × $1.10
= $11.00

b. whole life premium = number of units × table value
= 10 × table value of whole life at age 25
= 10 × $19.30 = $193.00

c. 20-year limited pay premium = number units
$\times$ table value for age 25
$= 10 \times \$29.80$
$= \$298.00$

d. 20-year endowment = number of units
$\times$ table value for age 25
$= 10 \times \$48.70$
$= \$487.00$

Learning objective
Calculate the cash surrender value of an insurance policy.

All forms of insurance mentioned above, except term insurance, have a **cash surrender value**. Cash surrender value is similar to a savings account. The insured's premium payments earn savings while providing insurance protection. If the insured cancels (surrenders) the policy after a certain time period (usually at least 3 years) money earned is paid to her or him. The amount earned and paid to the insured upon surrendering the policy is called the *cash surrender value*. Table 16.3 shows typical 20-year limited payment cash surrender values.

Example 7

Assuming Arnie Johnson purchased a $10,000 20-year limited pay life policy at age 25, what will be the cash surrender value of the policy at the end of (a) 5 years? (b) 10 years? (c) 20 years?

Solution

We calculate the cash surrender value in much the same way we calculated the premium cost.

Step 1: First we determine the number of $1,000 units of face value of insurance Arnie bought.

$$\text{number of units} = \frac{\text{face value of policy}}{\$1{,}000} = \frac{\$10{,}000}{\$1{,}000} = 10$$

Table 16.3

Cash surrender value for 20-year limited payment life

	End of year						
Age	**1**	**2**	**3**	**5**	**10**	**15**	**20**
20		12	32	73	190	320	480
25		16	36	85	213	355	530
30		20	43	97	238	395	582
35		26	52	110	263	435	636
40		32	60	123	288	475	690
45		38	69	135	313	515	741

Step 2: Next, we determine cash surrender value by multiplying the number of units by the table value corresponding to Arnie's age at the time he purchased the policy and the number of years for which Arnie has paid the premiums on the policy.

$$\text{cash surrender value} = \text{number of units} \times \frac{\text{table value for age}}{\text{and years paid}}$$

a. $\text{cash surrender value} \atop \text{at end of 5 years}$ $= 10 \times \$85 = \$850$

b. $\text{cash surrender value} \atop \text{at end of 10 years}$ $= \begin{array}{l} 10 \times \text{table value for} \\ 25 \text{ years and 10 years} \end{array}$
$$= 10 \times \$213$$
$$= \$2,130$$

c. $\text{cash surrender} \atop \text{at end of 20 years}$ $= \begin{array}{l} 10 \times \text{table value for} \\ 25 \text{ years and 20 years} \end{array}$
$$= 10 \times \$530$$
$$= \$5,300$$

Notice that if Arnie pays his fixed premium of $298 each year for 20 years, he will have $10,000 worth of life insurance protection for each of those years. If he dies before the 20-year period is completed, his beneficiaries will receive $10,000. If he survives the 20-year period, he will have accumulated a savings of $5,300 in the policy.

Term life insurance provides protection *only*, without the savings benefit, but the premiums are much lower, which provides the same or greater protection at lower cost. Although term life insurance may cost less for the same amount of face value protection, the premiums do increase when the policy is renewed at the end of the specified term. **Decreasing term life insurance** is an alternate form of term insurance for which the premium remains the same throughout the life of the policy, but the face value decreases at the end of each specified term (see Tables 16.4 and 16.5).

Table 16.4

20-year decreasing term life premium per $1,000 face value

Age	Premium
20	$ .90
25	1.00
30	1.15
35	1.50
40	2.25
45	3.60
50	6.00

For Your Information
How inflation affects insurance values

The graph shows the purchasing power of a $100,000 life insurance policy at successive 5-year intervals, assuming a 5% per year rate of inflation. The original $100,000 of purchasing power is reduced to $78,350 5 years later, $61,390 10 years later, and to less than half the original purchasing power after 15 years.

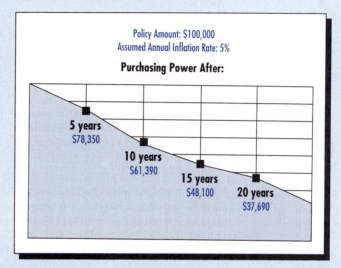

Policy Amount: $100,000
Assumed Annual Inflation Rate: 5%

Purchasing Power After:

5 years $78,350

10 years $61,390

15 years $48,100

20 years $37,690

Insurance companies recommend that the face value of a life insurance policy be 6 to 10 times the insured's yearly income. This factor is designed to help offset inflation's effect on purchasing power.

Source: Teacher Insurance Annuity Fund and the College Retirement Equity Fund. Used with permission.

Table 16.5

20-year decreasing term face value for $100,000

Year	Face value
1	$100,000
5	91,000
10	75,000
15	50,000
20	36,000

Example 8

A 35-year-old male purchased $100,000 of decreasing term insurance for 20 years. Determine (a) his premium, (b) the face value of the policy at age 40, and (c) the face value at age 50.

Solution   *a.*   The amount he would pay is a premium of 100 units × $1.50 per unit = $150 per year for each of the 20 years in the life of the policy.

b.   At age 40 the face value of his coverage would be $91,000 (determined from Table 16.5 for year 5 since he would have had the policy for 40 − 35 = 5 years).

c.   At age 50, 15 years after the original purchase of the policy, the face value would be $50,000.

Decreasing term life insurance provides greater protection early in the life of the policy, and the benefit of a fixed premium throughout the life of the policy. A family with young children might prefer such a policy since it will provide high coverage when the children are young and lower coverage as the children mature and become less dependent on their parents.

Underwriters (persons or companies in the insurance business) are providing an increasing number of variations on the basic types of life insurance we noted. Actuaries working for insurance companies use computers to "customize" policies to accommodate customers' needs for protection, savings, investment, and retirement.

CHECK YOUR KNOWLEDGE

Life insurance

Solve the following problems. Round dollar amounts to the nearest cent.

1.   Jake Malone is 35 years old and wants to purchase $20,000 face value of life insurance. Use Table 16.2 to determine the premium Jake will have to pay for each type of insurance: (a) 5-year renewable term life, (b) whole life, (c) 20-year limited pay life, and (d) 20-year endowment life.

2.   Marsha Sorensen purchased $50,000 face value of 20-year limited pay life insurance when she was 25 years old. Now, at age 30, she intends to surrender the policy. Use Table 16.3 to determine the cash surrender value.

3.   Frank Zajac purchased a $100,000 20-year decreasing term life insurance policy 15 years ago at age 25. (a) Use Table 16.4 to determine Frank's yearly premium for the policy. (b) Use Table 16.5 to determine the current face value of Frank's policy.

Answers to CYK: *1.*   a. $28; b. $502; c. $732; d. $1,002   *2.* $4,250.00   *3.*   a. $100; b. $50,000

16.2 EXERCISES

Solve problems 1–9 using Tables A–D below. Round dollar amounts to the nearest cent.

Table A

Annual premiums for $1,000 face value of life insurance

Age	5-year renewable	Whole life	20-year limited pay	20-year endow- ment
20	$1.21	$19.25	$30.00	$53.13
25	1.21	21.23	32.78	53.57
30	1.28	24.10	36.40	54.56
35	1.54	27.60	40.26	55.10
40	2.13	32.56	44.22	56.98
45	3.19	38.60	50.71	57.53
50	5.50	47.40	59.75	62.15

Table B

Cash surrender value for 20-year limited pay life insurance

	End of year						
Age	1	2	3	5	10	15	20
20		19	39	82	199	329	489
25		25	45	94	222	364	539
30		29	52	106	247	404	591
35		35	61	119	272	444	645
40		41	69	132	297	484	699
45		47	78	144	322	524	750

Table C

Decreasing term life insurance premium per $1,000 face value

Age	Premium
20	$1.05
25	1.15
30	1.30
35	1.65
40	2.40
45	3.75
50	6.15

Table D

20-year decreasing term life insurance face value for $100,000

Year	Face value
1	$100,000
5	92,000
10	77,000
15	52,000
20	38,000

1. Jim Smith is 30 years old and plans to purchase $40,000 face value of life insurance. Determine the premium Jim will have to pay for each type of insurance: (a) 5-year renewable term life, (b) whole life, (c) 20-year limited pay life, and (d) 20-year endowment life.

2. Sam Harris is 45 years old and plans to purchase $28,000 face value of life insurance. Determine the premium Sam will have to pay for each type of insurance: (a) 5-year renewable term life, (b) whole life, (c) 20-year limited pay life, and (d) 20-year endowment life.

3. Diran Abdul is 25 years old and plans to purchase $39,000 face value of life insurance. Determine the premium Diran will have to pay for each type of insurance: (a) 5-year renewable term life, (b) whole life, (c) 20-year limited pay life, and (d) 20-year endowment life.

4. Sara Hedges purchased $20,000 face value of 20-year limited pay life insurance when she was 20 years old. Now, at age 40, she intends to surrender the policy. Determine the cash surrender value.

5. My-Lin Sing purchased $40,000 face value of 20-year limited pay life insurance when she was 30 years old. Now, at age 45, she intends to surrender the policy. Determine the cash surrender value.

6. Jack Marmin purchased $100,000 face value of 20-year limited pay life insurance when he was

25 years old. Now, at age 40, he intends to surrender the policy. Determine the cash surrender value.

7. Arthur Levinson purchased a $100,000 20-year decreasing term life insurance policy at age 30. Determine (a) his yearly premium for the policy and (b) what the cash value of the policy is now that his age is 50.

8. Ann Michels purchased a $100,000 20-year decreasing term life insurance policy at age 20. Determine (a) her yearly premium for the policy and (b) what the cash value of the policy is now that she is 35 years old.

9. Cesar Escobar purchased a $100,000 20-year decreasing term life insurance policy at age 25. Determine (a) his yearly premium for the policy and (b) what the cash value of the policy is now that his age is 45.

16.3   PROPERTY INSURANCE

Economic loss due to damage to property we own or are purchasing is another form of risk that must be considered. Damage to real estate by fire, theft, vandalism, or other dangers could be economically devastating in terms of repair or replacement costs.

FIRE INSURANCE

Learning objective
Calculate the premium for a fire insurance policy.

Fire and lightning pose very definite risks to the loss of a building. Whether we consider the protection of our home or our business structures, physical loss of either could result in a corresponding risk of economic loss to us.

The premium paid for fire insurance is based on many factors regarding the structure to be insured. A structure built with fire resistant materials such as concrete or steel would cost less to insure than a structure made of wood and less fire resistant materials. Structures with sprinkler systems or that are near fire hydrants or in close proximity to fire departments would also have a lower premium than structures without such features.

Fire insurance premiums are usually based on each $100 of property valuation. A rate per $100 is determined based on an inspection of the property to be insured (for example, $.46 per $100 valuation) and the premium calculated.

Table 16.6

Rate discount percentages

Number of years	1-year premium
1	100%
2	185%
3	270%
4	355%

Example 9

Determine the annual premium for a $200,000 building at a rate of $.46 per $100.

Solution

$$\text{premium} = \frac{\$200,000}{\$100} \times \$.46 = 2,000 \times \$.46 = \$920$$

Insurance companies provide incentives to purchase insurance for long terms such as 2, 3, or 4 years by providing long-term rate discounts (Table 16.6).

Consequently, a 2-year premium in Example 9 would be

2-year premium = 1-year rate × percent for 2-year term
= $920 × 1.85
= $1,702

rather than $1,840 ($920 × 2). For a 3-year policy, the premium would be:

3-year premium = 1-year rate × percent for 3-year term
= $920 × 2.70
= $2,484

rather than $2,760 ($920 × 3 = $2,760).

Example 10

Determine the fire insurance premium on a $120,000 building with a rate of $.54 per $100 valuation for (a) 1 year, (b) 2 years, and (c) 3 years.

Solution

    a.   premium for 1 year $= \dfrac{\text{value of property}}{\$100} \times$ rate per \$100

$$= \dfrac{\$120,000}{\$100} \times \$.54$$

$$= 1,200 \times \$.54$$

$$= \$648$$

    b.   premium for 2 years = premium for 1 year
                                   × multiple year premium for 2 years
                               = \$648 × 1.85
                               = \$1,198.80

    c.   premium for 3 years = premium for 1 year
                                   × percent for 3-year term
                               = \$648 × 2.70
                               = \$1,749.60

COINSURANCE CLAUSE

A fire insurance policy usually includes a **coinsurance clause** that states the minimum amount the building must be insured for so that a claim will be fully paid by the insurance company. Although a building may be valued at \$120,000, it is unlikely that it will be totally destroyed. Most likely, the foundation, at least, will be left intact. The coinsurance clause requires the owners to insure a certain percentage, often 80%, of the value of the structure.

Learning objective
Calculate the amount of claim covered using the coinsurance clause.

Example 11

Determine the required amount of fire insurance for a \$120,000 building if the coinsurance clause requires 80% coverage.

Solution

An 80% coinsurance clause would require the owners of the \$120,000 building to carry \$120,000 × .80 = \$96,000 of fire insurance in order to receive 100% coverage of a claim filed.

    The amount of a claim that would be covered by the insurance company if the owners insured the building for *less* than the required 80% is determined by the following formula:

Coinsurance clause formula	$$\begin{array}{c} \text{amount of claim} \\ \text{to be paid} \end{array} = \dfrac{\text{amount of insurance carried}}{\begin{array}{c}\text{amount of insurance required}\\\text{by coinsurance clause}\end{array}} \times \begin{array}{c}\text{amount}\\\text{of claim}\end{array}$$

Example 12

Bob McClosky owns a building valued at $200,000. He purchased $120,000 of fire insurance with an 80% coinsurance clause. Three months later, Bob suffered $80,000 worth of fire damage to the building. (a) How much insurance should Bob have purchased in order to have been fully covered? (b) How much of the $80,000 claim will the insurance company pay?

Solution

a. To determine the amount of insurance Bob should have purchased, we multiply the percentage of the coinsurance clause by the value of Bob's building:

amount of insurance should carry = .80 × $200,000 = $160,000

b. To determine the amount of Bob's claim that the insurance company will pay.

Step 1: We determine the ratio:

$$\frac{\text{amount of insurance carried}}{\text{amount of insurance that should be carried}} = \frac{\$120,000}{\$160,000} = .75$$

Step 2: We then multiply this factor by the claim of $80,000.

amount of claim insurance company will pay = .75 × $80,000
= $60,000

So, Bob will have to pay the $20,000 difference.

Notice that if Bob had carried the required $160,000 of insurance, the amount of the claim paid by the insurance company would have been:

$$\frac{\$160,000}{\$160,000} \times \$80,000 = 1 \times \$80,000 = \$80,000$$

and Bob's loss would have been fully covered.

CHECK YOUR KNOWLEDGE

Property insurance

Solve the following problems. Round dollar amounts to the nearest cent.

1. E.J.'s Electrical Supply company owns a $300,000 warehouse. The rate for fire insurance on the structure is $.53 per $100. (a) How much will a 1-year premium for the insurance cost? (b) Use Table 16.6 to determine the cost of a 2-year premium and a 4-year premium.

2. Marney Hill owns a building valued at $350,000. She purchased $250,000 of fire insurance with an 80% coinsurance clause on the structure, and had a fire that caused $200,000 of damage. (a) How much should Marney have insured the building for according to the coinsurance clause? (b) How much of the $200,000 claim will be covered by the insurance company?

16.3   EXERCISES

Solve the following problems. Round dollar amounts to the nearest cent.

1. Abe's Plumbing supply owns a retail/wholesale complex valued at $600,000. Ann Jones's Independent Insurance Agency has quoted a rate of $.49 per $100 for fire insurance to cover the complex. How much will a 1-year premium for the insurance cost? Use Table 16.6 to determine the cost of (a) a 2-year premium, (b) a 3-year premium, and (c) a 4-year premium.

2. Alexandra's Greenery Service decorates commercial malls with decorative plantings. She has a $250,000 combination greenhouse/warehouse where she stores her supplies and plantings. Alex's fire insurance rate on the building is $.45 per $100. How much will a 1-year premium for the insurance cost? Use Table 16.6 to determine the cost of (a) a 2-year premium, (b) a 3-year premium, and (c) a 4-year premium.

3. Amy Felton has purchased a single-family home in her town of Belleville and has converted the downstairs into the Yarn Shoppe and small office, and the upstairs into a two-bedroom apartment. The value of her commercial enterprise is $125,000. She has been quoted a rate of $.42 per $100 for fire insurance to cover the complex. How much will a 1-year premium for the insurance cost? Use Table 16.6 to determine the cost of (a) a 2-year premium, (b) a 3-year premium, and (c) a 4-year premium.

4. Sally Feldman owns a building valued at $400,000. She purchased $300,000 of fire insurance with an 80% coinsurance clause on the structure. She recently had a fire that totally destroyed the building. How much should Sally have insured the building for according to the coinsurance clause? How much of the $400,000 claim will be covered by the insurance company?

Answers to CYK: *1.*   a. $1,590; b. $2,941.50; $5,644.50   *2.*   a. $280,000; b. $178,571.42

5. Harbinger Real Estate owns a building valued at $350,000. The firm purchased $250,000 of fire insurance with an 80% coinsurance clause on the structure. The building had a fire that caused $180,000 damage to the building. How much should Harbinger have insured the building for according to the coinsurance clause? How much of the $180,000 claim will be covered by the insurance company?

6. The B'ville Ambulance Corps houses its emergency equipment in a building valued at $275,000. The Corps purchased $200,000 of fire insurance with an 80% coinsurance clause on the structure. They recently had a fire that totally destroyed the building. How much should the Corps have insured the building for according to the coinsurance clause? How much of the $275,000 claim will be covered by the insurance company?

7. Abe's Plumbing Supply, in exercise 1, purchased $400,000 of fire insurance with an 80% coinsurance clause on its building. A fire to-

tally destroyed the building causing $600,000 damage. How much should Abe's have insured the building for, and how much of the $600,000 claim will the insurance company be responsible to cover?

8. Alexandra's Greenery Service, in exercise 2, purchased $200,000 of fire insurance with an 80% coinsurance clause on her building. A fire damaged the Greenery Service building causing $175,000 damage. How much should Alex have insured the building for, and how much of the $175,000 claim will the insurance company cover?

9. Amy Felton, in exercise 3, purchased $80,000 of fire insurance with an 80% coinsurance clause on her building. A fire destroyed part of the building causing $50,000 damage. How much should Amy have insured the building for, and how much of the $50,000 claim will the insurance company be responsible to cover?

16.4   **AUTOMOBILE INSURANCE**

Learning objective
Calculate liability insurance coverage of an automobile.

Automobile insurance provides protection to offset financial losses due to liability and collision claims involving the insured's vehicle when used for either business or personal transport. Vehicles used for commercial (business) purposes pay a different premium rate than vehicles used strictly for personal purposes.

Liability automobile insurance provides benefits to offset costs due to accidents that cause bodily harm to others, or physical damage to others' property. Liability insurance on an automobile is often stated in a three-number sequence, such as, 25/50/10. The first number indicates the maximum level of medical coverage to be paid by the insurance company for medical expenses incurred as a result of an accident to a passenger in the insured's vehicle (in this example, $25,000); the second number indicates the maximum total medical costs the insurance company will pay for a single accident (here, $50,000); the third number indicates the maximum amount to be paid for physical damage to the property of others caused by the insured's vehicle (here, $10,000).

**Automobile
insurance
quotation**

$$\underset{\text{payments per person}}{\text{maximum medical}} \bigg/ \underset{\text{payments per accident}}{\text{maximum total medical}} \bigg/ \underset{\text{payments per accident}}{\text{maximum total property}}$$

$$25/50/10$$

$$\$25,000/\$50,000/\$10,000$$

Example 13

Wendy Willis had an automobile accident for which she was responsible. She had two passengers, Antoine and Cassie, who were injured. Antoine's medical costs totaled $23,000, and Cassie's were $8,000. Wendy's auto caused $3,000 worth of damage to the parked auto with which she collided. Wendy's auto was insured with 20/40/10 liability coverage. (a) How much of the total costs will be covered by insurance? (b) How much of the total costs will not be covered by insurance?

Solution

a. Insurance will cover $20,000 of the $23,000 medical claim of the first person injured. Insurance will cover all of the $8,000 claim of the second person injured. Since the total costs of the medical injury claim is $28,000 for medical costs and Wendy's coverage for medical costs is $40,000, the insurance company will pay $28,000 for medical costs. Since Wendy is covered for a maximum of $10,000 property damage, the $3,000 claim would be totally covered by insurance.

$$\begin{aligned} \text{total insurance coverage of costs} &= \$20,000 + \$8,000 + \$3,000 \\ &= \$31,000 \end{aligned}$$

b. The total costs for the accident were

$$\text{total costs} = \$23,000 + \$8,000 + \$3,000 = \$34,000$$

The insurance company will not be responsible for paying the $3,000 beyond the $31,000 limit.

$$\text{uninsured costs} = \$34,000 - \$31,000 = \$3,000$$

In addition to liability insurance, automobile owners can purchase extended protection in the form of *collision* and *comprehensive* insurance. Automobile *collision* insurance provides benefits to cover all or part of the cost of damage to the *insured's vehicle*. *Comprehensive* insurance provides additional coverage for other physical damage to the insured's vehicle due to theft, vandalism, and so on. The cost of premiums for collision and comprehensive is based on where the vehicle is registered, its value, and the purpose for which it is used (personal or commercial). Premiums for these forms of insurance are determined in much the same way as other types of insurance already covered in this chapter.

CHECK YOUR KNOWLEDGE

Automobile insurance

Solve the following problem. Round dollar amounts to the nearest cent.

- Sally Mack's automobile liability policy is for 15/30/10. She had an accident and subsequent medical liability claims of $9,000, $8,500, $7,000, $5,500, and $1,500 for other people hurt in the accident; and $13,000 for damage done to other people's property. How much will the insurance company pay? How much will insurance not have to pay of the costs of the accident?

16.4 EXERCISES

Solve the following problems. Round dollar amounts to the nearest cent.

1. Tanya Magoon's auto liability policy is for 10/20/5. She had an accident and subsequent medical liability claims of $3,000, $4,500, and $1,500 for other people hurt in the accident; and $4,000 for damage done to other people's property. How much will the insurance company pay of the costs of the accident?

2. Marty Gale's auto liability policy is for 10/20/10. He had an accident and subsequent medical liability claims of $5,000, $4,500, and $12,000 for other people hurt in the accident; and $4,000 for damage to other people's property. How much will the insurance company pay of the costs of the accident?

3. Jan Sargent's auto liability policy is 10/20/5.

She had an accident and subsequent medical liability claims of $500, $1,500, and $1,200 for other people hurt in the accident, and $7,000 for damage to other people's property. How much will the insurance company pay of the costs of the accident?

4. Bob Jackson's auto liability policy is for 25/500/20. He had a one-car accident in which his car left the road and destroyed several road signs, shrubbery, and a small storage building. Four passengers in Bob's car were injured. Bob is faced with the possible loss of his license for driving while intoxicated; he has medical liability claims of $2,500, $6,500, $9,000, and $7,500 for other people hurt in the accident; and $30,000 for damage to other people's property. How much will the insurance company pay of the costs of the accident?

Answers to CYK: Insurance will cover $30,000 of the medical costs and $10,000 of the property loss; insurance will not cover $1,500 of the medical costs and $3,000 of the property loss.

16.5   HEALTH INSURANCE

Health insurance provides protection to offset economic losses due to injury or illness. Health insurance provides payment of benefits for

a.   health care expenses incurred from illness or injury (medical insurance)

b.   loss of income from inability to work caused by injury or illness (disability insurance).

Health insurance is provided by two types of insurers, government insurers and private insurers. The social, or government, type of insurance includes "Old Age, Survivors, Disability, and Health Insurance (OASDHI)" often referred to as social security insurance, and worker's compensation insurance.

Private health insurance companies provide a broad spectrum of coverages including

a.   medical insurance to cover costs of health professionals, hospitals, medications, and medical laboratory work

b.   disability income insurance to cover loss of earnings while a wage earner is unable to work due to illness or injury.

Health insurance, medical and disability income, is provided by both individual and group plans. Usually, group insurance plans cost less than individual plans. The larger number of people paying premiums into the company help to offset the costs of claims paid out by the insurance company, much the same as our earlier example concerning life insurance (Example 5). It is also less expensive for the insurance company to write a single policy to cover a large group than it is to write a separate policy for each person in the group. Other factors, such as the type of work or life-style of the group, may affect premium costs as well. A group of workers engaged in a hazardous line of work would be more likely to have higher premium costs than a group of people whose work is less dangerous and less likely to lead to illness or injury.

Actuaries determine premium costs based on a variety of statistical information pertaining to the expected payout of claims for a particular group of insureds. People in different age groups, occupations, or living circumstances have a different likelihood of making claims on their policies, and the amount of those claims will vary. Insurance actuaries gather statistical data describing these different characteristics and determine premium costs accordingly, similar to the way we noted for determining life insurance premiums.

16.6   BUSINESS INSURANCE

The basic concepts discussed earlier in this chapter apply to commercial (business) insurance. The *risk manager* in a business is responsible for establishing and maintaining a plan of action of (1) controlling risk and (2) risk financing. The risk manager wants to protect the assets and income of the business by providing protection against the risks of accidental loss. The risk manager of a company is not only responsible for determining ways to reduce risk in the company, but is also responsible for the company's insurance program of risk protection.

Business insurance includes a wide variety of protection plans.

- **Employee protection plans** including medical, disability, life, retirement, and social security insurance.

- **Transportation insurance**, including ocean marine and inland marine insurance, covers sea perils of ships and cargoes, and inland transportation by rail, motor truck, and other methods of transport.

- **Liability insurance**, including bodily injury, property damage liability, worker's compensation, and criminal and civil wrongs liability insurance, protects the company in the event it violates contract or tort law (e.g., intentional acts, omissions, or negligence).

- **Crime insurance** protects against nonemployee acts such as theft or vandalism, and *suretyship* protects against an employee failing to fulfill an obligation.

Other forms of insurance to protect a business, its employees, and its customers from the many risks due to uncertainty are available as well.

EXPRESS YOUR THOUGHTS

Compose one or two well-written sentences to express the requested information in your own words.

1.   Define risk, in the business sense.

2.   What is risk management?

3.   Describe how you would calculate the probability of choosing a girl's name from a box containing seven girls' and nine boys' names.

4.   Describe the difference between term life insurance and endowment life insurance.

5. Describe the difference between five-year term life insurance and decreasing term life insurance.

6. What is cash surrender value?

7. Describe how you would calculate the amount of claim to be paid on a $10,000 fire insurance claim if a coinsurance clause required $100,000 of insurance, but the owner purchased only $75,000 of insurance.

8. Explain the coverage of a 30/60/15 automobile liability policy.

Case exercise   A basic insurance program for an individual

Marti Svedman owns and operates her own pharmacy in her hometown of Parma Heights. Marti is a 35-year-old single parent with a 10-year-old daughter, Cindy.

Marti has met with her insurance agent to discuss insurance policies that might assure her daughter's financial future through college to age 23 in the event that Marti might die before that time. Marti's agent has recommended that she include some or all of the following:

1. A $250,000 5-year term life insurance policy that would provide high face value at the lowest premiums. This would guarantee sufficient funds for Cindy's livelihood and education.

2. A 20-year limited pay policy with a $20,000 face value to provide Marti with insurance that would cover incidental costs and debts that might be outstanding at the time of her death. She could pay for this policy during her most productive work years and continue to have the coverage the rest of her life.

3. A $10,000 20-year endowment policy that would provide a stable component of Marti's investment plan for her retirement program (Marti has established an investment program of stocks and bonds).

4. Marti's agent also suggested that she consider a universal life policy that she could tailor to fit her changing needs for immediate high coverage while Cindy is still young, and which could then be modified to suit her retirement needs after Cindy finishes college.

After considerable thought, Marti has decided to purchase the first three recommendations that her agent made. However, she has decided against the universal life policy since she feels she has a good retirement program that would not be enhanced by that part of the recommendation.

Marti's insurance agent has offered Marti a 5% discount on the life insurance premiums if she will insure her $300,000 store building with his company at a rate of $.52 per $100 and an 80% coinsurance clause.

A. Use Table 16.2 to determine what Marti's premiums will be if she adopts the first three recommendations suggested by her agent. Determine the premiums for each part of the program, and what the total of the premiums will be.

B. Determine what Marti's premium would be on her business if she took the minimum amount required by the coinsurance clause.

C. Determine what Marti's life insurance premiums would be if she received the discount offered.

SELF-TEST

A. Terminology review

Complete the following items using the key terms presented at the beginning of the chapter. Check your responses against the answer key at the end of the test.

1. The uncertainty of financial loss was our definition of _____.

2. _____ is the attempt to minimize loss by controlling risk and using insurance to compensate for accidental losses.

3. $$\frac{\text{number of outcomes an event occurs}}{\text{total number of outcomes in experiment}} = \underline{\qquad}$$

4. The _____ _____ of a policy is the amount of money that would be paid to the beneficiary in the event of the death of the insured.

5. _____ life insurance provides protection for the insured's entire life, whereas _____ life insurance covers the insured for a specific time period.

6. Decreasing term life insurance policies have the feature that the _____ amount remains the same as time passes, but the _____ _____ of the policy decreases.

7. _____ life insurance policies have the feature that, if the insured survives through the life of the policy, the insurance pays a regular periodic payment to the insured for the remainder of his or her life, or for a specified period of time.

8. _____ life insurance pays the insured a fixed sum of money if he/she survives the life of the policy.

9. If a person cancels a policy, the policy may have a _____ _____ value, which is a cash savings that the policy earned while the premiums were paid.

10. A _____ clause for a property insurance policy specifies the amount of insurance that should be purchased in order for losses to be fully covered by the insurance.

B. Calculation review

The following concepts and short problems are designed to test your understanding of the objectives identified at the beginning of the chapter. Answers are provided at the end of the test.

11. The "Surfer's Club" membership at Surefun College has 9 members who are in their teens, 15 in their 20s, and 7 in their 30s. If one person is chosen at random from the group, what is the probability the person's age is (a) in the 20s? (b) in the 30s? (c) in the teens? (d) not in the teens?

12. Use Table 16.1 to determine the probability that a person in each of the following age categories would have died in 1987: (a) a 17-year-old, (b) a 9-year-old, (c) a 50-year-old, and (d) a 23-year-old.

13. Sam Harris is 45 years old and plans to purchase $28,000 face value of life insurance. Use Table 16.2 to determine the premium Sam will have to pay for each type of insurance: (a) 5-year renewable term life, (b) whole life, (c) 20-year limited pay life, and (d) 20-year endowment life.

14. Miguel Espinoza purchased $20,000 face value of 20-year limited pay life insurance when he was 30 years old. Now at age 45, he intends to surrender the policy. Use Table 16.3 to determine the cash surrender value.

15. Jake Nichols purchased a $100,000 20-year decreasing term life insurance policy at age 30. Determine (a) what his yearly premium for the policy is and (b) what the cash value of the policy is now that his age is 50. (Use Tables 16.4 and 16.5.)

16. Sally Feldman owns a building valued at $400,000. She purchased $300,000 of fire insurance with an 80% coinsurance clause on

the structure. She recently had a fire that totally destroyed the building. How much should Sally have insured the building for according to the coinsurance clause? How much of the $400,000 claim will be covered by the insurance company?

17. Tanya Magoon's auto liability policy is for 10/20/5. She had an accident and subse-

quent medical liability claims of $3,000, $4,500, and $1,500 for other people hurt in the accident, and $4,000 for damage done to other people's property. How much will the insurance company pay of the costs of the accident?

APPENDIX A:
REFERENCE TABLES

Rate = .5%

N	A Future Value	B Present Value	C Ordinary Annuity	D Sinking Fund	E Present Annuity	F Amortization
1	1.005000	0.995025	0.999999	1.000001	0.995028	1.004997
2	1.010025	0.990074	2.005005	0.498752	1.985109	0.503751
3	1.015075	0.985149	3.015018	0.331673	2.970243	0.336673
4	1.020151	0.980248	4.030109	0.248132	3.950501	0.253133
5	1.025251	0.975371	5.050254	0.198010	4.925871	0.203010
6	1.030378	0.970518	6.075526	0.164595	5.896402	0.169595
7	1.035529	0.965690	7.105875	0.140729	6.862068	0.145729
8	1.040707	0.960885	8.141423	0.122829	7.822967	0.127829
9	1.045911	0.956105	9.182119	0.108907	8.779072	0.113907
10	1.051140	0.951348	10.228040	0.097770	9.730423	0.102770
11	1.056396	0.946615	11.279180	0.088659	10.677040	0.093659
12	1.061678	0.941905	12.335590	0.081066	11.618950	0.086066
13	1.066986	0.937219	13.397270	0.074642	12.556170	0.079642
14	1.072321	0.932556	14.464260	0.069136	13.488730	0.074136
15	1.077683	0.927917	15.536550	0.064364	14.416620	0.069364
16	1.083071	0.923300	16.614250	0.060189	15.339940	0.065189
17	1.088487	0.918707	17.697310	0.056506	16.258650	0.061506
18	1.093929	0.914136	18.785810	0.053232	17.172790	0.058232
19	1.099399	0.909588	19.879720	0.050303	18.082360	0.055303
20	1.104896	0.905063	20.979140	0.047666	18.987440	0.052666
21	1.110420	0.900560	22.084020	0.045282	19.887980	0.050282
22	1.115972	0.896080	23.194480	0.043114	20.784100	0.048114
23	1.121552	0.891622	24.310420	0.041135	21.675700	0.046135
24	1.127160	0.887186	25.431990	0.039321	22.562900	0.044321
25	1.132796	0.882772	26.559140	0.037652	23.445660	0.042652
26	1.138460	0.878380	27.691940	0.036112	24.324040	0.041112
27	1.144152	0.874010	28.830390	0.034686	25.198050	0.039686
28	1.149873	0.869661	29.974560	0.033362	26.067710	0.038362
29	1.155622	0.865335	31.124450	0.032129	26.933060	0.037129
30	1.161400	0.861030	32.280060	0.030979	27.794090	0.035979
31	1.167207	0.856746	33.441430	0.029903	28.650810	0.034903
32	1.173043	0.852484	34.608650	0.028895	29.503300	0.033895
33	1.178909	0.848242	35.781690	0.027947	30.351540	0.032947
34	1.184803	0.844022	36.960600	0.027056	31.195570	0.032056
35	1.190727	0.839823	38.145400	0.026215	32.035390	0.031215
36	1.196681	0.835645	39.336130	0.025422	32.871030	0.030422
37	1.202664	0.831487	40.532830	0.024671	33.702530	0.029671
38	1.208678	0.827351	41.735510	0.023960	34.529890	0.028960
39	1.214721	0.823235	42.944150	0.023286	35.353100	0.028286
40	1.220795	0.819139	44.158890	0.022645	36.172260	0.027645
41	1.226898	0.815064	45.379670	0.022036	36.987310	0.027036
42	1.233033	0.811008	46.606590	0.021456	37.798330	0.026456
43	1.239198	0.806973	47.839620	0.020903	38.605310	0.025903
44	1.245394	0.802959	49.078830	0.020375	39.408270	0.025375
45	1.251621	0.798964	50.324230	0.019871	40.207230	0.024871
48	1.270490	0.787098	54.097900	0.018485	42.580360	0.023485
60	1.348851	0.741372	69.770100	0.014333	51.725610	0.019333
72	1.432045	0.698302	86.408920	0.011573	60.339550	0.016573
84	1.520370	0.657735	104.074000	0.009609	68.453090	0.014609
120	1.819398	0.549633	163.879500	0.006102	90.073500	0.011102
240	3.310207	0.302096	462.041500	0.002164	139.580800	0.007164
360	6.022583	0.166042	1004.517000	0.000996	166.791700	0.005996

Rate = 1%

N	A Future Value	B Present Value	C Ordinary Annuity	D Sinking Fund	E Present Annuity	F Amortization
1	1.010000	0.990099	0.999999	1.000001	0.990099	1.010000
2	1.020100	0.980296	2.010000	0.497513	1.970393	0.507513
3	1.030301	0.970590	3.030098	0.330022	2.940983	0.340022
4	1.040604	0.960980	4.060400	0.246281	3.901965	0.256281
5	1.051010	0.951466	5.101002	0.196040	4.853428	0.206040
6	1.061520	0.942045	6.152010	0.162549	5.795473	0.172548
7	1.072135	0.932718	7.213533	0.138628	6.728191	0.148628
8	1.082857	0.923483	8.285666	0.120690	7.651675	0.130690
9	1.093685	0.914340	9.368515	0.106741	8.566011	0.116740
10	1.104622	0.905287	10.462210	0.095582	9.471303	0.105582
11	1.115668	0.896324	11.566830	0.086454	10.367630	0.096454
12	1.126825	0.887449	12.682500	0.078849	11.255070	0.088849
13	1.138093	0.878663	13.809320	0.072415	12.133740	0.082415
14	1.149474	0.869963	14.947420	0.066901	13.003700	0.076901
15	1.160969	0.861350	16.096890	0.062124	13.865050	0.072124
16	1.172579	0.852821	17.257860	0.057945	14.717870	0.067945
17	1.184304	0.844378	18.430440	0.054258	15.562250	0.064258
18	1.196148	0.836017	19.614740	0.050982	16.398270	0.060982
19	1.208109	0.827740	20.810890	0.048052	17.226010	0.058052
20	1.220190	0.819545	22.018990	0.045415	18.045550	0.055415
21	1.232392	0.811430	23.239180	0.043031	18.856980	0.053031
22	1.244716	0.803396	24.471570	0.040864	19.660370	0.050864
23	1.257163	0.795442	25.716290	0.038886	20.455810	0.048886
24	1.269735	0.787566	26.973450	0.037073	21.243380	0.047074
25	1.282432	0.779769	28.243170	0.035407	22.023140	0.045407
26	1.295256	0.772048	29.525630	0.033869	22.795200	0.043869
27	1.308209	0.764404	30.820870	0.032446	23.559600	0.042446
28	1.321291	0.756836	32.129090	0.031124	24.316440	0.041124
29	1.334504	0.749342	33.450380	0.029895	25.065780	0.039895
30	1.347849	0.741923	34.784880	0.028748	25.807700	0.038748
31	1.361327	0.734577	36.132730	0.027676	26.542280	0.037676
32	1.374941	0.727304	37.494050	0.026671	27.269580	0.036671
33	1.388690	0.720103	38.868990	0.025727	27.989680	0.035727
34	1.402577	0.712973	40.257680	0.024840	28.702660	0.034840
35	1.416603	0.705914	41.660260	0.024004	29.408580	0.034004
36	1.430769	0.698925	43.076860	0.023214	30.107500	0.033214
37	1.445076	0.692005	44.507630	0.022468	30.799500	0.032468
38	1.459527	0.685154	45.952700	0.021762	31.484650	0.031762
39	1.474122	0.678370	47.412230	0.021092	32.163030	0.031092
40	1.488864	0.671653	48.886350	0.020456	32.834680	0.030456
41	1.503752	0.665003	50.375200	0.019851	33.499670	0.029851
42	1.518790	0.658419	51.878980	0.019276	34.158110	0.029276
43	1.533978	0.651900	53.397750	0.018727	34.809990	0.028727
44	1.549317	0.645446	54.931740	0.018204	35.455450	0.028204
45	1.564811	0.639055	56.481050	0.017705	36.094500	0.027705
48	1.612226	0.620261	61.222580	0.016334	37.973950	0.026334
60	1.816696	0.550450	81.669630	0.012244	44.955030	0.022244
72	2.047099	0.488496	104.709900	0.009550	51.150380	0.019550
84	2.306722	0.433516	130.672200	0.007653	56.648440	0.017653
120	3.300386	0.302995	230.038600	0.004347	69.700510	0.014347
240	10.892540	0.091806	989.254400	0.001011	90.819410	0.011011
360	35.949590	0.027817	3494.959000	0.000286	97.218330	0.010286

Rate = 1.5%

N	A Future Value	B Present Value	C Ordinary Annuity	D Sinking Fund	E Present Annuity	F Amortization
1	1.015000	0.985222	0.999999	1.000001	0.985221	1.015001
2	1.030225	0.970662	2.014995	0.496279	1.955879	0.511279
3	1.045678	0.956317	3.045217	0.328384	2.912192	0.343384
4	1.061363	0.942184	4.090890	0.244446	3.854374	0.259446
5	1.077284	0.928261	5.152250	0.194090	4.782629	0.209090
6	1.093443	0.914543	6.229528	0.160526	5.697167	0.175526
7	1.109845	0.901027	7.322972	0.136557	6.598195	0.151557
8	1.126492	0.887711	8.432810	0.118584	7.485903	0.133584
9	1.143390	0.874593	9.559298	0.104610	8.360494	0.119610
10	1.160540	0.861668	10.702680	0.093435	9.222154	0.108435
11	1.177948	0.848934	11.863220	0.084294	10.071090	0.099294
12	1.195617	0.836388	13.041160	0.076680	10.907470	0.091680
13	1.213552	0.824028	14.236780	0.070241	11.731500	0.085241
14	1.231755	0.811850	15.450320	0.064724	12.543340	0.079724
15	1.250231	0.799852	16.682080	0.059945	13.343200	0.074945
16	1.268985	0.788032	17.932310	0.055765	14.131230	0.070765
17	1.288019	0.776386	19.201290	0.052080	14.907610	0.067080
18	1.307340	0.764912	20.489300	0.048806	15.672520	0.063806
19	1.326950	0.753608	21.796640	0.045879	16.426130	0.060879
20	1.346854	0.742471	23.123580	0.043246	17.168590	0.058246
21	1.367056	0.731499	24.470430	0.040866	17.900090	0.055866
22	1.387562	0.720688	25.837480	0.038760	18.620770	0.053760
23	1.408376	0.710038	27.225040	0.036731	19.330810	0.051731
24	1.429501	0.699545	28.633410	0.034924	20.030350	0.049924
25	1.450944	0.689207	30.062910	0.033264	20.719560	0.048264
26	1.472708	0.679021	31.513840	0.031732	21.398570	0.046732
27	1.494798	0.668987	32.986550	0.030315	22.067570	0.045315
28	1.517220	0.659100	34.481340	0.029001	22.726660	0.044001
29	1.539978	0.649360	35.998550	0.027779	23.376010	0.042779
30	1.563078	0.639763	37.538520	0.026639	24.015780	0.041639
31	1.586524	0.630309	39.101600	0.025574	24.646090	0.040574
32	1.610322	0.620994	40.688120	0.024577	25.267070	0.039577
33	1.634477	0.611817	42.298440	0.023642	25.878890	0.038642
34	1.658994	0.602775	43.932910	0.022762	26.481660	0.037762
35	1.683878	0.593867	45.591900	0.021934	27.075530	0.036934
36	1.709137	0.585091	47.275770	0.021152	27.660620	0.036152
37	1.734773	0.576444	48.984900	0.020414	28.237060	0.035414
38	1.760795	0.567925	50.719660	0.019716	28.804980	0.034716
39	1.787207	0.559532	52.480460	0.019055	29.364520	0.034055
40	1.814015	0.551263	54.267660	0.018427	29.915780	0.033427
41	1.841225	0.543117	56.081660	0.017831	30.458890	0.032831
42	1.868843	0.535090	57.922880	0.017264	30.993980	0.032264
43	1.896876	0.527183	59.791730	0.016725	31.521160	0.031725
44	1.925329	0.519392	61.688590	0.016210	32.040550	0.031210
45	1.954209	0.511716	63.613910	0.015720	32.552260	0.030720
48	2.043474	0.489363	69.564910	0.014375	34.042480	0.029375
60	2.443213	0.409297	96.214180	0.010393	39.380190	0.025393
72	2.921147	0.342331	128.076500	0.007808	43.844590	0.022808
84	3.492575	0.286322	166.171700	0.006018	47.578560	0.021018
120	5.969288	0.167524	331.285800	0.003019	55.498390	0.018019
240	35.632390	0.028064	2308.826000	0.000433	64.795710	0.015433
360	212.699900	0.004701	%14113.330000	0.000071	66.353230	0.015071

Rate = 2%

N	A Future Value	B Present Value	C Ordinary Annuity	D Sinking Fund	E Present Annuity	F Amortization
1	1.020000	0.980392	0.999999	1.000001	0.980392	1.020000
2	1.040400	0.961169	2.019996	0.495051	1.941556	0.515051
3	1.061208	0.942322	3.060395	0.326755	2.883879	0.346755
4	1.082432	0.923846	4.121596	0.242624	3.807718	0.262625
5	1.104081	0.905731	5.204028	0.192159	4.713449	0.212159
6	1.126162	0.887972	6.308103	0.158526	5.601415	0.178526
7	1.148685	0.870561	7.434261	0.134512	6.471974	0.154512
8	1.171659	0.853491	8.582944	0.116510	7.325462	0.136510
9	1.195092	0.836756	9.754599	0.102516	8.162215	0.122516
10	1.218994	0.820349	10.949690	0.091327	8.982563	0.111327
11	1.243374	0.804264	12.168680	0.082178	9.786826	0.102178
12	1.268241	0.788494	13.412050	0.074560	10.575320	0.094560
13	1.293606	0.773033	14.680290	0.068119	11.348350	0.088119
14	1.319478	0.757876	15.973890	0.062602	12.106220	0.082602
15	1.345867	0.743015	17.293360	0.057826	12.849230	0.077826
16	1.372785	0.728447	18.639230	0.053650	13.577680	0.073650
17	1.400240	0.714163	20.012010	0.049970	14.291840	0.069970
18	1.428245	0.700160	21.412240	0.046702	14.992000	0.066702
19	1.456810	0.686431	22.840490	0.043782	15.678430	0.063782
20	1.485946	0.672972	24.297290	0.041157	16.351400	0.061157
21	1.515665	0.659777	25.783240	0.038785	17.011180	0.058785
22	1.545978	0.646840	27.298890	0.036632	17.658010	0.056632
23	1.576897	0.634157	28.844870	0.034668	18.292170	0.054668
24	1.608435	0.621722	30.421760	0.032871	18.913890	0.052871
25	1.640604	0.609532	32.030190	0.031221	19.523410	0.051221
26	1.673416	0.597580	33.670790	0.029699	20.121000	0.049699
27	1.706884	0.585863	35.344210	0.028293	20.706860	0.048293
28	1.741022	0.574375	37.051080	0.026990	21.281230	0.046990
29	1.775842	0.563113	38.792100	0.025778	21.844340	0.045778
30	1.811359	0.552072	40.567940	0.024650	22.396420	0.044650
31	1.847586	0.541247	42.379280	0.023596	22.937650	0.043596
32	1.884537	0.530634	44.226870	0.022611	23.468290	0.042611
33	1.922228	0.520230	46.111400	0.021687	23.988520	0.041687
34	1.960672	0.510029	48.033620	0.020819	24.498540	0.040819
35	1.999886	0.500029	49.994290	0.020002	24.998570	0.040002
36	2.039883	0.490224	51.994160	0.019233	25.488800	0.039233
37	2.080681	0.480612	54.034040	0.018507	25.969410	0.038507
38	2.122294	0.471188	56.114710	0.017821	26.440590	0.037821
39	2.164740	0.461949	58.237010	0.017171	26.902540	0.037171
40	2.208035	0.452891	60.401740	0.016556	27.355430	0.036556
41	2.252195	0.444011	62.609770	0.015972	27.799440	0.035972
42	2.297239	0.435305	64.861960	0.015417	28.234750	0.035417
43	2.343184	0.426770	67.159200	0.014890	28.661520	0.034890
44	2.390047	0.418402	69.502360	0.014388	29.079920	0.034388
45	2.437848	0.410198	71.892420	0.013910	29.490110	0.033910
48	2.587064	0.386539	79.353180	0.012602	30.673070	0.032602
60	3.281020	0.304783	114.051000	0.008768	34.760840	0.028768
72	4.161124	0.240320	158.056200	0.006327	37.984010	0.026327
84	5.277307	0.189491	213.865400	0.004676	40.525480	0.024676
120	10.765090	0.092893	488.254600	0.002048	45.355360	0.022048
240	115.887200	0.008629	5744.360000	0.000174	49.568550	0.020174
360	1247.536000	0.000802	62326.810000	0.000016	49.959930	0.020016

Rate = 2.5%

N	A Future Value	B Present Value	C Ordinary Annuity	D Sinking Fund	E Present Annuity	F Amortization
1	1.025000	0.975610	0.999999	1.000001	0.975609	1.025001
2	1.050625	0.951814	2.024999	0.493828	1.927424	0.518827
3	1.076891	0.928599	3.075624	0.325137	2.856023	0.350137
4	1.103813	0.905951	4.152513	0.240818	3.761971	0.265818
5	1.131408	0.883854	5.256324	0.190247	4.645825	0.215247
6	1.159693	0.862297	6.387730	0.156550	5.508120	0.181550
7	1.188686	0.841265	7.547426	0.132495	6.349387	0.157496
8	1.218403	0.820747	8.736110	0.114467	7.170134	0.139467
9	1.248863	0.800729	9.954510	0.100457	7.970860	0.125457
10	1.280084	0.781199	11.203380	0.089259	8.752060	0.114259
11	1.312087	0.762145	12.483460	0.080106	9.514203	0.105106
12	1.344889	0.743556	13.795540	0.072487	10.257760	0.097487
13	1.378511	0.725421	15.140430	0.066048	10.983180	0.091048
14	1.412973	0.707727	16.518940	0.060537	11.690900	0.085537
15	1.448298	0.690466	17.931910	0.055766	12.381370	0.080766
16	1.484505	0.673625	19.380210	0.051599	13.055000	0.076599
17	1.521618	0.657195	20.864710	0.047928	13.712190	0.072928
18	1.559658	0.641166	22.386330	0.044670	14.353350	0.069670
19	1.598650	0.625528	23.945990	0.041761	14.978880	0.066761
20	1.638616	0.610271	25.544640	0.039147	15.589150	0.064147
21	1.679581	0.595387	27.183250	0.036787	16.184540	0.061787
22	1.721571	0.580865	28.862820	0.034647	16.765400	0.059647
23	1.764610	0.566697	30.584400	0.032696	17.332100	0.057696
24	1.808725	0.552876	32.349000	0.030913	17.884980	0.055913
25	1.853943	0.539391	34.157730	0.029276	18.424370	0.054276
26	1.900292	0.526235	36.011680	0.027769	18.950600	0.052769
27	1.947799	0.513400	37.911970	0.026377	19.464000	0.051377
28	1.996494	0.500878	39.859760	0.025088	19.964880	0.050088
29	2.046406	0.488662	41.856250	0.023891	20.453540	0.048891
30	2.097566	0.476743	43.902660	0.022778	20.930280	0.047778
31	2.150006	0.465115	46.000220	0.021739	21.395400	0.046739
32	2.203756	0.453771	48.150230	0.020768	21.849170	0.045768
33	2.258850	0.442703	50.353980	0.019859	22.291870	0.044859
34	2.315321	0.431906	52.612830	0.019007	22.723780	0.044007
35	2.373204	0.421371	54.928150	0.018206	23.145150	0.043206
36	2.432534	0.411094	57.301350	0.017452	23.556240	0.042452
37	2.493347	0.401067	59.733880	0.016741	23.957310	0.041741
38	2.555681	0.391285	62.227220	0.016070	24.348590	0.041070
39	2.619573	0.381742	64.782910	0.015436	24.730330	0.040436
40	2.685062	0.372431	67.402480	0.014836	25.102760	0.039836
41	2.752188	0.363347	70.087530	0.014268	25.466110	0.039268
42	2.820993	0.354485	72.839730	0.013729	25.820600	0.038729
43	2.891518	0.345839	75.660710	0.013217	26.166430	0.038217
44	2.963806	0.337404	78.552230	0.012730	26.503840	0.037730
45	3.037901	0.329175	81.516030	0.012268	26.833010	0.037268
48	3.271487	0.305671	90.859460	0.011006	27.773140	0.036006
60	4.399785	0.227284	135.991400	0.007353	30.908650	0.032353
72	5.917220	0.168998	196.688800	0.005084	33.240070	0.030084
84	7.958001	0.125660	278.320100	0.003593	34.973610	0.028593
120	19.358110	0.051658	734.324300	0.001362	37.933680	0.026362
240	374.736300	0.002669	%14949.450000	0.000067	39.893260	0.025067
360	7254.184000	0.000138	%290127.400000	0.000003	39.994490	0.025003

Rate = 3%

N	A Future Value	B Present Value	C Ordinary Annuity	D Sinking Fund	E Present Annuity	F Amortization
1	1.030000	0.970874	0.999999	1.000001	0.970872	1.030002
2	1.060900	0.942596	2.029999	0.492611	1.913468	0.522611
3	1.092727	0.915142	3.090898	0.323531	2.828610	0.353531
4	1.125509	0.888487	4.183626	0.239027	3.717099	0.269027
5	1.159274	0.862609	5.309133	0.188355	4.579705	0.218355
6	1.194052	0.837484	6.468407	0.154598	5.417190	0.184598
7	1.229874	0.813092	7.662459	0.130506	6.230281	0.160506
8	1.266770	0.789409	8.892333	0.112456	7.019691	0.142456
9	1.304773	0.766417	10.159100	0.098434	7.786107	0.128434
10	1.343916	0.744094	11.463880	0.087231	8.530201	0.117231
11	1.384234	0.722421	12.807790	0.078077	9.252622	0.108077
12	1.425761	0.701380	14.192020	0.070462	9.954001	0.100462
13	1.468534	0.680951	15.617780	0.064030	10.634950	0.094030
14	1.512590	0.661118	17.086320	0.058526	11.296070	0.088526
15	1.557967	0.641862	18.598910	0.053767	11.937930	0.083767
16	1.604706	0.623167	20.156880	0.049611	12.561100	0.079611
17	1.652847	0.605017	21.761580	0.045953	13.166120	0.075953
18	1.702433	0.587395	23.414430	0.042709	13.753510	0.072709
19	1.753506	0.570286	25.116860	0.039814	14.323800	0.069814
20	1.806111	0.553676	26.870370	0.037216	14.877470	0.067216
21	1.860294	0.537549	28.676470	0.034872	15.415020	0.064872
22	1.916103	0.521893	30.536770	0.032747	15.936910	0.062747
23	1.973586	0.506692	32.452870	0.030814	16.443610	0.060814
24	2.032794	0.491934	34.426460	0.029047	16.935540	0.059047
25	2.093778	0.477606	36.459260	0.027428	17.413150	0.057428
26	2.156591	0.463695	38.553030	0.025938	17.876840	0.055938
27	2.221289	0.450192	40.709620	0.024564	18.327030	0.054564
28	2.287927	0.437077	42.930910	0.023293	18.764100	0.053293
29	2.356565	0.424346	45.218830	0.022115	19.188450	0.052115
30	2.427262	0.411987	47.575400	0.021019	19.600440	0.051019
31	2.500080	0.399987	50.002650	0.019999	20.000430	0.049999
32	2.575082	0.388337	52.502750	0.019047	20.388760	0.049047
33	2.652335	0.377026	55.077820	0.018156	20.765790	0.048156
34	2.731905	0.366045	57.730160	0.017322	21.131830	0.047322
35	2.813862	0.355383	60.462060	0.016539	21.487220	0.046539
36	2.898278	0.345032	63.275930	0.015804	21.832250	0.045804
37	2.985226	0.334983	66.174200	0.015112	22.167230	0.045112
38	3.074783	0.325226	69.159430	0.014459	22.492460	0.044459
39	3.167026	0.315754	72.234210	0.013844	22.808210	0.043844
40	3.262037	0.306557	75.401230	0.013262	23.114770	0.043262
41	3.359898	0.297628	78.663270	0.012712	23.412400	0.042712
42	3.460695	0.288959	82.023160	0.012192	23.701360	0.042192
43	3.564516	0.280543	85.483850	0.011698	23.981900	0.041698
44	3.671451	0.272372	89.048370	0.011230	24.254270	0.041230
45	3.781595	0.264439	92.719820	0.010785	24.518710	0.040785
48	4.132251	0.241999	104.408400	0.009578	25.266710	0.039578
60	5.891601	0.169733	163.053400	0.006133	27.675560	0.036133
72	8.400014	0.119047	246.667100	0.004054	29.365090	0.034054
84	11.976410	0.083497	365.880300	0.002733	30.550080	0.032733
120	34.710960	0.028809	1123.699000	0.000890	32.373020	0.030890
240	1204.851000	0.000830	%40128.360000	0.000025	33.305670	0.030025
360	%41821.530000	0.000024	%1394018.0000000	0.000001	33.332540	0.030001

Rate = 3.5%

N	A Future Value	B Present Value	C Ordinary Annuity	D Sinking Fund	E Present Annuity	F Amortization
1	1.035000	0.966184	0.999999	1.000001	0.966183	1.035001
2	1.071225	0.933511	2.034998	0.491401	1.899692	0.526401
3	1.108718	0.901943	3.106223	0.321934	2.801635	0.356935
4	1.147523	0.871442	4.214937	0.237251	3.673075	0.272251
5	1.187686	0.841973	5.362460	0.186482	4.515049	0.221482
6	1.229255	0.813501	6.550145	0.152668	5.328548	0.187668
7	1.272279	0.785991	7.779398	0.128545	6.114537	0.163545
8	1.316809	0.759412	9.051674	0.110477	6.873948	0.145477
9	1.362897	0.733731	10.368480	0.096446	7.607678	0.131446
10	1.410598	0.708919	11.731380	0.085241	8.316597	0.120241
11	1.459969	0.684946	13.141970	0.076092	9.001543	0.111092
12	1.511068	0.661784	14.601940	0.068484	9.663324	0.103484
13	1.563955	0.639405	16.113010	0.062062	10.302730	0.097062
14	1.618694	0.617782	17.676960	0.056571	10.920510	0.091571
15	1.675348	0.596891	19.295650	0.051825	11.517400	0.086825
16	1.733985	0.576706	20.971000	0.047685	12.094110	0.082685
17	1.794674	0.557204	22.704980	0.044043	12.651310	0.079043
18	1.857488	0.538362	24.499650	0.040817	13.189670	0.075817
19	1.922500	0.520156	26.357140	0.037940	13.709830	0.072940
20	1.989787	0.502566	28.279630	0.035361	14.212390	0.070361
21	2.059430	0.485571	30.269420	0.033037	14.697960	0.068037
22	2.131510	0.469151	32.328840	0.030932	15.167110	0.065932
23	2.206113	0.453286	34.460360	0.029019	15.620400	0.064019
24	2.283326	0.437958	36.666460	0.027273	16.058360	0.062273
25	2.363243	0.423147	38.949780	0.025674	16.481500	0.060674
26	2.445956	0.408838	41.313020	0.024205	16.890340	0.059205
27	2.531564	0.395013	43.758980	0.022852	17.285350	0.057852
28	2.620169	0.381655	46.290540	0.021603	17.667000	0.056603
29	2.711875	0.368749	48.910700	0.020445	18.035750	0.055445
30	2.806790	0.356279	51.622580	0.019371	18.392030	0.054371
31	2.905028	0.344231	54.429360	0.018372	18.736260	0.053372
32	3.006704	0.332590	57.334380	0.017442	19.068850	0.052442
33	3.111968	0.321343	60.341090	0.016572	19.390190	0.051572
34	3.220856	0.310477	63.453020	0.015760	19.700670	0.050760
35	3.333586	0.299977	66.673880	0.014998	20.000650	0.049998
36	3.450261	0.289833	70.007450	0.014284	20.290480	0.049284
37	3.571020	0.280032	73.457700	0.013613	20.570510	0.048613
38	3.696005	0.270562	77.028730	0.012982	20.841070	0.047982
39	3.825365	0.261413	80.724730	0.012388	21.102490	0.047388
40	3.959253	0.252573	84.550080	0.011827	21.355060	0.046827
41	4.097827	0.244032	88.509330	0.011298	21.599090	0.046298
42	4.241250	0.235780	92.607150	0.010798	21.834870	0.045798
43	4.389694	0.227806	96.848390	0.010325	22.062680	0.045325
44	4.543333	0.220103	101.238100	0.009878	22.282780	0.044878
45	4.702349	0.212660	105.781400	0.009453	22.495440	0.044453
48	5.213578	0.191807	120.388000	0.008306	23.091230	0.043306
60	7.878070	0.126935	196.516300	0.005089	24.944730	0.040089
72	11.904300	0.084003	311.551400	0.003210	26.171340	0.038210
84	17.988200	0.055592	485.377300	0.002060	26.983090	0.037060
120	62.063990	0.016112	1744.685000	0.000573	28.111080	0.035573
240	3851.939000	0.000260	%110026.800000	0.000009	28.564010	0.035009
360	%239066.700000	0.000004	%6830448.000000	0.000000	28.571310	0.035000

Rate = 4%

N	A Future Value	B Present Value	C Ordinary Annuity	D Sinking Fund	E Present Annuity	F Amortization
1	1.040000	0.961539	0.999999	1.000001	0.961538	1.040001
2	1.081600	0.924556	2.039999	0.490196	1.886094	0.530196
3	1.124864	0.888997	3.121597	0.320349	2.775088	0.360349
4	1.169859	0.854804	4.246462	0.235490	3.629893	0.275490
5	1.216653	0.821927	5.416319	0.184627	4.451821	0.224627
6	1.265319	0.790315	6.632972	0.150762	5.242135	0.190762
7	1.315932	0.759918	7.898289	0.126610	6.002053	0.166610
8	1.368569	0.730690	9.214220	0.108528	6.732742	0.148528
9	1.423312	0.702587	10.582790	0.094493	7.435328	0.134493
10	1.480244	0.675564	12.006100	0.083291	8.110891	0.123291
11	1.539454	0.649581	13.486340	0.074149	8.760472	0.114149
12	1.601032	0.624597	15.025800	0.066552	9.385071	0.106552
13	1.665073	0.600574	16.626820	0.060144	9.985642	0.100144
14	1.731676	0.577475	18.291900	0.054669	10.563120	0.094669
15	1.800943	0.555265	20.023570	0.049941	11.118380	0.089941
16	1.872981	0.533908	21.824510	0.045820	11.652290	0.085820
17	1.947900	0.513374	23.697490	0.042199	12.165660	0.082199
18	2.025816	0.493628	25.645390	0.038993	12.659290	0.078993
19	2.106848	0.474643	27.671200	0.036139	13.133930	0.076139
20	2.191122	0.456387	29.778050	0.033582	13.590320	0.073582
21	2.278767	0.438834	31.969170	0.031280	14.029160	0.071280
22	2.369918	0.421956	34.247940	0.029199	14.451110	0.069199
23	2.464714	0.405727	36.617850	0.027309	14.856840	0.067309
24	2.563303	0.390122	39.082570	0.025587	15.246960	0.065587
25	2.665835	0.375117	41.645870	0.024012	15.622070	0.064012
26	2.772468	0.360690	44.311700	0.022567	15.982760	0.062567
27	2.883366	0.346817	47.084160	0.021239	16.329580	0.061239
28	2.998701	0.333478	49.967540	0.020013	16.663060	0.060013
29	3.118649	0.320652	52.966230	0.018880	16.983710	0.058880
30	3.243395	0.308319	56.084880	0.017830	17.292030	0.057830
31	3.373131	0.296460	59.328270	0.016855	17.588490	0.056855
32	3.508056	0.285058	62.701400	0.015949	17.873550	0.055949
33	3.648378	0.274094	66.209450	0.015104	18.147640	0.055104
34	3.794313	0.263552	69.857830	0.014315	18.411190	0.054315
35	3.946086	0.253416	73.652140	0.013577	18.664610	0.053577
36	4.103929	0.243669	77.598230	0.012887	18.908280	0.052887
37	4.268086	0.234297	81.702150	0.012240	19.142570	0.052240
38	4.438810	0.225286	85.970240	0.011632	19.367860	0.051632
39	4.616362	0.216621	90.409040	0.011061	19.584480	0.051061
40	4.801016	0.208289	95.025400	0.010524	19.792770	0.050524
41	4.993057	0.200278	99.826410	0.010017	19.993050	0.050017
42	5.192779	0.192575	104.819500	0.009540	20.185620	0.049540
43	5.400489	0.185168	110.012200	0.009090	20.370790	0.049090
44	5.616509	0.178047	115.412700	0.008665	20.548840	0.048665
45	5.841169	0.171199	121.029200	0.008262	20.720040	0.048262
48	6.570521	0.152195	139.263000	0.007181	21.195130	0.047181
60	10.519610	0.095061	237.990300	0.004202	22.623490	0.044202
72	16.842230	0.059375	396.055800	0.002525	23.515640	0.042525
84	26.964950	0.037085	649.123700	0.001541	24.072870	0.041541
120	110.662200	0.009037	2741.556000	0.000365	24.774090	0.040365
240	%12246.130000	0.000082	%306128.200000	0.000003	24.997960	0.040003
360	%1355184.000000	0.000001	%33879570.000000	0.000000	24.999980	0.040000

Rate = 4.5%

N	A Future Value	B Present Value	C Ordinary Annuity	D Sinking Fund	E Present Annuity	F Amortization
1	1.045000	0.956938	0.999999	1.000001	0.956937	1.045001
2	1.092025	0.915730	2.044998	0.488998	1.872667	0.533998
3	1.141166	0.876297	3.137022	0.318774	2.748963	0.363774
4	1.192519	0.838561	4.278188	0.233744	3.587524	0.278744
5	1.246182	0.802451	5.470705	0.182792	4.389974	0.227792
6	1.302260	0.767896	6.716888	0.148878	5.157870	0.193878
7	1.360862	0.734829	8.019146	0.124702	5.892699	0.169702
8	1.422100	0.703185	9.380007	0.106610	6.595884	0.151610
9	1.486095	0.672905	10.802110	0.092575	7.268787	0.137575
10	1.552969	0.643928	12.288200	0.081379	7.912715	0.126379
11	1.622853	0.616199	13.841170	0.072248	8.528912	0.117248
12	1.695881	0.589664	15.464020	0.064666	9.118577	0.109666
13	1.772196	0.564272	17.159900	0.058275	9.682848	0.103275
14	1.851944	0.539973	18.932100	0.052820	10.222820	0.097820
15	1.935282	0.516721	20.784040	0.048114	10.739540	0.093114
16	2.022369	0.494470	22.719320	0.044015	11.234010	0.089015
17	2.113376	0.473177	24.741690	0.040418	11.707190	0.085418
18	2.208478	0.452801	26.855060	0.037237	12.159990	0.082237
19	2.307859	0.433302	29.063540	0.034407	12.593290	0.079407
20	2.411713	0.414643	31.371400	0.031876	13.007930	0.076876
21	2.520240	0.396788	33.783110	0.029601	13.404720	0.074601
22	2.633651	0.379701	36.303350	0.027546	13.784420	0.072546
23	2.752165	0.363350	38.936990	0.025683	14.147770	0.070683
24	2.876012	0.347704	41.689160	0.023987	14.495470	0.068987
25	3.005432	0.332731	44.565170	0.022439	14.828200	0.067439
26	3.140677	0.318403	47.570600	0.021021	15.146610	0.066021
27	3.282007	0.304692	50.711280	0.019719	15.451300	0.064719
28	3.429698	0.291571	53.993280	0.018521	15.742870	0.063521
29	3.584034	0.279015	57.422980	0.017415	16.021890	0.062415
30	3.745315	0.267000	61.007010	0.016392	16.288890	0.061392
31	3.913854	0.255503	64.752320	0.015443	16.544390	0.060443
32	4.089978	0.244500	68.666180	0.014563	16.788890	0.059563
33	4.274027	0.233971	72.756150	0.013745	17.022860	0.058745
34	4.466358	0.223896	77.030180	0.012982	17.246750	0.057982
35	4.667343	0.214255	81.496520	0.012270	17.461010	0.057270
36	4.877374	0.205028	86.163870	0.011606	17.666040	0.056606
37	5.096856	0.196199	91.041240	0.010984	17.862240	0.055984
38	5.326214	0.187751	96.138090	0.010402	18.049990	0.055402
39	5.565893	0.179666	101.464300	0.009856	18.229650	0.054856
40	5.816359	0.171929	107.030200	0.009343	18.401580	0.054343
41	6.078095	0.164525	112.846600	0.008862	18.566110	0.053862
42	6.351609	0.157440	118.924600	0.008409	18.723550	0.053409
43	6.637430	0.150661	125.276200	0.007982	18.874210	0.052982
44	6.936116	0.144173	131.913700	0.007581	19.018380	0.052581
45	7.248240	0.137965	138.849800	0.007202	19.156340	0.052202
48	8.271446	0.120898	161.587700	0.006189	19.535610	0.051189
60	14.027390	0.071289	289.497500	0.003454	20.638020	0.048454
72	23.788780	0.042037	506.417400	0.001975	21.288080	0.046975
84	40.342940	0.024787	874.287600	0.001144	21.671390	0.046144
120	196.767600	0.005082	4350.391000	0.000230	22.109290	0.045230
240	%38717.490000	0.000026	%860366.400000	0.000001	22.221650	0.045001
360	%7618347.000000	0.000000	%169296600.000000	0.000000	22.222220	0.045000

Rate = 5%

N	A Future Value	B Present Value	C Ordinary Annuity	D Sinking Fund	E Present Annuity	F Amortization
1	1.050000	0.952381	0.999999	1.000001	0.952380	1.050001
2	1.102500	0.907030	2.049997	0.487806	1.859408	0.537806
3	1.157625	0.863838	3.152495	0.317209	2.723245	0.367209
4	1.215506	0.822703	4.310117	0.232012	3.545945	0.282012
5	1.276281	0.783526	5.525623	0.180975	4.329472	0.230975
6	1.340095	0.746216	6.801902	0.147018	5.075687	0.197018
7	1.407100	0.710682	8.141993	0.122820	5.786366	0.172820
8	1.477454	0.676840	9.549089	0.104722	6.463204	0.154722
9	1.551327	0.644609	11.026540	0.090690	7.107813	0.140690
10	1.628893	0.613914	12.577870	0.079505	7.721725	0.129505
11	1.710338	0.584680	14.206760	0.070389	8.306405	0.120389
12	1.795855	0.556838	15.917090	0.062826	8.863241	0.112826
13	1.885647	0.530322	17.712940	0.056456	9.393562	0.106456
14	1.979929	0.505069	19.598590	0.051024	9.898630	0.101024
15	2.078926	0.481018	21.578520	0.046342	10.379650	0.096342
16	2.182872	0.458112	23.657430	0.042270	10.837760	0.092270
17	2.292015	0.436297	25.840300	0.038699	11.274060	0.088699
18	2.406616	0.415521	28.132310	0.035546	11.689580	0.085546
19	2.526946	0.395735	30.538920	0.032745	12.085310	0.082745
20	2.653293	0.376890	33.065870	0.030243	12.462200	0.080243
21	2.785958	0.358943	35.719160	0.027996	12.821140	0.077996
22	2.925255	0.341851	38.505110	0.025971	13.162990	0.075971
23	3.071518	0.325572	41.430360	0.024137	13.488560	0.074137
24	3.225093	0.310069	44.501870	0.022471	13.798630	0.072471
25	3.386348	0.295303	47.726960	0.020953	14.093930	0.070953
26	3.555665	0.281241	51.113300	0.019564	14.375170	0.069564
27	3.733448	0.267849	54.668960	0.018292	14.643020	0.068292
28	3.920120	0.255094	58.402400	0.017123	14.898120	0.067123
29	4.116126	0.242947	62.322520	0.016046	15.141060	0.066046
30	4.321932	0.231378	66.438630	0.015051	15.372440	0.065051
31	4.538028	0.220360	70.760560	0.014132	15.592800	0.064132
32	4.764929	0.209867	75.298570	0.013280	15.802670	0.063280
33	5.003175	0.199873	80.063500	0.012490	16.002540	0.062490
34	5.253333	0.190355	85.066660	0.011755	16.192890	0.061755
35	5.515999	0.181291	90.319990	0.011072	16.374180	0.061072
36	5.791798	0.172658	95.835970	0.010434	16.546840	0.060434
37	6.081388	0.164436	101.627800	0.009840	16.711280	0.059840
38	6.385457	0.156606	107.709200	0.009284	16.867880	0.059284
39	6.704729	0.149148	114.094600	0.008765	17.017030	0.058765
40	7.039965	0.142046	120.799300	0.008278	17.159080	0.058278
41	7.391963	0.135282	127.839300	0.007822	17.294360	0.057822
42	7.761560	0.128840	135.231200	0.007395	17.423200	0.057395
43	8.149638	0.122705	142.992800	0.006993	17.545900	0.056993
44	8.557118	0.116862	151.142400	0.006616	17.662770	0.056616
45	8.984974	0.111297	159.699500	0.006262	17.774060	0.056262
48	10.401230	0.096143	188.024600	0.005318	18.077150	0.055318
60	18.679090	0.053536	353.581800	0.002828	18.929290	0.052828
72	33.544930	0.029811	650.898600	0.001536	19.403790	0.051536
84	60.241810	0.016600	1184.836000	0.000844	19.668010	0.050844
120	348.908400	0.002866	6958.168000	0.000144	19.942680	0.050144
240	%121737.100000	0.000008	%2434721.000000	0.000000	19.999840	0.050000
360	%42475080.000000	0.000000	%849501600.000000	0.000000	20.000000	0.050000

Rate = 5.5%

N	A Future Value	B Present Value	C Ordinary Annuity	D Sinking Fund	E Present Annuity	F Amortization
1	1.055000	0.947867	0.999999	1.000001	0.947867	1.055001
2	1.113025	0.898453	2.054997	0.486619	1.846317	0.541619
3	1.174241	0.851614	3.168019	0.315655	2.697930	0.370655
4	1.238824	0.807217	4.342259	0.230295	3.505146	0.285295
5	1.306960	0.765135	5.581082	0.179177	4.270280	0.234177
6	1.378842	0.725246	6.888039	0.145179	4.995524	0.200179
7	1.454678	0.687437	8.266878	0.120965	5.682960	0.175965
8	1.534686	0.651599	9.721555	0.102864	6.334559	0.157864
9	1.619093	0.617630	11.256240	0.088840	6.952187	0.143840
10	1.708143	0.585431	12.875330	0.077668	7.537617	0.132668
11	1.802091	0.554911	14.583470	0.068571	8.092528	0.123571
12	1.901206	0.525982	16.385560	0.061029	8.618508	0.116029
13	2.005772	0.498561	18.286760	0.054684	9.117070	0.109684
14	2.116089	0.472570	20.292520	0.049279	9.589638	0.104279
15	2.232474	0.447934	22.408610	0.044626	10.037570	0.099626
16	2.355260	0.424582	24.641080	0.040583	10.462150	0.095583
17	2.484799	0.402447	26.996340	0.037042	10.864600	0.092042
18	2.621462	0.381467	29.481130	0.033920	11.246060	0.088920
19	2.765643	0.361580	32.102590	0.031150	11.607640	0.086150
20	2.917753	0.342730	34.868230	0.028679	11.950370	0.083679
21	3.078229	0.324862	37.785980	0.026465	12.275230	0.081465
22	3.247531	0.307926	40.864200	0.024471	12.583160	0.079471
23	3.426145	0.291873	44.111730	0.022670	12.875030	0.077670
24	3.614583	0.276657	47.537870	0.021036	13.151690	0.076036
25	3.813384	0.262234	51.152440	0.019549	13.413920	0.074549
26	4.023120	0.248563	54.965820	0.018193	13.662490	0.073193
27	4.244392	0.235605	58.988940	0.016952	13.898090	0.071952
28	4.477833	0.223322	63.233320	0.015814	14.121410	0.070814
29	4.724113	0.211680	67.711150	0.014769	14.333090	0.069769
30	4.983938	0.200645	72.435250	0.013805	14.533740	0.068805
31	5.258055	0.190184	77.419180	0.012917	14.723920	0.067917
32	5.547247	0.180270	82.677210	0.012095	14.904190	0.067095
33	5.852345	0.170872	88.224460	0.011335	15.075060	0.066335
34	6.174224	0.161964	94.076790	0.010630	15.237020	0.065630
35	6.513806	0.153520	100.251000	0.009975	15.390540	0.064975
36	6.872064	0.145517	106.764800	0.009366	15.536060	0.064366
37	7.250027	0.137931	113.636900	0.008800	15.673990	0.063800
38	7.648778	0.130740	120.886900	0.008272	15.804730	0.063272
39	8.069460	0.123924	128.535600	0.007780	15.928660	0.062780
40	8.513279	0.117464	136.605100	0.007320	16.046120	0.062320
41	8.981509	0.111340	145.118400	0.006891	16.157460	0.061891
42	9.475491	0.105535	154.099800	0.006489	16.262990	0.061489
43	9.996642	0.100034	163.575300	0.006113	16.363030	0.061113
44	10.546460	0.094819	173.571900	0.005761	16.457840	0.060761
45	11.126510	0.089875	184.118400	0.005431	16.547720	0.060431
48	13.065210	0.076539	219.367400	0.004559	16.790200	0.059559
60	24.839640	0.040258	433.448100	0.002307	17.449850	0.057307
72	47.225260	0.021175	840.459300	0.001190	17.796820	0.056190
84	89.784920	0.011138	1614.271000	0.000619	17.979320	0.055619

Rate = 6%

N	A Future Value	B Present Value	C Ordinary Annuity	D Sinking Fund	E Present Annuity	F Amortization
1	1.060000	0.943396	0.999999	1.000001	0.943396	1.060001
2	1.123600	0.889997	2.059998	0.485437	1.833391	0.545437
3	1.191016	0.839619	3.183597	0.314110	2.673010	0.374110
4	1.262477	0.792094	4.374612	0.228592	3.465103	0.288592
5	1.338225	0.747258	5.637088	0.177397	4.212361	0.237397
6	1.418519	0.704961	6.975312	0.143363	4.917321	0.203363
7	1.503630	0.665057	8.393828	0.119135	5.582378	0.179135
8	1.593847	0.627413	9.897457	0.101036	6.209790	0.161036
9	1.689478	0.591899	11.491300	0.087022	6.801688	0.147022
10	1.790847	0.558395	13.180780	0.075868	7.360082	0.135868
11	1.898298	0.526788	14.971630	0.066793	7.886870	0.126793
12	2.012195	0.496970	16.869920	0.059277	8.383839	0.119277
13	2.132927	0.468839	18.882110	0.052960	8.852676	0.112960
14	2.260902	0.442301	21.015040	0.047585	9.294979	0.107585
15	2.396556	0.417265	23.275940	0.042963	9.712243	0.102963
16	2.540350	0.393647	25.672490	0.038952	10.105890	0.098952
17	2.692770	0.371365	28.212840	0.035445	10.477250	0.095445
18	2.854336	0.350344	30.905610	0.032357	10.827600	0.092357
19	3.025597	0.330513	33.759940	0.029621	11.158110	0.089621
20	3.207132	0.311805	36.785530	0.027185	11.469920	0.087185
21	3.399560	0.294156	39.992670	0.025005	11.764070	0.085005
22	3.603533	0.277505	43.392230	0.023046	12.041580	0.083046
23	3.819745	0.261798	46.995750	0.021279	12.303370	0.081279
24	4.048929	0.246979	50.815490	0.019679	12.550350	0.079679
25	4.291865	0.232999	54.864420	0.018227	12.783350	0.078227
26	4.549377	0.219810	59.156280	0.016904	13.003160	0.076904
27	4.822339	0.207368	63.705660	0.015697	13.210530	0.075697
28	5.111679	0.195630	68.527980	0.014593	13.406160	0.074593
29	5.418380	0.184557	73.639660	0.013580	13.590720	0.073580
30	5.743482	0.174110	79.058030	0.012649	13.764830	0.072649
31	6.088090	0.164255	84.801500	0.011792	13.929080	0.071792
32	6.453376	0.154958	90.889590	0.011002	14.084040	0.071002
33	6.840578	0.146186	97.342960	0.010273	14.230230	0.070273
34	7.251012	0.137912	104.183500	0.009598	14.368140	0.069598
35	7.686073	0.130105	111.434500	0.008974	14.498240	0.068974
36	8.147236	0.122741	119.120600	0.008395	14.620980	0.068395
37	8.636070	0.115793	127.267800	0.007857	14.736780	0.067857
38	9.154233	0.109239	135.903900	0.007358	14.846020	0.067358
39	9.703486	0.103056	145.058100	0.006894	14.949070	0.066894
40	10.285700	0.097222	154.761600	0.006462	15.046290	0.066462
41	10.902840	0.091719	165.047300	0.006059	15.138010	0.066059
42	11.557010	0.086528	175.950100	0.005683	15.224540	0.065683
43	12.250430	0.081630	187.507100	0.005333	15.306170	0.065333
44	12.985450	0.077009	199.757500	0.005006	15.383180	0.065006
45	13.764580	0.072650	212.743000	0.004701	15.455830	0.064701
48	16.393830	0.060999	256.563900	0.003898	15.650030	0.063898
60	32.987580	0.030314	533.126300	0.001876	16.161430	0.061876
72	66.377460	0.015065	1089.624000	0.000918	16.415580	0.060918
84	133.564400	0.007487	2209.407000	0.000453	16.541880	0.060453

Rate = 6.5%

N	A Future Value	B Present Value	C Ordinary Annuity	D Sinking Fund	E Present Annuity	F Amortization
1	1.065000	0.938967	1.000001	0.999999	0.938968	1.065000
2	1.134225	0.881659	2.065002	0.484261	1.820628	0.549261
3	1.207950	0.827849	3.199229	0.312575	2.648478	0.377575
4	1.286467	0.777323	4.407179	0.226903	3.425801	0.291903
5	1.370087	0.729881	5.693647	0.175634	4.155683	0.240634
6	1.459143	0.685334	7.063734	0.141568	4.841017	0.206568
7	1.553987	0.643506	8.522879	0.117331	5.484524	0.182331
8	1.654996	0.604231	10.076870	0.099237	6.088755	0.164237
9	1.762571	0.567353	11.731860	0.085238	6.656108	0.150238
10	1.877138	0.532726	13.494440	0.074105	7.188835	0.139105
11	1.999153	0.500212	15.371580	0.065055	7.689048	0.130055
12	2.129098	0.469683	17.370730	0.057568	8.158730	0.122568
13	2.267489	0.441017	19.499830	0.051283	8.599747	0.116282
14	2.414876	0.414100	21.767320	0.045940	9.013846	0.110940
15	2.571843	0.388826	24.182200	0.041353	9.402674	0.106353
16	2.739013	0.365095	26.754040	0.037378	9.767769	0.102378
17	2.917049	0.342812	29.493060	0.033906	10.110580	0.098906
18	3.106657	0.321889	32.410110	0.030855	10.432470	0.095855
19	3.308590	0.302244	35.516770	0.028156	10.734720	0.093156
20	3.523648	0.283797	38.825360	0.025756	11.018510	0.090756
21	3.752686	0.266476	42.349020	0.023613	11.284990	0.088613
22	3.996611	0.250212	46.101700	0.021691	11.535200	0.086691
23	4.256391	0.234941	50.098320	0.019961	11.770140	0.084961
24	4.533056	0.220602	54.354710	0.018398	11.990740	0.083398
25	4.827705	0.207138	58.887770	0.016981	12.197880	0.081981
26	5.141506	0.194496	63.715480	0.015695	12.392380	0.080695
27	5.475704	0.182625	68.856990	0.014523	12.575000	0.079523
28	5.831625	0.171479	74.332700	0.013453	12.746480	0.078453
29	6.210681	0.161013	80.164330	0.012474	12.907490	0.077474
30	6.614375	0.151186	86.375010	0.011577	13.058680	0.076577
31	7.044311	0.141959	92.989390	0.010754	13.200640	0.075754
32	7.502191	0.133294	100.033700	0.009997	13.333930	0.074997
33	7.989834	0.125159	107.535900	0.009299	13.459090	0.074299
34	8.509173	0.117520	115.525800	0.008656	13.576610	0.073656
35	9.062270	0.110348	124.034900	0.008062	13.686960	0.073062
36	9.651318	0.103613	133.097200	0.007513	13.790570	0.072513
37	10.278650	0.097289	142.748500	0.007005	13.887860	0.072005
38	10.946770	0.091351	153.027200	0.006535	13.979210	0.071535
39	11.658310	0.085776	163.974000	0.006099	14.064990	0.071099
40	12.416100	0.080541	175.632300	0.005694	14.145530	0.070694
41	13.223150	0.075625	188.048400	0.005318	14.221150	0.070318
42	14.082650	0.071009	201.271600	0.004968	14.292170	0.069968
43	14.998020	0.066675	215.354200	0.004644	14.358840	0.069644
44	15.972900	0.062606	230.352200	0.004341	14.421450	0.069341
45	17.011140	0.058785	246.325200	0.004060	14.480230	0.069060
48	20.548600	0.048665	300.747600	0.003325	14.635920	0.068325
60	43.749960	0.022857	657.691800	0.001520	15.032970	0.066520
72	93.147920	0.010736	1417.660000	0.000705	15.219450	0.065705
84	198.321000	0.005042	3035.708000	0.000329	15.307040	0.065329

Rate = 7%

N	A Future Value	B Present Value	C Ordinary Annuity	D Sinking Fund	E Present Annuity	F Amortization
1	1.070000	0.934579	1.000001	0.999999	0.934580	1.069999
2	1.144900	0.873439	2.070001	0.483092	1.808019	0.553091
3	1.225043	0.816298	3.214903	0.311051	2.624318	0.381051
4	1.310796	0.762895	4.439947	0.225228	3.387214	0.295228
5	1.402552	0.712986	5.750743	0.173891	4.100199	0.243891
6	1.500731	0.666342	7.153297	0.139796	4.766543	0.209796
7	1.605782	0.622750	8.654029	0.115553	5.389293	0.185553
8	1.718187	0.582009	10.259810	0.097468	5.971302	0.167468
9	1.838460	0.543934	11.978000	0.083486	6.515236	0.153486
10	1.967152	0.508349	13.816460	0.072377	7.023585	0.142377
11	2.104853	0.475093	15.783620	0.063357	7.498678	0.133357
12	2.252193	0.444012	17.888470	0.055902	7.942691	0.125902
13	2.409846	0.414964	20.140660	0.049651	8.357655	0.119651
14	2.578536	0.387817	22.550510	0.044345	8.745471	0.114345
15	2.759034	0.362446	25.129050	0.039795	9.107919	0.109795
16	2.952166	0.338734	27.888090	0.035858	9.446652	0.105858
17	3.158818	0.316574	30.840260	0.032425	9.763228	0.102425
18	3.379935	0.295864	33.999080	0.029413	10.059090	0.099413
19	3.616531	0.276508	37.379010	0.026753	10.335600	0.096753
20	3.869688	0.258419	40.995550	0.024393	10.594020	0.094393
21	4.140566	0.241513	44.865240	0.022289	10.835530	0.092289
22	4.430407	0.225713	49.005810	0.020406	11.061240	0.090406
23	4.740536	0.210947	53.436220	0.018714	11.272190	0.088714
24	5.072373	0.197146	58.176760	0.017189	11.469340	0.087189
25	5.427439	0.184249	63.249130	0.015810	11.653590	0.085810
26	5.807360	0.172195	68.676580	0.014561	11.825780	0.084561
27	6.213876	0.160930	74.483950	0.013426	11.986710	0.083426
28	6.648848	0.150402	80.697830	0.012392	12.137120	0.082392
29	7.114267	0.140563	87.346660	0.011449	12.277680	0.081449
30	7.612266	0.131367	94.460940	0.010586	12.409040	0.080586
31	8.145126	0.122773	102.073200	0.009797	12.531820	0.079797
32	8.715284	0.114741	110.218400	0.009073	12.646560	0.079073
33	9.325354	0.107235	118.933600	0.008408	12.753790	0.078408
34	9.978129	0.100219	128.259000	0.007797	12.854010	0.077797
35	10.676600	0.093663	138.237100	0.007234	12.947670	0.077234
36	11.423960	0.087535	148.913700	0.006715	13.035210	0.076715
37	12.223640	0.081809	160.337700	0.006237	13.117020	0.076237
38	13.079300	0.076457	172.561400	0.005795	13.193480	0.075795
39	13.994850	0.071455	185.640700	0.005387	13.264930	0.075387
40	14.974490	0.066780	199.635500	0.005009	13.331710	0.075009
41	16.022700	0.062411	214.610000	0.004660	13.394120	0.074660
42	17.144290	0.058328	230.632700	0.004336	13.452450	0.074336
43	18.344400	0.054513	247.777100	0.004036	13.506960	0.074036
44	19.628500	0.050946	266.121500	0.003758	13.557910	0.073758
45	21.002500	0.047613	285.750000	0.003500	13.605520	0.073500
48	25.728970	0.038867	353.270900	0.002831	13.730480	0.072831
60	57.946600	0.017257	813.522800	0.001229	14.039180	0.071229
72	130.506900	0.007662	1850.099000	0.000541	14.176250	0.070541
84	293.926700	0.003402	4184.668000	0.000239	14.237110	0.070239

Rate = 7.500001%

N	A Future Value	B Present Value	C Ordinary Annuity	D Sinking Fund	E Present Annuity	F Amortization
1	1.075000	0.930233	1.000001	0.999999	0.930233	1.075000
2	1.155625	0.865333	2.075001	0.481927	1.795566	0.556927
3	1.242297	0.804960	3.230627	0.309537	2.600528	0.384537
4	1.335469	0.748800	4.472925	0.223567	3.349328	0.298567
5	1.435630	0.696559	5.808395	0.172165	4.045887	0.247165
6	1.543302	0.647961	7.244026	0.138045	4.693849	0.213045
7	1.659050	0.602755	8.787328	0.113800	5.296604	0.188800
8	1.783478	0.560702	10.446380	0.095727	5.857306	0.170727
9	1.917239	0.521583	12.229860	0.081767	6.378889	0.156767
10	2.061032	0.485194	14.147100	0.070686	6.864084	0.145686
11	2.215610	0.451343	16.208130	0.061697	7.315428	0.136697
12	2.381781	0.419854	18.423740	0.054278	7.735281	0.129278
13	2.560414	0.390562	20.805520	0.048064	8.125842	0.123064
14	2.752446	0.363313	23.365940	0.042797	8.489156	0.117797
15	2.958879	0.337966	26.118390	0.038287	8.827122	0.113287
16	3.180795	0.314387	29.077270	0.034391	9.141509	0.109391
17	3.419355	0.292453	32.258070	0.031000	9.433962	0.106000
18	3.675807	0.272049	35.677420	0.028029	9.706011	0.103029
19	3.951493	0.253069	39.353230	0.025411	9.959081	0.100411
20	4.247855	0.235413	43.304730	0.023092	10.194490	0.098092
21	4.566444	0.218989	47.552590	0.021029	10.413480	0.096029
22	4.908928	0.203710	52.119030	0.019187	10.617190	0.094187
23	5.277097	0.189498	57.027960	0.017535	10.806690	0.092535
24	5.672879	0.176277	62.305060	0.016050	10.982970	0.091050
25	6.098346	0.163979	67.977950	0.014711	11.146950	0.089711
26	6.555722	0.152539	74.076290	0.013500	11.299490	0.088500
27	7.047402	0.141896	80.632020	0.012402	11.441380	0.087402
28	7.575957	0.131997	87.679410	0.011405	11.573380	0.086405
29	8.144154	0.122787	95.255380	0.010498	11.696170	0.085498
30	8.754966	0.114221	103.399500	0.009671	11.810390	0.084671
31	9.411589	0.106252	112.154500	0.008916	11.916640	0.083916
32	10.117460	0.098839	121.566100	0.008226	12.015480	0.083226
33	10.876270	0.091943	131.683600	0.007594	12.107420	0.082594
34	11.691990	0.085529	142.559900	0.007015	12.192950	0.082015
35	12.568890	0.079562	154.251900	0.006483	12.272510	0.081483
36	13.511560	0.074011	166.820700	0.005994	12.346520	0.080994
37	14.524920	0.068847	180.332300	0.005545	12.415370	0.080545
38	15.614290	0.064044	194.857200	0.005132	12.479410	0.080132
39	16.785370	0.059576	210.471600	0.004751	12.538990	0.079751
40	18.044250	0.055419	227.256900	0.004400	12.594410	0.079400
41	19.397590	0.051553	245.301200	0.004077	12.645960	0.079077
42	20.852410	0.047956	264.698800	0.003778	12.693920	0.078778
43	22.416340	0.044610	285.551200	0.003502	12.738530	0.078502
44	24.097570	0.041498	307.967500	0.003247	12.780030	0.078247
45	25.904890	0.038603	332.065100	0.003011	12.818630	0.078011
48	32.181570	0.031074	415.754200	0.002405	12.919020	0.077405
60	76.649420	0.013046	1008.659000	0.000991	13.159380	0.075991
72	182.562100	0.005478	2420.828000	0.000413	13.260300	0.075413
84	434.823000	0.002300	5784.307000	0.000173	13.302670	0.075173

Rate = 8%

N	A Future Value	B Present Value	C Ordinary Annuity	D Sinking Fund	E Present Annuity	F Amortization
1	1.080000	0.925926	1.000001	0.999999	0.925926	1.080000
2	1.166400	0.857339	2.080001	0.480769	1.783265	0.560769
3	1.259712	0.793832	3.246401	0.308033	2.577098	0.388033
4	1.360489	0.735030	4.506114	0.221921	3.312128	0.301921
5	1.469328	0.680583	5.866604	0.170456	3.992711	0.250456
6	1.586875	0.630170	7.335933	0.136315	4.622882	0.216315
7	1.713825	0.583490	8.922808	0.112072	5.206372	0.192072
8	1.850931	0.540269	10.636630	0.094015	5.746641	0.174015
9	1.999005	0.500249	12.487570	0.080080	6.246890	0.160080
10	2.158926	0.463193	14.486570	0.069029	6.710084	0.149029
11	2.331640	0.428883	16.645500	0.060076	7.138966	0.140076
12	2.518171	0.397114	18.977140	0.052695	7.536080	0.132695
13	2.719625	0.367698	21.495310	0.046522	7.903778	0.126522
14	2.937195	0.340461	24.214940	0.041297	8.244239	0.121297
15	3.172171	0.315242	27.152140	0.036830	8.559481	0.116830
16	3.425944	0.291890	30.324310	0.032977	8.851371	0.112977
17	3.700020	0.270269	33.750250	0.029629	9.121640	0.109629
18	3.996022	0.250249	37.450270	0.026702	9.371889	0.106702
19	4.315704	0.231712	41.446290	0.024128	9.603601	0.104128
20	4.660960	0.214548	45.762010	0.021852	9.818149	0.101852
21	5.033837	0.198656	50.422960	0.019832	10.016810	0.099832
22	5.436544	0.183940	55.456800	0.018032	10.200740	0.098032
23	5.871468	0.170315	60.893350	0.016422	10.371060	0.096422
24	6.341186	0.157699	66.764830	0.014978	10.528760	0.094978
25	6.848480	0.146018	73.106000	0.013679	10.674780	0.093679
26	7.396360	0.135202	79.954500	0.012507	10.809980	0.092507
27	7.988068	0.125187	87.350850	0.011448	10.935170	0.091448
28	8.627113	0.115914	95.338920	0.010489	11.051080	0.090489
29	9.317282	0.107327	103.966000	0.009619	11.158410	0.089619
30	10.062670	0.099377	113.283300	0.008827	11.257780	0.088827
31	10.867680	0.092016	123.346000	0.008107	11.349800	0.088107
32	11.737100	0.085200	134.213700	0.007451	11.435000	0.087451
33	12.676060	0.078889	145.950800	0.006852	11.513890	0.086852
34	13.690150	0.073045	158.626900	0.006304	11.586940	0.086304
35	14.785360	0.067634	172.317000	0.005803	11.654570	0.085803
36	15.968190	0.062625	187.102400	0.005345	11.717190	0.085345
37	17.245650	0.057986	203.070600	0.004924	11.775180	0.084924
38	18.625300	0.053690	220.316200	0.004539	11.828870	0.084539
39	20.115320	0.049713	238.941500	0.004185	11.878580	0.084185
40	21.724550	0.046031	259.056900	0.003860	11.924610	0.083860
41	23.462510	0.042621	280.781400	0.003561	11.967240	0.083561
42	25.339520	0.039464	304.244000	0.003287	12.006700	0.083287
43	27.366680	0.036541	329.583500	0.003034	12.043240	0.083034
44	29.556010	0.033834	356.950200	0.002802	12.077080	0.082802
45	31.920500	0.031328	386.506200	0.002587	12.108400	0.082587
48	40.210630	0.024869	490.132900	0.002040	12.189140	0.082040
60	101.257300	0.009876	1253.216000	0.000798	12.376550	0.080798
72	254.983100	0.003922	3174.789000	0.000315	12.450980	0.080315
84	642.091100	0.001557	8013.639000	0.000125	12.480530	0.080125

Rate = 8.5%

N	A Future Value	B Present Value	C Ordinary Annuity	D Sinking Fund	E Present Annuity	F Amortization
1	1.085000	0.921659	1.000001	1.000000	0.921660	1.084999
2	1.177225	0.849455	2.085001	0.479616	1.771116	0.564616
3	1.277289	0.782908	3.262227	0.306539	2.554023	0.391539
4	1.385859	0.721574	4.539518	0.220288	3.275599	0.305288
5	1.503657	0.665045	5.925378	0.168766	3.940644	0.253766
6	1.631468	0.612945	7.429036	0.134607	4.553590	0.219607
7	1.770143	0.564926	9.060503	0.110369	5.118516	0.195369
8	1.920605	0.520669	10.830650	0.092331	5.639186	0.177331
9	2.083857	0.479879	12.751250	0.078424	6.119065	0.163424
10	2.260985	0.442285	14.835110	0.067408	6.561351	0.152408
11	2.453169	0.407636	17.096100	0.058493	6.968987	0.143493
12	2.661688	0.375701	19.549270	0.051153	7.344689	0.136153
13	2.887932	0.346269	22.210960	0.045023	7.690958	0.130023
14	3.133406	0.319142	25.098890	0.039842	8.010100	0.124842
15	3.399746	0.294140	28.232300	0.035420	8.304240	0.120420
16	3.688724	0.271096	31.632050	0.031614	8.575336	0.116614
17	4.002266	0.249858	35.320780	0.028312	8.825194	0.113312
18	4.342459	0.230284	39.323050	0.025430	9.055479	0.110430
19	4.711568	0.212244	43.665510	0.022901	9.267723	0.107901
20	5.112052	0.195616	48.377090	0.020671	9.463339	0.105671
21	5.546577	0.180291	53.489140	0.018695	9.643630	0.103695
22	6.018036	0.166167	59.035720	0.016939	9.809798	0.101939
23	6.529569	0.153149	65.053750	0.015372	9.962947	0.100372
24	7.084583	0.141152	71.583330	0.013970	10.104100	0.098970
25	7.686773	0.130094	78.667910	0.012712	10.234190	0.097712
26	8.340149	0.119902	86.354690	0.011580	10.354090	0.096580
27	9.049062	0.110509	94.694850	0.010560	10.464600	0.095560
28	9.818234	0.101851	103.743900	0.009639	10.566460	0.094639
29	10.652780	0.093872	113.562200	0.008806	10.660330	0.093806
30	11.558270	0.086518	124.214900	0.008051	10.746850	0.093051
31	12.540720	0.079740	135.773200	0.007365	10.826590	0.092365
32	13.606690	0.073493	148.314000	0.006742	10.900080	0.091742
33	14.763260	0.067736	161.920700	0.006176	10.967820	0.091176
34	16.018130	0.062429	176.683900	0.005660	11.030240	0.090660
35	17.379680	0.057538	192.702100	0.005189	11.087780	0.090189
36	18.856950	0.053031	210.081800	0.004760	11.140810	0.089760
37	20.459790	0.048876	228.938700	0.004368	11.189690	0.089368
38	22.198880	0.045047	249.398500	0.004010	11.234740	0.089010
39	24.085780	0.041518	271.597400	0.003682	11.276260	0.088682
40	26.133070	0.038266	295.683200	0.003382	11.314520	0.088382
41	28.354380	0.035268	321.816300	0.003107	11.349790	0.088107
42	30.764510	0.032505	350.170700	0.002856	11.382290	0.087856
43	33.379490	0.029959	380.935200	0.002625	11.412250	0.087625
44	36.216760	0.027612	414.314800	0.002414	11.439860	0.087414
45	39.295180	0.025448	450.531500	0.002220	11.465310	0.087220
48	50.191320	0.019924	578.721300	0.001728	11.530310	0.086728
60	133.593600	0.007485	1559.925000	0.000641	11.676640	0.085641
72	355.584500	0.002812	4171.583000	0.000240	11.731620	0.085240
84	946.455100	0.001057	%11123.000000	0.000090	11.752280	0.085090

Rate = 9%

N	A Future Value	B Present Value	C Ordinary Annuity	D Sinking Fund	E Present Annuity	F Amortization
1	1.090000	0.917431	1.000000	1.000000	0.917431	1.090000
2	1.188100	0.841680	2.090001	0.478469	1.759112	0.568469
3	1.295029	0.772183	3.278102	0.305055	2.531296	0.395055
4	1.411582	0.708425	4.573132	0.218669	3.239721	0.308669
5	1.538624	0.649931	5.984714	0.167092	3.889653	0.257092
6	1.677101	0.596267	7.523339	0.132920	4.485921	0.222920
7	1.828040	0.547034	9.200441	0.108690	5.032954	0.198690
8	1.992563	0.501866	11.028480	0.090674	5.534821	0.180674
9	2.171894	0.460428	13.021050	0.076799	5.995249	0.166799
10	2.367365	0.422411	15.192940	0.065820	6.417660	0.155820
11	2.580428	0.387533	17.560310	0.056947	6.805193	0.146947
12	2.812667	0.355535	20.140740	0.049651	7.160727	0.139651
13	3.065807	0.326178	22.953400	0.043567	7.486906	0.133567
14	3.341729	0.299246	26.019210	0.038433	7.786152	0.128433
15	3.642485	0.274538	29.360940	0.034059	8.060690	0.124059
16	3.970309	0.251870	33.003430	0.030300	8.312560	0.120300
17	4.327637	0.231073	36.973740	0.027046	8.543632	0.117046
18	4.717124	0.211994	41.301380	0.024212	8.755627	0.114212
19	5.141666	0.194490	46.018510	0.021730	8.950116	0.111730
20	5.604416	0.178431	51.160180	0.019546	9.128547	0.109546
21	6.108814	0.163698	56.764590	0.017617	9.292245	0.107617
22	6.658607	0.150182	62.873410	0.015905	9.442427	0.105905
23	7.257882	0.137781	69.532010	0.014382	9.580208	0.104382
24	7.911092	0.126405	76.789910	0.013023	9.706612	0.103023
25	8.623090	0.115968	84.700990	0.011806	9.822581	0.101806
26	9.399169	0.106392	93.324090	0.010715	9.928973	0.100715
27	10.245090	0.097608	102.723300	0.009735	10.026580	0.099735
28	11.167150	0.089548	112.968400	0.008852	10.116130	0.098852
29	12.172200	0.082154	124.135500	0.008056	10.198280	0.098056
30	13.267700	0.075371	136.307700	0.007336	10.273660	0.097336
31	14.461790	0.069148	149.575400	0.006686	10.342800	0.096686
32	15.763350	0.063438	164.037200	0.006096	10.406240	0.096096
33	17.182050	0.058200	179.800600	0.005562	10.464440	0.095562
34	18.728440	0.053395	196.982700	0.005077	10.517840	0.095077
35	20.414000	0.048986	215.711100	0.004636	10.566820	0.094636
36	22.251260	0.044941	236.125100	0.004235	10.611760	0.094235
37	24.253880	0.041231	258.376400	0.003870	10.652990	0.093870
38	26.436730	0.037826	282.630300	0.003538	10.690820	0.093538
39	28.816030	0.034703	309.067000	0.003236	10.725520	0.093236
40	31.409480	0.031838	337.883100	0.002960	10.757360	0.092960
41	34.236330	0.029209	369.292500	0.002708	10.786570	0.092708
42	37.317600	0.026797	403.528900	0.002478	10.813370	0.092478
43	40.676190	0.024584	440.846500	0.002268	10.837950	0.092268
44	44.337050	0.022555	481.522800	0.002077	10.860510	0.092077
45	48.327390	0.020692	525.859800	0.001902	10.881200	0.091902
48	62.585380	0.015978	684.282000	0.001461	10.933580	0.091461
60	176.031800	0.005681	1944.797000	0.000514	11.047990	0.090514
72	495.118600	0.002020	5490.207000	0.000182	11.088670	0.090182
84	1392.603000	0.000718	%15462.260000	0.000065	11.103130	0.090065

Rate = 10%

N	A Future Value	B Present Value	C Ordinary Annuity	D Sinking Fund	E Present Annuity	F Amortization
1	1.100000	0.909091	1.000000	1.000000	0.909091	1.100000
2	1.210000	0.826446	2.100001	0.476190	1.735538	0.576190
3	1.331000	0.751315	3.310001	0.302115	2.486853	0.402115
4	1.464100	0.683013	4.641001	0.215471	3.169866	0.315471
5	1.610510	0.620921	6.105101	0.163797	3.790788	0.263797
6	1.771561	0.564474	7.715612	0.129607	4.355262	0.229607
7	1.948717	0.513158	9.487173	0.105405	4.868420	0.205405
8	2.143589	0.466507	11.435890	0.087444	5.334927	0.187444
9	2.357948	0.424098	13.579480	0.073641	5.759024	0.173641
10	2.593743	0.385543	15.937430	0.062745	6.144568	0.162745
11	2.853117	0.350494	18.531170	0.053963	6.495062	0.153963
12	3.138429	0.318631	21.384290	0.046763	6.813693	0.146763
13	3.452272	0.289664	24.522720	0.040779	7.103357	0.140779
14	3.797499	0.263331	27.974990	0.035746	7.366689	0.135746
15	4.177249	0.239392	31.772490	0.031474	7.606080	0.131474
16	4.594974	0.217629	35.949740	0.027817	7.823709	0.127817
17	5.054472	0.197845	40.544720	0.024664	8.021554	0.124664
18	5.559919	0.179859	45.599190	0.021930	8.201413	0.121930
19	6.115911	0.163508	51.159110	0.019547	8.364921	0.119547
20	6.727502	0.148644	57.275020	0.017460	8.513564	0.117460
21	7.400253	0.135131	64.002530	0.015624	8.648695	0.115624
22	8.140278	0.122846	71.402780	0.014005	8.771541	0.114005
23	8.954306	0.111678	79.543050	0.012572	8.883219	0.112572
24	9.849736	0.101526	88.497360	0.011300	8.984744	0.111300
25	10.834710	0.092296	98.347090	0.010168	9.077041	0.110168
26	11.918180	0.083905	109.181800	0.009159	9.160945	0.109159
27	13.110000	0.076278	121.100000	0.008258	9.237222	0.108258
28	14.421000	0.069343	134.210000	0.007451	9.306566	0.107451
29	15.863100	0.063039	148.631000	0.006728	9.369606	0.106728
30	17.449410	0.057309	164.494100	0.006079	9.426914	0.106079
31	19.194350	0.052099	181.943500	0.005496	9.479014	0.105496
32	21.113790	0.047362	201.137900	0.004972	9.526376	0.104972
33	23.225170	0.043057	222.251700	0.004499	9.569432	0.104499
34	25.547680	0.039142	245.476800	0.004074	9.608575	0.104074
35	28.102450	0.035584	271.024500	0.003690	9.644159	0.103690
36	30.912700	0.032349	299.127000	0.003343	9.676508	0.103343
37	34.003970	0.029408	330.039700	0.003030	9.705916	0.103030
38	37.404370	0.026735	364.043700	0.002747	9.732652	0.102747
39	41.144800	0.024304	401.448000	0.002491	9.756956	0.102491
40	45.259280	0.022095	442.592800	0.002259	9.779050	0.102259
41	49.785210	0.020086	487.852100	0.002050	9.799137	0.102050
42	54.763740	0.018260	537.637300	0.001860	9.817397	0.101860
43	60.240110	0.016600	592.401100	0.001688	9.833998	0.101688
44	66.264110	0.015091	652.641100	0.001532	9.849088	0.101532
45	72.890530	0.013719	718.905300	0.001391	9.862808	0.101391
48	97.017310	0.010307	960.173100	0.001041	9.896926	0.101041
60	304.481900	0.003284	3034.819000	0.000330	9.967158	0.100330
72	955.594900	0.001046	9545.948000	0.000105	9.989536	0.100105
84	2999.067000	0.000333	%29980.670000	0.000033	9.996666	0.100033

APPENDIX B: ANNUAL PERCENTAGE RATE — FINANCE CHARGE PER $100 OF AMOUNT FINANCED

Number of Payments	10%	10¼%	10½%	10¾%	11%	11¼%	11½%	11¾%	12%	12¼%	12½%	12¾%	13%	13¼%
1	0.83	0.85	0.88	0.90	0.92	0.94	0.96	0.98	1.00	1.02	1.04	1.06	1.08	1.10
2	1.25	1.28	1.31	1.35	1.38	1.41	1.44	1.47	1.50	1.53	1.57	1.60	1.63	1.66
3	1.67	1.71	1.76	1.80	1.84	1.88	1.92	1.96	2.01	2.05	2.09	2.13	2.17	2.22
4	2.09	2.14	2.20	2.25	2.30	2.35	2.41	2.46	2.51	2.57	2.62	2.67	2.72	2.78
5	2.51	2.58	2.64	2.70	2.77	2.83	2.89	2.96	3.02	3.08	3.15	3.21	3.27	3.34
6	2.94	3.01	3.08	3.16	3.23	3.31	3.38	3.45	3.53	3.60	3.68	3.75	3.83	3.90
7	3.36	3.45	3.53	3.62	3.70	3.78	3.87	3.95	4.04	4.12	4.21	4.29	4.38	4.47
8	3.79	3.88	3.98	4.07	4.17	4.26	4.36	4.46	4.55	4.65	4.74	4.84	4.94	5.03
9	4.21	4.32	4.43	4.53	4.64	4.75	4.85	4.96	5.07	5.17	5.28	5.39	5.49	5.60
10	4.64	4.76	4.88	4.99	5.11	5.23	5.35	5.46	5.58	5.70	5.82	5.94	6.05	6.17
11	5.07	5.20	5.33	5.45	5.58	5.71	5.84	5.97	6.10	6.23	6.36	6.49	6.62	6.75
12	5.50	5.64	5.78	5.92	6.06	6.20	6.34	6.48	6.62	6.76	6.90	7.04	7.18	7.32
13	5.93	6.08	6.23	6.38	6.53	6.68	6.84	6.99	7.14	7.29	7.44	7.59	7.75	7.90
14	6.36	6.52	6.69	6.85	7.01	7.17	7.34	7.50	7.66	7.82	7.99	8.15	8.31	8.48
15	6.80	6.97	7.14	7.32	7.49	7.66	7.84	8.01	8.19	8.36	8.53	8.71	8.88	9.06
16	7.23	7.41	7.60	7.78	7.97	8.15	8.34	8.53	8.71	8.90	9.08	9.27	9.46	9.64
17	7.67	7.86	8.06	8.25	8.45	8.65	8.84	9.04	9.24	9.44	9.63	9.83	10.03	10.23
18	8.10	8.31	8.52	8.73	8.93	9.14	9.35	9.56	9.77	9.98	10.19	10.40	10.61	10.82
19	8.54	8.76	8.98	9.20	9.42	9.64	9.86	10.08	10.30	10.52	10.74	10.96	11.18	11.41
20	8.98	9.21	9.44	9.67	9.90	10.13	10.37	10.60	10.83	11.06	11.30	11.53	11.76	12.00
21	9.42	9.66	9.90	10.15	10.39	10.63	10.88	11.12	11.36	11.61	11.85	12.10	12.34	12.59
22	9.86	10.12	10.37	10.62	10.88	11.13	11.39	11.64	11.90	12.16	12.41	12.67	12.93	13.19
23	10.30	10.57	10.84	11.10	11.37	11.63	11.90	12.17	12.44	12.71	12.97	13.24	13.51	13.78
24	10.75	11.02	11.30	11.58	11.86	12.14	12.42	12.70	12.98	13.26	13.54	13.82	14.10	14.38
25	11.19	11.48	11.77	12.06	12.35	12.64	12.93	13.22	13.52	13.81	14.10	14.40	14.69	14.98
26	11.64	11.94	12.24	12.54	12.85	13.15	13.45	13.75	14.06	14.36	14.67	14.97	15.28	15.59
27	12.09	12.40	12.71	13.03	13.34	13.66	13.97	14.29	14.60	14.92	15.24	15.56	15.87	16.19
28	12.53	12.86	13.18	13.51	13.84	14.16	14.49	14.82	15.15	15.48	15.81	16.14	16.47	16.80
29	12.98	13.32	13.66	14.00	14.33	14.67	15.01	15.35	15.70	16.04	16.38	16.72	17.07	17.41
30	13.43	13.78	14.13	14.48	14.83	15.19	15.54	15.89	16.24	16.60	16.95	17.31	17.66	18.02
31	13.89	14.25	14.61	14.97	15.33	15.70	16.06	16.43	16.79	17.16	17.53	17.90	18.27	18.63
32	14.34	14.71	15.09	15.46	15.84	16.21	16.59	16.97	17.35	17.73	18.11	18.49	18.87	19.25
33	14.79	15.18	15.57	15.95	16.34	16.73	17.12	17.51	17.90	18.29	18.69	19.08	19.47	19.87
34	15.25	15.65	16.05	16.44	16.85	17.25	17.65	18.05	18.46	18.86	19.27	19.67	20.08	20.49
35	15.70	16.11	16.53	16.94	17.35	17.77	18.18	18.60	19.01	19.43	19.85	20.27	20.69	21.11
36	16.16	16.58	17.01	17.43	17.86	18.29	18.71	19.14	19.57	20.00	20.43	20.87	21.30	21.73
37	16.62	17.06	17.49	17.93	18.37	18.81	19.25	19.69	20.13	20.58	21.02	21.46	21.91	22.36
38	17.08	17.53	17.98	18.43	18.88	19.33	19.78	20.24	20.69	21.15	21.61	22.07	22.52	22.99
39	17.54	18.00	18.46	18.93	19.39	19.86	20.32	20.79	21.26	21.73	22.20	22.67	23.14	23.61
40	18.00	18.48	18.95	19.43	19.90	20.38	20.86	21.34	21.82	22.30	22.79	23.27	23.76	24.25
41	18.47	18.95	19.44	19.93	20.42	20.91	21.40	21.89	22.39	22.88	23.38	23.88	24.38	24.88
42	18.93	19.43	19.93	20.43	20.93	21.44	21.94	22.45	22.96	23.47	23.98	24.49	25.00	25.51
43	19.40	19.91	20.42	20.94	21.45	21.97	22.49	23.01	23.53	24.05	24.57	25.10	25.62	26.15
44	19.86	20.39	20.91	21.44	21.97	22.50	23.03	23.57	24.10	24.64	25.17	25.71	26.25	26.79
45	20.33	20.87	21.41	21.95	22.49	23.03	23.58	24.12	24.67	25.22	25.77	26.32	26.88	27.43
46	20.80	21.35	21.90	22.46	23.01	23.57	24.13	24.69	25.25	25.81	26.37	26.94	27.51	28.08
47	21.27	21.83	22.40	22.97	23.53	24.10	24.68	25.25	25.82	26.40	26.98	27.56	28.14	28.72
48	21.74	22.32	22.90	23.48	24.06	24.64	25.23	25.81	26.40	26.99	27.58	28.18	28.77	29.37
49	22.21	22.80	23.39	23.99	24.58	25.18	25.78	26.38	26.98	27.59	28.19	28.80	29.41	30.02
50	22.69	23.29	23.89	24.50	25.11	25.72	26.33	26.95	27.56	28.18	28.80	29.42	30.04	30.67
51	23.16	23.78	24.40	25.02	25.64	26.26	26.89	27.52	28.15	28.78	29.41	30.05	30.68	31.32
52	23.64	24.27	24.90	25.53	26.17	26.81	27.45	28.09	28.73	29.38	30.02	30.67	31.32	31.98
53	24.11	24.76	25.40	26.05	26.70	27.35	28.00	28.66	29.32	29.98	30.64	31.30	31.97	32.63
54	24.59	25.25	25.91	26.57	27.23	27.90	28.56	29.23	29.91	30.58	31.25	31.93	32.61	33.29
55	25.07	25.74	26.41	27.09	27.77	28.44	29.13	29.81	30.50	31.18	31.87	32.56	33.26	33.95
56	25.55	26.23	26.92	27.61	28.30	28.99	29.69	30.39	31.09	31.79	32.49	33.20	33.91	34.62
57	26.03	26.73	27.43	28.13	28.84	29.54	30.25	30.97	31.68	32.39	33.11	33.83	34.56	35.28
58	26.51	27.23	27.94	28.66	29.37	30.10	30.82	31.55	32.27	33.00	33.74	34.47	35.21	35.95
59	27.00	27.72	28.45	29.18	29.91	30.65	31.39	32.13	32.87	33.61	34.36	35.11	35.86	36.62
60	27.48	28.22	28.96	29.71	30.45	31.20	31.96	32.71	33.47	34.23	34.99	35.75	36.52	37.29

Number of Payments	13½%	13¾%	14%	14¼%	14½%	14¾%	15%	15¼%	15½%	15¾%	16%	16¼%	16½%	16¾%
1	1.13	1.15	1.17	1.19	1.21	1.23	1.25	1.27	1.29	1.31	1.33	1.35	1.38	1.40
2	1.69	1.72	1.75	1.78	1.82	1.85	1.88	1.91	1.94	1.97	2.00	2.04	2.07	2.10
3	2.26	2.30	2.34	2.38	2.43	2.47	2.51	2.55	2.59	2.64	2.68	2.72	2.76	2.80
4	2.83	2.88	2.93	2.99	3.04	3.09	3.14	3.20	3.25	3.30	3.36	3.41	3.46	3.51
5	3.40	3.46	3.53	3.59	3.65	3.72	3.78	3.84	3.91	3.97	4.04	4.10	4.16	4.23
6	3.97	4.05	4.12	4.20	4.27	4.35	4.42	4.49	4.57	4.64	4.72	4.79	4.87	4.94
7	4.55	4.64	4.72	4.81	4.89	4.98	5.06	5.15	5.23	5.32	5.40	5.49	5.58	5.66
8	5.13	5.22	5.32	5.42	5.51	5.61	5.71	5.80	5.90	6.00	6.09	6.19	6.29	6.38
9	5.71	5.82	5.92	6.03	6.14	6.25	6.35	6.46	6.57	6.68	6.78	6.89	7.00	7.11
10	6.29	6.41	6.53	6.65	6.77	6.88	7.00	7.12	7.24	·7.36	7.48	7.60	7.72	7.84
11	6.88	7.01	7.14	7.27	7.40	7.53	7.66	7.79	7.92	8.05	8.18	8.31	8.44	8.57
12	7.46	7.60	7.74	7.89	8.03	8.17	8.31	8.45	8.59	8.74	8.88	9.02	9.16	9.30
13	8.05	8.20	8.36	8.51	8.66	8.81	8.97	9.12	9.27	9.43	9.58	9.73	9.89	10.04
14	8.64	8.81	8.97	9.13	9.30	9.46	9.63	9.79	9.96	10.12	10.29	10.45	10.62	10.78
15	9.23	9.41	9.59	9.76	9.94	10.11	10.29	10.47	10.64	10.82	11.00	11.17	11.35	11.53
16	9.83	10.02	10.20	10.39	10.58	10.77	10.95	11.14	11.33	11.52	11.71	11.90	12.09	12.28
17	10.43	10.63	10.82	11.02	11.22	11.42	11.62	11.82	12.02	12.22	12.42	12.62	12.83	13.03
18	11.03	11.24	11.45	11.66	11.87	12.08	12.29	12.50	12.72	12.93	13.14	13.35	13.57	13.78
19	11.63	11.85	12.07	12.30	12.52	12.74	12.97	13.19	13.41	13.64	13.86	14.09	14.31·	14.54
20	12.23	12.46	12.70	12.93	13.17	13.41	13.64	13.88	14.11	14.35	14.59	14.82	15.06	15.30
21	12.84	13.08	13.33	13.58	13.82	14.07	14.32	14.57	14.82	15.06	15.31	15.56	15.81	16.06
22	13.44	13.70	13.96	14.22	14.48	14.74	15.00	15.26	15.52	15.78	16.04	16.30	16.57	16.83
23	14.05	14.32	14.59	14.87	15.14	15.41	15.68	15.96	16.23	16.50	16.78	17.05	17.32	17.60
24	14.66	14.95	15.23	15.51	15.80	16.08	16.37	16.65	16.94	17.22	17.51	17.80	18.09	18.37
25	15.28	15.57	15.87	16.17	16.46	16.76	17.06	17.35	17.65	17.95	18.25	18.55	18.85	19.15
26	15.89	16.20	16.51	16.82	17.13	17.44	17.75	18.06	18.37	18.68	18.99	19.30	19.62	19.93
27	16.51	16.83	17.15	17.47	17.80	18.12	18.44	18.76	19.09	19.41	19.74	20.06	20.39	20.71
28	17.13	17.46	17.80	18.13	18.47	18.80	19.14	19.47	19.81	20.15	20.48	20.82	21.16	21.50
29	17.75	18.10	18.45	18.79	19.14	19.49	19.83	20.18	20.53	20.88	21.23	21.58	21.94	22.29
30	18.38	18.74	19.10	19.45	19.81	20.17	20.54	20.90	21.26	21.62	21.99	22.35	22.72	23.08
31	19.00	19.38	19.75	20.12	20.49	20.87	21.24	21.61	21.99	22.37	22.74	23.12	23.50	23.88
32	19.63	20.02	20.40	20.79	21.17	21.56	21.95	22.33	22.72	23.11	23.50	23.89	24.28	24.68
33	20.26	20.66	21.06	21.46	21.85	22.25	22.65	23.06	23.46	23.86	24.26	24.67	25.07	25.48
34	20.90	21.31	21.72	22.13	22.54	22.95	23.37	23.78	24.19	24.61	25.03	25.44	25.86	26.28
35	21.53	21.95	22.38	22.80	23.23	23.65	24.08	24.51	24.94	25.36	25.79	26.23	26.66	27.09
36	22.17	22.60	23.04	23.48	23.92	24.35	24.80	25.24	25.68	26.12	26.57	27.01	27.46	27.90
37	22.81	23.25	23.70	24.16	24.61	25.06	25.51	25.97	26.42	26.88	27.34	27.80	28.26	28.72
38	23.45	23.91	24.37	24.84	25.30	25.77	26.24	26.70	27.17	27.64	28.11	28.59	29.06	29.53
39	24.09	24.56	25.04	25.52	26.00	26.48	26.96	27.44	27.92	28.41	28.89	29.38	29.87	30.36
40	24.73	25.22	25.71	26.20	26.70	27.19	27.69	28.18	28.68	29.18	29.68	30.18	30.68	31.18
41	25.38	25.88	26.39	26.89	27.40	27.91	28.41	28.92	29.44	29.95	30.46	30.97	31.49	32.01
42	26.03	26.55	27.06	27.58	28.10	28.62	29.15	29.67	30.19	30.72	31.25	31.78	32.31	32.84
43	26.68	27.21	27.74	28.27	28.81	29.34	29.88	30.42	30.96	31.50	32.04	32.58	33.13	33.67
44	27.33	27.88	28.42	28.97	29.52	30.07	30.62	31.17	31.72	32.28	32.83	33.39	33.95	34.51
45	27.99	28.55	29.11	29.67	30.23	30.79	31.36	31.92	32.49	33.06	33.63	34.20	34.77	35.35
46	28.65	29.22	29.79	30.36	30.94	31.52	32.10	32.68	33.26	33.84	34.43	35.01	35.60	36.19
47	29.31	29.89	30.48	31.07	31.66	32.25	32.84	33.44	34.03	34.63	35.23	35.83	36.43	37.04
48	29.97	30.57	31.17	31.77	32.37	32.98	33.59	34.20	34.81	35.42	36.03	36.65	37.27	37.88
49	30.63	31.24	31.86	32.48	33.09	33.71	34.34	34.96	35.59	36.21	36.84	37.47	38.10	38.74
50	31.29	31.92	32.55	33.18	33.82	34.45	35.09	35.73	36.37	37.01	37.65	38.30	38.94	39.59
51	31.96	32.60	33.25	33.89	34.54	35.19	35.84	36.50	37.15	37.81	38.46	39.12	39.79	40.45
52	32.63	33.29	33.95	34.61	35.27	35.93	36.60	37.27	37.94	38.61	39.28	39.96	40.63	41.31
53	33.30	33.97	34.65	35.32	36.00	36.68	37.36	38.04	38.72	39.41	40.10	40.79	41.48	42.17
54	33.98	34.66	35.35	36.04	36.73	37.42	38.12	38.82	39.52	40.22	40.92	41.63	42.33	43.04
55	34.65	35.35	36.05	36.76	37.46	38.17	38.88	39.60	40.31	41.03	41.74	42.47	43.19	43.91
56	35.33	36.04	36.76	37.48	38.20	38.92	39.65	40.38	41.11	41.84	42.57	43.31	44.05	44.79
57	36.01	36.74	37.47	38.20	38.94	39.68	40.42	41.16	41.91	42.65	43.40	44.15	44.91	45.66
58	36.69	37.43	38.18	38.93	39.68	40.43	41.19	41.95	42.71	43.47	44.23	45.00	45.77	46.54
59	37.37	38.13	38.89	39.66	40.42	41.19	41.96	42.74	43.51	44.29	45.07	45.85	46.64	47.42
60	38.06	38.83	39.61	40.39	41.17	41.95	42.74	43.53	44.32	45.11	45.91	46.71	47.51	48.31

APPENDIX B

Number of Payments	17%	17$\frac{1}{4}$%	17$\frac{1}{2}$%	17$\frac{3}{4}$%	18%	18$\frac{1}{4}$%	18$\frac{1}{2}$%	18$\frac{3}{4}$%	19%	19$\frac{1}{4}$%	19$\frac{1}{2}$%	19$\frac{3}{4}$%	20%	20$\frac{1}{4}$%
1	1.42	1.44	1.46	1.48	1.50	1.52	1.54	1.56	1.58	1.60	1.63	1.65	1.67	1.69
2	2.13	2.16	2.19	2.22	2.26	2.29	2.32	2.35	2.38	2.41	2.44	2.48	2.51	2.54
3	2.85	2.89	2.93	2.97	3.01	3.06	3.10	3.14	3.18	3.23	3.27	3.31	3.35	3.39
4	3.57	3.62	3.67	3.73	3.78	3.83	3.88	3.94	3.99	4.04	4.10	4.15	4.20	4.25
5	4.29	4.35	4.42	4.48	4.54	4.61	4.67	4.74	4.80	4.86	4.93	4.99	5.06	5.12
6	5.02	5.09	5.17	5.24	5.32	5.39	5.46	5.54	5.61	5.69	5.76	5.84	5.91	5.99
7	5.75	5.83	5.92	6.00	6.09	6.18	6.26	6.35	6.43	6.52	6.60	6.69	6.78	6.86
8	6.48	6.58	6.67	6.77	6.87	6.96	7.06	7.16	7.26	7.35	7.45	7.55	7.64	7.74
9	7.22	7.32	7.43	7.54	7.65	7.76	7.87	7.97	8.08	8.19	8.30	8.41	8.52	8.63
10	7.96	8.08	8.19	8.31	8.43	8.55	8.67	8.79	8.91	9.03	9.15	9.27	9.39	9.51
11	8.70	8.83	8.96	9.09	9.22	9.35	9.49	9.62	9.75	9.88	10.01	10.14	10.28	10.41
12	9.45	9.59	9.73	9.87	10.02	10.16	10.30	10.44	10.59	10.73	10.87	11.02	11.16	11.31
13	10.20	10.35	10.50	10.66	10.81	10.97	11.12	11.28	11.43	11.59	11.74	11.90	12.05	12.21
14	10.95	11.11	11.28	11.45	11.61	11.78	11.95	12.11	12.28	12.45	12.61	12.78	12.95	13.11
15	11.71	11.88	12.06	12.24	12.42	12.59	12.77	12.95	13.13	13.31	13.49	13.67	13.85	14.03
16	12.46	12.65	12.84	13.03	13.22	13.41	13.60	13.80	13.99	14.18	14.37	14.56	14.75	14.94
17	13.23	13.43	13.63	13.83	14.04	14.24	14.44	14.64	14.85	15.05	15.25	15.46	15.66	15.86
18	13.99	14.21	14.42	14.64	14.85	15.07	15.28	15.49	15.71	15.93	16.14	16.36	16.57	16.79
19	14.76	14.99	15.22	15.44	15.67	15.90	16.12	16.35	16.58	16.81	17.03	17.26	17.49	17.72
20	15.54	15.78	16.01	16.25	16.49	16.73	16.97	17.21	17.45	17.69	17.93	18.17	18.41	18.66
21	16.31	16.56	16.81	17.07	17.32	17.57	17.82	18.07	18.33	18.58	18.83	19.09	19.34	19.60
22	17.09	17.36	17.62	17.88	18.15	18.41	18.68	18.94	19.21	19.47	19.74	20.01	20.27	20.54
23	17.88	18.15	18.43	18.70	18.98	19.26	19.54	19.81	20.09	20.37	20.65	20.93	21.21	21.49
24	18.66	18.95	19.24	19.53	19.82	20.11	20.40	20.69	20.98	21.27	21.56	21.86	22.15	22.44
25	19.45	19.75	20.05	20.36	20.66	20.96	21.27	21.57	21.87	22.18	22.48	22.79	23.10	23.40
26	20.24	20.56	20.87	21.19	21.50	21.82	22.14	22.45	22.77	23.09	23.41	23.73	24.04	24.36
27	21.04	21.37	21.69	22.02	22.35	22.68	23.01	23.34	23.67	24.00	24.33	24.67	25.00	25.33
28	21.84	22.18	22.52	22.86	23.20	23.55	23.89	24.23	24.58	24.92	25.27	25.61	25.96	26.30
29	22.64	22.99	23.35	23.70	24.06	24.41	24.77	25.13	25.49	25.84	26.20	26.56	26.92	27.28
30	23.45	23.81	24.18	24.55	24.92	25.29	25.66	26.03	26.40	26.77	27.14	27.52	27.89	28.26
31	24.26	24.64	25.02	25.40	25.78	26.16	26.55	26.93	27.32	27.70	28.09	28.47	28.86	29.25
32	25.07	25.46	25.86	26.25	26.65	27.04	27.44	27.84	28.24	28.64	29.04	29.44	29.84	30.24
33	25.88	26.29	26.70	27.11	27.52	27.93	28.34	28.75	29.16	29.57	29.99	30.40	30.82	31.23
34	26.70	27.12	27.54	27.97	28.39	28.81	29.24	29.66	30.09	30.52	30.95	31.37	31.80	32.23
35	27.52	27.96	28.39	28.83	29.27	29.71	30.14	30.58	31.02	31.47	31.91	32.35	32.79	33.24
36	28.35	28.80	29.25	29.70	30.15	30.60	31.05	31.51	31.96	32.42	32.87	33.33	33.79	34.25
37	29.18	29.64	30.10	30.57	31.03	31.50	31.97	32.43	32.90	33.37	33.84	34.32	34.79	35.26
38	30.01	30.49	30.96	31.44	31.92	32.40	32.88	33.37	33.85	34.33	34.82	35.30	35.79	36.28
39	30.85	31.34	31.83	32.32	32.81	33.31	33.80	34.30	34.80	35.30	35.80	36.30	36.80	37.30
40	31.68	32.19	32.69	33.20	33.71	34.22	34.73	35.24	35.75	36.26	36.78	37.29	37.81	38.33
41	32.52	33.04	33.56	34.08	34.61	35.13	35.66	36.18	36.71	37.24	37.77	38.30	38.83	39.36
42	33.37	33.90	34.44	34.97	35.51	36.05	36.59	37.13	37.67	38.21	38.76	39.30	39.85	40.40
43	34.22	34.76	35.31	35.86	36.42	36.97	37.52	38.08	38.63	39.19	39.75	40.31	40.87	41.44
44	35.07	35.63	36.19	36.76	37.33	37.89	38.46	39.03	39.60	40.18	40.75	41.33	41.90	42.48
45	35.92	36.50	37.08	37.66	38.24	38.82	39.41	39.99	40.58	41.17	41.75	42.35	42.94	43.53
46	36.78	37.37	37.96	38.56	39.16	39.75	40.35	40.95	41.55	42.16	42.76	43.37	43.98	44.58
47	37.64	38.25	38.86	39.46	40.08	40.69	41.30	41.92	42.54	43.15	43.77	44.40	45.02	45.64
48	38.50	39.13	39.75	40.37	41.00	41.63	42.26	42.89	43.52	44.15	44.79	45.43	46.07	46.71
49	39.37	40.01	40.65	41.29	41.93	42.57	43.22	43.86	44.51	45.16	45.81	46.46	47.12	47.77
50	40.24	40.89	41.55	42.20	42.86	43.52	44.18	44.84	45.50	46.17	46.83	47.50	48.17	48.84
51	41.11	41.78	42.45	43.12	43.79	44.47	45.14	45.82	46.50	47.18	47.86	48.55	49.23	49.92
52	41.99	42.67	43.36	44.04	44.73	45.42	46.11	46.80	47.50	48.20	48.89	49.59	50.30	51.00
53	42.87	43.57	44.27	44.97	45.67	46.38	47.08	47.79	48.50	49.22	49.93	50.65	51.37	52.09
54	43.75	44.47	45.18	45.90	46.62	47.34	48.06	48.79	49.51	50.24	50.97	51.70	52.44	53.17
55	44.64	45.37	46.10	46.83	47.57	48.30	49.04	49.78	50.52	51.27	52.02	52.76	53.52	54.27
56	45.53	46.27	47.02	47.77	48.52	49.27	50.03	50.78	51.54	52.30	53.06	53.83	54.60	55.37
57	46.42	47.18	47.94	48.71	49.47	50.24	51.01	51.79	52.56	53.34	54.12	54.90	55.68	56.47
58	47.32	48.09	48.87	49.65	50.43	51.22	52.00	52.79	53.58	54.38	55.17	55.97	56.77	57.57
59	48.21	49.01	49.80	50.60	51.39	52.20	53.00	53.80	54.61	55.42	56.23	57.05	57.87	58.68
60	49.12	49.92	50.73	51.55	52.36	53.18	54.00	54.82	55.64	56.47	57.30	58.13	58.96	59.80

Number of Payments	20½%	20¾%	21%	21¼%	21½%	21¾%	22%	22¼%	22½%	22¾%	23%	23¼%	23½%	23¾%
1	1.71	1.73	1.75	1.77	1.79	1.81	1.83	1.85	1.88	1.90	1.92	1.94	1.96	1.98
2	2.57	2.60	2.63	2.66	2.70	2.73	2.76	2.79	2.82	2.85	2.88	2.92	2.95	2.98
3	3.44	3.48	3.52	3.56	3.60	3.65	3.69	3.73	3.77	3.82	3.86	3.90	3.94	3.98
4	4.31	4.36	4.41	4.47	4.52	4.57	4.62	4.68	4.73	4.78	4.84	4.89	4.94	5.00
5	5.18	5.25	5.31	5.37	5.44	5.50	5.57	5.63	5.69	5.76	5.82	5.89	5.95	6.02
6	6.06	6.14	6.21	6.29	6.36	6.44	6.51	6.59	6.66	6.74	6.81	6.89	6.96	7.04
7	6.95	7.04	7.12	7.21	7.29	7.38	7.47	7.55	7.64	7.73	7.81	7.90	7.99	8.07
8	7.84	7.94	8.03	8.13	8.23	8.33	8.42	8.52	8.62	8.72	8.82	8.91	9.01	9.11
9	8.73	8.84	8.95	9.06	9.17	9.28	9.39	9.50	9.61	9.72	9.83	9.94	10.04	10.15
10	9.63	9.75	9.88	10.00	10.12	10.24	10.36	10.48	10.60	10.72	10.84	10.96	11.08	11.21
11	10.54	10.67	10.80	10.94	11.07	11.20	11.33	11.47	11.60	11.73	11.86	12.00	12.13	12.26
12	11.45	11.59	11.74	11.88	12.02	12.17	12.31	12.46	12.60	12.75	12.89	13.04	13.18	13.33
13	12.36	12.52	12.67	12.83	12.99	13.14	13.30	13.46	13.61	13.77	13.93	14.08	14.24	14.40
14	13.28	13.45	13.62	13.79	13.95	14.12	14.29	14.46	14.63	14.80	14.97	15.13	15.30	15.47
15	14.21	14.39	14.57	14.75	14.93	15.11	15.29	15.47	15.65	15.83	16.01	16.19	16.37	16.56
16	15.14	15.33	15.52	15.71	15.90	16.10	16.29	16.48	16.68	16.87	17.06	17.26	17.45	17.65
17	16.07	16.27	16.48	16.68	16.89	17.09	17.30	17.50	17.71	17.92	18.12	18.33	18.53	18.74
18	17.01	17.22	17.44	17.66	17.88	18.09	18.31	18.53	18.75	18.97	19.19	19.41	19.62	19.84
19	17.95	18.18	18.41	18.64	18.87	19.10	19.33	19.56	19.79	20.02	20.26	20.49	20.72	20.95
20	18.90	19.14	19.38	19.63	19.87	20.11	20.36	20.60	20.84	21.09	21.33	21.58	21.82	22.07
21	19.85	20.11	20.36	20.62	20.87	21.13	21.38	21.64	21.90	22.16	22.41	22.67	22.93	23.19
22	20.81	21.08	21.34	21.61	21.88	22.15	22.42	22.69	22.96	23.23	23.50	23.77	24.04	24.32
23	21.77	22.05	22.33	22.61	22.90	23.18	23.46	23.74	24.03	24.31	24.60	24.88	25.17	25.45
24	22.74	23.03	23.33	23.62	23.92	24.21	24.51	24.80	25.10	25.40	25.70	25.99	26.29	26.59
25	23.71	24.02	24.32	24.63	24.94	25.25	25.56	25.87	26.18	26.49	26.80	27.11	27.43	27.74
26	24.68	25.01	25.33	25.65	25.97	26.29	26.62	26.94	27.26	27.59	27.91	28.24	28.56	28.89
27	25.67	26.00	26.34	26.67	27.01	27.34	27.68	28.02	28.35	28.69	29.03	29.37	29.71	30.05
28	26.65	27.00	27.35	27.70	28.05	28.40	28.75	29.10	29.45	29.80	30.15	30.51	30.86	31.22
29	27.64	28.00	28.37	28.73	29.09	29.46	29.82	30.19	30.55	30.92	31.28	31.65	32.02	32.39
30	28.64	29.01	29.39	29.77	30.14	30.52	30.90	31.28	31.66	32.04	32.42	32.80	33.18	33.57
31	29.64	30.03	30.42	30.81	31.20	31.59	31.98	32.38	32.77	33.17	33.56	33.96	34.35	34.75
32	30.64	31.05	31.45	31.85	32.26	32.67	33.07	33.48	33.89	34.30	34.71	35.12	35.53	35.94
33	31.65	32.07	32.49	32.91	33.33	33.75	34.17	34.59	35.01	35.44	35.86	36.29	36.71	37.14
34	32.67	33.10	33.53	33.96	34.40	34.83	35.27	35.71	36.14	36.58	37.02	37.46	37.90	38.34
35	33.68	34.13	34.58	35.03	35.47	35.92	36.37	36.83	37.28	37.73	38.18	38.64	39.09	39.55
36	34.71	35.17	35.63	36.09	36.56	37.02	37.49	37.95	38.42	38.89	39.35	39.82	40.29	40.77
37	35.74	36.21	36.69	37.16	37.64	38.12	38.60	39.08	39.56	40.05	40.53	41.02	41.50	41.99
38	36.77	37.26	37.75	38.24	38.73	39.23	39.72	40.22	40.72	41.21	41.71	42.21	42.71	43.22
39	37.81	38.31	38.82	39.32	39.83	40.34	40.85	41.36	41.87	42.39	42.90	43.42	43.93	44.45
40	38.85	39.37	39.89	40.41	40.93	41.46	41.98	42.51	43.04	43.56	44.09	44.62	45.16	45.69
41	39.89	40.43	40.96	41.50	42.04	42.58	43.12	43.66	44.20	44.75	45.29	45.84	46.39	46.94
42	40.95	41.50	42.05	42.60	43.15	43.71	44.26	44.82	45.38	45.94	46.50	47.06	47.62	48.19
43	42.00	42.57	43.13	43.70	44.27	44.84	45.41	45.98	46.56	47.13	47.71	48.29	48.87	49.45
44	43.06	43.64	44.22	44.81	45.39	45.98	46.56	47.15	47.74	48.33	48.93	49.52	50.11	50.71
45	44.13	44.72	45.32	45.92	46.52	47.12	47.72	48.33	48.93	49.54	50.15	50.76	51.37	51.98
46	45.20	45.81	46.42	47.03	47.65	48.27	48.89	49.51	50.13	50.75	51.38	52.00	52.63	53.26
47	46.27	46.90	47.53	48.16	48.79	49.42	50.06	50.69	51.33	51.97	52.61	53.25	53.89	54.54
48	47.35	47.99	48.64	49.28	49.93	50.58	51.23	51.88	52.54	53.19	53.85	54.51	55.16	55.83
49	48.43	49.09	49.75	50.41	51.08	51.74	52.41	53.08	53.75	54.42	55.09	55.77	56.44	57.12
50	49.52	50.19	50.87	51.55	52.23	52.91	53.59	54.28	54.96	55.65	56.34	57.03	57.73	58.42
51	50.61	51.30	51.99	52.69	53.38	54.08	54.78	55.48	56.19	56.89	57.60	58.30	59.01	59.73
52	51.71	52.41	53.12	53.83	54.55	55.26	55.98	56.69	57.41	58.13	58.86	59.58	60.31	61.04
53	52.81	53.53	54.26	54.98	55.71	56.44	57.18	57.91	58.65	59.38	60.12	60.87	61.61	62.35
54	53.91	54.65	55.39	56.14	56.88	57.63	58.38	59.13	59.88	60.64	61.40	62.16	62.92	63.68
55	55.02	55.78	56.54	57.30	58.06	58.82	59.59	60.36	61.13	61.90	62.67	63.45	64.23	65.01
56	56.14	56.91	57.68	58.46	59.24	60.02	60.80	61.59	62.38	63.17	63.96	64.75	65.54	66.34
57	57.26	58.04	58.84	59.63	60.43	61.22	62.02	62.83	63.63	64.44	65.25	66.06	66.87	67.68
58	58.38	59.18	59.99	60.80	61.62	62.43	63.25	64.07	64.89	65.71	66.54	67.37	68.20	69.03
59	59.51	60.33	61.15	61.98	62.81	63.64	64.48	65.32	66.15	67.00	67.84	68.68	69.53	70.38
60	60.64	61.48	62.32	63.17	64.01	64.86	65.71	66.57	67.42	68.28	69.14	70.01	70.87	71.74

Number of Payments	24%	24$\frac{1}{4}$%	24$\frac{1}{2}$%	24$\frac{3}{4}$%	25%	25$\frac{1}{4}$%	25$\frac{1}{2}$%	25$\frac{3}{4}$%	26%	26$\frac{1}{4}$%	26$\frac{1}{2}$%	26$\frac{3}{4}$%	27%	27$\frac{1}{4}$%
1	2.00	2.02	2.04	2.06	2.08	2.10	2.12	2.15	2.17	2.19	2.21	2.23	2.25	2.27
2	3.01	3.04	3.07	3.10	3.14	3.17	3.20	3.23	3.26	3.29	3.32	3.36	3.39	3.42
3	4.03	4.07	4.11	4.15	4.20	4.24	4.28	4.32	4.36	4.41	4.45	4.49	4.53	4.58
4	5.05	5.10	5.16	5.21	5.26	5.32	5.37	5.42	5.47	5.53	5.58	5.63	5.69	5.74
5	6.08	6.14	6.21	6.27	6.34	6.40	6.46	6.53	6.59	6.66	6.72	6.79	6.85	6.91
6	7.12	7.19	7.27	7.34	7.42	7.49	7.57	7.64	7.72	7.79	7.87	7.95	8.02	8.10
7	8.16	8.25	8.33	8.42	8.51	8.59	8.68	8.77	8.85	8.94	9.03	9.11	9.20	9.29
8	9.21	9.31	9.40	9.50	9.60	9.70	9.80	9.90	9.99	10.09	10.19	10.29	10.39	10.49
9	10.26	10.37	10.48	10.59	10.70	10.81	10.92	11.03	11.14	11.25	11.36	11.47	11.58	11.69
10	11.33	11.45	11.57	11.69	11.81	11.93	12.06	12.18	12.30	12.42	12.54	12.67	12.79	12.91
11	12.40	12.53	12.66	12.80	12.93	13.06	13.20	13.33	13.46	13.60	13.73	13.87	14.00	14.13
12	13.47	13.62	13.76	13.91	14.05	14.20	14.34	14.49	14.64	14.78	14.93	15.07	15.22	15.37
13	14.55	14.71	14.87	15.03	15.18	15.34	15.50	15.66	15.82	15.97	16.13	16.29	16.45	16.61
14	15.64	15.81	15.98	16.15	16.32	16.49	16.66	16.83	17.00	17.17	17.35	17.52	17.69	17.86
15	16.74	16.92	17.10	17.28	17.47	17.65	17.83	18.02	18.20	18.38	18.57	18.75	18.93	19.12
16	17.84	18.03	18.23	18.42	18.62	18.81	19.01	19.21	19.40	19.60	19.79	19.99	20.19	20.38
17	18.95	19.16	19.36	19.57	19.78	19.99	20.20	20.40	20.61	20.82	21.03	21.24	21.45	21.66
18	20.06	20.28	20.50	20.72	20.95	21.17	21.39	21.61	21.83	22.05	22.27	22.50	22.72	22.94
19	21.19	21.42	21.65	21.89	22.12	22.35	22.59	22.82	23.06	23.29	23.53	23.76	24.00	24.23
20	22.31	22.56	22.81	23.05	23.30	23.55	23.79	24.04	24.29	24.54	24.79	25.04	25.28	25.53
21	23.45	23.71	23.97	24.23	24.49	24.75	25.01	25.27	25.53	25.79	26.05	26.32	26.58	26.84
22	24.59	24.86	25.13	25.41	25.68	25.96	26.23	26.50	26.78	27.05	27.33	27.61	27.88	28.16
23	25.74	26.02	26.31	26.60	26.88	27.17	27.46	27.75	28.04	28.32	28.61	28.90	29.19	29.48
24	26.89	27.19	27.49	27.79	28.09	28.39	28.69	29.00	29.30	29.60	29.90	30.21	30.51	30.82
25	28.05	28.36	28.68	28.99	29.31	29.62	29.94	30.25	30.57	30.89	31.20	31.52	31.84	32.16
26	29.22	29.55	29.87	30.20	30.53	30.86	31.19	31.52	31.85	32.18	32.51	32.84	33.18	33.51
27	30.39	30.73	31.07	31.42	31.76	32.10	32.45	32.79	33.14	33.48	33.83	34.17	34.52	34.87
28	31.57	31.93	32.28	32.64	33.00	33.35	33.71	34.07	34.43	34.79	35.15	35.51	35.87	36.23
29	32.76	33.13	33.50	33.87	34.24	34.61	34.98	35.36	35.73	36.10	36.48	36.85	37.23	37.61
30	33.95	34.33	34.72	35.10	35.49	35.88	36.26	36.65	37.04	37.43	37.82	38.21	38.60	38.99
31	35.15	35.55	35.95	36.35	36.75	37.15	37.55	37.95	38.36	38.76	39.16	39.57	39.97	40.38
32	36.35	36.77	37.18	37.60	38.01	38.43	38.84	39.26	39.68	40.10	40.52	40.94	41.36	41.78
33	37.57	37.99	38.42	38.85	39.28	39.71	40.14	40.58	41.01	41.44	41.88	42.31	42.75	43.19
34	38.78	39.23	39.67	40.11	40.56	41.01	41.45	41.90	42.35	42.80	43.25	43.70	44.15	44.60
35	40.01	40.47	40.92	41.38	41.84	42.31	42.77	43.23	43.69	44.16	44.62	45.09	45.56	46.02
36	41.24	41.71	42.19	42.66	43.14	43.61	44.09	44.57	45.05	45.53	46.01	46.49	46.97	47.45
37	42.48	42.96	43.45	43.94	44.43	44.93	45.42	45.91	46.41	46.90	47.40	47.90	48.39	48.89
38	43.72	44.22	44.73	45.23	45.74	46.25	46.75	47.26	47.77	48.29	48.80	49.31	49.82	50.34
39	44.97	45.49	46.01	46.53	47.05	47.57	48.10	48.62	49.15	49.68	50.20	50.73	51.26	51.79
40	46.22	46.76	47.29	47.83	48.37	48.91	49.45	49.99	50.53	51.07	51.62	52.16	52.71	53.26
41	47.48	48.04	48.59	49.14	49.69	50.25	50.80	51.36	51.92	52.48	53.04	53.60	54.16	54.73
42	48.75	49.32	49.89	50.46	51.03	51.60	52.17	52.74	53.32	53.89	54.47	55.05	55.63	56.21
43	50.03	50.61	51.19	51.78	52.36	52.95	53.54	54.13	54.72	55.31	55.90	56.50	57.09	57.69
44	51.31	51.91	52.51	53.11	53.71	54.31	54.92	55.52	56.13	56.74	57.35	57.96	58.57	59.19
45	52.59	53.21	53.82	54.44	55.06	55.68	56.30	56.92	57.55	58.17	58.80	59.43	60.06	60.69
46	53.89	54.52	55.15	55.78	56.42	57.05	57.69	58.33	58.97	59.61	60.26	60.90	61.55	62.20
47	55.18	55.83	56.48	57.13	57.78	58.44	59.09	59.75	60.40	61.06	61.72	62.39	63.05	63.71
48	56.49	57.15	57.82	58.49	59.15	59.82	60.50	61.17	61.84	62.52	63.20	63.87	64.56	65.24
49	57.80	58.48	59.16	59.85	60.53	61.22	61.91	62.60	63.29	63.98	64.68	65.37	66.07	66.77
50	59.12	59.81	60.51	61.21	61.92	62.62	63.33	64.03	64.74	65.45	66.16	66.88	67.59	68.31
51	60.44	61.15	61.87	62.59	63.31	64.03	64.75	65.48	66.20	66.93	67.66	68.39	69.12	69.86
52	61.77	62.50	63.23	63.97	64.70	65.44	66.18	66.92	67.67	68.41	69.16	69.91	70.66	71.41
53	63.10	63.85	64.60	65.35	66.11	66.86	67.62	68.38	69.14	69.90	70.67	71.43	72.20	72.97
54	64.44	65.21	65.98	66.75	67.52	68.29	69.07	69.84	70.62	71.40	72.18	72.97	73.75	74.54
55	65.79	66.57	67.36	68.14	68.93	69.72	70.52	71.31	72.11	72.91	73.71	74.51	75.31	76.12
56	67.14	67.94	68.74	69.55	70.36	71.16	71.97	72.79	73.60	74.42	75.24	76.06	76.88	77.70
57	68.50	69.32	70.14	70.96	71.78	72.61	73.44	74.27	75.10	75.94	76.77	77.61	78.45	79.29
58	69.86	70.70	71.54	72.38	73.22	74.06	74.91	75.76	76.61	77.46	78.32	79.17	80.03	80.89
59	71.23	72.09	72.94	73.80	74.66	75.52	76.39	77.25	78.12	78.99	79.87	80.74	81.62	82.50
60	72.61	73.48	74.35	75.23	76.11	76.99	77.87	78.76	79.64	80.53	81.42	82.32	83.21	84.11

Number of Payments	$27\frac{1}{2}\%$	$27\frac{3}{4}\%$	28%	$28\frac{1}{4}\%$	$28\frac{1}{2}\%$	$28\frac{3}{4}\%$	29%	$29\frac{1}{4}\%$	$29\frac{1}{2}\%$	$29\frac{3}{4}\%$	30%	$30\frac{1}{4}\%$	$30\frac{1}{2}\%$	$30\frac{3}{4}\%$
1	2.29	2.31	2.33	2.35	2.37	2.40	2.42	2.44	2.46	2.48	2.50	2.52	2.54	2.56
2	3.45	3.48	3.51	3.54	3.58	3.61	3.64	3.67	3.70	3.73	3.77	3.80	3.83	3.86
3	4.62	4.66	4.70	4.74	4.79	4.83	4.87	4.91	4.96	5.00	5.04	5.08	5.13	5.17
4	5.79	5.85	5.90	5.95	6.01	6.06	6.11	6.17	6.22	6.27	6.33	6.38	6.43	6.49
5	6.98	7.04	7.11	7.17	7.24	7.30	7.37	7.43	7.49	7.56	7.62	7.69	7.75	7.82
6	8.17	8.25	8.32	8.40	8.48	8.55	8.63	8.70	8.78	8.85	8.93	9.01	9.08	9.16
7	9.37	9.46	9.55	9.64	9.72	9.81	9.90	9.98	10.07	10.16	10.25	10.33	10.42	10.51
8	10.58	10.68	10.78	10.88	10.98	11.08	11.18	11.28	11.38	11.47	11.57	11.67	11.77	11.87
9	11.80	11.91	12.03	12.14	12.25	12.36	12.47	12.58	12.69	12.80	12.91	13.02	13.13	13.24
10	13.03	13.15	13.28	13.40	13.52	13.64	13.77	13.89	14.01	14.14	14.26	14.38	14.50	14.63
11	14.27	14.40	14.54	14.67	14.81	14.94	15.08	15.21	15.35	15.48	15.62	15.75	15.89	16.02
12	15.51	15.66	15.81	15.95	16.10	16.25	16.40	16.54	16.69	16.84	16.98	17.13	17.28	17.43
13	16.77	16.93	17.09	17.24	17.40	17.56	17.72	17.88	18.04	18.20	18.36	18.52	18.68	18.84
14	18.03	18.20	18.37	18.54	18.72	18.89	19.06	19.23	19.41	19.58	19.75	19.92	20.10	20.27
15	19.30	19.48	19.67	19.85	20.04	20.22	20.41	20.59	20.78	20.96	21.15	21.34	21.52	21.71
16	20.58	20.78	20.97	21.17	21.37	21.57	21.76	21.96	22.16	22.36	22.56	22.76	22.96	23.16
17	21.87	22.08	22.29	22.50	22.71	22.92	23.13	23.34	23.55	23.77	23.98	24.19	24.40	24.61
18	23.16	23.39	23.61	23.83	24.06	24.28	24.51	24.73	24.96	25.18	25.41	25.63	25.86	26.08
19	24.47	24.71	24.94	25.18	25.42	25.65	25.89	26.13	26.37	26.61	26.85	27.08	27.32	27.56
20	25.78	26.03	26.28	26.53	26.78	27.04	27.29	27.54	27.79	28.04	28.29	28.55	28.80	29.05
21	27.11	27.37	27.63	27.90	28.16	28.43	28.69	28.96	29.22	29.49	29.75	30.02	30.29	30.55
22	28.44	28.71	28.99	29.27	29.55	29.82	30.10	30.38	30.66	30.94	31.22	31.50	31.78	32.07
23	29.77	30.07	30.36	30.65	30.94	31.23	31.53	31.82	32.11	32.41	32.70	33.00	33.29	33.59
24	31.12	31.43	31.73	32.04	32.34	32.65	32.96	33.27	33.57	33.88	34.19	34.50	34.81	35.12
25	32.48	32.80	33.12	33.44	33.76	34.08	34.40	34.72	35.04	35.37	35.69	36.01	36.34	36.66
26	33.84	34.18	34.51	34.84	35.18	35.51	35.85	36.19	36.52	36.86	37.20	37.54	37.88	38.21
27	35.21	35.56	35.91	36.26	36.61	36.96	37.31	37.66	38.01	38.36	38.72	39.07	39.42	39.78
28	36.59	36.96	37.32	37.68	38.05	38.41	38.78	39.15	39.51	39.88	40.25	40.61	40.98	41.35
29	37.98	38.36	38.74	39.12	39.50	39.88	40.26	40.64	41.02	41.40	41.78	42.17	42.55	42.94
30	39.38	39.77	40.17	40.56	40.95	41.35	41.75	42.14	42.54	42.94	43.33	43.73	44.13	44.53
31	40.79	41.19	41.60	42.01	42.42	42.83	43.24	43.65	44.07	44.48	44.89	45.30	45.72	46.13
32	42.20	42.62	43.05	43.47	43.90	44.32	44.75	45.17	45.60	46.03	46.46	46.89	47.32	47.75
33	43.62	44.06	44.50	44.94	45.38	45.82	46.26	46.70	47.15	47.59	48.04	48.48	48.93	49.37
34	45.05	45.51	45.96	46.42	46.87	47.33	47.79	48.24	48.70	49.16	49.62	50.08	50.55	51.01
35	46.49	46.96	47.43	47.90	48.37	48.85	49.32	49.79	50.27	50.74	51.22	51.70	52.17	52.65
36	47.94	48.42	48.91	49.40	49.88	50.37	50.86	51.35	51.84	52.33	52.83	53.32	53.81	54.31
37	49.39	49.89	50.40	50.90	51.40	51.91	52.41	52.92	53.42	53.93	54.44	54.95	55.46	55.97
38	50.86	51.37	51.89	52.41	52.93	53.45	53.97	54.49	55.02	55.54	56.07	56.59	57.12	57.65
39	52.33	52.86	53.39	53.93	54.46	55.00	55.54	56.08	56.62	57.16	57.70	58.24	58.79	59.33
40	53.81	54.35	54.90	55.46	56.01	56.56	57.12	57.67	58.23	58.79	59.34	59.90	60.47	61.03
41	55.29	55.86	56.42	56.99	57.56	58.13	58.70	59.28	59.85	60.42	61.00	61.57	62.15	62.73
42	56.79	57.37	57.95	58.54	59.12	59.71	60.30	60.89	61.48	62.07	62.66	63.25	63.85	64.44
43	58.29	58.89	59.49	60.09	60.69	61.30	61.90	62.51	63.11	63.72	64.33	64.94	65.56	66.17
44	59.80	60.42	61.03	61.65	62.27	62.89	63.51	64.14	64.76	65.39	66.01	66.64	67.27	67.90
45	61.32	61.95	62.59	63.22	63.86	64.50	65.13	65.77	66.42	67.06	67.70	68.35	69.00	69.64
46	62.84	63.49	64.15	64.80	65.45	66.11	66.76	67.42	68.08	68.74	69.40	70.07	70.73	71.40
47	64.38	65.05	65.71	66.38	67.06	67.73	68.40	69.08	69.75	70.43	71.11	71.79	72.47	73.16
48	65.92	66.60	67.29	67.98	68.67	69.36	70.05	70.74	71.44	72.13	72.83	73.53	74.23	74.93
49	67.47	68.17	68.87	69.58	70.29	70.99	71.70	72.41	73.13	73.84	74.56	75.27	75.99	76.71
50	69.03	69.75	70.47	71.19	71.91	72.64	73.37	74.10	74.83	75.56	76.29	77.02	77.76	78.50
51	70.59	71.33	72.07	72.81	73.55	74.29	75.04	75.78	76.53	77.28	78.03	78.79	79.54	80.30
52	72.16	72.92	73.67	74.43	75.19	75.95	76.72	77.48	78.25	79.02	79.79	80.56	81.33	82.11
53	73.74	74.52	75.29	76.07	76.85	77.62	78.41	79.19	79.97	80.76	81.55	82.34	83.13	83.92
54	75.33	76.12	76.91	77.71	78.50	79.30	80.10	80.90	81.71	82.51	83.32	84.13	84.94	85.75
55	76.92	77.73	78.55	79.36	80.17	80.99	81.81	82.63	83.45	84.27	85.10	85.93	86.75	87.58
56	78.53	79.35	80.18	81.02	81.85	82.68	83.52	84.36	85.20	86.04	86.89	87.73	88.58	89.43
57	80.14	80.98	81.83	82.68	83.53	84.39	85.24	86.10	86.96	87.82	88.68	89.55	90.41	91.28
58	81.75	82.62	83.48	84.35	85.22	86.10	86.97	87.85	88.72	89.60	90.49	91.37	92.26	93.14
59	83.38	84.26	85.15	86.03	86.92	87.81	88.71	89.60	90.50	91.40	92.30	93.20	94.11	95.01
60	85.01	85.91	86.81	87.72	88.63	89.54	90.45	91.37	92.28	93.20	94.12	95.04	95.97	96.89

APPENDIX C:
6.2% SOCIAL SECURITY EMPLOYEE TAX TABLE FOR 1992, FOR WAGES FROM $58.63 to $99.92

6.2% Social Security Employee Tax Table for 1992

Note: *Wages subject to social security are generally also subject to the Medicare tax. See page 50.*

Wages at least	But less than	Tax to be withheld	Wages at least	But less than	Tax to be withheld	Wages at least	But less than	Tax to be withheld	Wages at least	But less than	Tax to be withheld
58.63	58.80	3.64	69.92	70.09	4.34	81.21	81.38	5.04	92.50	92.67	5.74
58.80	58.96	3.65	70.09	70.25	4.35	81.38	81.54	5.05	92.67	92.83	5.75
58.96	59.12	3.66	70.25	70.41	4.36	81.54	81.70	5.06	92.83	92.99	5.76
59.12	59.28	3.67	70.41	70.57	4.37	81.70	81.86	5.07	92.99	93.15	5.77
59.28	59.44	3.68	70.57	70.73	4.38	81.86	82.02	5.08	93.15	93.31	5.78
59.44	59.60	3.69	70.73	70.89	4.39	82.02	82.18	5.09	93.31	93.47	5.79
59.60	59.76	3.70	70.89	71.05	4.40	82.18	82.34	5.10	93.47	93.63	5.80
59.76	59.92	3.71	71.05	71.21	4.41	82.34	82.50	5.11	93.63	93.80	5.81
59.92	60.09	3.72	71.21	71.38	4.42	82.50	82.67	5.12	93.80	93.96	5.82
60.09	60.25	3.73	71.38	71.54	4.43	82.67	82.83	5.13	93.96	94.12	5.83
60.25	60.41	3.74	71.54	71.70	4.44	82.83	82.99	5.14	94.12	94.28	5.84
60.41	60.57	3.75	71.70	71.86	4.45	82.99	83.15	5.15	94.28	94.44	5.85
60.57	60.73	3.76	71.86	72.02	4.46	83.15	83.31	5.16	94.44	94.60	5.86
60.73	60.89	3.77	72.02	72.18	4.47	83.31	83.47	5.17	94.60	94.76	5.87
60.89	61.05	3.78	72.18	72.34	4.48	83.47	83.63	5.18	94.76	94.92	5.88
61.05	61.21	3.79	72.34	72.50	4.49	83.63	83.80	5.19	94.92	95.09	5.89
61.21	61.38	3.80	72.50	72.67	4.50	83.80	83.96	5.20	95.09	95.25	5.90
61.38	61.54	3.81	72.67	72.83	4.51	83.96	84.12	5.21	95.25	95.41	5.91
61.54	61.70	3.82	72.83	72.99	4.52	84.12	84.28	5.22	95.41	95.57	5.92
61.70	61.86	3.83	72.99	73.15	4.53	84.28	84.44	5.23	95.57	95.73	5.93
61.86	62.02	3.84	73.15	73.31	4.54	84.44	84.60	5.24	95.73	95.89	5.94
62.02	62.18	3.85	73.31	73.47	4.55	84.60	84.76	5.25	95.89	96.05	5.95
62.18	62.34	3.86	73.47	73.63	4.56	84.76	84.92	5.26	96.05	96.21	5.96
62.34	62.50	3.87	73.63	73.80	4.57	84.92	85.09	5.27	96.21	96.38	5.97
62.50	62.67	3.88	73.80	73.96	4.58	85.09	85.25	5.28	96.38	96.54	5.98
62.67	62.83	3.89	73.96	74.12	4.59	85.25	85.41	5.29	96.54	96.70	5.99
62.83	62.99	3.90	74.12	74.28	4.60	85.41	85.57	5.30	96.70	96.86	6.00
62.99	63.15	3.91	74.28	74.44	4.61	85.57	85.73	5.31	96.86	97.02	6.01
63.15	63.31	3.92	74.44	74.60	4.62	85.73	85.89	5.32	97.02	97.18	6.02
63.31	63.47	3.93	74.60	74.76	4.63	85.89	86.05	5.33	97.18	97.34	6.03
63.47	63.63	3.94	74.76	74.92	4.64	86.05	86.21	5.34	97.34	97.50	6.04
63.63	63.80	3.95	74.92	75.09	4.65	86.21	86.38	5.35	97.50	97.67	6.05
63.80	63.96	3.96	75.09	75.25	4.66	86.38	86.54	5.36	97.67	97.83	6.06
63.96	64.12	3.97	75.25	75.41	4.67	86.54	86.70	5.37	97.83	97.99	6.07
64.12	64.28	3.98	75.41	75.57	4.68	86.70	86.86	5.38	97.99	98.15	6.08
64.28	64.44	3.99	75.57	75.73	4.69	86.86	87.02	5.39	98.15	98.31	6.09
64.44	64.60	4.00	75.73	75.89	4.70	87.02	87.18	5.40	98.31	98.47	6.10
64.60	64.76	4.01	75.89	76.05	4.71	87.18	87.34	5.41	98.47	98.63	6.11
64.76	64.92	4.02	76.05	76.21	4.72	87.34	87.50	5.42	98.63	98.80	6.12
64.92	65.09	4.03	76.21	76.38	4.73	87.50	87.67	5.43	98.80	98.96	6.13
65.09	65.25	4.04	76.38	76.54	4.74	87.67	87.83	5.44	98.96	99.12	6.14
65.25	65.41	4.05	76.54	76.70	4.75	87.83	87.99	5.45	99.12	99.28	6.15
65.41	65.57	4.06	76.70	76.86	4.76	87.99	88.15	5.46	99.28	99.44	6.16
65.57	65.73	4.07	76.86	77.02	4.77	88.15	88.31	5.47	99.44	99.60	6.17
65.73	65.89	4.08	77.02	77.18	4.78	88.31	88.47	5.48	99.60	99.76	6.18
65.89	66.05	4.09	77.18	77.34	4.79	88.47	88.63	5.49	99.76	99.92	6.19
66.05	66.21	4.10	77.34	77.50	4.80	88.63	88.80	5.50	99.92	100.00	6.20
66.21	66.38	4.11	77.50	77.67	4.81	88.80	88.96	5.51			
66.38	66.54	4.12	77.67	77.83	4.82	88.96	89.12	5.52			
66.54	66.70	4.13	77.83	77.99	4.83	89.12	89.28	5.53			
66.70	66.86	4.14	77.99	78.15	4.84	89.28	89.44	5.54			
66.86	67.02	4.15	78.15	78.31	4.85	89.44	89.60	5.55			
67.02	67.18	4.16	78.31	78.47	4.86	89.60	89.76	5.56			
67.18	67.34	4.17	78.47	78.63	4.87	89.76	89.92	5.57			
67.34	67.50	4.18	78.63	78.80	4.88	89.92	90.09	5.58			
67.50	67.67	4.19	78.80	78.96	4.89	90.09	90.25	5.59	Wages	Taxes	
67.67	67.83	4.20	78.96	79.12	4.90	90.25	90.41	5.60	100	$6.20	
67.83	67.99	4.21	79.12	79.28	4.91	90.41	90.57	5.61	200	12.40	
67.99	68.15	4.22	79.28	79.44	4.92	90.57	90.73	5.62	300	18.60	
68.15	68.31	4.23	79.44	79.60	4.93	90.73	90.89	5.63	400	24.80	
68.31	68.47	4.24	79.60	79.76	4.94	90.89	91.05	5.64	500	31.00	
68.47	68.63	4.25	79.76	79.92	4.95	91.05	91.21	5.65	600	37.20	
68.63	68.80	4.26	79.92	80.09	4.96	91.21	91.38	5.66	700	43.40	
68.80	68.96	4.27	80.09	80.25	4.97	91.38	91.54	5.67	800	49.60	
68.96	69.12	4.28	80.25	80.41	4.98	91.54	91.70	5.68	900	55.80	
69.12	69.28	4.29	80.41	80.57	4.99	91.70	91.86	5.69	1,000	62.00	
69.28	69.44	4.30	80.57	80.73	5.00	91.86	92.02	5.70			
69.44	69.60	4.31	80.73	80.89	5.01	92.02	92.18	5.71			
69.60	69.76	4.32	80.89	81.05	5.02	92.18	92.34	5.72			
69.76	69.92	4.33	81.05	81.21	5.03	92.34	92.50	5.73			

APPENDIX D: THE METRIC SYSTEM

METRIC UNITS OF MEASUREMENT

Throughout history systems have been devised to express units of measure. Most of the early systems were based on the human anatomy. For example, the inch as we know it today was originally the length between the knuckle and the tip of the thumb. A foot was the length of a person's foot, and a yard was the distance between the chin and the tip of the thumb when the arm was stretched outward from a person's body. The Romans later divided the foot measurement into twelve equal parts called *unciae*, and defined the mile as *milia passuum*, or a thousand paces. The pace was not accepted as a standard length, so the *milia passuum* was later defined as a furlong, which eventually led to the mile of 1,760 yards or 5,280 feet.

Many years later the English refined and expanded the Roman system. The **English system**, which includes such units of measure as anglicized ounces, pounds, pints, quarts, pecks, bushels, inches, feet, and miles, was eventually also adopted as the system of weights and measures of the United States. This system, also called the **U.S. Customary Measurements**, has been used by the U.S. business community to determine the quantity of sale and the unit price of sale for more than two hundred years. However, due to the complexity of converting U.S. customary measurements (e.g., inches to feet, feet to yards, pints to quarts, quarts to gallons, etc.) the metric system is being adopted by most American industries as their official system of weights and measures.

Following the French Revolution in 1789, the French created a new unit of length based upon a natural measurement. This new unit was called the *metre*, which means measure. The **metric system** has become the official system of measurement of every major industrialized country in the world, except the United States. In 1975, the Metric Conversion Act was enacted by the U.S. federal government to encourage a complete conversion from the English system to the metric system, but that goal has not been realized and a dual system of measurement continues to exist in the United States. Many individual companies have converted to metric, especially those involved in international trade. In addition, the entire automobile, tool, beverage, and pharmaceutical industries have gone almost completely metric. It is not uncommon to see both metric and English units on food labels, or receive weather reports in both Celsius and Fahrenheit. While the conversion has not been as rapid as originally anticipated, the metric system will most likely become the official system of weights and measures of the United States in the future.

The metric system is a system of weights and measures based on decimals and powers of 10. Therfore, each unit of metric measure (e.g., meter, liter, gram) can be multiplied or divided by factors of ten to get larger or smaller units. For example, in the English system short lengths are expressed in inches, or feet, and longer lengths are expressed in yards or miles. But in the metric system, short lengths are expressed in millimeters, decimeters, and centimeters, while longer lengths are expressed in meters dekameters, hectometers, or kilometers. Notice that each of the metric measures of length contains a prefix that indicates its power of ten. The primary prefixes of the metric system are shown in Table A.1. These prefixes are used not only with **meter**, measuring length, but also with **liter**, the metric measure for volume, and **gram**, the metric measure for weight.

Table A.1

Metric prefixes

Prefix	Power	Multiple	Symbols
kilo	10^3	1000.0	km, kl, kg
hecto	10^2	100.0	hm, hl, hg
deka	10^1	10.0	dkm, kal, dag
meter, liter, gram	10^0	0.0	m, l, g
deci	10^{-1}	.1	dm, dl, dg
centi	10^{-2}	.01	cm, cl, cg
milli	10^{-3}	.001	mm, ml, mg

TEMPERATURE

In the metric system temperature is measured in degrees **Celsius**. On the English temperature scale water freezes at 32° and boils at 212° Fahrenheit. In comparison, on the metric scale water freezes at 0° and boils at 100° Celsius. To convert from degrees Celsius to degrees Fahrenheit we use the formula

$$F° = \frac{9}{5} C° + 32°$$

For example, if the Celsius temperature is 20°, the equivalent Fahrenheit temperature can be calculated as follows:

$$F° = \frac{9}{5} C° + 32°$$

$$F° = \frac{9}{5} (20°) + 32°$$

$$= \frac{180°}{5} + 32°$$

$$= 36° + 32°$$

$$= 68°$$

Conversely, to convert from degrees Fahrenheit to degrees Celsius we would use the formula

$$C° = \frac{5}{9} (F° - 32°)$$

So, for a Fahrenheit temperature of 68°,

$$C° = \frac{5}{9} (68° - 32°)$$

$$C° = \frac{5}{9} (36°)$$

$$C° = \frac{180°}{9}$$

$$C° = 20°$$

The scale on page 693 illustrates some comparative temperatures on Celsius and Fahrenheit thermometers.

Fahrenheit		Celsius	
212	—	100	water boils
194	—	90	
176	—	80	
158	—	70	
140	—	60	
122	—	50	
98.6	—	37	normal body temperature
86	—	30	
68	—	20	typical room temperature
50	—	10	
32	—	0	water freezes
14	—	−10	
0	—	−18	
−28	—	−30	
−40	—	−40	

METRIC CONVERSIONS

The metric system of measurement will some day be as familiar to U.S. consumers as is the English system. As the United States proceeds with the transition from the English system to the metric system, there is an ongo-

Table A.2

Metric–English conversion table

Metric to English			English to metric		
Metric measure	English measure	Conversion factor	English measure	Metric measure	Conversion factor
Length			**Length**		
centimeter	inch	0.4	inch	centimeter	2.5
meter	foot	3.3	foot	meter	0.3
meter	yard	1.1	yard	meter	0.9
kilometer	mile	0.6	mile	kilometer	1.6
Weight			**Weight**		
gram	ounce	0.035	ounce	gram	2.8
gram	pound	0.002	pound	gram	454.0
kilogram	pound	2.2	pound	kilogram	0.454
Volume			**Volume**		
milliliter	ounce	0.03	ounce	milliliter	30.0
liter	pint	2.1	pint	liter	0.47
liter	quart	1.06	quart	liter	0.95
liter	gallon	0.26	gallon	liter	3.8

ing need for conversion from one system to the other. To simplify this procedure, conversion tables such as Table A.2 provide approximate conversions between the two systems. For example, to convert from meters to feet the approximate conversion factor from Table A.2 is 3.3. In other words, there are approximately 3.3 feet in one meter. So to convert 15 meters to approximate feet, we would calculate as follows

$$15 \text{ meters} \times 3.3 \frac{\text{feet}}{\text{meter}} = 49.5 \text{ feet}$$

ANSWERS TO ODD-NUMBERED EXERCISES

CHAPTER 1

Section 1.1

1. $(1 \times 1000) + (3 \times 100) + (4 \times 10) + (5 \times 1)$

3. $(2 \times 100,000) + (5 \times 10,000) + (0 \times 1,000) + (3 \times 100) + (4 \times 10) + (5 \times 1)$

5. $(3 \times 1) + (0 \times .1) + (0 \times .01) + (4 \times .001) + (5 \times .0001)$

7. seventy-five thousand, two hundred fifty

9. sixty-four and three hundred twenty-seven ten thousandths

11. 750

13. 1,700

15. 12,481.37

17. 100,000

19. 63.0050

21. $35.05

23. $200 (10 + 40 + 60 + 90)$

25. $70 (100 - 30)$

27. $2,700 (900 \times \$3.00)$

29. 44.4

31. $200,000

33. $11.00

35. 200

Section 1.2

1. $\frac{4}{8}$

3. $\frac{50}{120}$

5. $\frac{10}{105}$

7. $\frac{35}{40}$

9. $\frac{35}{56}$

11. $\frac{1}{2}$

13. $\frac{2}{7}$

15. $\frac{7}{18}$

17. $\frac{10}{11}$

19. $\frac{8}{49}$

21. $\frac{11}{21}$

23. $9\frac{1}{2}$

25. $33\frac{1}{3}$

27. $11\frac{3}{8}$

29. $44\frac{5}{6}$

31. $^{10}/_3$

33. $^{132}/_5$

35. $^{29}/_{10}$

37. $^{282}/_7$

39. $^{21}/_4$

Section 1.3

1. .667

3. 148.141

5. .4

7. ½

9. $^4/_5$

11. ⅛

13. 30%

15. 150%

17. 5%

19. .06

21. .005

23. .20

25. 25%

27. 68.8

29. 70%

31. $6^2/_5$

33. $^1/_{200}$

35. .20, 20%

37. $^1/_{25}$, .04

39. 17.5, 1,750%

41. .250

43. 65.769

45. 95.287

47. 119.19

49. $^{19}/_{25}$, $^1/_5$, $^1/_{25}$

51. $^5/_2$

53. $136.92

55. $^1/_3$, $30,000

CHAPTER 2

Section 2.1

1. -5

3. -36

5. 36

7. -4

9. 4

11. -8

13. -40

15. -2.5

17. -16.5

19. -2.1

Section 2.2

1. 7

3. 8

5. 2

7. 9

9. 10

11. -51.5

13. -25

15. -38

17. 12

19. -62.4

21. 1,296

23. 343

25. 0

Section 2.3

1. $100, $350

3. $480

5. $90, $270

7. $2,071.44

9. 3 hours 45 minutes

11. $94,000

13. 20

15. 18,000

CHAPTER 3

Sections 3.1, 3.2, 3.3, 3.4

1. 75

3. $6.93

5. 1,696.99

7. 16,000

9. 250

11. 30%

13. 66.7%

15. 11%

17. 800

19. $340

21. 12.5%

23. 25%

25. 6.5%

27. 3,400

29. 800

31. $4,462.50

33. 1,600%

35. 7.5

37. 5,000

39. $1,000 (6% = $900)

41. 40

43. $8,880

45. 86.7%

Section 3.5

1. $.42 decrease, 31.8% decrease

3. 1,215, 18.8% decrease

5. 3.45 decrease, 26.6% decrease

7. 65%, 3.4% increase

9. 16,250 decrease, 6.5% decrease

11. 0%

13. 12.8% decrease

15. 17.4% increase

17. 30% increase

19. 21.4% increase

21. 19.2% decrease

23. 4.8% decrease

25. (a) 17.8%; (b) $52.99

CHAPTER 4

Sections 4.1 and 4.2

1. 37, $385.54

3. 35, $337.75

5. 24, $213.60

7. 40, 6.5, $12.15, $324, $78.98, $402.98

9. 40, 8, $10.20, $272, $81.60, $353.60

11. 40, 6.75, $11.40, $304, $76.95, $380.95

13. 4,686, $9.22, $13.83, $405.81, $55.34, $461.15

15. 484, $10.55, $15.82, $421.84, 0, $421.84

17. 1316, $11.76, $17.63, $505.50, $52.90, $558.40

19. $11.40, $314.40

21. 0, $263.30

23. $442.05

25. $552.10

27. $468.20

29. $92.24

Section 4.3

1. $400, $433.33, $866.67, $10,400

3. $322.50, $698.75, $1,397.50, $16,770

5. $784.62, $1,569.23, $1,700, $3,400

7. $51,225, $2,254.63

9. $42,050, $1,698.00

11. $22,005, $20,805, $338.08, $550, $888.08

13. $39,270, $38,070, $618.64, $550, $1,168.64

15. $460.89, $507.50

17. $2,925.25

19. $2,340.81

Section 4.4

1. $2.26, $9.68

3. $6.10, $26.09

5. $27.90, $6.53

7. $0.00, $45.60

9. $36.00

11. $74.00

13. $39.00

15. $40.91

17. $290.87

19. $140.86

21. $77, $14.65, $62.65, $709.40

23. $204, $17.99, $76.93, $779.43

25. $29.09, $5.77, $24.65, $309.69

27. $22.25, $7.67, $32.80, $400.75

29. (a) $94.29; (b) $22.05

31. $66

33. (a) $565.59; (b) $162.75; (c) $47.13

35. $291.87

Section 4.5

1. $414.62, $96.97, $53.50, $280.87

3. $239.64, $56.05, $30.92, $162.34

5. $325.33, $76.09, $2.50, $13.13

7. $247.39, $57.86, $25.08, $131.66

9. (a) $3,100; (b) $725; (c) $400; (d) $2,500

11. $50.65 ($31 + $7.25 + $12.40)

13. (a) $2,212.50; (b) $32.08; (c) $137.18; (d) $17.70; (e) $95.14

15. (a) $1,404.43; (b) $328.43; (c) $41.20; (d) $180.24; (e) $7,340.55

CHAPTER 5

Section 5.1

1. $21,688

3. $31,795

5. $76,515

7. current liabilities

9. owner's equity

11. fixed asset

13. fixed asset

15. current asset

17. fixed asset

19. $39,570

21. $61,005

23. $25,800

25. $148.975

Section 5.2

1. $27,500, 9,150, 2,600

3. $4,625, 152,648, 72,142

5. $51,375, 42,625

7. $73,970, 36,520

9. $35,220

11. $170,130

13. $6,300

15. $4,265

Section 5.3

1. net purchases 1993, 44.7; 1992, 44.5 gross margin 1993, 55.9; 1992, 56.6 total operating expenses 1993, 25.6, 1992, 22.8 net income (1993), 15.1; (1992), 16.8

3. total current assets ($3,500), (4.6)% total assets ($3,850), (1.5)% total liabilities $2,100, 1.9% total equity ($5,950), (4.1)%

Section 5.4

1. $3/15 = 1/5 = .20 : 1$

3. $36/108 = 1/3 = .33\ 1/3 : 1$

5. $120/15 = 8/1 = 8 : 1$

7. $72/12 = 6/1 = 6 : 1$

9. $7/100 = .07 : 1$

11. .6 : 1 two-bedroom, 4 : 1 one-bedroom

13. 15,000, 20,000, 25,000

15. (a) $27,855 cash; (b) $46,425 accounts receivable

17. (93) .91 : 1, (92) .88 : 1

19. (93) .45 : 1, (92) .5 : 1

21. (92) 9.23 times, (93) 8.29 times

23. (92) 23 days, (93) 23.3 days

25. (92) 70.2%, (93) 4.5%

27. $285,000

29. $108,857.14

CHAPTER 6

Section 6.1

1. $32.85
3. $32.50
5. $16.50
7. $170.85
9. $617.50
11. $1,337.50
13. $390.00
15. $137.50
17. $216.25
19. $1,952.00
21. $7.28
23. $43.50
25. $3.50

Section 6.2

1. $225, $1,275
3. $286, $1,014
5. $1,406, $5,994
7. 33%
9. 10%
11. 85%, .85
13. 78%, .78
15. 83%, .83
17. .80, $2,800
19. .70, $504
21. $300, $1,700, $170, $1,530, 23.5%
23. $70, $280, $42, $238, 32%
25. $165, $385, $19.25, $365.75, 33.5%
27. .765, 23.5%
29. .459, 54.1%
31. .68, $2,040, $960
33. .57375, $516.38, $383.62
35. .7691, $6,922.08, $2,077.92
37. .72675, .27325
39. .66348, .33652
41. $168.75, $506.25
43. $39

45. $1,461.91
47. (a) $2,275.88; (b) $2,380
49. .2147

Section 6.3

1. June 10, June 30
3. April 10, April 30
5. Dec. 10, Dec. 30
7. April 15, May 30
9. Jan. 15, March 1
11. March 31, April 20
13. Oct. 20, Nov. 9
15. July 7, July 27
17. April 3, May 18
19. Aug. 30, Oct. 14
21. April 20, May 10
23. Oct. 25, Nov. 14
25. Dec. 25, Jan. 14
27. July 1, July 21
29. April 10, May 30
31. May 25, July 14
33. (a) Oct. 12; (b) Nov. 11; (c) Dec. 11
35. (a) $8,245; (b) $8,500
37. $916.50
39. $765.33
41. $3,350
43. $2,516.64
45. $4,320

Section 6.4

1. $31.43
3. $215.08
5. $194.04
7. $845.94
9. (a) $1,054; (b) $9,946
11. $7,842.74
13. (a) $721.05; (b) $78.95
15. (a) $383,475.95; (b) $416,900.95

CHAPTER 7

Section 7.1

1. $33.00, $5.00
3. $510.00, ($9.00)
5. ($300), ($625)
7. $12.50, 100%
9. $125.25, 35.8%
11. (a) $600; (b) $360; (c) $240
13. $120.15
15. $4.76
17. $7.81
19. 53.1%
21. $4.52
23. $1.75
25. $239.15

Section 7.2

1. $24.00, $6.00
3. 16.74%, $164.50
5. $190.85, $284.85
7. $6,00, 50%, 33.3%
9. $174.23, $414.83, $72.4%
11. 16.7%
13. 33.4%
15. 67.6%
17. (a) $27,634.75; (b) $3,517.15
19. $8.00
21. 100%
23. $6.12

25. (a) $20,730; (b) $7,750; (c) 37.4%
27. (a) 59.1%; (b) 37.1%

Section 7.3

1. $5.85, $13.65
3. 25%, $.20
5. $9.48, $6.32
7. 40%, $9.60
9. $15.00, $17.50, $2.50
11. $11.90, 0
13. $2,100
15. $267.75
17. $301.67
19. $1,500

Section 7.4

1. $30.60, $.92, $31.52
3. $7.35, $.51, $7.86
5. $97.44, $5.85, $103.29
7. $342.00, $345.42, $352.33
9. $1,165.50, $1,182.98, $1,242.13
11. $248.40
13. $9.62
15. $10,710
17. $11,587.50
19. (a) $682.50 fed.; (b) $937.50 state; (c) $7,822.50

CHAPTER 8

Section 8.1

1. $960
3. $382.50

5. $650
7. $920.31
9. $219.52

11. $12,960
13. $2,637.50
15. $11,625
17. (a) $612.50; (b) $8,112.50
19. $38,333.33

Section 8.2

1. $6,000
3. $2,250
5. $13,000
7. 7.5%
9. 10.5%
11. 2
13. 1
15. 1.5
17. $614.25
19. $201.67
21. 7.4%
23. $20,492.33
25. $2,666.67

Section 8.3

1. $427.40
3. $407.93
5. $98.19
7. $99.56
9. $233.33
11. 90
13. 184
15. 97
17. Dec. 23
19. Dec. 15
21. $292.60
23. $1,273.42
25. $1,017.12
27. (a) Aug. 30; (b) $3,147.95

Section 8.4

1. $1,311.75, $9,688.25
3. $36, $864
5. $1,848, $10,152
7. $550, $1,650
9. $425.25, $5,874.75
11. $10,434.78
13. $6,944.44
15. $8,750
17. $34,736.84
19. $20,800; 30.77%
21. $25,722.67; 13.28%
23. $20,152; 15.72%
25. $16,121.67; 16.34%
27. (a) $2,291.25; (b) $21,208.75; (c) $23,500
29. (a) $4,180; (b) $3,451.67; (c) 12.11%
31. $67,567.57

Section 8.5

1. $13,368.75
3. (a) $21,137.12; (b) 13.31%
5. $41,221.47
7. $71,563.54
9. $76,427.08

Section 8.6

1. $7,800
3. $8,520
5. $6,862.50
7. $7,035
9. $6,918
11. $1,229.92
13. $2,735.09
15. $5,108.33
17. $207.58
19. $1,135.09

CHAPTER 9

Section 9.1

1. .04; 18
3. .005; 120
5. .025; 60
7. $8,671.77, $1,671.77
9. $1,250.61, $250.61
11. $10,509.45, $509.45
13. $9,070.09
15. $8,954.24
17. $9,096.98
19. $9,030.56
21. $17,339.86
23. $15,643.11
25. $14,644.40
27. $1,179.22
29. $85,223.44
31. $11,716.59
33. $50,789.39

Section 9.2

1. 804.96
3. 5,759.06
5. $69,907.41
7. 2,768.38
9. 5,254.52
11. $4,312.62
13. $13,857.69
15. $11,572.77
17. $8,892.77
19. $334.11
21. $2,280.57
23. $34,857.94
25. $5,836.53
27. $4,852.66
29. $14,378.79
31. $21,467.56

Section 9.3

1. 18.81%
3. 19.56%

5. 15.87%
7. 19.68%
9. 10.38%
11. 11.30%
13. 6.17%
15. 8.33%, $832.78

Section 9.4

1. $3,038.59
3. $14,578.37
5. $5,900.42
7. $9,721.56
9. $228,102.00
11. (a) $244,077.61; $104,077.61
13. (a) $255,446.40; (b) $55,446.40
15. $1,397,983.60
17. $37,278.46
19. $88,485.73

Section 9.5

1. $777.93
3. $11,348.33
5. $6,387.05
7. $101,147.17
9. $174,313.93
11. $44,378.12
13. $341,942.87
15. $45,409.71
17. $185,000
19. $7,594.79

Section 9.6

1. $113.06
3. $327.34
5. $153.82
7. $160.95
9. $1,131.74
11. $3,660.66
13. $7,761.96
15. $786.99

Section 9.7

1. $2,590.10
3. $5,753.60
5. $378.15
7. $1,000.98

9. $7,173.50
11. $360,820
13. $1,497.50
15. $223,400

CHAPTER 10

Section 10.1

1. (a) $201.70; (b) $274.90; (c) $364.50
3. $3.82
5. $463.11
7. (a) $600.98; (b) $712.63; (c) $983.51
9. $12.75
11. $279.57

25. $8,787, $183.06
27. $1,062, $35.40
29. $13,116, $273.25
31. (a) $891; (b) $89.10; (c) $245.03
33. $108.10
35. $300
37. $787.50

Section 10.2

1. $700
3. $120
5. $550
7. $400
9. $420
11. $350
13. $786
15. $475
17. $4,680, $195
19. $6,080, $168.89
21. $8,074, $672.83
23. $74,245, $206.24

Section 10.3

1. $99.64
3. $44.65
5. $491.71
7. $588.66
9. $334.37
11. $642.73
13. (a) $222.44; (b) $3,346.40
15. (a) $149.77; (b) $594.48
17. $550.55
19. $514.30
21. $53,016

Section 10.4

1.

n	Principal	Interest	Payment	Principal payment	New principal
1	$4,500.00	$90.00	$614.30	$524.30	$3,975.70
2	3,975.70	79.51	614.30	534.79	3,440.91
3	3,440.91	68.82	614.30	545.48	2,895.43
4	2,895.43	57.91	614.30	556.39	2,339.04
5	2,339.04	46.78	614.30	567.52	1,771.52
6	1,771.52	35.43	614.30	578.87	1,192.65
7	1,192.65	23.85	614.30	590.45	602.20
8	602.20	12.04	614.30	602.26	0

3.

n	Principal	Interest	Payment	Principal payment	New principal
1	$2,400.00	$120.00	$472.84	$352.84	$2,047.16
2	2,047.16	102.36	472.84	370.48	1,676.68
3	1,676.68	83.83	472.84	389.01	1,287.67
4	1,287.67	64.38	472.84	408.46	879.21
5	879.21	43.96	472.84	428.88	450.33
6	450.33	22.52	472.84	450.32	.01

5.

n	Principal	Interest	Payment	Principal payment	New principal
1	$12,000.00	$240.00	$1,638.12	$1,398.12	$10,601.88
2	10,601.88	212.04	1,638.12	1,426.08	9,175.80
3	9,175.80	183.52	1,638.12	1,454.60	7,721.20
4	7,721.20	154.42	1,638.12	1,483.70	6,237.50
5	6,237.50	124.75	1,638.12	1,513.37	4,724.13
6	4,724.13	94.48	1,638.12	1,543.64	3,180.49
7	3,180.49	63.60	1,638.12	1,574.52	1,605.98
8	1,605.98	32.12	1,638.12	1,606.00	.02

7. $8,844.74; $6,712.91; $3,556.60; $2,417.93

9. $10,583.67; $5,607.39; 0

11. $2,372.34; $1,673.00; $885.90; $231.39

13. $4,751.21; $3,348.05; $1,771.46; $911.53

15. $953.64

17. $1,595.30

19. $8,827.20

Section 10.5

1. (a) $1,396.52; (b) $653.31; (c) $176.55

3. (a) $4,237.41; (b) $2,490.41; (c) $1,165.06; (d) $314.84

5. (a) $232.40; (b) $109.09; (c) $30.24

7. (a) $1,183.81; (b) $560.01; (c) $371.27; (d) $157.72

9. $43.32

11. $91.17

13. $59.44

15. (a) $61.10; (b) $35.64; (c) $16.97; (d) $1.70

17. (a) $190.93; (b) $89.10; (c) $25.46

Section 10.6

1. $1,651.65

3. $1,543.30

5. $1,321.32

Section 10.6 *continued*

7. (a) $822.88; (b) $216,236.80

9. (a) 440.44; (b) $65,705.60

11. (a) $130,000; (b) 1,337.18; (c) $351,384.80

13. (a) $20,000; (b) 222.04; (c) $6,644.80

15. (a) $175,000; (b) $1,049.30; (c) $202,748

17. (a) $18,915.44; (b) $6,284.56

19. (a) $4,655.30; (b) $744.70

Section 10.7

1. 26%

3. 19%

5. 10%

7. 11%

9. 27%

11. 10%

13. 15%

15. 17.5%

17. 20.25%

19. 12.5%

21. 22%

23. (a) $2,513.10; (b) $413.10; (c) 28%

CHAPTER 11

Section 11.1

1. $9.50
3. $16.40
5. $21.00
7. $42.61
9. $1,345.65
11. pay to the order of Sutter's Hardware
13. for deposit only
15. $2,382.22
17. $77.28
19. $87.12 (Visa), $64.04 (MasterCard)
21. $4.33 (Visa) + $15.56 (MasterCard) = $19.89

23. $9.40
25. $8.23
27. $24.64
29. $506.86

Section 11.2

1. $791.95
3. $25,309.23
5. $1,626.94
7. $2,923.75
9. $419.95
11. $1,478.70

CHAPTER 12

Section 12.1

1. $2.50; $62.50
3. $.40; $40
5. $4; $80
7. $10.50; $20; $280,300; $10.125 $1.375
9. $99.375; $9.25; $42,000 $98; −$1.375
11. $60.125; $1.20; $117,300 $55.75; $4.75
13. $73.25; $.04; $2,293,400 $72.625; $8
15. $17.25; $.32; $58,431 $16.50; $.50
17. $2,487.50; $74.625; $2,562.125
19. $37,646.50; $36,550; $1,096.50
21. $6,111; $6,300; $189
23. $21,370.31; $22,031.25; $660.94
25. $14,259; $14,700; $441
27. $154.50
29. $11,310 gain

31. −$2,230.50
33. −$1,067.48
35. −$1,555.20
37. (a) $51; (b) $108,171; (c) $55.75; (d) $115,904.25; (e) $7,733.25
39. −$1,202

Section 12.2

1. (a) $1993; (b) $93.75
3. (a) $2009; (b) $93.75
5. (a) $2005; (b) $72.50
7. (a) $2011; (b) $57.5
9. (a) $1991; (b) $121.25
11. $93.75; $1,030; $9
13. $93.75; $1,050; $8.9
15. $72.50; $625; $11.6
17. $57.50; $850; $6.7
19. $121.25; $1,010; $12
21. $6.88; $1,006.88; $966.88
23. $15.63; $5,278.15; $5,078.15
25. $38.33; $8,546.64; $8,226.64

27. $6.56; $12,918.72; $12,438.72
29. $34.90; $1,054.90; $1,014.90
31. $10,137.50; $9,937.50
33. $41,961.60; $42,121.60
35. $5,469.50; $5,251.50; $248

Section 12.3

1. $204,000; $258,000; $138,000
3. $12; $3,600; $11,400; $16.29
5. $625; $250; $375; $1,250
7. $2,400; $1,600; $800; $3,200
9. $4,545.45; $2,272.73; $1,363.64; $1,818.18

11. $68,832.60; $103,248.89; $151,431.71; $105,933.37; $70,533.41
13. $9,263.16; $5,789.47; $6,947.37
15. $8.25; $8,250; $71,750; $8.97
17. $335; $165
19. $252.27; $302.73
21. $435.41; $204.90; $253.56; $256.12
23. $285.71; $142.86; $171.43
25. $923.08; $646.15; $1,430.77
27. $2,701.49; $189.10; $109.41
29. $140; $114.83; $147.95; $165.62; $72.87; $198.74

CHAPTER 13

Section 13.1

1. $3,000
3. $6,000
5. $19,170.83
7. $5,240; $10,480; $20,520
9. $5,240; $20,960; $10,040
11. $1,500; $8,800
13. $11,000; $342,000
15. $1,080 annual depreciation expense

Section 13.2

1. $4,250
3. $4,196.88
5. $9,025
7. $5,880
9. $2,881.20
11. $3,600; $8,400
13. $71,000; $60,350
15. $2,000

Section 13.3

1. $.08950; $290.86
3. $.8566978; $5,500.00
5. $.2885; $4,858.34
7. $21,335.34

9. $6,786.57
11. $2,787.20
13. $66,921.55
15. $6,000

Section 13.4

1. $3
3. $15
5. $5
7. 38%; $1,900
9. 5%; $12,250
11. 9%; $6,525
13. $6,742.50; $10,248.60; $9,978.90
15. year 1 book value $12,750
     year 3 book value $6,300
     year 5 book value 0
17. year 1 book value $78,625
     year 3 book value $38,350
     year 5 book value 0
19. $166,400

Section 13.5

1. $5; $19.20
3. $3; $44.45
5. $5; $11.52
7. $20; $4.462

9. $18,500; $5; $20; $3,700; $14,800
11. $85,250; $20; $3.750; $3,196.88
    $82,053.12
13. $125,000; $15; $5; $6,250; $118,750
15. year 1 book value $41,655
    year 3 book value $21,253
    year 5 book value $10,843
    year 7 book value $4,340
17. $49,500 cost recovered
    year 1 book value $39,600
    year 3 book value $14,256
    year 5 book value $2,852

19. year 1 book value $108,000
21. year 1 book value $332,500
23. year 1 book value $332,500.00
    year 3 book value $262,503.19
    year 5 book value $192,520.24
    year 7 book value $122,519.10
    year 9 book value $52,509.23
25. year 1 book value $842,129
    year 3 book value $778,153
    year 5 book value $734,177

CHAPTER 14

Section 14.3

1. $7,105
3. $26,900
5. (a) $948.09; (b) $1,105; $785
7. (a) $469.26; (b) $680; (c) $326
9. (a) $160; (b) $120; (c) $170
11. (a) $21,875; (b) 22,500.00; (c) $21,250,000

Section 14.4

1. $56,925
3. $135
5. $429,000

Section 14.5

1. $.725
3. $.6
5. $43,500
7. $306,000
9. $91,000
11. $140,000
13. $9,000
15. $30,000

CHAPTER 15

Section 15.1

1. 1.5; 1; 1
3. 150; 195; 220
5. 3,100,000; 800,000; 800,000
7. 3.5; 3; 2
9. 63

Section 15.2

1. 12, 17, 30.43, 5.516
3. 25; 10; 20.5; 4.53
5. 6; 1.5; 3.13

7. 29.6; 29
9. $v = 9; s = 3.58$
11. yes
13. 76
15. 10.25
17. 7
19. $v = 4.386; s = 2.09$

Section 15.3

1. 3
3. chart

5. no

7. 7.5

9. chart

11. yes

Section 15.4

1.
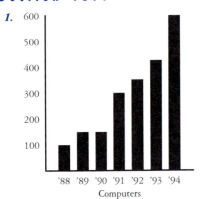
Computers

3.
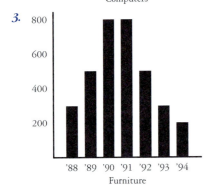
Furniture

5.
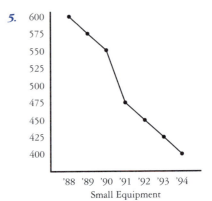
Small Equipment

7.
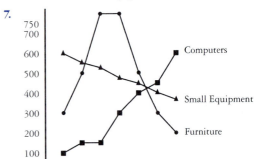

9.

Department	Amount		Percent	Degree
Computer	$ 150,000 ÷ 1,500,000 =		.10 × 360° =	36°
Office Equipment	550,000 ÷ 1,500,000 =		.37 × 360° =	133
Furniture	800,000 ÷ 1,500,000 =		.53 × 360° =	191
	$1,500,000		1.00	360°

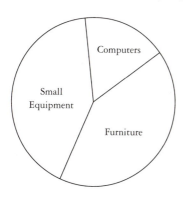

CHAPTER 16

Section 16.1

1. (a) ¼; (b) ¼; (c) ²⁄₄; (d) ²⁄₄; (e) ¼

3. (a) ¹³⁄₃₀; (b) ¹⁷⁄₃₀

5. (a) ¼; (b) ¼; (c) ¾; (d) 0

7. (a) ⁷⁄₂₄; (b) ⁵⁄₂₄; (c) ²⁄₂₄; (d) 0

9. (a) .0009;(b) .007896; (d) .0012

11. (a) 1,487; (b) $11,896,000; (c) $150.51; (d) .0188; (e) $150.40 (same)

Section 16.2

1. $51.20; $964; $1,456; $2,182.40

3. $47.19; $827.97; $1,278.42; $2,089.23

5. $16,160

7. $130; $38,000

9. $115; $38,000

Section 16.3

1. $5,439; $7,938; $10,437

3. $971.25; $1,417.50; $1,863.75

5. $280,000; $160,714.29

7. $480,000; $400,000

9. $100,000; $40,000

INDEX